THE PINKERTONS

Allan Pinkerton (center), Robert A. Pinkerton (left), and William
A. Pinkerton (right)

"WE NEVER SLEEP."

THE PINKERTONS ★

The
Detective
Dynasty
That
Made
History

by
JAMES D. HORAN

Crown Publishers, Inc.   New York

BOOKS BY JAMES D. HORAN

Fiction
KING'S REBEL
SEEK OUT AND DESTROY
THE SHADOW CATCHER
THE SEAT OF POWER
THE RIGHT IMAGE

Nonfiction
ACTION TONIGHT
The Story of the Destroyer O'Bannon

DESPERATE MEN
THE PINKERTON STORY
(with Howard Swiggett)

DESPERATE WOMEN
CONFEDERATE AGENT
PICTORIAL HISTORY OF THE WILD WEST
(with Paul Sann)

MATHEW BRADY:
Historian with a Camera

ACROSS THE CIMARRON
THE WILD BUNCH
THE D.A.'S MAN
THE MOB'S MAN
THE GREAT AMERICAN WEST
C.S.S. SHENANDOAH:
The Memoirs of Lieutenant Commanding James I. Waddell

THE DESPERATE YEARS
AMERICA'S FORGOTTEN PHOTOGRAPHER:
Timothy O'Sullivan

THE PINKERTONS:
The Detective Dynasty That Made History

© 1967 by James D. Horan
Library of Congress Catalog Card Number: 68-9098
Manufactured in the United States of America
Published simultaneously in Canada by
General Publishing Company Limited

Designed by Shari de Miskey

FOR GERTRUDE,
WHOSE TYPEWRITER NEVER SLEPT

Contents

Foreword

History offers few families as controversial as the Pinkertons, Allan, the father, and his sons, William and Robert. Their lives and the world-famous dynasty of detectives they founded are woven into the tapestry of our history with threads of many colors, some lurid. Their story begins with twenty-year-old Allan marching with the Chartists of Glasgow in the Monmouth Castle Raid of 1839, and it ends with William ruling a powerful international private police organization still described by London's newspapers as "America's Scotland Yard."

One startling fact has emerged from my years of research on this unique American trio and the events in which they played major roles: Our confused national political picture, our social unrest, riots, racial hatred, and urban crime—all these have happened before. During the Civil War, New York City was controlled by mobs protesting the unfairness of the draft. About one thousand people were killed, thousands were injured, and twenty-six persons, most of them Negroes, were lynched, some to the telegraph poles on Fifth Avenue. The police were helpless, and the army was called in to restore order. In the 1880's, labor and big business engaged in sporadic wars in which both sides used unbelievable violence. The events of Homestead in 1892 shook the country, influenced a presidential election, and resulted in Senate and House hearings. Washington issued many reports and made many promises, but Congress actually did little to correct the prevailing abuses.

Racial disturbances swept the land in the 1880's and 1890's, with immigrant Italians as the target of mob violence. Eleven men were lynched in New Orleans, several more in western mining camps, while posses and dogs hunted whole families in southern hills. The intense nationalism was unprecedented. Immigration quotas were tightened. Frightened, desperate immigrants in their ghettos battled mobs whose members, ironically, were separated by only a few years from the steerages that had brought their parents and grandparents from Europe.

Crime was a national threat in almost every large American city from shortly after the end of the Civil War to the outbreak of World War I. In 1866, the Methodist Bishop of New York revealed in a sermon that there were more gangsters and prostitutes than Methodists in the community. Most Americans were afraid to walk their city's streets after twilight. In the notorious Five Points section of Manhattan, citizens vanished without a trace. Years later, when the rabbit warrens of the tenements were demolished, their bones were found. Gunmen fought daylight battles in city streets. Witnesses were too terrorized to testify. Organized crime was so powerful that jury lists were in the hands of gangsters before they were turned over to the courts.

By 1880, the Mafia was an old story in the United States. The ancient terrorist society controlled the waterfront of New Orleans and the hiring of longshoremen, along with vice and prostitution. Municipal corruption was incredible. Driven out of the city, Mafia gunmen took over the limestone quarries of Pennsylvania until the early 1900's, forcing immigrant workers to pay tribute. They murdered potential witnesses, defied and terrorized rural law officers, and virtually controlled the quarries at a time when America was building its cities.

We can also find a political analogy to our times. In 1864, the country was war-weary. Casualty lists were long; the conflict seemed to have reached an impasse. Groups who advocated peace at any cost were getting stronger. In the spring of that year, the leaders of the Republican Party debated about forcing the withdrawal of Lincoln as their chosen nominee in favor of a "more vigorous candidate." By midsummer Lincoln was at odds with his party over his war aims and reconstruction, and had offended his Congress. Horace Greeley's opinion was, "Mr. Lincoln is already beaten." General McClellan's star burned brightly all that dark summer of 1864. Pinkerton's jubilant prediction that McClellan would be the next President was shared by many Washington leaders. Shortly before the Democratic Convention met in August to make McClellan their candidate, Lincoln was so sure he would be replaced by his former general that he wrote a memorandum promising to "co-operate with the president-elect to save the Union between the election and the inauguration." As he later revealed to his Cabinet, he intended to call McClellan to Washington "to raise as many troops as you possibly can . . . and I will devote my energies to assist and finish this war. . . ."

Then conditions changed dramatically. After a bitter floor fight, the Democrats allowed a "peace plank" to be inserted into their platform. This action, which completely misjudged the temper of the people, only stirred national resentment. Then Sherman took Atlanta, giving Lincoln

the major war victory he had needed for so long. This was followed by
Republican victories in Maine and Vermont. By mid-September, Lincoln's national popularity had risen sharply, and he won the election
with a majority of 400,000 over McClellan.

In every instance the Pinkertons were involved, thus making the history of this dynasty far more important than a simple tale of skillful
detectives and colorful criminals. They were on the frontier of the 1850's,
in the abolitionist underground, and with John Brown. They were
superb espionage agents, but incredibly incompetent military intelligence
forces in the Civil War. Allan Pinkerton frustrated an assassination plot
on the life of President-elect Lincoln in 1861. They broke the Molly
Maguires, played important parts in the great Burlington Strike of 1888,
and gained the everlasting hatred of labor at Homestead. They were the
first American law-enforcement agency to battle and defeat the Mafia in
this country. They solved the dynamite murder of former Governor
Steunenberg of Idaho, and were principals in the trial of Big Bill Haywood and the officials of the Western Federation of Miners—a trial that
featured two future giants—William E. Borah for the prosecution and
Clarence Darrow for the defense.

They were the nineteenth-century prototype of the present Federal
Bureau of Investigation, and a forerunner of Interpol. By 1872, they had
established a liaison with the important police organizations of Europe,
for the exchange of information about international crime and criminals,
and most of the frontier sheriffs and heads of metropolitan police in the
United States sought their assistance. Though it is a little-known fact,
the Pinkertons' pioneering Rogues' Gallery formed the basis for the
modern FBI's Criminal Identification Bureau, the largest in the world.

Many historical figures of their lifetime were either friends or enemies:
McClellan, Grant, Stanton, Welles, Andrew Johnson, Carnegie, Frick,
Debs, Haywood, the Vanderbilts, the Belmonts, Lord Kitchener, and every
President from Lincoln to Coolidge. In response to a cablegram from
his old friend Winston Churchill, Home Secretary, William Pinkerton
went to London in June, 1911, to assist Scotland Yard during the
coronation of Edward VII.

They helped to tame the Wild West, and they chased outlaws and
train robbers from the Great Plains to the rain jungles of Bolivia. They
captured, killed—and had their own men killed—in their hunt for international rogues of the Victorian Age. The techniques and methods they
developed influenced modern state and federal police throughout the
world.

Before William Pinkerton died in 1924, they were legendary and world
famous—their names synonymous with detectives. Their early trademark
(The Eye That Never Sleeps) became "private eye" and part of the
language. Father and sons had a Bourbon cast of mind: they were
opinionated and sometimes unbearably touchy, and they were feared,

hated, admired, respected, denounced, and praised from Capetown to the Orient. While they possessed a venom and a fury that numbed suspected assailants, they could also be generous and gentle, and they had insights into other people's characters and motives that were shrewdly perceptive.

Americans and Europeans, whether they admired, respected, hated, or despised them, could never ignore the Pinkertons. They always appeared in Paul Bunyan's class—outsize.

This is the first complete, documented history of the three Pinkertons and the activities of their world-famous Agency. It is based on material that I have gathered for years, both in the United States and abroad. A great deal of it will be new—even to the Pinkertons. I have resisted using the expression "hitherto unpublished" in the text, because there is so much that is unpublished it would soon become tiresome. The reader can consult my voluminous notes and sources of material.

I have always believed that the social incidents in which the Pinkertons played historic roles should not be separated from their times, and I have endeavored to present them in that perspective.

That my search for material was so often successful must be attributed to the assistance and cooperation of many persons. High on that list are: Vincent Dougan of Barrhead, Scotland; Joseph Meehan and Robert Blair Wilkie of Glasgow; and my friend and colleague of past newspaper days, John Dolan, now of Dublin; and the wonderful staff of the Mitchell Library, Glasgow. In London, the staff of the Public Records Office and T. E. Heron, Department of Public Records, The New Scotland Yard.

In Canada, the staff of the Historical Archives of Canada's Royal Mounted Police; George T. Bates, Provincial Land Surveyor and Secretary of the Halifax Historical Society; Evelyn M. Richardson, President, Cape Sable Historical Society, Barrington, Nova Scotia; and T. Regehr, Head, Public Records Section, Manuscript Division, Public Archives of Canada.

In the United States, many individuals and the staffs of federal, state, and local historical societies assisted me in unearthing old documents, records, newspapers, and photographs. I wish to thank the following for their graciousness, courtesy, and cooperation: Charles G. Eubanks and his fine staff of the Newberry Library, Chicago, where the voluminous and carefully documented files of the Illinois Central and Chicago, Burlington & Quincy Railroad are stored; Clement M. Silvestro, Director; Archie Motley, Manuscript Historian; Grant Talbot Dean, and Mrs. Paul M. Rhymer, Curator of Prints of the Chicago Historical Society; Collin B. Hamer, Jr., head, Louisiana Division, New Orleans Public Library; G. McDonald, Chief, American History Room, The New York Public Library; James Heslin, Director, The New-York Historical Society; Virginia Daiker and the staffs of Prints and Photographs and the Manuscript divisions, Library of Congress; the staffs of Prints and Photographs and the Manuscript Division, National Archives.

Surviving neighbors of Allan Pinkerton's "The Larches" and local historians contributed anecdotes, legends, and facts about the Pinkerton showplace estate in Onarga, Illinois. I should like to thank Pearl Parkinson, F. Myrtle Weber, Russell Palmer, now of Enterprise, Florida; Major Edward L. Davis, (Ret.) of Onarga, who has led a campaign to save The Larches; Mrs. Margaret Johnston, copublisher of the Piper City (Illinois) *Journal,* an enterprising newspaperwoman who pointed out to me Timothy Webster's grave in Onarga; Dorothy M. Long, Milford, Illinois, who has dug deeply into the local history of the Pinkertons and sent me a copy of the paper she prepared for the Iroquois County Historical Society; and Leslie Bork, Sr., and his sons, present owners of the land and the surviving weatherbeaten remains of the Villa—and Teressa Przeniczny of Carpentersville, Illinois.

The officials of the Pinkerton Agency, now Pinkerton's Inc., were always gracious and cooperative in granting my many requests for material. Heading the list must be the late Robert Pinkerton II, great-grandson of the founder; Edward J. Bednarz, the first non-Pinkerton to be President of that organization; Coleman J. Graham, Executive Vice-President; Bernard F. Boyce, Howard W. Nugent, Assistant Executive Vice-President, Investigations; George O'Neill, Director, Public Relations; and William H. Smyth, retired.

I should like to express a particular note of thanks to my son, Brian Boru Horan, B.S., M.A., a member of the Faculty of St. Peter's College, Jersey City, New Jersey, for his recommendations and suggestions on social Darwinism, Populism and the Agrarian concept, so much a part of the world in which the Pinkertons lived, that world so sadly misnamed "The Gilded Age."

BOOK 1
Barrelmaker, Revolutionist, and Detective, 1819-1850

CHAPTER 1
Glasgow, 1819-1842

On August 25, 1819, a son was born to Isabella and William Pinkerton in their third-floor tenement flat on Muirhead Street, Glasgow. The area on the Clyde's left bank, known as the Gorbals, was a section of filthy, airless lanes and narrow streets, crowded on each side by buildings dating from the time of the Reformation, and packed from cellar to garret with families of the poor. Crime of every description could be found in the district. The number of brothels and "shebangs" was staggering, and legend has body snatchers with chloroform-soaked pads lurking in the doorways waiting for victims. That year the city jail held a record three thousand prisoners, and as a London visitor noted—temporarily forgetting his city's own terrifying Shoreditch and The Jago—a gentleman was a fool to pass through the Gorbals and not be armed with a club or a pistol to fight off the footpads.

A few weeks after the child had been born, his parents brought him to the local Scotch Baptist Church and, in the high vaulted baptistery, named their son Allan, after his grandfather, the Gorbals' blacksmith. It was perhaps appropriate that the greatest detective of his age should be born surrounded on all sides by the crime, violence, and social injustice that would fill his controversial lifetime.[1]

The family was well known in the Gorbals. For years "Pinkerton the blacksmith" had been a familiar sight to the brewer's helpers, hand loomers, spinners, patternmakers, and butchers who passed the smithy that was always hazy with acrid coal smoke, and echoed from dawn to dusk with the measured clang of hammers. William Pinkerton, as his

Birthplace of Allan Pinkerton, at Muirhead Street and Ruglen Loan, Gorbals, Glasgow, Scotland. *Pinkerton's, Inc.*

Glasgow Bridge, looking north from the Gorbals toward Trongate. Pinkerton was born some two hundred yards southeast of this bridge, and would cross it daily to and from work. *Old Glasgow Museum*

famous son would recall, was a former handloom weaver who became a trusty in the Glasgow City Jail, a curious occupation for an inhabitant of the Gorbals. He was slender but strong, about six feet tall, taciturn, and a strict disciplinarian. His first wife had died after giving birth to seven children, three girls and four boys, two of whom died in their infancy. A proper mourning period was observed; then William Pinkerton married again, this time Isabella McQueen, a pretty Glasgow girl who worked in a spinning mill. Isabella gave birth to four sons. The first two, Allan and Robert, survived; the others died within a year.

The infant Allan fought off the countless diseases that periodically swept the Gorbals, and grew up in the tenement and the twisting, noisy streets. More than a half century later he would recall the third-floor dwelling as noisy and filled with the tensions of two families existing in a few rooms. His half brothers were "unruly," but his strict father "refused to be ruled by them." One enlisted as a soldier, "but after a few years had to be bought off." The oldest boy, James, "almost broke his father's heart" —how, we do not know. His half sisters, he remembered, left home in their teens to marry a headwaiter in a Glasgow restaurant, a miner, and a butcher.

Allan was about eight years old when his father died. A legend that has hardened by repeated telling has the older Pinkerton suffering fatal wounds in an uprising, but a search of the Glasgow police records fail to uncover such an incident.

Pinkerton also destroyed the myth that he came from a deeply religious family. As he wrote: "They [his parents] were obliged to take their children to church to be baptized, but otherwise they never went to church; they were what is called Atheists, which I and your mother are. . . ."

After the death of his father, young Pinkerton left elementary school and went to work, a way of life for most of the district's children. England's Factory Law, which supposedly limited the working hours of children up to twelve, was unknown in the Gorbals. For three years he worked from dawn to dusk for pennies as an apprentice in the pattern-making shop of his father's friend Neil Murphy. At night he would wait on the corner of Muirhead Street for his mother, who worked in a spinning mill. It is significant that one of the few specific details he recalled of those bitter years was his mother bringing home a precious egg.

Allan Pinkerton never acknowledged the irretrievable loss of childhood's warmth and mystery, but there is little doubt that the memory of his family's searing poverty never left him and that it helped to cast the mold of the man who would one day especially order 170 trees to be sent from Glasgow to adorn his American estate. It is evident that young Allan was fiercely protective of his mother and that during his formative years, with the "unruly" stepbrothers and stepsisters gone, he and his brother, Robert, and their mother were very close.

Allan was never defeated by life in the Gorbals. Even as a child apprentice he knew where he was going and what he was doing. When he was twelve he displayed the aggressiveness and enormous self-confidence that would shape his whole life. Because he found patternmaking "a dreary existence," he gave Murphy notice, and apprenticed himself to William McCauley, a Glasgow cooper. Pinkerton always recalled December 26, 1837, as one of the memorable days of his life. In a ceremony at "Richard O'Neil's Public House, opposite King William's statue," the eighteen-year-old apprentice received his journeyman's card as a full member of the Coopers of Glasgow and Suburbs Protective Association. From 1837 to 1838, Pinkerton became a tramp cooper, as they called the itinerant workers who went about the countryside making barrels, kegs, and casks by the day or week. He kept just enough to live on, and sent the rest home to his mother.[2]

At some time in 1838, Allan returned to Glasgow, and in the following year became devoted to Chartism, the revolutionary democratic "agitation" sweeping Great Britain. The heart of the movement was the "People's Charter," the name given to a bill containing the six famous points—equal electoral areas, universal suffrage, payment of members, no property qualifications, vote by ballot, and annual parliaments. Almost from their beginning the Chartists were not unanimous about the means of gaining social equality. They were split between the "moral force" faction, who preached against violence, and the "physical force men," who sought insurrection to gain their goals.

The ultimate aims of the Chartists were summed up in the London *Democrat's* editorial of 1839: ". . . that all shall have a good house to live in with a garden back or front, just as the occupier likes; good clothing to keep him warm and make him look respectable and plenty of good food and drink to make him look and feel happy. . . ."

To young Pinkerton, who had one worn suit and a pair of shoes he treasured, this sounded like Utopia. In the spring the Glasgow coopers appointed him to be their representative at the Chartist Convention held at Birmingham. Though a general strike was voted, and took place, it failed because of poor planning. In July, when Commons rejected the demands of the Chartists, the moderates lost control and the physical-force leaders took over.

In the fall of 1839, a secret military expedition was formed under the former mayor and justice of the peace John Frost to free Henry Vincent, the eloquent Chartist orator who had been arrested and jailed in Monmouth Castle at Newport. Meetings were held on the windswept moors, with Frost and the other physical-force leaders making their plans and shouting their defiance of the government, while Pinkerton and the Glasgow coopers held high their torches and listened intently. As he recalled, he was then about twenty, and the most ardent Chartist in Scotland.

The plan was for three columns of Chartists to unite at Risca, six miles from Newport. On the night of November 3, 1839, Pinkerton and his Glasgow delegation marched behind the mounted Frost through an all-night downpour to reach Risca early the next morning. They huddled in a field for hours, listening to speeches and waiting for the other two columns. Finally Frost, his red tie soggy, raised his collier's pick and shouted that they would take Monmouth Castle by themselves. They gave him a cheer, and then the men and boys filled the road, ancient muskets, axes, picks, iron bars, or sledges slung over their shoulders, their rough voices filling the damp dawn with the song of the Chartists.

At that time Pinkerton was of medium height, with powerful shoulders and arms that could swing a ten-pound hammer for hours without tiring. A man who knew him described the young cooper as a quiet, rather serious lad. But he remembered most of all the searching, cool blue-gray eyes that never left your face when he spoke to you, and the intense drive that animated him. He was known in the Gorbals as an earnest, hard-working barrel-maker who seemed to have little interest outside his job at McCauley's Cooperage, the Chartists and the singing societies that made up most of Glasgow's—and the Gorbals'—social life. Years later, when he was asked if he had sung in those days, he laughed and said he sang "about as much as the precentor's bull." Though he was devoid of social graces, he was filled with an enormous energy and a driving ambition. He was taciturn, a rather solid sort, but well liked among his fellow coopers. That day, marching behind Frost, a cooper's hammer over his shoulder, Allan Pinkerton was striking his first blow in the cause of social justice. It would not be the last. Yet his character was so paradoxical that with apparently no twinge of conscience he could still become a fierce reactionary. But this was in the future, years away from this dreary morning when, like the others, filled with great ideals and excitement, he roared out the words of the stirring Chartist ballad:

> May the Rose of England never blow,
> The Clyde of Scotland never flow,
> The Harps of Ireland never play,
> Until the Chartists gain their day!

Upon reaching the rise of a small hill, they saw the quiet town of Newport below them. Men who were there that memorable morning, many of them with tattered blankets tied about their shoulders for protection against the weather, never forgot the scene: They poured down the road by the thousands, gaunt and famished, an army of human scarecrows, their clothes in rags, their shoes tied together with string, many of them barefoot, the vanguard of England's starving millions. The older men looked weary and footsore but most of Frost's army were, like Pinkerton, young workers from the mills, factories, and mines.

THE SCOTTISH PATRIOT.

SPIRIT OF THE MOVEMENT.

GLASGOW UNIVERSAL SUFFRAGE ASSOCIATION.

On Tuesday evening, the weekly meeting of the Directors, along with Delegates from Trades, Shops, and Factories, was held in the Hall, College Open.

Mr Allan Pinkerton rose and said—Previous to withdrawing from the Association, he would trouble them with a few remarks as to the late proceedings in the Lyceum, on the subject of petitioning. These proceedings, he was sorry to say, had led to very unpleasant results. An Association had been formed in Glasgow, under the title of the "Northern Democratic Association." (Hear) Mr P. here proceeded, at some length, to refer to the proceedings in the Lyceum, when himself and a few others had endeavoured to carry an amendment to the motion almost unanimously come to by the meeting, in favour of petitioning. That amendment, he remarked, only asked the Association to wait until England had been consulted. It was not against petitioning. He then alluded to the recommendation of the Central Committee, and proceeded to stigmatize that body for giving out any such recommendation before testing the country. The Democratic Association coming into the field was not intended to divide, but to unite Radicals, and its motto would be, "We are determined to carry the People's Charter peaceably if we may, forcibly if we must." (Hear, hear, and a hiss.)

Mr M'Fadyen wished to know from Mr Pinkerton, what means the new Democratic Association meant to use to carry the Charter, if they did not agree with petitioning? (Hear, hear, and a laugh.)

Some conversation, through the Chairman, between Messrs Colquhoun and Pinkerton, ensued about the proceedings of the Central Committee, when Mr Ross rose to defend himself, as a member of the Central Committee, from the aspersions attempted to be cast upon it by Mr Pinkerton, and wished to know from Mr P. the names of the individuals in that Committee who had acted inconsistently, as he could not charge himself with any thing of the kind.

servations, the substance
Mr Pattison's remarks.

Mr Proudfoot, anoth
Committee, thought they
to such a meeting as tha
had a much wider consti
of opinion, however, tha
tion. Supposing that h
majority of his Chartist t
vour of petitioning, how
appear, if he were to go
up an Anti-Petitioning A
most ridiculous. If tha
holding the name of C
work, then he would say
for the Charter. Now, h
show a better mode of o
country (as some peopl
anxious for it), except b
were not to agitate and o
do? These men would r
their principles were, an
tives for setting up anothe
part, whatever his princi
solved to obtain the Char
onet, he would not seek t
blind his fellow-men, or
He would lead no man in
pared to share in, and if
take their rights by force
cloak his intentions, but
as well as advise, when th

The Delegate from To
said they did not blam
said the inhabitants of th
of petitioning. They onl
a little too zealous and
come to such a resolution
meeting on an early day
they had as yet come to
waited until they saw if n
to them, or if there w
adopted with a greater
versal Suffrage.

The Scottish Patriot, December 7, 1839 (the Chartist newspaper): Report of a meeting of the Universal Suffrage Association at which Pinkerton airs some views before withdrawing from the association. *Mitchell Library, Glasgow*

Unknown to Frost, word had preceded them, and the Mayor of Newport had summoned the King's 42nd Foot from the nearby barracks. The soldiers had taken up positions in windows of the Westgate Hotel facing the town square, and the shutters were closed. As the Chartists entered the square, the shutters slammed open, and the redcoats fired. The front line of the Chartists returned a brief volley, then charged with their drills and picks. It was a massacre, and soon the cobbled square was filled with the dead and dying. The Chartists broke and ran. Pinkerton and his delegation, ducking under a hail of bullets, made their way out of Newport.

"It was a bad day," Pinkerton said of that morning. "We returned to Glasgow by the back streets and the lanes, more like thieves than honest workingmen."

Frost and the other leaders, captured a short time after the raid, were tried and condemned to death, but their sentences were changed to deportation. However, they were all released under public pressure and a struggle for control began between the moral-force group and the physical-force faction.

A survey of Glasgow's newspapers of the period shows how active Pinkerton was in this bitter fight that split families and friendships. After the abortive march on Newport, he joined the Glasgow Universal Suffrage Association, and was soon elected a director. When he failed to defeat a resolution to consult England on a policy of petition, Pinkerton resigned to join the newly formed Glasgow Northern Democratic Association, composed of dissident members of the less militant groups. Pinkerton was a strong advocate of the organization's policy "to use force if necessary to gain the charter."

In December, 1839, Pinkerton became embroiled in a controversy over a letter he had written to a Glasgow newspaper, in which he described "in scurrilous terms" a meeting of the directors of the Universal Suffrage Association. The letter caused a sensation in the city. A few weeks later the directors made an angry reply to Pinkerton in the *Scottish Patriot,* but more important events in the national movement overshadowed the local conflict, and it was forgotten as the year turned.

In February, 1840, Pinkerton was back in the news as the head of a committee that brought the noted Chartist leader Julian Harney to Glasgow to speak at the city's Lyceum Theatre. For a time it appeared that a brawl might break out when Pinkerton's old foes from the Universal Suffrage Association challenged Harney, demanding to know by what right he was speaking in Glasgow. Pinkerton jumped to his feet and shouted angrily that it was by his invitation and that Harney would speak and no one in the theatre could stop him. For a few minutes there was a tense confrontation between the young cooper from the Gorbals and the Universal Suffrage delegation; but cooler heads prevailed and Harney addressed the packed theatre.

Young Pinkerton's championship of Harney is startling in view of Pinkerton's later denunciation by American labor as one of its bitterest enemies, an ultraconservative whose mercenaries served the robber barons of the nineteenth century. Harney, who was Pinkerton's age at the time of the Chartist uprising, was the enfant terrible of the movement. Physically he was frail, handicapped, as one writer stated, "by congenital quinsy and impaired hearing." In his teens Harney was a well-known street radical who had been in and out of London jails. Chartism in Great Britain was too parochial for his continental and universal conception of the movement. He was the precursor of the modern dedicated Communist, a superb orator with a fine command of language, who became a familiar figure on Glasgow's streets. A crowd was never too small for him to address, and he usually ended his bitter, forceful speech by circulating a petition to be signed by his listeners, endorsing the Chartists' Charter. Harney was on good terms with Marx and Engels who, however, regarded him merely as an agitator and referred to him as "Citizen Hip, Hip Hooray" because of his eagerness to endorse any revolutionary movement.

They made a strange pair in Glasgow: the taciturn, muscular, intense young cooper, ready to use his fists and boots to insure that the magnificent voice of the frail, white-faced Harney would be heard by the street crowds. Almost a quarter of a century later, Harney would be replaced in Pinkerton's life by the fanatical John Brown, and later the polished, urbane George Brinton McClellan. Pinkerton's career is a graphic illustration of the influence of one's situation on one's beliefs.

From the winter of 1839, after the Newport raid, until the spring of 1842, Glasgow newspapers reveal that while Pinkerton was far from being a major leader of the Chartists, he was a forceful and well-known figure among the Glasgow physical-force groups, as he would be a decade later among the more aggressive elements of the American abolitionists. It would appear that Pinkerton selected his causes, not for their goals and philosophies, but because they suited his opinionated, narrow, explosive character, and were tinged with a romantic glow of the righteous correcting social wrong. When he looked back on his early days in Glasgow, it was almost with relish that he recalled the street battles and blows struck —never the moral gains. His memories of his abolitionist activities usually centered on the fanatical John Brown and the violent men who surrounded him.

In 1842, some coherence appeared in the Chartist movement when the National Charter Association, technically an outlaw group, was formed in Glasgow. Pinkerton continued to work with the physical-force groups. There were many nights when the tiny flat on Muirhead Street was filled with patternmakers, coopers, spinners, and handweavers, all debating with the intense young barrelmaker the motives and benefits of the various leaders trying to gain control of the Chartists.[3]

During a spinners' strike in Glasgow, Pinkerton, as treasurer of his union, was delegated to arrange a series of "strikers' concerts" to raise money for the workmen. The Welsh and Scots, with their great love of song, were always ready to buy tickets to a "concert" to get a few pounds "for the Charter boys." The choir of the Unitarian Church on Center Street was fast becoming known as one of Glasgow's best singing groups, so Pinkerton visited Dr. Harris, the choirmaster, who agreed to bring his group to the back parlors of O'Neil's Public House for an evening of song.

All that week Pinkerton and his coopers sold tickets. On a Thursday night, dressed in his best, his one pair of boots gleaming and his mother on his arm, he sat in the front row in O'Neil's "parlors" and listened to the Unitarian singers fill the room with the rousing songs of Scotland. The evening was a big success. The rooms were packed to the doors, and the overflow filled the small square, with spectators sitting on benches in the small park under the iron scowl of King William.

The hit of the evening was the group's soprano, and the public house shook under the cheers and stamping of boots when she finished the forbidden song of the Chartists. Pinkerton couldn't take his eyes off the slender young woman who stood near the piano as Dr. Harris played. When the evening was over and his mother was gossiping with the neighborhood women, Pinkerton sought out his friend Robbie Fergus, a printer's apprentice and his boyhood chum from the Gorbals.

It was one of Robbie's last nights in Glasgow. He had been active with Pinkerton in the Chartists, and had been warned he was about to be put on the king's list to be arrested. Some of the other leaders had left for America, and Robbie was soon to join them to open a "public" printing shop in a place called Chicago. Fergus told Pinkerton that the young singer's name was Joan Carfrae and that she was "a bookbinder's apprentice from Paisle." [4]

There were other concerts promoted by the Glasgow unions that featured the Unitarian Choir and the pretty young soprano. Pinkerton attended every one. As he said: "I got sort of hanging around her, clinging to her so to speak, and I knew I couldn't live without her." It soon became accepted that he and no one else would escort her home from every concert and rehearsal.

The year turned. In the winter of 1842 a policeman named Miller at Glasgow Police Headquarters flipped through a number of king's warrants he had received for Chartists, and among the names was that of Allan Pinkerton. Several arrests were made, but when Miller walked up the creaky stairway in the Gorbals tenement, he found that the young barrelmaker had fled.

"I had become an outlaw with a price on my head," Pinkerton said.

For months friends hid him in various places in Glasgow. When Joan heard the news she went to the Coopers' union and begged some of

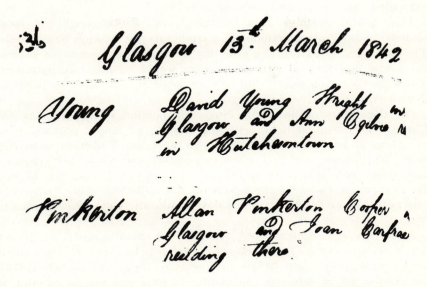

Copy of Marriage Register, 13th March 1842. *Mitchell Library, Glasgow*

his friends to take her to him. They agreed. A half century later Pinkerton recalled that meeting:

> When I had the price set on my head, she found me where I was hiding, and when I told her I was all set up to making American barrels for the rest of my life and ventured it would be a pretty lonesome business without my bonnie singing bird around the shop, she just sang me a Scotch song that meant she'd go too, and God bless her she did.[5]

On March 13, 1842, Joan Carfrae and Allan Pinkerton were married secretly in Glasgow. On the night of April 8th, after a hurried goodbye to his mother, Pinkerton and his bride were smuggled aboard a ship by Neil Murphy, his former patternmaker employer.

The ship sailed on the morning tide, April 9, 1842. To pay for their passage, Pinkerton signed on as the ship's cooper; he slept with the crew, and Joan was given a space in steerage. But after they were a few days out, some of the passengers heard they were newlyweds, and insisted that the captain let them have a "snug apartment as man and wife."

After a stormy four-week passage, the ship arrived off Nova Scotia, where she became entangled in the ice. She slipped her anchor, struck a rock, and began to fill. Pinkerton and his bride, along with the other passengers, took to the lifeboats and rowed to safety. They finally booked passage on a coastal mail steamer for Quebec, and from that city to Montreal, where they landed some time in May, 1842, with what Pinkerton called, "our health and a few pennies." [6]

They found lodgings in a boardinghouse, and through the local coopers' union Pinkerton obtained a temporary job making beef barrels. The job lasted a few months. One day the union representative warned the young Scot that in a few days there would be no more barrels to make. As Pinkerton said, "I all at once made up my mind to jump to that thriving little city of Chicago."

On the following morning Pinkerton bought steamer tickets for Chicago. He returned home with the tickets and empty pockets. Joan gave him a distressed look, and began weeping. Pinkerton soon discovered the reason; she had placed a small deposit on a "wee bonnet," and, thrifty Scot that she was, refused to leave the deposit. She begged her husband to exchange the tickets for the following week. Perhaps in the meantime he would get a few days' work, and they could claim the bonnet?

Pinkerton, as he remembered, "roared like anything but I finally let her have her way." The tickets were exchanged, and Pinkerton got a week's work. The night before they were to sail, Joan silently spread the evening paper before her husband. On page one was an account of the sinking of the steamer they had been scheduled to sail on during the previous week. A boiler had exploded; there were no survivors.

"I tell you my wee wife has had her way about bonnets ever since," Pinkerton said.

Evidently there was a change of plans, and instead of Chicago they arrived in Warsaw, Illinois, where Pinkerton said they were robbed of almost everything they had, how we do not know. We next find them in Chicago, then a thriving frontier town of about twelve hundred citizens and twenty-six business houses. The streets were deeply rutted and muddy, the bawling of the cattle in the yards as constant as the prairie wind. There was a vigorous, aggressive air about Chicago that appealed to Pinkerton; here, he decided, was a place of new beginnings. With the few pennies he had left, he hired a room and went looking for "auld Bobbie Fergus" from the Gorbals.

There weren't many printers in Chicago, and he soon found Fergus, who introduced him to the foreman in Lill's brewery. Pinkerton was hired that day as a cooper. Fergus insisted they stay with him until they were settled. In the summer Fergus and the Pinkertons attended a Scotch revival meeting. The feature of the evening was a well-known Scottish singer, who thrilled the lonely and heartsick Scots who crowded the meetings with ballads of their homeland.

The imaginative Fergus decided to collect the ballads and print them.

Mrs. Pinkerton folded the sheets as they came off the handpress, while Pinkerton trimmed them with a shoemaker's knife and punched holes for the stitches with an awl. Then the Pinkertons together stitched every copy of Fergus's songbook of "old country ballads"—one of the first songbooks printed in Chicago.

The following spring, 1843, Pinkerton heard of a small settlement of Scots on the beautiful Fox River, fifty miles northeast of Chicago. It was a thriving dairy section with a village named Dundee after their "own bonnie city." As Pinkerton recalled: "It was a fair and lovely spot, with its murmurous rivers, splendid farms, forests, noble hills, sunlit valleys and opulent herds in the district."

He told his wife: "I'm going to Dundee, Joan. I'll make their barrels, churns and tubs. You bide here with Fergus. I'll get a roof over my head and then I'll send for you, wife."

Joan walked her husband to the end of Lake Street, then the outskirts of Chicago where a small pontoon bridge crossed the river. On the other side a path disappeared into man-high reeds and grass. Beyond it was Father Marquette's "endless leagues of prairie," silent except for the soft morning breeze that moved across the reeds like invisible surf. Neither Pinkerton nor his wife ever forgot that goodbye. He kissed his wife, slung the bag of tools over his shoulder, and crossed the swaying bridge. On the other side he turned and waved. To reassure his wife, he began whistling a Scottish ballad as he disappeared into the tall reeds.

As Joan remembered: "I could na bear it when the great grass swallowed him up so quick. But I keen's from the brave whistle I could hear, long after I could na see him any longer, that there'd be a wee home soon for us." [7]

In Dundee, Pinkerton toured the farms, and found the prospects good for establishing a cooperage in the settlement. He built a one-story cabin and adjacent shed on the rise of a small hill about three hundred yards from the bridge that spanned the Fox River. It was an excellent spot. Cattle dealers and farmers going to market, freighters hauling grain to the Chicago market and lumber merchants could not help noticing the newly painted sign that read "Allan Pinkerton, Cooperage."

When Pinkerton finished his cabin, he returned to Chicago for Joan. He always thrived on hard work, and his tiny shop echoed from dawn to dusk with sawing and hammering and the dull thud of the "driver" upon the hoops as they were driven into place. There was never drinking, dancing, or smoking in Pinkerton's house, either in the tiny cabin on the Fox River or in the later palatial mansions. He developed a routine in Dundee that he never varied for the rest of his life: to bed at eight thirty and up at four thirty, seven days a week. Before the lamp was lowered, he perhaps read a chapter from *Eugene Aram,* which he considered the greatest novel ever written. As one old friend said, "He didn't think much of you if you disagreed with him on that." Such was Pinkerton's literary taste.

It was a good life in Dundee. The frontier was opening, and Chicago was expanding rapidly to become one of the great grain markets of the world. When Bobbie Fergus, later one of the most important printers and publishers in the history of the Midwest, came for a visit on a Sunday, he, Pinkerton, and Joan sat by the river, listening to Fergus tell how Chicago was changing; how land values were booming, more than half a million bushels of grain were moving into the city, and elevators now rose higher than the masts of the schooners that lined the shores of the lake.

The city had over sixteen thousand residents. Now that the Illinois and Michigan Canal had been opened, barges were coming down from the lakes and freighting lumber out across the treeless prairies.

By 1847 there were more farms, the settlement had grown, and Pinkerton's cooperage prospered. As he said, "by industry and saving [I] had gradually worked into a comfortable business at my cooper's trade and now employed eight men." Pinkerton's employees were Germans who lived on the other side of the river, but there was no love lost between the Scots, English, and the newly arrived German immigrants, and although there would be proposals that both communities unite into one, it never happened. There were always West Dundee and East Dundee.

Joan considered those placid days the best of her life. As she once told a friend: ". . . in the little shop at Dundee, wi' the blue river purling down the valley, the auld Scotch farmers trundling past with the grist for the mill, or their loads for the market and Allan, with his rat-tat-tat on the barrels whistling and keeping tune with my singing, were the bonniest days the good father gave me in all my life. . . ."

CHAPTER 2
How Allan Pinkerton Became a Detective

During the year 1847, Allan Pinkerton made a discovery that helped to shape his destiny. The small yard in front of his cooperage was usually stacked with staves and hoops for his casks and barrels. One day a workman pointed out that the supply was running low. Lumber was still scarce and costly on the frontier, and Pinkerton had found that the trees on a tiny island in the Fox River, a few miles above Dundee and a short distance from the village of Algonquin, were ideal for hoops, staves, and poles. Barefoot as usual, he poled to the island on a small raft.

He had spent most of the morning selecting, cutting down, and trimming his lumber, when he stumbled on the remains of a cooking fire and evidence that someone had been using the island. As Pinkerton said, "There was no picnicking in those days, people had more serious matters to attend to and it required no great keenness to conclude that no honest men were in the habit of occupying the place."

Pinkerton's curiosity was aroused. He returned to the island several times. When the island remained deserted during the day, he came back at night. Finally his patience was rewarded; late one night he heard the unmistakable rasp of oars. As he crouched in the shore grass, he watched a rowboat move in the moonlight downriver to the island. Several figures scrambled ashore, and in a short time he saw the faint flickering light of a fire.

15

The next day Pinkerton notified Luther Dearborn, Sheriff of Kane County. Together they watched the island. One night, "in the right quarter of the moon," as one account had it, Pinkerton and Dearborn, heading a posse from the settlement, raided the island and arrested a band of counterfeiters, along with "a bag of bogus dimes and the tools used in their manufacture."

The arrest of the gang gave Pinkerton some local publicity. He told the story until he grew weary to every farmer and cattle dealer who came to the shop for barrels and casks. Gradually, to Pinkerton's relief, it died down. From that time, the island was known locally as Bogus Island.

One July afternoon Pinkerton was in his shop when a boy ran in and said that H. E. Hunt, who operated a general store in the town, wished to see him at once. Pinkerton, dressed in a checkered shirt and denim overalls almost white from Joan's many washings, and barefoot as usual, walked into town to see Hunt. With the store owner when Pinkerton arrived was I. C. Bosworth, another village store owner. Hunt soon explained to Pinkerton why they wanted to see him; they wanted him to do "a little job in the detective line."

"Detective line!" Pinkerton said with a laugh. "My line is the cooper business. What do I know about that sort of thing?"

"You helped to break up the 'coney men' and horse thieves on Bogus Island," Hunt said. "We're sure you can do work of this sort if you only will."

Hunt explained that they were sure a counterfeiter was in the village, but admitted they had no evidence, only their suspicions, which had been aroused when a well-dressed stranger rode into the settlement and asked directions to Old Man Crane's place. Pinkerton knew Crane by reputation. He lived in Libertyville, in adjoining Lake County, about thirty-five miles away. For a long time he had been suspected of distributing worthless money along the frontier. Sheriff Dearborn had questioned Crane several times, and searched his old farmhouse, but without finding any evidence of his alleged counterfeiting.

The country was flooded with "wildcat" money at the time, and the only scrip the settlements trusted was "George Smith's money," the currency of the Wisconsin Marine and Fire Insurance Company, owned by George Smith, one of the most famous frontier bankers. Smith was noted for his toughness, shrewdness, and integrity, and his money was in demand everywhere. However, his bills were simple and easily counterfeited. As Hunt told Pinkerton, at least two counterfeit Smith ten-dollar bills had been passed in the settlement.

"Ten-dollar bills!" Pinkerton explained. "How would I know they were counterfeit? I never saw a ten-dollar bill in my whole life."

Hunt went behind the counter of his store and returned with a bill. Pinkerton studied it and returned it.

"What am I to do?" he asked.

"Do anything," Hunt urged him, "but there's no time to lose; this man is down at Eaton Walker's harness shop, having his saddle repaired."

Pinkerton, shoeless and in overalls, strolled into Walker's shop. The saddlemaker was sitting on a bench. He nodded to Pinkerton, and went on working. Hitched outside was a sleek roan. After Walker had repaired the saddle, he sent a boy to the local tavern to notify the owner. When he appeared, Pinkerton went outside and casually patted the horse. Out of the corner of his eye, he ticked off the stranger's description; about sixty-five, gray-haired, swarthy complexion, keen gray eyes, and a plain gold ring on his left hand.

The roan was saddled, and the stranger mounted. He eyed Pinkerton for a moment, then bent over and asked if he knew the direction "to Old Man Crane's house." Pinkerton gave him detailed instructions, and added in a low voice that as far as he was concerned Crane was a man who certainly could be relied on: "As good as cheese," as he put it. This led to a cautious conversation about a gunsmith in Elgin. When Pinkerton said he knew the smith, the rider asked the young cooper to meet him in a ravine just outside Dundee.

That afternoon Pinkerton and the stranger met again. He closely questioned Pinkerton, who decided there was no sense in lying—the man could easily ascertain the facts from a town loafer—and told him that he had been working at the cooperage for the last few years but that, with hard money not easy to find, he was looking for something that would bring in cash, "a good scheme."

The horseman identified himself as John Craig, a farmer from Fairfield, Vermont. He and Old Man Crane, he explained, had "done a great deal of business together."

As he and Pinkerton sat in the grassy ravine, mutually suspicious, Craig asked sharp questions, with Pinkerton playing the role of a man not averse to earning a safe, if crooked, dollar. Finally Craig agreed to give Pinkerton fifty $10 bills for 25 percent cash. The meeting was to take place in the unfinished Elgin Academy on a hill overlooking East Elgin. Pinkerton walked the five miles to Dundee, where Hunt and Bosworth gathered the money to pay Craig for the counterfeit bills. That same afternoon, in the rough basement of the academy, Pinkerton, still barefoot, gave Craig $125. The cautious counterfeiter asked Pinkerton to leave the basement for a few minutes, and when the young cooper returned he found the fraudulent bills under a rock.

Because Pinkerton knew the bills had to be found on Craig when he was arrested, he made another date to make a bigger purchase in Chicago. There Craig was arrested by Pinkerton and a Cook County deputy sheriff. A few weeks later the cooper-turned-detective had his first experience with official corruption. Craig was turned over to the Kane County authorities for trial and indicted on Pinkerton's grand jury testimony, but he escaped from the local jail, "leaving behind a certain law officer much richer than he had been," as Pinkerton recalled.

Back in Dundee, Pinkerton discovered that the righteous have responsibilities. The two village merchants, Hunt and Bosworth, told Pinkerton it was his duty to go to Chicago and demand that George Smith, the banker, pay Pinkerton's expenses.

Pinkerton, boots polished, his pants and shirt ironed by Joan, rode into Chicago. After waiting for some time in an anteroom of the bank, Pinkerton was admitted to Smith's office. The banker listened to Pinkerton's story, then leaned forward in his chair.

"Have ye nae mair to say?"

"Not anything," Pinkerton replied.

"Then I've just this tae speak: ye was not authorized tae do this wark, and ye have nae right t' a cent. I'll pay this, I'll pay this; but mind ye noo," and Pinkerton remembered how Smith shook his finger at him "in no pleasant way," then continued, "if ye ever do work for me ag'in that ye have nae authorization for, ye'll get ne'er a penny, ne'er a penny."

Smith paid Pinkerton, but he also gave him his first lesson in business: First get a contract or an agreement before you undertake an assignment.[1]

It was a lesson Pinkerton never forgot.

CHAPTER 3

The Frontier Abolitionist and the Move to Chicago

After the arrest of John Craig, life was never the same in the one-story frame building that housed Pinkerton's cooperage and living quarters. As Pinkerton recalled, "The country being new and great sensations scarce, the affair was in everybody's mouth, and I suddenly found myself called upon from every quarter to undertake matters requiring detective skill." One of the "matters" was the post of deputy sheriff of Kane County. When Sheriff Dearborn offered him the post, Pinkerton accepted immediately. At a time when law enforcement on the frontier was haphazard or incompetent, Pinkerton's tenacity and integrity were impressive. He still maintained his cooperage, laying aside his tools only to join Dearborn in an occasional chase after a horse thief, to serve court papers, and settle trivial community disputes.

In 1844, making barrels and casks and wearing his deputy's badge became secondary to Pinkerton's abolitionist activities. He served as "agent" for Elisha Dyer, Philo Carpenter, and the other Chicago abolitionist leaders, with the Pinkerton house an important stop on the Underground Railroad from the South to Canada. That year his abolitionist activities embroiled him in a bitter church controversy. Stubborn, quick-tempered, and obstinate, Pinkerton's approach was typical: he waded into the fight, figuratively sending deacons and church elders sprawling in all directions.

19

The controversy was both ludicrous and serious; Pinkerton, a teetotaler, was accused by Elder M. L. Wisner, pastor of the Dundee Baptist Church, of atheism and selling "ardent spirits." [1] The faded pages of the old "Church Book" in Dundee give a hint of the story, which has never been told before. Years prior to the arrival of Pinkerton, the Baptists of Dundee had organized their church at the farmhouse of a settler from New England. The original congregation was made up chiefly of these pioneers from the East, plus a few of the Scotch families who retained their Presbyterian faith for a time, then joined the Congregationalists. The New England members were of the element of the church known at the time as "general" Baptists, who believed in universal salvation as against those of their church brethren who limited the hope of heaven to the baptized in their own flock. The old "Church Book" reveals many instances wherein members accused of violations of strict frontier denominational beliefs were placed on "trial," exonerated, or officially rebuked as a matter of regular church discipline.

Some of the violations or accusations were breaches of orthodoxy, such as gossiping about church sisters, the slandering of or quarreling with one's neighbors of the same church. "Ardent spirits" were the cause of many of these churchly judicial sessions. The church members put on trial humbly accepted the verdicts of the jury of church elders—that is, until the tough young deputy of Kane County was tagged by Pastor Wisner for having a too liberal religious philosophy for the "general" Baptists of Dundee.

While there were churchly rumblings about young Pinkerton, who drove to Sunday services with Joan in a farm wagon, nothing came out in the open until the spring of 1847, when Pinkerton was a candidate in Kane County of the Abolitionist Party. What the office was for is not known, but it probably was for sheriff. The frontier was shocked one day to read a letter in the *Western Citizen,* a Kane County newspaper published in Batavia, challenging Pinkerton's fitness for public office. The letter was signed by Pinkerton's pastor, Elder Wisner. The following issue of the paper published a "collective protest" against the pastor's article, signed by a number of young Scots. There was nothing left for Wisner to do except file charges against Pinkerton and demand that he be put on trial in the Dundee Baptist Church.

The religious storm that followed shook the frontier from Dundee to Detroit. Supporting Pinkerton were the young Scots who had settled in Dundee; on the pastor's side were the older, more conservative, New England settlers. Then Wisner made additional charges that Pinkerton was using "ardent spirits." Pinkerton, with his low boiling point, was outraged. He quickly organized a committee and sent messengers to the Scots in Elgin, Detroit, and Crystal Lake to gather witnesses who could testify he had never tasted liquor, had never allowed it in his house, and had never smoked.

But Pinkerton was well aware that Wisner's charges were superficial: The growing issue of slavery that would someday divide his church and his adopted country was beginning to split families, friends, and business partners in the frontier settlements.

After several weeks of heated sessions in the beautiful little church of Dundee—one session was devoted to the charge that Pinkerton had circulated a book that stated Christ was an illegitimate child—a jury of church elders "vindicated" Elder Wisner. The verdict led to the withdrawal of Pinkerton and a number of Scots from the Dundee congregation. Soon similar arguments and church trials, essentially over abolitionism, would split the American Baptist Church into its northern and southern identities. The trial and subsequent withdrawal of Pinkerton and his neighbors disrupted life in the pastoral settlement along the river. Old friends looked away when they passed; women no longer paused to exchange the latest bits of gossip; and there was a strained formality even in business dealings.

Pinkerton became restless. The pettiness, trivialities, and frontier feuds were frustrating to the aggressive, ambitious Scot; even running the cooperage, so important a few years ago, had become monotonous. His family was growing; he now had a son, named William after his father, and his business was increasing, but Pinkerton was restless. Dundee was still quiet and beautiful, but could not be compared with Chicago, the magic city the whole frontier was talking about. In his cooperage Pinkerton heard stories of the expanding railroads, the mushrooming business houses, the unbelievable number of homes that were being built, the fleet of ships lining the lake shores. He heard such tales from drovers, lumber freighters, farmers returning from delivering their wheat, and lonely horsemen. Robbie Fergus was also writing brief letters glowing with descriptions of the city. He told Pinkerton he now had a partner, and more business than they could handle.

The pastoral serenity, the long, monotonous days of making barrels and casks, were beginning to make Pinkerton moody and irritable. Joan, with a woman's intuition, phrased it best when, recalling those days in Dundee, she added, almost wistfully, "They were bonnie days, but Allan was a restless one."

When William L. Church, Sheriff of Cook County, offered Pinkerton a deputyship, the Scot accepted—"immediately," as he said. He sold his cooperage, packed their household goods on a wagon, and left for Chicago. Though Dundee, despite that bitter year, would always remain in his memory, Pinkerton had little time for romance and sentimentality. Hard-nosed practicality was more to his bent.[2]

CHAPTER 4

Chicago and the Beginning of the Agency, 1850-1860

The Chicago that Pinkerton entered a short time after he and Joan left Dundee had changed enormously from the crude settlement they remembered. The muddy streets were now crowded with people. Ther were new hotels, new churches, new theatres.

As Pinkerton's wagon lurched down the rutted streets with Joan hanging onto her seat, the afternoon was filled with the sound of sawing, hammering, and the shouts of workmen. With a woman's eye, Joan recalled the striped buntings hanging from the dry-goods shops; Pinkerton, the born detective, studied the business signs and the rough, tough faces he saw in passing. As Joseph Jefferson, the famous actor, wrote that year, there were outlaws of every description in Chicago, "white, black and red," and the rate of crime was increasing daily. Canvas-covered freighters rumbled in at more than two hundred a day, all loaded with wheat for the elevators that lined the shores of the lake, built to store the grain until the spring arrival of the endless number of barges, schooners, and brigs. When Pinkerton arrived, more than a million bushels a year were stored. There were numerous abattoirs for hogs and cattle that had been driven across the grassy prairies. Pork and beef were now being sent to all parts of the country and as far as London. Hundreds of stores and small businesses were established along Lake and Clark streets, together with lumberyards, shipyards, and warehouses.

Later, Bobbie Fergus would proudly boast to Pinkerton that the city now had more than sixteen thousand residents.[1]

Pinkerton and Joan stayed with Fergus until they found their own home, the usual clapboard frame house, painted white, which the carpenters called "balloons" because of the swiftness with which they were erected. On the North Side were the red brick homes of the gentry, each separated by brick walls and gardens. The social life of the city was a mélange of the "flippery" of the East, backwoods crudities, New England ideals, education, and religion, and frontier ribaldry.

Pinkerton took to Chicago. Evidently Church found him satisfactory, because he recommended that he be kept on when C. P. Bradley took over as sheriff. Pinkerton, with his intense drive, ambition, and aggressiveness, soon established a reputation as an honest, tough lawman, and about 1849, newly elected Mayor Boone appointed Allan Pinkerton as Chicago's first detective. The husky, young Scot soon made a reputation with his fists and by his defiance of armed thugs, and acquired a number of enemies. There were several attempts on his life, and one almost succeeded. On a September evening in 1853, he was walking up Clark Street to his Adams Street home when a gunman fired at him from out of the darkness. Fortunately, Pinkerton had a habit of putting his left hand behind him, under his coat, as he walked along, deep in thought.

The Chicago *Daily Democratic Press* reported: "The pistol was of large calibre, heavily loaded and discharged so near that Mr. Pinkerton's coat was put on fire. Two slugs shattered the bone five inches from the wrist and passed along the bone to the elbow where they were cut out by a surgeon together with pieces of his coat." The newspaper also praised Pinkerton as Chicago's most efficient and courageous law officer, one who had done a great deal in keeping the community free of thugs and killers "who are on the run." [2]

Pinkerton stayed on as Chicago's sole detective for a year, resigning, as he later recalled, "because of political interference." He was not without a badge for long. The United States Post Office appointed him Special United States Mail Agent to solve a series of post office thefts and robberies plaguing Chicago.

The Postmaster of Chicago and the office of the Postmaster General in Washington had been deluged with complaints from Midwestern business firms that bank drafts and postal money orders sent to them had never arrived. Pinkerton employed the technique he had used in obtaining the evidence against Craig the counterfeiter—he played a role.

Pinkerton arranged to be hired as a clerk in the Chicago Post Office. After several weeks of tossing mailbags and loading mail cars, he discovered that a young clerk, Theodore Dennison, had a brother, Perry, who had once been arrested for pilfering mail in another city. Pinkerton, who assumed the role of a jolly, simple-minded transient, found out that the Dennisons were nephews of the postmaster. Characteristically, he included this in his first reports to Washington, which maintained an embarrassed silence.

Pinkerton finally concentrated on making the acquaintance of young Dennison, breaking the ice by observing how "swift" the clerk distributed letters and packages. One night, several days later, Dennison boasted to Pinkerton that his fingers were "so sensitive he knew when a letter contained a penny or a dollar." Pinkerton maintained a watch over Dennison from behind a mound of packages, and several times he saw the light-fingered clerk slip envelopes into his pocket.

One Saturday morning Pinkerton and a Cook County deputy arrested Dennison as he left the building. He attempted to flee but was downed by Pinkerton. After he had been booked and his family connections revealed, the postmaster grimly told Pinkerton he had better produce evidence to support his charges. Pinkerton and two deputies searched Dennison's room in a boardinghouse. Hours were spent carefully examining beds and chairs, ripping up the carpet and even the floorboards. As the *Press* reported: "The search was nearly concluded without finding any trace of Dennison's crimes when Officer Pinkerton decided to continue the search and took the pictures from the walls. On removal of the backs, several bank bills, to the amount of $3,738 were found concealed, many of them of large denominations." The account pointed out that the picture of the Virgin Mary held the highest amount, $1,503.

The solution of the robbery and the prominence of the defendant caused a sensation in Chicago. Its importance was emphasized when W. J. Brown, United States General Agent of the Postal Service, was sent from Washington by the Postmaster General to help Pinkerton obtain a confession in the delicate case. But by the time Brown arrived, Pinkerton already had the signed confession.

As the *Press* reported: "For three weeks Mr. Pinkerton scarcely has had repose in the devotion with which he has followed up the criminals. Complaint after complaint poured into the department and call after call came from Washington to Pinkerton to redouble his efforts, until body and brain were nearly exhausted. As a detective, Mr. Pinkerton has no superior, and we doubt if he has any equal in this country."

In the early 1850's, Pinkerton decided to open his own private detective agency. It was becoming clear to the ambitious, hardworking detective that there were fertile fields for an honest, dedicated law officer in this expanding city and on the frontier. Chicago was emerging from its awkward stage; it was now an impressive prairie metropolis whose grain towers and brawling steers cast impressive shadows across the land as the mighty gateway to the West. The strands of the Illinois Central and Rock Island would soon tie into an iron knot to grip the Midwest to Chicago. Mile-long columns of wagons creaking under their load of grain stretched along the shore, waiting to unload in the elevators. Cattle and hogs in their pens made the nights hideous with their bawling. The white "balloon" houses were going up so rapidly that painters with dripping brushes worked on the heels of the carpenters. Everywhere was exuberance of life—hustle and bustle, new faces, new people, more business.

And with the wealth were more criminals. Warehouses were robbed. The new express companies reported that the doors of their iron cars were broken and that cash, bonds, and merchandise had been taken. There were reports of outlaws boarding trains in the northern part of the state to rob and kill expressmen and passengers. The rural sheriffs were either corrupt or didn't have the experience to cope with such criminal acts; and in the cities the police were either too busy, paid off, politically dominated, or restricted by local jurisdiction in their pursuit of thieves. It was a time that begged for vigorous, honest law enforcement.

Pinkerton and a young Chicago attorney, Edward A. Rucker, formed what Pinkerton called the North-Western Police Agency. The Agency insists the date was 1850, but that date is debatable. The partners opened a small office on the second floor of 89 Washington Street, on the corner of Dearborn, then the heart of the city. Branch offices were located in Wisconsin, Michigan, and Indiana. Pinkerton appears to have been the senior partner. An early letterhead reads:

> Allan Pinkerton and Edward A. Rucker, under the style of Pinkerton & Co., have established an agency at Chicago, Illinois for the purpose of transacting a General Detective Police Business in Illinois, Wisconsin, Michigan and Indiana; and will attend to the investigation and depredation, frauds and criminal offenses; the detection of offenders, procuring arrests and convictions, apprehension or return of fugitives from justice, or bail; recovering lost or stolen property, obtaining information, etc.

We know little of Rucker; newspaper accounts describe him as "well-known attorney of Chicago," the usual flowery description accorded to every attorney, law officer, merchant or railroad man of the time who agreed to grant an interview. In one of his early books Pinkerton also lists Rucker as Clerk of the Cook County Court. Tradition has Rucker leaving after a year, but an 1856 letter by Pinkerton is written on stationery bearing Rucker's name. But Attorney Rucker, partner or not, soon disappeared. He remains only a name on a yellowing letterhead.[3]

Pinkerton's firm was not the first private detective agency in the world as some historians have insisted. Eugene Francois Vidocq, Europe's most celebrated detective, founded his Bureau des Renseignements—Information Office—in 1832. In the United States, two St. Louis police officers opened an agency when Pinkerton was still working his Dundee cooperage and assisting the Kane County sheriff to catch counterfeiters. On June 5, 1846, the St. Louis newspaper announced that "Mr. McDonough, late captain of the city guard, and Mr. Breuil, late lieutenant of the same, have established an independent police." The long account described McDonough as "so well known in the community that it is almost useless to say anything about him . . . he has been engaged for some years in ferreting out rogues." Breuil was called "an efficient and assiduous officer." The newspaper also indicated that McDonough and Breuil were not the first of their kind: "This kind of police has been tried in nearly all the Eastern cities and has been found to be much more efficient than the regularly appointed police."

However, a search of the major newspapers of the Eastern cities of the time failed to produce any mention of private police or detective agencies. The St. Louis newspaper may have been referring to the private-guard service established in Boston as early as 1821 after the city watchmen failed to halt a series of burglaries. In time these guards came to be known as "specials," a term still in use.

Pinkerton founded his agency at a time when the public was admiring the exploits of the private detective. Stories of crime chasing were nationally popular in nineteenth-century American literature; the detective was always pictured as the hero. The best known and the most sensational of the time was Vidocq's memoirs, the French detective who had risen from a police informer to found the Sûreté in 1811. Originally published in France in 1829, Vidocq's memoirs were issued in many editions in the United States and Great Britain. He was the first to popularize the slogan "set a thief to catch a thief"—not a new technique to American lawmen who had been giving protection to professional criminals in exchange for information and assistance since the 1820's. The penny press—"the penny dreadfuls"—founded in Boston in 1831 and read and reread in the word-hungry rural and frontier sections helped to establish the popular image of the private detective as relentless, resourceful, and courageous. The *Police Gazette,* founded in 1845, constantly glorified the "Eye"—the early Pinkertons—in its accounts of outlaws and celebrated criminals of the Victorian age.

However, Pinkerton played a far more important role in his country's history than did Vidocq; the Frenchman was occupied all his life with crime and criminals, whereas the Pinkertons were an important factor in the social growth of the United States. At the time that Pinkerton formed his Agency, the nation's rural law enforcement consisted of entrepreneurs, bounty hunters, rural marshals, and sheriffs with casual deputies. Big-city police departments were mostly undermanned, politically dominated, and usually corrupt. There was no centralized, federal police agency. Urban police, in addition to incompetence and corruption, were faced with jealously guarded jurisdictional boundaries of local, county, and state governments. For example, the effectiveness of the Philadelphia police was seriously hampered because they could not pursue the numerous thieves and robbers who emerged from their hiding places, then robbed, looted, and fled. The police were forced to stop at a county line. In addition, the railroads of America had far outstripped the law of the land. Unlike Canada, New Zealand, and Australia, which first introduced federal, centralized law to their frontiers, the railroad lines and public carriers of America, like the express companies of the 1840's and 1850's, had spread rapidly across America's open frontiers long before the law was firmly established to protect their property and the communities they had produced. Robbery, assault, and murder were commonplace along the Mississippi, especially in New Orleans. Local gangs were beginning to prey on the Illinois Central and its affiliate railroads.

What was needed at the time to fill the niche between the lack of rural law and the incompetence of corrupt urban law-enforcement organizations, was a private police force that could move across local, county, and even state boundaries in the pursuit of criminals. This is what Pinkerton established. Like Vidocq, Pinkerton proved to be the right man at the right time. His business expanded at a rapid pace. He decided to hire eight employees, five detectives, a secretary, and a few clerks. His first employee and his most loyal was George Bangs, a tall, slender man with luxurious black sideburns. Bangs, who traced his family to the *Mayflower*, had the cold, aloof air of a successful city banker considering the loan application of an unsuccessful businessman. Bangs soon demonstrated to Pinkerton he not only possessed a precise, imaginative mind and an awesome tenacity but was also an excellent office manager. Like Pinkerton, he liked order, neatness, courtesy, Old World manners—and profit. The following year he would be the Agency's first general manager.

On one of his first trips to New York City, in 1853, Pinkerton, like most western tourists, visited the Crystal Palace. He saw the exhibits, but he was more interested in the small police force inside the hall. A young sergeant, courteous and efficient, caught Pinkerton's eye. He made inquiries about the guard, and learned that his name was Timothy Webster. Captain—later Inspector—James Leonard, one of the famous names of the early New York Police Department, who knew Pinkerton, introduced the two men. Pinkerton discovered that Webster had been born in New Haven, Sussex County, England, in 1821, and had immigrated to the United States in 1833, with his parents, to settle in Princeton, New Jersey. He told Pinkerton that he had come to New York to try for an appointment to the New York Police force but had discovered that he needed political influence. Through Leonard, a maverick on the force, and a man hated by politicians, he had obtained a job as a guard at the Palace, and was soon made a sergeant.[4]

Pinkerton, who had an excellent instinct for selecting the right people to work for him, offered Webster a job in his Agency as a detective.

Pinkerton detective George H. Bangs.   Timothy Webster. *Library of Congress*
Pinkerton's, Inc.

Webster accepted, and Pinkerton paid his fare to Chicago and told him to report to Bangs. Pinkerton had made another fine choice, as Webster would prove to be not only a fine detective but a shrewd, courageous espionage agent as well.

After Webster came two more Englishmen, Pyrce Lewis and John Scully. Lewis, a former book salesman, was among the élite of Pinkerton's early staff. He was a dapper, handsome, and intelligent man, then about twenty-five. Like Webster, he would become a superb espionage agent behind enemy lines. Scully, who had a weakness for the bottle, would play a grim and tragic role in the lives of both Webster and Lewis.

Also on Pinkerton's early staff was John H. White, who, Pinkerton said, looked more like a confidence man than like a detective; John Fox, a cheery, garrulous New Englander; a young man named Rivers who would one day jog twelve miles rather than lose sight of a suspect's carriage; and Adam Roche, a stolid, pipe-smoking German, who once worked on a lumber barge.

None of these men came from law enforcement. They were former clerks, ship officers, farmers, merchants and, in Fox's case, an expert watchmaker and repairman. Pinkerton and Bangs taught them the art of "shadowing," disguise, and playing a role. From an early account, the Chicago office at times resembled the backstage of a theatre, with Pinkerton and Bangs demonstrating to an operative ready to go out on an assignment how to act like a "greenhorn just off the boat," a bartender, horsecar conductor, or gambler. Pinkerton kept a large closet in his private office filled with various disguises. First came the preliminary facts on a case, mainly interviews and data from a client, then a conference with Bangs. When they had agreed on the role, the operative would be summoned to Pinkerton's office, given the facts and the disguise, and sent out into the field.

Pinkerton also hired the nation's first female detective. As he recalled, it was on an afternoon in 1856 when his secretary said that a young woman wished to see him about employment. When Pinkerton stood up to greet her, he saw a slender, brown-haired woman, "graceful in her movements and self possessed. Her features, although not what could be called handsome, were decidedly of an intellectual cast . . . her face was honest, which would cause one in distress instinctly to select her as a confidant. . . ."

She introduced herself as Mrs. Kate Warne, a widow, and she said very candidly she wished to become a detective. Though Pinkerton had never heard of a female detective, he leaned back in his chair and asked why she thought she could be of value. Mrs. Warne carefully detailed how she could "worm out secrets in many places to which it was impossible for male detectives to gain access."

The idea interested Pinkerton, who asked her to return the next day. He stayed up a great deal of the night mulling over the idea, and the more he thought about it, the more he liked it. When Kate appeared the next afternoon, he hired her as the nation's first female detective. A few days later he assigned her to a case, and we know from Pinkerton's recollections that "she succeeded far beyond my utmost expectations."

Kate was an extraordinary woman. She would stay with Pinkerton for years; and, as he recalled, "Mrs. Warne never let me down."

Pinkerton was determined that the public view his firm as a profession rather than as a business. He was the Principal or Founder, and his investigators "operatives" rather than detectives, which in those times had the connotation of a palm extended to be greased. His office staff was neat and courteous. A client was expected to produce credentials, identification, and just cause before Pinkerton would sit down for an interview. If the case was accepted, a "journal" was prepared. This was the basic record, containing the client's problems and requirements, together with the detailed plan of operation from which the fieldman was instructed. The procedure is virtually the same today.[5]

Now that his agency was started, Pinkerton decided he would operate only under a code of ethics. He closeted himself in his office for a few days, then turned a sheaf of foolscap over to his secretary, who copied the pages in the beautiful copperplate handwriting of the time. Pinkerton's *General Principles* are still in existence, not only as a historical document but also as the guide rules for the modern Agency. Time and experience have added certain rules, but none of the original ones have been relaxed.

The Agency will not represent a defendant in a criminal case except with the knowledge and consent of the prosecutor; they will not shadow jurors or investigate public officials in the performance of their duties, or trade-union officers or members in their lawful union activities; they will not accept employment from one political party against another; they will not report union meetings unless the meetings are open to the public without restriction; they will not work for vice crusaders; they will not accept contingent fees, gratuities, or rewards. The Agency will never investigate the morals of a woman unless in connection with another crime, nor will it handle cases of divorce or of a scandalous nature. These were and still are Pinkerton's original rules.

In describing the role of the detective in American society as a "high and honorable calling," Pinkerton warned that the criminals of the 1850's were "powerful of mind and strong of will, who if they had devoted themselves to honest pursuits would undoubtedly have become members of honorable society." The detectives who had to gather the evidence and arrest these criminals, Pinkerton wrote, "must be men of high order of mind and must possess clean, honest, comprehensive understanding, force of will and vigor of body." Criminals, he insisted, eventually reveal their secrets, and a detective must have the necessary experience and judgment of human nature to "know the criminal in his weakest moment and force from him, through sympathy and confidence, the secret which devours him."

Pinkerton always maintained an unshakable confidence in his theory that a detective of "considerable intellectual power and knowledge of human nature as will give him a quick insight into character" would crack any criminal.

It was a question of playing a role, "acting it out to the life," as he put it, as he probed and analyzed the character of the man he was attempting to bring to justice.

One iron-strong philosophy ran through all the yellowing pages: "the ends justify the means, if the ends being for the accomplishment of Justice."

There were no high court rulings in the 1850's restricting the gathering of evidence, but Pinkerton warned his staff never to use statements or testimony of witnesses or defendants who were intoxicated. "Such statements when brought into court, tend to shake the strength of evidence," he wrote, "and it is not considered that such statements are as much entitled to reliance as those drawn from sober moments!"

For all his hate and contempt for crime and criminals, Pinkerton's original principles insisted that his staff, once they brought the criminal to jail, do all in their power to elevate and enable him, because sometime in the future he most probably will again come out into the world and take the chances of life. If Criminals are treated as men, capable of moral reform and elevation, if they were instructed in their duties and responsibilities—as good citizens—and better still, perhaps, if they could be taught some useful handicraft, whereby they might secure an honest livelihood when they return to society and maintain an honest and reputable character; no one can calculate the great service that would thereby be rendered to them and to humanity. Unfortunately, under our present system this is too little thought of.

The young Scot, a few years separated from the barefooted immigrant cooper, was now a strange combination of the puritanical manhunter and twentieth-century criminologist.

Pinkerton's success in the next few years was meteoric. As he wrote to his old friend Henry Hunt, the Dundee shopkeeper, "I am overwhelmed with business."[6]

It has become almost commonplace for historians to credit Pinkerton's success in Chicago to his friendship with George Brinton McClellan, later his wartime commander. While his association with McClellan, who was vice-president of the Illinois Central, was clearly advantageous, the voluminous archives of the line reveal that Pinkerton was protecting the railroad two years *before* McClellan appeared in Chicago. The never-before published contract between Pinkerton and the Illinois Central, signed on February 1, 1855, shows the detective was guarding the line rolling stock as early as 1854, at a yearly retainer of $10,000, a large sum at the time. The agreement, a landmark in the history of American business, may have been the first time a railroad had contracted with a private agency for police protection. The contract also reveals that in addition to the Illinois Central, Pinkerton protected the Michigan Central, Michigan Southern and Northern Indiana, Chicago and Galena Union, Chicago and Rock Island, Chicago, Burlington & Quincy railroads.

It was an enormous undertaking for an infant business. Pinkerton had to expand his operations to cover most of the midwestern frontier and be "devoted to the service and business of these corporations, even to the exclusion of all other business if necessary."

The railroads, however, apparently underwrote the expenses for the expansion of Pinkerton's Agency. As a clause pointed out, the railroads "have severally agreed to guarantee and pay to said Pinkerton and Co. the several sums hereinafter specified for the first year, to aid them in organizing and putting into effective operation the said Agency."

The annual retainer was $10,000: Michigan Central, $2,000; Michigan Southern and Northern Indiana, $2,000; Chicago and Galena Union,

$2,000; Illinois Central, $2,000; Chicago and Rock Island, $1,000; Chicago, Burlington & Quincy, $1,000.

Under the contract Pinkerton agreed to have on hand, in Chicago,

> a sufficient number of reliable, active and experienced assistants, to enable them to respond to the call of any; or either of the said companies without delay; and in case the business of either of them shall be of an unusually urgent character, and needing either more assistants or those having different qualifications than those then in their employ, they shall procure as soon as practical as many as may be needed . . . they are to give their personal attention to the investigation of the preliminary facts and maturing and adopting the plan of action . . .

The contract also permitted Pinkerton to continue as "mail agent" for the United States Post Office, investigating thefts and pilferage from mail cars and post offices in the Midwest. The contract agreed that "calls of the said department [Post Office] are to stand of the same class and priority or preference as those of said companies."

The services of Pinkerton's Agency were divided into three classes:

> according to their skills and abilities, having in view also the personal risk of the employment, and the charges for the first class, besides necessary expenses and disbursements shall not exceed ten dollars a day; the second class not to exceed seven dollars per day; and the third not over three and a half dollars per day. For such special assistants or special and sudden exigencies may render necessary, there shall be charged what they have to pay therefore, and a reasonable sum for their personal supervision of them when necessary.[7]

Free railroad passes and blank tickets were also issued to Pinkerton and his men. In July of that year the express car—later the target of frontier outlaw gangs from 1866 to the turn of the century—was born in the West when the American Express Company signed a contract with the Illinois Central and Chicago and Galena railroads to hire sections of their baggage cars to ship "express material." Under the contract, 128 feet of each baggage car leaving Chicago was partitioned "and equipped with a door in each side of suitable size to admit convenient loading and unloading merchandise and a stove for warming the same in cold weather."

The express company agreed to pay $324 a month to the Galena line and $180 to the Illinois Central for the use of the cars. However, this was not an added responsibility for Pinkerton; under the agreement American had to assume "all risks of injury and damage of any kind arising from any cause to their messenger or agents, and also all losses of bank bills, gold and silver coins and jewelry and valuable papers in said trains."

Articles of Agreement, made this first day of February 1855, between Allan Pinkerton & Co of the one part, and the *Michigan Central Railroad Company,* the *Michigan Southern Railroad & Northern Indiana Railroad Companies,* the *Illinois Central Railroad Company,* the *Chicago and Galena Union Railroad Company,* the *Chicago & Rock Island Railroad Company,* the *Chicago Burlington and Quincy Railroad Company,*

Witnesseth, whereas, the said Pinkerton and Company propose to establish a Police Agency, the office of which is to be at Chicago, but which is to operate in the neighbouring States; and whereas it is to be primarily and principally devoted to the service and business of the above named companies, (even to the exclusion of all other business if necessary to the prompt and efficient performance of their business); and whereas, in consideration thereof the said Compa-

Contract between the Illinois Central R.R. Company (and other railroads) and Pinkerton & Co. *Chicago Historical Society*

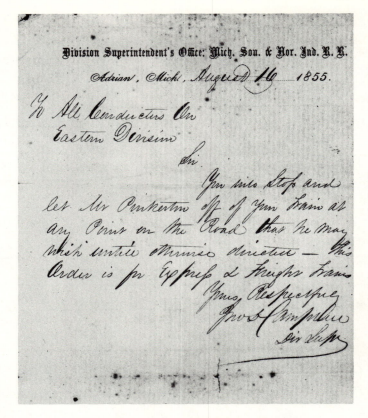

Some of Allan Pinkerton's pre-Civil War railroad passes.

Eventually American Express also became a client of Pinkerton's, not under an exclusive contract such as he would have with the Adams company in the East, but on individual cases.

Letters and reports in the vast historical archives of the Illinois Central disclose the extent of the lawlessness prevailing in sections of the frontier where the lines were extending their tracks. Payrolls were stolen and foremen brutally beaten by outlaw bands. Communities became helpless with the breakdown of local law enforcement either through corruption, fear, or sympathy with the desperadoes. One particularly brutal murder of a superintendent near La Salle, Illinois, may have prompted the railroad officials to seek outside protection for its property and employees.

An assistant superintendent's report, delivered to the president's office in Chicago, vividly describes how a band of outlaws had besieged a construction camp. Some of the workers fled or were killed, until the superintendent and his clerk were forced to take shelter in a wooden shack where they traded shots with the gang for hours. The outlaws, using a telegraph pole, smashed in the door. The wounded clerk got away while the superintendent shot his way through to a horse and rode to a nearby barn. The gang followed and stormed the barn. The superintendent, ammunition exhausted and severely wounded, was beaten to death and his body dragged about the yard.

The report reads:

> The sheriff is here today but is so completely frustrated and frightened that he can do nothing. I have advised him and all parties concerned to muster a good force in the morning and go out and clear the bluff of any vistage of them [the outlaws] and commence entirely now. . . . I have offered to lead the force and shall do all I can to get a posse that will follow. . . .

In addition to protecting the railroads, Pinkerton was also busy solving cases of fraud, murder, and counterfeiting. In 1857, through clever police work, Pinkerton and Bangs arrested Jules Imbert, a famous French forger. Since the thief had been looting the Belmonts and other New York financiers, the feat brought Pinkerton a great deal more than local fame.

In January of that same year, George Brinton McClellan, the Illinois Central's new vice-president and engineer in chief appeared. From the beginning, there was an immediate rapport between the dashing West Pointer and the detective. McClellan's letter books of the late 1850's show that he and Pinkerton held many meetings with William Henry Osborn, the line's president, discussing methods of expanding protection for the line. On December 2, 1858, McClellan was asking Pinkerton to assign "a smart detective to hunt out the sundry small thefts of segars, wines, etc." that occurred along the line. The line's attorney, a tall, rawboned, wryly humorous man from Springfield, also had met Pinkerton. His name was Abraham Lincoln.

The idea of a uniformed guard force was probably growing in Pinkerton's mind, for we find George Power, secretary to McClellan, writing to Pinkerton on December 22, 1858, to commit to paper the ideas he had orally given to McClellan "for a special police force to protect the line; the number of men, expenses and general particulars."

From 1857 to the outbreak of the Civil War, and for many later years, Pinkerton and McClellan were close, socially and in business. It was one of the strangest relationships of their time: the grim, almost humorless detective from the one-room frontier cooperage and the slum tenement in Glasgow and the handsome West Pointer, an observer in the Crimea, a brilliant engineer, and a friend of the great and near great. The motivation for Pinkerton's lasting loyalty and affection was probably very simple: McClellan represented everything Pinkerton ever wanted.

Pinkerton's fervent loyalty and affection for McClellan are sometimes bewildering because McClellan's political beliefs were poles apart from Pinkerton's. This relationship points up the inconsistency in his character. There were times when Pinkerton seemed two men, each with his own belief and philosophy. One could embrace the ideas of the most violent of the abolitionists, while the other could admire and form intimate friendships with financiers and railroad executives who were certainly never the champions of the slaves. The approaching war would bring this duality of Pinkerton's character into startling relief.

CHAPTER 5
Allan Pinkerton and John Brown

During these busy, formative years of building his business, Pinkerton was away from home for long periods, chasing bank robbers, tracing missing persons, solving murders, supervising his growing guard and security force, and personally attending to every trivial office detail. It was his wife, Joan, who managed the large family in the clapboard house on Adams Street, between Fifth and Franklin streets.

They now had another son and daughter—Robert and his twin sister, Joan, who inherited her mother's name, dark beauty, and her father's iron will and Emersonian independence, which were typical of all Pinkertons. Although the records are vague, and Pinkerton never mentioned it in his letters, he had brought his mother and brother, Robert, to the United States to live with him. Burial records show that death and tragedy were no strangers to the Pinkerton family in those years. In 1854, Pinkerton's mother and a two-year-old daughter, Mary, died. Two years later another daughter, seven-year-old Joanna, was fatally stricken with a fever. Another young daughter, named after Pinkerton's mother and called Belle by the family, was ill most of the time, and required her mother's constant care.

Many years later, in a moving letter to his wife, Pinkerton recalled her deep grief and fortitude of those bitter days. He described her as a woman of great courage and enormous devotion to her family. He might have added that she was also a woman of infinite patience. In addition to the duties and responsibilities of raising her family almost singlehandedly, she continued to hide and feed the many runaway slaves who crowded her attic, cellar, and kitchen. When prominent abolitionists were in Chicago, the house on Adams Street was one of their first stops. The free Negro leader John Jones, whom Pinkerton always called "my good friend," was a frequent visitor, as were the emissaries from John Brown and Frederick Douglass, who were assisting slaves to reach Canada. When Pinkerton wasn't home, it was Joan who took and passed on the messages of the Underground and who, when her own home was crowded, sought out neighbors, friendly to the abolitionist cause, to feed, hide, or clothe the frightened runaways.

For all his recollections "of the old happy days in Chicago," Pinkerton was a strict disciplinarian and irascible father who ran his home as he ran his business—"with an iron hand," as he once informed a new employee. He wrote: "I must get my way in all things . . . if I am right, I am right, if I am wrong I will take the consequences."

In his books and newspaper interviews, Pinkerton tried to create the image of a father constantly at the beck and call of his family, but his early correspondence shows that he devoted almost every working hour in the late 1850's to his business and his abolitionist activities.

He was intensely self-disciplined, his daily regimen almost military. He was in bed early and up before sunrise; a cold bath and a brisk walk followed, "and I was dictating to my secretary by seven." He was struggling to control an expanding business, the recruiting of new operatives —he was precise in their qualifications—checking bills, expenses, retaining fees, new contracts, and "raising business," as he called it, in the developing parts of the country.

Joan appears to have been a careful mother and obedient wife who looked up to her husband and accepted his will without question. In later years, tension and conflict would disrupt the household as Pinkerton's children rebelled against his domestic tyranny, but in the late 1850's, when the children were small, there were peace and harmony on Adams Street, with only the usual eruptions of a growing family.

By 1858, Pinkerton was one of the most rabid abolitionists in Chicago. The house on Adams Street now held more slaves than had the Dundee cooperage. As Lloyd Lewis observed: "While Pinkerton's right hand caught lawbreakers, his left hand broke the law. But his conscience was, of course, clear as that of any Quaker patriot out on the long Underground route that ran to the Ohio and Mississippi Rivers."[1]

Pinkerton didn't leave behind an inspirational tract or philosophical pamphlet detailing his motives, but there is little doubt he was impelled by memories of the gaunt-faced, starving men and women who had marched with him that long-ago rainy day into the square of Monmouth, beneath the muskets of the king's troops.

As he said in *Spy of the Rebellion*: "I detested slavery. . . . This institution of human bondage always reclined [*sic*] my earnest opposition . . . believing it to be a curse to the American nation. . . ."

John Brown with his blazing blue-gray eyes, John Henry Kagi, the violent pamphleteer and perhaps the best educated of Brown's followers, and Aaron Dwight Stevens, the soldier of fortune who died on the gallows with Brown, were no strangers to the Pinkerton household. By 1855, Brown was well known through the "Pottawatomie Massacre," in which his followers cold-bloodedly killed five proslavery settlers in retaliation for the killing of five free-state men. In August of that same year, Brown, with a small number of supporters, fought a bloody engagement with a superior proslavery force at Osawatomie. In the winter of 1859, Pinkerton played an important and little-known role in one of the most dramatic incidents in the life of the Middle Border zealot.

It was Brown's celebrated Missouri slave raid, the "war into Africa," as he called it. Brown, who had adopted the name of Shubel Morgan, let two bands into Missouri. After they had crossed the border, he took command of one, Stevens the other. Horse thieves and "adventurers" in his party liberated not only slaves but also watches and jewels, horses, oxen, saddles, and provisions. During the raid, Stevens killed a prominent farmer and drove off his stock of horses and wagons.

The murder of the elderly farmer shocked the frontier, with both Kansas and Missouri newspapers denouncing Brown and Stevens as bandits. Vacillating President Buchanan finally placed a reward of $250 on Brown's head, and the Missouri legislature matched the sum.[2]

In January, 1859, Brown led a wagon train with eleven slaves escorted by a small party of armed followers on the long road to Canada, where they had established a "Provisional Constitution and Ordinances for the People of the United States," with eleven white and thirty-five Negro followers. It was a bitter journey across the windswept frozen prairies. One of his men recalled, the shoes of the "old man," as they called Brown, fell apart, and his hands and fingers were frozen. They bluffed their way past the Topeka posses, the famous "Battle of the Spurs," swam swollen creeks and rivers, and staggered at last into Tabor, Iowa. The settlement had always been friendly to Brown, but the killing by Stevens and reports of Brown's men stealing horses on their raids—the cardinal sin of the frontier—had changed the settlers' attitude. Brown found "a curious but cold crowd to meet him." They moved on. In Iowa City a posse rode in to find "that damned nigger thief from Kansas," but Brown, Stevens, and Kagi had slipped out with the slaves. At Springdale, when they heard another posse was approaching, Stevens begged Brown to stay and fight, insisting, "Just give me a house and I'll defend them against forty." Some of the young Quakers of Springdale, forgetting they were peace-loving, loaded their rifles and rode out with Stevens to meet the posse, which fled when they heard Brown's men were ready to fight and die for the eleven slaves hidden in the tiny settlement.

The wagon train creaked across the frontier that January and February. In early March, Kagi, Stevens, and Brown put the slaves in a boxcar that a "conniving" railroad agent hooked to the Chicago train. At 4:30 A.M., on March 11, 1859, Brown, Kagi, and Stevens, followed by the slaves, now numbering twelve—a child had been born on the journey—walked up Adams Street and banged on Pinkerton's front door.

Pinkerton, a revolver in one hand, came down and opened the door. They weren't strangers, and there wasn't any need for explanations; Pinkerton herded the slaves into his kitchen, where his wife gave them breakfast. Within an hour, Pinkerton had "distributed the slaves and got them under cover." The "free Negro" John Jones took in Brown, while Stevens and Kagi stayed at the Pinkerton house. When Brown told Pinkerton he was "without a dollar" and needed money, the detective assured him he would raise the money to get the slaves to Canada.

Later that same morning Pinkerton called at the home of Jones. The Negro leader's wife recalled how Brown greeted the detective "warmly, more than that, brother to brother." As he was leaving, Pinkerton told Jones and Brown: "There is a Democratic meeting in the city today. I'll go down and make them give me enough money to send you and these slaves to Canada."

The meeting was the Chicago Judiciary Convention, with the main item on the morning's agenda the selection of a candidate for Cook County circuit judge. Pinkerton made up a "subscription list," as he called it, and visited Colonel C. G. Hammond, superintendent of the Illinois Central, "also a good friend of the colored people." Pinkerton told Hammond that Brown and a party of slaves were in town and that he "must see them through to Canada and what is to be done must be done quickly." Hammond agreed to have a railroad car ready at the Chicago depot at 4:45 P.M., but he told Pinkerton he had to supply the provisions.

The detective next visited the convention hall, sending in two friends "with my subscription list because I was too well known as being an anti-slavery man and I thought my absence from the meeting would be the best thing." The two men soon came out with the news that "the delegates refused assistance." As Pinkerton recalled: "I decided that I must have the money. I was willing to pay something myself but I could not pay the whole." He took the subscription list, and walked into the meeting "while there was a great deal of caucusing going on about the time." He was now well known, and a hush fell over the hall as he walked up to the platform.

"Gentlemen, I have one thing to do and I intend to do it in a hurry," he said in a loud voice that carried about the quiet hall. "John Brown is in this city at the present time with a number of men, women and children. I require aid and substantial aid I must have. I am ready and willing to leave this meeting if I get this money, if not, I have to say this. I will bring John Brown to this meeting and if any United States

To Dr Thomas Featherstonhaugh. with Compliments James E. Taylor

John Brown arraigned before the court at Charlestown.

John Brown is arraigned before the court. *Library of Congress*

Marshal dare lay a hand on him he must take the consequences. I am determined to do this or have the money."

There was a long moment of silence. Pinkerton was too well known for his vigorous, sometimes violent, support of his abolitionist ideals for anyone to doubt he would do as he threatened. Years later, men who had been there that morning told how John Wilson, a well-known Chicago politician and later a judge, walked up to the platform and handed Pinkerton a $50 bill. Pinkerton took off his hat and held it out as other delegates silently came forward with bills. Within a few minutes he had between $500 and $600.[3]

"Thank you, gentlemen," Pinkerton said, and left the convention with his hat filled with money. Promptly at four o'clock Pinkerton, carrying a pistol under his coat, with his son William, and Kagi, put the slaves who had been hidden in the Pinkerton house into a wagon, then toured the city, collecting the others in the homes of Pinkerton's fellow abolitionists. The last stop was at the Jones house.

Pinkerton and Jones shook hands with Brown and said goodbye; then, almost abruptly, Brown said, "Friends, lay in your tobacco, cotton and sugar because I intend to raise the prices." It was Brown's warning of the Harpers Ferry raid not too many months away.

Fifteen minutes later Brown and his men had escorted the slaves aboard the special car. The abolitionist waved his last goodbye, the blinds were drawn, and the diamond-stacked engine chugged out of the depot.

"Look well upon that man, Willy," Pinkerton told his son as the cars clicked down the rails: "He is greater than Napoleon and just as great as George Washington."[4]

Before the slaves had left, the Pinkertons had listened to their stories: One young girl described her life under six masters, and four of the field hands had served sixteen owners. Pinkerton, in his violent bitterness against slavery, never questioned a runaway's story. This eagerness to believe the worst against the South would seriously impair his objectivity as a front-line military intelligence chief.

Six hours after Brown's party had left Pinkerton's home on Adams Street, they arrived safely in Canada, "rejoicing in the safety of the Union Jack," as Pinkerton put it. It was the end of a remarkable journey for this tiny band led by Brown and his men. For eighty-two days they had traveled six hundred miles in a covered wagon in the dead of winter. In Pinkerton's memories it would always be a spiritual odyssey.

In the following year Brown was holding public meetings in which he described the terrible journey to Canada "and asked help to prosecute the work on a larger scale." In Boston he raised $2,000, but Bronson Alcott, "a venerable Don Quixote," as Carlyle called him, noted there was now a "touch of insanity" in those glass-hard eyes. Brown's grand tour of the East brought almost $4,000, and those close to him knew his next target: the federal arsenal at Harpers Ferry. That spring and summer, Brown toured the East and Midwest soliciting money for his "great plans."

On the morning of October 16, 1859, John Brown walked out into the Sunday-morning stillness of the yard of a house, five miles from Harpers Ferry, and told his followers: "Men, get on your arms; we will proceed to the Ferry."

With these words Brown, "Commander-in-Chief of the Provisional Army," set in motion his famous raid. The events that took place are all too familiar: the bloody assault on the arsenal, the siege, capture, trial, and finally the death of Brown and his followers on the gallows.

Legend has Brown stopping off at Pinkerton's Chicago home en route to Harpers Ferry, with the detective giving him $500 for railroad tickets and arms. Some historians have accepted it as a fact, confusing the incident with Pinkerton aiding Brown and the slaves to Canada the previous March. Yet there is indication that Pinkerton was considering some kind of jail delivery after Brown's arrest.[5] In Chicago he had raised funds, obtained McClellan's help to aid Brown, wrote and telegraphed to many of the nation's leaders, urging them to obtain the release of the Middle Border fanatic. There is no evidence that Pinkerton traveled to Harpers Ferry, but in 1883 he said, "had it not been for the excessive watchfulness of those having him [Brown] in charge, the pages of American history would never have been stained with the record of his execution. . . ."

CHAPTER 6

Pinkerton and the Expressman: The Nathan Maroney Investigation

Epochs began and ended with the year 1849, one of the three great milestones of our history. Within fifteen years, the gold dug out of California, the westward movement it encouraged, and the expansion of the railroads and public carriers changed the United States from a weak, economically dependent country to a world power. No longer were we forced to buy gold from Europe at a premium; now we dug it out of the earth like potatoes or washed it in tin trays in cold mountain streams. The result, in the expansion of our wealth, industry, and commerce, is almost incredible. Between 1850 and 1860 our foreign trade doubled, from $317,885,232 to $687,192,176, while our shipping rose from 1,439,694 tons to 2,347,396. The domestic picture also changed drastically. Telegraph and railroad lines now linked states; the color of the raw gold changed our politics and our politicians; transatlantic liners appeared; the new millionaires began to build their stately mansions.

With the new affluence came crime, not the footpads or the street robbers, but highwaymen, train and stagecoach robbers. The amounts they stole shocked the country, particularly the totally unprepared East. Law enforcement throughout the nation was incredibly weak, corrupt, or politically dominated. There was no national police force, no federalized central clearinghouse for the distribution of criminal information. Few cities had Rogues' Galleries. Justice was usually decided by neighborhood vigilante groups or by the barrel of a man's Colt.

As the Pinkerton Agency grew, Allan plunged into every case with grim intensity. In 1858 and 1859, he was writing to sheriffs and marshals in the larger cities and along the frontier, advising them to be on the lookout for Isaac S. King, president of one of Chicago's wealthiest commission firms, who had vanished while "partially deranged." Pinkerton advised the police that the family had offered $250 for information leading to King and that in addition all expenses would be paid. He emphasized that the rule of his Agency was never to accept rewards. Evidently Pinkerton by now had established his pioneering Rogues' Gallery; enclosed with a letter was a daguerreotype of King and a facsimile of his handwriting.

Pinkerton's letter is an excellent example of his early police work. His two-page letter not only gives a detailed physical description of the missing man but also points out that he was fond of music, "expertly played the violin and bass viol, is temperate in all of his habits, likes to see a good horse, would be examining and pricing grain of all kinds, and probably expressing an opinion of the same. He is quiet and rather reserved in demeanor and would be rather shy of strangers."

Several months later he was writing to his friend Henry Hunt that he was "so fatigued I never removed my clothes this evening but fell across my bed. . . . I am out all hours. . . ." [1]

In the late 1850's, the express and public-carrier business, which had boomed with the growth of our industrial and economic history, decided they needed private police to protect their shipments. The two largest companies were Adams and American. Their lines and branches crept across the infant country until they had linked the East and the West coasts by stage, train, and pony express riders. Adams dominated southern New England, and from New York pushed southward and southwest, even to southern Ohio, Indiana, and Illinois. American Express gradually entered northern New England, then Canada, and followed the Great Lakes into the Midwest and Northwest.[2]

Adams Express Company, one of the largest carriers, and the one closely linked with Pinkerton's early career and successes, did not really begin to expand until 1843, when Adams took over an express line connecting Philadelphia and New York. In the merger, Edward S. Sanford, one of the pioneers of the express business, joined Adams as vice-president. He was to occupy a warm and special niche in Allan Pinkerton's memories.

In 1850, Sanford and S. N. Shoemaker, Sanford's old partner and now supervisor of the Adams Express Company, had extended the company's services over the New York and New Haven Railroad, paying an unprecedented $1,000 a month for space in express cars. A short time later, after the line was extended, the fee was raised to $1,700, an indication of the company's growth. As the New York *Herald* commented, "No set of men have ever displayed more spirit and enterprise. They have become a marked feature of America."

Adams soon was sending freight from New York to St. Louis by rail, wagon, and canalboat. By 1850, a St. Louis merchant could hope to receive his shipment from New York within ten days (slightly longer if the lakes were frozen), an extraordinarily short time, considering the primitive forms of transportation.

By 1854, Adams had annexed southern New England, New York, New Jersey, Pennsylvania, the Ohio River country, and the southeastern states, whose main offices were in Augusta, Georgia, and Montgomery, Alabama. This huge carrier now controlled the most densely populated and industrialized parts of the Union. Adams had an advantage over American Express, its closest competitor, in that its winters were milder than those of the other's more northerly sections and less likely to be impeded by snow and ice.

It was about this time that Pinkerton received a rather bulky letter from the Adams Express Company's New York office at 32 Broadway. He glanced through it hurriedly. It was from Edward S. Sanford, vice-president, describing the loss of $10,000 from a locked money pouch somewhere between their Montgomery, Alabama, headquarters and a branch office in Augusta, Georgia. Sanford wrote that he was sending on the details of the case at the suggestion of Robert Boyer, a New York detective Pinkerton had met on the Imbert forgery investigation.

Sanford rather naïvely said he hoped Pinkerton would identify the thief. As Pinkerton later recalled, he wondered what sort of firm the Adams Company was, and who Sanford was, who thought he could solve a case while sitting in his office halfway across the country. He was tempted to return to the problems of his expanding uniformed-guard department, but a strict sense of courtesy and appreciation of Boyer's "unselfish recommendation" led him to spend the weekend in his office answering Sanford's letter. On Monday he wrote a nine-page report on the case that was copied by his secretary and sent on to New York. Without any more details, and based only on his analysis of Sanford's letter, he advised the Adams Company official that Nathan Maroney, manager of the Montgomery office, was the thief. While he couldn't offer legal evidence from a distance of hundreds of miles, he advised Sanford to keep Maroney "under strict surveillance before he bites you twice."

There was no answer from New York, and Pinkerton forgot the case. Then one Saturday night, a year later, he received a telegram:

"Can you send a man, half horse, half alligator? I got bit once more. When can you send him? Edward S. Sanford."

Pinkerton debated with himself over the weekend whether he should accept Sanford's assignment. His Agency now had more work than he could handle, but the challenge interested him. In addition, he now knew that the Adams Company was one of the biggest public carriers in the East, with indications that it would soon be the nation's biggest. He told

Bangs they were accepting the case, and made arrangements to meet Sanford in Montgomery, Alabama.

The Maroney investigation is an outstanding and little-known pre-
Civil War criminal case. It brought Pinkerton and his Agency to the
attention of big business in the East, and helped him to bring about the
national expansion of his organization. The Maroney case also demonstrates Pinkerton's tenacity, imagination, and organizational ability—
characteristics that would help him a few years later in the Civil War—as
well as his pioneering efforts in American criminology, which greatly influenced our early law-enforcement methods. Because of its importance
in these fields, the Maroney case and Pinkerton's techniques should be
examined. Some were crude, others ludicrous; but many are still used by
modern police.

It is almost unbelievable that Allan Pinkerton should have been ignorant of the reputation of the Adams Company when he received Sanford's
letter asking him to meet him in Montgomery to discuss the robbery. As
Pinkerton said, "I knew very little about the Adams Company at the
time, as they had no office in the West." This lack of knowledge under-
scores Pinkerton's provincialism. He was now a true Westerner: anything
beyond the Mississippi wasn't worth knowing or caring about.

In his meeting with Sanford in Montgomery, Alabama, Pinkerton
learned that Sanford, acting on the detective's early analysis of the previous robbery, had had Maroney arrested and charged with the $40,000
robbery. The large amount of money stolen and the subsequent arrest of
Maroney, a popular young man in the social circles of the beautiful
cotton city of Montgomery, was a sensation of its time. Maroney was
released in $40,000 bail, raised by the city's leading citizens, and Sanford
and his company were denounced for prosecuting the express-office
manager.

At his preliminary arraignment, the company had offered such flimsy
circumstantial evidence that Maroney's bail was reduced to $4,000 and
the case set for trial in the fall session of circuit court. It was then that
Sanford, harassed by the adverse publicity and the fear he might have
arrested the wrong man, had sent for Pinkerton.[3]

Pinkerton organized a team of operatives, headed by himself and
George Bangs, and established headquarters in Philadelphia. His staff included Kate Warne, Roche, his "flying Dutchman"; John Fox, the garrulous former watchmaker; John H. White, whom Pinkerton recalled
as a "shrewd hand"; and several others.

The techniques Pinkerton used were often ludicrous and melodramatic
—but they were effective. Roche, dressed as a stolid, "dull witted Dutchman" in baggy pants, an old cap, and smoking a heavy curved pipe,
followed Mrs. Maroney as she toured the South from Atlanta to New
Orleans and back again to Montgomery to find out if she was being

shadowed as a suspect in the robbery. As the woman transferred from train to stagecoach and carriage, Roche kept Philadelphia informed by coded telegrams. When she dropped a letter in her hotel's outgoing mailbox, Roche read the Jenkintown, Pennsylvania, address, and sent it to Philadelphia.

Pinkerton supplied Fox with a box of watch parts, and the operative set up shop in the Pennsylvania village. He soon discovered that Maroney's relatives lived there. When Mrs. Maroney arrived in Jenkintown, Kate Warne, posing as the wife of a wealthy forger in order to establish a common bond, was living at the local boardinghouse, impressing the village with her fine clothes and regal manners. Her assignment was to cultivate Mrs. Maroney.

The first important break in the investigation came when Bangs copied the address of a letter Maroney sent to New York City. It turned out to be the shop of a locksmith who was copying a key for Maroney. When Bangs examined the key, he discovered that it belonged to the Adams Company. Pinkerton predicted to Sanford that it would be part of Maroney's defense that employees other than office managers had keys to the mail pouches.

In midsummer, the Adams attorney notified Sanford that they did not have a strong case against Maroney and that there was a good possibility he would be acquitted. Pinkerton proposed to Sanford that they rearrest Maroney on a conspiracy charge and have John White become his cellmate. The detective was aware that Maroney was broke and would not be able to furnish bail. White, Pinkerton explained, would be arrested as a big city forger, and would have George Bangs as his "attorney." Their assignment would be to break down Maroney. Sanford agreed, and both Maroney and White were arrested and placed in the Eldridge Street prison in New York City.

Pinkerton began by sending anonymous notes to Maroney, advising him his wife was being wooed by an attractive stranger—also a Pinkerton operative—in Jenkintown. When she visited her husband in prison, Mrs. Maroney—who, Pinkerton recalled, had an "attractive bust"—denounced the anonymous gossip but admitted she was seeing a good-looking stranger in Jenkintown.

White and Bangs also put on a fine show, with White ordering sumptuous suppers that he shared with Maroney as he listened and sympathized with the express manager who told how he feared his wife was being seduced. When Bangs visited his "client," he was loud in his contempt for the law and the courts, who could be fixed easily if you had the "right kind of money." Maroney listened and brooded. One day Bangs swept into the cell waving a release for his client. Plagued by thoughts of an unfaithful wife sharing the stolen money with a lover while he, Maroney, lingered in jail, Maroney broke, and begged White to help him. When the operative told him it would take money, Maroney sent orders to his wife to turn the stolen loot over to White, who was on his way to Jenkintown.

Mrs. Maroney took Kate—still playing the role of the forger's wife—into her confidence. Should she give the stolen money to a total stranger her husband had met in jail? Kate assured her it was the only way, and promised that after the bonds had been cashed "they could go down to Texas and live high."

Mrs. Maroney then dug up the Adams Express Company pouch and gave it to White, who appeared in Jenkintown as a bookseller. A few hours later White, Pinkerton, Bangs, Kate Warne, and Sanford were in a suite in New York City's Astor House, counting the money. It was only $400 short of the original $40,000.

But the investigation was not finished, Sanford told Pinkerton. The Adams Company was determined to put together an airtight case against Maroney and his wife, and send them to prison as an example. Pinkerton kept most of his operatives working; Kate returned to Jenkintown; Bangs and White kept up their masquerade with Maroney, while the other detectives fanned out across the South to tie up loose ends.

In September, Maroney went on trial in Montgomery. He was the lion of the hour with the young bloods who crowded the courtroom, ready to appear as his character witnesses. On the first day the state laid the groundwork of its case with the testimony of a number of Adams employees. Then, on the morning of the second day, the court attendant called the day's first witness:

"John H. White."

Maroney looked, unbelieving at first. Then, as Operative White walked out of a nearby room, Maroney swayed and sank back into his chair. Before White could testify, Maroney's attorney interrupted the trial to announce that his client wished to plead guilty. Maroney was immediately sentenced to ten years at hard labor in the state penitentiary, while his wife later received a suspended sentence.

Sanford was particularly impressed with the intelligence, integrity, and skill with which the detective had organized his investigative teams. That fall, he persuaded Adams to follow the example of the Illinois Central, and put Pinkerton on a retainer.

If the railroads and public carriers of the East had not been aware of Pinkerton's Agency before, they were now. By 1860, Pinkerton was firmly recognized as the protective arm for the nation's biggest railroads and public carriers. McClellan of the Illinois Central, Samuel Felton, president of the Philadelphia, Wilmington & Baltimore Railroad (now the Pennsylvania); Edward Sanford, vice-president of Adams Express Company, now president of the American Telegraph Company, sang the praises of this detective who not only maintained an impressive record of arrests and convictions but who also recovered the stolen loot. Outlaws on the frontier and big-city thieves were becoming increasingly wary of touching the safes or rolling stock protected by the Agency.

It was now an established fact that the "Eye," as they called Allan Pinkerton, would follow you to the ends of the earth to arrest you, and then spend every available dollar to put you behind bars. In addition, either the Eye or his operatives, nine times out of ten, would somehow find the place where you had hidden the stolen money. The image of a staring, unblinking eye seeking out evildoers became a comforting symbol to the utilities and business firms of the 1850's; it gave outlaws and thieves an uneasy feeling that someone was peering over their shoulders as they touched off a charge of black powder to blow a safe or stacked logs across tracks to halt a train.

The early records of Pinkerton's Agency were burned in the Chicago Fire, but based on his Civil War reports, he must have had a small clerical staff and at least fifteen operatives working out of the Chicago office in the late 1850's. He and his men chased lawbreakers on horseback, in carriages, wagons, on trains, and stagecoaches. They were on the expanding frontier and in big cities. Pinkerton never gave one of his operatives an assignment he couldn't handle himself. At times, dissatisfied with the progress of an investigation, he either took over himself or assigned George Bangs.

There was a great deal of old-fashioned dignity in the Pinkertons, but no easy graciousness, no savoir-faire. Their fortune and their business were the product of their elemental vigor, restlessness, drive, and above all their partisanship. It would dominate Allan Pinkerton and his sons in their personal and business relationships, in politics—even in their choice of underworld informants. You were either with them, completely, entirely, absolutely, without question—or you were against them and their world. The reward for unquestioning loyalty was their unswerving, never-ending friendship: "to storm the gates of Hell for you," as one old friend said of Allan Pinkerton, "but cross him and he'd leave you to burn in there."

Allan Pinkerton's fame appears meteoric, but behind the newspaper headlines and the acclaim of utilities executives like Sanford and McClellan was a stern devotion to the Protestant ethic: Work hard, make money, and save it. He worked incredibly long hours, faced a great deal of personal danger, and served his clients with almost fanatical devotion. Pinkerton was not only the founder of his Agency; he was also its hardest worker. But while he was busy making money protecting big business, he was also pioneering in American criminology.

In his time there was no central federal law-enforcement clearinghouse such as the present FBI files and laboratory—the finest in the world—so Pinkerton devised the earliest central clearing headquarters for the distribution of photographs of criminals, as well as pertinent information about them and their *modus operandi,* to state, local, and government law-enforcement agencies. It operated in a manner similiar to that of today's Federal Bureau of Criminal Identification. The letters, telegrams, and reports of the early days of the Agency show an amazing exchange of information about crimes and criminals, ranging from police officials of large eastern cities to the obscure frontier sheriff laboriously writing with the stub of a pencil.

The Pinkerton Rogues' Gallery portraits followed the art of photography. In the beginning were daguerreotypes; then tintypes were used. When the wet-plate process entered the Civil War period, the Agency mounted their prints, and listed on the reverse side permanent data concerning the criminal. Some of it now appears hilarious. We find a bank robber who had a scar on his left hand, "speaks Mex," and lives with "a Hooker named Frisco Ann"; or a forger who "spits frequently as he talks," "works East St. Louis," and is a friend of the Scratch (Charles Becker, the world-famous forger of banknotes of the 1880's).

When the Pinkertons were involved in an arrest, they insisted that the prisoner be stripped in police headquarters and that every scar, mole, and physical deformity be listed.

The early Pinkertons also developed an excellent system of gathering underworld information. After the first criminal had whispered into his ear, Allan Pinkerton issued an order protecting informants. Each one had a code name that was used by the early Agency officials, even the Pinkertons themselves, in letters and telegrams.

By the time the Civil War began, Allan Pinkerton had established an excellent relationship with police of large cities—not only because they valued the Agency's cooperation but also because they were now aware that the Pinkerton Agency never accepted a reward, but always stepped aside to let the local authorities collect.

In 1860—some early accounts claim the idea was McClellan's—Pinkerton organized the nation's first guard service to protect Chicago's packing plants and commercial houses.[4] The force consisted of six uniformed men. Since then, guards have always been a major part of the Agency's business. There would come a time when these uniformed police would be accused by labor of being scabs, strikebreakers, and even "Cossacks." Almost the only hostile comment on the Agency's business has risen from this employment of guards. Today, if there is a strike in premises guarded by the Agency, the Pinkertons will withdraw the guards unless, as has happened many times, they are requested to remain by mutual agreement with the labor union. If workers are imported, the Agency's guards will withdraw.

The Agency's vast guard business began in Chicago when Pinkerton and Bangs, after "inspecting" the six uniformed men under Captain Paul Dennis, sent them off on their assignments. Those six men have now become 20,000, within a $75,000,000-a-year business that protects every type of American industry.

BOOK 2

Allan Pinkerton and the Civil War, 1861-1865

CHAPTER 7
The Baltimore Plot

If it had not been for Allan Pinkerton, Lincoln could have been assassinated before he was sworn in as President of the United States.

The attempt to murder the President-elect in April, 1861, in what history calls the Baltimore Plot, is one of the most controversial incidents of the Civil War. For more than a century, historians, amateur and professional, have debated whether Pinkerton, by courage and ingenuity, saw Lincoln safely to Washington to become one of America's greatest Presidents, or whether he was a shabby fabricator who concocted the plot to further his own ambitions and gain glory.

The story has been told before, but the discovery of Pinkerton's little-known Record Book of 1861, and detailed letters he had written of the account, shed new light on the part Pinkerton and his men played in Baltimore. The daily entries in the Record Book bolster the detective's claim that an actual plot existed, and they also give a startling insight as to why Pinkerton was first denounced as a liar by Ward Lamon, Lincoln's former associate and biographer—charges that are repeated to this day.

The events that brought Pinkerton to Baltimore began on the morning of January 19, 1861, when a letter was delivered to his Chicago office. It was from Samuel Morse Felton, president of the Philadelphia, Wilmington & Baltimore Railroad, asking him to come to New York City on a matter of the greatest importance.

At their meeting Felton explained he had received many threats of sabotage and destruction to his line, rolling stock, bridges and tunnels by secession sympathizers around Baltimore. In the event of war, the road that connected New York with the Capital would be the nation's most vital carrier of troops and ammunition. The critical question being discussed everywhere that January day when Pinkerton was meeting with Felton was whether Maryland would secede, cutting Washington off from the North, or remain in the Union.

Public opinion was fiercely divided, and Mason and Dixon's Line was its northern boundary. Pinkerton returned to Chicago to think it over, and not until the twenty-seventh did he write to Felton that "should the suspicion of danger still exist" he would come to Baltimore with four to six of his operatives, ascertain whether there was a disloyal organization, and if so, work his men into it. The letter is seven pages, sketching the methods he hoped to employ of "increasing shadow," stressing the "tedious and very frequently slow" operations the Agency used "to attain a controlling power over the mind of the suspected parties." He emphasized the importance of secrecy to Felton, and on no consideration would he "consider it safe for myself or my operatives were the facts of my operating known to any politician, no matter of what school or of what position." It is important, in view of questions raised later, to realize that the letter makes no plea for business. In fact, the letter ends very curtly with "I have other matters pressing on me." [1]

Felton agreed at once. In the last days of January, Pinkerton and several operatives left Chicago for Baltimore. Timothy Webster and Hattie Lawton were assigned to Perrymansville, about nine miles south of Havre De Grace, where Webster had heard "a Rebel company was organizing." Pinkerton himself, under an assumed name, opened a brokerage office across the hall from a secessionist named Luckett. Pinkerton and his operative, Harry N. Davies, began mingling with the crowds in the taverns and restaurants where Confederate sympathizers were openly denouncing Lincoln and the Union.

Pinkerton, in the field, could be a jovial, friendly man, a direct contrast to his usual unsmiling, dour appearance. He disliked whiskey, but would become a social drinker if a role demanded it. He made sure he met Luckett on the street or in the hallways to call out a cheery greeting. Soon they were exchanging confidences "over a glass." Luckett introduced Pinkerton to Cypriano Ferrandini, "one of the leading spirits" in the plot to kill Lincoln. Ferrandini, a follower of Felice Orsini, Italian revolutionist who had been executed in 1858 for trying to assassinate Napoleon III, was a wild-eyed fanatic who insisted to Pinkerton that "murder of any kind is justifiable and right to save the rights of the Southern people."

While Pinkerton was dining and drinking with the fiery Italian revolutionist who worked as a barber in Barnum's Hotel, Baltimore, his operative Davies was cultivating a young aristocrat named Howard, "who was willing to die to rid his country of a tyrant, as he considered Lincoln to be."

Davies located Howard in a bar at the fashionable Fountain Hotel, and they did the town. After attending a concert, Howard brought Davies to the biggest brothel in the city to visit an attractive prostitute who had just arrived. It was a delicate situation, but Davies convincingly played the role of a young man numbed by whiskey while Howard and his woman "kissed and hugged each other for an hour." But later they talked of secession and murder, and how Ferrandini would organize a group of assassins to kill the President-elect as he walked through a narrow tunnel to the waiting Washington express.

Webster joined the Confederate cavalry to learn from a group of officers a scheme to murder Lincoln. After the assassination, telegraph lines were to be cut, bridges blown up, and tracks destroyed to prevent troops from taking over the city. As Pinkerton admitted, the schemes were "wild" and the conspirators "reckless," but it was evidence that could not be ignored.[2]

Pinkerton now reported to Felton, as he recalled in 1866:

"Judging from the reports of my detectives and allowing they were even imperfectly posted, I had no doubt that there would be an attempt to assassinate Mr. Lincoln and his suite by probably not over fifteen or twenty men. Mr. Felton approved of what I said."

Given the conditions in Baltimore, with the Baltimore police chief himself a suspected Confederate sympathizer, the hearsay nature of the evidence, the lack of a secret service, and the boiling hatreds aroused by Lincoln's election, preventive arrests were impossible.

By now the wild threats had become so common in Baltimore that persons other than Pinkerton thought the President-elect wise to avoid the town. Dorothea Dix, the lecturer, was so horrified by the open threats against Lincoln's life that she sent word to Lincoln's party, urging them to bypass Baltimore and go direct to Washington.

Lincoln arrived in Philadelphia. Pinkerton by now had additional evidence that a murder conspiracy had been formed when he received a note from the master mechanic of Felton's railroad advising him that "the son of a distinguished citizen had taken an oath to assassinate Mr. Lincoln before he gets to Washington, and they may attempt it while he is passing over our road."

In Philadelphia, Pinkerton and Felton fought their way through the huge crowds to reach Norman Buel Judd, one of Lincoln's personal friends who was in charge of the presidential party. Judd, a short, stout man with a florid face, who had a great deal of influence with Lincoln, was remembered by the Washington correspondents as someone who had gone out of his way to make himself indispensable, "a character of much more tact than talent, who is fully impressed with the onus of the mysterious position he occupies in relation to the President-elect."

In Judd's room Pinkerton and Felton outlined the Baltimore situation. In answer to Judd's plea for advice, Felton urged that Lincoln go quietly to Washington that night. Judd predicted Lincoln would not agree, as he had to be in Philadelphia the next day, February 22nd. The reason was that Kansas had been admitted to the Union as a free state on January 29th, adding a new star to the flag. Washington's birthday had been chosen as the day for its first unfurling, and Lincoln was to do so at Independence Hall. It would be a political disaster to change the plans. By 10:15 P.M. the crowd had thinned enough for Pinkerton to get to Lincoln's suite and ask him by note to join them. Ten minutes later Lincoln, gaunt and weary, appeared. Judd outlined what Pinkerton and his men had uncovered. Pinkerton says:

"Mr. Lincoln listened very attentively, but did not say a word, nor did his countenance, which I had watched very closely, show any emotion."

Lincoln asked Pinkerton for more details. His account, written at the time, says in part:

> If there was an Escort it would be by a Disloyal Police, and the slightest sign of discontent would be sufficient to raise all the angry feeling of the Masses, and that then would be a favorable moment for the conspirators to operate: that again, as by the published route, he (Mr. Lincoln) in taking the Northern Central Rail Road from Harrisburg to Baltimore, would arrive at the Calvert Street depot, and would have about one mile and a quarter to pass through the city in an open carriage, which would move but slowly through the dense crowd, and that then it would be an easy matter for any assassin to mix in with the crowd and in the confusion of the moment shoot Mr. Lincoln if he felt so disposed; that I felt satisfied in my own mind that if Mr. Lincoln adhered to the published programe of his route to Washington that an assault of some kind would be made upon his person with a view to taking his life. After I concluded Mr. Lincoln remained quiet for a few minutes apparently thinking, when Mr. Judd inquired, "If upon any kind of statement which might be made to him [Lincoln] would he [Lincoln] consent to leave for Washington on the train tonight." Mr. Lincoln said promptly, "No, I cannot consent to this. I shall hoist the Flag on Independence Hall tomorrow morning [Washington's Birthday] and go to Harrisburg tomorrow, then I [Lincoln] have fulfilled all my engagements, and if you [addressing Mr. Judd], and you, Allan [meaning me], think there is positive danger in my attempting to go through Baltimore openly according to the published programe—if you can arrange any way to carry out your views, I shall endeavor to get away quietly from the people at Harrisburg tomorrow evening and shall place myself in your [hands]."
>
> The firmness of tone in which Mr. Lincoln spoke shewed that there was no further use in arguing the proposition, and Mr. Judd inquired of me what I thought best to do in the emergency and I said if Mr. Lincoln could manage to get away unobserved, from the people at Harrisburg by about dusk tomorrow evening that I thought we could

get a special Train on the Pennsylvania Rail Road to bring him from
Harrisburg to Philadelphia in time for the train going South on the
Philadelphia, Wilmington and Baltimore Rail Road, when we could
secure seats in the sleeping car which goes directly through to Washington and thus save us from being observed at Baltimore, as we would
not require to get out of the car.

This was finally after some discussion agreed upon, and I promised
to see the Superintendent of the Pennsylvania Rail Road in regard to
procuring the special train, and making all the arrangements for the
trip. I requested Mr. Lincoln that none but Mr. Judd and myself should
know anything about this arrangement. He said that ere he could leave
it would be necessary for him to tell Mrs. Lincoln and that he thought
it likely that she would insist upon W. H. Lamon going with him
(Lincoln), but aside from this no one should know.[3]

Lincoln, for some reason, never revealed to Pinkerton, Judd, or Felton
that Seward, who was to be his Secretary of State, had that night sent his
son to Lincoln with information forewarning him to the same effect,
which he had received from General Winfield Scott in Washington.

At Lincoln's request, Pinkerton outlined his plan. After the Philadelphia flag-raising on the morning of the twenty-second, Lincoln would
proceed to Harrisburg for a meeting with the Pennsylvania legislature
and to attend a banquet. Then he and his party would return to West
Philadelphia on a special Pennsylvania Central Railroad train. Simultaneously a professional wire climber of the American Telegraph Company
would cut all lines controlled by the PCRR out of Harrisburg. This
would take place after Judd had telegraphed Pinkerton that Lincoln's
special train had departed. The message would be in code. Pinkerton
was Plums, Lincoln Nuts, and the telegraph Sumac. It was an unfortunate
choice of words that would help to ridicule Pinkerton.

Pinkerton would meet Lincoln at Philadelphia and escort him by carriage from the Pennsylvania Central Railroad tracks to the Philadelphia,
Wilmington & Baltimore depot, where a sleeper would be waiting. Felton,
in the meantime, was to arrange with the conductor that the train must
not leave until a package addressed to E. J. Allen (Pinkerton's wartime
pseudonym) at Willard's Hotel had been delivered to him. Only after he
had received the package was the conductor to give the signal for the
train to depart for Washington.

When Lincoln agreed to the plan, "placing himself entirely in my
hands," as Pinkerton wrote, Kate Warne hired two rear sleepers of the
Washington train "for a sick friend and party" while Pinkerton assigned
every operative he could spare to positions along the route. Each one was
instructed to flash a light as the train passed to signal to Pinkerton on
the rear platform that the tracks were clear.

At ten that night Pinkerton met Lincoln and Ward H. Lamon, Lincoln's former associate, at the West Philadelphia train shed. It was a

marvelous scene from history: the bearded, hard-eyed detective chewing on a cigar, impatiently listening to Lamon offering the greatest son of the frontier a Bowie knife and pistol—an offer that was smilingly declined—in the huge empty shed filled with the panting of the engines and their acrid coal smoke. In the sleeping car, Kate Warne carefully drew the curtains and charmed the curious conductor.

Pinkerton was indignant at Lamon's ridiculous offer of the Bowie knife. As he wrote:

"I would not for the world have it said that Mr. Lincoln had to enter the capitol armed. If fighting has to be done it must be done by others than Mr. Lincoln."

Pinkerton in his Record Book abruptly dismissed Lamon as a "brainless, egotistical fool" [4]—a remark that would haunt Pinkerton and help distort his role in the Baltimore plot for more than a century.

Lincoln, as the detective recalled, wore "an overcoat thrown loosely over his shoulders without his arms being in the sleeves, and a Black Kossuth hat, which he told me someone had presented to him."

Some historians have accepted the tale of Pinkerton "disguising" Lincoln in a "Scotch hat," but a member of Lincoln's party insisted that Joseph Howard, Jr., the New York *Times* correspondent, writing from Harrisburg after Lincoln's appearance before the legislature, "invented" the story of the Scotch hat "because he said he must get up some sort of a story for his paper." This description of what Lincoln wore agreed with Pinkerton's recollections.[5]

After Lincoln and his party settled down in the sleeper, there was a momentary delay. Pinkerton mingled with the unsuspecting crowd that milled about the station, listening with growing apprehension to the wild talk. When he came back to the car, Lincoln was telling some of his marvelous stories, but Pinkerton was so occupied with details he completely forgot them, something few men did who had ever been captivated by that wonderful drawling, wry humor.

The trip to Washington was uneventful. They arrived at 6:00 A.M., and Pinkerton went to Willard's, where he sent that unfortunate telegram: "Plums arrived with Nuts this morning," to Judd, still in Harrisburg and to Felton and Sanford, who were both waiting with George Bangs in the Agency's Chicago office. The excited Lamon wanted to telegraph the story to the Chicago *Journal*, but Pinkerton dissuaded him.

After he had a bath and breakfast, Pinkerton saw Lincoln, who thanked him while Seward and a congressional delegate waited. That same afternoon Pinkerton returned to Baltimore, where he met Luckett, the stockbroker, who was cursing the "d——d spies who had betrayed us."

Mrs. Lincoln passed through Baltimore, and Joseph Howard's New York *Times* story of Sunday, February 24th, gives an indication of the violence in the city. Howard's story describes "the shocking abuse and disregard for personal comfort . . . oaths, obscenity, disgusting epithets

Inauguration of President Lincoln. *Library of Congress*

and unpleasant gesticulations were the order of the day. . . ." At one point the men in Mrs. Lincoln's car had closed the windows to shut out the shouts of a mob surrounding the car, but the windows were forced open for the frightened wife of the country's new President to hear "the dirty and foul language."

So impressed was Howard with the violence he had witnessed, the lead of his story reads:

"It is well Mr. Lincoln went as he did—there is no doubt about it." [6]

On March 19th, Pinkerton submitted his bill to Samuel Morse Felton, president of the Philadelphia, Wilmington & Baltimore Railroad. For his thirty-five days in Baltimore at $10 a day, Pinkerton charged the company $350. For five operatives, at $6 a day, the cost was $1,050, or a total of $1,400. Pinkerton informed Felton he had charged himself "with $229.38 for expenses which I deemed necessary to expend in the operation, yet not such as I considered should be charged to your company."

Pinkerton apologized for the "unusually large amount of expenses," but he explained "that such was the expensive habits of the characters we had to operate upon, that even with my own unremitting personal attention to Business, I found it impossible for my operatives to maintain their standing with the parties we had to associate with, without incurring an unusually heavy expense."

On April 12th Fort Sumter was shelled, and the Civil War began. The next day an obviously angry Pinkerton wrote to Felton demanding assistance from the railroad president in tracking down the source of an article on the Baltimore Plot that had appeared in the Albany *Evening Journal*. As Pinkerton pointed out, the details in the story were so accurate they could have come only from a person "well posted." He added:

> I have the pledge of President Lincoln and all to whom it was entrusted, that it [the Baltimore Plot] should forever be treated as strictly confidential. Whoever has furnished this information should be known. It could not have come from this Agency, without it having come from myself, as the important documents are in my possession and have been. It could not have come from my operatives as the information in this article which no one of my operatives could give. It would have required the reports of all to furnish it. If it is at all possible to find out who the writer is, I would very much like to know it. . . .[7]

There is no record of what Felton did, if anything. Then, in 1867, Benjamin Lossing, the historian, published a book on the war in which he quoted a long statement from John A. Kennedy, Chief of Detectives of the New York City Police, that he, and not Pinkerton, uncovered the plot to kill Lincoln in Baltimore. Lossing used Kennedy's statement, completely overlooking Kennedy's letter to George P. Kane, the Baltimore police chief and a Confederate sympathizer, that he did not believe an attempt would be made on Lincoln's life and that the men he had sent to Baltimore had informed him that "the city is safe."

Pinkerton was outraged by the leak. He had Bangs collect every report in the Agency's files, while he wrote a series of letters to the various officials and friends of Lincoln who had taken part in the events of that midnight journey. One of the first persons Pinkerton wrote to was Ward Lamon, who had offered the Bowie knife and pistol to the President-elect, to Pinkerton's disgust.

When he did not receive a reply, Pinkerton's Record Book shows that he wrote a second time. Another silence. Many came to his aid with signed statements, letters, and documents—but not Lamon. Pinkerton was bewildered at his silence, but privately published his now rare pamphlet, *History and Evidence of the Passage of Abraham Lincoln from Harrisburg, Pa., to Washington, D.C. . . .*

Nothing more was heard of the Baltimore Plot until 1872, when Lamon announced that there had never been a conspiracy to kill Lincoln in that city and that the whole thing "was a mare's nest gotten up by a vain glorious detective." Lamon described Pinkerton as "being intensely ambitious to shine in a professional way," and he charged Pinkerton had "discovered the plot" to further his own ambitions.

Pinkerton was shocked by Lamon's accusations. He wrote, demanding an explanation, but did not receive a reply. Until the day of his death Pinkerton never knew the reason for Lamon's seemingly unexplainable hostility. Apparently Lamon's political philosophy was simple: Don't get mad; get even.

However, twenty-three years later, in his *Recollections of Abraham Lincoln,* Lamon without any explanation changed his mind to admit:

> It is now an acknowledged fact that there was never a moment from the day he [Lincoln] crossed the Maryland line up to the time of his assassination that he was not in danger by violence, that his life was spared until the night of April, 1865, only through the ceaseless and watchful eyes of the guards thrown around him.

The conflicting statements from the one man who was in a better position to judge if there had been a plot than any other of Lincoln's biographers, puzzled and confused historians.

The reason for Lamon's statement of Pinkerton's "mare's nest" is revealed in Pinkerton's Record Book, in which he describes Lamon as "a brainless, egotistical fool." This was a strictly personal observation, but one day Lamon read these lines.

This is how Pinkerton's book came into his possession. Immediately after the assassination, Lincoln's old friend William Henry Herndon began to collect Lincolniana, a project that would take the rest of his life. He carried on a fantastic correspondence with persons who had known Lincoln; he traveled, and interviewed anyone who had the remotest story to tell about the Great Emancipator. This soon proved not only time-consuming, but also expensive, so he set his clerk, John G. Springer, to copying every letter and comment he collected. By 1868, Herndon had over 1,700 pages of transcript.

When Lamon heard about the plan, he had visions of a fortune to be made. His friend Chauncey F. Black convinced Lamon he was the logical man to write the definitive work on Lincoln: Lamon would contribute his knowledge, Herndon his documents, and young Black would be the writer.

The three entered a partnership. Black later insisted that Lamon, who received all the glory as the author of *The Life of Abraham Lincoln from his Birth to His Inauguration in Washington,* did not compose "one line of it or furnish the data upon which five lines were based." The book was written from Herndon's collections.

Pinkerton had lent Herndon his Record Book but insisted that all mention of Lamon must be kept confidential. Springer, the clerk, copied

> I should for ever remain unknown as having any thing whatever to do with it, All I could say to Mr. Lamon however appeared to be futile – regardless of all consequences he was determined to make a "Splurge" and have his name figure largely in it. The movement had been endorsed by Gov. Seward, and "it must be right", and Lamon would act upon no reasoning of mine. He talked so foolishly that I lost patience with him and set him down in my own mind as a brainless egotistical fool – and I still think so.

Published here for the first time is Pinkerton's denunciation of Ward Lamon, taken from his 1861 Record Book. *The Huntington Library*

the Record Book, including Pinkerton's descriptions of Lamon. Herndon, forgetting his promise to Pinkerton, gave Lamon and Black the copied Record Book. It was after Lamon discovered Pinkerton's harsh entry that he publicly declared the plot was a figment of Pinkerton's imagination.[8]

For more than a century controversy over the events of that night have raged; scarcely a year passes that some historical quarterly doesn't contain an impassioned article supporting Lamon's views. Yet, despite the revelations in the Record Book, it seems unlikely that Lincoln, a shrewd judge of men, would, shortly after Baltimore, sanction McClellan's choice of Pinkerton to head the Secret Service of the Army of the Potomac. If Pinkerton had manufactured the "mare's nest" of a plot to murder the President-elect, we must assume that he had deceived Lincoln's close friend Judd, along with Felton and Sanford, both heads of two of the nation's largest and most powerful corporations. Furthermore, these men were his clients. Certainly men in their positions, knowing a detective employed by them was capable of such a gigantic fraud, would have got rid of him at once, purely out of business prudence.

There is more evidence to consider: Timothy Webster, Kate Warne, Scott, and all the others would have known if the whole tale had been a monstrous fake. One must doubt that Webster would have gone to the gallows, sending his last message to a man he knew as a pious fraud.

CHAPTER 8
Behind Enemy Lines, 1861

After delivering Lincoln to Washington, Pinkerton returned to Chicago and his business. On April 19th, Colonel Elmer E. Ellsworth was killed at the head of his troops in Baltimore, and the violence that Pinkerton had predicted erupted. Railroad bridges leading into Baltimore were destroyed, and saboteurs cut the telegraph lines to the Capital. In Chicago, Norman Judd, who had been an eyewitness to the President-elect's passage to Washington, wrote to Lincoln, urging him to use Pinkerton and his forces to obtain military intelligence information. Addressing the President with the rather brusque "Dear Lincoln," Judd pointed out that Pinkerton had an experienced force prepared

> to go anywhere. I believe that no force can be used to so good advantage in obtaining information. His men can live in Richmond and elsewhere with perfect safety. Of course profound secrecy is the keynote to success. If you approve, Pinkerton can come to Washington and arrange the details. I have no doubt the importance of this, surrounded as you are by traitors . . . our people expect you will call out immediately 300,000 men and that they will not remain cooped up in Washington waiting for events but that your active military will be in Virginia with Richmond for its seat. Aggression is the only policy now . . . our people are crazy with excitement and furor. . . .[1]

On the same day, April 21st, Pinkerton wrote a letter to Lincoln offering his services. It was calmer, less hawklike than Judd's, and it sketched

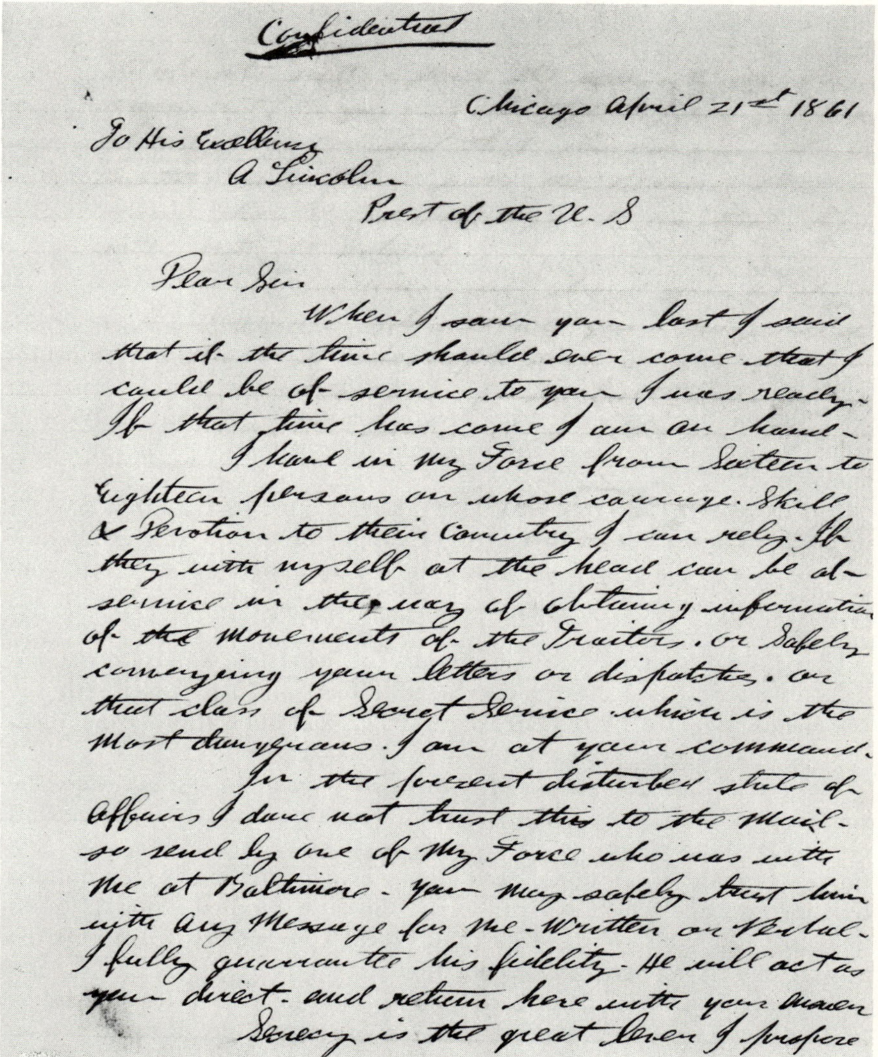

Confidential

Chicago April 21st 1861

To His Excellency
A Lincoln
Prest of the U. S

Dear Sir

When I saw you last I said that if the time should ever come that I could be of service to you I was ready. If that time has come I am on hand.

I have in my Force from Sixteen to Eighteen persons on whose courage, Skill & Devotion to their Country I can rely. If they with myself at the head can be of service in the way of obtaining information of the movements of the Traitors, or Safely conveying your letters or dispatches, or that class of Secret Service which is the most dangerous, I am at your command.

In the present disturbed state of Affairs I dare not trust this to the Mail—so send by one of my Force who was with me at Baltimore—you may safely trust him with any Message for me—Written or Verbal—I fully guarantee his fidelity—He will act as you direct—and return here with your answer

Secrecy is the great lever I propose

Pinkerton's letter of April 21, 1861

for the President his force of "from sixteen to eighteen persons on whose courage, skill and devotion to their country I can rely. If they, with myself at the head, can be of any service in the way of obtaining information of the movements of the Traitors or safely conveying your letters or dispatches or that class of Secret Service which is the most dangerous, I am at your service."

As Pinkerton said, he did not trust the "disturbed state of affairs" to deliver his letter by mail, but would entrust it "to one of my Force who was with me in Baltimore, you may safely trust him with any message for me, written or verbal. . . . Secrecy is the great lever I propose to operate with. Hence the necessity of this movement (if you contemplate it) of being strictly Private."

Pinkerton also included a copy of a cipher that he advised the President to use in telegraphing him.

Pinkerton's messenger was Tim Webster, who finally reached Washington after many adventures in Baltimore and Perrymansville. Lincoln, in turn, gave him a message for Pinkerton, asking him to come to Washington, "for his services are greatly for the government." [2] Webster rolled the messages into a tiny ball, and hid them in a hollow walking cane.

In response to Lincoln's message, Pinkerton came to Washington. At a meeting with the President and his Cabinet, Pinkerton was asked how he would go about keeping watch on the innumerable southern sympathizers in the nation's Capital. As Pinkerton remembered it in his *Spy of the Rebellion:*

"Accordingly I stated to them my ideas which I had entertained upon the subject . . . and after I concluded I took my departure, with the understanding that I would receive further communications from them in a few days." [3]

He waited for a few days, but nothing happened. In evident pique he started back for Chicago. Years later he explained that he had seen all along that "the confusion in government had been too great for anything systematic to be done." But it was evident he had been wounded by Lincoln's neglect. "I felt confident," he later recalled, "that I would be required to wait a longer time than I could conveniently spare from my business." And so he struck off for home.

Stopping off in Philadelphia to pick up mail forwarded from Chicago, he found a letter from McClellan, who was preparing to assume command of the new military Department of the Ohio, with his headquarters in Cincinnati. McClellan wanted Pinkerton to come at once, and come secretly, using only his first name. Pinkerton hurried to Ohio. As he explained it:

"Anxious as I was to serve my country in this, the hour of her need, I sought the first opportunity that presented itself and I left at once to comply with the instructions contained in this message of General McClellan."

En route to Ohio, Pinkerton's office alerted him that Webster was in a Pittsburgh jail after having escaped being lynched as a Confederate spy. Fortunately, Pinkerton knew the chief of police, and had his operative released. Pinkerton decided to take Webster with him, and the next day they were ushered into the parlors of McClellan's big house on Ludlow Street.

McClellan, by order of General Scott, now commanded the Department of the Ohio, consisting of the armed forces of Ohio, Indiana, and Illinois. Sixteen miles northwest of Cincinnati was Camp Dennison, the largest camp in the state, where most of the recruits of that time were getting their basic training.

McClellan proposed to Pinkerton that he organize a secret service for his department. Pinkerton pointed out that Lincoln had proposed the same idea but that he had left Washington "without arriving at any definite understanding with the President."

When McClellan insisted, Pinkerton agreed if McClellan would get permission from General Scott, which McClellan said he would do. A telegram was sent, and Scott endorsed the project.

For several days Pinkerton and Webster organized a Secret Service Department for the army, setting up headquarters in an office building in downtown Cincinnati. His most experienced operatives, including Kate Warne and Hattie Lawton, were summoned, along with Sam Bridgeman, a native of Virginia, Mexican War veteran, and former New York and Chicago detective; George Bangs, who would be Pinkerton's chief assistant in their Civil War operations; John C. Babcock, a veteran of the Sturgis Rifle Corps of Chicago, who would remain in the Secret Service until the war's end; G. H. Thiel, who would later form his own agency and become a bitter rival; Seth Paine, a slender daredevil, one of the best of Pinkerton's "scouts" behind Confederate lines; and John Scully, the Englishman. At the time that Pinkerton moved most of his personnel to Cincinnati, Pryce Lewis, his handsome, articulate English operative, was working in Mississippi on a murder investigation. Heading the staff of operatives was Tim Webster.

Pinkerton's first assignment from McClellan was to gather military information in the bordering Confederate states. Webster was the first operative to go behind enemy lines. Pinkerton sent him to Louisville with instructions to move southward to Memphis, Bowling Green, and Clarksville. Within the week he had dispersed his entire staff, singly and in pairs, to various towns and depots in the Confederacy. Absolute secrecy was the order of the day, with Pinkerton adopting the nom de guerre of Major E. J. Allen, with "my true name known only to General McClellan."

Webster's trip was a huge success. Still posing as a violent pro-Confederate Marylander, this quiet, intelligent man made many friends in the small towns and cities along the way. It was commonplace for him to be invited to inspect the rawest camp or a newly erected earthworks.

In mid-May the Virginia Convention passed its secret order of secession; but when Governor John Letcher ordered recruiting teams into West Virginia, they reported that the area was mostly pro-Union and that there was danger of Union forces along the Ohio taking over.

McClellan sent two regiments across the river at Wheeling to protect the Baltimore & Ohio Railroad bridges. Burned bridges were repaired, and more troops moved in.

In Cincinnati, Pinkerton had his staff working day and night to serve his general. The detective idolized McClellan so completely and unquestioningly, his usual good common sense always appeared to be badly tilted. He soon took on the role of McClellan's protector, with no protest from the general. In June, 1861, for the first time Pinkerton came to his general's defense against the Washington "cabal," as he called it.

In Washington, McClellan was under attack for reportedly entering into a secret agreement with General Simon Buckner of Kentucky, in which he promised not to occupy or enter that state. Pinkerton telegraphed directly to Lincoln, condemning the report as "completely untrue. . . . I have personal knowledge of this." He would have more confrontations with the cabal.[4]

His office emptied of operatives, Pinkerton himself went behind the Confederate lines to gather intelligence when McClellan asked him for information "on the general feeling of the people residing south of the Ohio River in Kentucky, North Carolina, Mississippi and Louisiana."

Representing himself as a "gentleman from Georgia," Pinkerton bought a "splendid bay," and began his dangerous tour. After some close calls—he was once recognized by a German barber he had known in Chicago who almost gave him away—Pinkerton returned to Cincinnati and wrote his report. It fills many pages of precise, eyewitness information:

> The Rebels have sunk two boats loaded with stone at the mouth of the Kanawha River near the Red House Shoals twenty or thirty miles from Charleston, and they are now erecting a battery of two six pounders concealed by bushes . . . there are fifteen hundred troops in the Kanawha Valley about one thousand near Charleston, say about one mile below on the level ground by the river and about five hundred at the mouth of the Cold below Charleston . . . there are only fifty soldiers at the Red House . . . they had little ammunition at either of the above places . . . the soldiers are equipped with muskets and poor rifles and with the exception of the Kanawha Rangers, (100 strong) were very poor specimens of mortality, many not exceeding fifteen years of age. . . .

THE MAGNETIC TELEGRAPH COMPANY.
PRINTING AND MORSE LINES.
DIRECT TO ALL STATIONS IN THE UNITED STATES AND BRITISH PROVINCES.

OFFICES.—432 Pennsylvania Av., U. S. CAPITOL, Willard's, and NATIONAL Hotels, Washington, D. C.

Terms and conditions on which Messages are received by this Company for Transmission.

The public are notified that, in order to guard against mistakes in the transmission of messages, every message of importance ought to be repeated by being sent back from the station at which it is to be received to the station from which it is originally sent.— Half the usual price for transmission will be charged for repeating the message, and while this company will as heretofore use every precaution to ensure correctness, it will not be responsible for mistakes or delays in the transmission or delivery of repeated messages beyond an amount exceeding five hundred times the amount paid for sending the message, nor will it be responsible for mistakes or delays in the transmission of unrepeated messages from whatever cause they may arise, nor for delays arising from interruptions in the workings of its telegraphs, nor for any mistake or omission of any other company over whose lines a message is to be sent to reach the place of destination. All messages will hereafter be received by this company for transmission subject to the above conditions.

J. KENDALL, Gen'l Sup't.　　　　　　　　**E. S. SANFORD, Pres't,**
145 BROADWAY, N. Y.　　　　　　　　　　145 BROADWAY, N. Y.

Dated Cincin June 26 1861

Rec'd, Washington, 27th 1861, o'clock, min. M.

To Abraham Lincoln Pres't
Washington

The report of compact having been made with Buckner of Kentucky by Genl. McClellan stipulating not to occupy or enter that state is completely untrue. Buckner has been profuse in offers to keep secession troops out of Ky. but Genl McClellan has offered him no consideration in return. I have personal knowledge of this.

Allan Pinkerton —

Pinkerton's telegram to Lincoln denying the alleged agreement with Buckner. *Library of Congress*

Pinkerton also toured Confederate breastworks, and included in his report were the thickness, height, type of lumber used, and location of the batteries. He also described the landing of the Confederates near Gauley Bridge and the amount of provisions entering the district around Charleston. He located and described for McClellan a "pretty good wagon road" on the south side of the Kanawha River, and included the names of Unionists who could "furnish experienced help."

A few weeks later, he returned behind the Confederate lines and subsequently wrote a report on the condition and locations of the roads that crossed or touched the Kanawha Turnpike, the number of bridges, the depth and width of streams, the types of bridges, thickness of their timbers and the possibility of their destruction by explosives. This time Pinkerton sought out "loyal Union men," a dangerous proposition in unfamiliar territory to any experienced secret agent, which Pinkerton was not. Either by luck or by shrewd observation Pinkerton was able to report to McClellan the location of a group of mountaineers "armed with their rifles and ready to act at a moment's notice for the government."

In this report Pinkerton also included his evaluation of the temper and qualification of a Colonel Tompkins, the local Confederate commander who headed the forces in the Kanawha Valley. Tompkins, he wrote, was a West Pointer, had military experience, was well liked by his neighbors, had the respect of his men, "and lives in a fine residence a few miles from Gauley Bridge." Pinkerton described his secret rendezvous with a "Colonel Dickerson, one of the wealthiest men in the district who is a strong Union man." Dickerson's son, about thirty-five, was a Unionist, and could act as a guide, "as he knows all the roads and paths in the vicinity." [5]

Relying on what he saw or heard, Pinkerton was an excellent spy behind the lines, but as a front-line analyzer of the reports of other agents, he would prove to be totally incompetent.

In July, 1861, in addition to his duties as a spy master, McClellan asked Pinkerton to investigate a ring of thieves who were looting army warehouses in and around Parkersburg. Pinkerton made several arrests. In a letter summing up the results of this investigation, Pinkerton reveals his total dedication to McClellan, even to the point of lying to his President. In his earlier telegram to Lincoln, Pinkerton had denied McClellan's agreement with Buckner. Now he wrote to McClellan:

> Buckner's letter of his understanding of the "arrangements" with you creates no feeling here [Cincinnati]. All are satisfied with your denial. My advisers in Washington say you are all right with the President and Cameron [Secretary of War]. I fear the Blairs would like to grind an ax at your expense. If you can only have one good brush with the Rebels it will put a wet blanket on all such.

General McClellan and staff. *Library of Congress*

It would not be the first time Pinkerton would gently try to prod his beloved general into action.[6]

The arrival of Pryce Lewis from the South coincided with McClellan's request to Pinkerton for additional intelligence on topography, position, and designs of Confederate fortifications and plans of attack in western Virginia. Lewis had just returned from a murder investigation in Jackson, Mississippi, to which he had been assigned before the outbreak of hostilities. During his five months in the towns and villages, he had had an excellent opportunity to observe that state's preparation for war. On his journey back to Chicago, he had also seen Confederate military activities in other states. Lewis arrived in Chicago on June 11, 1861. When he heard that Pinkerton and most of the Agency were in Cincinnati with McClellan, he went there to report on the murder case, which ironically absolved the principal suspect.

Pinkerton, now interested in espionage, not murder, questioned Lewis closely about his observations. Lewis, observant and intelligent, gave Pinkerton an impressive military report. On Pinkerton's instructions he wrote a detailed memorandum that was turned over to McClellan, who sent a copy on to Secretary of War Cameron. For Pinkerton, the problem of who should go to western Virginia was solved: Lewis was the man.

Pinkerton gathered as many maps of the area as possible, and with Lewis, Bangs, and Webster went over a number of possible routes. It was Pinkerton's idea that Lewis would play the role of an English peer on a combined cotton-buying and pleasure trip. Because the estate of a Lord Tracy had been near Lewis's home in England, he proposed that he "assume the personality of one of his sons. I was to go in a carriage with a footman, and my ostensible objective points as a tourist were the

Allan Pinkerton and General McClellan in private consultation.
From an engraving in Pinkerton's book Spy of the Rebellion

Pinkerton and a group of his agents. *Library of Congress*

Pryce Lewis. *From a photograph by O. F. Weaver, Chicago, in the Mary Lewis collection*

Brigadier General Henry A. Wise of Virginia (CSA). *Library of Congress*

White Sulphur Springs, Natural Bridge, Hawk's Nest, the Gauley Mountains, and other natural wonders of the old Dominion."

Pinkerton, who always insisted that an operative could successfully play a role only if the trappings were authentic, bought a coach "with a spacious boot" and a team of the finest bay horses he could find in Cincinnati. There was also a genuine George III English army chest "showily strapped behind the vehicle." Pinkerton's enthusiasm overcame his frugality, and he stocked the "boot" of the coach with several boxes of imported champagne, the best "segars," and a case of port. Sam Bridgeman was assigned the role of the footman. Bridgeman, according to Lewis, "handled the reins in a style worthy of a turnout in **Pall Mall** or Picadilly." More importantly, he had been born in Virginia.

There was one last touch: Pinkerton handed over his gold watch and diamond ring to Lewis with a fervent plea to watch over them.

In the early evening, June 27, 1861, in Cincinnati headquarters, Pinkerton gave his fraudulent peer and footman a final, admiring inspection. This tall, handsome operative, with his luxuriant sideburns carefully trimmed, was dressed in the finest broadcloth "of the latest English style." Across his chest was the heavy gold chain of Pinkerton's watch, and on his finger the diamond ring. Topping it all off was a gleaming stovepipe hat. His purse "bulged with an abundance of English sovereigns"; and inside his coat was "a handsome segar case with the British lion in ivory conspicuously embossed on it."

Allan Pinkerton's Spy in a Top Hat was now ready to start on his rollicking journey behind enemy lines, one of the most dramatic stories of the Civil War.

CHAPTER 9
Spy in a Top Hat

Pryce Lewis ("Lord Tracy") and his footman (Operative Sam Bridgeman) left Cincinnati on a riverboat in June, 1861. As additions to his stovepipe hat and his latest English-cut clothes, Lewis wore Russian-leather red shoes. Sam, a short, squat man of about fifty, with a florid face and pale-blue eyes, was also dressed for his role. They had their first test at Guyandotte, which they reached the following morning. As Lewis recalled, he signed the hotel register "as though I was a Lord traveling incognito." [1]

On the road to Sulphur Springs by way of Charleston, they were stopped by a Confederate cavalry patrol. Lewis was taken to a farmhouse, where he was questioned by a young officer who introduced himself as "Colonel Patton." Patton—grandfather of the World War II general—accepted Lewis's story that he was a traveling Englishman on a grand tour of the South, and they shared the first bottle of champagne that Sam Bridgeman removed from the silver-embossed box in the carriage. But Patton insisted that Lewis had to see General Henry A. Wise. As Lewis recalled, "I thought the hair on my head was standing straight." Wise, as the North remembered, had sent John Brown to the gallows. [2]

After a few bottles of champagne had been emptied, Patton invited Lewis to inspect his fortifications, which he boasted could stand off ten thousand Yankees for ten years. Lewis, forcing himself to remain calm and casual, toured the important Coal Mouth fortifications, at the junction of the Coal and Kanawha rivers, one of the chief entrances to Virginia.

At the Kanawha House in Charleston, Lewis heard for the first time how the Confederates had defeated the forces of the Union at Big

Bethel. He finally was interviewed by Wise, who questioned him in a "savage manner" while he denounced any Englishman who would attempt to make a tourist's tour of a country at war. But Lewis stood up to the fierce-eyed old Confederate, coolly informing him he would go over his head to the British consul in Richmond for a pass. For a time it looked as if Wise would have Lewis and Bridgeman arrested, but he didn't. Bridgeman pleaded with Lewis to abandon their roles and flee, but the young Pinkerton operative decided to stay. He believed that if they fled, they would be easily captured in enemy country, and hanged immediately as spies. In the hotel bar that night, Lewis felt his heart pound furiously when a young officer laughingly told him Wise considered him "a West Pointer sent here to make a map of the country." Lewis laughed weakly and ordered another round.[3]

The days passed, with one narrow escape following the other. It was natural, as Lewis later told Pinkerton, that he felt eyes were following him and that the strange men who turned into side streets or alleys were always Wise's detectives. Bridgeman also became a serious problem. With this frightened, cringing man weeping and talking about his wife and children every night, it is surprising that Lewis's nerve didn't break, sending them both into the woods for a quick capture and execution. Sam's love for the bottle was another grave danger; one night, while drunk, he kept shouting in a crowded bar that the Union would surely win and send them all to the gallows or the dungeons as traitors. A deadly stillness fell over the bar until Lewis fiercely berated his "servant," made sweeping apologies, and spent most of Pinkerton's gold pieces buying whiskey for everyone.

They crossed streams and creeks, the now battered coach rattling down into deep gullies and struggling up almost inaccessible mountain trails. Lewis recalled years later how the stolid mountain men, with their dreary wives and barefoot children, watched in awe as the stately coach passed with the stranger in the stovepipe hat bowing and waving. In one town, Lewis delivered a lecture on the war in the Crimea and what England's role would be in the War Between the States. To a troop of volunteers ready to march to fight the Yankees, he painted a vivid picture of how England's "iron clad fleets" were ready to "thunder" across the ocean to sweep the Union blockaders from the seas. Surely it was one of the strangest scenes in this war: the Pinkerton spy standing on a chair outside the country hotel, hynotizing the enemy with his fantastic tale, and then, when he had finished, given three cheers and a rousing tiger, led by the colonel, who called him a "fine speechifier."

For nineteen days, Lewis and Bridgeman toured the Rebel lines. Finally they made their way over the mountains to ford the Big Sandy River and enter Kentucky. Before noon they rolled up before Pike County Court House. Realizing he had to get his report into the hands of Allan Pinkerton, Lewis told Sam to use the whip on the horses. They drove at breakneck speed all that day until the fine bays were staggering. Ironton was seen through a cloud of dust. Catlettsburg was reached with the team on the verge of collapse. Both Lewis and Sam took time out only to eat, then continued on to Cincinnati, where they arrived on the morning of July 18th. In Cincinnati, the haggard pair reported to Pinkerton, who rushed Lewis's report to McClellan, then at Cheat Mountain, West Virginia. The general wired Pinkerton to have Lewis report at once to General Jacob D. Cox, who had his headquarters near Red House on the Kanawha River.

At noon of July 21st, Lewis arrived at Red House. He found Cox at his headquarters aboard a boat tied to the wharf. When Cox heard that Lewis had just come from Wise's camps, he seemed not to believe it. He brought in his adjutant general, and made Lewis go over his story of his trip, his conversations with General Wise and Colonel Patton, his visit to Charleston camps, and his estimate of the quality and number of the Confederate troops.

Lewis told Cox that Wise had about 5,500 troops, including those under Patton and Browning, gave the number of rations issued for troops at Charleston, and the number of pieces of artillery at Charleston. He warned Cox that in going to Charleston he would encounter opposition at the junction of the Coal Mouth and the Kanawha, the Elk River Suspension Bridge.

When he had finished, Cox "appeared astonished." When Lewis suggested that he be allowed to make a tour of his camps to compare them with those of General Wise, Cox jumped at the idea.

When Lewis returned he told Cox: "You have not as many troops as Wise, but they are better equipped. Your artillery is much finer."

Two days after he had received Lewis's report, Cox ordered a reconnaissance force sent to the Coal Mouth. Some of the troops were to go by water, some by land. Lewis asked permission to accompany the force, and Cox granted his request.

Lewis accompanied the transports that moved up the Kanawha River to within a mile of Coal Mouth. In the distance they could see a tower of smoke and hear the distant sound of musketry. Word came that Wise's troops were falling back and had burned the bridge near the junction. The troops disembarked on the shore of the Kanawha. During the trip up the river, Lewis had struck up an acquaintance with two regimental surgeons, and was standing with them, watching the troops move up the road into the direction of the battle, when a federal cavalryman came up.

"Where are the surgeons?" he cried.

"Here, boy," one of them called out. "What is it?"

"We have the Rebel commander at their headquarters, sir; my colonel asks that you come right away."

"Very well, lad. Where is he?" one of the surgeons asked.

The cavalryman pointed up the road. "It's only a short distance, sir," he said. "He's in a farmhouse around the bend."

The surgeons started up the road, inviting Lewis to go along. Lewis hesitated. He was to remember the strange foreboding that hung so heavily about him. He hesitated, then reluctantly accepted. In a few moments they were walking up the road, listening to the young cavalryman tell them how the Confederates had fallen back with heavy losses. Large numbers of prisoners had been taken, the cavalryman said, including the Rebel commander, who had been badly wounded in the arm.

They had gone only a short distance when the cavalryman pointed through the trees. "That's the farmhouse, sir," he said. "The Rebel's there."

Lewis looked across the fields and saw "the stately farmhouse" where he had shared his champagne with Colonel Patton. He could see a company of federal troops camped on the lawn, and sentries pacing up and down the porch.

"I think I'll go back," Lewis said to the surgeons. "I don't fancy watching an operation now."

He never waited to hear what the surgeons said in reply. Turning abruptly, he returned to the transport.

That evening one of the surgeons returned.

"Was the Rebel commander badly wounded?" Lewis asked.

"Yes," the surgeon replied, "in his left shoulder. He was in no condition to be moved."

"Who was he?" Lewis asked, almost anticipating the name.

"Colonel Patton," the surgeon replied.

Lewis turned away, glad that he had not gone into the farmhouse to face the man whose gentlemanly confidence he had won so completely.

That night, when Lewis returned to Red House, he was immediately summoned to appear before Colonel Cox. He found the Union commander pacing up and down the deck of the steamboat he was using as headquarters. Without any preliminaries, Cox informed Lewis that a message had come in from a Colonel Guthrie in a camp several miles away that "two good Union men, Virginians," had come into his camp with reports that Wise had 60,000 troops and was firmly entrenched on the road to Charleston.

Lewis replied that he was convinced that Wise had no more than 5,500, and described the reports of "the two good Union men" as "a falsehood."

"I warned you, Colonel, you would have two good fights, one at Coal Mouth and the other at the Elk Suspension Bridge," he said. "Your men have forced the Rebels to evacuate Coal Mouth, which Colonel Patton predicted he would hold ten years. The bridge is burned, and Colonel Patton is a prisoner in your hands."

"That is true, Mr. Lewis; that is true," Cox said hastily.

"Wise guards his camps most vigilantly," Lewis went on. "Those two men have been lied to, and are repeating the lies to Guthrie. They are nothing but flying rumors. I'm no soldier, General, but I promise you that with the men you have here, you could be in Charleston within twenty-four hours."

The next morning, at eleven, Lewis left for Cincinnati. The last person he saw was Colonel Cox.

"We're striking tents for Charleston, Lewis," he said. "I believe in you."

"You'll be in Charleston within twenty-four hours, sir," Lewis said, and they shook hands.

That afternoon Lewis reached Parkersburg, to find the city humming with the news of the Union defeat at Bull Run. The next morning he reached Cincinnati.

At breakfast the following day a man hurried into the dining room, shouting that Colonel Cox was in Charleston and that Wise was in full retreat to the Gauley Mountains. Western Virginia was now completely in Union hands.

But Lewis had no time for self-congratulations—he was on his way to Washington to join Allan Pinkerton and the other operatives for his next assignment.

Pinkerton next sent Lewis to the hotbed city of Baltimore. Sam Bridgeman was to accompany Lewis, but before they could leave Cincinnati, Bridgeman went on a spree. Pinkerton was furious and fired Bridgeman, who begged Lewis to intercede. Lewis recalled Bridgeman shaking from the whiskey, swearing "he would never let liquor again touch his lips." Pinkerton relented, and after a blistering lecture rehired Bridgeman, and the pair left for Baltimore.

While his operatives were moving about Baltimore, Pinkerton had uncovered the momentous news that W. L. Yancey, one of the Confederate political agents in Europe, was coming home through the North. His capture, of course, would be a great prize. On July 19th, from Cincinnati, he wrote to Lincoln:

> To His Excellency, Abraham Lincoln
> President, U.S.
> Sir:
>   I have positive information from a reliable source of T. Butler King, of Georgia, now in England, being on his return home—W. L. Yancey is expected to be with him. They are to pass through the Northern States in disguise.

Cincinnatti July 19th 1861

To His Excellency Abraham Lincoln
Prest U.S.

Sir

I have positive information from a reliable source of J Buttz King of Georgia. Now in England, being on his return Home - W.L. Yancey is expected to be with him. They are to pass through the Northern States in disguise.

Should you desire it I can manage to have them arrested at some convenient point in the Loyal States.

It occurred to me that it might be advisable to have a few such Hostages, should the Rebels undertake to carry out their threats of retaliating on Loyal their men their Prisoners

It is essential to success in this matter that I should have a reply at as early a moment as possible. As I have much mental machinery to move before my plans are perfected. And the Traitors are expected soon

The source of my information is such that if you can consistently keep this matter to yourself, you would

Pinkerton-Lincoln letter of July 19, 1861. *Library of Congress*

Should you desire it, I can arrange to have them arrested at some convenient point in the Loyal States.

It occurred to me that it might be advisable to have a few such hostages should the Rebels undertake to carry out their threats of retaliating on Loyal men now their prisoners.

It is essential to success in this matter that I should have a reply at as early a moment as possible as I have much Mental machinery to move before my plans are perfected. And the traitors are expected soon.

The source of my information is such that if you can consistently keep this matter to yourself you would oblidge me.[4]

On the surface it might appear that Pinkerton was putting little trust in his President and was acting with a great deal of presumption in advising the Chief Executive. But Pinkerton was aware of the lack of security in Washington and the complete absence of presidential privacy. There is no record of a reply from Lincoln, but three months later Pinkerton would learn that his informant had been reliable. How Pinkerton in remote Cincinnati discovered the arrival of Yancey has never been known, but undoubtedly it was the result of his intensive efforts to collect every scrap of intelligence. Some of the reports from his operatives—especially Timothy Webster—were voluminous. Pinkerton's task in Cincinnati was correlating the material and selecting fact from gossip or rumor. Evidently he was doing an excellent job that summer.

McClellan, then in Wheeling, West Virginia, on his Kanawha River campaign, was suddenly called to Washington. He wrote to Pinkerton:

MY DEAR SIR:

I enclose the draft properly signed. I informed my successor Genl. Rosecrans of the position of affairs and would be glad to have you communicate with him.

Keep me fully posted and be prepared to hear from me that I need your services elsewhere. I do not know what exactly the position is that I am to occupy in Washington.

Thank you for your good wishes,

E. J. ALLEN ESQ.
Cincinnati

Very truly yours,
GEO. B. McCLELLAN, MAJ. GNL.[5]

When McClellan wrote that he did not know what his next assignment would be, his doubt was as to whether he was to succeed Winfield Scott or command the Army of the Potomac. He reached Washington to learn it was the latter.

One of the first things McClellan did was to write to Pinkerton in Cincinnati and ask him to come to Washington and set up a secret service for the Army of the Potomac. Pinkerton recalled:

I was to have as much strength of force as I required. It was arranged I was to go whenever the army moved. I was to go forward with the General, so that I might always be in communication with him. My corps was to be continually occupied in procuring from all possible sources, information regarding the strength, position and movements of the enemy. All spies, counter brands, deserters, refugees and prisoners of war coming into our lines from the front were to be carefully examined by me, and their statements taken in writing.

Pinkerton was to serve under Colonel Andrew Porter, of the 16th United States Infantry, who had been appointed Provost Marshal of Washington. Later he would report directly to Assistant Secretary of War Thomas A. Scott.

Pinkerton closed his Cincinnati headquarters, and left for Washington after first sending Webster back into Tennessee for a long tour before joining him in the wartime Capital. On trains, in bars, on street corners, the handsome and engaging Timothy Webster struck up acquaintances with Confederate army officers and civilians, who usually told him what he wanted to know. Every night in his hotel room Webster wrote it all down: "An army officer from Fort Dover in the Cumberland River said 500 men well armed and with 4 32-pounders (iron) were there to guard the river. . . ." [6]

The parenthesis (iron) is typical of Webster's care for security details. From Memphis he wrote, "No one is allowed to leave Memphis without a passport from General Polk's agent (Mr. Morgan on Main Street)." He reported the Rebel capture of 3,000 Yankee handcuffs at Bull Run, then followed up another report of troop trains leaving Richmond jammed with 5,000 troops, about 4,000 of them armed. After he had casually questioned a clerk in a Nashville hotel who had just returned from the battlefields of Missouri, he hurried to his room and sent a report to Pinkerton. Another several pages went into details of how trading with the enemy was still going on, and described provision trains waiting to move out. Again his information was precise; the cars contained beans and bacon packed in Cincinnati.

Using a "passport" signed by Confederate Secretary of War Judah Benjamin, Webster came out of Kentucky at New Albany, and reported to Pinkerton in Washington.

From his Record Books and reports, Pinkerton was, as he wrote to his Chicago office, "out in the streets all hours of the day and night." Vouchers he had submitted for his services in the Department of Ohio had not yet been honored, although they had been approved by Mc-Clellan, so he had to get an advance of $1,000 from his own office in Chicago. Before the month was out, he reported to Chicago that the first draft "was now getting pretty low" and that he needed an additional

$500. This was sent, and Pinkerton distributed the cash among his operatives, some of whom were penniless.

Washington's bureaucracy, as ponderous a century ago as it is today, soon inundated Pinkerton with paper work. Every influential politician or businessman who sought out McClellan was passed on to Pinkerton. The president of the Ohio Valley Bank insisted that the Secretary of the Treasury be alerted to his bank's "facilities." Pinkerton did so, and wrote to the bank's president: "Secretary Chase desired me to say that the Bank of Ohio Valley should be duly remembered." A railroad superintendent for some long-forgotten reason demanded to know the schedule of one of his trains, and Pinkerton looked it up and sent on the times of the arrivals and departures. The official was "A. Carnegie, Pittsburgh," the man who would involve the Agency in its worst day thirty years later.

When the War Department learned that a detective named E. J. Allen had been assigned to McClellan, they began sending him complaints they were receiving about food and the commissary. It was the usual Washington round robin, with its voluminous complaints, tips, and information, that finally ended on Pinkerton's desk. The trivia and routine must have been maddening, but Pinkerton stolidly and faithfully looked into every complaint. All received an answer: A Chicago packer supplying beef for the army "is weighing in fifty pounds of manure with very light cows." Another was butchering cows that were almost "skeletons and steers with thirteen wrinkles on their horns." One deadpan report had an informant interviewed by Pinkerton insisting "complicity to the Hon. Simon Cameron, Secretary of War." "The Washington City Jail was a miserable, filthy loathsome place," and "guarding it is not the best school for a soldier." [7]

It is clear from the reports of McClellan, Cameron, and Pinkerton that they soon agreed on a roundup of potential agents in Baltimore. Webster, Mrs. Lawton, Lewis, and Bridgeman were reporting the growing danger in the city. What had been loose and disorganized was now an underground organization. The leaders and their headquarters were unknown, but reports insisted its members could soon be armed.

Webster, because of his excellent connections in Perrymansville and Baltimore, was sent back to that city to infiltrate the secret society. Hattie Lawton was ordered to work with Webster, while Lewis and Sam Bridgeman returned to Washington to help Pinkerton trap Rose O'Neal Greenhow, the Confederacy's most important agent in Washington.

CHAPTER 10
Pinkerton and the Wild Rose: The Washington Spy Ring, 1861-1862

At forty-four, Rose O'Neal Greenhow was tall and striking. Her flashing dark eyes, patrician nose, and slightly thin lips were framed by dark, thick black hair, drawn back in the severe fashion of the time. She had the manner of a woman born to the blood royal, which irritated Allan Pinkerton, who considered her nothing more than a flamboyant, dangerous woman who was trading her favors for important military information.

Mrs. Greenhow's battle with Pinkerton was on the grand scale. She and her lady spies raced about Washington in carriages and on foot, trying to dodge his "shadows"; she taunted him as "that German Jew detective," and denounced his operatives as "ruffians" and "lawless men." She had enormous influence with men holding high offices in Lincoln's administration, and although she pulled every wire she could, she never defeated Pinkerton. For months the detective and his operatives relentlessly followed Rose and her spies, day and night, until the widow and her lady agents were jumpy and fearful. Mrs. Greenhow's seductive smiles and soulful dark eyes left the puritanical Pinkerton cold.

Memoirs and recollections of politicians, generals, and statesmen help to establish Rose as a striking beauty. Alexander Gardner's photograph of the Confederate spy and her daughter in Old Capitol was taken

Rose O'Neal Greenhow. *Library of Congress*

by Gardner after she had spent some time in that dusty, badly ventilated boardinghouse turned into a prison. What woman would not show the ravages of months of sharing a tiny room with a peevish child in the musty halls of Old Capitol? The black dress accentuated her worn face, but despite the fatigue, the photograph also shows a woman of great dignity, pride, and breeding, who sits with queenly dignity on a plain chair, with a barred window and a whitewashed wall as a backdrop.[1]

Rose was not only a magnetic woman; she was also cultured and well educated. Men were drawn to her: statesmen, lawmakers, naval and army officers, politicians, clerks, blockade runners, and spies. Allan Pinkerton and his detectives never forgot her. Some recalled her "regal manners"; Colonel William E. Doster, Provost Marshal of Washington, thought they bordered on the "theatrical," a shrewd observation. Evidently Rose thought it was effective to talk in a regal manner to those she considered her inferiors. This included Wiliam P. Wood, the superintendent of Old Capitol Prison, Surgeon General Stewart, Union soldiers, Black Republican dogs, and Allan Pinkerton. Greeley's New York *Herald* classified her as "a dangerous and romantic spy," while the Washington *National* insisted that Rose was "dangerous but beautiful."

Rose was born in Montgomery County, Maryland, about 1817. Her sister, Ellen Elizabeth, married James Madison Cutts, a nephew of Dolley Madison. In her formative years, Rose was placed in the charge of an aunt who ran the Congressional Boarding House, actually in the Old Capitol Building.

In her teens she was the belle of every Washington ball, always surrounded by groups of admiring men. It was the older but handsome Tennessean, Dr. Robert Greenhow, artist, author, linguist, and physician, who finally captured her hand. Their home and gardens on H Street were soon the scene of the city's most elaborate dinners and receptions.

The men who later ruled the Confederacy were her husband's friends and many times her honored guests: Jefferson Davis, John C. Calhoun, James A. Seddon, later the Secretary of War; Robert Barnwell Rhett, the South Carolina secessionist; Robert M. T. Hunter, the dashing Virginian and later Davis's Secretary of War; and Turner Ashby, who would ride with Stonewall Jackson. James Buchanan—Old Buck, as his friends called him, then the Senator from Pennsylvania and later President—also lost his heart to Rose. In 1845, when he was Minister at the Court of St. James's, we find him writing to Rose, signing his letters "your ancient and devoted friend." When the great Calhoun died, it was Rose who stayed during the last hours to close the old man's eyes.

In 1857, Greenhow died in an accident in San Francisco, and Rose, not too long after the funeral, sued the city and collected an unknown sum. When Buchanan was President, she was seen so much in his company that the New York *Herald* called her "Queen of the Rose Water Administration."

Brigadier General Thomas Jordan of Virginia (CSA).
Library of Congress

While Pinkerton was shepherding Brown's small party of slaves to Canada, the parties continued, and the carriages lined up outside Mrs. Greenhow's red brick house on Sixteenth and I streets to discharge the belles in their low-cut evening gowns, and their beaux. In her parlor the brilliant sashes of naval officers mixed with the broadcloth of the statesmen.

The Washington female spy ring had been organized by Colonel Thomas Jordan, a handsome West Pointer who had been William T. Sherman's roommate. Before he had left Washington to become General P. G. T. Beauregard's adjutant general, Jordan had enlisted Rose and had given her a simple cipher he had devised, telling her to address her dispatches and notes to Thomas J. Rayford, the alias he had selected for himself. Though Rose insisted in her memoirs that she was motivated purely by patriotism, Colonel Doster revealed, many years after the war, that Jordan had once told him he knew Rose was having an affair with a powerful figure in the Senate—probably Henry Wilson, Chairman of the Military Affairs Committee—and that Jordan also "had established relations with the widow on the same footing."

Jordan knew that the widow's great value was her easy access to men who possessed important military, political, and diplomatic knowledge. He was also aware that Rose was so devoted to the Confederacy that she would use her charm and obviously her sex to gain information.[2]

Colonel Jordan wisely kept his lady spies apart, sending them notes of congratulations and making each one feel that the Confederacy would rise or fall on her efforts alone. Gradually he included professional men, government clerks, politicians, bankers, and army officers who relayed Rose's dispatches to Richmond or acted as her couriers. In time the ring spread as far as Texas.

Pinkerton's first assignment in Washington from Assistant Secretary of War Scott was to investigate Mrs. Greenhow's suspected activities. He found that she had been apparently operating with immunity. In July, 1861, she had sent word to Beauregard, commanding the Confederate forces, that Union General Irvin McDowell, "with 55,000 troops will advance this day from Arlington Heights." At Bull Run the Rebels had scattered McDowell's forces to send them fleeing back into Washington.

A conference was held with McClellan and Scott at which Pinkerton detailed the results of his preliminary investigation of the Confederate spies in Washington. It was obvious that some counterintelligence group had to be formed immediately, and McClellan asked Pinkerton for his views. A few days later the detective sent his general a letter in which he outlined his plans for a secret service agency:

> I propose to test suspected persons in various ways. I shall seek access to their homes, clubs and places of resort, managing that among members of my force shall be ostensibly representatives of every grade of society, from the highest to the most menial. Some shall have the entree to the gilded salon of the suspected aristocratic traitors and their honored guests, while others will act in the capacity of valets or domestics of various kinds, and try the efficacy of such relationships with the household to gain evidence. Other suspected ones will be tracked by the "shadow" detective, who will follow their every footstep and note their every action.

With approval of both Scott and McClellan, Pinkerton personally took over the investigation of Mrs. Greenhow; his agents were Pryce Lewis, San Bridgeman, and John Scully, who had been brought back from Baltimore.

While Pinkerton organized his department, Rose and her ladies were active on several fronts. When a company of militia delivered some Rebel prisoners to Old Capitol, Rose had baskets of food delivered to the men in tattered gray. Her arrogance was insufferable. When she walked into the prison yard and found Superintendent Wood lecturing the prisoners about the treason of the South, Rose calmly interrupted to inform the prisoners that the South "has prisoners 100 to 1 if the North wants to retaliate." The weary prisoners gave her cheers and a tiger, and left Wood sputtering with rage. Pinkerton, of course, heard from Wood that same afternoon.[3]

After the disaster at Bull Run, the officer commanding the city's defenses was her next victim. As she relates, she soon had the plans, plus blueprints of Fort Corcoran and Fort Ellsworth. To familiarize herself and her ladies with the Union plans, she took them on a Sunday-afternoon grand tour of the fortifications. She returned with one of the most fantastic schemes of the war.

At the signal of attack, her ladies would cut the telegraph wires to the War Department, kidnap McClellan, and spike the guns of Ellsworth and Corcoran. With the Capital in a state of fear and chaos following the Bull Run disaster, and War Department officials bewitched by this attractive and fanatical woman, who can say that the plan might not have been successful—at least in part?

Rose sent the blueprints of the forts and reports of military strength in Washington on to Jordan. Her report can be seen today in the National Archives. Several pages long, dated August 1, 1861, it details with surprising military perception the Washington key defense plan. Each fort is examined minutely; secret weaknesses in the earthworks are described; the number, caliber, and range of all field pieces are given.

When Rose suspected they were being tailed, she and her ladies made a game of trying to lose the detectives. But for all their games, Pinkerton finally discovered the young officer who was supplying Rose with important military information. On the night of August 21, 1861, Pinkton, Pryce Lewis, Sam Bridgeman, and John Scully followed the young officer about the city. It was warm and sultry, with the threat of rain in the air as they slipped through the shadows after the hurrying young man. The rain was falling in sheets when the officer suddenly darted into the Greenhow house on Sixteenth Street.

Pinkerton and his men took shelter under the dripping trees in front of St. John's Church across the street. When a lamp was lighted in the front room, they moved across the street. Pinkerton took off his boots and climbed on the "husky shoulder" of Lewis and Bridgeman to peer through the blinds. In what he recalled as an "elaborate room lined with valuable pictures and statuary," he saw the officer hand Mrs. Greenhow a map, and heard him, above the hiss of the rain, carefully describe for her the strength of the fortification on the map.

While Pinkerton's "blood boiled with indignation," Mrs. Greenhow and the officer left the room, "returning within an hour arm in arm." She walked him to the front door, and the detectives heard what Lewis recalled "sounded like a kiss."[4]

Pinkerton told Lewis and Bridgeman to keep watch on the house while he followed the officer. Suspecting he was being followed, the officer ran through the rain. Pinkerton took after him in stocking feet. At the barracks door the officer shouted for the provost, who arrested the detective, shoeless, mud-splattered, and dripping. Pinkerton refused to identify himself, and was thrown into the jail. He managed to bribe a guard to take a message to Scott, who had him "delivered to the War Department for personal interrogation."

Pinkerton, who recalled he looked more like something dragged out of the Potomac than like the Washington spy master, described to Scott what happened. The young officer was summoned by Scott. Faced with Pinkerton's report, he confessed. A search of his room uncovered, as Pinkerton recalled, "sufficient evidence to prove he was engaged in furnishing sufficient information to the enemy." He was arrested and sent to Fort McHenry, where he committed suicide.

Pinkerton and his men kept a round-the-clock watch on Rose, her house, and the activities of her agents. Every visitor to Sixteenth Street was investigated. Pinkerton left nothing out of his reports, and Scott was embarrassed to learn that some of the Union's leaders were seeing Rose in her "elaborate room."

Scott finally issued an order for her arrest. Pinkerton led Lewis, Bridgeman, and Scully to the Greenhow house. In the handsome parlor, they found Mrs. Greenhow, "a brunette, richly dressed," reading. Pinkerton was all business. "Lewis, you take charge of this lady," he said. "Detain her here. Scott, Bridgeman, you come with me."

While Pinkerton and his "uncouth ruffians," as Rose called them, searched her house, gathering boxes of secret reports, letters, and official documents, many classified, Rose chatted with Lewis on what he said "was a number of impersonal subjects." She closed her book, carefully took Lewis's measure, then poured on the charm. At one point she begged him to allow her to go upstairs. Lewis hesitated. At last he agreed if he could accompany her.

"It is my imperative duty to go with you, madam," he told the spy, who angrily flounced upstairs.

In her room, Rose snatched up a pistol from a mantel. In a typically theatrical gesture she whirled about, pointed the gun at Lewis, and cried:

"If I had known who you were when you came in, I would have shot you dead."

Lewis, with wry humor, smiled, and replied, "Madam, you will first have to cock that pistol to fire it."[5]

When she surrendered the weapon, Lewis suspected that Rose "was not as dangerous as she talked."

Though Rose might have been entertaining Pryce Lewis with her melodramatics, for Pinkerton it was a grim and deadly business. Boxes, drawers, and niches about the house were slowly yielding voluminous material: technical reports, in minute detail, concerning movements of troops, sizes and quantities of ordnance; the flaws and weaknesses of men she had charmed into committing treason; information on the morale of troops, the rumors current among certain regiments; the incidence of sickness; types of insubordination—nothing escaped Rose. It was evident she was too good for the amateurs in Richmond; they simply did not know how to use or evaluate the important information she was sending them.

Pinkerton gradually discovered the scope of her spy ring and her "secret conveyance" that passed her information from hand to hand until it reached Richmond. One letter, torn to scraps and carelessly tossed into a fireplace, was carefully pasted together by Pinkerton:

"Regt. Evansport Landing. Send to Col. W. B. Bates, camp near Evansport Landing—ask him to send to Chapman by Mr. Ray of his Regt. Nat Chapman will deliver it to Dr. Wyvill who will bring it here so that I can get it."

Pinkerton also found her small red diary, which listed her couriers and fellow agents, some of them well-known Washingtonians. Jordan's cipher was also in the book. From her captured documents Pinkerton put together the jigsaw of the spy ring.[6] He and his men shadowed and arrested a weird collection of army officers, politicians, professional men, government clerks, opium smokers, psychopaths, and a group of charming, attractive women, all recruited by Jordan before he left for Richmond.

There were a number of arrests in August and September. James G. Berret, Mayor of Washington, found himself in Fort Lafayette after Pinkerton successfully broke up a plot to ram through an act of secession in the Maryland legislature.

Pinkerton wisely kept Rose under guard in her house—"The Greenhow Prison," as the Washington newspapers dubbed it—while he continued his investigation. Mrs. Augusta Morris, "a gay and sprightly widow," as Pinkerton described her, an important courier for the ring, was next arrested.

When Pinkerton found Jordan's cipher, he had Kate Warne rewrite one of Mrs. Greenhow's dispatches, substituting useless or false information, and sent it on to Jordan, hoping to "entice Richmond into a correspondence." But Jordan was a crafty agent. He and his staff closely examined the letter, and came to the conclusion that it was too risky. He advised Beauregard that the old cipher was useless and that a new one had to be sent on to Washington, adding that he had heard that Washington had offered a large reward for anyone who could break the Confederate cipher. This most practical of spies wrote to his general: "I am inclined to furnish a key to a friend of mine in Washington and let him have the consideration."

In Washington the government juggled the explosive problem of what to do with Mrs. Greenhow. There were numerous conferences between Pinkerton, Secretary of War Stanton, and Secretary of State Seward as to what to do with this obviously dangerous woman. Men in high office were plotting to have her released. One must also consider her high connections: Her brother-in-law was James Madison Cutts, second Comptroller of the Treasury. He and his wife were the parents of Rose Adele Cutts Douglas, the widow of Stephen A. Douglas, who had taken her aunt's place as the most beautiful matron of Washington's society. Mrs. Greenhow had known nine Presidents, and had been the intimate adviser to one—President Buchanan. She had powerful friends at Queen Victoria's court as well; William Lowndes Yancey, the Confederate diplomatic agent in London, was spreading her fame there. In New York City, Washington, London, and Paris the newspapers were calling her America's most beautiful and dangerous spy. In Richmond her name was spoken with reverence.

Pinkerton refused to compromise. He stared down the emissaries who came to his office to plead, promise, or try to cajole him into abandoning the investigation of Mrs. Greenhow. When Colonel T. M. Key, McClellan's own aide-de-camp, visited Mrs. Greenhow, Pinkerton gave him a "stern" lecture on security.

In the first few days of her arrest, two of her most important agents rang her bell and walked into the sitting room, to be greeted by Pinkerton. One was William J. Walker, a clerk in the Post Office Department, and a direct link to Jordan. Michael Thompson, a South Carolina lawyer whom Pinkerton described as "a man of subtle intellect, finished education, practical energy, polished manners and an attractive address," was also arrested. His home yielded a storehouse of dispatches and reports ready for Richmond. A copy of Jordan's cipher, used by Rose, was also found.

The trail led from suspect to suspect. Before Pinkerton had finished his investigation, evidence he uncovered showed the ring had spread from Washington to Richmond and as far south as New Orleans and west to Texas. Members of the prominent family of Fontaine Maury, the famous oceanographer, were arrested, with one cousin, Rutson Maury, Jr., admitting he had delivered more than a thousand letters from the South, many of them from agents abroad.

Rutson Maury's arrest by Pinkerton as a spy recalled the role Rutson had played as a courier in delivering letters addressed to Lord Russell under a British seal, some dealing with Maury's plan to transfer cotton from the South to England. This had led Charles Francis Adams to charge that the British government had been engaged in secret negotiations to recognize the Confederacy, a charge Lord Russell was forced officially to deny.

The arrest of Michael Thompson, or Colonel Empty, as he was known to the Confederacy, led Pinkerton to William T. Smithson, a well-known Washington banker, a major figure in the Washington spy ring, and a close friend of Mrs. Greenhow. Pinkerton and his operatives trailed Smithson until mid-January, 1862, when Pinkerton took the banker into custody.

Old Capitol Prison in Washington

In his investigation of Smithson, Pinkerton discovered that the banker had a unique means of getting military information to Richmond—rolling it up and hiding it in a plug of tobacco. Another of Smithson's plans was to use a Sister of Charity from the Providence Hospital in Washington as a courier. Smithson's captured dispatches revealed that he and Mrs. Greenhow operated the upper level of the ring, with the banker addressing his information only to Secretary of War Benjamin. Pinkerton, after he had sent Smithson to Old Capitol, described him as "one of the most prominent and dangerous Rebel sympathizers in Washington." Over Pinkerton's objections, Smithson was released within three months. However, in the spring of 1863 he was taken into custody again, charged with conducting illicit banking operations for the Confederacy.

The documents and coded messages captured by Pinkerton showed that Rose and her spies were using all the traditional trappings of the nineteenth-century spies: hollowed-out tobacco plugs, hollow canes, messages sewed into the linings of gowns and waistcoats or hidden in the thick tresses of beautiful women. But despite these primitive methods of delivery, Pinkerton established the huge scope of the ring and the shocking amount of military, political, and diplomatic information its agents had smuggled into Richmond.

Pinkerton's insistence on confining Rose in Old Capitol Prison, along with the other spies, finally prevailed. Assistant Secretary of War Scott signed the order, and Pinkerton informed Rose that she and her daughter were to be moved. Pinkerton tried to keep the transfer secret, but Rose did not. The young officer in carge of the "rifles" guarding her house had long been charmed into bringing her fruit and taking out messages—which Pinkerton didn't know until much later—and Rose undoubtedly used him to spread the word.

Rose O'Neal Greenhow and her daughter in Old Capitol Prison, by Alexander Gardner. *Library of Congress*

For a time it was feared that Ben Butler, later the "Beast of New Orleans," would have his way when he tried to get the War Department to place Rose in his care at Fortress Monroe, where he would "put her through such an ordeal she would never again endanger the loyalty of Union officers." But Butler was boasting. Wood, the superintendent of Old Capitol, later told Pinkerton he would rather handle a cage full of hungry lions than one Wild Rose.

Before she left "the Greenhow Prison," Rose made a tour of her house with Pryce Lewis, denouncing Pinkerton and his "unwashed ruffians" for leaving footprints on her rugs. On a Saturday afternoon, with Pinkerton, "the German Jew detective," as she described him to a newspaperman, at her elbow, she left her home for the last time. Mrs. Greenhow was her own image maker; the streets were filled with spectators eager to catch a glimpse of Washington's most dangerous woman. Men and boys clung to tree limbs and lampposts. Even to a less theatrical person than Rose, this was a dramatic moment. She stood on the porch calmly looking down at the sea of faces, her dark eyes cold and contemptuous. With a disdainful look at Pinkerton, she took her young daughter's hand and majestically walked down the steps. At the bottom she said to the young lieutenant, "I hope in the future your men will have a nobler employment."

In a few minutes Rose and her daughter were on their way to Old Capitol Prison.

Old Capitol, one of the most famous of Civil War prisons, was a long, three-story hodgepodge of brick and wooden buildings situated on the corner of East Capitol and Carrol streets. In the center of this cluster of buildings was an open yard. A high wooden fence ran the length of the extensions on Carrol Street. It was, as Colonel Doster recalled, "one of the many makeshifts to which an unexpected war had driven the authorities." Originally the main building had been the Old Congressional Boarding House Rose had known as a child.

William P. Wood, the superintendent of Old Capitol, had served in Mexico, was in Nicaragua with William Walker, and was employed as a "model maker" in Washington. As an expert witness in a famous patent case, he had met Edwin Stanton. In his memoirs, Doster gives a good picture of Wood, a shadowy but powerful figure in Civil War Washington:

> He was in many respects a remarkable man—short, ugly and slovenly in dress while in manner affecting stupidity and humility, but at the bottom the craftiest of men. For some reason, which no one could fathom, he was deeper in the War Department than any man in Washington, and it was commonly said that Stanton was at the head of the War Office and Wood was at the head of Stanton.

During the time he was in Washington, Pinkerton worked very closely with Wood, but was cautious in his relationship with the prison superintendent, "a rather crafty man" as he once called him.

When Pryce Lewis and Sam Bridgeman delivered Rose and her daughter, Wood welcomed them in his "receiving room." He was undoubtedly surprised to have little Rose greet him with: "You have one of the darnedest Rebels here you ever saw."

Pinkerton had selected a room on the second floor of the prison for Rose and her daughter. A solitary window looked into the dismal yard. The high board fence cut off all view of the street or the city where Rose had reigned so long. Though the room was plain—containing only a bed, chair, looking glass, and sewing machine—it was bitterly familiar to Rose. Knowingly or unknowingly, the prison cell Pinkerton had selected was the same room in which Rose had administered to the dying John C. Calhoun. It would be her home for five weary months.

The most stunning disclosure—totally embarrassing to the Lincoln administration—Pinkerton had uncovered in the Greenhow correspondence was a thick package of love letters from Henry Wilson, Senator from Massachusetts, Chairman of the powerful Military Affairs Committee, and four years later Vice-President under Grant. The letters, known as the "H Letters," are terse, feverish love notes:

> You know I love you—and I will sacrifice everything on my own account. I do love you . . . I must see you tonight . . . I am sick mentally and physically . . . nothing would soothe me as much as an hour with you . . . at whatever cost I must see you tonight. . . .

I am in receipt of
your note. If you knew how
I suffered last night, and
am still suffering you could
find it in your heart to forgive
me. I had a burning fever the
whole night — I am now only able
to sit up because I *must* be
here. But sick or well I *will*
be with you tonight — and then
I will tell you again and again
that I love you, as I now do
and that too most truthfully
                        Eva Jone H

Letter from Senator Henry Wilson of Massachusetts, Chairman
of the Military Affairs Committee, and later Vice-President under
Grant. *The National Archives*

The letters are still marked "Love Letters from Henry Wilson, U.S.
Senator from Massachusetts." The words, "supposed to be" are inserted,
by caret, between "letters" and "from." [7]

The letters were turned over to McClellan and Scott. There is no
report of any official questioning of Wilson; certainly Pinkerton was
never called in. But Rose in her memoirs recalls that her seized papers
had come under discussion at a Cabinet meeting, with Scott and Mc-
Clellan in attendance, and that "several Republican officials had been
summoned amongst the number Wilson of Mass. as being implicated in
my information."

There is little doubt that the story of the Cabinet meeting is true. How Wilson met this trying hour is not known, but he was cleared, perhaps on the theory that he had done nothing to endanger the security of his country. If it had been a crime to fall under Rose's spell, many of the same Cabinet members might have joined Wilson in a cell.

Wilson was still bedeviled by Rose, even behind bars. He visited her in Old Capitol—simply as a member of a senatorial committee, he stiffly informed Wood, who looked embarrassed at the man all Washington was calling Rose's lover. When Wood left them, Wilson told Rose that he was doing all he could to get her released, but that McClellan, influenced by Pinkerton, was insisting to Lincoln that she be kept in jail for the duration. The news that her fame had spread to the White House mollified Rose, but not before she had delivered a tirade against Pinkerton.

Wilson undoubtedly noticed the change that had come over the woman he had begged to see at all hours of the day and night: The flawless olive complexion was now sickly; the burning eyes were sunk deep; the black hair was streaked with gray.

With Rose O'Neal Greenhow in prison, Pinkerton and his operatives continued to tie up the loose ends of the Jordan-Greenhow spy ring. During the bitter days of that first wartime winter, Mrs. Greenhow's captured correspondence gave them invaluable tips and clues concerning Confederate sympathizers on the periphery of the ring. Most of them were Jordan's attractive middle-aged widows or the wives of prominent professional men with Confederate ties. Arrested and delivered to prison was Mrs. Phillip Phillips, the wife of a former Alabama congressman and Washington attorney. Her mother had been Fanny Yates of Charleston, her father Jacob Clavius Levy, both prominent southern families. Like Rose, Mrs. Phillips had been a Washington hostess and society beauty: "a bad, bad woman" as Mrs. Chesnut, the Confederate diarist, called her.

Pinkerton confiscated their papers, and found enough to send them all to prison. He soon discovered that the ladies were having interested visitors: Secretary of War Stanton, senators, congressmen, and Colonel Thomas Marshal Key, Judge Advocate and McClellan's aide-de-camp. Fortunately, the group was sent south within a short time. In New Orleans, Mrs. Phillips again landed in jail for jeering at the funeral cortege of a federal soldier and for teaching her children to spit at northern officers. Mrs. Phillips, as Pinkerton once told Key, was an unrelenting Rebel.

Politicians, statesmen, and military leaders continued to press for Mrs. Greenhow's release and parole, but Pinkerton was unbending and uncompromising. His opinion, blunt and forceful, was delivered to McClellan, Stanton, and Scott—Mrs. Greenhow was a dangerous enemy agent, a threat to the Union, and she must be confined until the end of hostilities.

He informed Assistant Secretary of War Scott that the evidence he had uncovered revealed Mrs. Greenhow's home had been the center of a vast spy operation and that through her seductive powers "she had gained important military information" which she had sent to Richmond:

> She has made use of whomever and whatever she could as mediums to carry into effect her unholy purpose . . . she has not used her powers in vain among the officers of the Army, Navy, not a few of whom she had robbed of patriotic hearts and transformed them into sympathizers with the enemies of the country which had made them all they are.

Mrs. Greenhow, he reported, "is a willing instrument in plotting the overthrow of the United States government."

A dreary winter passed. Pinkerton sent an operative into Old Capitol who charmed Mrs. Roberta Hasler, another of Mrs. Greenhow's spies, into giving him three dispatches she was trying to smuggle into Richmond. But Rose found out about it, and managed to warn Jordan.

Assistant Secretary of the Navy Gustavus V. Fox went to Rose to tell her she would be free to go to Richmond if she signed an oath of allegiance. Rose turned on her charm, or "irresistible seductive powers," as Pinkerton called it, actually to worm out of Fox the secrets of McClellan's next campaign. That same night, Rose wrote a dispatch and sent it on its way to Jordan, detailed information, Rose said, "from Fox of the Navy Department."

How Rose smuggled out the dispatches Pinkerton doesn't disclose, but he writes vaguely of the widow "engaging herself" at the time in "tapestry," using balls of colored wool that were delivered by the provost marshal's office. Her finished products were sent to her friends as gifts. Pinkerton did not know she had sent Fox's information to Richmond—that dispatch was found after Richmond had fallen—but Pinkerton and all Washington realized that she was still the Wild Rose, as they called her, when the Richmond *Whig* published a letter she had smuggled to Jordan. The Confederate spy master shrewdly realized its publicity value, and had the Richmond *Whig* publish the Greenhow letter in full. A short time later it was republished by Greeley's *Herald*.

The letter was a melodramatic account of how Pinkerton and his "ruffians" had "torn letters from my bosom," which of course was all nonsense. However, the letter was a sensation not only in New York and Washington but also in London. The letter was embarrassing to both Lincoln and his Cabinet.

Pinkerton dressed Wood down in a private interview, and discipline tightened. Little Rose, who had been allowed to play in the prison yard, was now confined to the room. All laundry was carefully searched. Even a sprig of Rose's favorite jasmine, which had "reached her without examination," sent Pinkerton into a cold fury. Then, with dramatic suddenness, Mrs. Greenhow was notified she would go on trial before General John A. Dix and Judge Edward Pierrepont, both prominent New Yorkers who had been appointed by Secretary of War Stanton to examine the numerous cases of men and women charged with disloyalty. Dix, Secretary of the Treasury under Buchanan, knew Mrs. Greenhow. More than once he and his wife had dined at her table.

The interrogation took place in one of the rooms of Senator William Gwin's showplace house at Nineteenth and L streets, whose dining room and parlors were well known to Rose. An hour's wait in a small, stoveless room didn't sweeten the widow's disposition.

Rose put on a great performance, sweeping into the hearing room, loftily advising Dix and his commissioners that they could take their seats. While Dix was considerate of old friendships, the evidence Pinkerton had uncovered was devastating: only a traitor would ignore the reports, dispatches, and coded messages, some now carefully pasted together. Dix was no traitor, and as the hours passed his attitude grew colder. Rose's vilification of Lincoln didn't help her. Dix declared that one of her letters intercepted by Pinkerton was "equal to declaring determined hostility to the government."

Weeks passed. Pinkerton linked the wife of former Senator Jackson Morton of Florida to Mrs. Greenhow's ring, and took Lewis and John Scully to the Morton mansion to search for incriminating evidence. Pinkerton and his men searched the house, floor by floor, for four days. Letters and documents indicating the Mortons' sympathy for the Confederacy were found, but nothing so important as the dispatches Pinkerton had uncovered in the Greenhow house.

During the search, Lewis and Scully became acquained with the senator's two young sons. One afternoon Mrs. Morton and her daughter served tea for the weary and dusty detectives who had been rummaging all morning in the attic. After the boxes of material were delivered to the provost marshal's office, the Mortons applied for a pass to leave Washington. It took several weeks for approval, and Lewis occasionally saw Mrs. Morton, her sons and daughters, "and passed a few words." [8]

In her dismal Washington prison room, Mrs. Greenhow continued to use her influential friends to try to gain her release. Recommendations for her parole usually ended on Pinkerton's desk. The detective doggedly reminded Assistant Secretary of War Scott, Secretary Stanton, and the others that his men were daily risking their lives behind enemy lines and that to release Rose would be an affront to their bravery. The hot, humid summer days merged into the fall. Alexander Gardner, Brady's former assistant, returned to his Washington gallery to develop a number of "war views" he and his staff had taken on the front. One day he received permission from the War Department to take a picture of Mrs. Greenhow and her daughter in the courtyard of Old Capitol. The glass plate showed how confinement was starting to tell on Rose. She looked weary, and the long, black bombazine dress was becoming shabby. But Gardner's portrait also reveals the iron in her makeup; she was still the Confederacy's Wild Rose.

The winter was bitter, and cold edged into the ancient wooden building, forcing Rose, her daughter, and all the inmates of Old Capitol to wear the tattered blankets, sweaters, and coats—which didn't help her disposition. But the cold, the miserable food, the monotony, and the long hours with a bored, peevish child would have been forgotten by Rose had she known how the folds of her spy ring, uncovered by Pinkerton, were ironically ensnaring Lewis, Scully, Tim Webster, and Hattie Lawton in distant Richmond.

Rose would eventually be released and passed through the lines to Richmond, where she reigned like an exiled queen. She later went to London to write her memoirs, which became a best seller. Returning to her beloved South, she was drowned trying to run the blockade.

CHAPTER 11

The Pinkerton Spies
in Richmond, 1861-1862

The investigation of the Jordan-Greenhow spy ring in Washington and the arrests of its members were only part of Pinkerton's work in the fall and winter of 1861-1862. His Record Books show him still burdened by voluminous complaints and suspicions sent on from the War Department about corrupt meatpackers, fraudulent cotton brokers, and thieves stealing military stores. It was also evident that the scope and powers of his organization were getting to be too much for his limited personnel and budget, as well as the intent of McClellan's original proposal. Lack of money was a constant irritation. The government was traditionally slow in honoring his drafts. Pinkerton was always telegraphing his Chicago office to send on money to pay the expenses of his secret organization.

Tim Webster and Hattie Lawton were still in Baltimore, and once Mrs. Greenhow had been remanded to Old Capitol, Pinkerton turned his attention to that troubled city. Webster was now established in Miller's Hotel in Baltimore, "representing himself as a gentleman of means and leisure." Pinkerton had equipped him with a team and carriage and plenty of pocket money for the bars. He and Hattie moved between Perrymansville and the city, and as Webster reported to Pinkerton, he had "developed numerous acquaintances." John Scully was their courier. On one trip, as a precaution, Webster and Scully visited a Baltimore photographic gallery to have a picture taken, with a Confederate flag between them. Webster made sure he had a copy in his wallet at all times.

There were some close calls. Once a city tough who had led an attack on Union troops denounced Webster as a spy because he had seen Webster lean out of a carriage and talk to "the chief of the Yankee detectives." Webster knocked the bully sprawling, and convinced the bar that the tough was a liar.

Webster continued to deliver letters from Richmond to Baltimore, establishing his own relays of friends along the route. He was now a trusted courier for Secretary of War Benjamin, even delivering Benjamin's personal letters. His role as a Confederate sympathizer and mail runner established, Webster started to seek out the secret underground organization. After several weeks he heard whispers of the meetings, names of its leaders. Webster was finally invited to a meeting of the Knights of Liberty, a fifth column, which, its leaders insisted, could raise seven thousand rifles.

Webster was brought to a midnight meeting with the usual mumbo-jumbo of passwords and countersigns. He became a member, and one of their best speakers. At first, Webster was skeptical of the group's boasting, but gradually the extent of the organization's plans and number of its members were revealed. The major plan was an attack on Washington. Richmond would give the signal, and ten thousand Baltimoreans would rise, the leaders insisted. Webster wrote to Pinkerton that he considered the number exaggerated, but the rifles they showed him were very real.

Webster slipped into Washington and reported to Pinkerton, spending most of the day outlining the scope of the organization and the conspiracy for an uprising. While both Pinkerton and Webster agreed that some aspects of the plot "sounded rather visionary," the evidence of the hidden arsenal could not be overlooked. As Pinkerton wrote: "The great object, of course, was to break up the organization and defeat the conspiracy in a manner that would not compromise Webster; but it was not deemed prudent to go about this with any inordinate haste."[1]

Pinkerton advised Webster to return to Baltimore, and continue attending the meetings "in the character of an active conspirator." In the meantime, he would send in two more agents, also assigned to infiltrate the organization. Pinkerton wisely decided that the additional agents would be unknown to Webster.

Webster returned to Baltimore and continued to attend the meetings of the Knights. In a few weeks, the two other operatives reported to Pinkerton that they had been accepted as members. By the rules of the underground organization, no one could enter the meeting rooms without passing two guards and giving the password. The guards were appointed from volunteers. Every few weeks the passwords were changed, and any member who failed to give the proper words was barred.

Secretary of War Judah P. Benjamin.
Library of Congress

Pinkerton instructed his two agents to volunteer as guards and to notify him what nights they would be at the door. They sent the date to Pinkerton, advising him that the speaker of the evening would be a notorious Confederate sympathizer—Timothy Webster. Pinkerton advised his men that the Knights would be raided on the night they were guarding the door, and he suggested they give the signal when Webster was at the peak of his speech. This was a shrewd touch to cast off any possible suspicion against Webster.

In Washington, Pinkerton conferred with McClellan and Secretary of War Cameron to make arrangements for the raid. He left with several of his operatives for a meeting at Fort McHenry with General Dix, who had tried Mrs. Greenhow. Dix assigned an officer as liaison with the civilians, and several companies of soldiers.

Army muskets would batter in the doors, but Pinkerton was running the show. After studying a city map he deployed the troops and operatives in a small area surrounding the meeting place. They waited in the darkness until they received a signal from the Pinkerton agents guarding the door. Webster was on a small platform, roaring out defiance of Lincoln and the Union, when the doors crashed in. The Knights were caught in their seats. There was some confused scuffling during which Webster escaped through a rear window. Pinkerton reported the success of the raid to Secretary of State Seward, pointing out that he had been acting under orders of Cameron and McClellan. In his dispatch he outlined how he, his staff, and the army units of the 4th United States Cavalry had obtained a number of arrest orders, made the raids, and arrested the leaders within fifteen minutes. "Their clothing [was] thoroughly searched and immediately they were forwarded to Fort McHenry in separate carriages."

Pinkerton informed Dix that the prisoners included Frank Key Howard, one of the editors of the Baltimore *Exchange,* and T. W. Hall, editor of *The South.* The writ of habeas corpus had been revoked by presidential order, but it is still shocking to discover Dix granting Pinkerton "sufficient warrants" to search the editorial and executive offices of both newspapers "and seizing the correspondence therein." But the raid did yield information that showed how near right was the information Pinkerton had forwarded to Lincoln about Yancey in July. An operative reported that "a messenger had arrived in Richmond from England with important dispatches from William L. Yancey, Confederate Minister or Commissioner to England, to Jeff Davis which gave highest assurance that by the 1st of November their independence [the South's] would be acknowledged beyond doubt. The messenger bearing these dispatches was stated to have come over in an English steamer and passed through Canada."[2]

After the roundup in Baltimore, Pinkerton returned to Washington; Webster went on to Richmond. He made his headquarters at the Spotswood Hotel, was almost a daily visitor in Benjamin's office, carried Rebel mail back and forth to Baltimore, and thus met John Beauchamp Jones, the Confederate War Clerk whose diary became a Civil War classic.

Webster did a superb job. One report to Pinkerton covers thirty-seven handwritten pages. In studying the faded, barely legible pages, one can only feel a deep admiration for a man who had the enormous patience and personal courage to prepare them. Assembling and copying the report took Pinkerton and two operatives all night, and left them exhausted. Yet Webster, ringed by the enemy, had seen and remembered the smallest military details, and wrote them down without one word about himself, his narrow escapes, or his precarious health. As always, Webster's eye for detail was amazing: breastworks were of "split pine logs with a 64 pounder with a traverse of 180 degrees . . . the Yorktown landing was "in front of a hill with a slope 5 feet above the beach"; the batteries ringing Richmond numbered seventeen, and there were also Enfield rifles. Sickness was spreading through the Confederate Army, which "suffered for overcoats, some for shoes, not many." Webster's information also included prices in Rebel money on articles from corn by the bushel to "hay—very scarce, all sorts of prices."[3]

Early in February, with Richmond shaken by the news of the surrenders of Fort Henry and Fort Donelson in Tennessee, there was a break in the almost daily reports from Webster. Then word reached Pinkerton that Webster was seriously ill with inflammatory rheumatism, and confined to his bed. Hattie Lawton, who had returned to Washington from Baltimore, was slipped into Richmond to nurse him. That took care of Webster's personal needs but not for continued intelligence. Someone had to go into Richmond. Pryce Lewis's earlier successful trip into western Virginia, when he had posed as the English peer, made him the logical candidate.

It was a bitterly cold day in February, 1862, when Pinkerton summoned Lewis and gave him the assignment, but the Englishman refused. He told Pinkerton that he was "finished with spying" and that if he had to do so he would resign and "pick up a musket." But Pinkerton was persuasive, and finally got Lewis to go. Lewis sincerely admired Webster, and it was his admiration, and not patriotism, that persuaded him to accept the dangerous assignment. However, the plan almost collapsed again when Pinkerton casually said that he would also send John Scully. It was too dangerous for two, Lewis told Pinkerton: "One man can remember a story and stick to it but two will be sure to suffer." Lewis finally agreed for the second time when Pinkerton told him that Scully would simply bring back Webster's reports and that Lewis could "go on alone to Chattanooga, ascertaining the conditions of the railroads and rolling stock and gathering information for General McClellan." Their cover story, he informed Lewis, was that they were traders in contraband and were delivering a letter to Webster from a secessionist friend in Baltimore.

What happened to Pinkerton's operatives—Lewis, Scully, Webster, and Hattie Lawton—behind the lines, is a fascinating chapter in the still-shadowy history of Civil War espionage.[4]

CHAPTER 12
Escape and Capture

The grand adventure of Pryce Lewis and John Scully began quietly on a February afternoon in 1862, when Allan Pinkerton shook their hands, wished them luck, and gave Lewis a note he had written to Joe Hooker at Cobb's Point on the Potomac. The note would allow them to pass through the Union lines and cross the river. Pinkerton had supplied each of them with a sack of gold coins, new suits, baggage, and a navy Colt.

After having dodged their own patrols and narrowly escaped drowning when their skiff was swamped in a storm on the Potomac, Lewis and Scully reached the Virginia shore. Before they abandoned the boat, Lewis wrapped Pinkerton's note to Hooker, and a few personal letters, around a rock and dropped them over the side. He told Scully to do the same. At a nearby village, they discovered that the ferry to Leesburg had been sunk by a federal gunboat but that another would arrive on the following day.

After several close calls with Confederate cavalry, the two Pinkerton operatives made their way into Richmond. There they found Webster, bedridden with acute rheumatism and attended by Hattie Lawton. Lewis and Scully registered at the Ballard House on February 26, 1862, and waited for Webster to complete "making up the mail," as they called their intelligence reports, for delivery to Pinkerton in Washington.

At four the following afternoon, they were visiting Webster when Captain Sam McCubbin, head of General John H. Winder's detectives in Richmond, walked into the room. Lewis recalls in his diary how his

103

blood chilled as he found his measure being taken by the cool-eyed young officer. But McCubbin was solicitous only of Webster's health, and left after a brief visit. Then capricious Fate opened the door to allow another of Webster's Confederate friends to enter. Behind him was the young son of former Senator Jackson Morton, whom Lewis and Scully had guarded in Washington when the Morton family had been arrested and confined to their home on Pinkerton's orders.

Lewis, fighting to remain casual, and Scully, almost stricken dumb with terror, tried to avoid the boy's stare. While the puzzled Webster wondered what was going on, they quietly left the room. However, before they could flee from the hotel, they were arrested. Questioned by General Winder and McCubbin, both Lewis and Scully insisted they were simply friends of Webster who were passing through Richmond, but Winder was convinced they were Union agents after Senator Morton's two sons identified Lewis and Scully as the Pinkerton operatives who had searched their father's house and held them prisoner for a week. Apparently Winder also had excellent intelligence: Lewis heard the general and McCubbin checking off the list of names of Pinkerton operatives. The names Lewis and Scully were on the list.

Henrico County Jail was their next stop. Lewis had not long been a prisoner when he attempted an escape. A "well tempered" kitchen knife was stolen, and for fourteen days they carefully filed through the thick iron bars. It was long and tedious work. During the day Lewis concealed the saw marks with a paste made of brown soap and ashes. Knives broke, and others had to be stolen from the kitchen. One day McCubbin and his men inspected the prison. While Lewis and the others held their breath, the Confederates brushed aside straw mattresses, looking for evidence of digging, and inspected the meager baggage and possessions. Fortunately, they merely glanced at the barred windows, and left.

On March 15, 1862, the sawing was finished. On the night of the 16th, Lewis and ten other prisoners broke out. They hurried down a back wooden stairway to the prison while the Negro inmates sang to cover the noise. After scaling the outer walls, they dodged the provost's patrols in the city, then took to the country. For what Lewis remembered as a "terrible hour," they made their way through a tangled swamp, slipping and falling in the icy water. The long confinement began to tell on some of the older inmates, and Lewis and another prisoner carried one man between them. Near the Chickahominy River they found a pit made by a large uprooted pine tree. They dried their clothes about a small fire, "and walked about to keep off the chill."

During the night they pressed on, and as the lemonish dawn streamed through the trees, they stretched out on brushwood beds, and slept. He awoke, as Lewis remembered, like a man encased in an iron suit; his still damp clothes had frozen on his body.

When it cleared, they set out again that night, their path lighted by a cold, polished moon. Once, as he was helping to carry one of the older prisoners, Lewis slipped into an icy creek. When he was pulled out, his teeth were chattering and his blood felt like ice water. A small fire was started, and the hungry, half-frozen men held out their hands to the tiny flames, and alternately dozed and awoke by starts.

On the next day they were captured on the Pamunkey River. On his return to prison, Lewis learned that they had been twenty miles from Richmond and were on the road to Fredericksburg when they had been sighted by the posse. The streets were crowded when the wagons carrying the "Yankee Jail Breakers" rumbled down the main street of Richmond. The *Times Dispatch* estimated that the crowd was larger than the one that had greeted the Prince of Wales on his visit.[1] Winder ordered them all put in irons. Lewis, whom he called the ringleader of the break, was the only one leg ironed, which, the Pinkerton operative recalled, left him "as helpless as a man could be."

CHAPTER 13
In the Shadow of the Gallows

In March, 1862, following his escape, Lewis was transferred from Henrico County Jail to Castle Goodwin, a verminous, dilapidated building that had at one time been a slave pen. Lewis's cell was a large, windowless room, his bed a small pile of filthy straw; his cellmates were Confederate deserters.

Lewis was in his cell less than an hour when he was part of another jailbreak attempt. The plan was simple. Some prisoners had dug a hole that led to the street. That evening, after supper, the last few feet were scooped out with a stolen spoon and knife. Guards heard the scraping, and rushed into the cell. Lewis, "the Yankee spy," was immediately charged with leading the escape. He was removed to another, smaller, cell, and again leg ironed.

A short time later, the guards told him that Scully had been tried and that decisions concerning both of them would be handed down at the same time. The civilian attorney assigned to Lewis not only took what gold coins he had left from Pinkerton's original stake but the navy Colt as well. He tried for Lewis's gold watch, but the Englishman promised to send the watch back to him "after you get me out of here."

Lewis's trial lasted three days, with the Mortons the most damaging witnesses. Mrs. Morton, her two sons, and her daughter testified how Lewis and Scully, under Pinkerton's direction, had placed them under arrest and spent days examining the family correspondence. Lewis took the stand to repeat the story that he and Pinkerton had concocted. Though his attorney made an impassioned plea, Lewis, studying the face

106

of Judge Crump, a Richmond lawyer who was president of the court-martial board, knew the game was up.

On the morning of April 1st, Lewis was taken to Scully's cell. One look at his fellow agent, and Lewis realized "he had given up all hope."

The court's verdict was read to them: They had been found guilty of spying, and were to be hanged on April 4, 1862, between 10:00 A.M. and 2:00 P.M.

As Lewis wrote: "It turned me to stone, but I did not betray my emotion. I did not notice Scully."

But Scully broke that night, moaning and tossing on his straw pallet. Lewis ignored him to pace the floor, a plan slowly forming in his mind. He and Scully were technically English subjects. With Richmond desperately hoping for recognition from Queen Victoria's government, and with Yancey, the Richmond agent in London . . .

In the morning, when the guards ushered in Father McMullen, the prison's Catholic chaplain, to hear Scully's final confession, Lewis went off to one side of the cell to write a brief note to the British Consul in Richmond, pointing out that they were both English subjects, and demanding the king's protection. When the priest left, he promised to mail the letter.

Their next visitor was Judge Crump, president of the court-martial board who cross-examined Lewis about jobs he had held in the North. When he left, Crump mumbled, "I wish you were Yankees." The phrase shook Lewis. As he recalled, Crump's words stayed with him all night as he huddled in a blanket, staring into a small fire as the damp cold edged into the room and rats scurried about the old warehouse.

Of his thoughts that night, Lewis writes: "I had no fear of dying. I felt sure the physical pain would not be greater than an instant's toothache, as to hereafter, I believed in a just God. I was in his power. If he was not just I could not help it. I was 27, strong as a lion, and physically without nervousness."

After another visit from Father McMullen—Pinkerton later insisted that the priest was a "decoy" used by the Confederates, but Lewis denied this—they had a visit from John Frederick Cridland, Acting British Consul in Richmond, "a short, fussy man," as Lewis remembered him.

Cridland asked several rapid questions of Lewis as to where he was born, if his parents were presently living in England, and the whereabouts of his brothers and sisters. Cridland told Lewis he didn't have much hope of saving him and Scully, quoting General Winder to the effect that the Confederate detectives had "evidence enough to hang a hundred Pinkerton detectives." But when Lewis asked Cridland if he had seen or examined the evidence, the British Consul admitted he had not.

"They won't show it to me," Lewis quoted him as saying.

When Lewis indignantly demanded that he insist on reviewing the evidence that had sentenced them to the gallows, Cridland promised he would make all efforts to do so.

Lewis was congratulating himself on his last desperate move when he noticed that Scully was weeping. As he tried to console him, Scully blurted out that he had sent a message to Winder through the Catholic priest that he would confess if he were pardoned.

As Lewis recalled: "The ground slipped from under my feet. I felt dizzy and hot. I had to sit down."

Of his contempt for Scully, Lewis wrote, "My feeling of pity for him was now changed to intense indignation."

A guard now entered with handcuffs, and Lewis was taken back to the officer's room he had occupied the day before. He had been there only a short time when he heard footsteps on the stairs. Through the window in the door he saw General Winder and a man who he later learned was Randolph Tucker, Virginia's state attorney, hurrying up to Scully's cell.

General Winder, as Lewis observed, "didn't let any grass grow under his feet." All that day and far into the night detectives hurried in and out of the jailhouse or leaped from carriages to rush up the stairs. Lewis felt the electric tension that seemed to hover around the building as the hours passed.

The storm broke about one o'clock. Lewis was standing at the window that looked out on the street when a buggy drew up at the jail entrance. Two men, whom Lewis recognized as Winder's detectives, stepped out. They turned to help a third man, who was well dressed, but looked "pale and ill." It was Tim Webster. And behind him was Hattie Lawton.

He could feel the rough noose settling gently about his neck. Scully had betrayed them all.

At four o'clock Lewis was removed to the condemned cell. It was a miserable damp room. He read until midnight, occasionally looking up and catching a glimpse of the passing bayonets of the guard detail. He managed a few hours of "a fitful sort of slumber, full of dreams," and then it was dawn, April 4, 1862. The guards told him he was to die at 11:00 A.M. The crowds started to stream into the city at the first light. At eight, Lewis heard hammering. He didn't have to ask what it was.

At "precisely" 11:00 A.M. Father McMullen opened the cell door. He was smiling. "I have good news for you, Lewis," he said softly. "President Davis has respited you for two weeks." The priest warned him, however: "It still looks dark for you. . . . I think you should tell the authorities all you know.

Lewis thanked him, and the priest left.

The Archives of the British Foreign Office in London tell how John Frederick Cridland, Acting British Consul in Richmond, had furiously worked in those last hours to save the lives of Lewis and Scully. Cridland had known most of the Confederate leaders since the 1840's, when he had first come to the South as a clerk in the Norfolk consulate. From May 1, 1861, to November, 1862, he was Acting Consul in Richmond while Consul Moore was in England.[1]

Cridland reported to Lord Lyons, the British Minister in Washington, that he filed a brief first with Judah Benjamin and then with Secretary of War Randolph, charging that "the prisoners had been tried and condemned to death at a moment when it was utterly impossible for either of them to obtain any evidence in their own favor from Washington." He also offered "to write to Lord Lyons in order to obtain evidence should the executions be postponed."

What Cridland brought to the attention of Benjamin, one of the most brilliant legal minds of his time, was a case that had all the characteristics of a "reversible error" (the prisoners had been tried and convicted before they could obtain evidence for their defense). Benjamin, who had a keen sense of justice, acted completely in character when he overruled the court-martial board to postpone the executions.

For thirteen terrible days Pryce Lewis endlessly paced his damp cell, wondering if he would eventually be hanged. On the morning of his stay of execution, he bribed a waiter to take a note to Scully, asking what he had done. The answer was devastating: Scully admitted he had confessed to Winder's detectives, and he advised Lewis to do the same.

Then General Wise was reported in Richmond. Lewis recalled how he had been interviewed by Wise in western Virginia during those rollicking days when he had rolled through the Confederate lines as the imperious Lord Tracy. If Scully told Winder's detectives about that trip, there no longer would be any hope.

Crump next summoned Lewis. In a long interview, the old jurist skillfully tried to put the blame for Lewis's arrest on Pinkerton, picturing Washington as a cold, unfeeling bureaucracy that had "abandoned a young, misguided man to his fate." But Lewis was of sterner stuff than the craven Scully. He stood up to Crump, and denied he knew Tim Webster was a federal spy who had been working for Allan Pinkerton. Lewis was taken back to his cell, and handcuffed. For days he played a cat-and-mouse game with Crump, finally half convincing the Confederate judge he had simply delivered a letter to Webster.

One morning he was taken from his cell to the Richmond courthouse, where he learned he was to testify in Tim Webster's case. Lewis was shocked at Webster's appearance. The stocky, handsome man was a shrunken skeleton who had to be helped out of his chair.

Lewis refused to play informer. He doggedly kept to his version that he had "heard a rumor" that Webster "carried mails" and had brought a letter to him from "a friend in Baltimore."

After the day's testimony, Lewis shared a cell in the building with Scully, who put all the blame on Pinkerton, "who lied to us."

Lewis shouted: "Damn Pinkerton! What about Webster? I would not suffer for Pinkerton, but I would for Webster!"

Scully then went on to tell Lewis that Winder's detectives already had Webster under suspicion when they had arrived in Richmond. A tip had come in from Baltimore, probably concerning the mischance meeting with the bully whom Webster had knocked down in the bar. As Scully said, when Winder's agents began investigating Webster, "they found he was so high placed they couldn't believe it at first."

"Damn you!" Lewis cried. "That's all the more reason you should have said nothing against him! You should have given him every chance to get away."

Scully wept. "It wasn't any use, Lewis; he was too sick to get away."

There was one bright hope, since Scully had not mentioned Lewis's trip to western Virginia as Lord Tracy.

"How could I?" he said. "I don't know anything about it."

A few days later a guard whispered that Webster had been found guilty and would hang. Hattie Lawton had been sentenced to one year in prison. Later, through Pinkerton's efforts, she would be exchanged. Lewis and Scully would languish in prison until 1863.

CHAPTER 14

The Execution of Timothy Webster

Allan Pinkerton was in the field with McClellan when he first heard his agents had been arrested and condemned to death. The news came from a Richmond newspaper he was reading in his tent. As he sat staring at the account, he recalls, "My blood seemed to run cold, my heart stood still. I was speechless." [1]

Pinkerton rushed to McClellan's tent. The general, "whose sorrow was as acute as though the men had been joined to him by ties of blood," promised to do everything within his power to get the trio exchanged. Pinkerton says he paced his tent that night until dawn. At sunup he telegraphed the harbor master at Fortress Monroe for news.

Messages flew back and forth all day until the late afternoon, when word came from Monroe that the death sentence of Lewis and Scully had been delayed but that Webster was to hang. The message was in error at least on one point: Both Lewis and Scully, it said, had turned informer and testified against Webster. Scully, of course, had told all; but Lewis was still insisting he didn't know Webster as a Yankee spy.

Pinkerton begged McClellan to send a flag of truce and bargain for the lives of his men, but the general refused, pointing out that to do so would be a tacit acknowledgment of their spy status and that they might all be executed without delay.

It was at last agreed that Pinkerton and Colonel Key, Mrs. Greenhow's hand-holding adversary from Old Capitol Prison, should rush to Washington and ask Lincoln to summon a special meeting of the Cabinet. Pinkerton and Key saw the President, who called a special Cabinet meet-

111

ing for that same evening. Pinkerton also saw Stanton, who promised to do everything in his power to save Webster's life, but "was little disposed to assist the others, who in Stanton's words, 'betrayed their companion to save their own lives.'"

The Cabinet authorized Stanton to send a flag of truce to Jefferson Davis with a dispatch pointing out Washington's lenient attitude toward Confederate spies: short terms in Old Capitol, and never a death sentence.

But the conciliatory dispatch had a grim ending: Hang our people and we will hang yours.

On the morning of April 23rd, Pinkerton and Key delivered the dispatch to Fortress Monroe. The text of the Cabinet's resolution, signed by Stanton, was telegraphed to Norfolk, who sent it on to Richmond under a flag.

The dispatch was received, but Davis refused to commute Webster's sentence: the Pinkerton agent had to die. When Captain Sam McCubbin brought the news, Webster made his last request. He begged to be shot, not hanged. McCubbin summoned General Winder, who refused on the grounds that he could not "alter the court's sentence."

Hattie Lawton, who was standing alongside Webster's bed, made an impassioned plea, as she later told Pinkerton, but Winder shook his head. Webster had to die by the rope. Hattie, who herself had been sentenced to a year in prison by the court-martial board, promised Winder that Tim Webster would show them all how a Union man could die, but warned the Confederates that Washington would never forget this bitter hour.[2]

Her threat echoed in Washington three years later when Richmond sent a plea under a flag to save the lives of John Y. Beall and Captain Robert Cobb Kennedy, two followers of Captain Thomas H. Hines, a Confederate agent. Both had been tried and found guilty by a court-martial in New York City. Stanton, who never forgave the Confederacy for hanging Webster, turned down Richmond's plea, and the Rebels were executed on Governors Island. Like Webster, their pleas to be shot were refused.[3]

Webster spent the last hours writing messages to his family and friends, which he gave to Hattie. Promptly at five they heard the measured tread of the provost patrol. Tim gently kissed Hattie, and said goodbye. As she later described his last hours for Pinkerton, Webster whispered, "Tell the major I can meet death with a brave heart and a clear conscience."

It is a scene overflowing with Victorian melodrama, but Captain A. G. Alexander, the tight-faced young officer who opened the door, his patrol that stood ramrod stiff in the gray light as he read the formal death warrant, were stark and very real that distant morning.

Both Hattie and Webster were shocked to hear that the execution was to be a public spectacle at Camp Lee, formerly the city's fairgrounds.

After a final goodbye, Webster stepped between the ranks of the patrol and hobbled out. Because it was obvious to Captain Alexander that Webster, in his weakened condition, could not march to the grounds, a carriage was ordered, and Mrs. Lawton was allowed to assist him. Flanked on both sides by the patrol, the carriage made its way down the crowded streets as the first songs of the birds greeted the new day. After Webster was delivered to Camp Lee, Hattie was returned to her cell.

Long before sunup the crowds had begun to stream into Camp Lee. There was a carnival air about the city. The roads were choked with wagons bringing farmers and their families. Richmond ladies, hair neatly coifed, black gloves buttoned over dainty wrists, goffered dresses flared over delicate hoops, light coats or shawls thrown over shoulders for protection against the chill of the early spring morning, chatted gaily as their liveried footmen guided the carriages in and out of the crowds. There were soldiers on leave, some boasting loudly that the Yankee would beg for mercy once he saw the rope; mounted officers who had just come in from the lines at Yorktown; peddlers hawking chestnuts roasted over small iron stoves on the side of the road leading to the old fairgrounds where Timothy Webster, the first American military spy to die on the soil of his own country since Nathan Hale, would walk up the gallows steps at 8:00 A.M.

Richmond had no official executioner, so Kapard, the jailer at Castle Thunder, was selected. The local newspaper account has Webster snarling and cursing at the jailers, "treating his approaching death with scorn and derision." Lewis saved some of the accounts, which he marked "grossly prededucted." One must agree with Lewis: the gallant Webster was not a man to scoff at death; he could die only with dignity. The accounts also picture Webster begging and crying for mercy; again we are inclined to accept Mrs. Lawton's version as she gave it to Pinkerton and what Lewis heard from the guards: Webster died well.

It was a terrifying execution. Spectators packed the grounds, while boys and men clung to the tops of lampposts and trees. On the edges of the crowd were the gentry in their carriages. The soldiers helped Tim up the steps, then stepped aside as Kapard adjusted the noose and tied his arms and legs. In the tense silence the voice of the clergyman rose to beg mercy on the soul of the condemned man. Then the trap fell with a crash that splintered the early-morning stillness.

But the hangman's noose slipped, and Webster fell to the ground. He lay there, a grotesque and tragic figure, feebly struggling, the end of the hawser wound around his waist.

The provost men carried him, still bound, back up the steps. They held him upright as Kapard tied another noose about his neck, this time so tight Webster's face became a dark red and he gasped, "I suffer a double death."

The execution continued with agonizing slowness. The hangman now measured the rope, and one of the officers below called up, "The rope is too short."

"It will do," the hangman replied in a casual way, examined the knot again, stepped back, and sprung the trap.

This time Webster died without a sound. As the *Examiner's* reporter wrote: "There was not a motion of the body or a quiver of a muscle." [4]

The corpse was left to dangle a half hour, then was cut down and brought back to Richmond in a wagon. The escorts were Winder's detectives, who, the *Examiner* said, had cut up the rope for souvenirs.

Hattie Lawton was notified of Webster's death by Captain Alexander, a former guerrilla and commandant of Castle Thunder. Lewis and other prisoners recall Alexander as a pompous fool who was either reciting his own horrible poetry or walking about his warehouse prison, a huge black dog trotting at his heels. When Winder granted Hattie's request to see the body, Alexander, in a brilliant red and gray uniform, escorted her to the local funeral parlor, where she arranged to have Webster's body placed in a metal coffin.

As Mrs. Lawton told Pinkerton, several Confederate officers were gathered about the body when she came into the room. When she denounced them as murderers, Alexander dramatically put his hand on the dead man's forehead and swore: "I did nothing to bring this about. . . . I simply obeyed orders to bring him from the prison to the place of execution."

Under a flag of truce, the grief-stricken Pinkerton tried to arrange with Winder to have the body sent through the lines but Winder refused. A second petition was sent to Richmond by Pinkerton, requesting that a vault be hired until the war ended, but this Winder also refused.

Late at night Winder's detectives buried Webster's body in an obscure corner of the paupers' section of the Richmond cemetery. There was no marker, and the earth was tramped down.[5]

In his front-line tent, Pinkerton vowed he would someday find Webster's body "and have it buried in northern soil." It was a vow he would keep.

CHAPTER 15
Too Many Bayonets

In the spring and summer of 1862, Allan Pinkerton's headquarters was in the field with the Army of the Potomac. Here he failed miserably both as a front-lines intelligence officer and as a political infighter. The best that can be said of him is that he should have remained in Washington, chasing spies.

During that period something happened to Pinkerton's usual hard-rock common sense. In March, McClellan had moved him and his staff to the front, where Pinkerton was totally out of his own world of spies, reports, and suspects. In the open field the armies were constantly on the move; almost hourly reports of military strength, equipment, and movements had to be evaluated. One of Pinkerton's most important assignments that spring was to determine the strategy and strength of General Joseph E. Johnson's Confederate army waiting in Virginia.

McClellan always worried a great deal about the strength of his enemy. He was particularly anxious this time, his maiden effort at full-scale warfare. He had regimental commanders send to Pinkerton's Secret Service for grilling, numbers of refugees, escaping contrabands (Negro slaves), prisoners, and deserters. McClellan had always been impressed by Pinkerton's success in civilian life, and he set great store by his reports. This was unfortunate, for Pinkerton was as wretched a military espionage agent as he was triumphant in his Washington spy work. His reports to McClellan were incredibly inaccurate. There were times when he overestimated the enemy strength by 100 percent. To a commander like

Group from the United States Secret Service, Army of the Potomac, Harrison's Landing, Virginia, July, 1862 (left to right): Seth Paine, G. H. Thiel, George H. Bangs, William Pinkerton. *Library of Congress*

McClellan, who had a strange inclination to exaggerate his difficulties, this information only compounded errors.[1]

General Johnson, one of the most penetrating military minds in the Confederacy, pinpointed McClellan in a terse sentence. He had been outbluffing McClellan and Pinkerton with dummy wooden cannons and thin gray lines stretched to the breaking point, when he said, "Nobody but McClellan would fail to attack."

The reasons for Pinkerton's deficiency in correctly evaluating the military information he received were his blind hero worship of McClellan, the investigative methods he had introduced in the field that had made his Agency so remarkable in civilian life, and his intense abolitionist fervor.

In Chicago, when he was on a case, Pinkerton's method was to assemble an infinite number of small details, which when put together gave a clue to the mystery. Pinkerton's operatives traditionally sent in reports every day, no matter how difficult it was to do so. In Chicago these reports were filed in a systematic fashion. This very system, which Pinkerton introduced on the battlefields, defeated him: It failed because the man making the final report was an amateur at war. Then there was Pinkerton's anti-slavery attitude. For years he had been helping slaves who came to him with the most touching stories. In the field, Pinkerton, in his sympathy, was uncritical of the excited, uneducated slaves who stood before him in his tent, twisting a ragged hat, shuffling their feet in the excitement of knowing that at last they were among friends and in sight of food and freedom. Though they were incapable of giving realistic information about what was happening on a grand scale behind Confederate lines, it is evident that Pinkerton believed everything they told him. He insisted for many years that "the force opposed to General McClellan before Richmond approximated nearer 200,000 men than irresponsible historians who have placed the strength of the Rebel forces below 100,000."

The phrase "irresponsible historians" shows Pinkerton's reports to be a shocking exaggeration of Confederate strength. The *Official Records* estimate that on June 26th the Union forces threatening Richmond were 200,000 strong, with 100,000 of them on the Peninsula under McClellan. Lee's strength was 68,000, augmented late in June by Jackson's 18,000.[2] Pinkerton simply did not have the military experience necessary to draw fairly reliable conclusions or summaries from the excellent information he was receiving from his agents behind the enemy lines. Pinkerton saw too many enemy bayonets.

However, if his competence in judging enemy forces was the only issue, the matter would be comparatively simple, and could be left there. But it may be said, at the risk of oversimplification, that mistaken numbers of the enemy governed McClellan's whole conduct in the war. At times such estimates seem to have been deliberately made by him for reasons still not clear. Much has been written about this strange young general of thirty-one, and much has been unfavorable. The issue is not that he was unique in refusing to move against an enemy with superior forces, nor was he the first general in our history to exaggerate the number of his foes. Only a few great captains have moved with the audacity of Washington at Trenton, Grant against Fort Donelson, Lee on the way to Gettysburg, or Jackson making his brilliant flanking movement at Chancellorsville. The fascinating question is: What caused this inner uncertainty in McClellan? What made him feel from the start that all Washington—the "Washington Cabal," as his self-appointed protector Allan Pinkerton called it—was plotting against him? Why did he welcome every scrap of information, every whisper, every note of gossip from Washington? even to the extent of sending Pinkerton away from the army to find it. We have no way of knowing, but there are many original letters from Pinkerton telling McClellan what he wanted to hear.

We find Pinkerton as early as October, 1861, insisting that the strength of the Confederates "between Washington and the Potomac was 150,000 strong, well drilled and equipped," a ridiculous figure, of course. He begged Stanton "leave to repeat the opinion that the Army of the Potomac should number no less than 300,000 men."

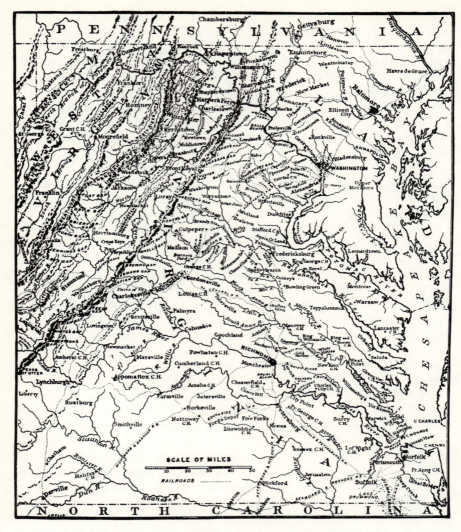

Peninsula Campaign, March, April, May, June, July, 1862

In the winter of 1862, McClellan proposed to Lincoln to move the Army of the Potomac against Richmond, by water to Urbana on the Rappahannock and then overland to Richmond before the Confederates under Johnson could move. After three months of debate—Lincoln favored the overland approach, and feared

for Washington's safety if the army moved away—Lincoln gave
in. But then Johnson moved back to Culpepper, and McClellan's
plan became inpracticable. He then proposed to Lincoln to
move his army to Fort Monroe and then up the peninsula against
Richmond. Reluctantly, Lincoln consented.

On April 4th, McClellan began moving up the peninsula. One
of the first faulty bits of information he received—probably from
Pinkerton—was that the Confederate fortifications at Yorktown
were concentrated in one position. When he arrived, he found
that they stretched across the peninsula. He received this news
on April 5th, the same day that he received word from Washington that Lincoln had canceled the order to General Mc-
Dowell for moving McDowell's troops by water to Fort Monroe
to join McClellan. The safety of Washington was more on
Lincoln's mind because of the movement of troops under Stonewall Jackson in the valley, a brilliant diversion for General
Johnson, who was massing his army to oppose McClellan.

After the siege of Yorktown, Johnson slowly retreated to Richmond. Heavy rains and muddy roads hampered McClellan, who
again had been outgeneraled.

In the valley, Jackson smashed General Banks, and Lincoln
again canceled orders to McDowell, who was supposed to be on
his way to join McClellan. McClellan, owing to Pinkerton's
faulty intelligence, did not know he outnumbered Johnson five
to three, and rested on his arms before Richmond instead of
storming into the city.

On June 26, 1862, Lee won a victory at Mechanicsville after
General Porter had gallantly fought unassisted for two days
while McClellan held his army inactive. On the twenty-seventh,
McClellan, probably in panic, ordered a retreat to the James
River, with Lee trying to employ his divisions in an attempt to
destroy the Union armies. But timidity, apathy, and lack of
teamwork on the part of some of his captains combined to
thwart his ambitions. Lee pulled back after the Battle of Malvern Hill, July 1, 1862, and McClellan retreated safely to Fort
Monroe. Lee had preserved Richmond and put McClellan to
flight. But the Army of the Potomac was still intact. Under a
more aggressive general, equipped with a better intelligence
officer than Pinkerton, the Union Army would have stormed
Richmond. In the series of battles from Mechanicsville to Malvern Hill, known to history as the Seven Days Battles, the
Confederates lost 20,000, the Union, about 16,000.

In February, 1862, the Comte de Paris, eldest son of King Louis Phillippe of France, and his brother, the Duc de Chartres, both acting as observers at McClellan's headquarters, estimated the Confederate strength around Richmond as 70,000, with 12,000 to 18,000 under Jackson in the valley. Freeman, basing his authority on the *Official Records,* found McClellan's strength as of March 1st to be 185,420, the Confederate strength, east of the Blue Ridge, as 74,000; but he points out that Jackson had only 5,000 to 6,000 in the valley. Yet on March 5th we find McClellan estimating the gray troops east of the Blue Ridge as high as 115,000.

In assaying Pinkerton's errors in evaluating the Confederate strength before Richmond, and in no way presenting alibis for his faults, McClellan's military experiences must also be considered. He had been an observer in the Crimea, and knew as much or more than any other American officer about war and large-scale tactics. It is certain from McClellan's letters and dispatches that he was constantly harping on the great strength of the enemy; Pinkerton, an amateur in military matters, could have absorbed this point of view. After all, didn't his general know more than anyone else in the army? Certainly McClellan's staff at headquarters never questioned his wisdom, at least until the Seven Days Battles in the Peninsular Campaign.

On May 9th, Johnson, with only 55,000 men, had fallen back up the peninsula before McClellan. Richmond was only thirty miles away, and the last barrier of the Chickahominy only fifteen. By the twenty-second, McClellan was crossing it at Bottom's Bridge, and if there had been a sudden breakthrough he might have been in the streets of Richmond within a few hours. Seldom in history had the requirement *à l'audace* been more needed.

On June 1st, Lee took command. McClellan halted to re-form and reorganize and waited. Not until the twenty-second did Jackson, ahead of his army, arrive at Dobbs House, Lee's headquarters.

On the twenty-fifth, McClellan reported that several contrabands had just arrived "to announce that Jackson's forces were in line; that even Beauregard had come up and that the Rebel forces were near 200,000 men." There is little doubt McClellan's report came from Pinkerton. Actually, with Jackson's troops, Lee now had 86,000 men, and McClellan 105,444, in the lines.

Pinkerton's admiration of McClellan is significant in analyzing his front-line failures. From his letters and dispatches one wonders if he was serving his friend, the former chief engineer of the Illinois Central, or Lincoln, his President and Commander in Chief. Two sentences in the preface of his war memoirs sum up his emotions:

"I followed the fortunes of General McClellan never doubting his ability or his loyalty, always possessing his confidence. I am this time proud and honored in ranking him foremost among my invaluable friends."

To Pinkerton, McClellan was not the victim of his political ambitions and a weird disinclination to close with Lee, but rather a man struck down at the peak of his career by "secret enemies who endeavored to prejudice the mind of the President against his chosen commander . . . wily politicians . . . jealous-minded officers. . . ."

From July, 1861, to March, 1862, Pinkerton had been at McClellan's elbow while he molded an army of a quarter of a million men into a trained fighting force organized upon European models, with a formidable fleet for support. As the Comte de Paris reported, McClellan was everywhere reviewing his troops with Lincoln and the Cabinet "boldly caracoling at the head. . . ." [3]

Pinkerton, like McClellan, believed the inexperienced Lincoln had begun to interfere with military affairs. The general found it "perfectly sickening" to be obliged to listen to the President's advice, and concluded that Lincoln was motivated by "hypocrisy, knavery and folly." When the President appeared to review the troops, McClellan's attitude was one of superiority, and showed what John Hay called in his diary "unparalleled insolence of epaulettes," in snubbing the President, writing complaining letters, and disregarding his official orders.

Pinkerton's tent, or Major E. J. Allen's, was always near McClellan's. By 1862, he had a formidable staff of scouts and spies operating along the front and behind the enemy lines. His teen-age son William, who had left Notre Dame to join his father, was a courier, and unconfirmed newspaper articles have him making a front-line flight with Professor T. S. C. Lowe, the Union balloonist. According to his Record Books, Pinkerton at this time was not only handling military intelligence and charges of espionage in Washington but was also chasing crooked contractors and bounty jumpers. Although he was at the front, the War Department still sent on to his headquarters the complaints and information it received. Court-martial boards and loyalty hearings demanded his presence and testimony. Defense attorneys sent him threatening letters. Politicians demanded introductions to McClellan. When Lincoln appeared to review the troops, only to find McClellan dashing off somewhere, the President would join "Major Allen" in his tent to reminisce of their railroad days in Chicago. [4]

One finds it ironical that Pinkerton, the rabid abolitionist, friend of John Brown and the man who had helped many runaway slaves gain freedom in Canada, should be unsympathetic with Lincoln in October, 1862. Unquestioningly he approved of the preliminary Emancipation Proclamation that Lincoln had issued nine days earlier, yet his sympathy for McClellan was so strong that he would not let Lincoln's antislaveryism dominate him. McClellan opposed freeing the slaves, and was the political favorite of the Democrats who were strongly opposing Lincoln's "inconstitutional" course.

At the time, Pinkerton was thinking more about military injustices suffered by his general than about Lincoln's attempts in behalf of the abolitionist cause the spy master had championed through the years. Pinkerton believed what McClellan believed about the Lincoln administration: that in baseless fears for the safety of Washington, it had withheld regiments McClellan could have used to crush the Confederate Army.

Civil War histories will forever differ on this question: If the forces had been taken from General McDowell and placed under a central command, with McClellan at its head (which was Pinkerton's dream), could they have taken Richmond? One school of thought argues that if McClellan had stormed into Richmond Lee might have driven into his rear, severed his communications, nullified his chance for naval support, then at Drewrys Bluff, near Richmond, and isolated his army. Lincoln and Stanton insisted that McDowell's army of 40,000 be kept between the two capitals. Ironically, McClellan's strategy was ultimately adopted by Grant.

Pinkerton was highly critical of the blunders he said Lincoln had committed in his hesitations between the advice of the McClellan and the anti-McClellan politicians in the Cabinet. Pinkerton insisted that the President, having once disclaimed knowledge of military affairs, should have allowed the conduct of the war to remain with McClellan. And Navy Secretary Welles, in his penetrating diary of his years in the Lincoln Cabinet, supports Pinkerton's insistence of "a cabal," led by Stanton, who undercut McClellan that tragic summer and fall. Welles reveals that he was shocked on an August Sunday to be approached by Secretary Chase, who wanted him to sign a "petition" against McClellan; the paper had been signed by himself and Stanton, demanding McClellan's dismissal. Although he knew of Chase's actions, the paradoxical Pinkerton was a close friend of Chase for many years.

A few weeks later the group, led by Stanton, again requested that Welles sign the petition. When Welles glanced at the document, he saw that Seward's name was absent. Then he knew why the Secretary of State had left Washington: "to be relieved from participation in this movement." Welles's diary gives a glimpse of the savage infighting among the Cabinet members. To Stanton you were either a McClellan man or a Stanton man.[5]

Pinkerton, now a part of the war fought in the rarefied air of the high policy makers of Washington, had about as much talent for this type of skirmishing as he had for evaluating military espionage.

CHAPTER 16
The Washington Cabal, 1862

In the summer and fall of 1862, Allan Pinkerton and General George B. McClellan were engaged in a second war in which the enemy was shadows, the gunfire whispers of intrigue. It was as savage a war as the one in the field, with "No quarter" the rallying cry. It was the Washington political war, and, shrewd and ruthless as Pinkerton was, he was constantly outmatched and outmaneuvered by the professionals. McClellan might have been idolized by his troops who hugged the haunches of his horse, but in Washington, like his chief of the Secret Service, he was an amateur.

Neither the general nor the detective covered himself with glory. Pinkerton's reports on the activities of Lincoln and his Cabinet to McClellan were, to say the least, questionable and unethical. But then he was doing what his general wanted—a case of mistaken loyalty again.

Pinkerton joined McClellan on the road to oblivion when Lee and Jackson joined forces for the defense of Richmond. Both armies met head on in the bloody Seven Days, June 25 to July 1, 1862. The great armies struggled as McClellan, retiring from the Chickahominy, changed his base from White House on the Pamunkey to Harrison's Landing on the James. Near Harrison's Landing, Malvern Hill, the final conflict of the Seven Days took place, and it proved to be one of the most terrible battles of the war. It was a McClellan victory, but had McClellan counterattacked, he probably would have defeated Lee and might have taken Richmond.

The reason for his refusal to counterattack may have rested with Pinkerton. McClellan was obsessed by the idea that Lee's forces were twice their actual number and that his beloved Army of the Potomac would have marched into a bloody trap—fears magnified by the reports of his intelligence chief.

Pinkerton's "Washington Cabal" had become the principal villain in McClellan's distorted imagination. On June 28, 1862, he wrote a bitter denunciatory letter to Stanton full of weird allusions about Washington's treachery because he had not received the fifty thousand reinforcements he had demanded. His main theme was the accusation that the "cabal" had sacrificed the Army of the Potomac.[1]

The problems on Lincoln's mind were enormous: the appointment of a general in chief—Henry W. Halleck got the post on July 11th—England's possible recognition of the Confederacy, compensated emancipation, the growing demand for a strike against slavery, rumblings of discontent in the North, and the anxiety for his party in the coming congressional election.

A letter to Pinkerton, written two years later by Colonel Key, McClellan's aide-de-camp, indicates that Pinkerton knew the contents of, or perhaps had helped McClellan to compose, the famous "Harrison's Landing Letter," which the general personally handed to Lincoln on July 7th. In the letter, which McClellan's critics denounced as a political document, he advised Lincoln on matters within the Presidency and Congress. In his war memoirs Pinkerton glosses over this damaging document. Pinkerton calls it simply "a review of McClellan's views on the conduct of the war," but it was far more than that. McClellan warned his President against aribitrary arrests, and counseled that the war must be conducted "upon the highest principles known to civilization." Certainly Pinkerton, that rabid abolitionist, must have winced when he read of McClellan urging Lincoln to avoid "forcible abolition of slavery" because a radical antislavery policy would result in the disintegration of the armies.[2]

Perhaps a man of stronger principles would have seen the light and ditched his general, but once again it was his intense, uncritical loyalty that made Pinkerton not only the Chief of the Secret Service of the Army of the Potomac, but also McClellan's private gumshoe at the courts in Washington. All that August, Pinkerton was reporting almost daily to McClellan, giving a good insight into the politics surrounding the army commands, the ignorance of the area commanders, John A. McClernand, John Pope, and Ambrose Burnside, and certainly the lack of any central war plan.

On August 20th, 21st, 23rd, and 25th, his letters to McClellan not only contained news of the army's reverses but inside political information as well. He reported how a delegation from Illinois had called on Lincoln, cautioning him against Pope . . . and I learned that he (L) intimated that he appreciated their sentiments. . . . I also learned last night that you are not to be placed under Pope, that Lincoln said to an Illinois friend that you should not be placed under Pope—that it would be a degradation, and he should not do it. . . . May this not account for the milk in the cocoanut?

[Burnside was] friendly but not communicative. He told me you were in Yorktown, and that your movements so far were satisfactory . . . that I might say to you that you are all right here [Washington] very satisfactory, just as if a cross word had never been spoken, and that you could have anything you asked for.[3]

In addition to the plots against his general, money was still a major problem to Pinkerton during those uneasy August days. He wrote that he was having a great deal of difficulty in getting the government to honor his drafts and that he refused to break the iron rule of his Agency never to reveal the names of his operatives, which the War Department was pressing him to do. "As I told the Assistant Secretary [of War], I would withdraw my bills rather than submit such a key to my force," he wrote. He ended with a gentle prod to McClellan to move: "If you give them one more battle you can assuredly route [sic] your enemies from the Cabinet Councils." [4]

But all Pinkerton's optimism and tactful prodding for action led nowhere. McClellan was replaced by Pope, whom the Washington radicals liked for his blunt criticism of McClellan's "incompetence." On August 29th, Lincoln telegraphed to McClellan for news of Pope, who at the time was being outgeneraled by Lee and Jackson. His general, instead of supplying front-line news, replied with advice. He told Lincoln that the government should adopt one of two courses: Concentrate all available forces to open lines of communication with Pope or "leave Pope to get out of his scrape," and dispose the available troops to secure Washington from attack. He then asked Lincoln what were his orders and what was his scope of authority. Lincoln coldly ignored this bid for complete command (which Pinkerton, of course, condemned as another grave presidential error), and advised McClellan that the decision would be up to General Halleck, "aided by your counsels." Lincoln was shocked by McClellan's statement about Pope, and told his secretary that McClellan seemed to want to see Pope defeated.[5]

On August 30th, Lincoln was exuberant when Pope telegraphed that he had engaged the Confederates and had driven them from the field. Based on the performances of his other generals who had lied to him in the past, Lincoln should have viewed Pope's news with suspicion. Then came the telegram announcing that Pope had been defeated at the Second Battle of Manassas, and was retreating. As T. Harry Williams notes in his study of Lincoln and his generals, Pope had many of Mc-

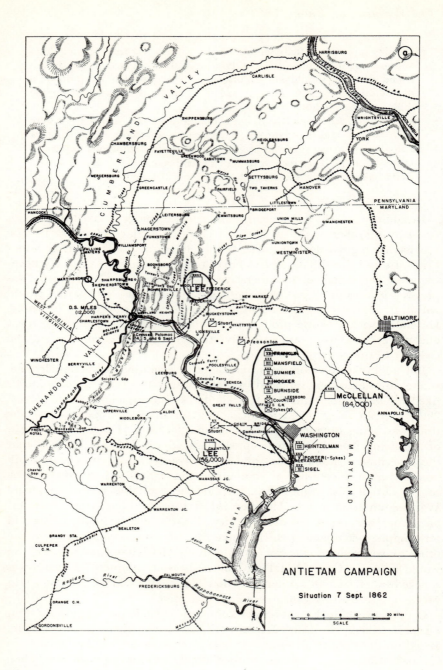

ANTIETAM CAMPAIGN

Situation 7 Sept. 1862

SCALE
4 0 4 8 12 16 20 Miles

Antietam Campaign, September, 1862

In early September, 1862, Lee, screened by Stuart's cavalry, crossed the Potomac and invaded the North. On the 7th he was at Frederick, Maryland. His reasons for the invasion were many. Among them was the need to keep the initiative on the battlefield, the chance that the South would gain recognition, and the hope of touching off a revolt inside Maryland. His goal was Harrisburg, Pennsylvania—to cut the North's major east-west railroads and then head toward Philadelphia, Baltimore or Washington.

On September 13th, Lee's "Special Order No. 191," which outlined the entire operation, was found wrapped about a cigar in D. H. Hill's abandoned camp. After an incredible delay of sixteen hours, McClellan moved. Jackson took Harpers Ferry, and when Lee heard that Jackson was on the way to meet him, Lee made a stand in defensive positions at Antietam Creek. On September 16th, McClellan hesitated again. Instead of smashing through Lee's inferior forces, he was content with skirmishing and making his plans. Later that day, Jackson and other forces joined Lee. On the morning of the 17th, troops under Joseph Hooker finally launched an offensive. Jackson's lines buckled but held. A savage counterattack checked the Union advance, and Hooker was wounded. In their fortifications before Sharpsburg, Lee's artillery was destroyed by the Union's more expert artillerymen. Hood's famous command of Texans was shattered, and most of Lee's lines held by sheer courage alone. One more strong Union attack and Lee's Army of Northern Virginia would have broken. When his generals, who had discovered the weakness in Lee's line before Sharpsburg, begged McClellan to attack, McClellan once more refused to exploit a glorious opportunity. Then A. P. Hill's troops smashed into the Union's flank under Burnside, and a furious battle ensued. On the eighteenth, with the arrival of reinforcements, McClellan could have driven Lee's army against the unfordable Potomac, but again he hesitated, remaining idle all that day. That night Lee made a skillful retreat.

The failure of McClellan to gain a decisive victory over Lee can be attributed only to McClellan's lack of imagination and aggressiveness along with Pinkerton's incompetence as a military intelligence officer. McClellan's officers had fought well, and his artillery had been superb. Only McClellan and Pinkerton had been lacking.

Clellan's faults in reverse: He was aggressive where McClellan was timid, rash where McClellan was cautious; neither could judge realities.

On September 1st, Pinkerton accompanied McClellan to Washington to see Lincoln, who demanded to know why McClellan's officers were not cooperating with Pope. McClellan denied this, and assured Lincoln that he would give the defeated commander his full support. To satisfy Lincoln he sent his headquarters a telegram ordering his generals to do so.

Partially satisfied, but still disturbed by McClellan's telegram about letting Pope get out of his own scrape, Lincoln reluctantly directed McClellan to take command of Pope's defeated forces as they streamed into the city's fortifications. Although Pinkerton later insisted that McClellan had been given a full field command by Lincoln, that was not true; as Lincoln informed Stanton and his Cabinet, McClellan was in charge only of the defense of Washington. Later, when Pope arrived in the city, he told Lincoln that McClellan, Porter, and other officers of McClellan's command were responsible for his defeat because they held back men and supplies.

Pope was sacrificed when Lincoln relieved him of command. The President was still angry at McClellan's refusal to aid Pope; but, as he told John Hay and Secretary of the Navy Welles, "We must use what tools we have . . . there is no other man in the army who can man these fortifications and lick these troops of ours into shape half as well as he . . . if he can't fight himself, he excels in making others ready to fight. . . ."

Lincoln's plan to make use of McClellan as an organizer rather than as a field commander was shattered when Lee moved his army across the Potomac and into western Maryland. It was obvious that the Army of the Potomac had to drive them from Union soil; Lincoln offered command of the Army of the Potomac to Burnside, who refused and who suggested McClellan. It was a bitter decision for Lincoln, but he finally returned McClellan to his old command. Pinkerton immediately returned to the field. George Bangs, Gus Thiel, and several other operatives were ordered to shadow Lee's army. On September 4th, two days after McClellan assumed command, Pinkerton reported to him that his men had found Lee's headquarters on the Aldie Turnpike near Dranesville, and Jackson's near Fairfax Courthouse.

McClellan came out of Washington to the wild cheers of his troops, and Pinkerton joined him at Rockville. Then, as John Masefield wrote in his fine study of Gallipoli, "great tactical combinations of modern wars have often been betrayed by very little things." In this case a private found Lee's orders, giving a disposition of his forces, wrapped about three cigars, lost by one of Lee's staff. The papers were rushed to McClellan.

"Here is a paper with which if I cannot whip Bobbie Lee, I will be willing to go home," he told one of his generals.

To delay McClellan until Jackson returned from Harpers Ferry, Lee stationed part of his army at South Mountain. It was only a delaying action, but the joyful McClellan telegraphed to Lincoln that it had been a great victory and that the Confederates were retreating. Lincoln in turn advised his Cabinet that McClellan was pursuing a retreating foe.

McClellan's premature joy was probably based on a combination of his refusal to recognize reality and Pinkerton's incompetent intelligence reports. Instead of leading a badly disorganized army, Lee had marched to Antietam Creek and dug in. On September 17th, McClellan crossed the creek, and attacked. He bent the Confederate right lines, but they did not break. On the left the Rebels were on the point of snapping when Jackson rode up and held the breach. At that point McClellan held not only his own but also Pinkerton's army career in his grasp. Had he sent in the reserve corps he had been holding back against the badly battered Confederate right, he could have swept Lee from the field and gained a tremendous victory. But he held back the reserves and broke off the attack for the day.

At the peak of the battle that afternoon, Pinkerton almost lost his life at the creek. He was accompanying a cavalry patrol when a Confederate battery discovered them. They were shelled as they galloped for the woods, but before they could reach shelter Pinkerton's favorite sorrel was shot from under him as he was crossing the stream. He was stunned but not seriously injured, although several cavalrymen were wounded by shell fragments. He struggled up behind another officer, and they galloped to the woods.

Pinkerton was with McClellan all through Antietam. On the day after the battle, Pinkerton's men reported that the Confederates had abandoned their positions, leaving behind nearly 3,000 dead, 13 guns, 39 colors, and 1,500 stands of small arms. Pinkerton reported a bag of 6,000 prisoners at the end of the campaign.

Pinkerton called Antietam a "brilliant victory," but once again we find his fanatical loyalty to McClellan blurring his common sense. It was true that McClellan had stopped Lee's offensive and "cleared Maryland of the presence of the enemy," as he proudly wired to Lincoln; but, considering to disparity of forces and the great stakes to have been won, this was a disappointing result.

Lee also had failed, for his ambitious and dangerous campaign had come to an inconclusive end. However, the Confederate general had, as Sir Frederick Maurice declares in his biography of Lee, retained "moral ascendancy." [6]

The by-passing of McClellan's army by Jeb Stuart, the beau sabreur of the Confederacy, did not enhance McClellan's prestige with Lincoln. When he wired Washington that his cavalrymen's horses were tired, Lincoln wired back a wry request to know what his horses had been doing since Antietam "to make them fatigued."

Group at Secret Service Department, Headquarters, Army of the Potomac, Antietam, October, 1862, by Alexander Gardner. *Chicago Historical Society*

Pinkerton charged that Washington, for ulterior purposes, did not push forward supplies for McClellan's army that October, but he fails to document or detail the charges. Like many other men in the past, and as many more would do in future wars, Pinkerton and his general were battling the mysterious "they"—the intangible enemies who were putting roadblocks in the path of every campaign, every plan, every move. To Pinkerton and McClellan, "they" were as concrete as Jackson's gaunt-faced troops.

On September 22nd, Pinkerton sent McClellan a long account of his talk with the President that morning. Few documents about Lincoln give so much insight into his horse sense or his deceptive readiness to believe what he was told. It is quite apparent that he did not accept all the explanations and excuses so completely as Pinkerton believed. But here is the letter in full, and whether Pinkerton knew it or not, Lincoln with his credulous questions, was making the case against McClellan that historians finally agreed upon:

GENERAL:

This forenoon I called at the President and saw my friend Hay, the Private Secy. He asked if I wanted to see the Pres. I said—no, not particularly. I have nothing new to say, but if the Pres. desired to see me,

I should be happy to tell him all I knew regarding matters in the _____.
Hay seen the Pres. and brought me an invitation to walk in.

Lincoln was very friendly at the start and continued so all the time.
He said he was glad I had called. That he wanted to learn all I knew
in relation to the movements of Genl. McClellan's Army—And that
before proceeding further, he would say that in talking with me whatever he might say was not meant to criticize anything relating to Genl.
McClellan, but simply for the purpose of eliciting what I knew or
supposed caused certain things to be done and not for the purpose of
seeking aught against you. That in reference to the Battle of South
Mountain & Antietam he thought those great and decisive victories—
victories achieved under great difficulty and in themselves of the greatest
value to the nation and that you had accomplished all you had set out
to do viz—to push the Rebels back of Maryland G____ and free the
Capitol from danger. Admitting that all this had been accomplished
and that he felt that to you, your officers and men, he and the nation,
owed you a deep debt of gratitude—and that he personally owed you
more. That you had taken the Command of the Army at a time of
great peril and when the army was suffering under great defeats. That
with the same army you had gone out to meet the same victorious foe—
that he owed you for this what he never could repay you, but that
placed as he is—he was desirous of knowing some things which he supposed from the pressure on your mind, you had not advised him on or
that you considered was of minor importance, not sufficiently worthy
of notice for you to send to him, and if I knew anything about these
matters and my duty to Genl. McClellan permitted of it—He would
like to ask me in relation to. I said that there was doubtless many
things transpiring in regard to the movements of the Army which you
did not deem of importance enough to report to him or trouble him
with. Skirmishes, reconnaissances and such as that you did not think of
importance enough. Except where important results followed to trouble
the Pres. with. So also with regard to the state of the Commissary or
Quartermaster Depts. or Ordnance or Ammunition, although all these
naturally affected the condition, position or progress of your Army. That
you relied upon having the full confidence of the President and relying
so, did not deem it necessary to burden him with such detail, etc., etc.

He then alluded to the surrender of Harpers Ferry and enquired if
everything had been done to _____ it _____ _____ _____. I assured
him it _____ _____ _____ _____ _____ _____ _____ movements
and efforts and also of _____ and informed him of your order to _____
_____ to _____ _____ frequently as they progress even though they
see nothing—So that the Commanding Officer at the Ferry might know
that your forces were covering them. I also happened to have one of the
dispatches you wrote to Col. Miles or the officer commanding Harpers
Ferry which you will recollect you wrote at Middletown and handed
to me to send. The Pres. was very much satisfied at this & did not fail
to express it so ____ed to be relieved. He said that many had endeavored
to impress him with the belief that you might have done more than you

had done for the relief of the Ferry. That he had always felt confident that you would do all in your power to aid the extrication of that force and when he knew you had done it he characterized the dispatch as evidently one which bore the stamp as having emanated from you—and breathing your spirit—as also recognizing your signature.

He next referred to the battle of Antietam, enquiring into the number of the enemy and condition, as also your numbers & condition. I stated the Rebel Force to be 140,000 and yours about 90,000. He said that he thought you had about 100,000 and admitted that he believed the rebels had the number I said. As for the condition of the two Armies I said that I believed the one was fully as anxious to fight as the other. I explained fully to him in relation to what had been done from the time you forced the enemy in position on the Antietam on Monday afternoon up till the time I left headquarters (Saturday P.M.) at least so far as I knew of them. He enquired the reason why the Army did not fight on Thursday and I explained to him the position of our Army on Wednesday evening after the battle had closed & the fact that the enemy still remained in line of battle all day Thursday—recalled to his mind the exhaused condition of our Army. The large number of dead & wounded which lay on the field and the necessity of disposing of them ere fighting the field over again. As also that large or long range ammunition was short and the fact that the enemy had punctured their line of battle well at [sic] the previous day and the necessity of great caution on your part or the largely superior force of the rebels might have obtained some partial success. I described _____ _____ indefatigable suspension of every disposition on the field—and he at once frankly said that he had no doubt—not any—but that you had fought the battle skillfully & frankly—much more so than any General he knew of could have done, and again repeated enquiring as he was about these details—he was not criticizing anything which you had done —for on the contrary you had his confidence, but he was seeking to learn all I could tell him—without betraying Genl. McClellan's confidence.

He next enquired regarding the Rebels escaping across the Potomac and I explained to him the position of the Rebel line of battle on Thursday in reference to the river. The stage of water. The fact that infantry and cavalry could cross almost anywhere. That the enemy had been _____ on the Maryland shore and the numerous fords in that vicinity which might be made available for crossing artillery on water. Also the fact that the citizens of Sharpsburg informed us that wave of the Rebels commenced crossing into Virginia until about 9 P.M. Thursday, but on the C___ t___. Some small portions of Rebel soldiers cruised into _____ on that day—arguing from this that if you had commenced the engagement you would have to have done it in the face of many very great obstacles. That all day Thursday was spent in burying the dead—Taking care of the wounded. Feeling the Rebel Army strength and _____ their position—as also in _____ up ammunition.

That on Thursday night the orders were given to _____ in their picket and bring on a general engagement which every person in camp expected would be _____.

I explained on Friday morning the rapid advance of your army to the shore and the crossing of Genl. Pleasonton's in rapid pursuit as also the movement of Banks Corps to occupy Maryland Heights & _____ march to Williamsport and assured him that you would drive them as rapidly as could be done.

He next spoke of the slowness of the advance from _____ to South Mountain, remembering that it was just eight days from the time you arrived at _____ until you fought at South Mountain. I recalled to his mind that on the day previous to your arrival at _____, the Rebels had occupied Frederick, pushing forward _____ _____ that point on the two succeeding days _____ _____ was _____ that you had before you the whole Rebel Army. And that it was necessary for you to keep your whole army together and more circumspectly and with great caution, but that _____ all this you had fought the Rebels and drove them every day from the time you left Washington— True, many of these engagements were but skirmishes, resulting probably in the loss of one, two or half a dozen men—and in others the Rebels fled without causing you any loss. Still all this showed that you had to move cautiously in order to do so successfully.

I must say General that I never saw a man feel better than he did with these explanations. He expressed himself as highly pleased and gratified with all you had done (_____ commending your caution) and frankly admitted that you had done everything which could or ought to be expected of you. The fact is all the other Generals are in the habit of _____ _____ of every skirmish—and when you do not, he naturally supposes you are doing nothing and your _____ try always to impress this _____ of it _____ him. For myself you know I am rather prejudiced against him—but I must confess that he impresses me more at this interview with his honesty towards you & his desire to do you justice than he has ever done before and I would respectfully suggest that whenever you can consistently give him information regarding his movements, skirmishes, _____, etc. it would be very acceptable. For instance, he knew nothing of the _____ of Antietam Creek which lay between you and the enemy except what he had learned from newspapers.

Previous to seeing the President I had seen Stanton at the Department. He saw me in the hall while waiting to see Eckert and invited me into his private room. He evidently wanted to talk—just as he has on one or two occasions done before—But feared to broach the topic, so after a few unimportant statements made by me, in reference to the _____ _____ the pursuit of the enemy, our conversation closed. I sat for about ten minutes without speaking, and on the entrance of some gentlemen, took the opportunity to leave. While with the President and just as I got through, Stanton came into the room. The Pres. asked him to be seated but S. said no—He supposed he (L) wanted to see Mr. Allen alone—and he left.

Allan Pinkerton, Lincoln, and McClernand at Antietam. *Library of Congress*

After Antietam, Lincoln issued his Emancipation Proclamation. This disturbed McClellan, who told Pinkerton he would resign if he had to serve a government that supported emancipation. But some of McClellan's more politically astute followers warned him he would have a much better chance at the polls in a race for the Presidency, if he approved. Finally, McClellan decided to say nothing publicly, but posted a notice for the Army of the Potomac, pointing out that in a democracy the military is subordinate to the civil authorities and the objectives of the war are not decided by the troops but by civilians. The remedy for "political errors," he pointed out, could be found at the polls. Pinkerton showed the weakness in his character when he, the onetme rabid abolitionist who had virtually obtained the train fare for John Brown and his runaway slaves by threats and intimidation of Chicago politicians, endorsed his general's egotistical, unbelievable order to the army.

In the weeks after Antietam, Lincoln and his Cabinet wanted to know what McClellan planned to do. As usual the general had excuses: He needed more men, supplies, horses. Lincoln wearily decided to see for himself. On October 1st he visited McClellan's front-line headquarters, and was squired about by Pinkerton, in his derby hat, and checkered shirt. Alexander Gardner—and not Mathew Brady—appeared to take a series of memorable pictures; one showed Pinkerton with the President and General McClernand.

All that October, telegrams were exchanged between McClellan's headquarters and Lincoln; the general was still finding reasons for delays; Lincoln was again prodding. As one of the President's secretaries noted, Lincoln kept poking sharp sticks under McClellan's ribs.

After several maddening weeks McClellan finally crossed the Potomac and grouped before Warrenton. Pinkerton's operatives reported that Longstreet was directly in front, while Jackson's and Hill's forces were near Chester and Thornton's Gap, west of the Blue Ridge.

McClellan's plan, according to Pinkerton, was "to divide the enemy, with the hope of forcing him to battle when it was believed an easy victory could be achieved." As McClellan wrote in his memoirs, the Army of the Potomac was in peak condition "to fight a great battle."

The battle was never fought. On November 5th, by presidential order, McClellan was relieved from command of the Army of the Potomac and ordered to turn it over to General A. E. Burnside. Just why Lincoln, who had been disappointed for so long in McClellan, should take this moment for dismissing him is somewhat of a mystery. To Pinkerton it was no mystery. "Stanton had at last accomplished his revenge and the political cabal in Washington had at last won," was his opinion.[7]

There were rumblings of mutiny in the army when word was released that "Little Mac" had been relieved of command, but McClellan spoke loyally of his successor, and asked his troops to give him their support.

It was unthinkable for Pinkerton to remain with the Army of the Potomac after McClellan had left. On November 7, 1862, on the same day McClellan received word he had been relieved, Pinkerton sent in his resignation as Chief, Secret Service, Army of the Potomac. He claims in his memoirs—and there is no reason to doubt it—that both Lincoln and Stanton urged him to stay on. But Pinkerton refused. It was evident by now that the responsibilities Washington was giving him were far beyond the abilities and resources of his small organization. He was still using his own money to pay the salaries of his operatives and their expenses. In 1862, McClelland had to approve—for the third time—a War Department draft for Pinkerton to get back cash he had put out during his 1861 investigation of fifth-column activities in Baltimore.

Before he left his headquarters at Warrenton, Pinkerton wrote a letter to Pryce Lewis in Castle Thunder, telling him he had resigned from the army and was "returning to the old stand in Chicago." He was still trying, and so was McClellan, he wrote, to get them exchanged. In Washington, where he was winding up his affairs, Pinkerton saw Stanton, and got a very weak promise from the Secretary of War to do what he could to get Pinkerton's agents released. But Stanton's mind had not changed: In his opinion, Lewis and Scully weren't worth an exchange.

Yet, despite any mistakes that he might have made politically, no matter whose toes his boots might have crushed, Pinkerton's abilities were still respected by both Lincoln and Stanton. After he had resigned, Stanton, with Lincoln's approval, assigned Pinkerton to investigate numerous claims filed against the government. Pinkerton accepted, and for the duration of the war he and his men worked on nonmilitary and nonespionage matters. In the spring of 1864, Pinkerton and his agents were transferred by Stanton to the Department of the Mississippi, under General Edward R. S. Canby, with headquarters in New Orleans.

Pinkerton's record of unearthing evidence of cotton frauds against the government is an impressive one. He obtained evidence that sent many crooked brokers to jail, and recovered a great deal of money for the government.

Apparently Pinkerton was also maintaining his private detective business. In 1863 the Philadelphia and Reading Railroad charged one of their conductors with embezzling funds and presented evidence prepared by employees of the Pinkerton Agency. During that same year and for the same line, Pinkerton investigated another conductor who, he had found, owned property valued at $50,000 acquired during nine years of employment as a $60-a-month conductor. The president of the railroad summoned the conductor to his office, confronted him with Pinkerton's evidence, and demanded repayment. The conductor turned over $18,000 in bonds, but later brought suit against the railroad, alleging he gave it under duress. The suit was heard but the conductor lost. A short time later the line, for the third time in the history of American jurisprudence, took to court a case of embezzlement uncovered by a private detective—Allan Pinkerton. Most of the dozen conductors, when faced with the evidence uncovered by Pinkerton, confessed and made restitution, but one fought the case and won.

He was constantly in touch with McClellan, and it is evident that they both yearned for the great days of 1861–1862. In February, 1863, we find him writing to his general, then living in Orange, New Jersey. McClellan answered:

ORANGE, NEW JERSEY,
July 17, 1863

MY DEAR ALLAN:
Yours of the 10th was delayed a little in reaching me on account of my absence from the city, but it came I think in due course of mail. I am much obliged to you for it. I can well imagine the state of affairs

you describe during the Battle of Gettysburg. I suppose, "How does it look now?" often passed over the wires. To be trapped like a rat? What you say about Meade having been some days in command before it was announced, is very new to me—and not yet improbable—what is to be done with Hooker now? [8]

The words "I suppose, 'How does it look now?' often passed over the wires," must have wakened many a memory of those Seven Days and the blood bath at Antietam.

In 1863, Pinkerton and his son William were in New Orleans when a telegram summoned them back to Chicago. His daughter Belle had died at nineteen. The death of this chronically ill but favorite child shattered Allan and Joan. In a mood of deep depression, he returned to New Orleans with William to continue the prosaic task of tracking down cotton thieves.

During the following year Pinkerton was in Washington. Grant's star was dimming after the Wilderness, and for a time Pinkerton thought his dream of McClellan returning in triumph to command the troops would become a reality. As he wrote to McClellan: "From what I could glean here there is intention of giving you command would you accept it."

Again it was only a dream, and Pinkerton returned to New Orleans to be joined by his son Robert, then seventeen, wro was sworn in as one of his father's assistants by a lieutenant of the New Orleans provost marshal's office.

CHAPTER 17
North to Freedom, 1863

In Castle Thunder, the Confederate prison in Richmond, the winter of 1863 seemed never to end for Pinkerton's agents, Pryce Lewis and John Scully. The warehouse filled and emptied with prisoners. There were as many as ten thousand and as few as ten. Eventually all had left—all except Lewis and Scully. Several times they were on the verge of leaving, once to the point of packing together their ragged belongings, but at the last minute orders had come rescinding their release.

One day, in 1863, Lewis heard from another prisoner that Humphrey Marshal of Kentucky, a former Confederate general, could be influential in obtaining a release from Castle Thunder. Marshal, a giant of a man, had opened a law office in Richmond after he had resigned his commission. The reason: The cavalry reported they couldn't find a horse strong enough to carry the general's weight.

Lewis asked that Marshal be allowed to visit him, and one day the huge man waddled into the commandant's office and asked to see Pryce Lewis. It was probably pity more than the promise of gold that persuaded Marshal to accept the case of this bent-over, shaggy, gray-haired man who looked to be a bag of bones clothed in greasy rags and a torn blanket. Was this the "daring Yankee spy" the Richmond papers had written about?

Lewis signed a note for $100 in gold as a retainer. As he said, "I would have signed a note for one hundred million dollars."

In early September, Marshal told Lewis their exchange had finally been approved. On the twenty-ninth, Lewis and Scully joined 150 Union soldiers and officers on a train to City Point. There, for the first time in twenty months, Lewis saw an American flag snapping in the morning breeze. "If before this moment I had any English feelings left," he recalled, "I was turned into a complete American at that time."

When the train pulled into the dock, they saw the exchange boat that was to take them to Annapolis. Lewis's description of what happened is moving: One-legged men, men with empty sleeves, some helping to carry stretchers, staggered down the long dock to the boat flying the American flag. When they reached the gangplank, they brushed aside the guards and poured onto the dock, where they jumped up and down in weird dances as they shouted and wept.

During the trip to Annapolis, Lewis, Scully, and an army sutler they had met slept on the deck. At the camp, Lewis, expecting to be greeted as a returning hero, was informed by the bored officer in charge that the army wasn't in the business of transporting civilians to Washington. Though Lewis protested, he got nowhere. Finally he sent the sutler and Scully to town with his jacket to pawn. They came back with three dollars that went for tickets to Washington and a slab of bread and cheese.

Late that night the ragged trio arrived at the Washington depot. The sutler shook hands and went off, leaving Lewis and Scully alone on the deserted platform. Pinkerton and McClellan were gone. Who was there to turn to? Lewis suddenly recalled Wood, the superintendent of Old Capitol, and they walked to the rambling old prison. When he was summoned by the night guard, Wood peered through the front grating at Lewis, but failed to recognize the haggard face beneath the shaggy gray hair that fell over the feverish eyes. Scully was just as bad; the flesh hung in folds from his neck, and he was clearly in a walking trance.

Wood was stunned when Lewis identified himself. He summoned a doctor and hurriedly ordered his commissary to supply a meal. Both men gorged themselves.

Wood almost wept as he watched them. "My God," he kept saying, "why didn't you telegraph me? I would have sent a special locomotive for you!"

The morning after their arrival in Washington, Wood brought Lewis and Scully to the War Department to see Stanton, but the Secretary refused to see them. To Stanton they were still informers who had sent another man to his death. It seems incredible, but Stanton dismissed both Lewis and Scully without ordering that they be interviewed by intelligence for firsthand reports on what was going on behind Rebel lines.

The embarrassed Wood tried to explain why Stanton wouldn't see them, but Lewis shrugged it off. It was evident to the Englishman that he and Scully had long been forgotten. They were receiving the usual treatment accorded captured spies of all times who returned home.

Wood telegraphed to Pinkerton, who was in Philadelphia on an investigation, informing him of the return of Lewis and Scully. Pinkerton immediately wired back a reply, which Lewis kept among his papers. Addressed to Wood, and signed "E. J. Allen," his wartime nom de plume, it reads:

> Many thanks for your kind information. Tell Scully and Lewis to come here. I cannot possibly leave just now. Should they require money to come please let them have it. I will return it to you. Give them my address here and tell them to avoid all publicity of their affairs until they see me.

Pinkerton apparently was uneasy that his bitter agents would blast him in a press interview. To Lewis's credit they avoided any "publicity," and left at once for Philadelphia. Unfortunately, Lewis did not leave any details of the meeting he and Scully had with Pinkerton in Philadelphia. He dismisses the confrontation as a "hot interview with the old man . . . and we did not spare him for his carelessness in getting us into the enemy's hands . . ." Lewis apparently was referring to a so-called "agreement" Pinkerton had with Stanton that Mrs. Greenhow or the other lady spies arrested by Pinkerton, were not to be released until Lewis and Scully were back in Washington.

A rare pamphlet issued by the Agency on the life of Timothy Webster casually explains that Mrs. Greenhow and the Morton family had been released from Old Capitol to return to Richmond because of a "terrible mistake" on the part of the War Department. The pamphlet was published when both Scully and Lewis were still alive. One wishes for their comments.

At the last meeting Lewis had with Pinkerton in Philadelphia, before he returned to Washington, Lewis got a firm promise from Pinkerton that he would send $100 in gold under a flag to General Marshal in Richmond who had gained their release. According to Lewis, Pinkerton never sent the money to Marshal. He claimed he finally raised $100 and gave it to an exchanged prisoner returning to Richmond. But General Ben Butler—"the Beast"—discovered the money when the prisoner was searched in Fort Monroe, and had it sent to the United States Treasury.

Lewis was in Philadelphia on government business soon after this, and met Pinkerton on Chestnut Street. He explained the circumstances of the return of the money. "I will be in Washington in a few days and I will see the Secretary of War and have the money forwarded again," Pinkerton promised him. But he never did.

Copy of the picture of Belle Boyd found among the papers of Pryce Lewis

It was Belle Boyd, the glamorous Confederate spy, who finally managed to get the gold past Butler and deliver it to Marshal. Lewis met her at Old Capitol Prison, and probably arranged with her to undertake the mission. No one could have been a better choice.

Captain James B. Mix, then in command of the guards at Old Capitol Prison, escorted Belle Boyd past General Butler on December 1, 1863. Mix had formerly been in command of Lincoln's bodyguards. He had once won Lincoln's gratitude when he incurred injuries by stopping the President's runaway horse. Politicians tried to oust him from presidential favor, but were never successful. While Mix was being politically attacked, Lincoln sent him a personal letter thanking him for his friendship, and expressing faith in his loyalty. Mix's post at Old Capitol was in the form of a sinecure after he was injured.

The world had certainly turned upside down that day: a notorious enemy spy carrying federal gold to an enemy general with an escort whom General Butler would not dare to question! [1]

Back in Washington, Lewis was appointed a bailiff by Wood in Old Capitol, and Scully left for Chicago, where he ended his days as a guard in Chicago's City Hall.

CHAPTER 18
Watch on the Western Rivers, 1865

In the summer of 1863, Pinkerton was still trying to collect his "drafts" from the government for money spent in his spying activities. In July the government auditors were writing to both McClellan and Pinkerton in connection with "monies paid out by the State of Ohio for Secret Service in 1861 and for which she claims reimbursement from the United States." Records showed that Pinkerton had spent $12,683, but "in his account, credits the state in amount of $12,000, leaving a deficiency for $683," according to R. J. Atkinson, "3rd Auditor" in the Treasury Department, who asked that both Pinkerton and McClellan "submit at the earliest practical period a reply." [1]

In a letter to his representative in New York City—he did not open a branch there until 1866—Pinkerton explained the "deficiency," and gave a fascinating glimpse of how spies were paid in the early days of the Civil War. According to Pinkerton, before he arrived in Cincinnati to take over as head of McClellan's Secret Service, the general "had sent out to Memphis and vicinity" three agents whom he had promised to pay $10 a day and their expenses:

They returned on May 19 and at the General's order reported to me. I took their statements and on the General's order settled their accounts with them. Taking—on direction of Major Marcy (now General Marcy) separate vouchers from each in duplicate, calculating their time at ten

142

dollars per day, including the 20th and expenses. Receiving from the General's personal check on the Commercial Bank, Cincinnati, for $419 which was the amount necessary to settle with them. The General had paid two of them since [*sic*] Marcy at starting out, which amount I included in the settlement. I think it likely you will find some receipt of this in my files or the General has it.

Please call on General McClellan at this office and he will give you the date when these men left, compute their time at ten dollars each day and divide the balance of the amounts paid by General McClellan prior to starting and the $419.00 and disbursed by me to them as for expenses to each $1000.

All these paid (to the agents) were paid by the General into his own funds, and the only way it appears to me is to include those charges in my bill and when the balance is paid I can repay the General. Thus my bill will be his (McClellan's) voucher for his operations in the "Department of Ohio" but in all make out the charges as the General directs and then deliver the bill to the General making a full Journal entry as regards total of the bill and balance.

In the following dark and bitter summer of 1864, Allan Pinkerton, for the last time, played a role in national events at the side of his flamboyant general. In the early weeks of that summer a strange movement had begun within the Republican Party to get rid of its chosen nominee, to force the withdrawal of Lincoln for a more vigorous candidate. Everything appeared hopeless. Grant semed to be accomplishing nothing; Lee looked invincible, the war endless; and the casualties were mounting daily. Early had almost seized Washington; Congress was offended by Lincoln's Reconstruction, and this saddest of Presidents was at odds with factions within his own party on his conduct of the war. The government's financial credit was sagging, and in the North, Captain Thomas Henry Hines, that most daring of Confederate agents, was desperately trying to organize a Copperhead fifth column. On August 9th, Greeley wrote:

"I firmly believe that, were the elections to take place tomorrow the Democratic majority in this state and in Pennsylvania would amount to 100,000 and that we should lose Connecticut also." [2] He also wrote: "Mr. Lincoln is already beaten. He cannot be elected."

Greeley's sentiments were echoed by men high in the Republican Party: David Dudley Flood, F. W. Davis, John Austin Stevens.[3]

Again it was McClellan's hour. As the summer passed, the campaign to make him the Democratic presidential candidate gained momentum. In Chicago, Pinkerton rallied influential friends in the railroads and utilities to "the General's support." But, like the Republicans, the Democrats were split by dissension. There were two factions now: the Peace Democrats and the War Democrats. Clement Vallandingham represented the peace-at-any-cost philosophy, and his followers were growing. Also in

Chicago, unknown at the time to Pinkerton, Confederate agents were desperately attempting to sow disunity for the coming covention. From the private diary and papers of Captain Thomas H. Hines, we learn that the insertion of a peace plank in the Democratic platform was one of his objectives.

McClellan was wooed by the "western advocates of slavery" at meetings in New York City, and there were fears the general might agree to a compromise peace plan. Colonel Thomas Key, McClellan's former aide and the man who once worked for the release of Rose O'Neal Greenhow in Old Capitol Prison, wrote of these fears to Pinkerton. In his letter he also mentions the Harrison's Landing Letter, written by McClellan when he "was with us."

Addressing Pinkerton as "My Dear Major," Key wrote:

> My friendship for McClellan, my hatred of Stanton & Lincoln, my Democratic views, my anti-slavery sentiments, my abhorrence of the war and the way it is carried on, all combined to separate me politically from everybody that I know but yourself.
>
> We were in the same condition when the Harrison Landing Letter was written, except that then McClellan was with us. What man in the Army but you and myself would have approved of his sending it. Yet [on] it and some military orders and Western and Eastern Va. rests his entire political fabric. . . .

Key's two-page letter urges Pinkerton to do all he can to protect McClellan from the Peace Democrats faction, with Key promising to write "my views fully and often."

He ends with a warning to Pinkerton: "This letter ought not be preserved. You will please burn it." [4]

The Democratic Convention was held in Chicago on August 29th. With Pinkerton at his side as always, McClellan was nominated for the Presidency to please the War Democrats, but the drafting of the platform was assigned to Vallandingham and the "peace faction." After referring to "four years of failure to restore the Union by the experiment of war," the platform demanded the immediate cessation of hostilities so that peace could be restored.

This was not a peace-at-any-price declaration that the Confederate agents hoped they could swing; it proclaimed reunion as the condition of peace. Its weakness lay, not in the aims and objectives that were visioned, but in the easy assumption that an undefeated Confederacy would consent to abdication by the Davis government, after having achieved an armistice on what could be termed a southern victory.

Shortly before McClellan's nomination, Lincoln had written a brief memorandum agreeing that there was a probability his administration would not be reelected. And if that came about, he intended to "sit down with McClellan and talk over with him and say, 'General, the election has demonstrated that you . . . have more influence . . . than I. Now let us together . . . with your influence and with the executive war [*sic*], try to save the country . . . you raise as many troops as you can and I will devote all my energies to assist and end the war.' "

But as McClellan had told Pinkerton a year earlier, he had firmly resisted all attempts to bring him into the peace party. Addressing Pinkerton as "My Dear Allan," he wrote:

> I presumed the association of my name with Vallandingham was abandoned—I take it for granted my letter effectually knocked on the head any ideas of bringing in the Peace Party. . . . I intend to destroy any and all pretense for any possible association of my name to the Peace Party.
>
> Many of my conservative friends regret that I wrote that letter [disassociating himself with the Peace Party].
>
> I did not. I tried to do what was right and I trust that the future will vindicate the wisdom of my course by showing that the letter in question did very much toward breaking up the Copperheads in the North.[5]

Pinkerton agreed; it was McClellan's finest hour. Pinkerton was as active as he could be in Chicago during the campaign. Until the beginning of September, it looked as if "the General" would be elected by an overwhelming majority. Pinkerton did not commit his secret hopes to paper, but the close relationship between him and McClellan surely can permit us to assume he was wondering what the future might hold for him in Washington should his man win.

Suddenly the tide of public opinion began to turn; the peace plank that McClellan feared was beginning to stir up resentment. The Republican orators were making good use of the plank and Vallandingham's name. The activities of Confederate agents in the North was another factor; they had fire-bombed a part of lower New York City, captured a gunboat on the lakes, and in Chicago, Captain Hines had barely escaped a patrol by disguising himself as a woman leaving a funeral parlor. In reality Hines and his men were only striking a match and not a torch, but the Republicans made much of it. Then followed the fall of Atlanta, giving Lincoln the one big military victory he needed, along with the Republican victories in Maine and Vermont. The anti-Lincoln radicals were appeased by the retirement of Montgomery Blair from the Cabinet and the appointment of William Dennison, war governor of Ohio, in his place.

The multitudes rushing to McClellan, which had given the Republicans so much concern, were now halted.

Only the Union states were counted; all except three (Kentucky, Delaware, and New Jersey) gave Lincoln their electoral vote, while in the popular vote Lincoln had a 400,000 majority over McClellan. Though the experts of the time hailed the election as a "Lincoln landslide," the large minorities in New York, Pennsylvania, Ohio, Indiana, and Illinois underscored the enthusiastic predictions the Democrats had made in August of a McClellan victory. An old friend of Pinkerton, John D. Caton of Illinois, in a letter to McClellan gives a shrewd analysis for the general's defeat: The Democrats were ambiguous in their platform; some of the leaders of the convention had questionable principles; they were loud in their cries for peace while they denounced all others as abolitionists; they organized secret societies such as the copperheads, and inserted an important plank to please a minority in the party that had assumed leadership only by its shrillness.[6]

One point Caton failed to make was the shrewd political image-making of the Republican propagandists of 1864, who placed strong emphasis on the "peace plank,"which in reality did not represent the majority of the party. If the Democrats had won the Presidency, they would have done so under McClellan, and not under the copperhead Vallandingham. Actually, all parties in the North of 1864 were Union parties. The Union (Republican) under Lincoln, the Democrats under McClellan, and the radical anti-Lincoln party under John C. Frémont, which vanished before the election, all had as their chief point resumption of the Union.

As for Allan Pinkerton, McClellan's defeat was just another victory for the Washington cabal. But Pinkerton was always a practical man who only occasionally allowed himself the pleasure of peering over his shoulder into the past. After the election, he turned all his vigor into directing the activities of his Agency. He still kept up his friendship with the general, writing him letters and never failing to visit him in Orange, New Jersey, when he came east on Agency business.

Until the day he died Pinkerton always viewed George Brinton McClellan as the Lochinvar who could have ridden out of the West on a fiery black charger to save the Union—that is, if the numskulls, the vicious cabal in Washington, had given him the chance. They never did.

Allan Pinkerton would play one final brief role in the days following Appomattox. He was in General Canby's New Orleans headquarters when the telegraph ticked out the shocking news that Lincoln had been shot by Booth in Ford's Theatre. Memories of the violent days in Baltimore overwhelmed him, and as his son William later recalled, his father wept bitterly as he crumpled the telegram in his hands.

Pinkerton immediately sent off a telegram to Stanton, placing himself and his staff at the disposal of the War Department. Stanton replied the following morning, still addressing Pinkerton by his wartime nom de guerre of Major E. J. Allen:

War Department
Washington City 23d
April 24

G. F. Allen Esq.
New Orleans

Accept my thanks for your telegram of the 19th received this evening. Mr Seward is still alive and there is a bare possibility of his recovery. His son case is hopeless. Booth and two of his accomplices ~~are still~~ Surratt and Harold are still at large. ~~The others~~ Some of the others have been secured. Booth may have made his way to the west with a view of getting to Texas or Mexico. I think he has tryto do so. You will please take measures to watch the western rivers and you may get him. The reward offered for him now amounts to One hundred thousand dollars or over. Ask ~~the Commanding officers of the Department~~ General Canby to give orders in his command for his arrest,

Edwin M Stanton Secretary of War

Stanton's April 24, 1865, letter to Pinkerton. *Pinkerton's, Inc.*

WAR DEPARTMENT
WASHINGTON CITY

April 24, 1865.

E. J. ALLEN, Esq.
New Orleans.

Accept my thanks of your telegram of the 19th, received this evening. Mr. Seward is still alive and there is a bare probability of his recovery. His son's case is hopeless. Booth and two of his accomplices, Surratt and Howard, are still at large. Some of the others have been secured. Booth may have made his way to the West with a view of getting to Texas or Mexico. I think he had tried to do so. You will please take measures to watch the Western Rivers and you may get him. The Rewards offered for him now amount to One Hundred Thousand Dollars or over. Ask General Canby to give orders in his command for his arrest.

EDWARD M. STANTON,
Secretary of War [7]

"If only I had been there to protect him as I had done before," Pinkerton wrote.

It is a fascinating might-have-been of history. For all his pettiness, political naïveté, hero worship, and amateurishness in military espionage, he was still the best detective of his time. It is hard to believe that had Allan Pinkerton been on duty that night in Ford's Theatre, John F. Parker, a city policeman with a "drunk and disorderly" record, would have been Lincoln's sole guard—he had also left his post outside the door of the presidential box to go downstairs to visit Taltavul's, a nearby tavern—or that John Wilkes Booth could have got close enough to fire the fatal shot.

BOOK 3

The Middle Border Outlaws, 1866-1877

CHAPTER 19
The Overture

The quiet scene in McLean's parlor at Appomattox slowly slipped into history. Weary men in gray returned to their homes and the Reconstruction, a period when industry rose to dominate agrarian forces in the American economy.

Lee's men came back to a ravaged land. Once-proud plantations were charred shells, and lands were devastated. Slave labor, representing billions, had been wiped away by emancipation measures, delivering a tremendous blow to the economy of the South. There was no capital, for banks had disappeared, and factories had been either burned or stripped. There is no need for words to describe the war-ravaged cities. The photographs by Civil War photographers like Alexander Gardner, Timothy O'Sullivan, and the Gibson brothers are powerful reminders that the Civil War was as brutal and devastating as any fought by Americans. Many of the people had no homes. As one witness recalled, there wasn't a pig, horse, or cow from Winchester to Harrisonburg, Virginia.

Yet, while the rebuilding of the South with its enormous special problems was important, vitalizing the economy was just as important to the North. There had been a slump immediately following the cessation of hostilities. A federal budget deficit of almost one billion dollars in the fiscal year of 1865, perhaps one-seventh of the national income, dropped to zero in the year following the surrender. The wartime speculating boom in wholesale prices had collapsed like a punctured balloon. For example, pig-iron contracts fell from a wartime requirement of 1,136 tons to less than 900 in late 1865.[1]

One and a half million men engaged in war had to be thrown on

150

the labor market, while the economy had to absorb a growing stream of 300,000 immigrants in each of the fiscal years 1866 and 1867. The contraction of the nation's economy which began in 1866 continued until 1867, but then the upturn began with bursts of prosperity. In ten years agricultural outlets doubled. Steel and oil emerged as giants of industry. With the introduction in the United States of the Kelly-Bessemer process of steel blasting in 1868, the great steelworks were born, with the Carnegie syndicate commissioning huge systems of steel mills, plants, and bridgeworks. In the year of Appomattox, a young man named John D. Rockefeller formed a Cleveland company, with a capital of about $1,000,000, which was reorganized as the Standard Oil Company of Ohio, five years later. In 1866, permanent electric communication between America and Europe was established on July 27th. Earlier, in 1858, a continuous cable was laid between Trinity Bay, Newfoundland, and Ireland, and Queen Victoria and President Buchanan transmitted congratulatory messages.

Most of the activities of the booming postwar period centered upon the railroads. Following the driving of the last spike at Ogden, Utah, to link East and West, railroad construction and expansion continued at a phenomenal rate. The outstanding men of the time turned to some form of railroading: Charles Francis Adams, McClellan, Robert Todd Lincoln, Ambrose Burnside, John A. Dix, and many others. Not only lines but extensive transportation systems were also built. The public carriers, like the Adams and American Express companies, so close to the rise of the Pinkertons, flourished during the flush period that followed the Civil War. But the influence of increasing national wealth and consequent greed among the carriers caused companies that had formerly been allies to become bitter rivals. The Adams and the Southern remained friendly allies in the fierce competition, but the American, United States, and Wells Fargo, all born from the same stock, became bitter enemies.

Harper's Weekly hinted that the express-company business had made at least fifty millionaries in the postwar period—only a slight exaggeration. As a national business it ranked second only to railroading, and the men it raised from log cabins to palatial mansions were many.[2]

One of Pinkerton's postwar investigations had to do with wiretapping, a term familiar to twentieth-century newspaper readers. Pinkerton was retained by William Orton, president of Western Union, to investigate a ring that was tapping the company's lines somewhere on the western frontier, intercepting important messages and forwarding to New York newspapers spurious stories that had seriously affected the New York stock market. Losses to investors were estimated in the millions. Railroad lines, banks large and small, shipping lines, notably the large Pacific Mail Steamship Company, had been driven to the brink of bankruptcy when false stories of major money losses and disasters had driven the stocks

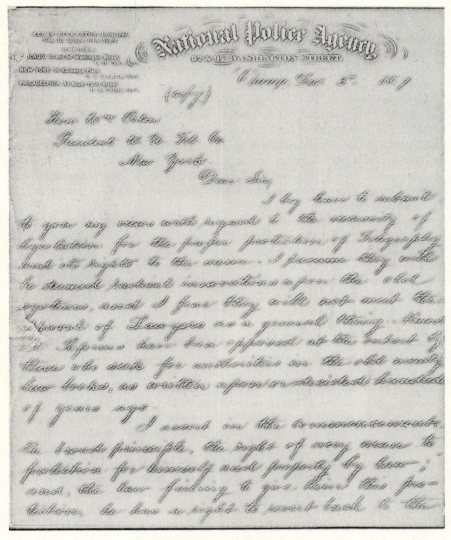

Letter from Allan Pinkerton to Western Union president, warning about wiretapping, in 1867. *Chicago Historical Society*

down. Stories of mine disasters in Colorado had almost wiped out some of the mining companies, and allowed speculators to buy large blocks of stock at prices far below their value. Suicide and murder had followed the plummeting stock market. On the West Coast a father of four had killed his family and himself after a sudden drop of the Pacific Mail stock had cleaned him out. In another city a hysterical investor had shot and killed his broker. When a newspaper had received the story of a major disaster, editors had asked for confirmation. Return messages had been signed by the newspapers' official correspondents with their private code numbers.

Pinkerton and Bangs, working with Western Union's General Manager Anson Stager, broke the ring in two months. They began by tailing messengers, and found one stopping off at the office of a Wall Street investment broker. A check by Pinkerton revealed that this broker, through fronts, had made a considerable amount of money by buying the tumbling stocks of the companies named in the disaster stories. The investigation led to San Francisco and to two brothers employed as operators by Western Union. Weeks of tailing the messengers, the brothers, and the broker paid off when conspirators met in New York to plan a major stock coup. The wiretappers were captured after they had tapped the Western Union wires on a remote section of the frontier to send a news story to the New York *Tribune* detailing the sinking of the Pacific Mail's crack liner with the loss of 800 lives and a $2,500,000 Wells Fargo gold shipment. The *Tribune* was alerted that the story was spurious, the gang was caught, and on Pinkerton's recommendation Orton reorganized the company's codes. A number of crooked messengers and operators from New York to San Francisco were also discharged.

After the investigation was concluded, Pinkerton outlined to Orton, in a twelve-page letter, his views on the need for federal legislation to protect the nation's telegraph lines. The letter, found among Pinkerton's papers in the Chicago Historical Society, contains suggestions that are being argued today in congressional and state legislative committees.

Telegraph lines, Pinkerton proposed, should be protected from the lawless, as should any utility of his time. He pointed out to Orton that American business in the future would make telegraph lines an indispensable part of America's economic life, and had to be protected by federal laws similar to those that protected the United States mail:

"The lines must be protected by Congress so that a man who stole communications from the wires was equally guilty as the man who stole letters out of the mail and opened them. . . ."

As the telegraph, railroads, and public-carrier business expanded, so did Pinkerton's National Detective Agency. In 1866, Allan Pinkerton opened a New York office, and a year later one in Philadelphia. After the war William had returned to Notre Dame with Robert; then both joined their father in the Agency. Robert was sent to the New York office, in charge of the eastern and southern sections of the firm's business; William made his headquarters in Chicago as supervisor of the Midwest and West. Allan, the founder, was still supreme.

The endless days and intense drive were beginning to tell on Allan in those postwar years. Photographs reveal how he had aged from the days he had occupied the tent next to McClellan's on the front and posed with Lincoln and his generals. His letters show he was becoming more irascible and demanding. He still insisted on knowing everything that was going on in every branch office; copies of reports of every investigation, from a minor case to a major robbery, had to be sent to him for approval. Faithful George Bangs, now the Agency's superintendent of the New York office, was frequently the target of his bitter and often unreasonable letters. But Bangs was a veteran of the wars; between him and the quieter, more complacent Robert, they managed to take most of the slings and arrows and still keep the offices, now so important in the mushrooming urban growth of the East, on an even keel.

There was more glory for the Agency in the postwar years when it solved a $90,000 robbery in the Adams Baltimore office—like the Maroney case, another inside job—and three years later cracked the nation's first big train robbery—but not holdup.

In that period the Adams Express "carried" between New York and Boston, leaving Twenty-eighth Street, Manhattan's main terminal, at about eight o'clock. It pursued an indirect course, turning north from New Haven, through Hartford to Springfield, then eastward over the Boston and Albany Railroad to Boston. It carried freight only for Hartford, Springfield, and Worcester, and the car was opened only at these cities. The express car, sheeted with iron plates and mounted on an iron frame, was supposedly theifproof. The assignment of the messenger who rode in the baggage car was to check the huge padlocks of the car at each stop. This had become such a seemingly useless precaution that it was often forgotten or ignored. On Saturday evening, January 6, 1866, the locked car had two Adams Express Company safes filled with currency. The train clicked along up through Rye, Greenwich, Stamford, Norwalk, and Bridgeport, until it reached New Haven, three hours later. There Moore, the messenger, noticed that one of the two doors of the iron car was ajar. He checked the safes, and found that they had been broken open and that $700,000 in cash, bonds, and jewels had been stolen. Somewhere along the route the hasp of the padlock had been forced and the safes pried open.

The robbery was the biggest of that period. The Pinkertons were summoned by Edward Sanford, president of Adams. Allan and William joined Robert in New York, and the investigation began. Moore, the messenger, admitted to Robert that he had checked the lock on the door facing the platform only at Bridgeport, and hadn't bothered to look at either door after that stop.

Allan Pinkerton flooded the area with operatives, doggedly questioning residents of towns and villages along the line, trackwalkers and railroad employees. The daring but rather stupid thieves had swung off the cars at Cos Cob. In the bushes alongside the tracks, a Pinkerton operative found a bag of $5,000 in gold coins that had been dropped by the jittery train robbers.

Livery stables in every town and village were checked. In Stamford, the Pinkerton operatives learned that two men had tried to hire a horse and buggy on the night of the robbery but that the stable owner refused because they were strangers. They then stopped overnight at a local hotel and took an early train eastward the next morning. Robert and William obtained a minute description of the men, and trailed them in a buggy to Norwalk. One man was identified as John Grady, a brakeman on the railroad. He had vanished, but the Pinkertons kept on his trail. From the Norwalk station their investigation led them to the home of an old man named Tristam, who lived on the outskirts of town. While William and his men combed the line, talking to employees and train riders who daily used the line, Robert looked into Tristam's activities. He discovered that the old man, on a trip to New York City, had been seen with a large parcel that he had refused to check, keeping it on his lap, "hugging it as he would a child."

In New York, the Pinkertons trailed Tristam block by block, until he entered a tenement on Division Street on the lower East Side. It was comparatively easy to find that the woman in the house was Tristam's married sister. The sequel was simple: The Pinkertons raided the apartment, and found $113,762 of the loot still in Adams Express bags. Tristam, picked up in a tavern, confessed to William Pinkerton. He implicated several others, including Grady the brakeman. Half the gang were amateurs, and even the thieves with records admitted to Pinkerton they had taken on a job far beyond their talents.

Pinkerton insisted that all members of the gang be taken into custody. When one escaped to Canada, William and Robert followed him to Montreal and Quebec and finally back to New York, where they nabbed him. One of the petty thieves, upon being persuaded by William to turn state's evidence, told how the job was pulled: Grady had watched the Adams messengers, and found that Moore was the most careless. When he was assigned to a run that carried a big haul, they waited until the safes were put aboard the Adams car, which as usual was rolled into the yard to await the makeup of the train. There, three of the gang, shielded by the noise of the panting engines, pried off the lock with a crowbar and marline spike, and hid in the car. The rest of the gang crouched in the bushes north of the Harlem River. The plan was to pull the signal cord, and, when the locomotive ground to a stop, fling open the door and roll out the safes to the gang in the bushes. But to their surprise, the signal cord in the express car was encased in an iron tube, and could not be touched. They battered open the safes, filled two suitcases, and then jumped out at Cos Cob. One bag was hidden in a pile of lumber and another was hidden behind a stone wall, a mile east of the bridge across Cos Cob inlet. They walked the three remaining miles to Stamford, where they unsuccessfully tried to hire a buggy. They went back the next night and retrieved the loot, part of which they buried east of Cos Cob. After the money and jewels were recovered, the publicity for the Agency was widespread in the East.

In the same year the Agency arrested a ring of forgers who, unlike the Cos Cob robbers, had carefully planned their robbery of the Adams Express Company by forged drafts. The thieves had established a real-estate office in Philadelphia, actually conducted some business, and then vanished after the robberies. The case was broken by the excellent detective work of Robert J. Linden, Pinkerton's assistant Philadelphia superintendent (who would play a key role in many of the Agency's major investigations), after he had discovered a scrap of blotting paper with a faint New York address. Linden, painstakingly using a mirror and magnifying glass, brought out the address and part of a name. The laborious investigation was similar to the Maroney case, with operatives, including Allan Pinkerton himself, "shadowing" suspects on trains, in wagons, or on horseback from Philadelphia to the South, then back to the North. The suspect was finally nabbed with the evidence, and what had been called a "perfect case" was broken.

Between supervising investigations of train robberies and forgery rings, the indefatigable Allan Pinkerton continued to take part in the historic events of that period. In the winter of 1867, impeachment of the President of the United States occupied most of the thoughts and plans of the radicals in Washington when it became evident that Andrew Johnson would not be bullied by Congress into forcibly imposing Negro suffrage on the South. In February, 1866, William Lloyd Garrison had startled a Brooklyn audience with his announcement that if he were in Congress his first order of business would be to "impeach Andrew Johnson." From then on, whenever Johnson displeased the radicals, there were cries of impeachment. The following winter, the Missourian Benjamin Loan, in a frenzied speech on the floor, charged Johnson with causing Lincoln's death for political reasons. Loan forced through an investigation by the Judiciary Committee, which sat behind closed doors. The notorious Lafayette C. Baker, who had taken over the chasing of wartime spies when Pinkerton left Washington, was the first witness. He set the tone of the entire proceedings by testifying that Johnson had conspired with Jefferson Davis to betray the Union.

Permit to attend the impeachment proceedings. *Library of Congress*

From February to December, Americans, high and low, humble and great, villain and hero, came to Washington to testify. The hearings were held in secret, with the apprehensive President Johnson and his supporters using every means to find out the nature of the new charges being concocted "against the criminal in the White House."

In desperation, Johnson or his friends turned to Allan Pinkerton, a friend of Johnson, for help. As George Fort Milton writes in his *Age of Hate:* "Through his [Pinkerton's] instrumentality, the President and his friends were informed every day as to the secret deliberations of the men trying to impeach him."

Pinkerton's "instrumentality" was a pretty girl who "made up" to the committee's stenographer (they were male in those days). She sent on verbatim reports of the hearings to Pinkerton in Chicago, who forwarded them to the White House.[3]

Apparently this is the only part Pinkerton played in the impeachment proceedings. Although the evidence against the President that he had violated the Tenure of Office Act by removing Secretary of War Stanton was insufficient, the Senate at the time was extremely partisan, and Johnson escaped conviction by only one vote (35 to 19; a two-thirds majority was necessary for impeachment) on May 16, 1868.

Allan Pinkerton next turned the resources of his Agency from the solemn impeachment proceedings of an American President to the lonely forests of the Middle Border, where the brief postwar depression, social unrest, and divided loyalties had produced the first of the nation's organized outlaw bands. The Jameses, Youngers, and Renos were blood brotherhoods that robbed small neighboring banks, county treasuries, and trains. Their victims were many times unarmed cashiers or innocent townspeople. The Pinkertons viewed the Renos simply as common criminals who had to be brought to justice because they had dared to rob a client—the Adams Express Company—or looted banks and county treasury offices who had retained the Agency when local law-enforcement bodies showed they were not capable of trailing or lacked the resources to capture the gangs.

But the Jameses and Youngers became personal foes of the Agency. They finally committed the unpardonable sin: they not only killed two Pinkerton operatives but the fear they inspired, along with official corruption and partisan politics, provided a wall the Pinkertons could never breach.

During Christmas week, 1868, Allan Pinkerton dictated a fifteen-page letter to George Bangs in his New York office. It is a violent, bitter document, sometimes abusive, in which Pinkerton reviews the accomplishments of the New York City branch during the two years it was established. Bangs had been having trouble with his New York staff, and of course had sent on this information to his employer, who then urged him to give those "incompetents the boot. Show your fist, let them be kicked downstairs as quickly as possible." There is one paragraph in which Pinkerton does not mention the Jameses, Youngers, or Renos but in which his philosophy certainly applied to the events that followed:

> I shall not give up the fight with these parties until the bitter end and the last die is cast whatever that may prove to be; life or death, prosperity or adversity, the present life of the eternity of darkness. I have told Mr. Davies [the new superintendent] how we stand and what his course must be; it must be war to the knife and knife to the hilt.
>
> You know my policy in such cases, it is no delaying the fight; if a fight has to come, let it come and let it come soon the sooner the better for all concerned—at all events at least for me. Delay no fight one moment—make all the attacks you can. Keep yourself right upon the attack with hands clean and with clear conscience you are sure to win . . . no power in Heaven or on earth can influence me when I know I am right . . . the right is mighty and must prevail and all we have to do is to manage our own affairs with discretion, with honor, with integrity and we must and we shall win. . . .[4]

The letter is clearly written by a person obsessed by his own opinions and rules; a harassed, exhausted man with a frightening tenacity and an almost fanatical devotion to his business. There must never be dissent;

the rallying cry was always "Success." It is surprising that Bangs, an astute man who knew Pinkerton perhaps better than Allan's own sons did, failed to detect the warning signals in this letter. The relentless drive, the exhausting energy, and the near-contempt for physical limitations were slowly taking their toll of Allan Pinkerton. But the hickory-tough Scot continued to ignore the blinding headaches that made him stop in the midst of dictating to his secretary, close his eyes, and grip his forehead. The only possible reason why no one alerted his sons or why they were not aware of the approaching breakdown in their father's health was that Pinkerton had impressed them all with his own image as the inexhaustible man of iron.

Now, out of the bitter social postwar upheaval rode, like the horsemen of the Apocalypse, the Renos of Indiana, to be followed by the Jameses and Youngers of Missouri, with robbery and murder in their wake, to provide one of the most lurid, melodramatic, and exciting chapters in the history of the Pinkertons.

CHAPTER 20
The Renos of Indiana

The American outlaws who committed our first train robbery were the Reno brothers of Indiana, not Jesse James and the Youngers. The Renos, like the Jameses and Youngers, rose out of the political, social, and economic unrest following the Civil War. Their reign was shorter than the sixteen years of Jesse James and his men, but more successful; the Renos carried away sums that were staggering in their time.

The Pinkertons, father and sons, took an objective view of the Renos; there is none of the intense, personal hatred of the Indiana bandits that is evident in the correspondence of the detectives when they wrote of the James boys and Youngers. At least thirty years after the gang had vanished into history, William Pinkerton demanded that a Midwest newspaper retract a description of Laura Reno, sister of the outlaws, as a desreputable woman. He wrote:

> She was a respectable girl, and although she probably knew as much about her brothers' activities as anybody, yet her virtue was never questioned. . . . I think they [the newspaper] should take back this part of their report, simply as a matter of justice to this woman, who, if living, this article might be a reflection on. . . .[1]

One factor that helped the Pinkertons break up the Renos was their ability to penetrate the outlaw community. Dick Winscott, a Seymour saloon owner, acted as Pinkerton's informer. We know little of him, but

Laura Reno. *Pinkerton's, Inc.*

Frank Reno, an early and rare picture. *Pinkerton's, Inc.*

he certainly was persuasive; on one occasion he talked John Reno, the gang's leader, and Franklin Sparks, the gang's horse holder, into posing for an itinerant photographer, also a Pinkerton operative. The photographs proved to be invaluable in identifying the outlaws, who often were just names, not faces.

In his rare autobiography, John Reno pictures his mother, Julia Ann Reno, as a "highly educated woman." This may be exaggerated and sentimental remembrance, but Jefferson County, Indiana, court records show she had a neat, legible handwriting. Wilkison Reno, the father of the outlaw breed, was born in Boyle County, Kentucky. The original name of the family is believed to have been Renault, and he was of French descent. The older Reno was an illiterate, who, John said, "could scarcely count his own money." The old man, however, possessed a shrewd investment sense that enabled him to gather a great deal of farmland. As the Jefferson County records show, the elder Reno was one of the biggest taxpayers.[2]

Frank Reno, oldest of the sons, was born on July 27, 1837, near Seymour, Jefferson County. John Reno, the second child, was born on July 23rd, two years later. The birthplace of Clinton and Laura, the only girl, are not known. Clinton, known to Indiana history as "Honest Reno," was never connected with the outlaws. Nor was Laura.

The other two Renos were Simeon, born on August 2, 1843, and William, born on May 15, 1848.

In 1816 the family settled on the White River bottomland, two miles northwest of the present city of Seymour, Indiana. John Reno, who, like Jesse James, had shown the traits of leadership in his boyhood, attended a log-cabin school on the corner of the Reno property. As he recalled he hated school, "thinking more of sport and excitement than I did of my lessons."[3]

After Appomattox, the Renos bought up sections of nearby Rockford, the scenes of so many mysterious fires that the Seymour *Times* described it as a ghost town. From the evidence, it appears that the Renos were the arsonists. The ravaged town, under control of the gang, soon became a postwar hideout for outlaws and counterfeiters.

Seymour, as one writer of his time called it, "was a carnival of crime." The Renos robbed, stole, and tortured from the fall of 1865 to the spring of 1866, when they raided the Clinton County, Indiana, Treasury. Though Frank Reno was arrested, he was soon acquitted.

On October 6, 1866, the Renos committed what is said to be the first formal train holdup in the United States. Three masked men, John and Simeon Reno and Franklin Sparks, boarded an Ohio & Mississippi train as it left Seymour depot. After slugging the Adams Express Company messenger, they pushed two safes from the car when they were three miles east of town. One safe held $15,000 in cash; the other, $30,000 in cash and gold. Pinkerton's subsequent investigation revealed that an accomplice had probably signaled to them the location where horses were tied. The area was desolate, and there was no citizen riding along a public road to be suspicious of hitched horses and waiting men. The robbers cracked open the safe and got the $15,000; the other, heavier and more strongly built, was abandoned.

The Adams people alerted Allan Pinkerton, who hurried to Indiana. It didn't take him long to discover that the Reno brothers were running the county by fear or bribery. Pinkerton's favorite theory—that a criminal enterprise could successfully be broken by infiltration—was employed. It is unfortunate we know nothing of Dick Winscott, who operated the saloon in Seymour, or the tall, ruddy-faced man with the cold eyes, luxuriant sideburns, and embroidered waistcoat of a riverboat gambler who made his headquarters at the saloon and announced he was ready for action. There was also a new hand working at the depot. All were Pinkerton operatives, "laying pipe with the outlaws." [4]

The Renos visited the saloon, and Winscott made sure they liked what they found. Winscott, of course, hinted he had been in some shady deals back East, leaving one jump ahead of the law. The saloon was a dingy, smoky place filled with the shadows cast by the oil lamps; the Renos and their riders sat at the tables or stood at the rough bar, drinking and making plans for their next strike while the hard-eyed gambler flipped out the cards and cashed the chips. When the "loose women" appeared, liquor flowed, and solemn reporters of their time recorded that the saloon became "wild and boisterous." It was during one such party that Winscott was able to persuade John Reno and Franklin Sparks to pose on a stool for a photographer. To the hilarious shouts and hoots of his gang,

Reno and Sparks, beer glasses in hands, grinned drunkenly into the lens. They failed to notice that Winscott kept the pictures, and soon there were new faces in the Pinkerton's Rogues' Gallery in Chicago.

Encouraged by the Renos' success at train robbery, two young thieves held up a train near Seymour, robbing the Adams Express car of $8,000. The Renos were outraged that their idea and territory had been appropriated. They summoned their riders, thieves, train robbers, and killers, and set out after the "two young men from Jackson County." They caught up with the buggy, thrashed the train robbers, hijacked the $8,000 and turned the pair over to the local sheriff of Jackson County. But John Reno recalled in his memoirs that there was another motive: One of the young men had been courting John's "fast woman"; robbing a train in Reno territory was just adding insult to injury.

The Renos' next strike was the Daviess County Treasury, Gallatin, Missouri, where they stole $22,065. Although the county treasury was not protected by the Agency, Weir, general manager of the Adams Express Company, asked Pinkerton to investigate the robbery. The Renos were soon identified as the outlaws. Pinkerton got in touch with Winscott and his other men in Seymour. All agreed any attempt by the Pinkertons to ride into Seymour to take John Reno and his brothers would surely result in a gun battle, with innocent lives endangered.

In Chicago, Allan and William Pinkerton decided that the only way to get John, the leader, to face justice was by kidnapping him. As William said, "It was kidnapping but the ends justified the means." Once again it was putting into action the philosophy that ruled the Agency in those rough, early years.

Allan Pinkerton wired to the sheriff of Daviess County to meet him in Cincinnati with a writ for the Indiana outlaw. Meanwhile, he led "six muscular men" aboard a special train he had hired in Cincinnati. The sheriff arrived with the writ, and Pinkerton sent a coded message to Winscott to get Reno on the depot platform on some pretext, then wired him the time and place.

The wood-burning engine and car "stood at the ready" for two days. Then the telegram arrived: John Reno would be on the platform "waiting for a friend." The train slowly chugged into Seymour station only a few minutes before the express was to arrive. From his window, Pinkerton saw Winscott laughing and talking to a husky black-haired man in a rumpled blue suit and crushed black hat. He glanced quickly at the pictures Winscott had sent into Chicago. "That's our man," he snapped.

The big iron wheels of the coal burner were still turning when Allan swung from the car, followed by his men. They moved quietly through the crowd that usually gathered to see the express go by. Suddenly the strangers had surrounded John Reno. The outlaw saw that he was in a trap, and lunged; but he was quickly overpowered, his arms pulled up behind him. While the crowd gaped, he was carried, shouting and squirming, into the car. Pinkerton leaped on the steps, waved his hand, and the train puffed out of the station. Inside the car, the detectives handcuffed and roped Reno until he looked like a steer ready for branding.

Back in Seymour, the alarm was sounded. The other Renos gathered together a force of the most desperate men in the county, and set out in pursuit of the Pinkerton train. But they never caught up, and the chase was abandoned.[5]

Reno was arraigned the following day in Gallatin before a judge who certainly didn't represent blind justice. When Reno was pushed before him, the judge leaned over to shout: "You're the one who did this work and we're going to hang you to the highest tree in Grand River bottoms if that money is not returned."

Reno was put into the "condemned cell" with a round-the-clock armed guard. Word of his arrest spread through the countryside with the speed of a prairie fire. As John recalled: "The natives began coming from all directions with their shotguns and coonskin caps and with their hair hanging down to their shoulders. Some of them had not taken the mess from their backs that had grown there during the war." John, of course, ignored or had forgotten his lengthy record as a bounty jumper.

On a Monday morning, January 18, 1868, John Reno, under heavy guard, was taken to the penitentiary. He later wrote: "When we arrived at the prison gate I looked up and read in large letters over the entrance: 'the way of the transgressor is hard; admission twenty-five cents.' But I was on the deadhead list and went in free." [6]

While John Reno was on his way to the penitentiary, his brother Frank, now in command of the gang, was feverishly making plans to free him by force. Three days after he had been admitted to the Indiana Penitentiary, John received a letter from Frank, explaining that "he had missed the connections at Quincy, or he would have been good as his word."

In defiance of the Pinkertons and the growing vigilante movement, Frank led his gang across the state, robbing county treasury offices, post offices, and trains. In February, 1868, the Renos robbed the Harrison County Treasury office at Magnolia, Iowa, of $14,000. It was a serious loss to the frontier settlement—a "public calamity," the local papers described it.

When Allan Pinkerton was asked by the county supervisors to take over the case, he sent William to Iowa. The oldest Pinkerton son, now twenty-two, a powerful younger version of his father, arrived in town with two assistants. Days of dogged, monotonous police work followed. Farmers, townspeople, passing travelers were questioned. When he discovered that the gang had fled on a handcar, Pinkerton followed the tracks to seven miles outside the village, where he found the abandoned handcar.

Hiring a buggy, William stopped at the farmhouses along the way to trace the outlaws to Council Bluffs. On a hunch, he ordered his men to find out if there was a "disreputable place" in town owned by a former resident of Seymour. When a saloon run by a former counterfeiter who had once lived in Seymour turned up, Pinkerton ordered a day-and-night watch kept on the place. The surveillance turned up one startling fact: A visitor to the saloon was Michael Rogers, reported to be one of "the wealthiest citizens of Council Bluffs and a pillar of the Methodist Church." Pinkerton sent a coded message to Chicago. The answer soon came back that Rogers had an old police record. In Iowa, Pinkerton carefully retraced Rogers' movements on the night of the robbery, discovering that Rogers had paid his taxes a short time before the county treasurer had closed his office. As Pinkerton deduced, Rogers had "cased" the office and tipped the Renos.

For the next several days and nights, a Pinkerton "shadow" stayed with Rogers. On the fourth day an operative reported that a dark-skinned man answering Frank Reno's description had visited the Rogers home. Just before dawn of the following day, four men, led by Frank Reno, slipped into the Rogers home by the rear door. It wasn't long before the frontier hummed with the news that the Mills County Treasury office safe had been cracked and $12,000 stolen.

Pinkerton decided to move in on the gang at the Rogers home. Local authorities, as he recalled, "laughed in my face at the thought Mr. Rogers was implicated." When Pinkerton and his men found another handcar used by the gang in its getaway, he showed it to the sheriff, who reluctantly granted him a search warrant.

Pinkerton and his men surounded the house, with William crashing down the door to find Frank Reno, Albert Perkins, and Miles Ogle, the nation's top counterfeiters, eating breakfast. Frank cursed Pinkerton out, and warned him that he would sue the Agency for damages. While an operative held the trio at pistol point, William led his men on a search of the house. He was returning to the kitchen with two sets of burglar tools when he noticed a wisp of smoke coming from the big iron stove in the kitchen. He yanked open the lid: $14,000 of the Magnolia loot lay smoldering on the coals. While one of the gang had diverted the attention of the Pinkerton guard, another had slipped the bills into the stove.

Reno, Ogle, Rogers, and Perkins were arrested and held in total bail of $11,000 at Council Bluffs. Pinkerton received a telegram the next day: the four had broken out of jail. Chalked in large letters over the hole they had punched in the mortar and brick wall were the words APRIL FOOL. It was April 1, 1868.[7]

The most famous and lucrative train robbery committed by the Renos was that of the Marshfield Express in 1868. The safes of the Adams Express netted the gang some $96,000 in governmnt bonds and gold on its way to the United States Treasury. Unlike the haphazard planning of Jesse James, the Marshfield affair seemed to have been carefully thought out and superbly executed.

The twelve-man gang was led by Frank Reno, with Simeon and William riding with him stirrup to stirrup. There were also Frank Sparks. the horse holder from their first train robbery; Michael Rogers, no longer an esteemed churchman; Charlie Anderson, a safe cracker from Windsor, Canada; Fril Clinton, who usually cased the out-of-town-robberies; Val Elliott, a dashing-looking bandit who was a former brakeman; Charlie Roseberry, a Union Army captain turned outlaw; Henry Jerrell, a house-painter who Pinkerton thought "had been led astray"; and John J. Moore, a local desperado whom Pinkerton described as a "desperate outlaw."

Moore had been the central figure in one of the most unusual cases on the frontier. Chased by police, he had stolen a locomotive but jumped from the cab as it entered a town. The runaway engine plowed up a length of track before it ground to a halt. Railroad officials, realizing they couldn't collect any damages from the penniless Moore, charged him with stealing a locomotive. Moore's attorney argued the defense of an ancient English law that held that a man could enter another man's home, remove his goods from one side to another, and be charged with damage but not theft. Therefore, he told the jury, as long as the locomotive had not been removed from the tracks it had not been stolen. It took the jury two minutes to acquit Moore.

The robbery took place at 9:30 P.M. on a Friday, May 2, 1868. The Ohio & Mississippi Valley train left Jeffersonville, Indiana, and stopped for water at Marshfield, then a fueling station, about fourteen miles south of Seymour. The outlaws suddenly appeared and knocked out David Hutchinson, the fireman; George Fletcher, the engineer, was clubbed into unconsciousness. As the engine, tender, and express cars were uncoupled and driven off, the conductor, Americus Wheeler, got off one shot before he was cut down by a volley.

Moore, the locomotive thief, was at the throttle. As the woodburner chugged through the darkness, followed by a plume of smoke and sparks, Frank Reno and the rest of the gang crawled over the top of the baggage car, dropped to the platform, and jimmied open the door. The Adams Express Company messenger was almost beaten to death, and his body hurled out into the blackness. Fortunately, he was discovered the following morning, barely alive.

The iron safes, four feet long and two feet wide, were forced open, and the $96,000 in cash and bonds poured into sacks. South of Seymour where Sparks had the horses, the train was abandoned.

Frank Reno, Charlie Anderson, Albert Perkins, Michael Rogers, and Miles Ogle escaped to Canada; Simeon and William Reno hid out in

Minneapolis, while Sparks, Jerrell, and Moore fled to Coles County, Illinois, twenty-seven miles west of Terre Haute, Indiana.

Five days after the robbery, July sixteenth, Pinkerton and five operatives hurried to the county seat of Coles County, then Mattoon, and with county law officers searched the countryside. Sparks was captured on a farm; Moore and Jerrell were arrested in a saloon in Aetna, Coles County. R. J. Dick Winscott, the Pinkerton informer who ran the saloon in Seymour, was one of the possemen. The bandit trio was taken to Indianapolis, ironically enough in the same baggage car they had robbed, which was still full of bullet holes.

There is no direct proof, but it seems evident that railroad employees, so long victimized and terrorized by the Renos were now cooperating with vigilantes who were also after the Renos. Never had the southbound train from Indianapolis to Seymour experienced such difficulties. Every few miles the engineer stopped his train to jump from his cab and carefully inspect the wheels and other parts of his engine. The stops at each station became longer and longer. The Pinkerton operatives guarding the three prisoners exchanged nervous glances. More than once they questioned the conductor about the delays, only to be answered with shrugs and the excuse of "necessary repairs." The westbound Ohio & Mississippi Valley train pulled out of the Seymour depot at 10:30, with the Pinkertons and their prisoners missing it by more than an hour.

It is not hard to imagine the consternation of the detectives when they realized that they were stranded on a dark night in a town that was both violently pro-Reno and just as violently anti-Reno. Anything could happen. Obviously, it was not a safe place to be. A wagon was quietly hired to bring the men to Brownstown. There Sheriff John Scott, a courageous law-enforcement officer who had once before defied the mob with his small brass cannon, could be asked for assistance. Sparks, Jerrell, and Moore, handcuffed and leg-ironed, were ordered to lie on the bottom of the wagon in a circle of six Pinkerton guards armed with rifles and navy Colts. Three miles west of Seymour, two hundred men wearing crimson flannel masks rose up out of the brush and overpowered the detectives, who were told to "get along and trot for Seymour." The three bandits were yanked to their feet and the nooses fastened about their necks. Only Moore was defiant, shouting at the mob that they were "a pack of mossback hoosiers." A moment later he was dangling on the end of the rope.

The bodies were cut down, and the verdict "hanged by persons unknown" closed the brief investigation. The three funerals, held simultaneously, had a carnival note. Again special trains were chartered, and carloads of morbid curiousity seekers jammed the town to view the three dead men.

After the hanging of Sparks, Jerrell, and Moore it was a race between the southern vigilante committee and the Pinkertons as to who would first get the Reno brothers. The vigilantes openly campaigned for funds for a war chest to hang the Renos publicly when and if they were captured.[8]

On July 22nd, William and Simeon Reno were arrested by William Stiggart, a Pinkerton operative, in Indiana. They were charged with the Marshfield robbery, and held in bail of $63,000, an enormous amount at the time; both were sent to the Lexington jailhouse, a small, flimsy structure. Laura Ellen Reno, fearful that the vigilantes would storm the jail and hang her brothers, offered to pay the expense of transferring her brothers to New Albany, which had a stronger jail, surrounded by an iron picket fence.

Large sections of southern Indiana were now terrorized by the mass meetings of vigilante committees or the threats of Reno sympathizers who vowed reprisals if anything happened to the outlaw leaders. Ohio and Mississippi Valley Railroad officials reported to Allan Pinkerton that a notorious counterfeiter at Osgood, Indiana, had openly threatened to derail all the trains in the neighborhood if the Renos were hanged by the vigilantes.

The prisoners were finally turned over to Sheriff Thomas J. Fullenlove, of Floyd County, who secretly brought the Renos aboard a steamboat, to land them fifty miles up the Ohio River at Madison, Indiana. Late that night, heavily armed deputies on horseback escorted them through the darkness to Lexington, eighteen miles north. A few days later, Sheriff William Wilson of Scott County informed Governor Baker by telegram that a state of insurrecton had arisen, and demanded additional arms. The state's chief executive ordered the state militia to march into Lexington with forty stands of arms.

The preliminary hearing of the Renos was set for July 30th at Lexington. The peaceful little town was an armed camp; soldiers were strung in a double line around the jailhouse; and the newspapers announced that "an army of hangmen is expected at any hour."

For a time it appeared that the vigilantes would ride into Lexington in full force and attack the militia. Crowds streamed into the city. The courthouse was jammed, and a moment after the judge took his place on the bench, a phalanx of militiamen, surrounding the Renos, dressed in black and wearing broad-brimmed black hats, pushed through the shouting, jeering crowd as Judge P. H. Jewett pounded vainly for silence. Finally the uproar subsided sufficiently for the county prosecutor to read the indictment and ask the prisoners, "How do you plead?"

The Seymour outlaws looked at one another. "Not guilty," they said in calm, even voices. Again the uproar broke out, and Judge Jewett restored order only after threatening to clear the courtroom. The Renos waived examination bail of $63,000, and the judge ordered that they be remanded. A warrant signed by Allan Pinkerton, charging the Renos with conspiracy to commit a felony on May 22nd, was then read. The Renos again put in a plea of not guilty. At this point the seething violence in the courtroom exploded. Men leaped over benches, clawing and kicking at the militiamen, who fought them off with rifle butts. Shouts, screams, and hoots filled the air. Judge Jewett jumped on his chair, crying: "Take those men back to jail quickly! At once! Clear the courtroom!"

He might just as well have ordered a hurricane to stand still. For twenty minutes the mob fought to get at the Renos, but were held off by the militiamen, who finally drove a wedge through the crowd with their bayonets.

On August 4th, the Reno brothers, guarded by the militia and several heavily armed deputies, secretly left Lexington for New Albany.

In September an attempt was made by the vigilantes to capture the Renos who, newspapers reported, were to be transferred from New Albany jail. The attempt failed when Allan Pinkerton telegraphed to Governor Baker of Indiana that he had located Frank Reno and some other members of the gang in Windsor, Canada. Rather than have his client and the county bear the expense of separate trials, he had suggested to Baker that all the train robbers be tried at one time. The jittery state officials agreed, and Baker wired the jailers at New Albany not to remove the prisoners. The red-masked night riders, who had controlled the entire countryside while they waited to capture and lynch the Renos as they were being transported along the dark roads, quickly disappeared into the night, with their leaders promising they would return with their ropes.

According to the letters of a Pinkerton operative who had been in the chase for the Renos, and to the memoirs of Langdon Moore, a famous bank robber of the 1870's, Windsor was a border Dodge City when Allan Pinkerton arrived with his men to take the Reno gang into custody. The Windsor Turf Club, a combination saloon and pool hall, had been taken over by the various American train robbers, safecrackers, thugs, and sneak thieves who were wanted in the States for every crime from murder to forgery. Two other gang strongholds were Manning's saloon and Rockford's near the Windsor ferry.

In the curious caste system of the underworld, the celebrated Renos were the undisputed leaders of Windsor. Pinkerton's operatives undoubtedly had discovered their hideout while chasing another outlaw combination that had held up a train near Garrison, New York, robbing the Union Express Company's safe of $11,000. Pat O'Neil, a young Pinkerton operative who was known to the gang as "The Pinkerton Kid," located Jack Friday, who drove the buggy for the Renos, in Rockford's saloon. In a fight, O'Neil was battered with a pool cue, and Friday escaped through a window, "taking the panels with him," as O'Neil wrote

Allan Pinkerton's letter to the Secretary of State requesting extradition of the Reno gang from Canada. *The National Archives* to Pinkerton.[9] Friday and the others planned to murder young Pat, but Tom Manning, the owner of the saloon, interfered, and told them, as O'Neil later reported to Allan Pinkerton:

"Pinkerton would never let them rest until he ran all of them down. They agreed to do this [assassinate Pat] and concluded not to have anything to do with me."

Frank Reno, Albert Perkins, Charlie Anderson, and Michael Rogers, the "churchman" turned outlaw, were finally arrested by Allan Pinkerton, who led a posse of his operatives, including young O'Neil and local deputies, in a raid on the outlaws' hideout, a small frame house on Windsor Avenue and Brant Street, Windsor. At their preliminary hearing, Rogers, who had assumed an alias, informed the court that his arrest was a case of mistaken identity. There were no known photographs of Rogers, and fingerprinting was unknown. Pinkerton described to the judge how Rogers had been arrested by his operative for the Magnolia robbery, but the court "reluctantly" released Rogers, who, Pinkerton predicted, would flee the court's jurisdiction. A few hours later, Rogers confirmed the detective's guess. While operatives searched for him in Windsor, he slipped across the border at night.

After the first arraignment, Pinkerton rushed back to Cincinnati to obtain extradition papers for Reno and Anderson. He sent a copy of the arrest warrants and a description of the crimes committed by the Reno gang to Secretary of State Seward, accompanied by a formal request for their extradition to Indiana. A few days later, Acting Secretary of State William Hunter wrote to Edward Thornton, British Minister in the United States, requesting that the Renos be turned over to Pinkerton. On the following day Thornton forwarded the extradition request to Governor-General of Canada Viscount Monck, and so informed the State Department.[10]

Pinkerton then returned to Windsor with L. C. Weir, an Adams Express Company official. In a second hearing, Frank Reno produced a number of witnesses, including his mother, who swore he was at home at the time of the Marshfield train robbery. While the hearing dragged on, Minister Thornton snagged the international machinery by informing Pinkerton that London had told him the United States had not followed proper diplomatic channels. Evidently Her Majesty's council had recently drawn up a new set of requirements for the extradition of criminals, which Washington was not aware of, or State had not been sent copies by its minister at the Court of St. James's.

While Washington and Downing Street exchanged polite notes, American desperadoes in Windsor held a meeting to plan the murder of Pinkerton. Dick Barry, a noted cracksman, was selected to assassinate the detective. Barry followed Pinkerton to Detroit. While the detective walked down the ferry ramp, Barry aimed a pistol at the back of Pinkerton's head. Pinkerton, who heard the revolver cock, whirled about, jammed his finger into the trigger guard, and twisted the gun from Barry's hand. After a brief, fierce struggle he subdued the safecracker. At pistol point he marched the handcuffed Barry through the streets of Detroit to the police station. A few days later the underworld again tried to kill Pinkerton. A train robber named Johnson fired a shot at Pinkerton, but missed. After a chase he was caught, disarmed, and delivered to the Wayne County police station. Two hours later Pinkerton was notified that Johnson had escaped. When he indignantly demanded an explanation, the deputy sheriff blandly explained that Johnson had escaped "while taking a buggy ride about the city."

When word of the attempted assassination reached Washington, Seward, a friend of Pinkerton from Civil War days, ordered a gunboat to Windsor. The vessel stayed ten days, and departed only after the Canadian government protested to Washington.

The extradition hearings dragged on for weeks. The case then took a weird turn, with Viscount Monck announcing that he had granted the extradition after interviewing Frank Reno in his cell and obtaining Reno's confession that he was one of the Marshfield train robbers.

There were more delays. The Reno attorneys obtained a writ on the ground that train robbery was not an extraditionable crime. This had to be argued, and the writ was finally dismissed. A curious note entered the case when Monck advised Pinkerton that William P. Wood, head of the United States Secret Service, had warned his office in a letter that the Renos should remain in Canada because they would be lynched if they were brought back to Indiana. Now a high Washington official was admitting that the forces of law and order had completely capitulated to the vigilantes, which, tragically, was correct. There was more mystery about Wood's connection with the Renos when Barry, the train robber who had tried to kill Allan Pinkerton, swore at his trial for attempted murder that he had been put up to it by Wood. In Washington, Wood indignantly denied the story, but Barry insisted from the witness stand that he was telling the truth.

While sensational developments continued to break one after the other in Canada and Washington, Frank Reno was using a more direct method: Magistrate McMickum publicly announced that Reno had tried to bribe his sixteen-year-old son by offering the boy $6,000 in gold "to influence his father in their behalf." [11]

The attempted assassinations of Pinkerton, the crude bribery moves, the endless wrangling and notoriety finally made Monck throw up his hands and tell Allan Pinkerton he could have the Renos, and bad luck to them all. Pinkerton exuberantly telegraphed to William that they had won. With young O'Neil he drove to the governor-general's office in a buggy to claim his prisoners.

But there were more formalities: Monck's office informed Pinkerton that the new rules of the Queen's Council had established that seven days had to pass before prisoners could be claimed by law officers of another country. The seven days passed. When Pinkerton returned to the governor-general's palace, he was told that this time London had cabled new provisions: now Pinkerton had to present written authority from the State Department, signed by the President of the United States. The weary, exhausted, fuming detective immediately telegraphed to Seward at his home. The Secretary of State, who was on his way to a funeral, wrote Hunter in Washington to prepare the necessary papers and send them to the White House for President Johnson's signature. From New York City, Seward wrote to Hunter:

> I reached home late on Sunday evening, and early Monday morning was appealed to to assist in procuring the extradition of two men in Canada, who have been there arrested on the charges of having robbed the Adams Express Company. They were the leaders of a gang in Indiana. The people in that state took care of the rest of the gang by hanging six of them. The two in Canada were examined before a Magistrate, under threats on the part of their friends to assassinate Allan Pinkerton, who is conducting the case on behalf of the Express Company. He appealed to me by telegraph to protect him. A telegram received from Pinkerton yesterday, advises me that the protection was promptly afforded and took the somewhat forcible appearance of a gunboat. So far it is all right. After the case has been submitted to the Magistrate, his son was offered $6,000 if he would procure his father to liberate the prisoners. This clinched the nail against the prisoners, and the justices decided yesterday to hold them. Pinkerton telegraphs, that under the treaty or statutes, seven days must elapse before the prisoners can be delivered to the custody of the agent of the United States. The Queen's counsel here advises him (and he has twice telegraphed the advice) that the prisoners cannot be safely held against a habeas corpus, unless the officials are fortified with a written paper from the State Department, under its seal and under the hand of its presiding officer, directing the reception of the prisoners by the agents named, and stating that the said authority is received and is conferred by the direction of the President of the United States. I do not know whether the Department regards this practice as correct, but inasmuch as it seems to be required by the authorities in Canada, I telegraphed yesterday, asking that such a paper as is requested to be made out, and I presume it will be all right if it is sent to General Averill to be delivered to Pinkerton. In my dispatch to Fred, I mentioned the names of the prisoners and the names of the Agents. You have, therefore, all the information necessary to prepare a paper directing the agents to receive, on behalf of the United States, under the treaty, the persons of the prisoners. If it is proper to execute such a paper, will you please send it to General Averill, and advise me that you have done so? I write to you about this matter for the reason that I am advised that both my Uncle and Fred have gone to Albany to attend the funeral of Mr. Wharton.[12]

With the newspapers of the Midwest reporting that vigilante leaders had publicly promised to storm any jail where the Renos were confined, and hang every member of the gang, the State Department found itself in a delicate position. It would be unthinkable for the Secretary of State to admit that the Renos, notorious outlaws, could not be returned to their own country to face an impartial justice. At a meeting in Washington, Hunter officially decided to transfer responsibility for the Renos' safety to the state officials of Indiana. A request was made to Ambassador Thornton to wire to Governor Baker of Indiana for assurances that the Renos would be given "the utmost physical protection." The governor, no doubt squirming on this diplomatic spot, could do nothing but answer that the outlaws would be protected at all times. The uneasy governor, perhaps as an afterthought, then telegraphed to Pinkerton, urging him to gather a strong escort of armed men to guard the Renos "day and night." It was also rumored at the time, though there is no official evidence, that Pinkerton was forced to put up $25,000 in cash to ensure the safety of the Renos.

The international legal machinery moved slowly. Hunter finally obtained the extradition papers, and had them signed by President Johnson. When they returned from the White House, Hunter sent them to General Averill, United States Counsel at Montgomery, by special courier. When Averill advised Pinkerton that the President's letter had arrived, the detective rushed to Montgomery, picked up the papers, then hurried back to Windsor to deliver them to Governor-General Viscount Monck, who finally signed the extradition papers putting the Renos into Pinkerton's custody. Monck also advised Pinkerton that the Canadian government would no longer be responsible either for his protection or for the safety of his prisoners.

Allan wired to William, who ordered a seagoing tug to Windsor. Aboard were Chief Patrick Foley, head of the Pinkerton's Guard Service; John Curtin, later to become one of San Francisco's most celebrated detectives; and a number of Pinkerton operatives, armed with pistols and rifles.

Frank Reno, Albert Perkins, and Charlie Anderson, handcuffed and leg ironed, were escorted to the tug by Allan Pinkerton with a navy Colt on his hip. It was sunup, October 7th, when the tug pulled out from the Windsor dock, a beautiful Indian-summer day, with scarcely a ripple on the river. The heavily armed detectives sat in the small galley, smoking and joking with the outlaws.

Suddenly the tug swerved sharply to one side. As Pinkerton and his men jumped to their feet, a steamer neatly sliced away the bow of the tug. Miraculously, neither the outlaws nor the lawmen were injured. But the tug sunk like an anvil. Reno and the others, weighed down by the irons and handcuffs, struggled to stay afloat. Pinkerton, Curtin, and Foley clung to the outlaws, desperately trying to hold their heads above water. The steamer, its bow dented but still watertight, swung about. After detectives and outlaws were pulled aboard, the steamer limped into Detroit, where it was met by a large crowd and another armed posse of Pinkerton men. Although the collision came in the wake of underworld threats, William Pinkerton always insisted that it was "an accident caused by a mistake in signals."[13]

After a change of clothing, Pinkerton, Curtin, Foley, and several armed operatives escorted the gang aboard a steamboat bound for Cleveland. From there they traveled in wagons and buggies to Louisville, where they stayed overnight. The following day, Pinkerton, exhausted and suffering from a heavy cold, delivered the train robbers to Floyd County Sheriff Thomas J. Fullenlove, who put them in the New Albany jail along with William and Simeon Reno, who shouted down a welcome from their cell on the second tier. Pinkerton inspected the jail, and warned Fullenlove that it appeared to be too flimsy to withstand a mob's attack. He urged Fullenlove to transfer the prisoners secretly to Indianapolis.

When it became known that the Renos were in the New Albany jail, the townspeople were terrified. It was an open secret that the vigilantes were making plans to storm the jail, while one newspaper correspondent from Fort Wayne reported that the remnants of the Reno gang "had held a convention resolving to lay Seymour in ashes if the Renos were hanged."

Feeling grew so intense that Fullenlove was forced to assure the citizens of his county publicly that if the vigilantes attempted to take his prisoners "they would be sure to meet a hot reception here and they had better keep at a safe distance."

A few days after Pinkerton had delivered his prisoners, the Democratic Party held a convention at New Albany. Fullenlove was offered $1,000 to "let the Seymour Committee get the Renos." Fullenlove, a courageous but vastly overconfident man, refused, and again publicly announced: "There will be no murder for any amount of money . . . the law must take its course."

That fall, desperadoes waged terrifying warfare on the community. Men were ambushed and left mutilated. Houses were surrounded, and men dragged from their beds to be given the "hanging torture." Rocks wrapped in paper with the warning "If the Renos are lynched you die" were hurled through the windows of the homes of county officials. Women were told that they would be kidnapped along with their children and that their throats would be cut if their husbands rode with the vigilantes.

Then, on December 7th, Flanders, the engineer who had been wounded in the train holdup, died. An ominous quiet lay over the county that week as temperatures plummeted and men and boys walked in the woods searching for Christmas trees.

At midnight, December 12, 1868, the town of Seymour, Indiana, was sleeping, the streets deserted. It was bitterly cold, and a frosty moon silvered the rooftops. The only sign of life was the yellow light in the New Albany jail where Tom Matthews, deputized by Sheriff Fullenlove, was dozing in the sheriff's office. Outside, at the curb, warming himself at a small fire, was another deputy, Luther (Chuck) Whitten. Inside the jail, the Reno gang slept soundly in their bunks.

Without headlights, bell, or whistle, the Jefferson, Madison, Indianapolis train quietly pulled into the Seymour station. In single file, men masked in red flannel lined up in a ragged military fashion. Leaders with numbers chalked on coats turned inside out issued brisk commands. The masked men, all armed with shotguns, Colts, and rifles, moved rapidly through the cold darkness. Small groups dropped off at street corners. A rider came up to report that the wires had been cut. New Albany was isolated from the rest of the state.

Number One raised his hand, his words echoing in the frigid darkness: "Ready men—Salus populi suprema lex!"

The columns snaked through the streets, moving in and out of the moonlight. Workmen, faces buried in their coat collars as they hurried home, suddenly found themselves pushed into doorways at pistol point. Down State Street the boots of the column made a steady, rhythmic, marching sound. Ahead in the moonlight loomed the two-story stone jailhouse where Chuck Whitten was standing by his tiny fire. Startled, he looked up into the pistols pointed at his head. He broke free from the ring of masked men and ran toward the jail, shouting the alarm. Two men grabbed Whitten and beat him to the ground with pistol butts.

Several of the mob took Fullenlove at gunpoint, but the sheriff ran from his house shouting, "I am the sheriff, the highest peace officer in the county . . . you must respect the law. . . ." As he reached the gate, several shots rang out. Fullenlove, who had warned any raiders they would get a "hot reception," stumbled and fell, one arm torn by the bullets.

"Don't kill him," Number One ordered. "Take him to his house."

Fullenlove was carried, bleeding and barely conscious, to his house and placed on a couch. His wife, made of stern stuff, defied the vigilantes when they demanded the sheriff's keys. Then she, her bleeding husband, and Whitten were locked in a bedroom. But the vigilantes found the keys and moved in on the jail. Matthews, behind the locked door leading to the cells, nervously fingered his navy Colt and shouted that he would shoot down the first man who stepped inside.

Number One held up five ropes; each had a hangman's noose. The vigilante leader tried the keys, but none worked. Not wishing to waste time on such a minor detail, he gave Matthews the choice of opening the door or having it battered down with a log and hanging along with the Renos. Realizing the helplessness of his situation Matthews opened the door and the mob rushed in.

"Bring the rope for Frank Reno," Number One ordered. The rope was passed from man to man; torches were raised, the wavering crimson light falling on the terrorized faces of the outlaws pressed to the cell bars. The key grated in the lock, and the raiders moved inside the cell. Frank, a powerful man, put up a fierce struggle, but he was quickly overpowered. The noose was flung over his head and around his neck. Still struggling, he was pulled out into the corridor.

One by one the cell doors were opened and the outlaws dragged outside. Ropes looped over ceiling beams with a menacing hiss. The struggling William was swung off the second tier. His body flopped pitifully, his eyes bulging from their sockets and blood gushing from his mouth. Someone grabbed his legs and snapped his neck. His body swung slowly, as Simeon was hauled from his cell. He had put up a fierce fight, but the butt of a navy Colt knocked him unconscious. The rope was tightened about his neck, and he was pushed off the tier. His bare feet barely touched the stone floor.

Charlie Anderson, the expert cracksman, begged and cried as the rope was fitted about his neck. "My soul, gentleman, my soul," he kept saying, "give me time to pray for it."

"Ain't worth praying for, Charlie," said Number One briskly. Then: "Let him go."

Charlie plummeted down, but the noose gave, and he slammed on the floor to lie there screaming and begging for mercy. But the vigilantes brought him back to the tier, again tightened the noose, and carefully lowered him into space, where he strangled, twisting and jerkng like a grotesque fish at the end of the line. Finally, he too was still, his body slowly turning at the rope's end.

"Any more?" someone called.

"Let's hang the whole damn lot," was the angry answer.

"Quiet!" snapped Number One. "We did what we came for; now let's go."

The ten other frightened prisoners, eyewitnesses to the lynchings, crouched in the darkness of their cells as the masked men left with a commissioner as a hostage.

They left behind a deadly silence, the bodies slowly twisting in the air, the purplish faces staring into the wavering lights of the dying torches. Then, as the horrified prisoners watched, the body of Simeon Reno began to twitch. The battling Reno had returned to consciousness. His eyes opened, and his mouth moved as he frantically gasped for air.

Simeon Reno fought desperately to live. Gradually the pandemonium died down as the ten prisoners watched in horrified fascination Reno's attempts to touch the floor with his toes. He died slowly and horribly. Finally, he too was still.

While Simeon fought for his life, the masked vigilantes marched to the station, pushing the commissioner before them. The shivering official was barefoot, with a coat thrown over his nightshirt. As they passed down the street, patrols fell in line. At the depot the train was ready, the cars still dark. Again in single file they boarded. Number One gave a city official the sheriff's keys, apologized for having had to shoot Fullenlove, then gave the signal to the engineer. Just before the train slowly moved out of the depot, the mob's leader stood on the steps of the car and shouted: "Salus populi suprema lex!"

The words hung for a moment in the cold night, then were lost as the big wheels ground on the rails. In a moment the train had disappeared in the darkness, a distant, defiant whistle echoing across the countryside. On the platform the shivering city official was joined by shadows armed with guns. But their newborn courage was too late. Then someone suggested they go back to the jail and get a doctor for Fullenlove. They left the station, hurrying down the street exchanging experiences in low, excited voices.[14]

Day was breaking when the town's firebell clanged frantically. Men and women in nightclothes flung up their windows to shout questions at those below in the streets. The answers came back: "The vigilantes have hanged the Renos. . . . They're back in the jail. . . . The sheriff was shot. . . ."

After the wires had been repaired, the news of the lynching spread across the countryside to villages and towns and finally to the capital. The governor's office alerted Allan Pinkerton, who hurried to Indianapolis with William. After a series of conferences, strong statements were issued and warnings made that those who had taken the law in their own hands would be found and punished. The words were meaningless. There was a token investigation of the lynching, but nothing came of it. Secretly, state and county officials breathed a sigh of relief that the reign of the Renos had finally been ended. No one, of course, pointed out to those officials that the actions of the vigilantes only underscored the total breakdown of law and justice in that section of the state.

In the Floyd County jail, the bodies had been cut down. A physician examining the dead men pointed out that Simeon must have lived a half hour as he vainly struggled at the end of the rope.

There was another sensaiton when Laura Ellen Reno, summoned from St. Ursula Academy at Louisville, was escorted through the mob surrounding the jail. The shouting and jeering died down as she hurried up the steps, her face white and drawn, her eyes red from weeping. When she was brought into the room where the bodies of the outlaws were laid out on planks, a deputy removed the handkerchief from Simeon's swollen, purple face. Laura screamed, then rushed to the window, shaking her fist in a frenzy at the sea of staring faces as she shrieked over and over that the blood of her brothers was on the heads of all of them.

Later in the day the doors of the jails were opened to let thousands view the bodies, now in plain pine coffins. In the penitentiary, John

Reno was told the news. As he recalled, "The awful news came near dethroning my reason but I was kept hard at work which may have saved me."

On the morning of December 21st, the residents of Seymour awoke to discover vigilante posters about the town listing all remaining members of the Reno gang and ordering them to leave at once. Hysteria gripped the county when officials, some known to be friendly to the gang, received warnings, while masked thugs disguised as vigilantes robbed and kidnapped. Then England, through the Governor-General of Canada, demanded an apology for the "shocking and indefensible lynching." Diplomatic relations were strained, while legal experts predicted that England would eliminate the extradition clause in the treaty, which would provide a haven in Canada for American desperadoes.[15]

A bill providing federal protection for extradited criminals was then introduced by an Illinois senator; Seward, in his apology to Downing Street, diplomatically enclosed a copy of the bill, which had been rushed through both houses.

After the Agency's "war" with the Renos, the Pinkertons were retained to solve three major bank robberies: Those at the National Village Bank of Bowdoinham, Massachusetts; the Beneficial Savings Fund of America, Philadelphia; and the Walpole, New Hampshire, Savings Bank. Operatives trailed and captured the bank robbers, and returned most of the stolen money. In Bowdoinham $80,000 was taken; the vaults of the Philadelphia savings bank yielded over $1,000,000 in cash and securities, and the New Hampshire bank $40,000.

George Bangs had also broken a difficult murder case in Edgewood, New Jersey. After Bangs had traced the suspected murderer to New York City, where he was employed as a shoemaker, he assigned Joseph Mendelsohn, an operative who had once worked as a shoemaker, "to work in the shop and gain the murderer's confidence." Bangs made sure the suspect knew he was being "shadowed," and the man begged Mendelsohn for money to leave the city. When the operative demanded some security, the murderer gave him a pawn ticket. Mendelsohn promised to go to his bank on his lunch hour and get the money. He and Bangs redeemed the pawn ticket and recovered the dead man's watch and jewelry. The shoemaker was arrested, and confessed before nightfall. He pleaded guilty and was sentenced to life.

CHAPTER 21
The Larches

In the winter and summer of 1868-1869, the compulsive need to work, to be occupied every waking hour with the problems of his business, coupled with his intensive drive, began to take toll of Allan Pinkerton. He became more irritable, demanding, unreasonable. His target was not only the long-suffering George Bangs but his son Robert as well. From their correspondence it is evident that they read the long, emotional letters from Chicago with weary sighs, and sent back soothing, conciliatory replies. There was no ignoring them; within a few days a stronger letter would arrive demanding to know why the letters and suggestions of the founder were ignored. Pinkerton was also becoming slightly paranoiac about the mysterious "powers" that were fighting the Agency. In his highly agitated state, bone weary and burdened with countless responsibilities, he started to see specters and goblins. In 1868, after a tour of his branch offices, he excoriated Bangs, his general manager, for the conditions he had found. Then he went on to discuss the "enemies" of his business:

> The year 1868 has been marked by a determined fight against us; at the close of that year that fight still continues but I tremble not before it. I feel no power on earth is able to check me, no power in Heaven or Hell can influence me when I know I am right. I think it cannot be long ere our enemies flee—that they are vanquished, it cannot be long if we persevere in the right and they are continually in the wrong. . . .[1]

Pinkerton might have added that the year of 1868 was one of the saddest of those dark years. In the early hours of January 1st, with the Chicago church bells welcoming the New Year and all its hopes for the war-weary nation, Kate Warne, the first female detective in her nation's history, died in her sleep after a long illness, with Allan Pinkerton at her bedside. A few hours later, telegrams were sent from Chicago to all superintendents, advising them of Kate's death. In New York, George Bangs made the melancholy observation that the "old group" was slowly dying off.

That year, Death was a relentless visitor. In May, Allan's brother, Robert, died. Apparently he had stayed with Allan, since he had accompanied their mother from Scotland to the United States. There are no records to show that he ever swung a hammer in the Dundee cooperage, took part in any abolitionist activities, or even met John Brown. He never joined the Agency, nor is there any hint of his occupation. He died a middle-aged man, indistinct, completely lost beneath the dominant shadow of his famous brother.

Though death and tragedy shook the family, they did not alter the Agency, which Pinkerton always insisted had to be divorced from his personal life. Business continued to flourish. The operating schedule of expenses of the year 1868–1869 found in the Agency's Record Book for that period shows that expenses for the Chicago, New York, and Philadelphia offices, in operation, salaries, expenses, office equipment, house expenses, and two-fifths of general expenses of the entire business, were over $1,000,000.[2]

Pinkerton's correspondence also reveals that Commodore Vanderbilt, congressmen, civic leaders, and officials of the New Haven Railroad were either meeting with Bangs in New York or sending Pinkerton letters in Chicago, urging him to accept the post of Superintendent of the New York City Police Department, and clean up that graft-ridden organization.

Pinkerton's replies were cordial but firm in his refusal to replace Superintendent Kennedy, who only that same year had denounced Pinkerton for making up the Baltimore Plot, forgetting, of course, that he had also warned the President-elect's party of the threatening violence in that city. It would have been sweet revenge; but, instead, Pinkerton, in a letter to Vanderbilt, praised Kennedy as a good police officer, and refused the appointment. As he later wrote to Bangs: "Political influence would only prevent the operation of the department in the manner in which I would want to conduct it, making necessary changes for the interest of efficiency."[3]

In the late summer of 1869, Pinkerton reaped his personal whirlwind; he was dictating to his secretary when he was stricken with a stroke—a "shock," as they called it in those days. In the months that followed, there is evidence that William and Robert did everything to perpetuate the image of their father as a physically invincible man, the all-knowing, all-powerful Eye That Never Sleeps, as the Agency's slogan claimed. The reports they issued were reassuring, not only for clients but for their jittery employees. The stroke was a slight one, their reports claimed, a description that has become accepted fact through repeated telling.

In reality, the stroke was physically devastating and almost fatal to Pinkerton. From 1869 to some time in 1871, he was paralyzed and could not talk. From a study of his personal letters, it took years before he was barely able to scrawl his name or dictate correspondence. One side would remain partially crippled, and when he became emotionally distraught he shook, as he put it, "with the palsy," and his speech became slurred.

Pinkerton's bitter fight to regain the use of his limbs and to recover his speech, his refusal to accept the verdict of his doctors, the best in the land, that doomed him to a wheelchair at best, is typical of his fierce determinaton and intensive drive. In a letter to an unnamed friend who may have been the victim of a stroke, Pinkerton describes for several pages his brush with death and his agonizing efforts to regain his health.[4]

For over a year he underwent treatment by the "best doctors" in New York. When they sent him back to Chicago as incurable, he turned in desperation to a primitive "spring" in the Midwest and an iron routine of baths and grueling exercise to help him walk and talk again. One can almost see this once robust man, now paralyzed, crawling into a crude frontier spring for months of daily "baths," then forcing himself to walk, the distance becoming longer each day, until he reached twelve miles.

Pinkerton heard about the "singular waters" of the spring in November, 1869, following his return from New York City with the doctors' verdict on his mind. After he had sent an operative to the village of St. Louis, Michigan, to obtain details, he forwarded a report to his New York physician, who cautiously advised him to try the spring but to send him weekly reports of his physical condition. Pinkerton traveled to Michigan in the spring of 1870 to try "the singular waters which had been discovered by men drilling for salt." For months Pinkerton took a series of daily baths, probably therapeutic. When he returned to Chicago, he reported to his friend, in his letter of September, 1870: "I can now talk very well but have to be slow and cautious. I walk every day eight, ten and twelve miles. . . ."

But Pinkerton, for all his boasting of having regained his health, was far from the tough Scot who had arrested counterfeiters in his bare feet, disarmed assassins, chased bank robbers, and masterminded a corps of counteragents. His signature at the bottom of this dictated letter is very shaky, with each letter carefully formed, like the guided handwriting of a very old man or the labored efforts of a small child.

It was during his period of convalescence that Pinkerton turned his attention to the building of "The Larches," an elaborate summer estate that became a showplace of the Midwest. Today, as the Illinois Central reaches Onarga, Illinois, eighty-three miles south of Chicago, a passenger studying the passing landscape might catch a glimpse of the weather-beaten, deserted clapboard house shadowed by the grove of stately trees.

A century ago this was the Villa, as it was known, or main house, gleaming as white and proud as the king's own, surrounded by 254 acres of rolling lawns and pastures where blooded livestock grazed. There were also carpenter shops, greenhouses, and huge barns with green and white trim. The Illinois Central's track ran through the estate, dividing it almost equally into east and west sections.

Pinkerton had bought the land on January 9, 1864, from the Illinois Central for $4,067.52, but it wasn't until his convalescence from the stroke that he turned to building his estate, patterned after one he recalled from his early days as a roving cooper in Scotland. Characteristically, he plunged into its planning and organizing with a fierce intensity. First came the name, "The Larches," after the Scottish trees he loved so much. Having settled on the name, he informed his patient Joan that thousands of larch trees had to be planted along the driveways. Letters and telegrams flew to George Bangs, the Agency's general manager in New York: "Find Larch trees." Bangs discovered that they couldn't be found in the United States, and so informed his employer. Pinkerton, now slightly reminiscent of the early Hearst, sent a terse answer:

"Then cable Scotland and order them."

Bangs carried out the order, and 85,000 larch trees, an entire shipload, were sent to New York City. It was a bitterly cold day when the ship docked. In the Exchange Place office of the Agency, Bangs and the New York agent who had arranged for the purchase of the trees completed arrangements to have them shipped to Chicago. From there a special Illinois Central train would deliver them to the gardener at the estate.

Between inspecting the trees on the windswept dock, the agent made several trips to a waterfront saloon to fortify himself against the subzero temperatures. One glass followed another; the agent, warmed by the whiskey and the camaraderie of the rough saloon, fell asleep. The next day the worried Bangs sent an operative to the pier. He returned with the news that the bitter cold had killed the dockload of saplings.

Bangs telegraphed Pinkerton the news. Back came the reply: "Fire the agent. Send to Scotland for another boatload of trees." [5]

Another load of 85,000 larch trees finally arrived, to be planted along the winding driveways and about the house. Then Pinkerton turned to the Villa. Neighbors recalled how he tramped about the place, a sturdy, stocky man with an iron-gray beard who seemed irritable that he was forced to lean on a heavy walking stick. Anger would bring out the Scottish burr as he shook his stick and growled, "He's a durrrty, durrrty dawg, that's what he is. . . ."

West Lane leading to the Pinkerton house. *The New York Public Library*

Pinkerton, whose beginning in the stark poverty of Glasgow's Gorbals may be cited as psychic explanation for his character and temperament, found serenity in the luxury of building The Larches. From a farm it became a showplace with an incongruous policeman's touch. There were three main entrances for the big house with its Negro attendants in spotless blue uniforms and gold buttons. Each entrance had a tiny guard-house with an armed guard.

Joan, who never forgot the fields and flowers of the Dundee country-side, insisted that if there were larch trees there must be flowers. Pinkerton had gardeners plant vast beds of riotous colors. On a warm day visitors could smell their fragrance as they entered the driveway.

There were also a racetrack, a beautiful little fishpond, a "camping grounds" where church revivals were held, and a large wine pavilion known as the Snuggery. In the 1870's Pinkerton had a deep tunnel dug that linked the wine pavilion and the main house; some called it the whim of an eccentric old man, but it was much more than that: Hired killers had tried to assassinate him several times, and, later, after the Molly Maguires' investigation, threats of murder and bombing were so strong, legend insists that he kept a six-shooter in a holster by his bed.

The heart of the estate was the Villa, a square building with a pillared porch on three sides and a cupola where riflemen swept the quiet country-side with glasses, seeking assassins. A wide hall ran the full length of the house. At night the hallway glowed with the light of four huge crystal chandeliers.

Pinkerton never forgot the great days when he was in the field with McClellan. He brought Paul Loose, an artist from Scotland, and commissioned him to do a series of panels depicting wartime events, along with his favorite scene of the Pennsylvania countryside. The original oils, admired by famous men and women of Pinkerton's time on their visits to The Larches, are now dark, stained, and torn. But some are still recognizable as "The Battle of Gettysburg," "Sherman's March to the Sea," "McClellan and His Staff," "Bull Run," and the "Secret Service Staff of the Army of the Potomac." In the latter panel Allan Pinkerton in his familiar bowler hat is surrounded by fifteen of his operatives. Over each door on the lower floor he had portraits in oil of the men he knew and admired: McClellan, Lincoln, Grant, and Sherman.

One large panel depicted a section of the countryside on the main line of the Pennsylvania, east of Harrisburg. The oil, entitled "Conewago Bridge," shows a high stone bridge spanning a river on which floats an Indian in a canoe. A wood-burning locomotive with a high stack is crossing the bridge.

The estate soon became a gathering place for Pinkerton's clients and friends. Before World War II, old men who had been boys at the time recalled Pinkerton bringing weekend guests to The Larches in a private Pullman car: "It was the big event of the town and we all used to troop down to see the gay crowd of men and women troop off the train. Pinkerton's carriage with four horsemen and a coachman in livery would be on hand and everything would be shined up." [6]

The once barefoot young cooper of Dundee now had as his guests the great names of his age: Henry Sanford, president of Adams Express; Commodore Vanderbilt, General Grant, August Belmont, Seward, Burnside, Chief Justice Salmon P. Chase. After an elaborate dinner, Joan would take the ladies on a tour of the estate in a buggy, while Pinkerton led the men to the Snuggery for a few glasses and, if they had been with him in the Civil War, to argue and refight the great battles.

An old man in Onarga remembered running across the fields of The Larches as a child and watching Allan Pinkerton and Joan walking slowly along the winding paths, the summer dusk heavy with the fragrance of the flowers that lined the graveled paths and lawns.

Mr. and Mrs. Allan Pinkerton about 1870–1875. *Chicago Historical Society*

Pinkerton always loved horses and dogs, and colts and blooded horses roamed in the pastures beyond the big house, and the yelping and barking of hounds in the kennels echoed across the countryside in the evening when Pinkerton brought them their food. Later on, there would be a small animal cemetery in the corner of one field where the favorites were buried, each with a tiny headstone.

Because the early West was an important part of the Agency's history, in the Snuggery were wall maps where Pinkerton would trace the movements of his operatives chasing the outlaw gangs. The tough western Indian ponies, half wild, struck a responsive chord in Pinkerton, and William and Robert never left one of the territories that he didn't give them specific instructions for buying a good horse. This probably accounts for the herd of western mustangs he brought to the estate "just for the sport of watching a good rider breaking them to the saddle." There were also several Shetland ponies and carts for the grandchildren and the children from the nearby farms. One recently remembered how they would ride around the estate with Pinkerton telling them stories of Lincoln and the far-off days of the front lines during the Civil War.

Finally the Villa was finished. Thousands of larch trees had been planted along the driveways. The famous scenes in oil on the walls gleamed in the soft light of the chandeliers. There were footmen in livery, uniformed guards, gardeners, fieldhands, and expert horsemen and grooms for the stables. It was important that the still vivid memories of the tenement on Muirhead Street be wiped out forever. For Allan Pinkerton, The Larches was more than a beautiful, midwestern farm—it was a symbol, his final triumph over the Gorbals.[7]

During his illness and convalescence Allan Pinkerton turned over the administration of his beloved Agency to his sons, William and Robert. As their father had done, they toured the branch offices, poring over the profit-and-loss ledgers, "raising" new business in the slowly recovering South, and personally conducting most of the major investigations. In 1871, Allan returned to his office in Chicago, slower, irascible, but still "A.P.," the Founder. He had been back at his desk only a short time when disaster struck with fury: The great Chicago fire wiped out most of Chicago, including the Pinkerton's National Detective Agency. Early records and his pioneering Rogues' Gallery were reduced to ashes. A major blow was the destruction of his Civil War files, which he was about to sell to the government for $100,000, a figure never officially confirmed.

Pinkerton had tried desperately to save his records. In February, 1872, he wrote a long letter to his old friend Chief Justice Chase, in Washington, describing how he and his staff tried to drag records from his Washington Street office, only to flee before the fast-moving inferno that jumped the river and roared up the streets with terrifying speed. As Pinkerton said, everything was reduced to ashes within fifty minutes, "including four volumes of my records of the Army of the Potomac, from the time McClellan took over the Army of the Ohio until the time he retired from the field . . . among these the history of Cameron and Stanton was fully portrayed."

However, the detective refused to be defeated. As he wrote to Chase, the buildings were still cooling when he hired a team of carpenters "and was soon made pretty comfortable with some lumber." Pinkerton even managed to turn the tables on disaster; he obtained contracts to guard "all the burned district and so I have done very well."

Pinkerton also revealed to Chase that he was still suffering from effects of the stroke and the rigid routine he was maintaining

> to beat the doctors. Sometimes I am troubled by an impediment in my speech but not all the time . . . bad weather troubles my limbs.
>
> But upon the whole I am better amazingly. In the morning at five o'clock I am up and into a cold bath from ten to eighteen minutes, then rub myself dry and by six out in the air for a walk for probably three quarters of an hour or an hour. Breakfast ready by seven, then walk to the office. In this manner I am beating all the doctors.[8]

Heartsick, still partially crippled, and weary from the long days and nights in the charred, foul-smelling area of burned-out buildings, Pinkerton began to rebuild his business. "I will never be beaten," he wrote to Bangs, "never. Not all the Furies of Hell will stop me from rebuilding immediately." He underscored the last word. It was during this period that Jesse James raided an Iowa bank. His "war" with the Pinkertons had begun.

CHAPTER 22

Dingus James and His Missouri Bravoes

Few men in any American age were more fiercely hunted or more fiercely determined to stay alive than Jesse Woodson James, the Middle Border train and bank robber whose sinister, alliterative name became synonymous with American outlawry. His deeds were prodigious, but mythmaking has distorted his story until at times it is no longer recognizable.

Jesse was no hero. His life, completely lacking in glamour, certainly cannot be held up as proof that sin is attractive. Yet, as Theodore Roosevelt recognized, Jesse will always be America's Robin Hood, the gallant, handsome outlaw who robbed the rich to help the poor. The facts, however, reveal that Jesse was a ruthless killer, a whining criminal who insisted that the social unrest following the Civil War had forced him and his followers into their outlaw roles. Serious works on frontier unrest and apologists still echo the gravedigger at Lee's Summit: "They was drove to it." [1]

But not all Missourians accepted this theory. William H. Wallace, the Jackson County prosecutor who had been elected on a platform of breaking up the gang and was near fulfilling his promise when Bob Ford pulled the trigger, pointed out in his memoirs:

> I remember distinctly of seeing Cole Younger in our neighborhood immediately after the war, and at a time when he was not in hiding,

189

Jesse James at seventeen Jesse James, from a daguerre- Frank James
otype made in 1875 at Ne-
braska City, Nebraska

and when he was not being molested—at least in no greater degree than others who had belonged to Quantrell's band. The people had a great deal of confidence in him and I believe if he had stayed at home he could have been elected to almost any office in Jackson County.

Of course when I saw him he wore two large pistols, as did scores of other Southern men immediately after the war, and this was doubtless necessary, but I have never known any man who presented any evidence that there was any greater danger for the Youngers and James immediately after the war than for the balance of Quantrell's men, many of whom I could now name, who settled down in Jackson Co. and went to work and have since led most honorable lives. One of these has held various positions of public trust in Jackson County.[2]

Yet no one can read the story of Jesse without feeling a sense of pity for the man who possessed such undeniable qualities of leadership, and in particular for the woman who bore him children and followed him faithfully until the very morning when Bob Ford sent her husband into the world of our folklore.

The Pinkertons, father and sons, hated Jesse James with an unyielding passion; that hate was returned with equal fervor. Two Pinkerton opera- tives died in their "war." One, hands tied behind his back, was shot from a horse, and his body was left for the wild hogs. The other died from wounds suffered in a standup fight after he had killed one of the Youngers.

The Pinkertons hunted Jesse and his men for years. A combination of sympathy for the former Quantrell riders, partisan politics, and the terror the gang inspired in Clay County defeated not only the Pinkertons but local and state law officers as well—at least those who had the courage to move against the gang. A correspondent of the Missouri *World*, writing from Appleton City in 1874, gives an indication of conditions in the Jesse James country: "So great is the terror that the Jameses and Youngers have instilled in Clay County, that their names are never mentioned save in back rooms and then only in a whisper." [3]

It was evident that most of Clay County's law officers were also afraid of the James gang. As William Pinkerton recalled when he tried to get a deputy to help him:

> He said he would deputize me and aid me secretly, but owing to the relatives and sympathizers of these men residing in the county he dared not lend me a hand openly; that I did not reside in the county and did not have to live there after the arrest had been made, but he did. He deputized me and one of our men whom I had brought with me, and that night he rode with me into the Missouri Bottoms, pointed out the house of the men we wanted, helped to surround the house and was ready to kill either of the men if necessary, providing it was not known that he had helped to do so. This man was a good officer and will do his duty but it would have been impossible for him to conduct a fight against these men alone. Had it been known that he was against them he would have been assassinated. [4]

The story of the robberies committed by the James-Younger gang is too well known as a part of our folklore to be repeated here in detail. They began by riding into Liberty, Missouri, on the morning of February 3, 1866. The gang, reportedly led by Jesse, and numbering among his riders his brother, Frank, Cole Younger, Arch Clements, George Shepherd, George White, Cell Miller, Jim Poole, Bud Pence, and Ed Miller, robbed the Clay County Savings Association of $70,000. A young college student was killed by the gang as they "hurrahed" the street. In October, they struck Alex Mitchell & Co., Lexington, Missouri, to take $2,000. The following year, in Savannah, Missouri, they robbed a bank, seriously injuring the banker. The gang met strong opposition when they held up the Hughes and Wasson Bank in Richmond, Missouri, on May 22, 1867. Mayor John B. Shaw, Franks, Griffin, and the latter's father were killed in the exchange of gunfire. Two more banks in Russellville, Kentucky, and Gallatin, Missouri, followed. In the latter robbery, the leader of the gang, believed to have been Jesse James, murdered the cashier John Sheets, with the explanation that he looked like a Union man who had chased them during the war. On June 3, 1871, Jesse and Frank James, the Youngers, Jim Cummings, Charlie Pitts, and Ed Miller rode to Corydon, Iowa, to rob the Ocobock Bros. Bank of about $6,000. For the next few years the gang would ride across the Midwest, robbing trains and looting banks. If Robert Pinkerton's memory was correct, the

Bob Younger two weeks before his
death

Agency briefly took up the trail of the James gang after they had been
retained by the Corydon, Iowa, bank, following the 1871 robbery. Evidently the Pinkertons did not return to Missouri until three years later.[5]

The years 1871 to 1874 were trying for the Pinkertons. Allan, still in-
capacitated, was slowly regaining his ability to speak and to walk. The
Chicago fire had left their business in ashes, and the Agency almost collapsed in the worldwide depression of 1872. The Agency was also stretch-
ing its manpower thin. In the East, operatives were chasing bank robbers
who were stealing sums that the entire career of the Middle Border
bandits would never total. Disciplinary hearing records reveal that in the
late 1860's and 1870's, Pinkerton undercover operatives were being used
by railroads and streetcar companies to obtain evidence of cheating by
conductors. The Agency's offices in New York City, Chicago, and Philadelphia were also occupied with almost every aspect of American crime
from insurance murder for profit to locating missing persons, the everyday routine of large metropolitan police organizations.

Despite his personal disasters, Allan Pinkerton relieved George Bangs
of his administrative responsibilities in 1871—Bangs held one of the most
responsible posts in the Agency's executive structure—and ordered him
to Richmond to locate Timothy Webster's body, have it disinterred, and
brought back to Illinois for reburial. His personal world could be crumbling about him, his business on the brink of disaster, yet he could detach
his most important employee and spend money he could not afford, to
keep a six-year-old promise he had made to a dead man.

Bangs's expense sheet shows that he left New York City on April 25, 1871, and arrived in Richmond two days later, where he engaged "a team and a buggy to tour the cemeteries to obtain information of Webster's remains." On the twenty-ninth, he finally located Webster's grave, and hired a local undertaker "to box the remains for the express office." Unfortunately, there was no correspondence between Bangs and Pinkerton after the body arrived in Chicago. For almost a century it has been assumed Webster was buried in the Pinkerton plot in Chicago's Graceland Cemetery, under a monument with the story of his service to the Union and his education chiseled on one side. However, cemetery records show that the body was sent to Onarga, where Pinkerton buried Webster in the Onarga Cemetery beside Webster's young son, who had been killed in the war shortly before the cessation of hostilities.[6]

In April and May, 1872, Jesse and his gang robbed the Columbia, Adair County, Kentucky, Bank, a theft during which Cashier R. A. C. Martin was brutally murdered, and the Ste. Genevieve, Missouri, Savings Bank. Existing records do not disclose if the Pinkertons were hired by these banks and had sent operatives into Missouri. But what Allan Pinkerton's correspondence of that period does show is that the fate of his business, and not the activities of the Missouri bravoes, occupied almost every waking hour.

In the spring of 1872, depression had crept slowly across the land like an ugly, crippling disease. It was the time of the brownstone front, morally edifying tales of Horatio Alger, atrocious plaster-cast statues, Currier and Ives, stained-glass windows, and sprawling, ugly cities. *The Nation* has since called is our chrome civilization, while Walt Whitman saw it as "cankered, crude, superstitious and rotten . . . never perhaps was there more hollowness of heart."

It followed a period in which the North, its wealth and energy intensified by the war, pushed frantically and unashamedly to create a new, postwar America of giant finance and capitalism. The stench of corruption in Grant's administration was beginning to seep from under the Washington lids, as former Senator James W. Grimes wrote to Lyman Trumbull. While the campaign of 1872 was at its height, the country was shocked to learn of the wholesale corruption that had been rife during the construction of the Union Pacific. The promoters of the railroad had formed a construction company, the Credit Mobilier of America, which was awarded incredible construction contracts. The line was pushed to the brink of bankruptcy, while the credit company paid dividends of 348 percent! Exposure of the credit company's stock deals disgraced many Republican leaders, including Vice-President Colfax and Pinkerton's wartime foe, Senator Henry Wilson of Massachusetts.

The year 1872 had barely turned when Pinkerton was after Bangs to watch the expense bills of his operatives. Bangs replied that he was stressing honesty to all his men, "but you know what difficulty we have had with our best men in the matter of expenses, and in fact with nearly all our men and while such is the fact, it is not very creditable to ourselves that they seem to get more expenses the longer they are with us . . . the matter of expenses is one that cannot be given too much attention and positive control. . . .[7]

A little more than two months later, J. G. Horne, the Agency's auditor —and from his correspondence a tight man with a penny—was again after Bangs to forward New York's expense bills. Bangs did so, hastily pointing out that the bills for Operative Des Rossiers, one of his best, "does not have board charged. It is occasioned by the fact that he is getting his board free at present at the American House for services tendered them." A Mrs. Packard, another operative, had a bill for $2.15, and Bangs himself had a bill for $2.65 for "treating" three important witnesses in saloon in Rome and Atlanta in early January. A few days later Bangs sent a long report to Pinkerton, describing how he had managed to cultivate the friendship of one of Jim Fisk's agents "who got information as regards the Erie stockholders and he [is used] as a Lobbyman."

Pinkerton was evidently after Bangs to try for a retainer from the Erie, which was plagued by cheating conductors. Bangs met Fisk's man in Delmonico's on Broad Street, and after several dinners and drinks finally learned that the New York Central "was contemplating having us but after they heard what it cost the Hudson River road to keep their conductors honest it was claimed that our bill was more than the conductors would steal in three years." Bangs pointed out, "This shows what has been used against us." Bangs also reported to his employer that Fisk's agent "conceded our system was the most thorough, but few railroads would use our operations because of the expense. . . ."[8]

A tightening up had begun, and as Bangs reported to Chicago, layoffs were spreading on the railroads in the East. In the late spring the depression widened; in Chicago, Pinkerton found that contracts for guards and property security were canceled; business houses that had been his clients for years closed their doors. Then he discovered that his own credit rating was in jeopardy. In May, Bangs was beginning to worry. The Agency had been retained, possibly by the Cuban government, to investigate the activities of General Peralta, the rebel commander of the revolutionary army, and as Bangs informed Warner in Chicago, who wanted one of New York's best men, "We have been keeping our force down so low during this dull period we have few experienced men left."[9]

Then money became so tight that Pinkerton assigned his superintendents to act as collecting agencies, ordering them to go out and bring in all monies due on old accounts. On August 15, 1872, Pinkerton wrote Bangs: "I suppose there is no hope for anything paying in New York. God knows what I am to do two days from this date."[10] On the same date he was writing to a Chicago representative that his business "is in great want of money, on every hand I am in debt, yet I cannot get a person to help me, for everyone to whom I owe a shilling are calling on me for it . . . it is nearly Saturday and you know I have to pay everyone. I must have money for they must have money. I would not for anything allow them to go without their wages, but how am I going to get the money unless you and the others do your duty and bring in the money?" [11]

Apparently the superintendents dunned their clients, and enough money came in that late summer to meet the Agency's payroll, but by October, Pinkerton was feeling the breath of financial ruin. He wrote to Bangs, imploring him to "collect all your bills without one moment's delay, things are coming right on us. Let business stand for the moment—go to work and collect bills, sacrifice everything to get money, discount at any price . . . any day whatever there may be a crash around us that we little suspect." [12]

A month later Pinkerton was still floundering financially. He appealed again to Bangs in New York to dun their clients. Bangs went to the New York office of the Adams Company and managed to collect various sums from $1,200 to $75, which he sent on to J. G. Horne, the Agency's accountant in Chicago. The money helped to settle some of the bills, but that month Pinkerton had his back to the wall. He was forced to sell some of his property and a substantial block of railroad stock to get cash to finance a new assignment the Agency had been offered by the Atlantic & Great Western Railroad.

Ties of old friendships were strained. Henry Sanford, of Adams, who had worked so feverishly with Pinkerton on the Maroney case and had been one of his greatest supporters, had made a loan to the detective, who reported to Bangs that Sanford had been abusive "and has insulted me in every way lately." [13]

On September 17, 1873, the banking house of Jay Cooke and Company closed. This was the firm that had financed the Civil War and the building of the Northern Pacific. Firm after firm fell, and the Stock Exchange, in an unprecedented move, closed its doors for ten days. As the panic broadened into a worldwide depression, and with European industry calling in their American loans, half the nation's railroads defaulted on their bonds.

In May, 1873, Pinkerton was writing to Bangs: "I can scarcely tell which way to go, and many a time I am perfectly bewildered what to do. . . ." Then came a confession that Pinkerton had never before made: "I am afraid." [14]

But it was a different man who faced his sons. The year before he had advised "Willie": "I will come out all right, by'n bye . . . my idea is never to lose heart, never think for a moment of giving up the ship. I am bound to go through sink or swim. Hold your head up. I will back you at all eternity." [15]

Without public welfare, and with the resources of private charitable organizations stretched thin by the frantic appeals of the starving and the jobless, the cities of the East witnessed their first breadlines. Tramps were common. Many became train robbers, forgers, and what the Agency's records describe as "yegg" burglars, or transient cracksmen who roamed the country from New York to San Francisco, breaking into the safes of small banks and county treasury offices. All that year and part of the next, Pinkerton fought off financial ruin. Then, in 1874, he sent his operatives back to Missouri to resume the Agency's "war" with the Jameses and the Youngers. They probably had again been retained by either the looted express companies or the banks.

The Pinkertons' first attempt at using their favorite method of infiltration was a disaster. In March, 1874, the body of John W. Whicher, a young operative who had begged William Pinkerton to send him to Missouri, was found on the side of a road in Jackson County, near Independence. There were wounds in his head, shoulder, and stomach. The last two shots had been fired at such close range that the muzzle blast had burned away clothing, skin, and hair. Part of the face had been chewed away by wild hogs. The body was removed to the county morgue, and a coroner's jury quickly returned a verdict of "death at the hands of some unknown party."

A New York *World* correspondent, assigned to investigate the Jesse James story, visited Clay County and wrote a review of the Whicher murder and the train and bank robberies that everyone in the area accepted as having been committed by the James gang. The New York newspaperman seemed startled that the Jameses and Youngers could kill and rob with such impunity, "although they live within an hour's ride of Kansas City, a town of 14,000 inhabitants." [16]

A few days later, Louis J. Lull, Annapolis student, Union veteran, and former captain in the Chicago Police Department, also a volunteer, went in after the gang. He was accompanied by John Boyle, a former St. Louis police officer recommended to William Pinkerton as a "reliable officer." Lull, using the name of W. J. Allen, and Boyle that of James Wright, traveled to St. Clair County, where Lull hired Edwin B. Daniels (also spelled Daniel), a former deputy sheriff. Although some historians insist Daniels was a regular Pinkerton employee, William Pinkerton wrote: "Daniels has been quoted as a Pinkerton man but he was never in our employ. He was deputy sheriff of St. Clair County and was an entire stranger to us up to the time of the meeting between him and Lull." [17]

The three men, posing as cattle buyers, by chance met John and Jim Younger on a small stony rise named Chalk Hill Road. It was just half past two on the afternoon of March 16, 1874. A few minutes after the outlaws had called out a command to the detectives to halt, there was a crash of gunfire. What happened in that bloody confrontation is best told in Lull's own words, taken as he lay dying in the Roscoe Hotel in nearby Roscoe. At the time he was still not known as a Pinkerton operative, and the clerk of the coroner's jury swore him in as W. J. Allen. The deposition, taken on the following morning, reads:

> Yesterday about half past two o'clock, the 16th of March, 1874, E. B. Daniels and myself were riding along the road from Roscoe to Chalk Level, which road runs past the house of one Theodore Snuffer, and about three miles from the town of Roscoe and in St. Clair County, Missouri. Daniels and myself were riding side by side, and Wright a short distance ahead of us; some noise behind us attracted our attention, and we looked back and saw two men on horseback coming toward us, and one was armed with a double barrel shot-gun, the other with revolvers; don't know if the other had a shot-gun or not; the one had the shot-gun cocked, both barrels, and ordered us to halt; Wright drew his pistol and put spurs to his horse and rode off; they ordered him to halt, and shot at him and shot off his hat, but he kept on riding. Daniels and myself stopped, standing across the road on our horses. They rode up to us, and ordered us to take off our pistols and drop them in the road, the one with the gun covering me all the time with the gun. We dropped our pistols on the ground and one of the men told the other to follow Wright and bring him back, but he refused to. I reached my hand behind me and drew a No. 2 Smith & Wesson pistol and cocked it and fired at the one on horseback, and my horse frightened at the report of the pistol turned to run, and I heard two shots and my left arm fell, and then I had no control over my horse, and he jumped into the brushes and the trees checked his speed, and I tried to get hold of the rein with my right hand, to bring him into the road; one of the men rode by me and fired two shots at me, one of which took effect in my left side, and I lost all control of my horse and he turned into the brush and a small tree struck me and knocked me out of the saddle. I then got up and staggered across the road and lay down until I was found. No one else was present.

Theodore Snuffer, a friend of the Youngers who lived nearby, gave another version. He quoted to the coroner the story Jim Younger had told him that he and his brother John were about to pass "the man on the white horse" (Lull) when the Pinkerton operative and Daniels opened fire. John fell off his horse and fired his double-barreled shotgun at Lull, then shot Daniels. The wounded Lull rode off, but the dying John Younger followed. They exchanged shots "until John fell dead." Another witness, G. W. McDonald, who had appeared after the first shots had been fired, testified that Jim turned over the body of his dead brother and, practical outlaw that he was, "took some revolvers off of him and a watch and something else out of his pocket. . . . I think James Younger took four revolvers off John Younger . . . he threw one over a fence and told me to keep it, then he told me to catch a horse and tell Snuffer's folks."

After the shooting, a Negro laborer carried Lull to his cabin. From

Cabin to which Lull was carried by a Negro laborer

there the operative was removed to the Roscoe Hotel. Allan Pinkerton wanted to hire a train and have him taken to Chicago, but D. C. McNeil, a local physician, telegraphed that Lull was too critical to be moved. Mrs. Lull, in the company of Robert Linden, the assistant superintendent of the Philadelphia office, rushed to Roscoe to stay with her husband until his death.

A. Ray, foreman of the coroner's jury, announced that "John Younger died of a pistol shot supposed to have been in the hands of W. J. Allen [Lull]," while Daniels "came to his death by a pistol shot supposed to have been in the hands of John Younger." The jury's report also revealed that the wounds of Lull and Daniels were "pretty large, indicating the ball was a pretty large size." [18]

Boyle or Wright, that "capable officer" who had galloped down the road when he had caught sight of the Youngers, displayed a bullet hole in his hat, and lamely insisted he had only ridden off for reinforcements, failing to explain why he had deserted Lull and Wright when the Youngers had been outnumbered. William Pinkerton never forgave Wright. As he wrote to his brother, Robert, "We were betrayed by a coward. . . . Captain Lull would be alive today if Wright had not run off. . . ."

But William Pinkerton wasn't the criterion of courage. A month after the killing of Lull and Whicher, Allan Pinkerton wrote a bitter letter to George Bangs in New York:

> I have no soldiers but all officers in my regiment—all are capital men to give orders, few will go forward unless someone goes ahead. I know that the James-Youngers are desperate men, and that if we meet it [sic] it must be the death of one or both of us . . . they must repay . . . there is no use talking, they must die. . . . Mr. Warner [Frank Warner,

superintendent of the Chicago office] and William refused to go with the men to Missouri, both declared they were not to be made a notch to be shot at . . . consequently I made no talk but simply say I am going myself. . . .[19]

What Allan Pinkerton probably had in mind when he was writing to Bangs was a vigilante posse to go into Clay County and attack "Castle James," as the newspapers were calling the Samuels place. Pinkerton's letters of the 1870's show how much he admired the Indiana vigilantes and the action they had taken against the Renos. Night riders and lynching suited his philosophy that the ends justify the means. In January, 1875, such a force was organized to raid the farmhouse and kidnap Jesse and Frank James. Time and the lack of records have obscured the details of that so-called "bomb raid," but the reminiscences and newspaper accounts supply the stark outlines of that bloody night. For years William and Robert Pinkerton denied they led the trainload of possemen. As late as 1892, the subject of the raid came up in the senatorial investigation of the Homestead Riots when Senator Vest, in a sharp examination of the Pinkertons, demanded to know if they had taken part in the raid. They replied: "When the house in which the robbers [Jesse and Frank James] lived was surrounded, none of the Pinkertons or watchmen were present . . . what was done was not done by our employees. . . ." Unfortunately, Vest didn't press to try to determine exactly *who* was there. Despite the Pinkertons' denials, newspaper accounts place William Pinkerton in Kansas City at the Northend Hotel before the raid, conferring with law-enforcement officials of Clay County whom he felt he could trust.

In a series of articles in the Kansas City *Sunday Sun,* an unidentified writer who claimed he was the telegraph messenger who delivered most of the messages between the sheriff and Pinkerton described the meetings: "The sheriff [of Clay County] assured the detectives that they could rely upon the sympathy and moral support of the majority of the best people of Clay County. A crafty scheme was mapped out and the proposals were therefore bright."

The next step was to "shadow" the small, rugged log cabin, the local residents had dubbed "Castle James." This was supposedly done by "ten trustworthy Clay County citizens and reports were wired to Billy Pinkerton three times a day." But Pinkerton should have known that in the widespread and intricate arrangements someone would talk; and they did, whether it was a railroad employee or one of the "trustworthy" Clay County residents, we shall never know. While the raiders were arriving at Union Station, and the local posse was moving in to surround Castle James, the outlaw brothers were galloping along the back roads "to a hideout at the farm of a friend."

It is said that William Westfall was the conductor on the train, and that may be true. He would one day die under the guns of the gang, and

Frank James would be tried for his murder. Another contemporary account of the raid appeared in the Kansas City *Times,* written by "Doctor" Munford, who accompanied the raiders for the *Times,* thus scoring a scoop over on "its loathsome competitor, the *Journal.*" The railroad officials supposedly didn't object to having Munford accompany them when he appeared in a long gray ulster "and slipped aboard without a word to anyone." Significantly, Munford doesn't mention any of the Pinkertons.

The train rattled over the Hannibal Bridge, then slipped into Clay County. It was a clear, cold night with a yellow wafer of a moon. There were no headlights on the engine, no lamps lighted in the coaches, no piercing whistle to echo over the silent countryside. There was only the monotonous *click-click* of the big iron wheels as the train chugged along the gleaming rails toward Castle James. When the raiders swung off the cars, "the detectives felt elated, the die was cast, there was no retracting of plans. The battle for law and order was at last to be fought and the country was to be electrified with the results on the morrow."

The night, as Munford wrote, was bitterly cold as the shadowy figures moved toward the Samuels place. Two men—they were never identified—crept to the west window of the house. In attempting to raise the sash, they awakened an old colored woman who had worked for the family for years. She quickly gave the alarm.

Then the "bomb" was tossed inside the house. In reality it was a small flare with an iron base, a copper top with two curved wicks, the type used by traveling medicine shows or "tonka" peddlers. Inside was cotton saturated with turpentine.

Occupying the house were Dr. Samuels, Zerelda, mother of the outlaws, and two small children. The room was filled with heavy smoke as Dr. Samuels ran into the main room, which had a big fireplace off to one side.

The plan, according to the reporters, was to capture Frank and Jesse, who, the raiders assumed, "would rush outside at this strange sight." Surrounding the house were the possemen armed with rifles and navy Colts. The two small children began screaming, but Mrs. Samuels, "true to her stern nature, began shouting orders and arranging to subdue the flames."

Dr. Samuels used the end of his cane to push the flare into the fireplace, which still had a bed of glowing coals. After a few minutes the flare exploded. The pieces of copper and iron flew like shrapnel, tearing Mrs. Samuels' arm to shreds, and critically injuring Jesse's half-brother, eight-year-old Archie. The room was a horror, with the children screaming, the woman injured, and the wall splattered with blood.

When it was evident that the outlaws were not at home, "the detectives withdrew, sullen and disappointed."

Mrs. Samuels lost her arm, and young Archie died a short time later. At Kearney, Munford aroused the local telegrapher and had him "raise" the Kansas City office to alert them he had "a special for the *Times*." Kansas City responded in a few minutes, and in the lamplight of the tiny station Munford wrote a bulletin with a postscript "to hold the forms open, he would bring the balance of the story on the returning train."

The vigilantes rolled into Union Station at two o'clock. Munford hurried to the *Times* office and wrote a dramatic four-column account that not only scooped the *Journal* but electrified the nation.

Archie was buried three days later, "and as the coffin was lowered there were curses, loud and deep, hurled at the Pinkertons."

In Chicago it was obvious that the great plans had backfired. The Pinkertons realized they had now replaced the outlaws as the popular villains; but, more importantly, the small but growing voices of opposition to the gang were silenced. For the first time in the Agency's history, news columns and editorial pages were hostile and abusive. When it became known that the local authorities were seeking murder indictments against the Pinkertons, Allan wrote to Robert in New York:

> I have but little to say about this subject; the fact is they are trying their best to get indictments against some of my men for the operation in Clay County where James' mother had met with a merited and fearful punishment. Also into West Virginia, Texas, Arkansas where they will undoubtedly try to get indictments against my men who have gone to these places to fight the battle. . . .

Pinkerton informed his son that he was sure Jesse and the Youngers "and their comrades" had been killed in their raids, a surmise which was as wrong as most of his planning in Missouri. Pinkerton also assailed some midwestern police chiefs who had criticized his Agency:

> I will gladly allow these people to go into Clay County or St. Clair County or Monegaw Springs as my men have done. I paid the penalty of having lost my men but I will not bandy words regarding those great men in the detective business at the present time. . . . 'Tis enough I must say I ask nothing from the Adams Express Company. I must say I spent money freely and I ask no reward. I must say my end is accomplished and in that I am content. . . .[20]

In response to the critical editorials, the Pinkertons denied that William had led the raiders, but they never told who did. In a letter to his Kansas City superintendent, J. H. Schumacher, Robert wrote: "It used to be charged that William Pinkerton led the raid [on the James house] but we have contradicted this statement so thoroughly and as frequently that it is hardly worth while to raise the question any further."[21]

The Pinkertons denied that a "bomb" had been hurled into the house, pointing out that it was a flare filled with cotton saturated with turpentine, "which on being thrown into the hot fire place caused the explosion." Explanations were lost in the editorial.

Jesse never forgave the Pinkertons. In an interview with a reporter for the *Courier-Journal* after Jesse's death, "Old George" Hite, uncle of the outlaws, revealed that following the raid, Jesse had traveled to Chicago to assassinate Allan Pinkerton. In between serving customers in his country store in Russellville, Hite told the story:

> He stayed there four months but he never got a chance to do it as he wanted to. "I could have killed the younger one [William?] but I didn't. I wanted him to know who did it," he said. "It wouldn't do me no good if I couldn't tell him about it before he died. I had a dozen chances to shoot him but the opportunity never came."
>
> He left Chicago without doing it but I have heard him say often: "I know God some day will deliver Allan Pinkerton into my hands."

Hite's interview was filled with intimate details of the outlaw gang, including Jesse's rather unglamorous methods of organizing a raid: "They decided on going somewhere, and then they'd send word to all the others —they always knew where they were—and then went and done it. That's all there was to it."

There is no way, of course, to confirm Hite's story of Jesse James's Chicago trip, but there is no reason to doubt the details of the interview.[22]

The disastrous raid also resulted in the first formal move to obtain amnesty for "the boys." On March 17th, Jefferson Jones of Callaway County, who would be a vigorous apologist for the Jameses and Youngers until he died, introduced a resolution in the Missouri House of Representatives, offering amnesty to Jesse and Frank James for any acts of lawlessness committed before and during the Civil War, and guaranteeing a fair trial on any charges or acts since the war. The resolution failed to win a majority, but the split vote showed the impact the gang had on Missouri politics.[23]

The Jameses and Youngers continued to ride roughshod over Missouri and the Middle Border states, but it was the guns and courage of the citizens of Northfield, Minnesota—and not the Pinkertons or the law of Missouri—that finally shattered the gang. On September 17, 1876, in seventeen action-packed minutes, the residents of Northfield, a quiet farming town, forced the so-called "greatest revolver fighters in the world" to leave their dead and flee, some of the outlaws riding double. Jesse would reorganize his gang, but it would never be the same. Then one day he stepped up on a chair to fix a picture, and Bob Ford fired the bullet that sent his leader into the hazy, distorted, but attractive world of American folklore.[24]

BOOK 4
The Crucial Years, 1874-1876

CHAPTER 23

The Molly Maguires

The depression still gripped the country, and money was scarce when Allan Pinkerton wrote to George Bangs, urging him to call on Franklin Benjamin Gowen, president of the Reading Railroad, "to suggest something to Mr. Gowen about one thing or another which could be feasible and I have no doubt he would give us work." [1]

Bangs followed his employer's suggestion, and went to Philadelphia to see Gowen. They were not strangers; the Pinkertons had worked for Gowen before to obtain evidence on cheating among conductors. Bangs could not have arrived at a more opportune time; violence was breaking out in the coalfields, with mine superintendents being beaten or murdered, railroad cars derailed, and coal tipples burned. After Bangs's visit to Philadelphia, Pinkerton operatives appeared in the vicinity of Pottsville where railroad property had been destroyed. Not long afterward, Allan Pinkerton's report to Gowen linked the Molly Maguires, a secret terroristic society, to the incidents of violence.

The growing number of derailed railroad cars, the burning of the large coal tipple west of Pottsville, and the intimidation of mine superintendents led to a meeting between Allan Pinkerton and Gowen. Pinkerton's own version has Gowen summoning him to Philadelphia. Starting with this initial meeting, Pinkerton and his Agency entered the long, fascinating, and many times incredible investigation of the Molly Maguires and its reign of terror in the Pennsylvania anthracite counties.

For over a hundred years writers and historians have written about the

Molly Maguires with fierce partisanship; either the Molly Maguires were killers, arsonists, or robbers or they were labor martyrs railroaded to the gallows by union-busting capitalists. There are also two versions of Gowen and the Pinkertons: The railroad president is either praised for his fearless campaign to rid the coalfields of a menace or he is pictured as the archvillain who created a dangerous society only to arouse a public opinion that sent the Molly leaders to their death because they were unifying labor in the minefields. The Pinkertons were either described as the serfs of capitalism who secured the convictions of honest men by fabricating evidence or they were hailed as courageous, ingenious detectives who had eradicated a group of murdering terrorists.

Francis P. Dewees, a Pottsville attorney living at the time of the Molly Maguire investigation wrote a surprisingly objective book on the subject that has become a source for many historians of the period. Dewees based his book on court testimony and a personal investigation of conditions. He claims that most of the Mollies belonged to labor unions, yet he states: "There is no proof that the labor union as a body helped or sympathized with the Molly Maguires." [2]

Anthony Bimba's version, generally accepted as the left-wing labor view, has "both organization and the name [Molly Maguires] invented by the mine owners to provide a convenient label for the militant miners in the Pennsylvania anthracite fields. After the label has been sufficiently fatal to send a man to the gallows, the mine owners proceeded to fasten the label upon all union leaders they wished to get rid of." [3]

Bimba is in error as to the origin of the name. The Molly Maguires was a clandestine society formed in Ireland to battle the landowners. Wayne G. Broehl, Jr., in his recent study of the Molly Maguires, traces the society back to 1845, when Thomas Foster, an English lawyer and journalist, mentioned the Molly Maguires in the London *Times*. From County Cavan, Foster wrote: "What is the Molly Maguireism which has disturbed this county? . . . it is the same as Ribandism, say the magistrates in their placards offering rewards for the apprehension of the Molly Maguires. . . ."

During the first half of the nineteenth century, the Irish arrived in large numbers in the Pennsylvania coalfields. Some of the miners who were members of the Mollies, or who took part in their activities, emigrated from Ireland before, during, or just after the 1846–1852 potato famine. Others were sons of Irish immigrants with strong cultural ties to the immediate past. There is little doubt that the shadowy society in the anthracite fields was a transplant from the Old Country. In Ireland their traditional foes were land agents; in Pennsylvania they were mineowners and mine bosses. The decisive involvement of the Roman Catholic Church was as strong—if unwilling—in Ireland as it was in America.

Beyond the stark conditions under which the miners of Pennsylvania existed, the elements of strife in the Molly Maguire story are more complex than those of simply good and evil men. Labor was at war with capital. Class warfare had violently erupted to face the nation for the first time. Democrats were warring against Republicans, Protestants against Catholics, natives against immigrants. Morals and ethics had sunk to an all-time low. Ambassadors, ministers, statesmen, and legislatures had been proved corrupt, and business practices were shocking.

Immigration was at a flood level, the immigrants bringing with them all the ancient feuds and hates. They were social radicals, as Pinkerton himself had been thirty years earlier, or ignorant, illiterate men. In both cases they were obsessed by dreams of a new life. They crowded the steerages, dreaming in the damp, stench-filled darkness of the glittering world in which thy would soon make their homes. When they found a life scarcely better than the one they had left behind, their bitterness and their hate increased.

In the minefields, conditions were particularly shocking. Miners, including the Mollies, went underground to hack out coal under primitive conditions. There was no local or federal legislation to protect them. In 1871, 112 men were killed in the anthracite mines, and 332 permanently injured. In seven years, 556 men had been killed and 1,565 maimed or crippled for life. Out of the 22,000 miners, more than 5,000 were sixteen years of age or under.

Take-home pay was uncertain; deductions were often arbitrary or at the whim of the owners by means of what was then called the "bobtail check." A typical week's wages for a miner at the time of the Molly Maguires was $35; expenses, including rent, groceries, and a new drill, came to $35.03.[4]

In the coalfields during the Civil War there had been violent demonstrations against the draft, and in some sections strong copperhead sentiments. Provost patrols roused the hatred of the people in the fields when they dragged miners from their homes, tied them to the saddles of cavalrymen, and marched them to Pottsville. Troops had to enforce the draft in Pottsville and Scranton. After a show of bayonets the local general telegraphed to Washington that the miners in the area "had no fear of God, the Devil or the State."[5]

In the following year murder and violence became commonplace, with the Molly Maguires blamed for the crimes. In July, 1864, Bishop James Frederick Wood of Philadelphia, one of the few Catholic leaders who denounced the secret societies of his time, ordered his pastoral letter read from every pulpit, "in which he denounced the Molly Maguires, the Buckshots [a local name for the Mollies] and others."[6]

The coal industry and the fields were hit by the recession that followed the end of the war. Prices fell, and miners were laid off only to find their ranks augmented by veterans coming back from the war. In January, 1868, the first strike hit the coalfields. Though it was brief, it resulted in the formation of a new coal union, the Workingmen's Benevolent Association of St. Clair, whose leader was John Sidney. Then a new figure appeared, Franklin Benjamin Gowen.

Just thirty-three, Gowen was a member of a wealthy Philadelphia family. At the excusive John Beck's Boys Academy his schoomates had been the sons of Virginia planters, Pennsylvania ironmasters, and Philadelphia bankers. In the late fifties he had tried his hand at coal, but in 1859 he sold out his operations and turned to the study of law. He soon became known as a dynamic courtroom figure, whose booming voice and lush rhetoric checkered with colorful phrases and classical references could hypnotize any audience.

His personal magnetism could be almost irresistible, even when his arguments were obviously preposterous. His greatest weakness appeared to be an incredible optimism and an apparent unwillingness to square his larger projects with the practical necessities of the moment. He also craved to be the center of the hard white light of publicity. Large meetings of the stockholders were usually held in public halls only for the purpose of allowing Gowen to make a long, florid speech, and when the applause raised a flush to his cheeks, he had the appearance of a man intoxicated by a magnum of champagne.

Pinkerton may have offered Gowen the opportunity for extraordinary publicity, as well as the plaudits of his community, for crushing the secret society that had terrorized the coalfields for so long and with such impunity, a state of affairs for which, ironically, Gowen himself was responsible. He had served two years as district attorney of Schuylkill County, resigning in 1864 to devote all his time to an expanding law practice. He did not leave behind an impressive record as prosecutor; in a county that was terrorized by riots, violence, and murder, the lack of convictions for major crimes in the county at the time he was D.A. is shocking. The reason is either politics—the rioters and murderers were usually Irish and Democrats, the party that had put him into office—or more likely the fact that he was an opportunist.

Gowen's next big step was his appointment as head of the Legal Department of the Reading Railroad. In 1866, he appeared in the state supreme court to win a victory over the Pennsylvania Railroad. Finally he was elected president of the line. In 1870, Gowen was appointed mediator between the striking Workingmen's Benevolent Association and the mine operators, formulating the famous "Gowen Compromise," in which he suggested that the miners' wages be linked to the rise and fall of the price of coal. When the prices fell during the postwar recession, the miners saw their pay dwindling. In the winter of 1870, when the northern miners went on strike and persuaded the southern WBA to join them, the coal industry was faced with the threat of a unified labor movement in the fields, a nightmare that became reality to the operators.

The strike began in January, 1871. Several of the operators, fearing financial ruin, attempted to sign with the WBA. But Gowen stunned both operators and union by raising the Reading's freight rates from $2 to $4 a ton—a 100 percent raise. When the miners demanded that Gowen's freight raise be investigated, a legislative committee was appointed. Gowen was an impressive witness. In his version the WBA was to blame for the conditions in the fields, and his booming voice graphically described how the Molly Maguires voted secretly at night "that men's lives should be taken and that they shall be shot before their wives, murdered in cold blood." [7]

Shortly before Pinkerton appeared, there was a new and unforeseen development. Operating through various fronts, Gowen purchased huge tracts of coal land, and also maneuvered a bill through the legislature which the governor signed, giving the Reading a monopoly in the fields. Gowen was later accused of bribery, but legal evidence was never produced to support the charge. By the end of 1874, the Reading owned 100,000 acres of coal land, more than double that owned by any other corporation.

After his conference with Gowen, Pinkerton felt that there was only one way to break up the Molly Maguires, and that was his traditional, usually successful—with the exception of the Jameses and Youngers—method of infiltrating. Four years later, Pinkerton described how he envisioned the operative he needed for this dangerous task:

> It is no ordinary man that I need in this matter. He must be an Irishman and a Catholic, as only this class of person can find admission to the Mollie Maguires. My detective should become, to all intents and purposes, one of the order, and continue so while he remains in the case before us. He should be hardy, tough and capable of laboring, in season and out of season, to accomplish unknown to those about him, a single absorbing subject.[8]

Better than most, Pinkerton knew from his days as a Chartist how bitterly an informer was hated. He realized that his Irish operative had to be an extraordinary man. As Robert Pinkerton observed:

> It required something more than mere pecuniary reward to secure the right sort of person for this task. The man had to feel that he was serving his church, his God, his race and his country; otherwise it would be impossible to get anyone to undertake a work which invited death by assassination.[9]

Everything would depend on the man selected. The choice apparently came in a flash of intuition. On a West Side streetcar in Chicago, while on his way to his office. Pinkerton saw one of his men, James McParland, acting as a conductor, doing a routine check for thievery. McParland,

Pinkerton detective James
McParland. *Pinkerton's, Inc.*

Pinkerton detective Robert J.
Linden. *Pinkerton's, Inc.*

who had been with the Agency for a year, was a twenty-nine-year-old
Ulster immigrant. He had worked at a variety of jobs that served as good
experience for a future detective: grocery-store clerk, teamster, meat-
wagon driver, deckhand, lumberman, private coachman, bartender, policeman, and owner of a liquor store and saloon in Chicago. After the 1871
fire had wiped out his business, he joined the Agency.

Pinkerton left a message at McParland's home, asking him to call
upon him. When he arrived, McParland was told of the nature of the
assignment, and informed that his status would not be injured if he
refused. McParland accepted.

On October 27, 1873, James McParland, posing as James McKenna,
a fugitive from a murder charge in Buffalo, set out for the Pennsylvania
coalfields. He hadn't shaved for ten days. A dirty reddish stubble covered
his jaws and chin. He wore stained old clothes, carried a worn carpet-
bag, and smoked a clay cutty pipe. For two and a half years he would be
engaged in an undertaking that, as J. Walter Coleman sums up in his
history of the Molly Maguires, "was of such a nature that even the most
calm recital of his deeds had all the aspects of the wildest fiction."

Pinkerton first assigned McParland to research the secret societies of
Ireland, their history, motivations, and activites. The tall, thin, red-
haired detective was given the order on October 8th. On the tenth he
turned in a long report—ten typewritten pages in the Reading Archives

—detailing the Molly Maguire movement. McParland's view of the Molly Maguire movement was of a clandestine religious society and not a protest movement organized to fight the landed gentry. Though there are errors in spelling and grammar, it demonstrates McParland's intelligence and ability.

McParland was then ordered to see Benjamin Franklin, Pinkerton's Philadelphia superintendent. There Franklin told McParland he was to send him as many reports as he could. Only the Pinkertons, Allan, William, and Robert, along with Bangs, Franklin, and Robert Linden, assistant superintendent in Chicago, knew McParland's identity. Gowen only knew his initials.

McParland moved from town to town, or "patches," as the smaller hamlets were called. Swatara, Tremont, Rausch Creek, Donaldson, and Tower City saw the lanky tramp. Stories spread from saloon to saloon of the happy-go-lucky redheaded tramp with the wonderful tenor voice, a bagful of songs, the ability to dance a lively jig, and a prodigious capacity for whiskey. McParland continued with his sensational exploits, disarming drunk-crazed ruffians, gracing social events, and gaining the confidence of all the better-known Irishmen in the region.

When he discovered that the Buckshots, or Mollies, were centered upon Pottsville, McParland moved eastward and finally arrived at the Sheridan House, owned by the giant Pat Dormer, which, as Pinkerton said, was the scene of many "drunken brawls and midnight orgies . . . three stories in height, having a long low extension in the rear, lightened by a sky light, and in which was located the well patronized ten-pin alley; the basement of the main structure was employed as a dining room, kitchen and laundry, and the first or business floor, a saloon. Just back of the latter was a card playing and bagatelle division. . . ."

McParland chose the place after he had heard that Dormer was a "Sleeper," another name for the Molly Maguires. He staged his entrance with the care of an actor making his first appearance in a play, bursting through the doors, to all appearances a wild-eyed drunk. A fiddler was sawing away in a dim corner, and McParland immediately leaped into an uproarious jig. Men who had turned from the bar with a frown of suspicion now slowly smiled. He drained a few glasses, then shrewdly lifted his strong tenor in a melancholy Irish air which he knew would capture them: the famous Molly Maguire ballad of Donegal.

McParland was accepted. He joined a euchre game, and then, in scene out of the Wild West, suddenly hurled back his chair, grabbed the hand of one of the players, Frazier, the "Pottsville Bully," and showed that the man had six cards instead of five. A fight followed in which McParland beat Frazier to his knees in five rounds, then shook hands, and invited him to the bar for a drink.

Dormer was won over. Upon questioning McParland, he heard the

"Muff" Lawler's barroom and residence, a Mollies' rendezvous, in Shenandoah, Schuylkill County, Pennsylvania. *From an old woodcut*

carefully coached story of James McKenna who had been forced to flee a murder charge in Buffalo, New York, and who had worked the mines in Colorado and had been a Union seaman during the war. "McKenna" also hinted that he had been a member of the Ancient Order of Hibernians in Ireland, but pointed out that it was so long ago, "I'm almost as ignorant as if I nivver had seen the inside of the affair."[10]

Dormer was captivated by the pugnacious, hard-drinking redhead. He invited McParland to stay, and the Pinkerton man accepted. Dormer's tavern was not only a center of Molly activities in the area but also a stopover point for Mollies from over the mountains, from Mahanoy City and Shenandoah. When McParland insisted that he must find work, Dormer gave him a letter to Muff Lawler, the leader, or "body master," of the Molly Maguires in Shenandoah, twenty miles north of Pottsville. From there he went on to Girardville to meet Jack Kehoe, owner of the Hibernian House, and one of the key figures in the Molly Maguires. Kehoe was then forty-three, a handsome, cold-eyed man who was related by marriage to many of the killers and gunmen of the organization.

"I see you know nothing of the present," Kehoe said when McParland failed to respond to a secret sign.

"It's a long time since I was within," McParland said, his throat suddenly dry under the searching eyes of the saloonkeeper. He knew Kehoe was no Dormer or Lawler.

McParland now realized he was on the brink of the inner circle of the Mollies. He was spending freely in Lawler's combination saloon and tavern, and as a cover story he hinted that his funds came from passing "the queer money." On some occasions he showed currency that he said was the work of a counterfeiter partner in upstate New York. This story, together with his magnetism and gaiety, his fine voice and repertoire of Irish airs, his ability to liven up the dim, smoky bars, and his fierce hatred of landlords and mine operators, made him a popular figure at Muff Lawler's place. He captivated Mrs. Lawler, a slattern who served the drinks. When the Lawlers invited him to stay, McParland accepted. From then on, Lawler's would be his base of operations.

McParland's most difficult task was to report to Franklin, who sent his material on to Pinkerton in Chicago. The hamlets were small, and everyone knew everyone else's moves. He had almost no privacy in the crowded, noisy Lawler tavern, and he shared his bedroom with another Molly. Franklin sent him postage, which he had to hide in his boot. He made his own ink from chimney soot and water until the day when his literacy helped him to overcome this obstacle. Lawler needed someone to write a letter, and when McParland acted as his scribe, the grateful body master allowed him to make ink with Mrs. Lawler's bluing.

McParland's reports were always sent secretly, at night, from other towns to which orders were addressed to him in code. In February, Lawler got McParland a job in the mines, and the detective was soon hauling twenty tons in a twenty-hour day at a wage of $10 a week. It was brutal, backbreaking work that left McParland so exhausted he could scarcely throw himself onto the hard pallet in the dirty bedroom that echoed with the drunken snoring of his bedmate.

Five days later his hands were mashed by a carload of coal, and he went back to the saloon to buy drinks for the regulars and entertain them with his singing and jigging. When McParland hinted to Lawler that he would like to join the Mollies, the body master held out some hope.

In February there was a murder in Centralia, and McParland was startled to learn that the Mollies suspected the Chain Gang, another secret society in the fields. By casual questioning he found that others existed: the Sheet Iron Gang, Iron Clads, or Iron Shields. All were splinter groups, none so tightly knit as the Mollies. He also learned that the men he drank with were all armed, either with revolvers, billies, or steel knuckles. Lawler's young nephew, Ed, was said to have shot and maimed four or five men. He was just twenty-one.

Finally, Lawler introduced McParland to Frank McAndrew, another miner, a man whom McParland sincerely liked and whom he viewed as above the ordinary brutal gunman of the Mollies. From McAndrew the detective learned that his name had been proposed as a member.

On April 13th the Mollies met at Lawler's, with McAndrew and McParland waiting downstairs. It was a tense night for the detective as he wondered if they were discussing his membership or arranging his execution as a spy. He had either broken through the gang or he had been found out and his number was up.

One of the members finally came down to lead him upstairs. There the oath of the Ancient Order of Hibernians was administered: "Friendship, unity and Christian charity . . . should I hear a member illy spoken of I will espouse his cause. . . ."

McParland took the oath on his knees, making the sign of the Cross and paying the treasurer $3. After he had received the signs, they all drank toasts to "the Emperor of France and Don Carlos of Spain." As McParland wrote triumphantly to Franklin, "The victory is won at last." [11]

But final victory was many grim months ahead. On May 4th, Lawler took McParland to see Barney Dolan, the highest Molly in the county, at Big Mine Run, "to get the goods" for the quarter.

The "goods" have been described by many writers as though they were a unique part of the Molly Maguires' history. Actually, they were the usual abracadabra of all secret societies, in some instances similar to the signs of the Knights of the Golden Circle, the fifth-column pro-Confederate organization of the Civil War.

Stopping off at a colliery, McParland got his first taste of Molly Maguire violence. While he and Lawler were drinking, a man came in armed with a gun, shouting that he intended to kill the saloonkeeper. Lawler fled, but McParland disarmed the man and stood him to a drink. It didn't do McParland any harm. Before nightfall another legend was being told about the laughing, singing, hard-drinking "Jim McKenna."

The unlimited drinking, late hours, poor food, and the terrible strain he was under began to tell on the Pinkerton operative. He came down with the "fever and ague." After a spell in bed, Lawler sent him to Wilkes Barre to "distribute the goods." He visited "bodies" in Kingston and Plymouth on the north bank of the Susquehanna, met dozens of members, and on the twenty-seventh, in Scranton, attended a "convention" of twenty-five body masters. Bishop William O'Hara of Scranton addressed the group, warning the lodge members that if they didn't mend their ways he would be forced to excommunicate them.

In September, 1873, the *Miners Journal* reported over three hundred pistols sold in Mahanoy City. The dull summer of 1874 seemed to have made the miners restless, and violent crimes mounted. A lit of "outrages" collected by Gowen for a legislative committee totaled ninety-four, including assault, arson, murder, robbery, and attempts to derail trains. Although Gowen drew up the list with a partisan viewpoint, it was no less indicative of the lawless conditions in the region. One murder that stirred the Mollies, and that would finally have an influence on McParland, was the slaying of a Molly by a Welshman, Gomer James, to whom we shall shortly return.

Economically, the coalfields were in dire trouble. The prices had slumped, primarily because of overproduction. Gowen, realizing this, gathered together the heads of the rail and coal companies in New York to fix coal prices at $5 a ton—certainly one of the first price-fixing devices in United States history. Gowen still had the WAB under his thumb, and in the spring of 1874, the union sullenly submitted to his demands.

Inside the Molly Maguires, McParland was listening to growing demands that Gomer Jones, who had killed the young Molly, be shot. Muff Lawler delayed naming an executioner. One night, McParland was stunned to discover that his name had been posted as body master of the Shenandoah lodge. The detective was worried: To take the post would make him part of the plan to commit murder. It took the Pinkerton man three days of wild drinking and talking to persuade the Mollies that he would be a better secretary and that McAndrew would be a better body master. The members at last saw the logic of his argument that he could read and write for McAndrew. This was another lucky stroke for McParland, who could now use his secretarial duties as a cover to write to Franklin in Philadelphia.

In McParland's reports and later testimony, one gets the impression that McAndrew was trying to do what he sincerely regarded as his duty. However, his intelligence was so limited that McParland found it difficult to teach him the simple prayers that opened the meeting.

As soon as McAndrew took the chair, pressure was put on him to kill Gomer James. McParland secretly advised Franklin in Philadelphia to have James taken in custody to save his life, or else urge him to leave the fields. McParland now was walking a tightrope: Too strong objections to murdering James could reach the suspicious Jack Kehoe and the least that could happen would be an order barring him from the inner councils where he now sat as an intimate of the men who ruled the society.

McAndrew hesitated; he plainly feared murder. He suggested that the killing be done by men "borrowed from another county." Letters came in from Kehoe asking why the "Gomer James removal hadn't been accomplished. McAndrew nervously had McParland reply.

Early in August, after Jack Kehoe had been elected as a body master, McParland and McAndrew had to visit him with the "goods." Not for the first time, McParland felt the chill of fear when he found Kehoe studying him while he suggested that McParland execute Gomer James. Again McParland went on a roaring drunk, with the hope of convincing Kehoe that McParland was not "the man for a clean job." On the way back to Shenandoah, McParland, shaky and hungover from both the whiskey and the strain, was horrified to have one of the Mollies whisper in his ear that he had better watch Jack Kehoe, a man who would slaughter his mother for more power among the Mollies.

In view of Kehoe's insistence that he would be a good man with a gun, McParland diversified his activities in the "patches" and villages to create a new image as a trainer of winning fighting cocks and pit dogs, a nurse and primitive doctor of gunshot wounds and knife cuts, a ready scribe with a fine hand. Through his secretarial duties he discovered that Kehoe was plotting to oust McAndrew for failure to murder James. In desperation, McParland again warned Franklin, and at last Gomer James vanished.

In September the detective stopped at the post office, where he was told by a clerk there was a letter for a James McParland that appeared to have been written by the same hand which had addressed his (McKenna's) letter.

"McParland?" McParland said, trying to keep his voice casual. "Oh, yeah. I know him. He's a friend of mine in Pottsville. I'll take it to him."

Miraculously, no one paid attention to the slip, but it shook McParland badly. He had seen the suspicion in Jack Kehoe's eyes, and the Gomer James murder plot hung over them all. By a ruse, McParland managed to slip into Philadelphia to see Pinkerton, who was shocked by his "lean and cadaverous face." Back in the fields, McParland discovered that one of his drinking companions had been brutally beaten for not obeying Kehoe's order to kill Gomer James. The inner tensions of the Mollies resulted in more violence as the weeks passed.

In October, a fire broke out in Mahanoy City, and the volunteer fire companies of the Mollies and their rivals, the Modocs, a gang of Welsh miners, rushed to the scene. A fight followed, and shots were fired. A town official was killed, and a Molly Maguire was charged with his murder. Feeling ran high in the coalfields. McParland's reports had Jack Kehoe raising a defense fund, with some of the money coming from the proceeds of robberies. The violence increased into November, with scarcely a day passing without a beating, assault, or shooting reported. The year turned with the fields alive with rumors that a strike was near. Gowen by now had organized the independent coal operators, and John Siney's WBA faced a solid bloc when he came up with new demands. Gowen and the owners' counteroffers shocked the miners: only pay cuts were placed on the table, with the threat that if a miner didn't accept he would be out of a job.

It was clear that the mine operators were committed to reducing wages in the coalfields and breaking the union. Pressure was put on the WBA when nonunion workers, the so-called northerly "Wyoming" miners, accepted the pay cuts and remained on their jobs. Miners in the Lehigh and southern fields now felt they had no alternative to striking. By Christmas week mines began closing; by the first of the year 1875, nearly all had suspended operations. One of the most critical strikes in the history of the Pennsylvania coalfields—the tragic "Long Strike"—had begun.

McParland's expense accounts show he was moving about the county in early January, 1875. When he attended the county Ancient Order of

Hibernians' convention in Pottsville to plan the St. Patrick's Day parade, he spent $6.20 buying drinks, a sizable amount of whiskey at the prices of the time.

McParland also sent on to Philadelphia an example of the "coffin notices" that were being posted on mine property. The WAB passed a formal resolution disavowing the "mean and cowardly acts," but the union could never shake off the shadow of the violence committed by the Mollies. That early winter McParland's reports told Gowen a great deal of what was going on among the strikers and inside the community. He sent on only what he saw or heard, without caring whether it would be palatable to the railroad president. One report bluntly informed Gowen that "all classes" of persons in the coal regions "are very much embittered toward your company and openly denounce the course you have taken." In the early days of the strike, he warned Gowen in February that violence against the operators was denounced but, as the strike continued, that "any violence against the operators was praised by all miners."

Jack Kehoe led his Mollies in the St. Patrick's Day parade after warning his men that he would stand for no drunkenness or disorder. This was an attempt, he told McParland, to "show the clergy and the public we don't deserve our bad name." But on the following Sunday, a Shenandoah priest read off a list of Mollies, and asked his congregation to pray for their lost souls. McParland, a deeply religious man, sat in the front pew and heard his name head the list.

This was not the first denunciation of the Molly Maguires from the pulpit. In a recently discovered letter, McParland disclosed that Archbishop Wood

> not only ex-communicated every member of the Molly Maguires that claimed to be a Catholic, but also denied to them the privilege of being buried in a Catholic cemetery. As evidence that Archbishop Wood's edict was carried out, I would simply cite one of many instances, a Molly named Brennan died in Shamokin. Father Koch (a local priest) refused to have him buried in the Catholic cemetery. Pat Hestor, [later executed] broke down the fence to get into the cemetery. The driver of the hearse refused to drive into the cemetery. Hestor drove in himself, assaulted Father Koch, in fact threw him out of the cemetery, and buried Brennan. . . .

Another example of how Archbishop Wood's order was carried out, McParland revealed, was the refusal of the Shenandoah pastor to accept Christmas or Easter offerings from known members of the Molly Maguires. "In fact he refused my offering," McParland wrote. "The priests of the diocese, if they knew it, refused to allow a Molly Maguire to stand sponsor for a child. I know this to be a fact because Father O'Reilly (of

Shenandoah) refused to allow me to stand sponsor for a child of Joe McCue, a Molly Maguire. . . ." [12]

But the denunciation of his Church and the pleading and warnings of the priests in the valley did not frighten Jack Kehoe. It was more important that he had been elected high constable of his home town of Girardville, which, as Allan Pinkerton reported to Gowen, gave him the power of arrest and custody of prisoners.

In an uneasy April, with the union still holding out, McParland found himself in another precarious situation. The Shenandoah Mollies came to him with a plan to blow up the railroad bridge on the Catawissa and Williamsport branch of the Reading to shut off the shipment of non-union coal. They insisted that McParland lead the expedition.

McParland was faced with the choice of committing a felony or refusing to do so, in which instance he would put himself under suspicion. In a dramatic scene, McParland and the conspirators met late at night on top of a mountain. It was a windy April, and the stark trees bent under the gusts, the faces of the miners tight and bitter in the wavering shadows of their lamps. McParland dramatically revealed that he had "absolute knowledge" that the railroad police had the bridge under constant surveillance and that it would be suicide for them to attempt to dynamite the structure. One can almost sense his relief when the Mollies, swayed by his vehemence, finally agreed. Less than a week later, a car loaded with iron slag was uncoupled, and the runaway only narrowly missed a passenger train. McParland worked steadily on the case until he finally got two of the Mollies to admit that they had uncoupled the car. The Pinkerton operative had solved his first Molly Maguire crime.

But admission by the Molly Maguires of a crime to McParland was of no legal use unless he could take the stand and testify in court. From the very beginning, Pinkerton had insisted that McParland never be named, not even to Gowen. At a meeting in March, McParland had also pointed out to Ben Franklin, the Philadelphia superintendent, that their lines of communication must be shortened. Even if he sent Franklin a telegram, it took hours for an answer to arrive, and was extremely dangerous. McParland had brought this problem up several times, and emphasized it at their March rendezvous.

After Pinkerton had received McParland's reports of the two Mollies who had confessed to him that they had uncoupled the car, he decided on a new move. In April, Pinkerton met with Gowen in the Philadelphia office of the Agency, and proposed, as Gowen recalled, "a flying squadron" of police to cover the coalfields. They would be ostensibly "coal and iron police," composed of six Pinkerton operatives with an equal number of picked railroad men, all under a Pinkerton lieutenant. The latter would be in direct touch with McParland, and between the two this mobile police force could be on the spot when a crime was committed to gather legal evidence for a conviction. Gowen quoted Pinkerton at the meeting:

"There would be but little difficulty in breaking off this association and when the arrest of a gang was made, the names and localities of all the known MM's in the County should be published and thus strike terror within their midst." [13]

Gowen agreed to the plan, and Pinkerton sent for Robert J. Linden, who had been his assistant superintendent in Chicago since 1871. Pinkerton described Linden as "about forty years of age, tall, powerful in frame and physical organization, with black, close-cropped hair, whiskers and mustaches of the same texture and color, blue eyes, which were expressive of confidence—just the kind of orbs to win the confidence of others."

On May 6th, Linden was inducted, along with another Pinkerton operative, into the "coal and iron police" at Pottsville. The next day McParland and Linden met secretly at Ashland, twenty miles west of Shenandoah. While Linden's presence gave him an ally, it also increased McParland's personal risk. However their meetings might be planned, there was always the possibility of a mischance, one human error that could result in McParland's murder.

On May 17th, McParland found himself in another desperate situation: McAndrew resigned as body master to go to Wilkes Barre to find work, leaving the detective in charge of the Shenandoah Mollies. In addition to finding himself leading a gang of cutthroats whose deeds were becoming more violent as the days passed, McParland also missed Mc-Andrew was an ally who agreed with the logic of his arguments. Without McAndrew, the pressure to go along with murder, robbery, and arson would be that much greater.

Now the Mollies came up with another plan: McParland was to write a letter to the company demanding that Gomer James be returned as watchman at the mines, and pointing out that he had proved himself a brave man, and, in addition, had reduced petty thefts. This letter was to go through the colliery superintendent and through channels to Philadelphia. But once again the twisted nature of the Maguire men came to McParland's aid. When Jack Kehoe sent for the detective, McParland feared it would be an absolute order for murder. To his surprise, Kehoe brought him to the kitchen at the rear of his bar, and vehemently told him that we was sick of being dictated to by the Shenandoah men and that the James murder had to be put off.

McParland had just given a silent heave of relief, when Kehoe went on to advise him that the English and the Welsh in Mahanoy City were forbidding the Mollies to enter the public square. To offset this order, he proposed to arm all the Mollies and conduct a reign of terror, "shooting down anyone we meet, sparing women and children." For this purpose he was calling a meeting in Mahanoy City, and he wanted McParland to summon the other body masters. When they met, the murder of still another man had become the principal item on the paranoiac Kehoe's agenda: McParland was given three days to arrange the death of a man named Bully Bill Thomas.

At this meeting, as McParland later described it in his court testimony, one of the Mollies was called to the room to show the others the bullet holes in his coat that he said had been the result of Bully Bill's erratic aim. McParland and two others were assigned the task of murdering Thomas, with Kehoe cold-bloodedly advising them that "the best plan was to get a couple of men well armed and go right up to him on the street and shoot him down in daylight or any time we could get him." [14]

Meanwhile the "Long Strike" was bringing tragedy to the coalfields. Traditional "credit stores" which in the past had taken strike risks as part of their business now began to refuse further credit to the miners, even though the union had passed a resolution that the store owners would be paid as soon as the strike was over. The past threat of starvation was now a reality. Coffin notices were commonplace, and in May, 1875, McParland was sending daily reports to Assistant Superintendent Robert Linden of planned acts of sabotage. Though the plots to blow up bridges, burn down coal depots, and derail trains never materialized, Linden took no chances: Every report he received from McParland was checked out, and precautions were taken.

In May it was obvious that the strike had failed. Desperate union leaders met with the operators to lay before them a plan that all sliding-scale and contract wages be eliminated in favor of a flat weekly wage of $15 for six eight-hour days. The operators, who knew they had won, rejected the terms. A few weeks later, the mineowners announced that they intended to reopen the mines, and they made it clear they would offer protection to any miner who wanted to work. On June 1, 1875, when the huge West Shenandoah Colliery was opened in Reading, the strike died with a whimper.

McParland's next report to Linden warned that a raid was to be made on the colliery and the "black legs" who had come to work. Nothing happened immediately, but as Linden was preparing to move out with his eighteen-man force of 'iron and coal police," he received word that a mob was moving in on the Shenandoah. Early in the morning of June 3rd, the shouting, angry miners swarmed down out of the hills and onto mine property. Leading the wide-eyed men who brandished clubs, iron bars, and pistols was McParland. In one hand he waved a large hickory club; a worn gray coat flapped about his knees, and two pistols were tucked into his belt. Tugging at the rope he held was a vicious bulldog. Facing the raised rifles and pistols of Linden and his men, the mob hesitated, then retreated, with McParland shouting curses over his shoulder.

Inflamed by liquor and emotions, the miners marched into Mahanoy City to be joined by striking miners from the Hazleton mines. The mob grew so large that store owners hastily locked their doors. Shootings followed, and Governor John F. Hartranft summoned the troops. Muskets and bayonets restored an uneasy calm. By the first week in June, the executive board of the WAB, in a frantic effort to save the union, appealed to Gowen for a compromise, but the triumphant Reading president refused. Though the power of the WAB was broken, the Mollies emerged stronger than ever.

The Bully Bill Thomas murder still ranked high on Kehoe's plans. When four armed gunmen appeared, McParland was able to persuade them to forget the shooting of Thomas because the city was filled with troops. "Any one of us is worth fifty of Bully Bills," he told them.

Fortunately, McAndrew appeared to take over. The furious drinking and the strain had hewn flesh from McParland's already thin frame. He had a severe cold and became ill. On the night of June 27th, three gunmen appeared at his boardinghouse. Bill Thomas was to be killed the next day.

Early in the morning of June 28, 1875, McParland was summoned to Ringtown Mountain, where three Molly gunmen told him how they had killed Thomas as he saddled a horse. When McParland brought McAndrew to the mountain hideout with bread, cheese and a pint of whiskey, the trio repeated their story.

Pinkerton's critics and the attorneys for the defense made much of the fact that McParland did not warn Pinkerton, Franklin, or Gowen, nor did he apprehend the gunmen in the act or try to warn the victim that his life was in danger. As Coleman insists in his history of the Molly Maguires, "Thomas was apparently to be sacrificed if the evidence is correct, in order that the men who plotted against him could be convicted of murder instead of the lesser crime of assault and conspiracy."

McParland's defense was simply self-survival. As he testified during the famous Molly Maguire trials, he was not only ill but his own life was in danger. With Molly gunmen dogging his footsteps, "it was as much as my life was worth to contact or have communicated the facts to Captain Linden." [15]

However, Bully Bill Thomas wasn't dead; one bullet had gone through his neck, narrowly missing the jugular vein; another chipped a rib to come out the other side. Miraculously, he survived. But the Molly Maguire gunmen were successful the following month. On July 5, 1875, they shot down Benjamin Yost and traded shots with Barney McCarron. Yost, a German, had had trouble with James Kerrigan, the body master of Tamaqua, and McCarron, an Irishman, also had gained the enmity of the Mollies. Both composed the police force of the community. Yost was murdered as he climbed a ladder to put out a streetlamp. McCarron exchanged shots with the killers but was unharmed. This time McParland knew nothing of the shooting. After the Yost murder, he reported to

Franklin that Kehoe and the other Molly leaders were beginning to sense a hardening of the public's attitude, even on the part of the Irish, toward the Mollies.

McAndrew now also was proving to be a burden to McParland. He insisted on the killing of a mine boss who was anti-Irish and refused to hire Mahanoy City men after the mines had been reopened. This time McParland managed to get word to Franklin, and the boss disappeared. The increasing threats McParland overheard were now becoming a major problem. Some were wild, some so serious they couldn't be brushed aside. But all added to the strain and tension under which McParland was working.

But he knew that one threat was very real: Jack Kehoe's determination that Gomer James, who had been brought back to his watchman's job, be killed. Again McParland sent word to Franklin, who notified Gowen. This time, the Reading president did not act.

After the Yost killing, McParland visited Tamaqua to learn the details and motivation for the Yost murder. A long report was sent on to Franklin. But because Jimmy Kerrigan, who was the triggerman, was absent, the Pinkerton operative waited—and for the first time romance enters the grim and violent story.

McParland desperately needed not only Kerrigan's confession of his part in the Yost murder but also his corroboration. Some months earlier, at a wedding, he had met Mary Ann Higgins, Kerrigan's sister-in-law, who lived with the Kerrigans. McParland liked this vivacious blue-eyed girl, and began "sparking," as he called it. According to his later testimony, it was a coldly calculated move to win a murder conviction: "It was not for the sake of throwing off suspicion on Kerrigan's part that I made love to his sister-in-law but to throw off any suspicion there might be as to my object in stepping around Tamaqua." [16]

While McParland "sparked"the pretty Mary Ann, he was also hunting for the Yost murder weapon. Kerrigan was back now, and he readily accepted the jovial, well-thought-of Jim McKenna who was holding his sister-in-law's hand on the porch these hot nights. McParland, who was armed with a .32, finally persuaded Kerrigan to show his own .32, which he admitted was the one "that fixed Yost." Kerrigan then boasted of the murder. Under McParland's casual questioning he soon spilled the intimate details. But there was also the problem of independent corroboration. On several occasions McParland managed to get Kerrigan out for a walk in the Tamaqua cemetery where Linden crouched behind some bushes, but the scheme never worked. All Linden got was numerous mosquito bites.

Then, in August, the tension in Girardville, Shenandoah, and Mahanoy City exploded in an orgy of murder and assault. McParland dropped Mary Ann's hand to hurry back. He found that not only had the justice of the peace been killed while his young daughter begged the gunmen not to hurt her father but also that Gomer James was now a corpse.

McParland quickly learned that the Molly Maguire gunman Tom Hurley, ringleader in the Bully Bill Thomas shooting, had killed James at a fireman's picnic. There was almost a slipup when someone saw McParland talking to Linden. The Pinkerton detective denied it, and Hurley told him that if he found Linden "speaking around Shenandoah" he would kill him himself. When McParland later repeated this threat to Linden, the Pinkerton superintendent had a choice bit of news himself: The Welsh and English had posted McParland as the next Molly to be murdered if anything else happened in the county. The only police action taken in the whole violent week was by Jack Kehoe. That incongruous high constable arrested the Molly who had murdered the justice of the peace, then let him go and arrested the killer's brother. When the killer fled the state, Kehoe released the brother "for lack of evidence."

This was an example of the local police action the Pinkertons had to contend with. McParland now had pinpointed the murderers of Yost, but Allan Pinkerton advised Gowen that they had insufficient evidence to get a conviction. The only evidence could come from McParland, and there were scores of Mollies to take the stand and deny his story. He had to await one more break, which now was not far off. But before it came, three men would die.

On August 25th a wild convention of the Mollies took place in a Tamaqua saloon where Jack Kehoe complimented Tom Hurley for "a neat job" of killing Gomer James. When Hurley demanded a reward for the murder, a Molly from Lost Creek stood up to charge that one of his gunmen had actually done the job. Incredibly, cold-bloodedly, Kehoe ordered that the "claims" be arbitrated. McParland and another body master were to act as arbitrators.

On his return to Shenandoah, McParland discovered that a Molly gunman now shared his room. The Molly casually explained a Smith and Wesson pistol on the washstand by saying that he was staying over because he had to go out to kill a mine boss that morning. While McParland sat on the edge of his bed, two other killers came into his room, and the three argued the best way to kill their victim. McParland tried to get word to Franklin or Linden, but the gunman clung to him. By the time he finally got a message to Philadelphia, the three killers had riddled the mine boss. A young miner who was a boarder in the house was also murdered; his crime was simply walking the boss to the colliery.

McParland had scarcely received the news when he was in the midst of another tight situation. He himself was assigned to kill a mine boss. With the other Mollies named to the killing, he took the train to Tamaqua to get pistols and ammunition. During a waiting period he managed to get off a long report to Franklin. For the first time McParland introduced the labor question, this time warning that if the union were completely broken in the fields it would mean only more violence and murder. Though the report certainly wasn't to Gowen's liking, Pinkerton ordered Franklin to send it along anyway.

Events now moved fast. Young Kerrigan, Mary Ann's brother-in-law and the killer of Yost, the policeman, became impatient with the officially designated killers—including McParland—who were assigned to do in the mine boss, so he shot the victim on the station steps of the Tamaqua depot. Kerrigan and two others were captured and jailed.

McParland was bitterly attacked at the trial for his failure to notify Pinkerton, Linden, or Franklin. Again his defense was survival: "In doing so I ran the danger of losing my life," he said. McParland's defense is unassailable. Had he tipped his hand, any one of the killers would have been suspicious. He could also prove that in early July he had warned Franklin and Gowen that the mine boss was the next one marked for death and that for a time security had been tightened about the boss. Only when it was relaxed had the Molly gunmen slipped into town and shot down their victim.

It was a wearying period for Allan Pinkerton. His health was precarious; he was beset on all sides by the problems of his Agency; and some of his most trusted employees, such as G. Thiel, who had served with him during the Civil War, had left to form their own detective agencies. To Pinkerton, this was unpardonable. With typical unreasonableness he ignored their long records of devotion to his firm. His Agency was also under attack by the country's most powerful newspapers, including the New York *Times,* for the attack on the Samuels farmhouse. Added to Pinkerton's burdens was the Molly Maguire investigation and the unalterable fact that for all the dangers and expenses incurred, the evidence McParland had gathered was still not enough to gain felony convictions.

As in Clay County, the law officers were either cowed, corrupt, or in sympathy with the Mollies. But unlike the farmers of Clay County, the residents of the minefields were growing bolder and more outspoken. Vigilante talk was in the air. In a letter to Bangs, Pinkerton sympathized with, if he did not actually advocate, vigilante action in the Molly Maguire country—surely a strange philosophy for a man who for so long had pictured himself as a defender of law and order.

Pinkerton told Bangs he had called in Frank Warner, his Chicago superintendent, and his son William to read McParland's reports and review his decision: "Whether they believed in the action I was determined to take or not, they assured me that it was perfectly right and they would act, disregarding all consequences."

Pinkerton's letter also reveals that there were other operatives now in the field who, Pinkerton assured Bangs, were all right, but "beer had been the cause" of all their trouble. Then came this incredible paragraph:

> The M.M. [Molly Maguires] are a species of thugs. You have probably read of them in India. Their religion taught them to murder, to make out their victims, and their plans by which they were to strike, and not to divulge anything even if they are brought to the stake. So it is with the M.M.'s. They are bound to stick by their oath and to carry out their revenge. He who they think does a wrong is marked out and he must die. It is impossible to believe that a jury in the mining districts would not give a verdict of guilty against the M.M.'s should they be brought to trial but I believe that someone on the jury would hang on and get the guilty men to escape. The only way then to pursue them as I see is to treat them as the Renos were treated in Seymour, Indiana. After they were done away the people improved wonderfully and Seymour is quite a town. Let Linden get up a vigilante committee. It will not do to get many men, but let him get those who are prepared to take fearful revenge on the M.M.'s. I think it would open the eye of all the people and then the M.M.'s would meet with their just deserts. It is awful to see men doomed to death, it is horrible. Now there is but one thing to be done, and that is, get up an organization if possible, and when ready for action pounce upon the M.M.'s when they are in full blast, take the fearful responsibility and disperse.
>
> This is the best advice I can give you. I would not keep this letter in Philadelphia, but if you want to preserve it send it over to New York. Place all confidence in Mr. Linden, he is a good man, and he understands what to do.
>
> If you think it is advisable, bring the matter before Mr. Gowen but none other than him.

The letter ends on this note: "In case of failure, bail may be required. Mr. Gowen will be able to furnish it by his understanding it." [17]

Evidently Bangs or the calmer Robert Pinkerton, who was in charge of New York, made sure no one followed this violent advice. In Shenandoah, McParland heard about the vigilante talk in the local papers and in the barrooms. The Mollies sneered at the threats, he said, promising to sack and burn the companies if the vigilantes rode. McParland himself was concerned by such talk because Linden again told him there were mutterings in Tamaqua about McParland, whom some people were calling "a bad Molly."

While Pinkerton's suggestion of vigilante action was shocking, his prediction to Bangs did come true. In October, there was another violent night when assaults and shootings took place in and around Shenandoah. The sheriff's office ordered a curfew, and asked for a posse to help him enforce it, but most of the law officers in Shenandoah were Irishmen who openly refused to arrest their countrymen.

McParland slipped out of the coal towns to meet Bangs in New York, where he compiled a huge report on the Mollies, listed the members by names, and noted their crimes. There were 374 names. An undated handbill lists the names and the crimes of the Mollies. Whether it was printed by the Agency is not known. But as Linden's reports reveal in October, he was touring the coal towns "with the view of giving necessary information to the leading citizens advising them as to who the parties are who have committed the recent assassinations." Was this in line with Pinkerton's suggestion to Bangs of vigilante action?

There was now talk in Shenandoah of an informer among the Mollies. Muff Lawler, McParland's old friend, insisted there was "a screw loose somewhere."

Then, in the early morning of Friday, December 10, 1875, masked men dressed in oilskins broke into the large duplex home of Widow Margaret O'Donnell in Wiggans Patch. After her husband died, Mrs. O'Donnell took into her home her married daughter, Ellen McAllister, her husband, Charles, and their infant son, and her two unmarried sons, James "Friday" O'Donnell and Charles O'Donnell. That night there were also four paying guests in the house: Tom Murphy, John Purcell, James Blair, and James McAllister, the brother of Charles.

Mrs. O'Donnell awakened when the vigilantes smashed in the kitchen door. Charles McAllister jumped out of bed and ran to the cellar. His wife followed, although McAllister warned her to go back to bed. One of the gunmen fired at the woman's white-clad figure framed in the doorway, killing her instantly. Two men burst into Mrs. O'Donnell's bedroom and pistol-whipped her. They tied up Purcell and Blair and threatened to kill Murphy. James McAllister was dragged downstairs, but fought his way free and ran into the yard. Though he was wounded in a fusillade of shots, he managed to make his way into the nearby woods. "Friday" O'Donnell also escaped, but his brother, Charles, was riddled with bullets as he tried to get out of bed. As the Shenandoah *Herald* reported, O'Donnell's head was crushed by "no less than fifteen bullets." [18]

Word of the murders reached McParland in Pottsville. That same day, Friday, December 10, he dashed off a bitter and sometimes inaccurate letter to Franklin. It read:

> This morning at 8 A.M. I heard that a crowd of masked men had entered Mrs. O'Donnell's house, Wiggans Patch, and had killed James O'Donnell alias Friday, Charles O'Donnell and James McAllister, also Mrs. McAllister whom they took outside the house and shot. Now as for the McDonnells I am satisfied they got their just deserves. I reported what those men were. I gave all information about them so clear, that the courts could have taken hold of their case at any time, but the witnesses were too cowardly to do so. I have also in the interest of God and humanity notified you months before some of the outrages

were committed, still the authorities took no hold of the matter. Now I wake up this morning and find that I am the murderer of Mrs. McAllister. What had a woman to do in this case? Did the Sleepers (Molly Maguires) in their worst time shoot down women? If I was not here, the Vigilante committee would not know who was guilty. And when I find them shooting women in their thirst for blood, I hereby tender my resignation to take effect as soon as this message is received. If there is another job in the Agency you may want me for I will accept it. Otherwise I will go home to Chicago as I am sure I am sold anyway by some of these men on the committee and it is through them the Hon. James R. Reilly has got his information that something is wrong. Now no doubt there will be man for man taken and I do not see which side will have the Sympathizers. As for myself I will remain here until you dispatch for me to go down which I hope will be as soon as this letter is received, it is not cowardice that makes me resign but just let them have it now. I will no longer interfere as I see one is the same as the other and I am not going to be accessory to the murder of women and children. Direct your dispatch to me at the Northwestern Hotel as it is not worth while leaving for a boarding house at the present when I am going away anyway. At 10:00 A.M. I got your letter and contents noted but as you see this alters states of affairs in general hence there is no further use of comments. Of course you may expect burning and murdering all over. Where we have had a little quietness and now innocent men of both parties will suffer and I am sure the Sleepers will not spare the women, so long as the Vigilantes have shown the example.

Respectfully submitted,
J McP
L.[19]

It is a remarkable letter written in the heat of indignation. In addition to revealing McParland's character, it also refutes the critics of the Pinkerton's work in the Molly Maguire investigations, who insist that his operatives did not submit information to the authorities. It also disposes of the many-times-repeated charge that McParland was an agent-provocateur.

Franklin's reply to Allan Pinkerton in Chicago said in part:

> This morning I received a report from "Mac" of which I sent you a copy, and in which he seems to be very much surprised at the shooting of these men; and he offers his resignation. I telegraphed "Mac" to come here from Pottsville as I am anxious to satisfy him that we had nothing to do with what has taken place in regard to these men. Of course I do not want "Mac" to resign.[20]

McParland's letter also raises the question. What vigilante action was he referring to? Was McParland aware of the inflammatory letter Allan Pinkerton had sent to Bangs in New York? Who were the killers in oilskins who left the O'Donnell house a bloody shambles? Without pardoning Pinkerton for his shocking suggestion, there were others in the Molly Maguire country who were openly advocating night riders and the rope to bring law and order to the fields, and this included the editor of the influential *Herald* and the publisher of the *Miners Journal*. There was already a citizens' committee in Tamaqua, and Captain Linden's "coal and iron police" who had faced the howling mob outside the gates of the colliery knew at first hand the violence and seething hate in the fields.

The murders also took on another shading during the impromptu coroner's jury inquest held in the O'Donnell living room by the Mahanoy City coroner. According to the reporter for the Shenandoah *Herald,* when the cornoner asked Mrs. O'Donnell if she had recognized any of the killers, Jack Kehoe rushed into the room and warned the witness, "I order you not to answer that question." The startled coroner demanded to know by what authority Kehoe issued this order. The Molly Maguire leader replied that he was the brother-in-law of both Charles O'Donnell and Ellen McAllister, through his wife, another of Mrs. O'Donnell's daughters. Then Kehoe said mysteriously, "This business will be settled in another manner."

Dewees, the earliest and one of the most reliable historians of the Molly Maguires, quoted John J. Slattery, who turned state's evidence in a later Molly Maguire murder trial, to the effect that the murders were committed at the order of Kehoe, after Charles O'Donnell "became restless and disturbed" over the part he had taken in a double Molly Maguire slaying. Dewees wrote: "O'Donnell's uneasiness remained, and it was feared by Kehoe that through him all the circumstances connected with the murder would be exposed. Slattery understood the state of affairs and knew of Kehoe's feelings."

Dewees then described how, on the morning of the day the murders had taken place, Slattery met a Molly gunman who told him that he was going to Mahanoy City that day and that a "job was to be done in Wiggans Patch that night." [21]

Reports were also published locally and in Philadelphia that the O'Donnells had been involved in a "clan fight." In Boston the influential Boston *Pilot* reported that the shooting "grew out of a previous shooting affairs, the facts of which the O'Donnells were aware of, and it is thought the murderers found it necessary to silence them for fear of damaging evidence in their possession." [22]

Vigilantes, Kehoe's gunmen, clan killers, or murderers seeking to silence potential witnesses—it is impossible to pinpoint them almost a century later. The fading lines of McParland's letter remain tantalizingly incomplete.

The murders in the O'Donnell house shook the Mollies. The realization that a traitor among them had put together a list of their membership and their crimes on a handbill was a shattering thought for all of them. McParland, who evidently had been persuaded to remain in the fields, reported: "The Mollies are now confident that there is a traitor in their midst."

Then Mrs. O'Donnell, the mother, swore that the leader of the murderers was Frank Wenrich, her butcher in Mahanoy City. Wenrich, a "most respectable man" in the eyes of the Philadelphia newspapers, was a first lieutenant in the National Guard. Charged with homicide, he was released on bail.

Kehoe was loud in his denunciation of the butcher. When feeling ran high, Wenrich was removed to Pottsville to a stronger jail. A few days later, during a habeas corpus plea by Wenrich's attorney, Mrs. O'Donnell was asked to identify Wenrich as one of the killers. After she had done so, the district attorney abruptly demanded to know if she had made the identification on the orders of Kehoe. The flustered widow looked frightened, then slowly answered, "Yes." The court promptly released Wenrich on nominal bail, and the butcher returned to Mahanoy City. Kehoe's attempt to send an innocent man to the gallows appears to strengthen the suspicion that he was involved in the murder of his wife's brothers.

Christmas and then another year turned for McParland in the Molly Maguire country.

The drunken singing, fiddling, and jigging that ushered in New Year's Eve had barely died away when shots cracked again. This time the target was a Molly gunman whom McParland had named in his reports as one of Constable Yost's killers. The ashen-faced Molly poked his fingers through the bullet hole in his coat for the benefit of the silent, apprehensive Mollies gathered in Kehoe's saloon.

It was evident that the hunters were now the hunted.

Then came the trials of Jimmy Kerrigan, Mike Doyle, and other Mollies for the murder of John Jones, a mine superintendent, on September 3, 1875. A severance had been granted, and the gunman Doyle, with the battered, scarred face of a punch-drunk, bare-fisted fighter, went on trial in Mauch Chunk. It was January, 1876, with Doyle's fate a burning question for all of them. It was the first time the law had locked in combat with the Mollies. In February the jury returned a verdict of guilty. Doyle was the first Molly to be convicted. Twenty-two days later a shocked, silent courtroom heard the judge sentence Doyle to be hanged.

But Doyle's sentence was lost in the uproar that greeted the latest news: Jim Kerrigan, McParland's companion in those futile twilight strolls in the lonely cemetery, and brother-in-law of Mary Ann, had turned informer. The news hit the coalfields with the impact of a bomb. In the smoky, foul saloons men stared silently into their glasses of cheap whiskey and beer or passed the news in frightened whispers, while inside his cell Kerrigan detailed the secrets of the Mollies. In Chicago,

Allan Pinkerton was jubilant. This was the big break they were all waiting for—now the Yost and other murders had corroborative state's witness.

As the names, dates, and other details spilled from Kerrigan's lips, Linden was ordered by Pinkerton to form a posse of lawmen and bring in the accused. In February, Molly Maguire gunmen were quietly plucked from their towns, one by one, and taken to the Pottsville jail. This time the local police, some Mollies themselves, never knew what had happened until a frantic mother, a father, or wife rushed into the sheriff's office demanding action.

There was talk about the Mollies storming the Mauch Chunk jail to free Kerrigan and the others, but it was all talk. In reality most of them were packing their carpetbags. As the Shenandoah *Herald* said contemptuously, "The exodus of the scum fills the air."

In February, Kerrigan had given them enough to solve the brutal murders of a mine boss, Thomas Sanger, and his boarder, William Uren, on September 1, 1875, at Raven Run. Linden gathered another posse, and four Molly gunmen were taken into custody.

McParland, meanwhile, decided to continue sparking Mary Ann Higgins, and dropped by the Kerrigan house with a pint in his pocket for "the old gentleman." He found the family gathered around the kitchen table, plotting how to manufacture evidence that Kerrigan had taken part in some of the murders. The scene, which could have been taken from any Liam O'Flaherty play of the 1916 Rebellion, was vivid evidence how the traditional Irish hatred of an informer had split one family in the fields so drastically it was plotting to send its own son to the gallows.

Mary Ann had no time for sparking this day, she told McParland. She was full of conspiracies. One plan she had was to get some shells from the revolver used in one of the murders and plant them in Kerrigan's drawer. "She was positive they would correspond with the one found in Yost's body," McParland reported. But even more startling was the news Mary Ann whispered to McParland: After Linden's posse had picked up the four Mollies for the Raven Run murders, some of the Mollies were saying that he—Jim McKenna—was the informer in their midst.

As the days passed, McParland began to realize that the deadly Jack Kehoe and his men were carefully putting together pieces of the jigsaw; and the picture that was forming as the pieces slipped into place was that of the gaunt face of the jovial, brawling Jim McKenna, whom they had elevated to their inner councils.

What happened in the weeks to come is an incredible story of McParland's courage and bravado, surely one of the most thrilling real-life stories in the history of American crime.[23]

It began on February 23, when he met Frank McAndrew, his friend and the Shenandoah body master, who told him gravely that the boys

were making bets that he, Jim McKenna, was the informer. Kehoe, he
said, had warned all the men "to beware of me, I was a detective, that
such was the report, that he Jack Kehoe had it from responsible
sources."

Instead of fleeing, McParland went to Girardville, strode into the
Hibernian House, and faced Kehoe in his own bar.

"What about these reports?" he demanded.

Kehoe shrugged. "Well," he said, "I have heard them, and I heard it
some time ago."

McParland replied angrily: "Well, I want someone to prove it. I am
willing to let the Society try me. I will stand a trial and find out. The
man that is lying about me, I will make him suffer, no doubt, to say I
am a detective."

Then Kehoe told him he had heard the story from a conductor who
had called him into a baggage car and told him. McParland again denied it, and insisted he be tried. Kehoe reluctantly promised to have a
county convention try him.

"Name the time and the place," McParland snapped.

Kehoe did: it would be in March, in Ferguson's Hall, Shenandoah.
Then Kehoe went behind the bar, and came back with some paper and
a pen. He tried to write, but couldn't. He handed the pen to McParland. "I'm too nervous to write," said the so-called King of the Mollies.
"You sign my name to each of the body masters in the county."

McParland took the pen and paper, went upstairs to the second floor,
wrote to the body masters, then addressed the envelopes. He returned
to the bar, showed Kehoe the letters, and both of them sealed, stamped,
and mailed them.

The incredible McParland stayed overnight with Kehoe. Back in Pottsville, another Molly leader told him bluntly that he was a detective and
that the Mollies were seeking action against him.

"Don't worry about me," the Pinkerton operative replied, "I will take
action against myself. There will be a fair trial."

Later, Kehoe came to Pottsville and told McParland that there was a
secret movement of over two thousand men who had banded together
for the purpose of destroying the Ancient Order of Hibernians and that
he had positive proof a detective was among them. "This detective," he
said, coldly studying McParland, "even gets money to go around and
spend amongst them to find out all their secrets, and then turn around
and either send them to the penitentiary or hang them."

The next day still another Molly bitterly accused McParland of being
a detective and said the new word was that he wanted to get them all together so Linden's posse would take them all in one sweep.

Next, McParland saw Linden, and begged him to keep out of sight
for a while. With an air of almost unbelievable self-confidence, he told
the superintendent to advise Allan Pinkerton that he was confident he

could "fight them right through and make them believe I am no detective."

On his return to Shenandoah, he caught his first glimpse of a stalking gunman. In one of the railroad cars, Jack Kehoe's wife suddenly became evasive and nervous. When he swung down at the Shenandoah station, he found it deserted in the harsh February twilight. This was the first time since he had been in the field that there weren't six or seven Mollies led by McAndrew to meet him "and give us the news." As he walked down the streets, McParland's hand crept inside his coat and touched the cold butt of his navy Colt. In a saloon, one of McParland's old hangouts, the saloonkeeper tried to pour a bottle of porter, but McParland noticed that his hand shook "as if with the ague." Later, McParland passed an old friend who stared right through him.

When he saw McAndrew, the body master was so vague about the trial that McParland was now sure he was ready to "get the black spot," the traditional mark for murder. That night he avoided his usual route, and instead slipped down the backpaths and side streets to his boarding-house. He stayed awake all night, his revolver near by, weary, exhausted, his nerves wound tight as a watch spring, sitting in the cold, dark wretched bedroom, staring through the tattered curtains out at the moonlight.

The next day, the body masters arrived, some drunk or feigning drunkenness, all armed. One man looked unbelieving when he saw McParland.

"My God, man, don't you know why you are here?" he asked McParland. When the detective said "No," the man hurried to the back of the saloon. When McAndrew arrived, they had some drinks, and McAndrew, visibly nervous, insisted they go for a ride in a "cutter" (sleigh). As they raced across the deep snow, McAndrew told him that in a cutter following them were two gunmen who had been assigned to kill him.

"Have you got your guns?" McAndrew, asked tersely.

"I have," McParland replied.

"Well, so have I," the body master said, "and I will lose my life for you. I do not know whether you are a detective or not, but I do not know anything against you. I always knew you were doing right and I will stand by you. Why don't they try you fair?"

Later, McAndrew told McParland that Kehoe had insisted on his death. He quoted Kehoe as saying, "McAndrew, for God's sake have him killed this night, or he will hang half the people in Schuylkill County."

"And what did you say to that?" McParland asked.

"I consented," was the reply.

The first plan of murder had twelve to fourteen Mollies gathered at the depot. They were to be armed with bars, axes, and tomahawks, "for they did not feel very much like shooting you," McAndrew said. He added wryly, "They felt it would make too much noise."

As they raced to outdistance the other sleigh, McAndrew asked, "What will you do now?"

"I'm going down to Kehoe's," McParland said.

In Girardville, McParland walked into Kehoe's bar. The boss of the Molly Maguires was stunned to see the man he had ordered murdered accompanied by the man who had promised to have it done. They discussed the trial, and Kehoe agreed with McParland there wasn't much use of having one. The strange conversation ended with Kehoe advising McParland to see Father O'Connor, the local priest. Apparently the clergyman had warned Kehoe that McParland was a detective. McParland knew he would never last the night in his boardinghouse bedroom, so he stayed away. The next day, McAndrew told him that three gunmen had surrounded the house, waiting all night for him to return.

Before he saw Father O'Connor, McParland conferred with Linden. "They [the Mollies] had a peek at my hand and the cards were all played," he told Linden. Although he knew that he was marked for death and that even McAndrew couldn't save him, McParland was determined to go back once more and to see Father O'Connor to find out who had betrayed him. Linden agreed, and kept a close "shadow" on McParland when he returned to the coal towns.

In a recently discovered letter, written years later, McParland recalled that dramatic meeting:

> On calling on Father O'Connor that memorable afternoon, which I will always remember as the last day I spent in the Anthracite Coal Fields until the prosecution was commenced, stating my objects to Father O'Connor, setting forth that he had done me an injustice by advising some parties I was a detective, he replied he had never heard of me, which was probably true. He stated that if I belonged to that gang, the curse of God was on my head and every possible member. I excused myself and the organization the best I could and still wanted to know why Jack Kehoe would send me to him. He said, "Well, Mrs. Kehoe is a very religious woman."
>
> This fact I was well aware of. Father O'Connor said, "She has called on me on several occasions to pray that her husband might quit this organization. I have done so and have sent for Kehoe on other different occasions and have labored with him for hours but to no avail. About two weeks ago I heard a rumor that a detective was investigating this band of murderers. I sent for Kehoe and after laboring with him for hours to no avail without making any impression, I told him what I had heard and reminded him that if the report was true, their deeds had been so open that a good detective would possibly get information to hang at least half of them if not all. Now, young man, (he said) if you belong to this accursed organization the sooner you give it up the better for yourself." [24]

McParland later testified that as he entered the rectory he had heard

Martin Dooley, "a member of the Order, speaking to the maidservant, asking for a chair. She gave him a chair and I heard the chair move right over beside the door. I was standing in front of this door but the door was closed."

McParland said he defended the Ancient Order of Hibernians "in a loud tone. . . . I stated it was a good society, that I had belonged to it for many years, that all the crimes that had been committed in the county were all crimes attributed to the society, that they were not guilty of these crimes. . . ."

McParland gave as the reason for his vigorous defense of the AOH that Dooley "should have the benefit of my observation to Father O'Connor and so I could get out of there with my life. . . ."

Later, this iron-nerved man sought out Dooley, who laughed as he told McParland how he had overheard his conversation with the priest.

"You gave the Society a pretty good lift," Dooley told him.

"I know I did," McParland replied.

"And you were telling the truth," the Molly Maguire said with a "satisfied" smile.

When McParland told Dooley and the other Mollies that he would be in Pottsville the following day, they told him "it would be a good thing." The Pinkerton operative read murder in their faces, and at last he told Linden he had tested his luck as much as he could.

The following morning, March 7, 1876, instead of going to Pottsville, and probably to his execution by the waiting gunmen, he left the county, "with Captain Linden shadowing me in the same car."

It was almost three years since he had first stepped into Pat Dormer's Sheridan House as the singing, jigging, brawling Jim McKenna.

After his escape from the Molly Maguire country, McParland was faced with the disturbing question of whether he should retain his anonymity or reveal his identity and testify as a state's witness—and perhaps be assassinated.

In Mauch Chunk a jury had sentenced another Molly gunman to the gallows, but then came the important trials of the murderers of Thomas Sanger and William Uren and of John Jones.

Jimmy Kerrigan, the Molly who had turned informer, was the people's principal witness in the Jones case, but he knew nothing of the Sanger and Uren murders. McParland alone held the key to the motivation for the murders, and while he had not been told beforehand of the double slaying, the murderers had described to him how they had shot down Thomas Sanger, the mine boss at Raven Run, a few miles west of Shenandoah, and William Uren, the young miner who boarded with the Sangers.

Gowen, now a special prosecutor aiding Schuylkill County District Attorney George Kaercher, put his problem before Allan Pinkerton. He told Pinkerton that he was well aware of their agreement that McParland would never be exposed on a witness stand but that it was now important to review the decision, for without McParland the case against the killers might collapse.

At the time, Pinkerton was a harassed man. Two of his operatives had been killed in Missouri by the Jameses and Youngers; the wave of unfavorable, even savage, editorial denouncements of the Pinkertons for their disastrous raid on the Samuels farmhouse was slowly subsiding. But now something sinister had reappeared in the Reno country that threatened to embroil the Pinkertons in another scandal—one they could ill afford during this crucial period.

After the Renos had been lynched by the vigilantes in Indiana, one of the operatives who had worked on the investigation had been fired by Allan Pinkerton for stealing money. He had promptly gone to work for a rival detective agency. In 1874, he was arrested on charges of fraud, and the head of the rival agency was determined to prosecute the man and send him to prison. This news was upsetting to Allan Pinkerton, but why it was is impossible to determine from his vague letters to Bangs in the fall of that year.

Pinkerton wrote to Bangs, "I suppose they will attempt to break me down and bleed me from anywhere from one dollar to $500,000, if I don't come down" (to New Albany, Indiana). He also vowed that "if they make any attempt to blackmail me they are sadly mistaken if they imagine they can make anything by the operation." Pinkerton's violent letter threatens to "make no halfway fight with the crowd . . . war to knife and the knife to the kill and let the best man win. . . ." [25]

All that month Pinkerton's correspondence dwelt on the problem, which despite his bombast, was obviously very disturbing to the detective. One letter indicates that the head of the rival agency was trying to make a deal with his thieving employee; in exchange for leniency, the agent would turn over damaging information about Pinkerton. What the information was is never made clear. Did the agent have any secret information concerning the Indiana vigilantes and Pinkerton? It is evident from the letters between Pinkerton and Bangs that nothing finally happened in Indiana. By Christmas the fury had disappeared from Pinkerton's letters, the matter was dropped, and he returned to the problems in Pennsylvania.

Gowen was pressing Pinkerton to try to persuade McParland to take the stand. Pinkerton approached McParland, who at first refused, and bluntly told his employer that as a witness he would surely be shot, perhaps even in the courtroom. The winter passed, and still McParland held out. But in April, he was pressured into taking the stand. The trial opened in Pottsville on May 4th. After the selection of the jury, the district attorney stunned the packed courtroom with the news that James

McParland, a Pinkerton detective known as Jim McKenna, would be the state's witness. As District Attorney Kaercher's words died away in the silent courtroom, all eyes swung to the defense table. The Mollies on trial were now white-faced; one man looked as if he couldn't catch his breath, another shook "like an aspen," while others appeared as if they had been struck over the head with a heavy drill.

There were more sensations that day. Linden's posse had swept across the county in a series of fast-moving raids, and eleven Molly Maguires, "all high in the Order," handcuffed and in chains, hobbled into the courthouse. This time Jack Kehoe led the group. On Saturday, May 6, 1876, James McParland took the stand. His appearance was a moment of high drama. When his name was called, he walked out of the rear door and up to the witness stand, escorted by Linden and two Pinkerton bodyguards. Gone was the sullen, red-eyed man with the ragged coat that flapped about his knees who had led the mobs at the colliery, holding back his vicious bulldog who snapped and growled at Linden—the man who now walked at his side. In place of McKenna was a lanky, shaven man dressed, as one reporter wrote, "in the height of fashion." [26]

As the days passed, it became evident from McParland's testimony that a secret group of terrorists had gained control of the area, intimidating its critics by murder or assault. It was not a question of a few isolated crimes: the design of the game was murder. He named names, gave minute details and was "considered to be the sharpest witness that ever occupied a chair in this court."

The defense tore into McParland, but could not shake his calm, straightforward account. Though he was made to go over and over each detail, his story was never shaken. The defense tried to impress on the jury that McParland had known beforehand that some of the murders were to be committed but had neglected to warn either the authorities in Philadelphia or Pinkerton in Chicago. When it was brought out that Jones, marked for murder, was only five miles away from McParland's boardinghouse, the defense attorney grimly asked why the detective hadn't saved "the life of the man you knew was going to be assassinated?"

"My reason was that I was afraid of being assassinated myself," was the detective's quiet answer. "I would not risk losing my life for all the men in this courthouse . . . walking five miles was nothing. . . . I would walk twenty, but it was the saving of my own life I was looking to."

At no time was McParland trapped or tripped by the defense attorney, nor was he ever contradicted by a defense witness. Under the legitimate but endless provocative questions about his motives and his past, he remained calm. Even when the defense brought out his Catholicism and asked if he had gone to confession or communion after he had joined the Mollies, he replied:

"I never did; it was sacrilegious, the idea of such a thing."

The trials continued, with the nation's newspapers devoting much space to the story. One after another, the Molly Maguire gunmen were found guilty and sentenced to die. As bits of information continued to come to Captain Linden, fugitives were flushed out of their hideouts in the black hills. But some slipped through the ring of possemen: Tom Hurley, the gunman; Friday O'Donnell, one of the killers of Sanger and Uren, who had escaped the bullets of the vigilante killers that bloody Friday night in Wiggans Patch; and others. Then another Molly turned informer in August. He was joined by Muff Lawler, the huge saloon owner who had first befriended McParland. Kehoe was named as a killer, and indicted.

In the winter of 1877, Jack Kehoe, "King of the Mollies," was found guilty. On April 16th, he was sentenced to be hanged. In June, 1877, nineteen of the Mollies went to the gallows; ten were executed at one time. All wore a rose and clutched a criucifix as they climbed the steps to the waiting hangman. Jack Kehoe fought a desperate legal battle; then he too died a particularly horrible death when the noose slipped, and he slowly strangled.

After the trials, Gowen returned to private law practice; his honest but disastrous management had brought the Reading to the brink of bankruptcy. He was in Washington to plead before the Interstate Commerce Commission in a rate case against Standard Oil when he was found dead in his room at Wormsley's Hotel, a pistol at his side. Linden, now Pinkerton's Philadelphia superintendent, rushed to Washington. At first it was assumed a Molly had finally given Gowen his "black mark." However, an investigation proved suicide. The living Mollies triumphantly insisted it was a case of his conscience catching up with him, but Professor Schlegal, Gowen's biographer, put it better when he wrote that after days of power, there was before him "only an empty future of obscurity."

After a long period of convalescence, McParland became Pinkerton's superintendent of the Denver branch of the Agency, and Pinkerton's field marshal in the long chases after the Western outlaw bands. We shall meet him again in the Governor Sturnenberg murder, which took place in another century, with a cast that was strangely familiar.

Did society profit from Allan Pinkerton's investigation of the Molly Maguires? Did he free an American community from the grip of a terroristic organization whose evil deeds had affected the lives of its women and children and destroyed its economy? Or was he in reality a nineteenth-century strikebreaker who destroyed the infant unions of the coalfields for the benefit of the railroad? Was James McParland an agent provocateur, a teller of tall tales, a liar of gigantic proportions?

These and innumerable other questions have been debated by historians, amateur and professional, for a century, and have provided the background for at least one novel, H. G. Wells's, *Valley of Fear*. Wells wrote his book after listening to William Pinkerton's stories of the investigation while both were traveling to London aboard a transatlantic liner.

Although there were shocking abuses on the part of capital in the anthracite coalfields of the period—the blacklist, depressed wages, and an unyielding antiunion attitude—no evidence was ever produced to indicate that the Molly Maguires were motivated by social injustice. And this is the greatest tragedy of the whole grim story: The murders, arsons, brutal assaults all came to nothing. After the last Molly had been hanged, the plight of the miners remained the same.

In his history of the investigation, F. P. Dewees bluntly describes the days of the Mollies as "a reign of blood . . . they held communities terror bound, and wantonly defied the law, destroyed property and sported with human life."

The American Law Review of January, 1877, praised the work of the Pinkertons: "The debt which the coal counties owe to these men cannot be overestimated, nor can the personal qualities of untiring resolution, daring and sagacity, in both principal and agents be too highly praised." The *Review* article on the Molly Maguires trials ended: "It was one of the greatest works for public good that has been achieved in this country and in this generation."

By this time the story of the Molly Maguires was slipping into history as one of the most violent chapters in the post–Civil War annals. As always, the mythmakers and the balladeers were busy: Jack Kehoe and his gunmen were being canonized as martyrs to labor, while the folklore tune about Jim Kerrigan, who became the first informer, was as popular as the one about Bob Ford, that dirty little coward who shot Mr. Howard. . . .

CHAPTER 24
Trials and Tribulations

In the United States and parts of Europe, the name Pinkerton was now synonymous with the protection of business and utilities by private police. William Pinkerton was in Europe cementing the Agency's connections with Scotland Yard, the Sûreté, Turkish and Belgian police, and, in the Caribbean, with the Cuban government. While it was a period of expansion and financial gain, there would be little peace and serenity during the next few years for Allan Pinkerton. It would be a time of slow physical deterioration and mental anguish. After years of bending to their father's tyrannical rule, William, Robert, and Joan finally rebelled.

Allan Pinkerton was now in his late fifties, but he looked older than his years. His hair and beard were gray. He wore spectacles, and was more irascible than ever. He had discovered that the "detective story" was loved by many Americans, and he ground out a series of books of his adventures that became best sellers of the 1870's and 1880's. Shortly after the conclusion of the Molly Maguire investigation, Pinkerton disclosed to his son, in 1876, that he had "seven writers working on my stories." As he told Robert, his method was to sketch the outlines of one or more investigations, then turn them over to the "writers" to expand with dialogue, and geographical and physical descriptions. The books, now collectors' items, are lurid, melodramatic, and filled with maudlin dialogue, but the investigative techniques are Pinkerton's. His book on the Molly Maguires sticks fairly close to the court transcript, and his wartime memoirs, *The Spy of the Rebellion*, while violently, blindly pro-McClellan, is fairly accurate, with some facts—nonpolitical—sifted from captured Confederate correspondence, especially Mrs. Greenhow's, now in the National Archives.[1]

Pinkerton produced eighteen volumes of about 3,000,000 words. Authorities on dime novels believe that Pinkerton was the inspiration for George Munro's *Old Sleuth, the Detective*, America's first fictional detective, who was introduced in 1872. Old Sleuth, a pontifical character, with a beard, spectacles perched on the end of his nose, and wearing a plug hat, became the synonym for "detective." Munro copyrighted the name, and for years no one could use the word "sleuth" in connection with a detective, although there were many attempts to break the copyright.

Pinkerton's new set of troubles began on the morning of September 2, 1875, when he opened a telegram from Henry W. Gavinner, an official of the Pennsylvania Railroad and one of the Agency's more important clients, complaining that George Bangs, Pinkerton's general manager, was drinking heavily.

The telegram read:

> I have just passed Mr. Bangs on Third Street between Walnut and Wellings Alley, drunk as a lord, reeling and staggering from side to side, trying hard to retain a cigar in his mouth, sustaining himself from falling by wildly catching all posts and rails and finally landing on a pile of building debris. He came out of a saloon near Wellings Alley, nine A.M. Mr. Boyd [another railroad official] said this is the second time he has seen Bangs in this condition and he reported to the offices of the company.[2]

Pinkerton exploded. He dashed off a letter to his son Robert in New York, repeating the telegram and ordering him to pay Bangs his salary up to that Saturday, and "not to give him another penny except as when you know it is necessary." He also told Robert that if Bangs had not returned to his office, to seek out Mrs. Bangs, "tell her the facts and try to find him."

On the same day Pinkerton wrote a blistering letter to Bangs, repeating in detail the telegram:

> My God, I was horror struck when I had finished reading it. . . . Oh, I cannot tell you what my feelings were; I was almost driven mad. George Bangs, I have known you for years and now what does all this mean? When is this going to end? Think of the railroad officials in Philadelphia who saw you "drunk as a lord." Oh, my God, I cannot stand this. Think of the General Superintendent of this Agency so miserably drunk as you were. And at nine A.M.! Yes, at nine A.M. I thought it might have been nine P.M., but no, it was nine A.M.! It was at a time when railroad officials were going to work!

Then Pinkerton lashed out as Bangs and the whole eastern office for not notifying him that Bangs has been "drunk as a lord" on another occasion. "You must look me square in the face, George—you were drunk as a lord once before and neither Franklin [Benjamin Franklin, superintendent of the Philadelphia office] nor my son, Robert, saw fit to inform me. What is going on?"[3]

For pages Pinkerton wept over Bangs and his terrible "condition." He reviewed their long years together, their many close calls in the war, and their fight to keep the business from floundering. Pinkerton apparently spent a good part of that day sending out letters to Bangs, Franklin, and his son Robert. He bitterly excoriated his Philadelphia superintendent and Robert for covering up Bangs's previous fall from grace. Then there is a hilarious exchange between Franklin and Pinkerton. In his report on the affair, Franklin accidentally placed Bangs "drunk as a lord" on September 31st. Back came a long, tedious letter from Pinkerton explaining that Bangs could not have been drunk on that day "because there is no such day in the year. . . . I said he was 'drunk as a lord' on August 31st."[4]

For days letters shuttled back and forth between New York, Chicago, and Philadelphia. Bangs contritely confessed all, and vowed never to take another drink. It wasn't until late that winter that the Agency's *cause célèbre* faded away.

A few months later Pinkerton happened to be in the Chicago office when a client came in and asked for an immediate "shadow" to tail someone. Pinkerton was horrified when a clerk summoned an operative. This led Pinkerton to issue a list of new and firm rules that "the principles of this Agency mean everything to be kept secret and all persons doing business with the Agency must do it through the General Superintendent, Superintendents, Assistant Superintendents or Chief Clerks, and the Patrons must not be allowed to speak or see the operatives . . . the business must be done strictly through the above parties." The executives of the various branches, he ordered, were to read again his *General Principles,* "where they will find their duties broadly set forth. . . ."[5]

Another crisis appeared in the winter of 1876 when Bangs, Robert, and Franklin banded together to urge Pinkerton not to hire "female detectives," a program the detective had ordered following the death of Kate Warne. A series of outraged letters and telegrams soon arrived from Chicago:

> It has been my principle to use females for the detection of crime where it has been useful and necessary . . . with regard to the employment of such females I can trace it back to the time I first hired Kate Warne, up to the present time . . . and I intend to still use females whenever it can be done judiciously. I must do it or falsify my theory, practice and truth. . . .

Then Pinkerton learned that Franklin's wife was advising her husband against the use of females in his office, apparently out of jealousy. One can see Pinkerton in his Chicago office, his hands shaking with emotion, his speech blurred and indistinct, as he furiously dictated to his secretaries:

> I cannot tolerate that a female should be consulted about this and under no circumstances will I allow my argument to be brought up on this subject . . . with me the question is whether I am right or am I wrong.` . . . I think I am right and if that is the case, female detectives must be allowed in my Agency.
>
> As for Mrs. Franklin, I hope that Mr. Franklin will realize what he is drifting into. . . . I don't like to lose Mr. Franklin but if I am driven to it I must discharge him. I shall be very sorry for it.[6]

To make sure his authority would not be questioned again, Pinkerton sent a Mrs. Angela Austin from Chicago to work in the Philadelphia office. Previous correspondence shows Mrs. Austin to have been an attractive former Texas actress. One wonders what Franklin did about her. But Robert could be as stubborn as his father. He immediately dispatched a terse note to Chicago that he didn't want Mrs. Austin or any other female under his jurisdiction. Back came a curt reply from his father, with his own letter enclosed:

> I return your letter as it is disrespectful to me as the Principal of this Agency.
>
> It is doubly so, yea, triply disrespectful to me as your father, therefore I return it to you. . . . If Mrs. Franklin is to become Superintendent of the Philadelphia office then I shall put another man in the place of her husband . . . this you can rely upon . . . if Mrs. Franklin is to be jealous of her husband this is nothing to me. I simply wish to extract from him the fulfillment of his duties, nothing more nothing less. For the last time I shall tell you that you have no right to interfere with the employment of any Agency, except those of New York, of which you are Superintendent. As for any trouble that may occur between me and my Superintendents leave that for me to settle. After I am dead and the sod is growing over my grave you will then learn that someone must take the management of everything, but while I live I mean to be the Principal of this Agency and I question much if you will prove to be a better Principal than I have been. . . .

Pinkerton was again driving himself to the limits of his physical capabilities. As he wrote to his son, between dictating the outlines for "my stories" and operating his business, "I am at work from half past four in the morning to nearly nine o'clock at night, and I have enough to do without getting any complaints from you."

Pinkerton made it clear, not only to his sons but also to Bangs and all the other executives, that the Pinkerton's National Detective Agency belonged to him, "and I mean to be the Principal of the whole and will continue to be until Death claims me as its own." [7]

Pinkerton's harsh letters irritated Franklin and undoubtedly his wife. In March, 1876, he wrote a long letter to Pinkerton, demanding that his salary be raised from $2,000 a year to $3,000. The letter reviewed his association with the Agency, emphasizing his work in the Molly Maguires investigation.

Pinkerton didn't wait. A letter written on the same day that he received Franklin's arrived on Robert's desk. Allan Pinkerton coldly reviewed Franklin's career as former head of the Philadelphia Police Department Detective Bureau, his long period of sickness, "when no one would hire him," and his five-year employment with the Agency.

"You, Robert Pinkerton, and I are the only ones who know what I have done for Benjamin Franklin," Allan wrote. "When he was sick only I could control him. . . . Mrs. Franklin had no more control over him than a child. . . ."

Pinkerton bluntly told Robert that if Franklin left, "Willie will take over the Philadelphia office and you two will make a good team." Then, apparently forgetting that he had almost fired Bangs for being "drunk as a lord," he proudly boasted to his son that they could always count on Bangs, "he will never leave me, he will stand with me and I will stand with him." [8]

After Robert wrote to Franklin, cautioning him not to press for his "advance," Franklin abruptly dropped his demands and wrote a long, friendly letter to his employer. Pinkerton coldly replied that for the record there was "only one man who broke the Molly Maguires and his name is James McParland."

That spring, cheating on expenses, which never failed to irritate Pinkerton, was again an issue, with Pinkerton writing fierce letters to his superintendents in New York and Philadelphia, ordering them to cut bills. Bangs, it appears, was one of the offenders. As Pinkerton wrote, "You have overdrawn your accounts by $225.36, a matter which pains me to bring to your attention." Overdrawing, he told Bangs, "must stop and stop immediately." He sent a duplicate of his letter to Robert with a curt order to "stop all overdrawing of salaries."

In the fall there was a scandal in the Chicago office when Pinkerton discovered that some of his executives in the guard and security forces were stealing. As he wrote to Bangs, someone had informed him his men were buying expensive jewels and furniture. He called in Horne, the Agency's accountant, who produced records showing that the Pinkerton Patrol Department had earned only $1,207 in 1875 and that for the nine months of 1876 there had been a loss of $46.30. In one case Horne, by double checking some of the accounts, found the head of the department working a racket by putting new subscribers on the "dead beat list," then pocketing the monthly fees.

Pinkerton seemed stunned by the dishonesty of his executives, some of whom had been with him since the 1850's. Although the accountant had produced uncontestable evidence of thievery, Pinkerton, as he informed Bangs, hesitated to fire them without gathering more evidence. With a curious consideration for the sensitivity of his crooked employees, Pinkerton suggested that rather than embarrass them, Bangs should send two strange operatives to Chicago to make a citywide check of all clients belonging to members of the Pinkerton's Patrol Service to find which one paid, when, and to whom.

> Should he ask what it is for, he [the operative] can say he is going to get up an article about it, say for the Chicago *Times* or *Tribune*. You and I, George, both know the growth of Chicago since the fire . . . something has been going on and to a large extent . . . the fact is I have lost almost ten thousand dollars some way or another. How? That is for me to solve.[9]

A few weeks later a major crisis erupted in the Pinkerton family that wiped out all thoughts of office thievery, Bangs's drinking, Franklin's threat to quit, and the East's refusal to use female detectives. It all revolved about the romance of Pinkerton's daughter, Joan, or, as her father called her, "Pussy."

Joan, a pretty and vivacious girl, was then in her early twenties. After attending the best schools in Chicago, she had returned home to help her mother keep house. From his letters, Pinkerton adored his daughter but refused to believe she had grown up and wanted a life of her own. When he was out of town, he continued to send her letters decorated with his tiny sketches of a kitten, eating, sleeping, or jumping rope. With his sons married, Pinkerton seemed to turn more to his daughter. His wife, a kind and gentle woman, accepted without question her husband's decisions and desires. But his daughter had more iron. As she grew older, she began to question the stern regimen of the Pinkerton household that saw lights out shortly after dark, early rising before sunup, with the women of the household preparing his breakfast while he took his twelve-mile walk and cold bath. It was a typical Victorian household: The father was the supreme being; the women belonged in the kitchen, in bed, and with the children. It was against this life that Joan rebelled.

Pinkerton's letters to his son Robert, who apparently had a more sympathetic ear than William who saw his father every day, reveal that when the conflict finally came to a head, it was a painful story of instinctive, passionate defiance against a selfish, domineering, iron-willed man by his daughter, who, if she was ever to find happiness, had to defy and defeat him. Pinkerton's wife acted the role of the loving, self-sacrificing mother

her daughter adored, but while she was outgoing and warm and had sympathy for her daughter's problems, her gentleness must have been battered to pieces in the struggle between the two determined persons she loved so dearly. At times her only defense was to take to her bed and announce that she was too distraught to go on.

It began with Joan's romance with William Chalmers, son of a distinguished Chicago family, whose sister was Joan's classmate. In the spring, summer, and fall of 1876, young Chalmers, who one day would become one of the nation's most famous industrialists, was an almost daily visitor to the Pinkerton house on Monroe Street, known locally as the "Pinkerton homestead," a large, rambling house surrounded by gardens and shrubs. Pinkerton, who was away most of the day and night, usually found "young Chalmers," as he called him, courting Joan.[10]

It is clear from his later letters that the thought of someone else supplanting him in the heart of his daughter disturbed Pinkerton a great deal. By the end of the summer, it was obvious that Joan had fallen in love. In an attempt to break up the romance, Pinkerton sent her on a tour of Europe. Joan, respecting her father's wishes, reluctantly agreed to go. Months later she returned, and, as she informed her mother, was still in love with Chalmers, "and could not lose that feeling."

At the time, Pinkerton was a fanatical believer in phrenology, the now-discredited science that judged a human's character and personality by the conformation of his skull. It was popular at the time, and Pinkerton's letters of the 1870's invariably referred to some police officer's or criminal's features as certain proof that he was either an idiot or a man of heroic character. In letters to Robert, Pinkerton went into great detail about the skull measurements of Napoleon, Garibaldi, and of course his eternal hero, McClellan, who was "brilliant." He also modestly put his measurements and those of his sons in the same class. But Chalmers, he wrote, just didn't have the necessary brain power, would surely fail his daughter as a husband.

In late November, Pinkerton wrote a long and "troubled" letter to Robert, describing how Joan had requested his permission to marry Chalmers. Pinkerton refused, and there was, as he put it, "a scene."

For the rest of the winter, an armed truce existed between Pinkerton and his daughter, with his wife nervously attempting to keep peace. Joan, as Pinkerton wrote to Robert, was listless and pale, "caring only to stay in her room." Weeks dragged by. Then, on a January night, 1877, friends visited the Pinkertons. In a letter Pinkerton wrote this significant line: "They vied with each other to please me and make me happy."

After Pinkerton and his wife went to bed—at eight o'clock—he was aroused by voices. When he went down to the living room and "turned up the gas," he saw his daughter saying good night to Chalmers. Pinkerton, as he said, was horrified when he discovered it was 1:15 A.M. "and with the gas turned low." As he described the scene to Robert, he said:

"What does this mean, Mr. Chalmers?" his voice slightly raised. "You must leave this house at once and never enter this door."

The embarrassed young man bowed, and left.

Almost a century later it all sounds ludicrous, the stuff from which the maudlin Victorian melodramas were made; but it was no badly written play to Pinkerton's heartbroken daughter. There was a bitter row that aroused her mother, who desperately tried to calm her husband and daughter.

Young Joan insisted that Chalmers and she were in love and intended to get married. Pinkerton bluntly informed her that he would make her a present of "some money" but that he would not be at the church. "If necessary your mother and I will travel about Europe until it is all over," he told his daughter.

Heartsick, Joan packed her bags, kissed her mother, and left for New York to stay with Robert, her twin.

It is clear from his letters to Robert that Pinkerton was more furious over his daughter's defiance of his iron rules than over her wishes to marry. All that winter he bombarded Robert with letters, repeating again and again his refusal to allow Joan to marry. Gradually the tenor of his demands weakened, until he was pointing out: "Joan must know the door is always open, all she has to do is walk in."

To add to his worries, his wife had begun to fail physically. For all his petty, domineering ways, Pinkerton deeply loved "my wee bonnie lass," as he still called her. As he wrote to Robert, he had cut down on his nightwork "to stay at your mother's side, listening to her every word."

Although Pinkerton evidently hoped Robert would persuade "Pussy" to return home, his daughter kept a dignified silence all that winter. By June, Pinkerton was picturing himself as the hurt but forgiving father who was ready at "any hour" to see his daughter.

But Joan was temporarily forgotten when Pinkerton received the news that his Philadelphia office had got religion. It was the time of the great revivalists Dwight Moody and Ira David Sankey, and their series of notable revival meetings were sweeping the country. He again reverted to the role of the domineering, completely unreasonable employer.[11]

"What is this?" Pinkerton wrote to Franklin in Philadelphia. "I should never have dreamt for a moment that the evil preachings which are spread throughout the U.S. by Moody and Sankey and others should have at length come into my Agency. . . . I would have hoped that my employees would have known better. . . ." For some pages Pinkerton, a self-styled atheist, went on to discuss the principles of his Agency. Then he issued the incredible order that instead of his employees going to church on Sunday, they would have to work:

> They are to give their whole time to my business without any reserva-
> tion whatsoever. The men are to remain on duty on Sunday until the

Superintendent sees fit to excuse them . . . none of them shall in any
way undertake to attend church on Sunday but shall be at the office
at 9 A.M.

Unfortunately, there is no correspondence to tell us the reaction of
Bangs, Robert, or Franklin to this order. Apparently they accepted it;
to have ignored it would have resulted in another series of directives
from Chicago.

The problem of Franklin came up again in March; the Philadelphia
superintendent still insisted he was worth $3,000 a year. Now he was
demanding retroactive pay for the last three months. Another series of
"confidential" letters went on to Bangs in New York in which Franklin's salary as chief of the Philadelphia detectives was reviewed, his last
raises, his frequent illnesses, his domineering wife, and his refusal to accept female detectives. The letter finally ended with a stern refusal to
give Franklin "another cent." Now, instead of William taking over, it
was Robert Linden, who had served under Franklin during the Molly
Maguire investigation. Franklin capitulated, and Philadelphia was again
silent.[12]

In mid-June, 1877, Pinkerton was joyously writing to Robert that Joan
was planning to return home, "my favorite child, the only girl I have."
However, a few days later he querulously wrote to Robert that the issue
had not been entirely solved: Pussy was demanding that "she have company until 11 P.M." Pinkerton stood firm: "I cannot see how it can be
done . . . as the slightest sound will awaken me and your mother, then it
is hard for us to fall asleep again. . . . I cannot see any reason for Pussy
having any company later than 10 P.M."

Evidently Robert persuaded his sister to accept ten o'clock as an ulti-
matum, and Joan returned home—probably more to care for her ailing
mother than to bow to her father's iron will.

The dreary fall days were brightened for Pinkerton when he received
the "glorious news" McClellan had been elected Governor of New Jersey.
Memories of the great days of the Peninsula, Antietam, the Chicago Convention, and the near victory of the Presidency in 1864 flooded over
Pinkerton. Through all these years he had never abandoned his fondest
dream that his beloved general would some day end in the White House.

In a long letter to McClellan, he reviewed the old days, and ended by
predicting that the "thousands of old soldiers and soldiers' children who
have loved and still love you" would someday put him into the White
House: "You must be sure as I, that I have no axes to grind, no favors
to ask. I merely come to you with these things as a friend, whom you
know and trust and as that friend I only ask that you shall place yourself
in the hands of able friends and their friends, so that all these things
may be consummated." [13] In many other letters to his son, friends, and
wartime comrades, Pinkerton would vainly hope that McClellan was at

last on his way to Pennsylvania Avenue "and the office that rightly belongs to him," but it always remained a dream.

Family and business affairs rode smoothly for several months. The Agency's business was becoming worldwide. Plans were drawn for opening another office in Boston; nearly every large railroad in the country was using Pinkerton operatives to spot cheating conductors; and the Agency was getting deeper into supplying guards for strikebound plants. Franklin had been stricken by a serious illness; and for all his criticism and blistering letters of the past, Pinkerton, in a sympathetic note, ordered Bangs to keep Franklin on the payroll as long as possible, and said that if Franklin's illness was so serious that he could never return to the Agency, to give Mrs. Franklin a lump sum of $1,000 "or whatever sum you think I would be justified in paying. . . ."

William also came in for his share of fatherly lectures on his father's favorite subject—expense accounts. Pinkerton instructed Bangs that if his son, then in New York, didn't stop spending so much money, he was to pay him an allowance "and nothing more." He cautiously warned Bangs that "when the cutting down part comes you will find some difficulty."

That year the Agency was engaged in making the ransom deal with the grave robbers who had stolen the body of A. T. Stewart, the famous New York merchant. When he reached an impasse in his investigation, Robert turned to his father for advice. From his desk fifteen hundred miles away, the old detective made some shrewd observations. Robert had outlined the case up to the point where one of the intermediaries had refused the Agency's offer for $25,000 for the return of the remains. As Pinkerton wrote to his son:

> The fact is Robert, from all this seeming correspondence I think the body is not far away. You will notice they talk about the annoyances of the Custom House officers in having the body brought from Canada, but they forgot to mention any annoyance to them whilst taking the remains to Canada. No, I do not think this story of the body being taken to Canada hangs well together; I think the remains may be in New Jersey or at farthest, in Pennsylvania . . . this man says he is in Montreal, although you have not been there, I think by your correspondence it has been clearly shown that no letters were ever delivered to this man at Montreal, as purported were sent to him. . . .[14]

Pinkerton's long-distance predictions were later proved correct when the crime was finally solved and the remains were recovered.

Then, in the spring of 1879, Robert kicked over the family traces; he not only wanted to resign from the Agency; he also insisted that he wanted to change his name. Robert, who had seen at close hand the growing wealth of the Agency, demanded a share of the profits, not a salary.

There was a brief, stunned silence; then came the letters from Chicago, recalling the old happy days in Chicago, the war, Scotland, and the never-ending cry, "You are my children . . . I love you . . . soon you will have everything."

Pinkerton still refused to believe that his children were grown and that they had families and increasing responsibilities. Although by now William and Robert operated a great deal of the business, whatever they did was evidently accomplished only after badgering their father with demands, pleas, and even threats. It was the classic story of sons entering their father's business and viewing all as archaic and old-fashioned. As Pinkerton sadly warned them, "Someday you will know the problems of this Agency and they are many. . . ."

Although he was momentarily stunned by his son's letter, Pinkerton lashed back with a strong reply "that if you wish to dissolve your connections with me, I am ready to supply your place *at once*. I am not too bothered with any of this nonsense; obey orders and you will be useful, otherwise nothing. . . . In regard to what you say of our name, I would advise you to petition the Legislature to permit you to change it, I pledge you I will not use any effort to stop it. . . ." [15]

There was more of an exchange between father and son; from their letters we can see Robert relenting, Allan forgiving. It had been just another bad month.

The Pinkertons' thirty-sixth wedding anniversary fell in March, 1877. In the countless number of letters Allan Pinkerton wrote during that decade, many of them petty, unreasonable, bombastic, sarcastic, self-pitying, the one he wrote to his wife that month is probably the most sincere. He was still getting up at four thirty, and we can picture him in his bedroom, the outside darkness filled with the moaning of the wind, laboriously getting dressed to make his own breakfast and be driven to his office. Now sixty, he had aged a great deal in the last few years, and his hands, as he wrote a friend, "still shake like the palsy." He was almost always irritable, and probably frustrated when anger slurred his speech. The years had not mellowed him; he was as stubborn, fiercely opinionated, and egotistical as ever. He was also worried about Joan, who was ill with a heart condition, and was confined to her bed.

In his office he slowly dictated a three-page letter to Joan, "My Dear Little Wife," reviewing their years together from the morning in 1842 "when we had pledged our faith, sailed from Scotland and wondered if we should ever look at fair Scotia again as we sailed down the Clyde." He recalled how their ship had foundered off Sable Island and their first glimpse "of the strange sights we saw that morning, on our first landing on the shores of America. . . ." Then the overland journey to Chicago, "which had been cleared of the Indians but I was not content and went on to Dundee . . . then after a few years we returned to make our home in Chicago. . . ."

He recalled the births of their "wee ones" and the death of Belle, their firstborn, in Chicago: "I felt it much but I know how deeply you felt it.

. . ." Other children were born and died in the rough frontier city, and as Pinkerton poignantly wrote, "We both remember the days of their birth as well as the last day we had them on earth. . . .

> I know, since you were eighteen years of age you have been battling with me, side by side, willing to do anything, to bear our children and work hard, yet you never found fault, you never said a cross word but was always willing to make our home cheery and happy. . . . Now Joan, on this day, I wish you to take things easy. When I can get home I will come and sit by you and talk to you and cheer you . . . this is a dark and gloomy day but wait, it will get to be brighter days and you will be able to go out again. . . . Let us wish we may be spared a few more years . . . enjoying happiness and health to ourselves, our children and our friends. . . .

The secretary had ended the letter "ever Yours," but Pinkerton had laboriously scrawled "Allan." [16]

BOOK 5
Other
Eminent
Victorians

CHAPTER 25
The Scott-Dunlap Ring

$\mathbf{T}$ he operation of the Agency slowly reverted to the control of William and Robert Pinkerton as the 1870's came to an end. The axis of the business was still Chicago, New York, and Philadelphia in that order, and while Allan remained the unyielding "Principal," his fading health made it necessary for him grudgingly to turn over to his sons the major cases that took them across the country, deep into Spanish Honduras, and to Europe. The Molly Maguires was the last important investigation Allan personally supervised and in which he made the sole decisions. While he still fired his barrage of orders and letters to his superintendents, a slow, almost subtle change took place in the hierarchy of the Agency. It wasn't spelled out, but William and Robert had taken over.

In 1877, the Agency assisted the United States Secret Service in finding and arresting the ghouls who had attempted to steal the body of Abraham Lincoln from its marble sarcophagus in the Springfield Memorial. The plan was to bury the corpse in the sands of the Indiana dunes and demand a ransom for its return. The plot was originally hatched by Big Jim Kinealy, midwestern counterfeiter, but a member of his five-man gang boasted to a woman "of dubious character" that he was going to "steal Lincoln's bones." She notified police, but Kinealy and his men escaped. Two other counterfeiters, Terence Mullen and John Hughes, who operated a notorious saloon called The Hub, decided to go through with the plan. They took in a fast-talking horse thief named Lewis C. Swegles, who was a "roper," the nineteenth-century underworld term for "stool pigeon." Swegles notified P. D. Tyrrell, a Chicago Secret Service operator. Tyrrell asked William Pinkerton for assistance, and after a conference with Robert Lincoln, two operatives were assigned to trail Hughes, Mullen, and Swegles to Springfield. Posing as tourists, the grave robbers visited the tomb, closely questioned John C. Power, custodian of the memorial, then left. After Mullen stole a rusty ax with which to smash the sarcophagus, he and Hughes "sat down in a saloon waiting for darkness." Swegles, meanwhile, was questioned by Tyrrell, Elmer Washburn, former chief of the Chicago police and former Chief of the Secret Service, and two Pinkerton operatives. Power was alerted to the plot late that afternoon.

Elaborate preparations were made to capture the grave robbers, but the combination of Swegles's inability to warn the detectives in time and an accidentally discharged pistol allowed the criminals to escape. They were arrested a short time later and sentenced to a year in prison. Because attorneys hired by Robert Lincoln could find nothing in the Illinois statutes to cover grave robbing, the pair was convicted of conspiracy to steal the coffin, which was valued at $75.[1]

A few years earlier, Allan Pinkerton would have personally shadowed the grave robbers and arrested them, even if it meant traveling across the country, but now his deteriorating physical condition prevented him from leaving Chicago. Lincoln's death still plagued him. As William recalled, his father said over and over that if he and his operatives had been guarding the President that night at Ford's Theatre, there would have been no assassination. It must have horrified Pinkerton to know ghouls were ready to steal Lincoln's corpse and hold it for ransom. That William and not his father supervised the investigation is an indication that the old detective's health was fading. Yet his Record Books show how he tried to cling to the reins of his business. To his superintendents he still dictated letters of approbation or praise or offering advice, and on rare occasions made inspection trips to New York or Philadelphia.

Crime continued to mount throughout the nation, and organized gangs fought wars to control sections of the larger cities. Footpads made it unsafe for citizens to travel the dimly lighted streets. In the teeming ghetto of lower New York City, victims disappeared without a trace. Years later, when the tenements in the notorious Five Points section were torn down, a number of skeletons were found. The police of the time appeared inadequate, corrupt, or incompetent. Existing records reveal that insurance companies, business firms, banks, and even local and state governments automatically called in the Pinkertons when they became victims of a major crime.

In the fall of 1878, operatives working under the direction of William Pinkerton broke the notorious Dr. Meyer "murder-for-profit" ring that claimed victims from New York to Chicago. Meyer, a sad-eyed, moustached physician, had poisoned a woman, two men, and a child to collect

Dr. Henry C. F. Meyer. *Pinkerton's, Inc.*

$10,000 in insurance claims, and was wooing and planning to murder other women in Canada, Detroit, New York, and Chicago before the Mutual Life Insurance Company called in the Pinkertons. After an accomplice of Meyer was arrested and confessed to William Pinkerton, operatives traced the physician, who was using a number of aliases, from New York to South Bend, Indiana, then to Canada, and finally to Detroit, where he was arrested by local police and the Pinkertons. He was convicted on a murder charge and sentenced to life imprisonment.

In the late 1870's the operations of the Pinkertons became worldwide when they began hunting some of the most colorful, ingenious, and little-known international criminals of the Victorian Age who robbed express cars, banks, and brokerage houses of millions of dollars. The Bank of England and investment and jewelry firms in France and Belgium were among the criminals' victims. Here the Pinkertons filled the role of a paid national police force that cooperated with the principal police organizations of Europe. Letters from criminal divisions of Scotland Yard, the

Sûreté, Turkish, and Cuban police, and our State Department showed they were sharing their knowledge of these colorful rogues in an informal, international pool of police information. The Pinkertons appeared to be a crude but effective Victorian Age Interpol.

Although they dutifully sent progress reports of their investigations to Allan in Chicago, it was William and Robert who made the final decisions in these cases and who traveled across the nation and around the world from Capetown to Constantinople. No door was closed to them, nor did they seek the sole company of policemen. Statesmen, diplomats, business leaders, aristocrats, fascinated by their profession, invited the Pinkertons to their dinner tables and in time accepted them as the law in America, a land they viewed as part frontier. Within a decade the Agency had changed from a unique private American firm of bounty hunters to a sophisticated organization of international law-enforcement officers.

The criminals they chased for years were strongly individualistic, talented, and intelligent. Forgers and counterfeiters like Charles Becker, alias "The Scratch," who was such a skillful artist he could copy an entire front page of a newspaper, were a daily menace to bank tellers in every American city and throughout Europe. Baron Maximilian Shinburn, who operated in the United States and on the Continent, spoke five languages and was an authentic connoisseur of art. Charley Bullard, the cracksman, was an accomplished pianist—he was Piano Charley to the underworld—and spoke French and Italian fluently. And Adam Worth, the master thief of the Victorian Age, toured the ports of Europe in a luxurious yacht.

They dressed in the best broadcloth, wore diamonds, pearl stickpins, and the finest "beavers." Their women were beautiful; one became a multimillionaire New York society leader, another a Broadway star. They invented tools and devices such as the "air pump" to plunder banks, many times shattering the economy of entire communities.

Jim Dunlap and Bob Scott must head the list of bank robbers. It was the considered opinion of William Pinkerton, in 1880, that if there is a niche for America's outstanding cracksmen, this pair must fill it. In the 1870's, the very names of Scott and Dunlap made most bankers look nervously over their shoulders and test the vaults and combinations of their safes. Their apprehension was not unfounded; in little more than three years Scott and Dunlap had emptied the vaults of some of the country's largest banks of more than $3,000,000, a staggering amount in those days.

They established a record for a single bank robbery that lasted until modern times. On January 25, 1876, the Ring, as it was called, stole $1,250,000 in cash and securities from the Northampton, Massachusetts, National Bank. Until the robbery of the Boston Brinks office in 1950, this crime was not surpassed.

Dunlap was usually the model of patience, planning, and resourceful-
ness, yet he seemed to be the favorite target of a capricious fate that
insisted on pulling the rug from under him and his men so that most of
their robberies became slapstick farces. Several of their "strikes," as the
Victorian thieves called bank or train robberies, could have supplied the
plots for half a dozen W. C. Fields or Marx Brothers movie scripts.

The activities of the Ring are important for several reasons: They offer
a classic example of the dogged, commonsense police work of the early
Pinkertons; but, more significantly, they help to illuminate the morals
and mores of the Gilded Age when bankers considered the return of
their stolen securities far more important than protecting society from
the criminals. They called it "compromise," or "working back," which
meant making a deal with the underworld to buy back their property
and that of their depositors. The secret negotiations usually took place
through a lawyer retained by the thieves. The unwritten rule of the game
was that no one would get hurt: The securities were returned to the
banks while the crooks retained their freedom along with a percentage
of the loot. To give the Pinkertons credit, they first put the thieves
behind bars before they did any dickering. They were often hamstrung
when the banks refused to prosecute.

In addition to establishing their dubious record for loot, Scott and
Dunlap established another first. Though expert cracksmen were roaming
all over the country, blowing bank vaults, Scott and Dunlap not only
sought out and corrupted a well-known key and safe expert to help them
pull off their biggest jobs but also had him make a schedule of the
nation's biggest and most vulnerable banks.

The leadership of the Ring was equally divided between Jim Dunlap,
a cool, blue-eyed Scottish brakeman, and Robert Scott, who was known
to the Mississippi River pirates as "Hustling Bob" because of his inability
to keep still. Any nervous tension showed in Scott's characteristic shrugging. As William Pinkerton once observed, "Scott looks like a man wearing a jacket two sizes too large."

In contrast, Dunlap was a calm, patient perfectionist. He had served
in the Civil War as a sergeant in an Ohio regiment. He was wounded
three times, the last time at Antietam. In a front-line hospital he threatened a surgeon with a heavy brass pitcher when the physician produced
saws and chloroform and announced that Dunlap's leg had to be amputated. The Scot saved his leg, but the Minié ball in his knee would
give him a slight limp in later years—a limp that he would use to good
advantage. After the war, Dunlap became a brakeman on the Chicago,
Rock Island & Pacific Railroad.

Dunlap was perhaps the smarter of the two. Where Scott was impulsive,
sometimes rash, Dunlap insisted on careful strategy and reconnaissance.
From time to time the best cracksmen of their time joined the Ring, but

its two other charter members were Red Leary, a huge pugilist and soldier of fortune whose challenge John L. Sullivan refused, and Billy Connors, a stout little man who wore a gleaming stovepipe hat and carried a yellow cane. A slight birthmark in the rough outline of a four-leaf clover on Billy's pudgy cheek made him very acceptable to the superstitious underworld.

The idea of the Ring was born in the early 1870's when Scott met Dunlap in New York City after he had been released from the Illinois Penitentiary where he had served five years for robbery. They were brought together by an oldtime burglar in Shang Draper's, New York City's Sixth Avenue saloon, the gathering place for the élite of the underworld. There was an immediate rapport between the two young thieves. Billy Connors was recruited, and the trio leisurely toured the South to select their first target. When another thief whispered that he had heard the Falls City Bank of Louisville, Kentucky, was brimming over with cash from the tobacco harvest, Jim Dunlap, posing as a New Yorker interested in investigating a tobacco plantation, opened an account. The bankers, impressed by his bank roll, diamond ring and stickpin, welcomed the new depositor. Dunlap came back to his associates to spend most of an evening in their boardinghouse, carefully making a sketch of the interior of the bank, which was a simple affair, its safe "little more than a tin cracker box." On this, their first job, they cleaned the vault of $200,000 in cash. The robbery had a severe effect on the community; the bank barely survived, and most of the tobacco farmers were in debt until the next harvest. Back in New York the Ring divided its loot. At the time, Scott and Dunlap did not care for "riotous living," as the newspapers called it. Instead of champagne and late suppers with the dancers from the Bowery Theatre, they invested their money in more mundane things like racehorses and potential champions who fought fifty rounds with bare fists on the Jamaica Bay barges. Billy Connors went in for diamonds and clothes. Even Jimmy Ryan, who operated the racehorse stables on Price Street, was heard to say that Billy the Pipe was becoming the fashion plate of Eighth Avenue.

Several months of idleness followed for Scott, Dunlap, and Connors. Then Connors reported he had heard that the Elmira, New York, National Bank held close to $500,000 in cash. The bank was on the ground floor of a two-story building. Above it was the headquarters of the Elmira Young Men's Christian Association. Pious and solemn as archbishops, Scott and Dunlap visited the YMCA's offices. Their story was that they had just completed a mighty struggle with Demon Rum and wanted to help others less fortunate than they. The dedicated young men of the association welcomed them. In between lectures on temperance, Dunlap sized up the rooms; the one directly above the bank vault was a file room. Once, he managed to pass through the room, and as he bent down to tie his shoelace he saw that the large flat lock was a Hall lock, one of the newest and strongest made. Dunlap and Scott left Elmira and returned to New York, where Connors joined them.

"We can't work it," Dunlap said. "Let's look somewhere else."

"We can work it if we get a party interested in locks," Scott said. "Try that lay, Billy, and see who has the keys." [2]

Connors returned with the information: The president of the YMCA had the keys.

In a few weeks Dunlap and Scott returned to Elmira as free-spending drummers for a shoe company. Through the hotel clerk they learned the address of the YMCA president. One night, equipped with rubber-soled shoes, masks, and glass cutters, they slipped out of their rooms and headed for the house of the YMCA president. They removed the sash of a bottom-floor window and tiptoed to the president's bedroom. For an hour they searched the bedroom, which echoed with the snorings and mutterings of the old man. As Dunlap later recalled, more than once they froze as he tossed and turned. They searched pants pockets, wallets, coats, dresser drawers, and even a shaving mug without finding the keys. Not until years later did they learn that the cautious YMCA president each night slid them under the edge of his bedroom carpet, where the flat keys made not the slightest bulge.

The disgruntled pair returned to New York. Only a knowledge of safes and vaults would help them, Dunlap said. The Ring invested what it had left of the profits of the Louisville robbery to equip Dunlap with an elaborate wardrobe so that he could play the role of a bank officer seeking an estimate for a complete new dial and vault system. With a gleaming new top hat, cutaway, and diamond stickpin, Dunlap toured New York City's biggest safe companies. He obtained a great deal of information, brochures, and had several fine lunches with eager salesmen, but he sadly informed Scott and Connors that it was all wasted effort because it would take him years to learn the secrets of the major safe and lock companies.

"We can't work it by ourselves," Dunlap told them. "We still have to get someone who knows keys and safes."

One night when Dunlap and Scott were pondering over methods to recruit a key-and-safe expert, Billy Connors excitedly rode up in a buggy to tell them he had been looking over Scott's new racehorse, Knox, in Jim Ryan's stables when he had heard someone mention the name of Herring & Company, one of the country's largest safe companies. Dunlap sent him back to find out more. The next night a triumphant Connors returned to Shang Draper's saloon. He carefully peeled off his gloves, laid his yellow cane and top hat on a chair, and told them the news. The horse next to Knox's stall was owned by William Edson, Herring & Company's expert on bank safes.

Dunlap leaned back in his chair, ordered another glass of beer, and for the rest of the evening he mapped their strategy to ensnare William

Edson. Connors was assigned to spend most of his spare time in the stables with Bob Scott. They raced Knox several times at Coney Island; and whenever Edson was inspecting his mare in the nearby stall, they made sure they were loud in their comments on the amounts of purses they had won. Soon they engaged Edson in a discussion of horseflesh, and one afternoon Scott invited Edson for dinner. Other dinners and champagne parties followed. Once, when Jim Dunlap was passing their table while they were in discussion at a midtown establishment, they invited him to join them. By the time the racing season was over, Dunlap knew a great deal about Edson: He liked everything that money could buy—good food, fine wines, women, and horses.

Dunlap cautioned the others not to become impatient. The grooming took several weeks, but one night, after Edson had irritably denounced his employers as cheapskates who were making a great deal of money from his talents, Dunlap casually mentioned that he knew a way to make "easy money" without too much effort. The greedy Edson leaped for the bait. They talked most of the night about the Elmira bank. When Dunlap returned to their rooms before dawn, he gleefully told Connors and Scott, "We have landed our fish."

Edson was out of town on business for some weeks. During this time Dunlap brought in Red Leary and John Berry, a famous New York cracksman, to round out the gang. He now announced his plan of robbing banks on a national scope. Either he, Billy Connors, or Edson would travel throughout the East, South, and West to select the banks with the most cash to be robbed. By the time Edson returned to New York in the fall of 1873, Dunlap had made a series of sketches of the interior of the YMCA office and the Elmira Bank. Connors was ordered to return to Elmira and survey the bank and YMCA office. He returned with the report that nothing had changed. Dunlap then arranged for Connors to send a letter to Herring & Company, requesting them to send a representative to Elmira to discuss a new safe estimate. As they knew he would be, Edson was sent upstate.

By this time the whole gang was in Elmira. Dunlap had hired an elderly woman—a well-known Baltimore shoplifter—to pose as his mother. They rented a small house on the outskirts of the city and furnished it with just enough furniture "to make a show." Connors, Scott, Leary, and John Berry hid in the house during the day.

Before Edson arrived in Elmira, Scott visited the YMCA and stuffed a small piece of paper into the Hall lock so it wouldn't work properly. The next day when he saw one of the clerks trying to make the lock work, he casually mentioned that Mr. Edson of Herring & Company was staying at his boardinghouse and that he would be glad to have him come over. Edson did, and left with a wax impression of the Hall lock. The way was now clear for the gang to enter the room of the YMCA that was directly over the vault of the bank.

Every night the crew left the house where the motherly shoplifter made a great display of keeping house, sweeping the steps and the yard with great vigor, and went to work at the YMCA office. First, the flooring was removed. Underneath they found a mortar, stone, and iron-beamed ceiling. Tons of stone were carried over the roof of the bank building to the roof of the taller Elmira Opera Building. It took the gang a week, working in teams, to carry away four feet of solid masonry and a layer of railroad iron. The last barrier was a one-and-a-half-inch steel plate. They were working on this when the bank's president, coming home late, impulsively decided to check his bank. He entered, held high a lantern, and was about to leave when he noticed that the floor near the vault looked white in the lantern light. He silently rubbed his finger along the floor, then looked up to the ceiling where by now cracks appeared. He slipped out the door and raced to police headquarters in his buggy.

At that time, the gang was resting. Dunlap, his face coated with plaster dust, had emerged from the hole. The others, stripped to shirt-sleeves, were stretched out on the floor, exhausted from their trips with the heavy baskets. Suddenly Billy the Pipe ran into the room with the alarm that the law was coming up the street in buggies.

Dunlap, like a fine commander, had his retreat prepared. Out the windows and across the roof to the Opera House, then down the drainpipes. They scattered like a disturbed flock of birds, fleeing across the rooftops and sliding down the iron pipes like trained acrobats. Within minutes the darkness had swallowed them. John Berry, who had decided to take his own escape route, was caught near the bank. By morning the house on the outskirts was strangely quiet, and the industrious elderly housekeeper had vanished.[3]

The First National Bank of Quincy, Illinois, was next on Dunlap's list. The loot totaled more than $700,000 in bonds and $120,000 in cash. During the robbery, Dunlap introduced the Ring to a small air pump, similar to a modern bicycle pump, which he and Edson had invented for blowing a vault. The purpose, Dunlap explained, was to suck air from the interior of the vault, then blow in a pound or more of powder. A small trigger device was attached to the train of powder, which was sprinkled on a sheet of stiff paper. When the trigger was snapped by a long cord held by someone hidden behind a barricade of desks or bank furniture, the powder inside the vacuum of the vault exploded with a tremendous outward force, splitting or shattering the vault doors. Edson had leased the pump to the Ring for $10,000.[4]

Some time that winter, romance entered Bob Scott's life. He discovered Mary Wood, a dark-haired girl who, William Pinkerton claimed, gave him more trouble than any other woman he had ever met in his lifetime. Mary would play an important part in the life and times of the Ring and the Pinkertons. Who she was or where she really came from may never be known. In her lengthy autobiographical stories and letters, published in Pulitzer's *World,* Mary insists she met Scott while she was a junior at Moravian Colege, Bethlehem, Pennsylvania. On May 15, 1871, over her parents' protests, they were married in Jersey City. "Thus the old adage, 'love laughs at locksmiths' was exemplified this time in our case," Mary wrote.[5]

William Pinkerton had another version: "It is all bosh about Scott taking her out of a seminary and eloping with her, and Scott being a college graduate, as he could scarcely write his name when he came to New York. He was originally a river thief on the Mississippi. She [Mrs. Scott] was the daughter of a butcher in Ellenville, named Wolf."

Pinkerton was prejudiced against Mary when he wrote this; at the time she was an able opponent of the Agency. There is little doubt she came from a wealthy upstate family. Later trial testimony revealed that she had been a promising pupil at the New York College of Music and a soloist at the First Presbyterian Church on Fifth Avenue, attended by the wealthy of the period. Mary also lived at 123 Fifth Avenue, a neighborhood of exclusive brownstones.

After their marriage, Mary and Hustling Bob moved to Number One Washington Square, a brownstone with glittering brass front-door fixtures and two servants. Bob, she later insisted, was content to sit in their sunny parlor, listening to her golden soprano, "because should anything happen to him he would know I would have the means of at least making a livelihood." Bob also seemed to have been infected with the need for culture; under Mary's urging he attended college three days a week, studying history, algebra, Latin, and art. There was a beautiful little garden in the rear of the house, and on warm spring evenings Bob and Mary would dine under the trees.

Scott invited the members of the Ring to the garden, where they had dinner; and later, while Mary sang in the parlor, they discussed ways and means of getting into the vaults of the country's major banks. Mary later insisted to William Pinkerton that she never suspected her handsome husband was a notorious criminal. Though the detective scoffed at this suggestion, it may have been true for two reasons: Hustling Bob was too much in love with his bride to let her know his real profession, and Jim Dunlap's iron rule was never to allow women to share their secrets.

In the summer of 1873, at a meeting in Scott's backyard, the Ring selected their next target: the Saratoga National Bank, which Billy Connors had been "piping" for three weeks and which he said was overflowing with cash and securities.

Dunlap and Scott met with Edson, who had got his air pump back, but the safe-and-lock expert gave them a cool reception. Either pay me the agreed $10,000 fee for the pump or count me out of all future operations, he told them. They were sitting in the rear of Red Leary's Fort Hamilton saloon when Edson gave them his ultimatum. Under the table, Scott nudged Dunlap, but the cold-eyed Dunlap needed no prompting. Edson later recalled how Dunlap toyed with his glass for a moment in silence, then said softly:

"I hear that John Berry up in Auburn wants to squeal. I'm the only one who can stop him, Edson. Suppose I let him go. Would you want your family and your employers to know of your disgrace?" [6] There was a long moment as Edson studied their faces. They were as cold as stone, and he knew Dunlap "would soon have me looking out of a grating if I didn't go along with him," as Edson told Robert Pinkerton.

Dunlap next led the Ring on a national tour to case banks. They followed their *modus operandi* of digging tunnels under houses adjacent to the banks at night, then removing the mortar and bricks in bags. During the day they posed as horse traders or land speculators, but not all were successful. The robbery of the First National Bank of Pittston, Pennsylvania, turned into a fiasco, with Scott and Dunlap touching off charge after charge to crack the huge iron vault. The two bank robbers, their clothes in shreds, their faces blackened, emerged from the bank barely able to stand from the effects of the blasts. The gang almost wept when they counted the torn currency and bonds: $500 in bills and $60,000 in bonds.[7]

In the winter of 1875, with the treasury of the Ring at its lowest ebb, Scott and Dunlap decided to rob the Northampton, Massachusetts, National Bank. The crime was Dunlap's greatest coup. The trial testimony reveals how meticulous he was in his year-long planning.[8]

In the spring of 1875, he invited Edson, the vault-and-lock expert to a meeting in Scott's Washington Square garden. On an April afternoon Edson, cold and distant, was ushered out among the trees by Mary, who later served them beer and sandwiches. Dunlap did his best to thaw Edson's hostility by promising to pay the $10,000 "fee" for the use of the air pump in the Covington, Kentucky, robbery along with a bonus. To show his good faith he gave Edson a few hundred dollars—actually, the last of the Ring's ready cash.

This meeting was followed by others every week or ten days. Dunlap was cautious in his dealings with Edson. When Scott became impatient, he begged his partner not to press the lock-and-vault man: "He is our fish; let us make sure we have him hooked," he told Scott.

Edson kept asking for money, but Dunlap managed to stall him. Under the trees in Scott's yard, on the sultry afternoon of July 29, 1875, Dunlap finally brought up the Northampton bank. The patient cracksman had first made a careful study of the town and the bank. It was now obvious to him that the three safes in the vaults held a large amount of cash and bonds. But the dials were brand new—in fact, they had been installed by Herring & Company, Edson's employer.

What he now wanted from Edson were the specifications for the vault lock. Edson went even further, and stole a sample lock and set of keys from Herring & Company. In the first two weeks of August, Dunlap built a miniature wooden vault and had Edson install the lock. For hours every day he and Scott would practice opening and closing the tiny door.

On weekends they traveled to Northampton to select a getaway route and a hideout, and, what was more important, to make a schedule of the movements of John Whittelsey, the bank's chief cashier. Whittelsey, they discovered, lived in a large white clapboard house on Elm Street, two-thirds of a mile from the bank. He was a quiet, meticulous man who apparently was devoted to business. He was at his desk at eight and retired promptly with his wife to their second-story bedroom at seven o'clock. There was a household of seven, including a housekeeper and a pretty Irish servant girl named Maggie.

All that blazing hot summer Dunlap and Scott shadowed Whittelsey from his bank to his home. As Dunlap later recalled, "We got up with him in the morning and put him to bed at night." Such close surveillance had its dangers. One night in August, the bank robbers were sprawled in the thick grass, under some bushes in the rear of the Whittelsey residence, when Scott heard footsteps. Both men hugged the ground as a man passed within a few feet, paused, and whistled softly. The rear door opened quietly, and Maggie slipped out.

For the next few hours, Maggie and her "beau" rolled about in the grass, grunting and groaning in the throes of their lovemaking. A few feet away, Dunlap and Scott fought to remain motionless as hordes of mosquitoes settled on their face and hands. Then a full summer's moon rose to bathe the backyard in its brilliant light. Nevertheless, Maggie and her boyfriend continued to roll about in the grass. Finally they got up and brushed the grass from each other. There was a last good-night kiss, with a fervent promise of enduring love, and Maggie slipped back into the house. Her exhausted boyfriend went down the road and disappeared in the darkness. Only then did Dunlap and Scott get up. Their bodies were covered with mosquito bites, and Scott had been stung so badly one eye was almost swollen shut.

At their next meeting, held in New York, Edson appeared with bad news. The combinations of the three safes and the keys to the vault and bank doors were divided among the employees of the bank. After he had questioned Edson, and learned that a young clerk shared the bank secrets, Dunlap advanced the idea to Edson that he should point out to the bank's officers the danger of entrusting such vital information to a young man. It would solve some of their problems if they could get the bank to put the combinations with one man, he told Edson. The keys were not much of a problem. All Edson had to do was return to Northampton and finish his assignment of regulating the dials of the safe. He would tell the bank president, Oscar Edwards, that the keys needed filing, and it would be a simple matter to make wax impressions of all keys.

Edson did his part. At his suggestion, James L. Warriner, vice-president of the bank, turned the keys and safe combinations over to one man—Whittelsey, the dedicated cashier.

The plan moved along without a hitch until November, when Edson told Dunlap that a former employee had warned the bank officers that the Herring safes were imperfect. He had been called back to the bank and had repaired some defects. Edson now had cold feet. This was as far as he would go, he told Dunlap. The bank was now talking of hiring guards, and that could mean violence. He told Scott and Dunlap, "I'm not a man for pistols," and said that the sight of blood made him faint.

Dunlap soothed Edson's fears, but after the safe man had left, he ordered Scott to summon the Ring. This was in early January, 1876. Dunlap set the target date as the twenty-fifth.

The members of the team he selected to accompany him and Scott were Red Leary, Billy Connors, Shang Draper, Big Jim Burns, and Bobby Howard. Howard was a skilled cracksman who had just arrived from England, where he headed Scotland Yard's list of major thieves. Big Jim, a smiling, jovial Irishman, was regarded with awe in the New York underworld. To celebrate robbing a downtown bank, he and his partner visited a saloon. After a wild champagne party Burns fell asleep. He awoke to discover that his partner had robbed him of his share. Burns denounced his fellow thief, and predicted that within a week he would "die in the gutter." Within a few days his former partner dropped dead while walking down Broadway.

To house his band of bank robbers, Dunlap selected the attic of the abandoned rural Bridge Street schoolhouse, set off the main road near a cemetery. The attic was stocked with blankets, whiskey, and food, mostly cooked chickens. The gang now concentrated on the movements of the two night watchmen who composed the Northampton police force. In the attic hideout, after he had studied the reports of their movements, Dunlap said they would have to kidnap the whole force and lock them in their cells while they raided the bank. This plan was abandoned when Billy Connors reported that the last police tour was four o'clock. From 4:00 to 7:00 A.M. the street was deserted. This would give them three hours to raid the bank. The final plan was to break into Whittelsey's house and hold the entire household captive while they forced the cashier to give them the combination.

At midnight they left the schoolhouse. Each man was dressed in a long linen duster or overalls, rubber-soled shoes, and wore a mask made from the legs of a man's winter underwear. They carried sledges, jimmies, crowbars, and dark lanterns.

At midnight they surrounded the house, smashed in the front door, and entered. Whittelsey was awakened by a nudge. When he sat up in bed, he found himself handcuffed to his bedpost. One by one the rest of the household were roused and brought into the bedroom. After a whispered consultation with the others, Dunlap ordered Whittelsey to dress. The bank robber was most considerate, even to helping the cashier select the correct vest. Whittelsey, now properly dressed, was escorted downstairs and seated in a chair. When he refused to give them the combinations of the safes, Leary reached over and let a hamlike hand slowly close about the cashier's neck.

In the dim light of the dark lantern, Scott drew a pistol and held it to Whittelsey's head. "It's no use to lie to us," the thief snapped.

Whittelsey noticed that the bank robber was nervously shrugging his shoulders as he prowled about the room, waving his pistol.

"Would you like some brandy?" Dunlap asked softly.

"No, I don't need it. I can stand it," Whittelsey replied.

"I'll twist his God-damn neck like a chicken's," Leary growled, holding his big hand before Whittelsey's face.

"I'm not going to allow any harm to come to him," Dunlap said firmly. Then, to Whittelsey, "It is best that you give us the combinations."

It was primitive psychology. Leary and Scott were acting the roles of villains; Dunlap was the gentle man trying to protect their helpless victim. Whittelsey finally gave in and recited the figures, which Dunlap wrote down. Now that the game was over, the gang became brisk and businesslike. Dunlap ordered Scott to return Whittelsey upstairs, handcuff him to the bedpost, and gag him and all the others. Whittelsey recalled that the clock struck four while he was being escorted back to his bedroom.

Dunlap and Scott left for the bank while Leary, Shang Draper, and the others remained in the house. Billy Connors piped outside, as always. There was a sliver of cold moon as Scott and Dunlap hurried down the deserted streets to the bank. After the vaults were opened, Dunlap squatted before the first safe. Carefully he spun the dial. After he reached the last number he yanked on the door handle, and the safe swung open. The cracksmen gasped as they saw the piles of stacked greenbacks and securities.

The second safe yielded still more cash and bonds. Dunlap and Scott were dumbfounded.

"My God, Jim, there must be over $500,000 in swag here," Scott excitedly whispered to Dunlap.

Actually, they stuffed $1,250,000 in cash and securities into pillowcases. The loot would have been far more if they had waited to open the third safe, which contained another million in securities belonging to Smith College. As the college authorities later stated, the loss would have been a catastrophe, and might have led to the closing of the college. But for some reason, probably because they had no more pillowcases, the two bank robbers failed to open the third safe. Their arms full of sacks bulging with a fortune in cash and securities, Scott and Dunlap ran back to the Whittelsey house. Connors whistled, and they all ran out. As they hurried back to the schoolhouse, Scott and Dunlap told the gang what had happened. They were dumbfounded when the crisp new bills and securities were dumped on the floor in the lantern light. There was no time to sort the loot, Dunlap said; it had to be buried. It was getting near seven o'clock, when the town's watchmen would begin their rounds.

"Where will we hide it, here in the attic?" Red Leary asked.

"No. In the cemetery," Dunlap replied.

The precise Dunlap had already selected a vault in a deserted section of the burial ground, and forced the door with a jimmy. The bonds and a large part of the cash, still in the pillowcases, were hidden in a corner of the darkened tomb.

When they scrambled over the graveyard fence, the church bells were tolling six—one hour for a getaway. Dunlap's orders were brief: Every man had to make his own way back to town. The next meeting would be held at Red Leary's saloon in Fort Hamilton, Brooklyn.

At seven o'clock Mrs. Whittelsey managed to push aside her gag and began screaming. A neighbor leaving for work heard her and summoned the watch. Whittelsey drove to the bank and found the dials broken off the safes. A telegram was set to Herring & Company, and Edson was summoned. He arrived later that day, attached a dial to the exposed spindles, and opened the safes. Edwards and Warriner, the bank's president and vice-president, both wept when the heavy doors swung open.

As Whittelsey later testified, "Most of it [the stolen money] belonged to private parties, and they lost their all."

The robbery was a national sensation. Reporters flocked to Northampton from New York, Boston, and as far as Chicago. Artists made sketches of the bank, Whittelsey, and his family. Days were spent making a list of the bonds, while outside in the streets depositors, who now realized that their life savings had vanished, watched the closed doors in numbed silence. Some weeks after the robbery, Robert Pinkerton was summoned by the bank's president, Edwards, who asked him to take over the investigation.

Pinkerton carefully went over the story of Whittelsey and his household again and again, dredging up minute details they had forgotten in their initial excitement. From both Mr. and Mrs. Whittelsey he finally discovered that one of the leaders of the gang constantly shrugged his shoulders. This man, the cashier now recalled, was impatient and impulsive; the other, the "general manager," as Mrs. Whittelsey called him, was "cool, gentlemanly and self-possessed."

The gang had left their masks, linen dusters, overalls, and iron sledges. From one mask Robert Pinkerton removed several strands of light brown hair. The dusters, overalls, and the masks made from winter underwear were obviously new, so Pinkerton assigned several operatives to question storekeepers within a fifty-mile area. Each operative had a duster, sledge, and mask. In less than a week, an operative had located two stores in

Springfield where the items had been purchased. The owners of the stores gave detailed descriptions of the two male customers. Pinkerton carefully underlined the phrase from Pinkerton operative Tom Gallagher's report: "E. A. Hall, a clothing dealer in Springfield, said one of the men shrugged almost constantly as he waited for him to wrap their purchases." With a map, Pinkerton sketched the logical route from Springfield to Northampton, and covered the area with the operatives. It was dogged, methodical police work. Witnesses recalled two men—one of whom had shrugged—who had waited for trains, hired teams, or stopped off for breakfast. Within a few weeks Pinkerton knew a great deal about the habits of the two very important strangers.

Pinkerton next met with Deputy Sheriff Henry F. Potter, and suggested that they make a search of all abandoned farmhouses in the area on the theory that the gang might have used one for a hiding place. Potter, who appears from Pinkerton letters to have been an alert and aggressive rural police officer, deputized some of the townspeople, and they searched the area around Northampton. In the schoolhouse attic they found horse blankets, scraps of food, an empty whiskey bottle, ropes and pulleys. The grease from the fried chicken had almost obliterated the name of the restaurant on the box but a Pinkerton operative spent a day laboriously tracing the name until it showed a New York City address. There was a torn page of a newspaper which Pinkerton traced to an issue of the New York *Sun*, December 22, 1875. He now had a general description of the gang's leaders, most of their movements in the winter of 1875–1876, and circumstantial evidence to indicate they were New York cracksmen.

Pinkerton now turned his attention to the bank and its equipment. When he questioned Whittelsey and discovered that Edson had been at the bank several times, had filed the vault keys, and in fact had been the man who had suggested that the combinations be entrusted to one bank official, Pinkerton decided Edson should be watched. A team of "shadows" were assigned to the lock expert, with orders to report his every move, day and night.

The investigation was still in its early stages when Edson met with Dunlap, Connors, and Scott on January 31st. He was given $1,200 and was told he would receive more when they finally divided up the loot. Edson protested that he needed more cash, but Dunlap soothed his fears by picturing the pillowcase full of money that he would get. Scott, he said, was going back to pick up the bonds from the cemetery vault.

In early February, Edson met Dunlap again. Scott hadn't returned yet, he was told. This time Edson left disgruntled when Dunlap admitted he didn't have any money for him. Scott, meanwhile, was on his way back to Northampton, but in Springfield he saw a story in the Springfield *Union* that told how the gang's hideout had been located in the schoolhouse and Pinkerton's theory that the bonds might have been hidden in the area. Scott, who had visions of opening the cemetery vault and finding a Pinkerton operative waiting with a navy Colt, returned to New York.

Dunlap now had another plan to use Edson as an intermediary. They summoned the lock expert and put it to him: "See what Edwards will pay," Dunlap told him.

Edson returned to Northampton and got in touch with Warriner, who met him in Springfield. By this time the bank officials were frantic; as far as they were concerned, the return of the bonds was all-important. Warriner told Edson he was "open" to any proposition.

Edson returned to New York for a meeting with Dunlap. They talked for some time, but, as Edson later testified: "Dunlap appeared not to notice what I was saying. Finally he took out his watch, looked at it, and said: 'I won't string you any longer. They are just about putting their hands on the stuff right now.' "

Then Dunlap stood up and told him bluntly: "There's no use talking about this any further. If the bank people want their property they know how to get it."

It was agreed that a personal ad in the New York *Herald*, "Idalia, F.N., Monday evening Eight sharp," would be the signal for the next meeting at Red Leary's saloon.

Edson returned to his job, always under the surveillance of the Pinkertons. One day Operative Tom Gallagher was surprised to follow Edson to Fort Hamilton, where he entered a saloon. Gallagher waited for some time, then trailed Edson back to New York City. He returned to the saloon, "leaving his sleigh nearby while he stopped off for a few drinks of cheap whiskey." The giant Red Leary was behind the bar. Gallagher was soon a regular customer who just happened to be on hand when Edson was taken into the rear by Leary for long discussions.

In the Exchange Place office, George Bangs and Robert Pinkerton slowly put the pieces together. Underworld informants had identified Hustling Bob Scott as a man who had a habit of shrugging when under pressure, and Jim Dunlap was his constant associate. Operatives now trailed members of the gang.

What Pinkerton didn't know at the time was that the bonds had been removed from the cemetery vault in February and hidden in New York. This had taken place before Pinkerton had been brought into the case by the bank officials. After Dunlap had told Scott that he no longer trusted Edson, the pair had traveled to Springfield, where they hired a buggy and team. They drove to the Northampton cemetery, removed the bonds, and brought them to New York. They spent days touring the city and its outlying sections, looking for another hiding spot. Scott finally found one: the belfry of the Church of the Redeemer, on Temple Avenue, Astoria.

Scott later confessed that he had selected this remote spot because the congregation was a wealthy one, and the property having recently been repaired, there was little chance of its being torn down. "By swinging the packages of cords over the bells there was little chance of them being discovered. It was also a dry place. The church was detached from other buildings so there was little chance of fire."

Only Red Leary was given the location of the new hiding place. Dunlap then printed a series of four letters to Edwards, suggesting that the bank "work back" its securities. While they waited for Edwards to reply through a personal ad placed in Greeley's *Herald,* they heard from Edson. Scott, Dunlap, Connors, and Leary met in the rear of Leary's saloon with the luscious Kate Leary, also a redhead, serving beer and sandwiches. This was one of the first mistakes to be committed by the usually cautious Dunlap; each man attending this meeting had been tailed to the saloon by a Pinkerton "shadow."

The meeting was stormy. Scott denounced Edson as an informer, and showed him the copy of the Springfield *Union,* quoting a bank officer, who in turn quoted Pinkerton, to the effect that the securities had been buried in the Northampton area. Edson protested he "didn't tell man, woman or child about their game" but the gang leaders refused to believe him, with Scott shouting they weren't going to pay him "a d——n cent."

In late November, 1876, Operative Gallagher tailed Edson back to Leary's saloon. This time Edson presented a proposition for Scott and Dunlap: The bank would pay up to $150,000 for the return of the securities.

"If they will pay that amount they will have the securities," Scott told Edson.

Billy Connors, the fashion-plate bank robber, was selected as the intermediary. Edson aranged for one of the bank officers to meet Connors in New York City. Apparently Edson had set the "compromise price" too high, and the bank balked at paying $150,000. Two other meetings followed, with Connors and Edson tailed constantly by the Pinkertons. At last Edson told the bank officer: "I am trying to effect a negotiation, but I am left by these men in a very bad light with their constant playing with you and me, after you take the trouble to come to New York. Now sir, if you don't reach a settlement at the next meeting, by G—d, I will tell you who the men are."

When he was told this, Robert Pinkerton made sure the next meeting also resulted in an impasse. As Edson left the hotel in a rage, he was picked up by Pinkerton and brought to his office. There was no "sweating" of Edson, as the police of that time called the third degree. Pinkerton quietly showed Edson how the case was building up against him, with the probability that he would spend the rest of his life in prison. Edson, then fifty-two, left troubled and trembling. The next day, and for several days after that, he was "invited" to see Pinkerton. The meetings, held in Robert Pinkerton's private office in the Exchange Place building, were long and leisurely. Edson often stayed "until the gas lights had to be turned on."

Pinkerton also made sure that Edson now knew he was being followed. The same "shadow" dogged his footsteps day and night. He was followed in the morning. At night a man in a buggy trailed him to his doorstep. When he peered through his curtains, he saw the same man standing under the gas streetlight. Again it was primitive psychology, but it worked.

Edson cracked. One afternoon he blurted out: "By God, I'll tell you the whole story, Pinkerton."

For hours details poured out, with the pen of the "shorthand man" racing across the page to keep up with his tale of planning and bank robbery on a national scale.

Operative Gallagher, Philadelphia Superintendent Ben Franklin of Molly Maguire fame, and his assistant Robert Linden had tailed Dunlap and Scott from New York to Philadelphia. At the Philadelphia depot Linden picked up a coded telegram from Robert Pinkerton. It was the order to arrest Scott and Dunlap.

The pair were returned to New York. A key found on Dunlap was traced to the Grand Central Hotel. In his room a trunk yielded bars of wax, screws, and burglar's tools. But there was no trace of the missing securities. When they were questioned, both Dunlap and Scott looked blank. Edson, of course, didn't know where the securities had been hidden.

Billy Connors, Red Leary, and Shang Draper were also arrested and lodged in the Ludlow Street Jail in lower Manhattan. They were confined only a few weeks before a turnkey found their cells empty. There was a great deal of explaining by the prison officials about how Leary had dug his way free, but Robert Pinkerton gave a terse, logical explanation for the trio's escape: "They used the golden key"—bribery.[9] Connors and Leary fled to Paris, where a New York *Times* corespondent reported they "were living a high and easy life."

Shang Draper, who was tipped off that the state didn't have a case against him, surrendered with an attorney. The grand jury handed down a "no bill," and he was released. But before he was released, Shang had bribed a guard to deliver a message to Dunlap and Scott, advising them the bonds had disappeared. Leary had climbed to the belfry and removed them. It was now clear how the Fort Hamilton saloon owner was financing his stay in gay Paris.

While Scott and Dunlap languished in jail in Cambridge, Massachusetts, in lieu of the astronomical bail of $500,000, Robert Pinkerton and his operatives carefully put together the state's case. Witnesses were located who had seen Scott and Dunlap in Northampton, once studying the house of Whittelsey, the cashier. The storekeeper who had sold the bandits the linen dusters, overalls, and winter underwear for the masks identified the purchases. A general-store owner who had sold the gang the sledges was found. In Springfield the livery-stable owner picked out a photograph of Dunlap as the man to whom he had rented a "fine team" the day before the cracksman retrieved the securities from the cemetery vault. A team of physicians also identified the strands of hair Pinkerton had removed from one of the masks as coming from Dunlap's thick, light brown hair.

Pinkerton also introduced a new gimmick into this investigation: a handwriting expert. He persuaded the district attorney to hire a New Yorker named Joseph E. Payne, "for the past ten years a professional expert in handwriting." Payne compared Dunlap's handwritten money order that Franklin had found in the bank robber's pocket with the names on the registers of the hotel and livery stable in Springfield, a telegraph receipt book, and the "superscriptions" of the four letters received by Oscar Edwards, the Northampton bank president, and announced they had all been written by one man, James Dunlap.

Scott and Dunlap went on trial in Northampton in the summer of 1877. Edson took three days to reveal the inner workings of the Ring, their other robberies, and, finally, how the Northampton raid was organized and pulled off. Column after column in the nation's big-city dailies repeated the testimony of Whittelsey, his wife, and the others in the household who had been held captive that night. As always in every sensational American trial, women fought to get seats in the courtroom. They reached out to tear buttons from the jackets of Scott and Dunlap, and tried to bribe the jailers for a lock of their hair.

After a twelve-day trial, a jury found the pair guilty of robbery, and both were sentenced to twenty years. After a fall and winter of repeated appeals, Scott and Dunlap finally entered the Massachusetts State Prison at Concord. Scott was a model prisoner, but within a year Dunlap had formed a small group of prisoners to take over a train that delivered supplies into the yard and escape by ramming it through the prison's huge iron gates. An informer told a guard, and Dunlap was sent to solitary. But he was soon back to take over a choice job as boss of the clothing mill.

Scott and Dunlap disappeared from the pages of the nation's newspapers, but they remained fresh in the public's memory. Women constantly wrote to the warden, requesting a lock of hair from the bandits' heads or a photograph. Scott, whose health was failing, didn't care about his public, but Dunlap, never a man to let a dollar slip past him, gained permission from the prison authorities to send out his carte de visite photograph for twenty-five cents. He reported a brisk mail-order business. When he found he was fast running out of his own locks of hair, he made a deal with the prison barber. In the 1870's scores of women proudly exhibited a lock of hair from the head of the dashing Jim Dunlap. If they had been put together, the curly locks would have made hair-pieces for a small army.

A steady, faithful visitor was Mary Scott. It was she who announced that her husband had died. She quoted his last words as: "Mary, never desert poor Jim. Be as a sister to him and do as much for him as you have done for me. Never cease in your efforts to obtain his pardon, for I am cause of his being where he is." [10]

The maudlin story, first published in the New York *World,* caught the fancy of the age. Women flocked to help Mary obtain the release of "poor Jim," who meanwhile was casually sorting his suits of long underwear, pairs of shoes, and rough overalls while he kept up his mail-order business of selling his photographs and locks of hair carefully swept from the prison barbershop floor. Mary was at first startled by the outburst of sympathy but she knew a good thing when it appeared on the horizon. She was soon a well-known figure on the lecture platform and in concert halls from New York to Chicago, pleading that "poor Jim" be released.

The amount of publicity she gained is unbelievable today. Scott's will was a tidbit for the press, and she added the lachrymose story of how Bob, on his deathbed, had handed her his cameo ring, with instructions to "place it on Jim's finger the day of his liberation."

Another sensation she revealed was Hustling Bob Scott's manuscript of a great drama he had written while in prison "which he had hoped to produce some day with success and profit to her." The drama, of course, was the "true story" of the great Northampton Bank Robbery.

Unbelievable as it may seem, Mary even enlisted the support of many of the nation's leading bankers to endorse Dunlap's parole. Heading the list was Oscar Edwards, president of the Northampton Bank! But Cashier Whittelsey wasn't among Mary's supporters. "I don't believe in letting bank robbers out of jail," was his stiff reply to a reporter's question.

But there was more on Robert Pinkerton's mind than poor Jim's parole. The detective had never given up hunting for the more than $1,000,000 in stolen securities that were still in Red Leary's possession. Operatives had trailed Leary for years throughout Europe, but the huge red-haired adventurer had dodged numerous traps from Paris to Constantinople. Legends grew about this strange man's journey to Europe: He was a mercenary attached to some sultan's army; he had fought fifty barefisted rounds with the English champion and had finally knocked him out; he had enlisted in the French Army as a sergeant when he found that the Pinkertons weer close at hand. Some of the tales were published after his death, but most of them seem apocryphal.

But Pinkerton realized Leary was now tired of running and wanted to return home to the Fort Hamilton saloon and his pretty red-haired wife, Kate. He also knew that Dunlap, who had refused in the past to try to approach Leary, was now smelling the fresh air of freedom through Mary Scott's efforts. Pinkerton approached Dunlap with his proposition: Get Leary back with the securities, and the Agency will favor your parole and help you to start a new life.

Dunlap agreed. His first letters to Leary resulted in a brief, penciled answer:

"You're on the inside, I'm on the outside. We no longer see things in the same light." [11]

But under Pinkerton's prompting, Dunlap continued to write to Leary. The letters were sent through a Midwest cracksman who had left the brotherhood to run a Chicago saloon. Dunlap's persistence finally won over Leary, who sent word he was returning to New York. The plan was to make a secret deal with Edwards to buy back the securities for $100,000. When Leary returned, Dunlap promptly informed Edwards and Pinkerton that the redhead could be found on the second floor of his Fort Hamilton saloon, being administered to by his ravishing Kate.

Leary's arrest took place on a snowy winter night, after Robert Pinkerton had chased Leary in a sleigh across what was then described as "the undeveloped part of Brooklyn." In an eastern version of the traditional Wild West scene, Pinkerton leaped from his sleigh to Leary's, and pulled the bank robber down into the snow. They rolled about for a while until Pinkerton clubbed Leary into submission with the butt of his revolver.

A few days later there was a daylight attempt by Leary's friends to free him on the steps of Jefferson Market Court when he was being transferred to Northampton for trial. It was another Wild West scene. Several husky "yegg burglars" rushed up the steps of the courthouse and tried to pull Leary from the grasp of a slightly built deputy sheriff. While Captain John Byrnes, later a famous New York City police inspector, held one of the gang leaders at pistol point, Robert Pinkerton, as the New York *World* reporter wrote, "dashed through the crowd of men on the steps, hurling them right and left until he stood between them and the deputy. Then he turned and faced the ruffians who were embarrassing each other in getting up the narrow steps. Pinkerton's face was deadly pale as he told them he would shoot down the first man who came an inch."

Byrnes, Pinkerton, and the deputy boxed in Leary and forced him back into the courthouse.

For the rest of the afternoon, the courthouse was under a state of siege by gangs of what the police called "desperate characters." Several coach-loads of policemen armed with pistols and rifles finally arrived. But the gangs still crowded the streets, waiting for Leary to come out. Winter twi-light was closing in when Pinkerton escorted the handcuffed and chained Leary across the inner yard of the courthouse and into a coach. Two other coaches were filled with armed police under Byrnes. At a signal the gate opened and the coaches emerged, the drivers laying their whips across the teams. As the *Herald* reporter wrote: "The pace was so rapid that one of the horses on the prisoner's carriage leaped over a trace and brought the cavalcade to a standstill on Fifth Avenue. The officers in the other carriages then surrounded Leary's carriage with their hands on their pistols." [12]

Leary was finally deposited in the Ludlow Street Jail, where the Pinkertons kept a twenty-four-hour guard to prevent Leary from finding another "golden key."

On the way up to Northampton with Leary, Pinkerton casually hinted at the state's strong case. He also made sure that a note from Dunlap, ostensibly smuggled out of prison, was slipped to Leary. The note threatened that Dunlap would appear as a state's witness if Leary did not return the securities to the bank. Pinkerton played the game for a week. Finally Leary gave in and told Pinkerton he had sent instructions to his wife where to find the buried loot. A few days later nearly a million dollars in musty-smelling securities were delivered to Pinkerton, who turned them over to Edwards, president of the bank.

Pinkerton made good his promises to Dunlap. In the fall of 1891, O. M. Hanscom, assistant superintendent of the Agency's Boston office, represented Robert Pinkerton at a hearing for Dunlap's parole. The Executive Council approved the parole, but Governor Russell unex-pectedly turned it down. He explained he had received numerous tele-grams and letters from residents of Northampton who "strongly objected to the liberation of Dunlap whom they regard as one of the most dangerous cracksmen in the country." [13]

When she heard the verdict, Mary Scott sniffed. "It's just a lot of old fogies who told Governor Russell Jim would start cracking safes as soon as he was released," she told the New York *World*. But Mary worked harder than ever the next year. The *World* was still on her side, and Pulitzer's reporters wrote long, sad stories about the "brave little woman" and her fight to free "poor Jim." Telegrams and letters poured into Governor William Russell's office that Christmas week of 1892.

"A Pardon in His Stocking," was the *World's* jubilant headline as it revealed that the great General W. T. Sherman had written a personal letter to the governor, asking leniency for his "old comrade in arms." [14] Veterans groups joined Sherman in asking for Dunlap's parole. The bank robber apparently decided to capitalize on his old-soldier status.

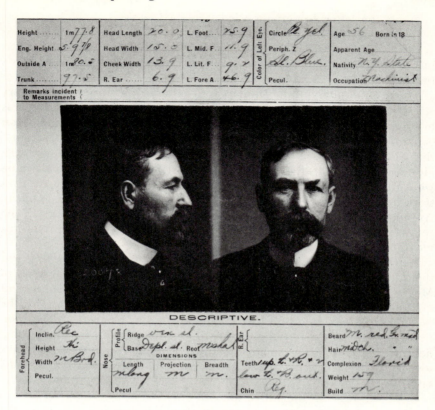

Height	1m 77.8	Head Length	20.0	L. Foot	25.9	Color of Left Eye	Circle *Re yel.*	Age	56	Born in 18
Eng. Height	5.9 7/8	Head Width	15.0	L. Mid. F	11.9		Periph. Z	Apparent Age		
Outside A	1m 80.5	Cheek Width	13.9	L. Lit. F	9.2		*Al. Blue.*	Nativity	*N.Y. State*	
Trunk	97.5	R. Ear	6.9	L. Fore A	46.9		Pecul.	Occupation	*Machinist*	

Remarks incident
to Measurements

DESCRIPTIVE.

Forehead	Inclin.	*Rec*	Nose	Profile	Ridge	*vin sl.*	R. Ear		Beard	*M. red. Gr. mix.*
	Height	*Hi*			Base	*Dept. sl. Root mshal*			Hair	*mdch.*
	Width	*mBrd.*				DIMENSIONS			Complexion	*Florid*
	Pecul.			Length	Projection	Breadth	Teeth	*up. L. vB. + r*	Weight	157
				mlong	*m*	*m.*		*low L. +B. out.*		
			Pecul.				Chin	*Reg.*	Build	*M.*

Profile and full face of James Dunlap, famous bank
robber of the 1880's. *Pinkerton's, Inc.*

The warden soon reported "old Jim" was limping from his Civil War
wounds. The *World* heard about it, and a reporter was sent into the
prison to interview Dunlap on his war experiences. Now the *World*
viewed him as a hero of that bloody day at Antietam.

On December 29, 1892, Governor Russell bowed under the pressure
of the growing campaign, and ordered Dunlap paroled. After a heady
press conference Jim and Mary left the prison in a hired carriage. Dunlap
was thinner and grayer, but he "could still turn a lady's head," as one
reporter noted. In New York the bank robber stared silently up at the
buildings. "My, they are certainly tall," he whispered to Mary as they
toured Manhattan.

By now Mary's press agentry was beginning to get under the skin of
both Pinkertons. "I see from a clipping from today's *Herald* that Mrs.
Scott has taken a great deal of credit to herself for Dunlap's release,"
William wrote to Robert. "The fact is, I really think this woman has
kept Dunlap in prison for the last five years with her blowing."

Across the letter Robert scrawled, "So do I."

Four days after his release, Dunlap paid a visit to Robert Pinkerton at the Exchange Place office. Informed by George Bangs that Robert was in the West, Dunlap left a note thanking Pinkerton for "all your efforts in my behalf."

Then, on January 13th, Dunlap was back on the front pages. Mary Scott disclosed to her favorite newspaper, the *World,* that Dunlap was to star in an elaborate production of the real story of the Northampton bank robbery. "The play is now being finished by an eminent playwright," she said. "It will be a true and exciting story of the robbery from beginning to end. Nothing will be held back. There will be some people who won't be happy when they see it." The *World* followed up with a story in its Sunday paper, revealing that the playwright was a Madison Avenue dentist "who has written several clever detective stories." The rest of the long story was devoted to virtually reviewing the dentist's maudlin play, act by act.

It was an exciting week for Dunlap and Mary. Reporters followed them wherever they went, and in the afternoon gathered on the stoop of Mary's fashionable brownstone at 123 Fifth Avenue. Her announcement of Dunlap's stage debut produced widespread editorial criticism, with the New York *Times* sternly advising Dunlap to stay away from the footlights and devote the rest of his years to a better way of life. The Springfield *Republican* wryly commented that Dunlap "had tried to make something in the original and failed. He may do better now. It's certainly safer."

Governor Russell, the Pinkertons, or the nation's bankers refused to recognize any great dramatic value in Dunlap's attempt to take to the boards and show the country exactly how a bank could be robbed of $1,250,000. Northampton Bank President Oscar Edwards wrote to Robert Pinkerton that he was horrified at the idea and that most of the bankers in New England were of the same mind. Evidently he had forgotten he had recommended Dunlap's parole. Robert sent back a three-page letter agreeing with him. Mary Scott, he said, was at the core of all the trouble.

The story of Dunlap's venture in the theatre was brief. When the reporters ran out of hard facts, they rehashed the old story of Mary's long fight to free "poor Jim." A cold, formal letter from Governor Russell abruptly made Mary agree that Dunlap was a better bank robber than an actor. The letter, delivered by hand to her Fifth Avenue residence, informed the bank robber that his parole would be revoked if he put on the greasepaint. Robert Pinkerton put it even more bluntly: There were still two indictments in Northampton that could be reactivated, he warned Dunlap.

Dunlap by now seemed to be weary of the aggressive Mary Scott. He paid Robert Pinkerton a visit to suggest that he help him open a saloon on upper Broadway. But Pinkerton pointed out that Chicago offered more opportunities: "We can keep a better eye on him out there," he wrote to his brother. It was now a question of money. Pinkerton, who recalled that Dunlap had served in the war, had an operative search out his war record. To the bank robber's surprise, he was eligible for $1,000 in pension rights. Dunlap, dodging Mary, went to Chicago, where he found a saloon for sale. He next appeared at William Pinkerton's office with his hand out.

"You pledged yourself to see that if I got out I made an honest living," he told Pinkerton. "So here I am, ready to do just that."

William, who boasted that he never broke his word "to any man, thief or clergyman," accompanied Dunlap to the saloon. The sale would require $2,000 more than Dunlap had. After an exchange of telegrams, William and Robert advanced Dunlap $2,000 to buy "a nice combination lunch and saloon."

"It will be principally a day trade, and his customers will be business people," William wrote to Robert. He also wrote to a member of the Massachusetts Parole Board, describing how they were setting Dunlap up in the saloon business. The letter reveals that for a worldly man he was either incredibly naïve or possessed a tremendous amount of faith in his fellowman—even bank robbers:

> You are aware I had pledged my brother and myself to see that if released he [Dunlap] should have an opportunity to make an honest living, and if necessary start him in some business. My brother and I let him have the money to open this place, and my brother who lives in Chicago, with other friends there whom we have caused to take an interest in Dunlap, will keep a lookout after him, and help and advise him in any way in our power. Personally I have the greatest confidence that James Dunlap will turn out alright. He is a man who does not drink to excess, is of steady habits, has ability and plenty of confidence in himself. Should you be visiting the World's Fair and can find it convenient to call in on Dunlap, I am sure he would be pleased to see you.

The man of such steady habits had engineered the most daring bank robbery of his age and had sent the Pinkertons chasing about the world after the loot he had stolen. . . .

Pinkerton also wrote to Oscar Edwards, the Northampton bank president, about Dunlap's new bar. The man whose bank almost crashed about his ears because of Dunlap's robbery was also invited to drop in to see the proud new owner of this saloon that catered "to only the first class trade." Pinkerton advised Edwards that before Dunlap opened his place, he had taken the precaution of bringing him around to Chicago police headquarters and introducing him, "so this will keep the detectives from following him up on his past reputation."

Pinkerton also acted as a drumbeater for Dunlap's new saloon. In a letter to Edward F. Hamlin, Executive Chief Clerk in the State House, Boston, who had helped Dunlap win his parole, the detective invited him to try the saloon's menu: "Should you be visiting Chicago during the World's Fair, and can find it convenient to call on Dunlap, I am sure he would be pleased to see you. The place he opened is in the business district and his trade should be businessmen. His intention is to serve a first class trade."[15]

Dunlap soon proved to be a better bank robber than a businessman. With every new problem he was at Pinkerton's doorstep. After several months Pinkerton wrote to his brother, "Although I am determined to keep our promise to help Dunlap start a new life, he is on the verge of distraction and frankly so am I." The saloon was failing, William wrote, at the rate of $14 a day. Finally, Dunlap's creditors were chasing him all over Chicago. His only refuge was in the Pinkerton office. William was in the West, chasing a band of train robbers, when the superintendent of his Chicago office sent a series of telegrams all along the frontier, trying to locate his employer, to get his approval to release the chattel mortgage Pinkerton's held on Dunlap's saloon and accept $500 for the saloon's fixtures and stock. "We have to act quickly," the superintendent wired. "This is the first of the month. Dunlap frantic. He has the whole office the same way."

The telegrams caught up with Pinkerton in a small western town in Utah. Saddle worn, and with two desperadoes in handcuffs, the detective sat down in the telegraph office and wearily gave his superintendent permission to accept $500.

On his return to Chicago, William wrote to Robert: "This ends the whole matter, and I think it will be a stone off our shoulders."

"So do I," was Robert's laconic reply.

But during the following month Dunlap was back at the Agency's Chicago office, offering Pinkerton another "business proposition." "A faro game! Think of that!" William wrote to Robert. "I would as soon think of buying him 'The Bowery' as I would anything of this kind. I haven't seen him since I turned him down and frankly I don't care if he never pays us a visit." [16]

But not long afterward, Dunlap suddenly reappeared. This time he silently held out the morning paper for William Pinkerton to read. It was a long interview with Mary Scott telling how she had come to Chicago to find "poor Jim." "Poor Jim," the cold, analytical outlaw, whom the nation's top bank presidents viewed as the most dangerous thief of their time, the man who could mastermind the biggest bank robbery in the history of his country, begged Pinkerton to give him the fare to get out of town. The sympathetic detective gave him the money to buy a ticket to Portland. The next day Mary, "full of beans," appeared at the Agency. When she demanded to know where "poor Jim" was living, Pinkerton told her bluntly his Agency didn't keep tabs on bank robbers for lady admirers, and ushered her out of the office.

In the following year Pinkerton, sending from Chicago the details of a crime ended his letter to his brother with the terse announcement: "Mrs. Scott is back in town with Jim Dunlap in tow. I saw him on the street the other day. He looks like he has a ring in his nose. I don't think we have to worry about him any more poor fellow. I wish we had a Mary Scott for Old Man Hope, Davey Cummings, Charley Becker and the others. A woman like this is more effective than ten police departments in keeping these fellows in line." [17]

But Dunlap, like the Bishop's Beggar, continued to haunt the Pinkertons. He appeared several times at the Chicago office of the Agency, always with his hand out and the reminder that it was the Agency which had helped him obtain his freedom and therefore was responsible for his livelihood. From his letters William Pinkerton now appeared resigned to being the eternal benefactor of the onetime bank robber. He dashed off angry letters to Robert, vowing he would have Dunlap barred from his office, but always he relented at the last moment and gave Dunlap either a small cash loan—which was never repaid—or help in obtaining a job. "We sit here and he tells me these great stories of how he intends to start in business! My God. When will the man ever learn he is no business man?" cried William in a letter to Robert.

Mary was still chasing the aging Dunlap, who no longer had the curly locks women once cherished. He was stooped, his face lined, his clothing worn. When he could trap the detective in his quiet office, he would spin tall tales for William, who simply didn't have the heart anymore to kick him out.

Dunlap was at the end of his rope when he turned to the one thing he really knew—bank robbery. But he had lost his touch, bungled a Chicago crime, and was sentenced to Joliet for twenty years. Then he was paroled, probably because of fading health.

Mary Scott, now rather plump, and her thick black hair streaked with gray, met Dunlap at the prison gates. They left hand in hand. Dunlap appeared to be happy to see her. She was all he had left.

CHAPTER 26

Adam Worth: The Other Napoleon

The most moving and fascinating chapter in the history of the Pinkertons' century of fighting international crime and criminals deals with the life and times of Adam Worth, whom a superintendent of Scotland Yard called "The Napoleon of Crime." Allowing for William Pinkerton's many times overblown characterization of criminals as the greatest, the cleverest, the most dangerous, he was not exaggerating when he called Worth the outstanding criminal of the Victorian Age.[1]

In over thirty-five years of crime, Worth stole an estimated $4,000,000 gross without once resorting to bloodshed or physical violence. He was arrested only twice and put in prison for a mere total of six and a half years. Though he had little formal education, he was highly intelligent, and operated halfway around the world in lands whose languages he couldn't speak. Versatile and inventive, he robbed millions from international banking firms, European businesses, and jewelry firms. He engineered the $400,000 Boyleston, Boston, bank robbery shortly after the Civil War, and moved across the world to Capetown to rob the Kimberly Diamond Mines of a fortune in uncut gems. He was daring and courageous, yet he could be cautious to the last degree. He made stealing an art, and the highlights of his lifetime were the occasions he outwitted Scotland Yard, the Turkish secret police, or the Sûreté. He died having only two friends, the greatest detectives of their time, who, he knew, wanted nothing more than to put him behind bars—William and Robert Pinkerton.

Worth was capable of planning for months a plot sufficiently complicated to furnish a Restoration comedy of intrigue for the purpose of embarrassing the superintendent of Scotland Yard, whom he passionately hated, while his sensational theft of the priceless Gainsborough painting "The Duchess of Devonshire" was accomplished with a minimum of effort. Worth kept "the London Lady," as he called the work of art, for twenty-five years in warehouses in Brooklyn, Manhattan, and Boston before he turned it over to William Pinkerton as a token of his respect. Taking into consideration certain inadequacies of the era as being in his favor—weak or nonexistent extradition laws, statutes of limitation, the extent of police corruption and/or inefficiency, ignorance of finger-printing, and flimsy bank vaults—Worth was still an extraordinary figure.

Physically he was a slight man, five foot seven inches, and never weighed more than 130 pounds. He had a sad, almost melancholy face, with large, luminous dark eyes, thick black hair and luxurious sideburns that gave him a distinguished, professorial appearance. He usually wore a frock coat, a gold watch chain, and a solitary pearl stickpin. He was vain about his appearance, and in his last days darkened his bushy eyebrows.

His associates, as he called them, were few and carefully chosen. He never suffered fools gladly, and had only contempt for cowards. The great love of his life was Kitty Flynn, a beautiful Liverpool barmaid who married his best friend, another international thief. She eventually married a millionaire and died in a New York mansion, and was described by the press of her day as a society leader and prominent philanthropist. Her once great beauty is still evident in fading newspaper cuts.[2]

Worth was never far from beautiful women. He used one to seduce a Constantinople jailer so Worth could obtain the keys and free his men from the dungeons of a Turkish prison, and another to frame his enemy, the noted John Shore, Superintendent of Scotland Yard. Worth and his men traveled only in style. Because commuting between New York and Paris was difficult in the 1870's, Worth purchased a yacht, which Kitty named *The Shamrock*. In Paris he opened and operated the first American nightclub, the American Bar in the Rue Scribe, which had the most popular faro game in all Europe. Worth lived well; he had a fine house in Piccadilly, with neighbors that were making history in society, literature, or politics. Worth was at 158, Lord Palmerston at 144; Nelson had stayed with the Hamiltons at 103; Apsey House, the home of the Iron Duke, was at 149, and Nathan Rothschild was at 107. There were afternoons when Worth bowed in passing to a man, dressed in somber broadcloth, who smiled and called a cheery time of day. Worth later discovered that the Eminence was Gladstone walking home along Picca-dilly to Jermyn Street from the House of Commons.

Piccadilly with the world's great figures as neighbors was far from Cambridge, Massachusetts, where Worth was born in 1844. In his lifetime he never discussed his family, although William Pinkerton once said that Worth's father had been a prosperous businessman and that Worth had attended a private "academy" before he ran away to New York. In 1861, at seventeen, Worth enlisted in the Union Army to become a bounty jumper in and out of the New York regiments. He was briefly in the Army of the Potomac and with McClellan on the Peninsula. When the Confederates offered to pay deserters with rifles $30 in hard money, Worth slipped through his lines, collected the money, and came back through West Virginia.

In 1864 he was arrested for the theft of a package from an Adams Express truck, and sentenced to three years in Sing Sing. This was his only arrest in the United States, and one of two in his life. Worth's prison job was handling nitroglycerine for the quarry gangs. He had the ticklish task of heating the explosive when it was frozen.

"I was a rather stupid young fellow" he once told William Pinkerton; "I never questioned the guard and I always wondered why he left when I put the brittle chunks in the stove. When one of the older inmates told me I could be blown to bits, I decided I had enough of prison."

Worth planned his escape with characteristic care. First he drew up a schedule of the changing of the guards at the quarry, and then, with split-second timing, slipped into a culvert to crawl past the guards, who had orders to shoot any prisoner attempting to escape. He had also made a schedule of the arrival and departure times of a working tugboat. He swam out to the craft, hid under some cargo, then noiselessly went over the side and swam to shore as the tug neared New York City.

In 1866, his brother John came from Boston to join him. Together they tried to steal $30,000 from the safe of the Atlantic Transportation Company, on Liberty Street, New York City. The attempt failed, and for the first time Worth became disillusioned with his ineffective brother. The next year Worth returned home briefly, not to see his family, but to rob an insurance company in Cambridge of $30,000. This time he worked alone, and the job was neat and workmanlike.

With the proceeds, Worth bought a wardrobe and took rooms at New York's Astor House, which he told William Pinkerton was "the only first class house in New York." He moved about the city in leisurely fashion, gradually entering the circle of the élite of the underworld to choose carefully the men he wanted. In a "sporting saloon" on Sixth Avenue, probably Shang Draper's, where the best of the cracksmen drank nothing but champagne and had late suppers, Worth met Charles Bullard, who could honestly be called a society Raffles. Bullard came from an old and wealthy New York family that, early newspaper accounts insisted, could trace its ancestors to an officer on Washington's staff. He drifted into crime in classic fashion. His father died and left him a small fortune which he dissipated in a short time. Bullard's carte de visite from the early Pinkerton Rogues' Gallery shows him to have been a handsome man with thick curly hair, sideburns and a thin, aloof, aristocratic face.[3]

With a young burglar named Ike Marsh, Bullard had pulled off a daring train robbery on May 4, 1868. The pair had knocked out John Putnam, the Union Express Company guard, in the baggage car of the Hudson River Railroad Express en route to Grand Central from upstate New York. When the thieves swung off the train at a point in the Bronx where the train slowed down for a signal, they had two carpetbags fiilled with $100,000 in cash and negotiable securities. Putnam was found unconscious, a thick froth about his mouth. Later he told railroad officials he was asleep when attacked. When the Agency was called in by the company, Robert Pinkerton assigned Robert Linden, assistant superintendent of the Philadelphia office, to the case.

Linden searched the car and found a cake of soap and a small piece of brass shaped like a hook which the thieves had obviously used to lift the door's inside latch. The hook had been inserted into a small hole whittled out about the lock. Linden examined the hole, and reported to Pinkerton that the thieves had apparently used a knife with a jagged blade. The hook and soap, the only clues, were brought to the Agency.

The Pinkerton operative finally identified the hook as a piece of ornamental brass used on expensive accordions. After Linden had made a list of all the city's musical shops, he visited each one. It took several weary days to find a repairman who had replaced a fitting on a fine accordion. However, there was no record of the owner's name, but the shopkeeper recalled that the woman who had picked up the instrument had been in a hurry: "I have twenty persons to feed this evening," she had explained in a heavy French accent. At a conference in the Agency's office, Robert Pinkerton and George Bangs agreed with Linden that the woman probably operated a boardinghouse. A team of operatives under Linden was assigned to visit every boardinghouse, then grouped in the same section of the city. In a few days an operative reported to Linden that he had found the boardinghouse, "quite fashionable on the East Side," run by a French woman who also gave French lessons.

Bangs put Katherine Brelsford, a French-speaking female operative, in the boardinghouse. She became friendly with the boardinghouse keeper, who described her husband as a "traveling man." By the simple process of watching the morning mail placed on a plate in the lower hall, the woman operative discovered that a letter had arrived from Toronto. The following day the boardinghouse keeper sold out her establishment, and vanished. The Pinkertons now centered their investigation in Canada, with Bangs and Robert Pinkerton setting up headquarters in a Toronto hotel. Circulars listing the serial numbers of the missing securities were distributed in every large city and town in the Dominion. One day a young American named Martin tried to cash a $4,000 bond in a Hamilton, Ontario, bank. An alert teller checked the serial number with the Pinkerton circular, detained Martin, and notified the police. The young thief insisted he had bought the bond from two Americans he had met in his hotel who told him "they had to leave for Boston before the banks opened the next day."

Though Martin was sent to jail, he was quickly released on a writ supplied by a lawyer who mysteriously appeared. Pinkerton ordered the attorney tailed. Operatives reported they had followed him into an elaborate faro game operating above a Toronto restaurant. Pinkerton selected a young operative who could play the part of a "wide and handsome spender," and sent him into the faro game to "get close" to the attorney. The operative, who posed as a "Boston blood," was soon dining with the attorney, who advised him to call if he needed legal advice.

"I have two hot clients who would be in jail right now, if it wasn't for me," he boasted.

One night the free-spending Pinkerton operative was invited to join the attorney for dinner in the restaurant below the faro game. With him were two other well-dressed Americans. Later, they were joined by a third. From the descriptions of the first two, Pinkerton concluded the pair appeared to be Ike Marsh and Charley Bullard. The third man was Martin, the young American who was still on bond for passing the stolen securities.

In New York, other operatives now had found a railroad laborer named Burns who had seen Bullard and Marsh, carrying the heavy carpetbags, jump from the car. Bangs brought Burns to Toronto, "dressed him in toff's clothes," and had his operative take him to the faro game.

"They are the two men I saw get off the train," Burns whispered when he saw Bullard and Marsh, who came in with Martin.

Later, a woman joined Martin and was introduced as his wife. When the operative reported to Bangs that the couple spoke French, operative Katherine Brelsford was rushed to Toronto. Martin's wife was quickly identified as the East Side boardinghouse-keeper.

One night, when the attorney, Bullard, Marsh, and the Martins were having dinner, the Pinkertons and the local police placed them under arrest. A search of Bullard's hotel room produced a knife with a jagged blade, the nicks matching the cuts on the express door. Most of the cash and securities were discovered in Bullard's false-bottomed trunk.

In New York, Robert Pinkerton turned over a detailed confession signed by John Putnam, the express-car guard, to the district attorney. Pinkerton had hammered away at one point in Putnam's earlier statement that identified the section of the Bronx where he had been slugged. As the detective had reasoned, how could the guard have known where he was if he had been sound asleep when attacked? Even if Putnam had been awakened only for a moment by the attack, the combination of the darkness, the excitement, and the express car's lack of windows would have prevented him from knowing exactly where the train was at the time. The soap, Putnam confessed, was used to make the froth on his mouth. Young Martin, faced with a long term in Sing Sing, also became a state's witness with Putnam.

In Toronto, Bullard and Marsh fought extradition. After extended court battles they were finally brought back to the United States, and lodged in the White Plains, New York, jail.

Bullard's parents hired one of the best criminal lawyers in the country to defend their son, but the man dropped the case when a lady pickpocket who had been visiting Bullard stole the attorney's retainer of $1,000 and returned it to Bullard. But the handsome young thief didn't need any legal advice: A week after he was in prison, friends—including the lady pickpocket—dug through the wall of the jailhouse to return Bullard and Ike to their champagne parties and late suppers.[4]

The crime and escape had made Bullard the most-talked-about thief in the underworld at the time he met Worth. There was an instant rapport between the two men. They both abhorred violence, admired beautiful women, liked good food, fine wines, and expensive living. In his suite at the Astor House, Adam Worth suggested to Bullard and Marsh that they join him in robbing the Boylston National Bank at Boylston and Washington streets in Boston. Worth had carefully reconnoitered the place; his plan was to dig into the bank from an adjacent building. He had made sketches, and Bullard and Marsh carefully examined the penciled drawings.

The bank was on the second floor, over the Reeves Furnishing Goods Store. In the next building, on the same floor, was a barbershop. Worth's plan was to buy out the shop and dig through the wall into the bank. Bullard liked good planning, and agreed to form a partnership with Worth. Ike Marsh, who followed Bullard like a shadow, enthusiastically seconded the idea.

In Boston, Worth and Bullard put up $500 to buy out the barbershop adjacent to the bank. A few days later Judson and Company, Dealers in Wine Bitters, opened for business; Worth always insisted on a convincing façade. He bought baskets of dark, mysterious-looking bottles to line the window. Next he hired a carpenter to erect a partition that divided the office; one section was for his partner, he explained. Desks and chairs were moved in before they started digging behind the shield of the partition. Work was done only at night. Worth insisted that before dawn the office be cleaned and made businesslike. Mortar and bricks were hidden behind a chimney in the room. At Worth's orders one member of the gang stayed in the office during the day, ready to write an order for bitters in case a curious neighbor dropped by.

Although Bullard had the reputation, he accepted Worth's leadership without question. But it wasn't all work those weeks. Adam and Charley, in their best frock coats, were familiar visitors at Boston's best restaurants and faro games. They were never alone, for a beautiful woman was always on their arms.

On a rainy night they finally broke through the wall and entered the bank. Thunder rumbled above the city while they blew the big iron safe; and $450,000 in cash and securities were poured into carpetbags.[5]

Back in Worth's Astor House suite, they read the account of the robbery in the New York *Times, World, Herald,* and other newspapers.

On the second day, when it was announced that Robert Pinkerton and Robert Linden were in Boston, Bullard suggested to Worth that they leave for Europe. Many years later, although he was still reluctant to discuss the Boston robbery, Worth wryly quoted for William Pinkerton, Charley's remark: "Those damn detectives will get on to us in a week. I don't want to be playing a piano in Ludlow Street [Jail]."

Bullard's remark was prophetic. The usual dogged police work by Robert Pinkerton and his operatives, the door-to-door search for witnesses, identification by carte de visite, Pinkerton Rogues' Gallery photographs, physical descriptions, and *modus operandi* had identified Bullard, Marsh, and Worth as the Boston bank robbers. But the Pinkertons were forced to stand aside until the bonds had been "compromised," or "worked back," through a New York lawyer for a percentage of their total value. Divided equally, deducting expenses and auxiliary charges, each man received about $15,000. Robert Pinkerton and his superintendent, Robert Linden, trailed Worth, Bullard, and Marsh to New York and the steamer on which they sailed for England. Their securities returned, the bank's officers, with the strange morality of the bankers of their day, decided that they had spent enough on the investigation, and called off the Agency. A master report was made on the robbery and on the chief suspects. Copies, including photographs, were sent to all branch offices and large city police departments. Steamship lines were alerted, and coded letters were sent to overseas informants. While the Pinkertons would not travel through Europe trailing criminals unless their expenses were paid, they periodically reviewed unsolved cases, and sought to find out if the suspects had returned to the United States.

In the Boston bank robbery investigation, Pinkerton and Linden arrived at the South Street pier to find their suspects on the high seas. It was a time when major American criminals had as their goals London, Paris, and other European capitals. The prizes there were vast, the competition less severe, and even the Pinkertons—the FBI of their day—were hampered in their manhunts by convenient borders and negligible extradition laws.

Adam Worth was now finished with crime in America. Like other and greater Americans, he would become a member of his country's growing army of expatriates. He and Bullard arrived in Liverpool, that dismal,

Adam Worth

Charles Bullard, alias Piano Charley

Kitty Flynn

soot-blackened city of the 1870's, only a short time after the arrival of
Henry James, who would become Worth's Piccadilly neighbor, and after
Henry Adams had left for London.

The prizes Adam Worth sought lay not in grimy Liverpool but in
London. Yet in that waterfront city Worth found the great love of his
life, only to have it taken away by Charley Bullard, the handsome,
charming bank robber whom, John Cornish, a famous Pinkerton superintendent, once said, "had fingers so sensitive he is one of the few burglars who can open a combination safe with his hands alone."[6]

Bullard now was posing as Charles Wells, a wealthy New York merchant, and Worth, with sly humor, had adopted the name of Henry J.
Raymond, after the founder of the New York *Times*. He would keep
this name and bequeath it to his son.

They stayed for a time at the American Hotel in Liverpool. On their
first night in the hotel's pub they met Kitty Flynn, the city's most-talked-
about beauty. Kitty, then about seventeen, was known to many American
travelers "who remembered her face and rather petite figure."

In later years Worth refused to discuss Kitty, gallantly insisting it was
ungentlemanly to mention a lady's past without her permission. Unfortunately, we don't know how Bullard wooed Kitty, but one account of
her life that seems factual says Charley fell in love with Kitty from the
first moment he saw her in back of the bar in the pub. He courted her
day and night with flowers, rides in a "trap," and late suppers. Finally
Kitty succumbed, and agreed to marry Bullard.[7]

The wedding took place on a Sunday afternoon in the hotel. Most of
Liverpool's best people were on hand, along with the curious, including
the city's famous fishmongers with their large bare feet and foghorn
voices, who stood outside and bellowed congratulations to Kitty, one of
their favorites. Adam Worth was Bullard's best man. They were both
dressed in the most expensive frock coats and beavers Liverpool could
offer. The room was filled with flowers, and the guests danced and drank
champagne until the early hours. There is no way of knowing Worth's
reaction, but there is little doubt he was deeply in love with Kitty, and
remained so until the end.

Bullard and Kitty left him for a honeymoon in Paris. Worth, bored
and alone, occupied himself with robbing a pawnbroker of £20,000. It
was a neat, simple job. Worth stole the keys to the man's vault, had them
copied, and returned them before they could be missed. There was a
great deal of petty crime in Liverpool, as the newspapers of the period
show, but Worth's coup shook the small police force and rocked the city.

Worth, who knew his abrupt departure would be suspicious, remained
in Liverpool for several weeks. No one, of course, suspected the dignified,
handsome American with the grave face and professional manners. "After
the storm blew over," Worth left for London, then Paris, to join Charley
and Kitty. He discovered the Bullards living in a luxurious house across

Henry Jarvis Raymond. *Library of Congress*

Lydia Chapman

the street from the apartments of former Queen Isabella. Kitty was full of news of how she and her bridegroom daily watched the queen depart in her magnificent carriage drawn by four white-plumed horses. For six months, life was a round of champagne parties, balls, and affairs. The Wellses (Bullards) and their distinguished friend Henry J. Raymond (Worth) were always welcome guests at the best American houses.

When he wasn't sipping champagne with Kitty and Charley, Adam was drinking with the assorted bank robbers and gentlemen forgers who were arriving from the States. A report on Worth's activities, written in the precise hand of a Scotland Yard detective, informed Robert Pinkerton that Worth, "now delights in the more aristocratic name of Henry Raymond [and] occupies a commodious mansion standing well back in its own grounds out of view of the too curious at the West Corner of Clapham Common and known as West Lodge."

In the United States, a trio of criminals whose ingenuity, daring, and intelligence came near to matching that of Worth and Bullard were preparing to flee to England with $100,000 in cash and bonds stolen from the First National Bank of Baltimore. Like Worth and Bullard, Charles Becker, "The Scratch," undoubtedly the cleverest and most skilled forger in the history of international crime, and handsome Joseph Chapman, another counterfeiter, also employed elaborate props for their robberies. For weeks they had operated a small business firm next to the bank. Every night the policeman on the beat marveled at the hard-working partners who took turns at the ledgers, under a solitary lamp. He never failed to tap on their window as he passed, and they never failed to give him a cigar. After he had passed, work on the tunnel to the bank vault would be continued. Their loot was mostly in cash and Baltimore & Ohio and North Central bonds. Robert Pinkerton had traced them to the Liverpool-bound steamer *City of Brussels,* and Lydia Chapman, the counterfeiter's dark-haired wife, to the S.S. *Cuba.*

Informants advised Robert Pinkerton that Becker and Chapman had registered at the Grosvenor Hotel in Liverpool. When Lydia arrived, Chapman met her, and together they traveled to London, where they leased a fine house at 103 Neville Road which Lydia immediately began decorating with their share of the Baltimore loot. Informants later told the Pinkertons that expensive crystal chandeliers and rolls of dark red carpeting were seen being delivered to the Chapman house.

When the Pinkertons learned that Worth and Bullard had been seen in Liverpool, Paris, and London, and alerted Scotland Yard, the Agency persuaded the Baltimore bank officials to send William to London in pursuit of the bank robbers. It was then that William Pinkerton's long friendship with John Shore, the famous superintendent of Scotland Yard, began.

Like Worth and Bullard, Chapman and the others had little to fear from the Pinkertons. They were safe from extradition; bank robbery, curiously, was not an extraditable crime, but Pinkerton had found an old charge of forgery against Chapman that was extraditable. Reports in the Agency's Record Books show William Pinkerton shadowing Chapman as the bank robber lived the life of a wealthy London gentleman, opening bank accounts, driving about the park in a "spanking trap," and patronizing expensive jewelers with Lydia.

Lydia Chapman was "one of the most beautiful women the underworld of the 1870's had ever known," a contemporary account insisted, with the thieves of the times viewing them as the ideal couple. "Joe Chapman had but one vice—forgery; and one longing passion—Lydia Chapman," as one writer solemnly put it.

Another international thief in London was Max Shinburn, alias The Baron. For years William Pinkerton chased, arrested, and jailed The Baron across Europe and in the United States. Prussian, arrogant, and unbearable, Shinburn's carte de visite bears a resemblance to the early Eric von Stroheim. He was Adam Worth's bitterest enemy. The only time

Worth mentioned violence, even in his old age, was when he spoke of Shinburn. "He is the only man I would gladly kill," Worth quietly told William Pinkerton years after the great days in London and Paris were fading memories.

When these two intelligent, masterful thieves fell out is not known. William Pinkerton, the realist, thought it had to be a difference over some stolen bonds. But Sophie Lyons, another international thief of the 1870's and 1880's who stole almost as much as Adam Worth in her day, had a more romantic explanation: They had quarreled over Shinburn's attention to Kitty.

However, the bitterness didn't develop until years after America's most dangerous and skillful thieves had gathered in Paris, Shinburn among them. Worth loved the gay, carefree life of Paris in contrast to dismal, austere London. The idea of opening an American club in Paris combining a bar, restaurant, and gambling setup slowly developed in his mind. He finally selected the fine-looking Regency-style house at 2 Rue Scribe for his club—the first American bar and nightclub to be opened in Paris.[8]

By this time did the beautiful Kitty realize that her husband and his close friend Adam Worth were notorious American criminals? In later years Kitty insisted she had believed their stories of affluent businessmen from the States seeking European markets. William Pinkerton, perhaps out of gallantry, said he believed Kitty. Her ignorance can be accepted when it is realized that Worth, Bullard, Shinburn, and the rest of these Victorian rogues dressed and talked like men of the international business world. They were polished, charming, and sophisticated. They were accepted both by society and by European financial circles. In their Paris club, high police officers—who came to be paid—appeared to be close friends.

Kitty thought it incongruous that two wealthy American businessmen would want to open a Parisian nightclub, but Worth and Bullard, glib and persuasive, sold her the idea that as a novelty it would be financially successful. During the time it operated, the American Bar was the busiest night spot in Paris. As the saying went in the 1870's, if you wanted to see any American of any importance, visit the American Bar in the Rue Scribe.

Early accounts, which William Pinkerton confirmed, had Bullard and Worth investing $75,000—an enormous sum at the time—equipping the bar with walled mirrors, dazzling crystal chandeliers, mahogany tables, thick carpets, fine glassware, and the services of a superb chef. The first floor of the house was fitted up as a clubroom. Worth insisted that a clerk be hired who could keep a file of current American newspapers and magazines such as *Harper's* and *Leslie's Weekly*. They also took on a bartender "skilled at making American drinks which at the time were unknown in Europe." As Worth told Bullard and Kitty, the club had to be a second home to traveling or lonesome American tourists and businessmen.

On the second floor they established an elaborate gaming room. One account has Worth importing croupiers and faro men from the States. This may be legend, but William Pinkerton, who knew the club—and who closed it with the help of the Sûreté—later told a magazine editor that American Bar's faro game room was the most luxurious he had seen on the Continent. The luxury of the place excited the curiosity of the Parisians, and immediately attracted wealthy American tourists and bored businessmen. Apparently Kitty was the hostess: "She was a beautiful woman and a brilliant conversationalist who dressed in the height of fashion. Her company was sought by almost all the patrons of the house. . . ." [9]

While Worth was organizing the American Bar and its faro game, the officers of the Third National Bank of Baltimore were getting restive about William Pinkerton's lack of success in arresting the thieves. As the five bank officers informed Bangs, "They would forget the benefit of another dividend if they could catch the guilty parties and convict them."

Bangs brought up the old extraditionable charge of forgery against Chapman. While he agreed there was a good possibility of getting the American bank robber behind bars, he also warned the bank officers that Chapman had probably been alerted that "extradition papers had been issued for his arrest."

Now, for the first time, William refused to obey a direct order from his father. Bangs had written to Allan Pinkerton with the suggestion that John Geary, an informer securely placed in the international underworld, be sent to London and Paris to help William. Allan cabled his son, ordering him not to make any move until Geary had arrived. William sent back a terse reply that he was capable of running his own show. Cables and letters from his infuriated father followed, but William ignored them. Allan's last cable was: "Have full confidence in Geary. If no clue you must take him or withdraw. Willie we must win. Never withdraw."

William ignored his father's cabled instructions, and instead wrote a letter to Bangs that he had picked up the trail of the Chapmans and was going to Brussels. Allan probably gave up the fight and let William have his own way, for the matter disappears from the daily Record Books. Geary never reached London or Paris—at least not on expenses provided by the Pinkertons.[10]

From Belgium, William notified Bangs that Joe and Lydia Chapman had fled back to London; the pair had been tipped off, William insisted. A quarter of a century later, Adam Worth confirmed the detective's suspicions when he revealed he had "bought" a French interpreter who kept the gang informed of the moves made by the Pinkertons and Scotland Yard.

Back in Paris, Pinkerton heard about Worth's American Bar. One night he sauntered in. Worth and Bullard were in the lower rooms speaking to a minor French government official—Bullard spoke French and Italian—when Worth glanced across the room and saw the big American detective. He nudged Bullard. "Billy Pinkerton," he whispered.

Bullard quickly disappeared, but Worth ushered the Frenchman to the bar, ordered a drink, and then walked back to Pinkerton. The two men, the huge Pinkerton dwarfing the slight Worth, greeted each other formally, then went to the bar for a drink. There was some inconsequential talk before Worth left, explaining he had to see some guests. Bullard, of course, had spread the word, and when Pinkerton came up to watch the faro game the visiting American criminals, all in evening clothes with their women in plumes, furs, and diamonds, nervously cashed in their chips.

In a memorable interview with William Pinkerton many years later, Worth said, with considerable understatement, "We were rather troubled at what had brought you to the club."

Pinkerton was looking for Chapman, whom he never expected to, find. After a tour of the club, Pinkerton said a grave good night to Worth, and left.

After the club had closed for the night, Worth, Charley Bullard, and the others met in Adam's private office to discuss excitedly what they should do. Nothing, Worth counseled. We're all bank robbers and burglars, and that crime isn't extraditable.

"But they dug up that old charge against Joe [Chapman]," Bullard said.

"Then Joe will have to look out for his own tail feathers," was Worth's reply.

It was typical. Worth, a realist, came to the rescue of his accomplices or forsook them as his own interests required.

At a meeting with the Sûreté Pinkerton described the criminal backgrounds of Worth, Bullard, Shinburn, Chapman, and Little Joe Eliott, another American criminal, who were seen nightly at the American Bar. As William Pinkerton suspected, nothing was done. The explanation was simple. Worth, many years later, confirmed Pinkerton's suspicions that before he had opened the American Bar he had bought off influential police officials "to avoid later difficulties." [11]

After the meeting with the Paris authorities, the Adam Worth-Chapman interests received an unexpected break. William Pinkerton was ordered by his father to London to join John Shore, Inspector of Scotland Yard, in the investigation of a million-dollar Bank of England robbery. (Eventually the Pinkertons would arrest the American forgers who staged the robbery—Austin Byron Bidwell, George Bidwell, and George McDonnell—in such diverse places as Havana, London, and New York.)

The absence of Pinkerton was a relief to Worth and Bullard, who were short of cash. They found their next target in a busy French diamond merchant who liked to drop by the club for a drink and a few hours at the faro table. There was no great planning to the crime. One night the merchant came in and, as was his custom, placed his leather bag of gems on the bar. When he asked Worth to cash a check, the bag was switched as Worth went to the safe. When the merchant found his bag of gems, valued at £30,000, stuffed with paper, he went to the police. Worth insisted the man was mistaken, but he was arraigned on a charge of theft.

At the preliminary hearing, Worth asked for an opportunity to question the merchant. Permission was given. With all the police arranged against him, Worth succeeded in so confusing the diamond merchant about whether he actually ever had a bag with him that night that the hapless man finally admitted to the magistrate he coud not be sure he might not have left the bag somewhere else. Worth was discharged.

There was a triumphant champagne party that night at the American Bar, but Worth was strangely morose, and not even Kitty could cheer him up. He didn't tell the others, but his paid informant in the Sûreté had warned him that William Pinkerton was writing to French officials, demanding that something be done about closing the American Bar. Pinkerton was now joined by Inspector Shore; this time the Paris police could not ignore the combined pressure of Pinkerton's Agency and Scotland Yard.

The imaginative Worth decided that they needed a vacation, so he bought a yacht. There was a hilarious ceremony at the shipyards, with Kitty breaking a bottle of vintage champagne across the ship's bow as she bestowed the name of *The Shamrock*. Old woodcuts show *The Shamrock,* a large vessel with one stack, steaming alone, a bone in its teeth, pennants stiff in the wind. There is much legend about *The Shamrock,* but the meager facts indicate that Worth and the rest of the gang furnished it lavishly with a gambling room, bar, elaborate dining room, complete with crew and captain. Allowing for the imagination of the reporters of the period, *The Shamrock* was probably a fair-sized vessel that took Worth and his band of rogues, scoundrels, and international criminals and their ladies on a grand tour of the Mediterranean. As always, Adam Worth had a dual purpose: In addition to a vacation away from the jittery Sûreté, he and Bullard carefully reconnoitered local banks, jewelry exchanges, and business firms in every city they visited. This cruise probably gave him the idea for his later grand-scale draft forgeries in Turkey and other parts of Europe.[12]

The money finally gave out. Worth sold the yacht, and they all returned to London. Then Charley vanished, appearing later in the States.

Kitty was heartbroken. Adam's personal code, almost puritanical when it came to women, refused to allow him to take advantage of Kitty, but it was inevitable that Kitty, lonesome, bewildered, and heartsick, should turn to Worth. It was an idyllic time. The testimony of his colleagues in crime that Kitty's two children were Worth's was so unanimous that it is hard not to credit. What may have helped to win Kitty was the contrast between Worth and Bullard. Worth was shrewd, polished, cool, and assured, as against Bullard, handsome and dashing, but now so unstable and full of moods that Kitty was getting weary of him and his soulful piano playing.

There are stories, repeated by William Pinkerton in later years, which found their way into newspaper accounts of the 1880's of Worth still maintaining his guise of a well-heeled American, and going nightly to a thieves' hangout in the East End of London without Kitty's knowledge. He would change his fine clothes for humbler garb to confer with his criminal colleagues, then seek out a railroad washroom to change back into his "gentleman's clothes" before stealing back to their bedroom as dawn was breaking.

The happy times ended when Charley suddenly reappeared in London. Worth always refused to tell what happened, but we do know he bowed out and left for Kingston, Jamaica. His state of mind is revealed in a report to the Pinkertons from the Colonial police in Kingston, telling how a simple warehouse robbery was bungled so badly the thieves fled in a hail of bullets. Three of the robbers were local, petty criminals, but the leader was believed to be an American. "Inspector Shore agrees with me this must be Adam Worth," William wrote Robert in New York. "It is surprising he should be engaged in such cheap crime."

The answer undoubtedly lay in Kitty. Worth was a deeply troubled man that year, and it shows in his haphazard wandering about South America. He committed no crimes, but gambled, drank heavily, and went from steamer to steamer. Kitty was the powerful magnet that finally pulled him back to London. But Kitty was gone, traveling to Italy with Charley, who apparently still held some of his old charm. However, Joe Chapman, Little Joe Eliott, and the famous "Scratch" Becker were there. With them was a new man, Carlos Sesisovich, Russian-born forger who had worked with Becker in America, and his Gypsy mistress, Alima. Worth, fundamentally a gentle man, instantly disliked the dark. intense Sesisovich, who had a savage temper.

It was a time for big plans: William Pinkerton was on the trail of the Bidwell brothers, who were hiding in Havana after successfully robbing the Bank of England of one million dollars. Since Worth had only contempt for Superintendent Shore and Scotland Yard, the field was open. Worth, still Henry J. Raymond, gathered his thieves together in his Piccadilly apartment to propose a plan of great range. This time it was semiglobal. Becker was to forge letters of credit such as were issued by the

London bankers Coutts & Company. With these letters, the working party, with Worth remaining in London, would proceed to Smyrna, and there draw and cash sight drafts under the credits.

The plan shows that a large part of Worth's criminal genius lay in his variety of plots. He could patiently tunnel through a building into a bank vault, or switch bags like a common confidence man, but he could also plan and carry out over long distances crimes that required an expert knowledge of large commercial businesses and the minutiae of drafts, warehouse receipts, and supporting documents. In this case, he proposed a crime in a faraway land whose customs and languages he didn't know, and without any knowledge, furthermore, of what the Otto-man Bank's practices were.

In Smyrna the drafts were successfully exchanged for over $400,000, with a good percentage flowing back to Worth in London. Worth sent them a message in code advising caution; but, lacking his combination of audacity and wariness, they were caught while advancing a large draft.

The Turkish secret police threw them into an unnamed prison, and ignored the American consul's protest and request for information. Years later Becker, who was eventually to be arrested by William Pinkerton, recalled their arrest: "Jail meant nothing to us as men of experience. It was the country not the jail that held us. We couldn't get out of the country."

There was a quick trial; the American thieves were convicted and sentenced to three years at hard labor. To make it more difficult, the Turkish police, who had learned of their previous records from John Shore, the Scotland Yard superintendent, shipped them off to the dungeons in the Constantinople prison. A confidential police circular at the time stated that they were to be held for Superintendent Shore, who would have them extradited to the United States. Shore, who had been in touch with his friend William Pinkerton, now had a criminal dossier on each man.

Sesisovich smuggled out a letter to his mistress, and somehow a copy found its way to Robert Pinkerton in New York. Addressed to "My Dearest Alima," Sesisovich, a veteran thief who had been in and out of American prisons, claimed that conditions in the Turkish prison were the worst he had ever encountered.

> I have had but bread once every twenty-four hours, no bed to sleep on but the bare plank floor, packed to the number of thirty-five or forty in a room not large enough for twenty. You can imagine the amount of filth and vermin there must exist. Actually the bread I eat would not suffice to feed the hungry bugs, fleas and lice which constantly gnaw at my naked flesh. [The thought of spending years in this confinement, Sesisovich confessed, had at last driven him to thoughts of suicide.] There is little hope, so little hope. . . .[13]

While his confederates were imprisoned in the dank cells in Constantinople, Adam Worth was safe and secure in his Piccadilly apartment. As Max Shinburn, the "Baron," told William Pinkerton many years later, Worth was never troubled by the fate of his partners. If they were not skilled enough to avoid arrest, so be it, was Worth's philosophy.

One night after Becker, Chapman, and Eliott had been sentenced to the dungeons, there was a knock on the door of Worth's Piccadilly house. A servant told him that "a lady from America" was calling. When he went out into the foyer, Worth found Lydia Chapman. In contrast to Kitty's blondeness, Lydia had a dark, sultry beauty. While there is no evidence there was ever an affair between them, Worth liked Lydia and admired her "cool nerve," as he called it. He ushered her into his library, poured a drink, and settled back to listen. Tears flowed as Lydia described how she had traveled to Constantinople, where the Turks refused to let her see her bank-robber husband. Even the American consul told her he was helpless to assist her. Lydia begged Adam to help her stage a jailbreak and free Joe and the others.

Worth's subsequent actions were many times cited by the legend makers in the underworld of his time as evidence of his great loyalty to his friends. There is nothing to indicate that this cool, resourceful man did what he did for anything but self-interest and, in this case, inordinate vanity to prove himself before a woman as beautiful as his beloved Kitty.

He told Lydia Chapman that he would set them all free, an audacious statement that reveals his enormous self-confidence. At the time neither he nor Lydia even knew in what prison Chapman and the others were confined. Worth and Lydia traveled first class to Smyrna, then on to Constantinople. There, in that great teeming, polyglot triborough city, he set out to find his partners in crime and free them from their dungeons.

He was in a city where forty languages, none of which he understood, were spoken on the bridge to Galata, across the Golden Horn, where every Friday troops lined the streets as Sultan Abdul-Aziz drove to his devotions. It was a city where time was out of joint. There were only a handful of Americans in Constantinople, most of them attached to the American Women's Board of Missions, and surely a group Adam Worth would not have been interested in knowing. One thing in Worth's favor was a revolt brewing against the sultan.

Somehow Worth discovered the prison where the Americans were held. Bribery had opened many doors in his past, and since bribes were a commonplace fact of life in Constantinople of that day, this is probably the answer to his success. He visited the prison, scattered money in fertile areas, and soon discovered that the head jailer, who had all the keys to the jail, liked attractive women. The beautiful Lydia was the obvious key. He managed to have her present in a coffeehouse when the head jailer was there, and of course arranged an introduction. He always refused to rush: There were more meetings, a dinner or two, and then on some occasion Lydia said, with a great deal of wide-eyed wonder, that she had never seen a prison. The Turkish jailer promptly invited her on a tour, and Lydia returned to the hotel with a set of spare keys she had lifted from his desk—just as Worth had known she would.

Fantastic as it may seem, Worth decided to return to London. His reasoning was that he, like all foreigners, was under surveillance, and for him to have a set of keys made would be suspicious. Therefore, even at the cost of time, he told the impatient Lydia he had to have keys made in London. He returned, and with bribery again paving the way, entered the prison. In the early hours of a January morning in 1875, he led Becker, Sesisovich, and Eliott out. There was one slip in his plans: Worth couldn't find Chapman. He had been isolated in another section after a fight with Eliott, who had accused him of trying to make a deal with John Shore, the Scotland Yard superintendent. Unfortunately, there are no details on the scene of the confrontation between Worth and Lydia when he broke the news to her that her husband had been left behind, but they couldn't wait any longer; all of them had to leave or else join Chapman.

Worth did manage to smuggle a letter from Lydia in to Chapman, who bribed a guard to send his answer, which gallantly insisted that Lydia forget him and leave at once for the United States. Years later, the bank robber would be released from the prison, a feeble, emaciated ghost of the once-handsome counterfeiter who liked nothing more than to stroll into an expensive jeweler's and buy a diamond necklace for Lydia.[14]

In London, Lydia virtually became a recluse in the Neville Road house she had so lovingly furnished. Worth was the only one Lydia visited. There were tears, recriminations, and even threats, but Worth, who admired the fierce love this dark-haired woman had for her man, never refused to see her. He sent Chapman money for bribes, wrote letters to George Baker, the American consul in Constantinople, trying to obtain a new hearing for his former partner; and hired a criminal lawyer, until at last he told Lydia there just wasn't anything more he could do.

The combination now broke up, with Becker, Eliott, and Sesisovich returning to the States. Becker took up his "work," as he called it. Sesisovich opened a fashionable saloon under Booth's Theatre that would rival the infamous Shang Draper's headquarters for international thieves and their ladies—and Little Joe went on to marry Kate Castleton, a glamorous star of the American theatre.

Joe was back from London only a short time when he visited San Francisco's famous Minstrels. Kate, "a rose cheeked girl," as William Pinkerton recalled her, was the star of the show. Joe, enchanted by her beauty, besieged her with bouquets of roses, champagne dinners, and diamond bracelets—usually the loot from some of his better strikes. He

Kate Castleton   Sophie Lyons

courted Kate for months, until she finally consented to marry him. The
marriage took place in New York's Little Church Around the Corner,
with the wedding party held at Delmonico's. The entire cast of *Crazy
Quilt,* then a Broadway hit starring Kate, were on hand "in their stage
clothing," as the *World* man reported. Their honeymoon was a grand
tour of Europe, with Adam Worth receiving the happy pair in Piccadilly.
After months, they returned to New York. Joe insisted that Kate leave
the stage, which she did, "and they settled down in an elegantly furnished apartment on Twenty-First Street."

As with Kitty, Worth's love, Kate was not aware of how her husband
made a living. When "a handsome young man about town informed
her of her husband's true character," Kate was horrified. She threatened
to leave Joe, but relented when he promised to go straight. Joe worked
at various jobs for a year, until he "became weary of the quiet life" and
was arrested for forging a $64,000 draft on the New York Life Insurance
Company. On the way to the Tombs he made a daring escape but was
captured in Poughkeepsie, where he was identified by the Pinkertons as
the man who had robbed a Boston jeweler of $4,000 in gems several
years earlier. He pleaded guilty, and was sentenced to five years in Sing
Sing. Kate remained loyal and visited him often. He was released on
good behavior, and went back to Kate. Their marriage lasted a year
before she divorced him.

Again Little Joe pursued Kate relentlessly, following her, as George Bangs reported to William Pinkerton in Chicago, "from city to city, wherever she is playing. He's probably in your town by now."

The roses, champagne suppers, diamond bracelets, and fervent promises to return to the "straight life" sapped Kate's resolutions never to see Joe again. There was another intense courtship. Finally Kate and Eliott were remarried on the road when Kate was starring in a national tour of *Crazy Quilt*. When they returned to New York, Joe worked at a variety of jobs. Then Charley Becker appeared. The schemes of The Scratch were too good to ignore. A forgery backfired, and the pair was arrested. This time Kate was unrelenting in her determination never to see the handsome Joe Eliott again.

After his release from jail, Joe went to London, where he tried to interest Adam Worth in some wild plans, but the master thief shrugged them off. Back in New York, Eliott found Kate starring in another Broadway hit. This time the roses and jewels were coldly returned. Joe soon discovered the reason: Kate was being escorted nightly by "a young man of wealth."

One night Joe waited at Herald Square for the actors to leave the theatre. As Kate and the young man approached, arm in arm, Joe stepped out of a doorway, and, as the *World* reporter said, "gave the young man a scientific chop behind the ear, then walked over him." Then, turning to Kate, without a word, he made a slight bow and disappeared into the crowd. A short time later Kate obtained her second divorce from Joe, and married the manager of her hit show. One wonders what happened to the "young man of wealth" who received the "scientific chop."

With Kate now forever lost, Joe and Becker returned to London. It was an opportune time. Adam Worth had completed plans for a series of large-scale bank and brokerage robberies, and was seeking professional help. The Scratch and Little Joe were greeted cordially. For the next year, this trio pulled off some of the largest robberies in the history of Europe.

As William Pinkerton once recalled, Becker was the only forger he had ever known who could forge a currency note freehand and have it pass "microscopic scrutiny." He did this many times, using a large array of camel's hair brushes and special pens. Once, to win a barroom wager, Becker, using a newspaper-size sheet of paper, copied a news story, including the headline, column rules and ten-point type. As a contemporary said, "for ghastly accuracy this feat had never been surpassed."

Little Joe was the "middleman who passed the queer." Well dressed, debonair, his engaging manners charming bank executives, tellers, and clerks in brokerage firms, he passed checks Becker had raised or stocks so skillfully copied that William Pinkerton said it was almost impossible to tell the authentic from the fraudulent. It had been a full year for major coups against the biggest banking and brokerage houses in Europe, their victims including the Banks of England and France.

Worth was still deeply in love with Kitty, who by now had finally left Charley Bullard after that final romantic interlude in Italy. With her two infant daughters, said to be Worth's, Kitty took up residence in New York, alternately running a "fashionable" boardinghouse, which was the thing to do for genteel widows or impoverished aristocrats of the 1870's, and hiring out as a ladies' companion. The girls went to the best finishing schools, their tuition paid by pawning the jewels Charley had given her and some of the furnishings she had removed from the American Bar when the Sûreté, prodded by Scotland Yard and William Pinkerton, had finally staged a raid.

Whenever one of the brotherhood arrived in London, Adam Worth's Piccadilly house was their first stop for an exchange of trade secrets, underworld gossip, new projects, and requests for loans, which Worth never refused. Worth's first question was always "How's Kitty?"

Sophie Lyons, the thief, who would become America's first society columnist, recalled in her memoirs: " 'How's Kitty?' would be Raymond's [Worth's] first question whenever we met in London. He would eagerly ask about her health, how she looked and how were the two children, which we all knew were Raymond's."15

Late in 1876, William Pinkerton returned to London. His assignment was twofold: Check on the activities of Worth and the other big-time American criminals operating in England, and tie up some loose ends on the Bidwell Bank of England forgeries that the Agency had finally solved. He again saw Worth, who apparently had developed a strong liking, or at least respect, for the American detective. One evening Pinkerton and Superintendent Shore strolled into the Criterion Bar, which Worth visited nightly. When he saw Worth, Pinkerton waved him over and introduced him to the man from Scotland Yard. "There were a few words passed between them," Pinkerton wrote his brother.

Twenty-five years later, Worth's recollection of his meeting with the superintendent was much more vivid:

"I told Shore he didn't know anybody but a lot of three-card monte men and cheap pickpockets, and he could thank God Almighty the Pinkertons were his friends or he would never have gotten above the ordinary street pickpocket detective."

Worth remained in London that winter. In April he heard that Lydia Chapman was ill in her luxurious house on Neville Road. Worth was shocked by her appearance. Worn and haggard, she told him of her endless days in Constantinople, wearily going from office to office, bribing, pleading, offering to do anything to get her husband released. Finally George Baker, the American consul, told her that the Turkish police were adamant in their refusal to parole Chapman. She saw her husband for the last time. At his insistence she had returned to London.

The striking dark beauty that had turned the head of the Constantinople jailer was now fading. Worth also noted that she was drinking heavily and taking pills, "for my nervousness," as she explained.

Worth learned that Carlos Sesisovich, the sinister thief, and "dearest Alima," his Gypsy mistress, now back in London, were daily visitors at. the Chapman place. Sesisovich insisted that Lydia had his share of the forged drafts, and demanded the money. The desperate woman, in turn, tried to force Sesisovich to return to Turkey in one last attempt to deliver her husband. Worth warned Lydia she was dealing with a violent man who possessed an almost insane temper. She laughed away his fears. One morning a servant found Lydia's body—she had been poisoned.

Violence was abhorrent to Worth, perhaps only because it was stupid. But altogether it was a tribute to him that neither William Pinkerton nor Superintendent Shore regarded him as implicated in any way in Lydia's death. Pinkerton easily established Sesisovich and his mistress as the likely suspects, and the Agency, in cooperation with the Yard, issued a circular for European distribution, naming the pair as the murderers.[16]

After Lydia's death, Worth led the quiet life of an English gentleman. His few friends were cultured, polished, and wealthy. Then Charley Becker and Little Joe Eliott appeared again in London. Months of high living had reduced their finances to a dangerously low ebb. The answer was simple: Another strike had to be made. As The Scratch once explained:

> Now it follows that if you want to get on quickly you must be rich or you must make believe to be so. To grow rich you must play a strong game—not a trumpery cautious one. No. No. If in the hundred professions a man can choose from and he makes a rapid fortune, he is denounced as a thief. Draw your own conclusions. Such is life. Moralists will make no radical changes, depend on that, in the morality of the world. Human nature is imperfect. Man is the same, at the top, the middle or bottom of society. You'll find ten bold fellows in every million of such cattle who dare to step out and do things, who dare to defy all things, even your laws. Do you want to know how to wind up in first place in the daily struggle? I will tell you. I have traveled both roads and know. Either by the highest genius or the lowest corruption. You must either rush a way through the crowd like a cannon ball or creep through it like a pestilence. I use the cannon ball method.[17]

Becker and Little Joe were all for trying for a big coup, but Worth cautioned them that William Pinkerton was in London and had warned the country's largest banks and brokerage houses to be on the lookout for Becker's perfect forgeries. Worth recommended a smaller draft of £13,500. Becker was to supply the drafts; Eliott would cash them; Worth would select the brokerage house. The small amounts were below Worth's talents, but their pleas appealed to his ego.

Perhaps another reason for Worth entering the modest fraud was the unexpected arrival of his brother, John. After Becker had forged the draft, and Eliott had cashed it in London, Worth sent his brother to Paris to "work" more of the forged drafts. But Becker had made a slight error in the serial numbers, and it was spotted by an alert clerk in the London office of Meyer & Co. On a hunch that the thieves might try to victimize his Paris office, Meyer, the firm's president, notified Shore. The Scotland Yard superintendent rushed a detective to Paris. John Worth entered the Paris branch of Meyer & Co. in Rue Saint-Honoré, cashed the forged draft, and was arrested. At first it appeared that the detection of the forgeries was brilliant work on Shore's part, but months later Adam Worth learned that it had been Meyer, the banker, who had tipped off Scotland Yard. Adam never forgot Meyer. Years later he would be ruthless in his revenge.

After he had pleaded not guilty in Paris, John was extradited to London. He was imprisoned in Newgate, where he wept bitterly in his cell, begging Adam to free him. For three feverish days Adam hurried about London, but no freeholder would go John's bail because he was an alien.

On the afternoon of May 27, 1876, as he strolled down London's Bond Street, Adam Worth was frustrated for one of the few times in his life. His companion that day was a gorilla of a man named Junka, or Jack, Phillips, one of the newest arrivals from the American underworld. Phillips' forte was putting an iron safe on his back and carrying it away to be blown open by black powder after jimmies or crowbars had failed to "spring a panel." From his photographs, Phillips was an enormous man with drooping moustaches, thick sideburns, a tangled beard, and wide black slashes for eyebrows. An early carte de visite photograph shows him roped to a post by police photographers. He looks like an aged Samson in broadcloth.

That afternoon, Worth, lost in thought, walked down Bond Street, listening half heartedly to Phillips' rumbling gossip. In front of a building a large crowd had gathered. Worth started to walk around the men and women who spilled into the street, then stopped and asked a man what was wrong. He was told that Gainsborough's painting "The Duchess of Devonshire," just sold at Christie's, was on exhibition. The address was that of Agnew and Company, one of the world's most famous private galleries. The painting was of the lovely Georgiana Spencer, who at the age of sixteen had married the fifth duke.

Worth silently turned away. Junka continued talking. After several blocks Worth stopped, turned to Junka, and startled the big man by saying simply that he was going to steal the painting that night and that he needed his help. Junka gulped, and nodded. They walked back to the gallery, and Worth told Junka to buy two tickets. Junka returned,

Gainsborough's "Duchess of Devonshire"

outraged at the price asked to see "only a picture," as he put it. Worth bought the tickets and they went inside to the second floor. Junka was bored, but Worth gazed for a long time in silent admiration at the lovely duchess.

Later that same afternoon, Worth enlisted the help of Little Joe, who was crushed by the idea of stealing a painting when there were so many banks to be robbed; but he went along as the lookout, after Worth pointed out that it was he who had freed Joe from a Turkish dungeon; now past favors had to be repaid. When the three met that night, Worth explained his seemingly mad scheme. He would cut out the canvas, leaving a small, jagged piece in one corner of the frame. The authentic painting could then of course be matched, and he would give it to his brother's attorney as a prize with which to bargain for his brother's freedom. The officials of Agnew would go John's bail to get back their Duchess.

Compared to all of Worth's crimes, this, his most famous, was his most casual. He simply stood on the giant Junka's shoulders, pried open the second-floor window of the gallery, and climbed inside. As Worth was busily cutting the priceless portrait from its frame, it was unfortunate that he could not hear the silent laughter of the ghost of Laurence Sterne, author of *Tristram Shandy,* whose portrait had been painted by Gainsborough and who had died in that very room. Sterne, too, knew robbery at first hand, for body snatchers had dug up his corpse and sold it for dissection.

The following morning Worth appeared at the office of John's attorney. Jubilantly, the lawyer told him that he had found a flaw in the indictment. John, held as a principal, could at worst only be charged as an accessory. The previous afternoon, while Worth had been silently admiring Gainsborough's painting in the Agnew Gallery, the attorney had brought this fact before the court. His Lordship, after examining the legal precedents, had dismissed the indictment. John would be freed that afternoon.

"Oh, and what do we have here?" the attorney asked, nodding at the rolled-up paper cylinder under Worth's arm.

"Just a trifle I picked up in a gallery," Adam replied casually, then changed the subject. As he left the office, he realized that he was carrying the world's largest white elephant.[18]

In his Piccadilly house he carefully opened the painting and sat in a chair, studying the Duchess. Though he was, as he said later, tempted to return her to the Agnew Gallery, he decided that perhaps "she would come in handy on some future day." He rolled her up in the paper cylinder and stored her in his trunk. The Duchess would not return to England for a quarter of a century.

Worth was at Newgate, greeting his brother, while Pinkerton was sitting in Shore's office at the Yard, trying to pinpoint the criminal who had stolen the Gainsborough painting. Beyond the fact that it was gone, there were no clues. Pinkerton told Shore there was only one man with enough nerve to pull off a crime such as this, but neither detective could establish motivation. Pinkerton said he was puzzled as to why Worth—if he was the thief—would steal a work of art so well known that no fence would touch it.

Worth's main fears now were of Junka Phillips and Little Joe Eliott. Both needed money. Worth paid the latter's passage to New York in June, 1876, but Junka was another matter. The huge, slow-thinking criminal began to dun Worth for money. Worth finally told him he had to sell the painting "for a bagatelle." (One can see Junka puzzling over the word.) By way of explanation, Worth gave him £50 and told him it was his share. It satisfied Phillips for a while; then he was back.

One night Junka tailed Worth to the Criterion Bar. He began to talk loudly. Worth, embarrassed as heads turned, tried to hush him, but Junka became increasingly belligerent. Then, in a bar mirror, Worth caught a glimpse of a familiar face, that of Inspector Greenham of Scotland Yard. It suddenly became clear: Phillips had turned informer, and was trying to get him to make an admission before a witness. When Phillips began to accuse him of making him an accomplice in the theft of the painting, Worth whirled about and crashed a champagne bottle over Phillips' head. The giant crashed to the rug like a cut oak. Worth carefully brushed his frock coat, placed a bill on the bar, stepped around Inspector Greenham, who was assisting Phillips, and walked out. He was never troubled by Junka again.

As the year 1878 dawned, Disraeli, now Lord Beaconsfield, went off to the Congress of Berlin, and the Prince of Wales visited Paris to start his friendship with the new French Republic. Worth, emulating the prime minister, turned his attention to the international field.

In the spring of that year, with an accomplice, a Captain George, a noted Parisian confidence man, he broke into the money car of the Calais-Paris Express and got away with Spanish and Egyptian bonds valued at 700,000 francs. It was a daring robbery committed during the train's run. Captain George, arrested in Paris, appealed to Worth for funds. In the captain's case, there was no beautiful Lydia Chapman to plead for him. When he failed to receive money, he made a full confession, naming Worth as the mastermind of the robbery. Worth was sentenced to twenty years *in absentia*.

When the French judge handed down his decision, Worth was on the high seas, returning to New York. He was still Henry J. Raymond, international financier, a slightly built, well-dressed man, whose courtly manners charmed the women passengers and whose skill at cards caused acute embarrassment to their wealthy husbands.

In a leather bag in his stateroom was the Duchess, still secure in her cylinder of brown wrapping paper. The morning after his arrival, Worth stored his trunk in a Brooklyn warehouse. Wrapped in an expensive hunting coat, "the very best of the lot," as he told Pinkerton, was the Duchess. Worth stayed in the States for three years, masterminding several large bank robberies and forgeries. The reports of Robert Pinkerton indicate that The Scratch and Little Joe Eliott were his favorite associates, and he sometimes asked Sophie Lyons to help push a forged note. When Sophie suggested that he drop by to see Kitty, Worth would silently shake his head and turn away.[19] Charley Bullard, still Kitty's husband, was now spending most of his time dodging the Pinkertons, who had warrants for him from Canada, Massachusetts, and New Jersey for bank robberies and forgeries. But it wasn't Bullard's absence that made Worth decide not to see Kitty: Though Sophie and other close friends in the underworld didn't tell him, someone did—Kitty was being courted by the wealthy young Juan Terry, heir to one of Cuba's largest sugar fortunes.

Terry, dark and handsome, with the startling blue eyes of his Irish father, was a favorite of the New York society of the 1870's. His father was Tomaso Terry, an Irish adventurer from Venezuela who went to Cuba in the 1840's to exchange cheap jewelry for tracts of land considered worthless. On one of his inland tours he met the daughter of a wealthy sugar planter. After a secret courtship he asked the planter for his daughter's hand. The enraged Cuban ordered his field hands to horsewhip him off his land. In a rare interview, Terry once recalled how he had sworn to "be as wealthy as he was—someday."

Terry left the jewelry business to cultivate his land. In a few years he became moderately successful. He remained loyal to Spain in the Cuban insurrection, and was rewarded with huge tracts of confiscated sugar plantations—one belonging to the planter whose field hands had horsewhipped him. This time, when Terry returned, the planter gladly turned over his daughter. In five years Terry owned the largest plantations in Cienfuegos, "which proved to be veritable gold mines."

When Tomaso Terry died, he left an estate valued at $50,000,000. It was divided equally between eight children, each child receiving between $6,000,000 and $7,000,000. In 1875, Juan, the youngest, came to New York with $900,000 in cash, and by shrewd bargaining and investing in sugar, left with $1,500,000. Juan returned to Cuba for a year, then settled in New York City, where he became "distinguished for his business ability, although he was also fond of a life of luxury and pleasure."[20]

There are two versions of how Kitty, the onetime Liverpool barmaid and bank robber's wife, came to meet Juan Terry. In her memoirs, Sophie Lyons has Kitty selling "an objet d'art" she had taken from the American Bar in Paris after the Sûreté had closed it, to help support her two daughters, and meeting Terry in the shop. The less romantic, but more plausible, story has Kitty running a fashionable lodging house and meeting Terry, who asked her to go to a society charity ball. While their meeting is obscured by the dust of a century, we do know that Kitty obtained a divorce from Charley Bullard in New York in the winter of 1880. The following spring she married Terry in the chambers of a Judge Parker in New York City's Jefferson Market Court. Adam Worth undoubtedly read the story of the wedding. Shortly afterward, William Pinkerton received word from Inspector Shore that he was back in London. In the one fascinating talk Worth had with William Pinkerton a short time before he died, he talked of many things, but refused to discuss Kitty.

"He would marry another woman in London," Sophie Lyons wrote, "but I am sure he never forgot the beautiful Irish barmaid who had captured his heart . . . had Kitty become his wife, I am confident the whole course of his life would have been changed." Sophie's memoirs were written in her old age, years after Worth, Kitty, Bullard, and all the others were dim, distorted memories. Her ghostwriter undoubtedly accepted everything she told him. Yet there is little doubt that Adam Worth loved Kitty deeply. However, as a realist, he undoubtedly knew he was deeply committed to his way of life, with no chance of turning back the clock.

Once back in London, Worth had little time for lost love; it was "back to the old stand," as Superintendent Shore wrote to William Pinkerton. But it was 1880, and England's bankers had become more sophisticated. On March 11, 1880, the board of directors of the Bank of England met privately in the bank's "parlors." First, a dividend of 4¾ was voted; then the chairman—as the bank later explained in a public statement— informed the members that because of the frequent forgeries by American bandits, "a combination of the artist, printer and chemist" had made alteration of their new checks impossible.

Worth may have been alerted to the new type of check, because it was then that he cut his ties with the international forgers and turned to the diamond mines of South Africa. Worth had researched carefully: The country was thinly populated; Capetown had thirty thousand people, Johannesburg three thousand, and Kimberly, in the diamond country, was a sandy veldt with a few thorn trees, very little water, dirt streets, and kaffir huts of sacking and paraffin tins. A tense political situation existed between the English and the Boers, who had proclaimed their republic in December, 1880. Pretoria was in the hands of Sir Theophilus Shenstone, eight British servants (Rider Haggard among them), and twenty-five police. The small police force and crisscross of legal jurisdictions was made to order for Worth. Settling down to study the situation, he found that the diamonds came down from the north under strong wagon convoy to Port Elizabeth. The timetable was worked out to the minute to have the wagons arrive at the same time that the steamer was to sail, and it had to take into account ferrying of rivers, breakdowns, floods, and highwaymen.

Worth had no liking for a western-frontier highway robbery. To him, that was a stupid, dangerous business. As always, he was determined to avoid violence. He stopped at the best hotel, spreading the word in the bar that he was in the ostrich-feather business. It was Boston all over again: He opened an office, hired a clerk, bought a shipment of feathers, and had them crated and sent to a London warehouse.

Hard-eyed guards with rifles rode the convoy of diamond wagons. Worth, to test their marksmanship, invited them to an old-fashioned American turkey shoot staged near the hotel. Ostriches were the targets, a bottle of good whiskey the prize. He swallowed hard when the guards casually shot the heads off the birds and walked away with the bottle of whiskey. Worth returned to his feather buying. To build up a background, he had his brother John and his wife come out to take a house. Worth's planning was canny and deliberate. He became friendly with some of the Boers who handled the convoy, and found that if a diamond shipment was delayed, the gems were transferred to the Port Elizabeth post-office safe to await the next steamer. Worth's plan was to bring a delay about.

Very carefully, he began to make friends with the postmaster of Port Elizabeth. There was a great deal of social drinking, entertaining, and chess, at which Worth was a master. As he had in Liverpool, Constantinople, and elsewhere, he managed to get the postmaster's keys, and made wax impressions of them. Worth's patience and timing were perfect. He had made the Boers' favorite expression, *Waacht-oen-Bietje* (Wait a bit), his own motto.

Worth finally selected the date for his raid on the diamond convoy. He carefully traveled their route several times, an incongruous figure wearing "gentleman's riding clothes" as he trotted along the narrow dirt road. Dusty and saddlesore, he explained to the bar's patrons on his return that he was seeking "inland agents" for his new business.

Worth finally found the most vulnerable link in the carefully timed route of the diamond-wagon convoy: the inn where it paused for refreshment, water, and to feed the mules, before crossing the river by an ancient cable ferry. At this stop, one or two guards were left on the wagons, while the majority rushed inside to the bar. Worth also observed that the men left on guard, weary and thirsty, were less than alert, their whole attention focused on the door of the pub, waiting for their relief to emerge.

Worth was in the inn's bar when the heavy wagons came to a halt. He greeted the guards whom he knew, stood them to a round, then slipped out and carefully shredded the ferry cable. The scheme had a dazzling simplicity.

When the convoy rumbled aboard the ferry, the heavy flatboat pulled out, snapping the weakened cable. The native ferrymen poled the boat back to shore, where the captain examined the cable and announced that it had either worn through or been cut. The wagons rolled back onto shore to travel to Port Elizabeth, where the boxes of gems were put into the postmaster's safe. That night Worth slipped out of his hotel, and down the dark rough streets to the post office. The old-fashioned safe, opened with the key Worth had copied, yielded £700,000 in uncut gems.[21]

The next day, after a preliminary investigation of the theft, the postmaster was jailed as a suspect, after it developed that he had been engaged in minor pilfering from money orders for some time. The unfortunate postmaster was in the prisoner's dock in the hot steamy courtroom when John Worth and his wife sailed for London, the Kimberly gems lodged in a false-bottomed trunk.

Worth, to avoid suspicion, remained in Kimberly for a month, then sailed for London. Before he disposed of the diamonds, Worth decided his brother John should get out of crime, take his wife back to the States, and open a business. As Worth told William Pinkerton in 1899: "John was a darn fool as a crook and I stopped him at it a long time ago. I gave him a considerable sum of money at the time of the African robbery and with that kept him clean and above board."

John Worth and his wife returned to the Bay Ridge section of Brooklyn. He kept clean and aboveboard, but they both later proved to be a bitter worry to Adam.

The Kimberly loot was in rough, uncut gems, but Worth had no intention of "working them back" at a discount. He took in as a partner Ned Wynert, another personable society thief. They opened a diamond-merchandising firm under the name of Wynert & Company in High Holborn, London, proceeding to sell the unidentifiable diamonds to regular dealers at attractive prices. Here again, Worth displayed his versatility in crime: He had no trouble in acquiring, almost immediately, knowledge and customs of trade in the valuable gem market. Worth and Wynert made careful sales, not in large quantities, and never at ridiculously low prices. William Pinkerton's estimate was that Worth cleared £32,000. We know little of Wynert, except what Shinburn, that underworld moralist, told Pinkerton: "Wynert is married to a lady of a very respectable family. He treats her shamefully, spending all his stealings on other women."

In 1881, Worth could have read in New York newspapers the account of a great ball given by Kitty Terry and her husband at their mansion in Long Branch, New Jersey. Reporters had discovered that she had been married to Charley Bullard, the bank robber; but instead of degrading her, the sensational disclosures made Kitty a glamorous, mysterious beauty. Terry was madly in love with her, all the accounts agreed, and whenever she appeared on his arm at society affairs, reporters were awed by her diamonds, pearls, furs, and clothes.

For the next two years Worth lived quietly in Piccadilly. Occasionally he masterminded a big forgery or theft of bonds and securities. He was finding it more difficult to find expert accomplices: Bullard, Becker, Little Joe Eliott, and the others were either in jail or dead. The handsome Ned Wynert had died in classic fashion: A society husband had come home at an inopportune time and killed Worth's old partner in his wife's bedroom as Wynert struggled to free himself from a tangle of bedclothes. On several occasions, Adam traveled alone throughout Europe, "laying work," as he told Pinkerton some years later. On a trip to Paris he was walking down the Rue Saint-Honoré when he suddenly saw the office of Meyer & Co., the banker who had informed on his brother, John, in 1876. Worth investigated, and found that the company's safe was filled. One night he cleaned it of 250,000 in francs. Meyer was ruined, his company went into bankruptcy, and Adam Worth had his revenge.

In London, Superintendent John Shore had never given up hope of finding evidence that would send Worth to prison. His detectives constantly shadowed the dapper little thief or loitered near his house. With the twisted logic of all criminals, Worth once bitterly told Pinkerton that Shore for years had "persecuted" him.

When the Scotland Yard man and the international criminal met in the Criterion Bar, Worth would give Shore a bitter, cold glance, then move away. Shore told Pinkerton he was sure that Worth had stolen the Gainsborough painting, but years of investigation had not produced a single clue. Shore kept up the pressure, assigning detectives to tail Worth day and night, and the tension began to tell on the thief. He had one small triumph when he was able to tip off an American bank robber that Shore's men were ready to raid his apartment and arrest him on an old extradition charge. The thief fled to Belgium. When underworld informers told Shore that Worth had warned the robber, the enmity between them rose to a blaze.

As William Pinkerton wrote to Robert: "Worth said if Shore had treated him in a half-decent manner the picture would have gone back long ago, but that Shore persecuted him like a human tiger."

Worth, weary of detectives, gave the Yard men the slip in 1886. In Brussels, he successfully robbed a shipment of jewels and cash that was being moved by tramway in Ostend. The loot was about $150,000, enough for Worth to travel in grand style to Canada for a holiday. Aboard the liner, unknown to Worth, was a well-known "steamship thief." The Canadians knew it, and were waiting for him at the pier in Montreal.

When the unsuspecting Worth's baggage was examined, the jewels and securities were found. The Montreal police at first believed that Worth was the steamship thief. Worth, traveling as a London broker, was righteously indignant, and rattled off a list of well-known Londoners who could vouch for him. He demanded an attorney, and was generally a problem to the perplexed Montreal police. Worth was finally let go with apologies, but the securities were impounded and placed in a railroad car. Worth, with his amazing faculties of observation and coordination, spotted the car number and its location. He paid a fine for not declaring his jewels, packed his bags, graciously accepted the apologies of the police, and registered at the best hotel. That night he stole into the railroad yards, found the numbered car, jimmied the door, repossessed his securities, and left the next day for the United States. He later told William Pinkerton that "at a small cost of a few thousand I was able to save my principal."

He remained in the States only a few months, moved the Gainsborough painting from the Brooklyn warehouse to one in New York, then returned to London. His restlessness may be explained by his fading health. He was listless, and now had a constant cough. Worth was back in London only a few days when Superintendent Shore resumed his pressure. Detectives began following him, and a constable was posted outside his door. The furious Worth decided he had to fix Shore once for all.

Worth knew an "old swell," as he later described him, a minor confidence man who had become a pitiful alcoholic. But, as Worth said, he still had exquisite manners and "could pass as a peer when he was sober."

Worth was aware that one of Superintendent Shore's principal informants was Nellie Coffey, a pretty prostitute who was friendly with every important thief in London and who "had a fund of information which was useful" to Shore. When she had a tip for the inspector, Nellie would send word to the Yard, and Shore "would meet her at the Rising Sun Inn, the foot of Fleet Street, a place which had private dining rooms."

Worth's plan was to pass spurious information on to Nellie. While she met Shore in the inn, Worth's "swell" was to hurry to the Yard's office, and charge Nellie with stealing an expensive piece of jewelry "when they were in a place of assignation." Then the swell would lead the Yard's police to the inn and surprise Shore and the pretty whore.

As Worth later told William, it took him weeks to sober up the old thief. He set him up in a small, expensive hotel, where he virtually kept the confidence man prisoner, lectured him on the evils of alcoholism, appealed to his pride, sense of family, and even love of country. After the ancient thief had "dried out," Worth fed him regular meals and took him for long walks. They retired early and rose at dawn. As Worth recalled, he was never healthier—and so was the thief. He now had a commanding presence, bristling Guards moustache, piercing blue eyes, and a superbly imperious manner. Worth took him to Saville Row and bought him a wardrobe. At last the stage was set.

The next step was to make sure Nellie received the information: Worth made up a story concerning his part in a fictitious bond robbery. Shore, he knew, would rise for the bait if he thought it would help him put Worth in prison. Worth knew underworld gossips who hung about "the drinking house of Bill Richardson, a resort for thieves in London." Very carefully, he fed them the concocted story. One night a bartender who was on Worth's payroll informed him that Nellie had sent a message to Shore. One of Adam's men tailed Nellie to the Fleet Street inn, and the jubilant Worth hurried to the small hotel where his principal player was waiting.

When Worth entered the room it was dark. Turning on the gas lamp, he found the Imperious Presence stretched out on the bed—dead drunk. Afterward, Worth admitted that he had felt like throwing the old thief out of the window but that, instead, recognizing the irony of the situation, he had sat down on the edge of the bed and laughed at himself. A few days later the old thief appeared at Piccadilly, trembling and apologetic. Worth gave him a few pounds, told him to keep the clothes, and sent him away.[22]

Years later, Pinkerton told him he thought such a waste of time, energy, and money to embarrass a police officer was beneath him; Worth's cold reply was that Shore was "an ordinary street pickpocket detective who deserved the worst."

It was during this period that Worth was married "to one of the little girls who lived in the lodging where I used to live" (in Piccadilly, over Fortnum and Mason's). Between 1888 and 1891, a son and daughter were born.

Things didn't go so well for some time, and Shore wrote to Pinkerton: "Adam Worth is fidgety over the ill-luck which is attending so many of his American clients." Charley Bullard, his favorite partner, had died in prison; Joe Chapman had finally been released from prison, only to die a shattered wreck.[23]

The feud between Worth and Superintendent Shore still blazed. It was on May 21, 1888, that Shore wrote to Pinkerton that he and his men had discovered Worth's new headquarters in West Lodge, Clapham Commons. After weeks of shadowing, they crashed in to find a hidden machine shop and a number of intricate burglar tools, neatly lined up on the shelves. But Worth had gone. Later, he appeared at the Yard with an attorney, indignantly denouncing Shore for raiding his "office" and demanding that his property be returned, very expensive machine tools, he called them. He actually forced Shore to appear in court, but the judge ruled against him.

Worth's next crime was a simple robbery of an express company's wagon on a quiet street in Liége, Belgium. The wagon was to be robbed on one of its stops while the helper delivered a planted package to Worth's hotel. The lock was to be broken, and Worth would step inside the wagon, select the packages of bonds, hand them to Peter Curtin, a fugitive American bank robber, and jump out. Curtin panicked, and Worth was caught. Under the name of Edouard Grau, he was convicted and sentenced to seven years in a Belgian penitentiary. A three-page circular sent to the Pinkertons by the Belgian police as a result of the Agency's interchange of information about international criminals sketched "Grau"'s criminal career and told how "for the past two years he has lived on proceeds of his thefts . . . he has sold diamonds for the firm of Wynert and Company in London." Apparently the Belgian authorities did not know that the London company belonged to Worth, that the diamonds were the proceeds of the Kimberly theft, and that Worth's partner was a notorious criminal.

The circular then described the difficulty the police and Belgian court were having in ascertaining Worth's true identity:

For family reasons he has refused to disclose his identity. The in-
. dividual speaks and writes very good English, speaks German and some
French with a British accent. The man is of sanguine temperament,
hair cut short, side whiskers, mustache in Russian style and has a commanding presence.

The undersigned judge herewith asks his associates and all police
officers to try their utmost to establish this man's identity.[24]

The touching line about "family reasons" for concealing his identity
must be taken with a grain of salt. Worth, an unconscionable rogue, was
only hoping the Belgian police would not discover he was the notorious
Adam Worth with a long criminal record. There are no copies of any
communications between the Pinkertons and the Belgian High Court.
The answer is that there was no existing charge against Worth in the
United States, with the exception of the Boston robbery. And for that,
with witnesses dead or gone, there was little chance of conviction.

Superintendent Shore, however, had written to Pinkerton that he suspected the Edouard Grau arrested in Liége might be Worth. Inspector
Byrne of the New York police had also cabled Liége that their prisoner
might be Worth. That the Yard and the New York police knew about the
arrest was enough for Pinkerton. But whatever the reason, Adam never
forgot that William Pinkerton "didn't knock me around when I was arrested in Liége."

Worth was released, and came home to find that his "little girl" had
been seduced by one of Worth's criminal "associates," introduced to
drink and narcotics, and was now lodged in a London asylum, judged
hopelessly insane. His son and daughter had been sent to his brother,
John, and his wife in Brooklyn.

Dissipation, imprisonment, and apparently a deep and sincere grief
had taken its toll of Worth's vitality. Symptoms of tuberculosis had
begun to appear. But in 1898, in a great burst of his early criminal
genius, Worth staged and led the robbery in the Gare du Nord in Paris,
where his twenty-year conviction *in absentia* still hung over him, and got
away with a million francs in securities and jewelry. Pinkerton once
asked him if it amounted to that much in collateral value. Worth said
No, for "it was worked back for £12,000, about 25 per cent of the face."

Late that year, William Pinkerton heard from Pat Sheedy, a famous
American gambler, that Worth was in the States and wanted to make a
deal with him to return the Gainsborough painting. The reward still
existed, and it was Worth's belief that the Agency would gladly arrange
the return of the painting and share the reward. Pinkerton made it immediately and abundantly clear to Sheedy that every principle of their
business and prestige prevented such a thing and that he could not partic-
ipate. He advised Worth to retain a lawyer. Sheedy next said that Worth
wanted to see Pinkerton, and the detective agreed that a meeting would

be held in confidence and without recourse. He put a coded personal ad in the Chicago *Daily News* as a sign that he accepted the terms of the meeting.

One day William received a call from "the gentleman from England." There are photographs of this pleasant end-of-the-century office, filled with pictures of dogs and horses and the memorabilia of Pinkerton's active life. It looked like a gentleman's study, where he could relax with his friends, and in that atmosphere Worth was received.

The man who came in was five feet five and a half, with rather long arms and carefully kept hands. He was well dressed in a frock coat, and wore a gold chain and cameo charm. In his scarf was a small pear-shaped pearl. His manner was genteel, and he spoke with a brisk British accent. Pinkerton saw little change in him in the twenty-five years since they had met.

William carefully explained that he would not make or try to make a deal on the Gainsborough painting. Worth listened, and accepted his reasons, saying, however, "I am putting myself in your hands." Then they "spoke very freely about matters in Europe for the past twenty-five years and Worth, without hesitation spoke of numerous robberies in which he had been engaged." [25]

There was no American crime against Worth except the Boylston Bank robbery in 1869, and Worth knew that case was dead. Pinkerton asked him casually if he had been in Boston, and Worth said, Yes, several times, adding that he always stopped at the Adams House and that he thought it was, besides New York's Astor House, "the best managed hotel in the United States." The Gainsborough had been moved from New York to Boston, and Pinkerton's questions may not have been so casual as Worth thought them to be.

When Worth spoke of his night sweats and sudden hemorrhages, Pinkerton quickly took the opportunity to measure and weigh him, finding that he weighed only 122 pounds. Gradually Worth began to speak of the "little girl" in the English asylum and his two children in Brooklyn. Surely a masterful criminal never made a stranger remark to a great detective than the following of Worth to Pinkerton: "I would like," he said, "to get the children a fox terrier puppy." The breed was popular in the late nineties. William said he would have one in a week and would send it to him. A general discussion of dogs and racehorses followed, and they spoke of old times, old crimes, detectives, underworld and sporting figures, most of them dead.

What seems to have been in each man's mind was this: Pinkerton, while unwilling to make a compromise or deal for the famous painting, was very anxious to return it to England. Apparently, they chatted for hours. William found himself, as he said, drawn to this strange criminal. At one point Worth was shaken by a deep tubercular cough, and Pinkerton offered to lend him money for medical treatment if he was short of cash. But Worth, his wallet filled with bills from the Gare du Nord robbery, said he had enough.

Worth did a bit of showing off, casually indicating he bought clothes only on Saville Row, and berating Inspector Shore and the other Yard detectives, who, Worth said, "were just not gentlemen." The most famous of Yard inspectors, plagued at the time with a wave of bank and bond robberies, would have roared at that remark. The American eagle was screaming at the time in Cuba and the Philippines, and the two Americans, thief and detective, discussed America's foreign policy and the "sticks" of Englishmen they had both known who managed to fumble everything in Downing Street.

Worth then told Pinkerton he was grateful that the Agency hadn't made it worse for him when he was arrested in Liége. William shrewdly sidestepped explanations, and waved aside Worth's gratitude. The meeting ended on a handshake. As William told Robert, he did not assign anyone to shadow Worth when he left the Agency's office, for "he seemed in good faith in everything he was doing, and if he thought I had broken faith with him and all, I would only scare him away."

Worth returned the next day. This time the visit was brief. "I would like to buy a house and settle down with my children," he said wistfully, and Pinkerton told him where in the city a man could best bring up children. Then Worth gave Pinkerton what he was waiting for—permission to inform Scotland Yard that the Gainsborough would be returned. He said quietly, "I think the Lady should return home, don't you?"

Pinkerton nodded, and said he couldn't agree more.

On January 16, 1901, Scotland Yard cabled to Pinkerton to take the painting "on Worth's terms." What they were we do not know, but probably immunity from arrest, because Worth returned to London within a few months.

The son of one of the Agnew partners arrived in Chicago on March 27, 1901. Word was passed to Worth. The next morning, with Pinkerton present in the Agnew suite, there was a knock on the door. A messenger silently handed William a cylinder rolled up in ordinary brown wrapping paper. It was the lovely Duchess, unmarred and unspoiled after twenty-five years in exile in warehouses in Manhattan, Brooklyn, Boston, and Jersey City. Pinkerton escorted Agnew and his wife—and the Duchess—to New York and to their stateroom on the steamer, where the Pinkertons watched over them until sailing time.

Very shortly afterward, the Duchess returned to America—the land her friend Charles Fox had admired so much. This time she was not in the trunk of a thief, but in the J. P. Morgan collection.

A few months later Pinkerton left for Hot Springs, Arkansas; with him was Worth. He had told Pinkerton, "If I can ever do you a favor on earth, outside of going right out and being a policeman, I want you to call on me."

In the weeks since he had arrived in New York, Worth's physical condition had deteriorated rapidly. On Pinkerton's insistence he had agreed to accompany William and Robert to Hot Springs. In a rare photograph, Worth is sitting in the famous Hot Springs Stage, facing Robert and William Pinkerton, the only two men, he admitted, he could trust. Dead were Charley Bullard, Shinburn, the famous Baron, Sesisovich, and his Gypsy mistress, and many "associates" who had robbed and looted across the world with Adam Worth as their leader.

Pinkerton urged Worth to buy a house in Hot Springs and settle down, but the little man, giving him a wan smile, said only that he would think about it. Both men knew it was hopeless. That winter, Worth returned to London. His last letter, on June 22nd, is about his children and the life that might have been. It ended: "I am a little better, not so much blood . . . but . . . the awful night sweats and cough . . ."

Pinkerton's reply urged Worth to take care of his health and to return to the States, to Colorado, "where the altitude is very beneficial for people suffering with pulmonary trouble." Worth never answered.

During the late summer, Worth's two children joined him. On January 8, 1902, as the early winter darkness closed over the London he loved, Adam Worth, the greatest criminal of the Victorian Age, died in his apartment in Regent's Park.

On January 24th, Worth's son, Henry, wrote to William Pinkerton, disclosing his father's death and advising the detective that he and his sister were now living with a cousin at 88th Street and Shore Road, Fort Hamilton, Brooklyn.[26]

Wiliam wrote to Robert from Chicago, "I am sorry indeed to hear of the little fellow's death. I think we were about the only people he trusted."

On February 7th, the story broke in the New York *Times,* the dispatch identifying the mysterious Henry Raymond (the *Times* did not use the initial) as America's most famous criminal. Almost immediately William Pinkerton received another letter from Worth's son, written from Brooklyn:

> My father left little or no money, and after paying the funeral expenses and our passages back to America we were practically penniless. I am now staying with my married cousin at the above address and so far so good. It seems too bad that my father should have left my sister and myself in the circumstances that he has, but now there is only one thing for me to do and that is to put my shoulder to the wheel and earn an honest living, which will always be my desire to do. My father often used to speak of you and mentioned several times about some safe alarm which I think was being made by a friend in Lon-

don and who was to send it over to you, perhaps he has mentioned something about this matter to you. My father's death was sudden and he
told me little or nothing about his affairs before his death; he was sick
for several weeks, but would consult no doctor, and it was not till after
his death that we knew that he had died of liver trouble. I left his room
to go down to my supper and he seemed to be in the best of spirits
but when I came back to his room he was as I thought sleeping; several
hours afterwards the landlady went into the room and came out to me
and said that she did not like the looks of my father and requested me
to go in and I did so but my father had quietly passed away without a
struggle. I would like Mr. Pinkerton very much the pleasure of meeting
you and if you will let me know when I can call on you or if you
prefer to come out to my cousin's house I will make it my duty to meet
you. You will no doubt be able to enlighten me to things regarding my
father that I do not know and that would interest me greatly. Assuring
you that I highly appreciate your kind offer of assistance and if you can
help me I shall be very grateful. Again thanking you for your kind
wishes which I can assure you are highly appreciated, believe me,

Yours respectfully,
Henry Raymond [27]

Pinkerton was very impressed by the letter, although he suspected it
was too mature to have been written unaided by a boy of fourteen. The
sentence "you will no doubt," and so on, evinces the natural curiosity
of a son about his father. Perhaps the boy had suspected his father of
being more than the wealthy London businessman, a role he always
played, and wanted confirmation more than information. If so, he had
written to the wrong man. Pinkerton's reply, which for its goodness of
heart, worldly wisdom, and noble deception has surely, in such circumstances, seldom been surpassed. It is the letter any boy of an honorable
father might receive in his bereavement from his father's close frind:

Henry L. Raymond, Esq.
c/o Mr. P. Strawson, 88th Street,
Shore Road, Fort Hamilton, Long Island.
. . . I do not recollect your father ever telling me of your age and the
age of your sister. I wish you would write and tell me the ages of both. I
am surprised to note that your father left you and your sister as badly
off as he apparently did. When I saw him last, eleven months ago, he
had some money, and I urged upon him to invest the same in securities
and leave the same in my care for your benefit. He said he thought
well of the plan, but thought he could invest to better advantage in
Europe, and of course took the money with him. I urged upon him at
that time to quit Europe and come back here in this vicinity and with
the means he had to settle down to some little business, and to give up
his ideas to speculation, which to my idea seemed quite wild. He took
seriously to the matter and thought he would like to locate at Hot

Springs, Ark., and I told him that would be a good idea and to bring yourself and your sister out here and with the means he then had he could easily have started himself in a nice little business at Hot Springs and make a good living for you all, and his health would have been much improved. I feared his return to London among genial companions would be too much for him in the state of health he was then in.

I know what a stubborn man your father was about consulting a doctor and even in this city I had to practically force him to go and see my family physician, who gave him some medicine which seemed to improve him quite a bit. I think what troubled him most were the pains in his head, which my doctor thought were caused by a tumor, but as to keeping his liver right that was a thing which could easily have been done, but he seemed anxious to get back to England to you and your sister and you were the constant theme of his conversation while he was here. I was very sorry to hear of his death, but am glad to know he passed away as peacefully and quietly as he did. I note your question in regard to the safe alarm he was working on. He explained something of his ideas to me and explained he was going to work further on it, and when it was completed he wanted me to see to the patenting of it in this country, which I promised to do, but he never wrote me on the subject again. In one of the four letters I received from him he said he was working on the matter, but what progress he had made he did not say. I have not heard from any of his friends, and there is no one in Europe I know to whom I could write in regard to this matter. He was a man of great inventive ideas and it is just possible that he may have perfected something of the kind for the protection of safes, but if he has some of his supposed friends in Europe have evidently taken advantage of it for their own benefit.

There is a man in this city who owes your father some money—$700 or $800, but he has nothing and owes everybody else. He took advantage of your father's kindness of heart both in this city and in Europe, but if he ever gets any money and I learn of it, I intend to make him pay up what he owes.

I do not know just when I will be in New York, but probably not before the summer, but you can depend on it when I do get there I will send word to you and have you come to the office to see me. In the meantime write and let me know in regard to your education and whether or not you wrote the letter yourself, because I want to say that if you did it is a remarkably fine letter for a boy of your years, and I think we could be able to find a better place for you.

I shall always have a kind remembrance of your father for while we had not met in years up until two years ago and then again a year later, still we always had a kindly feeling for each other and I would willingly do anything consistently in my power to aid either you or your sister. Let me hear from you whenever you have time to write, as I always will be pleased to know how you are getting along. Personal letters addressed to me here will always reach me because my personal mail is

always forwarded wherever I may be. With best wishes for yourself and
your sister, believe me dear Henry,

Sincerely yours,
WILLIAM A. PINKERTON [28]

This is noble deception not only in the complete absence of any hint
of his father's complicity in the world's biggest robberies and of his evil
life but also in reference to the "man who owes your father" $700 or $800.
The man Pinkerton was going to "make pay up" was William Pinkerton himself.[29] A few weeks later, Worth's son received a check for seven
hundred dollars.

BOOK 6
The Great Burlington Strike of 1888; Homestead, 1892

CHAPTER 27
The Death of Allan Pinkerton

In 1880, Allan Pinkerton was badly crippled, almost completely paralyzed, yet he refused to retire. Each morning his carriage brought him to the office on Washington Street, Chicago, where he carefully read the copies of reports neatly stacked on the desk, dictated for hours, then went home to spend most of the afternoon sitting in his gardens with Joan.

There was now peace in the family. Pussy had finally married "Young Chalmers," who was on his way to become an important midwestern industrialist. On Sundays, the big house echoed with the cries and laughter of grandchildren, but old friends were dying, and Joan, his "wee bonnie lass," was confined to her bed much of the time. One of the last projects that Pinkerton insisted be carried out was his favorite employment of "female detectives." He was still doggedly writing to Bangs in New York:

> I suppose you have not yet hired a female detective, but I think with some effort you will. I now give you a description of the class of woman you will require. Say a lady about 35 years old, about five feet six or seven inches high, hair dark, black or auburn. I don't think blonde would do. She should be either married or single, but if married her husband must be dead [!], face oval, forehead large and massive. Her hair should be worn plain or very little braided or banged, eyes should be large, whether black, blue or gray, her feet moderately small. An easy talker but careful and one who can keep her own counsel, yet be able to carry on a conversation on any subject and be always self possessed and natural, although assuming a character.

I am anxious to have such a female detective and if you are able to get such a one, I will be highly pleased. We will find plenty of work for her to do bye and bye. I am anxious for you to give this your strict attention and let me know what you are doing.[1]

A short time later Pinkerton dictated another letter to an old friend, publisher of a northern Illinois newspaper, enclosing a paid ad for a "female detective," and listing the same qualifications.

Then, in 1881, the letters to New York and Philadelphia began to dwindle; the fire died; he trembled more, and for the first time sought out his favorite seat in the garden rather than his desk. One day William came to see his father. They sat for some time exchanging comments on the business, with William faithfully presenting a progress report on the Agency's important cases. Then he told his father that the Chicago office had received a telegram that morning informing them that George Bangs had died. He recalled that his father barely nodded, but when William left, Allan was staring straight ahead, hands gripped tightly over the head of his cane, tears rolling silently down his cheeks.

One of the last letters Allan Pinkerton dictated was to William Gladstone, England's prime minister, when the British government was considering hiring the Pinkertons to assist Scotland Yard in the apprehension of the Fenian assassins who had murdered two British officials. Dated July 8, 1882, and labeled "Private and Confidential," Pinkerton's letter warned Gladstone that if his Agency was retained, "I differ very much in my ideas of detective work from the police of Ireland, England and Scotland. . . ." Gladstone was undoubtedly surprised to find this American detective advising him that investigators could only be "honest . . . bold in the truth, sleepless in energy and loyal in thought and act. . . ." It would be very difficult to find investigators possessing such qualifications Pinkerton informed His Lordship, "for it requires great caution to select these men and women." For three pages Pinkerton outlined the methods he would employ to select informers "from men of leisure or the laboring Irishman with the dudeen in his mouth."

Pinkerton also reminded Gladstone that the Agency had worked for the British government "in other matters"; unfortunately, he does not detail those assignments. For the first time in months, probably in deference to Gladstone's position, Pinkerton signed his name to a letter. It is barely discernible, and obviously written by a violently shaking hand. There are no known records of Gladstone's government retaining the Pinkertons, and apparently Scotland Yard persuaded the prime minister that they were quite capable of handling any amount of Fenian terrorism without any help from American detectives, even though the *Times* called them "America's Scotland Yard." [2]

While Allan was living out his last years in comparative serenity in his Chicago garden, Jesse James, the one symbol of lawlessness the Pinkertons

Bob Ford, slayer of Jesse James

"GOVERNOR, I AM FRANK JAMES, I SURRENDER MY ARMS TO YOU. I HAVE REMOVED THE LOADS FROM THEM. THEY HAVE NOT BEEN OUT OF MY POSSESSION SINCE 1864. NO OTHER MAN HAS EVER HAD THEM. I NOW GIVE THEM TO YOU PERSONALLY. I DELIVER MYSELF TO YOU AND THE LAW." *Frank James*
KANSAS CITY TIMES, OCT. 5, 1882

THE GOVERNOR ACCEPTED THE PISTOL AND BELT AND SAID, "YOU SHALL HAVE EVERY PROTECTION AFFORDED BY THE LAWS OF YOUR COUNTRY, AND AS FAIR A TRIAL AS THOUGH YOU WERE THE SON OF A PRESIDENT." *Thos. T. Crittenden*
GOVERNOR OF MISSOURI
SEDALIA DISPATCH, JEFFERSON CITY, MO. OCT. 5, 1882

Surrender of Frank James

could never shatter, rode back into the national headlines: On July 15, 1881, Jesse led his newly formed gang in robbing the Chicago, Rock Island & Pacific train near Winston in Daviess County. Two unarmed men were killed, a stonemason named Frank McMillan and the conductor, William Westfall, whom legend had on the Hannibal and St. Jo train that took the posse to the James farmhouse in 1875.

The brutal and senseless murders of the two men at Winston roused the state, with the Kansas City *Journal* editorially placing the responsibility on the Missouri Democratic Party. The *Post-Dispatch* and other leading papers in Missouri insisted that Governor Crittenden take steps to bring about the capture of Jesse James. In the absence of a law that would permit posting more than $500 in reward money, Crittenden called a meeting of representatives of the leading railroad companies in St. Louis on July 26th. On July 28th a proclamation was issued, offering $5,000 reward for the capture of Frank and Jesse James and an additional

$5,000 for their conviction. It was assumed the railroads would put up the money.

On September 7, 1881, Jesse and Frank led the gang in their last Missouri robbery, at Buel Cut in Jackson County, when the Chicago-Alton Express was held up. A political squabble took place after this robbery, with the Republicans and their newspapers insisting that the Democrats had not been aggressive enough in their pursuit of the James gang, that national publicity had held back immigration, and that the value of land had been reduced.

On April 3, 1882, Allan Pinkerton was at home when his Kansas City superintendent telegraphed to William that Bob Ford had shot down Jesse in his St. Joseph home. Ford and his brother, Charlie, were later indicted for murder and sentenced to hang, but Governor Crittenden granted both of them pardons.

In October, Frank James dramatically surrendered to Governor Crittenden in his office, telling the governor as he handed him his gun belt: "I have removed the loads from them. They have not been out of my possession since 1864. No other man has ever had them. I now give them to you personally. I deliver myself to you and the law." [3]

It was great playacting and high-flung dialogue, and the crowds loved James as he traveled to Independence. The reporter from the Sedalia *Dispatch* found him an ordinary-looking man, about five feet eleven inches, slightly bald, with a tired, worn face. Most of his interviews were sanctimonious claptrap, but there was one harsh truth from Frank James that could be the epitaph of all Western outlaws:

> I have literally lived in the saddle. I have never known a day of peace. It was one long, anxious, inexorable eternal vigil. When I slept it was literally in the midst of an arsenal. If I heard dogs bark more fiercely than usual, or the feet of horses in a greater volume of sound than usual, I stood to arms. Have you any idea of what a man must endure who lives such a life: no, you cannot. No one can unless he lives it for himself. . . .[4]

In his Chicago office, William Pinkerton read the lush, dramatic quotes, and was unimpressed. As he wrote to Robert: "I have read a great deal about Frank James surrendering to Governor Crittenden. There is a lot of noise about him now, but I doubt they will ever get him behind bars. There is too much sympathy in the state for those cold blooded killers." [5]

William Pinkerton's words were prophetic. James was indicted for murder, but before he could be put on trial Missouri's Supreme Court Justice John W. Henry proposed that he be pardoned. On August 21, 1883, Frank James was tried in Gallatin. The trial was given national attention, with the *Post-Dispatch* commenting that the outlaw's trial was attracting as much attention as that of Charles J. Guiteau for the murder of President Garfield.

To no one's surprise—and certainly not the Pinkertons—Frank James was acquitted. Putting aside the florid, Victorian language, one has only to read Prosecutor William Wallace's summation, in which he convincingly put together the people's case, to realize the intense sympathy that existed in the state for the James boys, a major obstacle in the efforts of the Pinkertons, state, and local lawmen to bring the outlaws into custody. The jury's findings were widely criticized. Some newspapers editorially underscored the political overtones of the jury. The St. Joseph *Gazette* and the Jefferson City *Daily Tribune* disclosed, before both sides had rested, that the jurymen were all Democrats. The St. Joseph *Herald* predicted that the best Wallace would get would be a hung jury—if that.

The political careers of both Prosecutor Wallace and Governor Crittenden were undoubtedly influenced by the James issue: Wallace was refused a congressional nomination by the Democrats, while Crittenden was not chosen by the state convention that selected John S. Marmaduke, the former Confederate general, for the governorship.

Gradually the story of the Missouri outlaws disappeared from the pages of the Chicago newspapers. In the summer of 1882, the Pinkerton household was stirred with the news that Allan was to be a guest of honor at a large reception to honor John Brown's widow. Pinkerton, whom the Chicago *Times* described as "one of the engineers of the underground railroad," was asked to supply his reminiscences, which would be read at the gathering. The reception was held in Farwell Hall, on August 31, 1882. Mingling with the crowds of curious who had come to see Brown's widow were politicians, members of the state and local judiciary, and civic leaders. A huge portrait of Brown dominated the bare stage, the bony face and deep-set eyes of the fanatic disturbingly realistic in the cold, hard glare of the stage lights. James B. Bradwell, a Chicago judge, introduced Mrs. Brown, Mrs. John Jones, widow of the Chicago Negro leader who had worked with Pinkerton; and the other old abolitionists who had come from the East, the West, and the border states to attend the reunion.

After Mrs. Brown—a quiet, white-haired woman—was introduced, the packed auditorium listened to Judge Bradwell read Pinkerton's memories of the stormy night in 1859 when Brown knocked on his door and asked for help in getting the slaves into Canada.

Mrs. Jones, introduced as "the widow of John Jones of African blood," described how Pinkerton had knocked on the door of her home "in the early hours of the stormy night of pitchy darkness which I shall ever remember." Brown, she said, "greeted Mr. Pinkerton that of friend to friend, yea, more than brother to brother. Then the three of them, my husband, Mr. Brown and Pinkerton had a talk together. I don't think I should divulge the secrets of that meeting even now of twenty-five years ago. Only one thing I will repeat. I remember Mr. Pinkerton saying: 'There's a Democratic meeting in town today. I will go right down and make them give enough money to send those slaves to Canada.' " [6]

A brief, poignant note ends this incident. In answer to a letter from an admirer in Boston, possibly a Negro, Allan Pinkerton replied:

> Your letter to my son, asking for my autograph has been received. I am not in the habit of giving my autograph to any persons, for particular reasons to myself, but in this instance for the purpose you wish it, I forward it to you. I have always been a friend to the colored man and will do anything to secure him his rights.

The letter was signed with a barely discernible signature. As William Pinkerton noted in a postscript: "The tremulousness observed in my father's signature is caused by the effects of a paralytic stroke." [7]

In the spring of 1884, it was evident that Allan Pinkerton was dying, but, iron-willed and as obstinate as ever, he insisted on trying to walk, even for a few feet. In the latter part of June, he fell, and never regained consciousness. He died on the afternoon of July 1st, with his wife, William, Robert, and Joan, his daughter, at his bedside. The obituaries were long and glowing, with columns in the big-city dailies retelling the Horatio Alger story of the young Chartist who had fled from Glasgow to frontier America, there to become a household word.

Pinkerton's will, filed on July 10, 1884, bequeathed his property to his wife, his books and copyrights to his daughter, Joan, and the Agency to his sons. He also ordered that Bangs's widow be placed on a $15-a-week pension and that the graves of Tim Webster, Kate Warne, and the other Pinkerton employees buried in Graceland Cemetery, Chicago, "never be sold, graveled or aliened in any manner whatsoever." Pinkerton's love for The Larches is also evident in his will. He requested that the showplace be kept in its present condition, be worked for seven years, then another seven, and if possible to remain in the family "forever." [8]

After Allan's death, life had little meaning for his wife, Joan—"my wee lass"—who had followed the intense, complex man she loved from Chartist Scotland across the prairie to the Dundee cooperage and then to the elaborate home in Chicago. As the months passed she gradually grew weaker. One night her sons and daughter were summoned. Just before dawn, she whispered to William that she was joining his father, then closed her eyes and passed on.

After the death of their parents, William and Robert Pinkerton managed the Agency in copartnership. Additional branch offices were opened in Seattle, Denver, Kansas City, and Boston; staffs were enlarged and business was expanded.When robberies of jewelry salesmen across the country reached alarming frequency, Robert proposed to the American jewelry industry that it organize itself into a Jewelers' Security Alliance, "a union of one for all, all for one," the first object of which would be the arrest and conviction of thieves without compromise of any sort. A crime against one firm would be a crime against all. Unlike the bankers of the 1870's who considered the recovery of cash, bonds, and securities to be foremost, the recovery of jewelry, often so tempting to its owners and at times vital for some to continue in business, would be secondary to capturing and punishing the thieves. The alliance was formed, and the work of the Pinkertons met with such success that shortly afterward the manufacturing jewelers of the nation formed a similar group, the Jewelers Protective Union, and it has been Pinkerton's client since that day. Agency detectives traveled around the world to arrest and return jewel thieves to the United States for trial.

During the 1880's and 1890's banks were principal targets of cracksmen and forgers. One of the greatest contributions to the suppression of crime by the Pinkertons was made through their services to the American Bankers Association in that period, and to individual banks, until crimes against national banking institutions, members of the Federal Reserve or Federal Bank Deposit Insurance, came under the jurisdiction of the FBI.

In the 1880's bank robberies were mostly the work of criminals the agency dubbed "yeggs." None had the ingenuity or finesse of major American criminals such as Adam Worth, Max Shinburn, or Charley Bullard. They came principally from hobo jungles, wandering the country like tramps, combining the brutality of the criminal with the habits and customs of the early American hobo. As tramps they moved mostly at night, in freight cars, the blind end of baggage cars, or on lonely roads through the woods, hiding by day in haystacks or barns and stealing their food. They used nitroglycerine or black powder on safes, selecting banks in small communities that had inadequate police protection. Faceless, homeless, many times with no criminal associates, disappearing after a strike into the dim tramp world, it had been almost impossible to trace and arrest them.

In the 1880's, the Pinkertons were convinced that if it were known that a centralized agency, acting for all banks, was after them and would stay on their trail until they were found, bank robbery would decline. The American Bankers Association subscribed to this service, and signs announcing that a bank was under the protection of the Pinkertons became commonplace in large American cities and smaller communities in the West and Midwest. The Pinkertons' record here is an impressive one. Up to 1909, there were 1,097 robberies, with a total cash loss of $1,489,-407.32 against banks without the Agency's protection. In the same period, there were 202 robberies with a cash loss of $154,544.48 against banks with the Agency's protection. During that time operatives arrested 697 bank forgers and presented evidence that convicted 558; 284 burglars were arrested, and the Agency obtained the same number of convictions—

with a total of 1,657 years meted out by the courts. So formidable did the Pinkertons' reputation become that there were occasions when thieves, after robbing a bank where the sign was not conspicuously displayed, anonymously returned the loot on learning that Pinkerton protection had been violated.

Another profitable phase of the Agency's business that continued to grow in those years was supplying watchmen for strikebound plants, mines, railroads, and corporations. The attitude of the Victorian industrialist was typical of the times: In a labor dispute it was the duty of local law-enforcement bodies or the government to protect the lives of nonunion employees and the company's property; and if the law or the government failed to do this properly, the employer was justified in hiring a private police force to provide protection. By the late 1880's the Pinkertons were well known in this field. From 1869 to 1892, groups of watchmen, ranging from twenty to three hundred, were hired out at $5 a day, in seventy-seven strikes during which three strikers were killed. As Robert Pinkerton would say: "We never looked for any strike work; it was something which has grown about our shoulders."

In 1888, the Pinkertons played an important role in the great Chicago, Burlington & Quincy Railroad strike, one of the most stubbornly contested labor struggles in American history. Terence V. Powderly, Grand Master Workman of the Knights of Labor, one of the Agency's bitterest enemies, would charge before Congress that in this strike the Pinkertons had incited riots, murdered strikers, and even set off dynamite charges for which the strikers were blamed. The vast archives of the Burlington Railroad, including reports of Pinkerton operatives, now in the Newberry Library, show Powderly's charges to be without foundation.

Hundreds of secret reports underscore the reason why the Pinkertons were there: The law-enforcement organizations of the small towns and sparsely populated villages on the fringe of the dying frontier, with their casual deputies and stringent municipal budgets, were unable to handle a major strike filled with such dangerous potential as the Burlington walkout.

A typical example of the incompetence of the local police is revealed in the report of a Pinkerton operative assigned to a Missouri railroad town. He arrived in the early evening to find "considerable excitement in the streets and a large crowd gathering at the depot." He quickly learned that two strikers had been arrested on the complaint of a nonstriking fireman, and had been fined $100 for assault. Though the strikers paid the fines, they had gathered a crowd "vowing vengeance against the man who had them arrested." The mob was growing ugly, shouting threats of what would happen to the fireman when shortly he had to appear to take out a train. The operative hurried to police headquarters and advised the lieutenant, who headed the two-man force, that the fireman was scheduled to appear within an hour and would have to pass through the mob to get to his train, which was waiting at the depot. The Pinkerton guards, he advised the officer, had no authority off the railroad property, and it was up to the local police to break up the crowd. When the lieutenant refused to act, the operative hurried through the town, searching for the two-man force. When he found the patrolmen, they informed him "they would not be on duty before 9 P.M." When the operative saw they "were indifferent to the matter," he gave them $3 each "for refreshments," and persuaded them to break up the mob, "as this would avoid trouble for once started no person could tell what might happen." [8]

The duties of the Pinkerton watchmen brought in by Charles Perkins, president of the Burlington road, in February, 1888, when the strike took place, were to patrol the yards, the rolling stock, and to protect "the loyal workers" who remained on their jobs. These included clerks or employees who had refused to obey the orders of the brotherhood or who were members of different unions. As Donald McMurry states in his exhaustive work on the strike, "No evidence has been found that in the strike Pinkerton guards ever acted as strikebreakers in the sense they did any of the strikers' work."

In all the strikes in which they participated in the 1880's and 1890's, the Pinkertons employed a particularly odious method of using the law to protect their activities. They insisted that before any of their watchmen could enter a strikebound plant, they first had to be sworn in by the sheriff. It was not unusual that this county official had been recommended for the post by the local railroad officials or the company that was strikebound. However, there were also occasions when this same post was held by officers who were in sympathy with the strikers and who conveniently left town—"on a case"—when trouble erupted. On March 1, 1888, as *Inter-Ocean* reported, not only the Pinkertons but other employees were deputized, "which gave the men a feeling of security by enabling them to protect their lives and the company's property in a lawful manner."

The first Pinkerton guards arrived in Omaha on March 1st, and the Omaha *Bee* thought they looked slightly decrepit in their dusty, worn uniforms. However, the second group of watchmen impressed the *Bee*'s reporter as hardy, young-looking fellows, "and they all wore, besides their uniforms of blue, wide, soft brimmed hats with gold cords. They formed smartly into platoons and marched off to the Windsor Hotel for supper. . . ."

The reports of the operatives, sent almost daily in code to William Pinkerton, then transcribed and sent to H. B. Stone, general manager of the CB&Q by William Pinkerton, show how they traveled about the midwestern railroad towns and cities, living in boardinghouses, playing pool, or drinking with strikers. It was both a boring and precarious life. One operative in a crowded saloon was spun about by a man who accused him of being a "d—— detective who wants to send us all to jail."

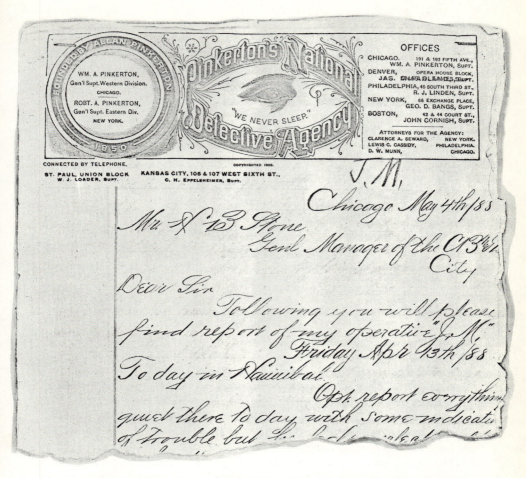

From William Pinkerton's report to H. B. Stone, general manager of the Chicago, Burlington & Quincy Railroad. *The Newberry Library*

The operative made his accuser apologize, and minutes after the confrontation, had the customers admiring his expertise with a pool cue and laughing at his jokes. On another night he was forced to accompany the elderly owner of the boardinghouse to the local opera house to attend a "musicale." As he explained, "I went along because the crowd was there and I thought I might learn something of value." He didn't. However, the long days and nights of traveling from town to town, living in ramshackle boardinghouses, playing countless games of pool, and drinking horrible frontier whiskey sometimes paid off. In the spring of 1888, one operative was able to send on to William Pinkerton the names

Typescript of June 12, 1888, report to H. B. Stone. *The Newberry Library*

of the strong-arm men who had savagely beaten a conductor with a rock, along with supporting affidavits of eyewitnesses.

The chief function of the undercover operatives was to act as an intelligence group for the company. They also described public sentiment, sometimes not favorable to management. One operative discovered that the engineers had hired a detective agency to find out what the company was doing and also to learn the plans of the firemen and switchmen. For a time it was a case of detectives tailing detectives.

The strike was only ten days old, when a mob at Clinton attacked a Pinkerton guard. The Clinton *Daily Herald* of March 8, 1888, quoted the sheriff as saying, "The pulse of the rough element was beating rapidly for the blood of a Pinkerton man this day." Another guard, attacked by several strikers, killed one and wounded two others. As the Chicago *Times* said, "He vanished just in time from being lynched." The guard was charged with homicide, but was acquitted.

Violence continued to erupt along the line. Switches were thrown, and passenger cars stoned as they passed through cuts; then trains were blown off the tracks. On April 16th, an operative reported to William Pinkerton in Chicago, "The strikers are getting desperate since they are beginning to realize they are beaten and more trouble is expected at any time."

The first intimation of the new "trouble" came when an operative discovered a union circular that recommended sabotaging locomotives. S. E. Hoge, chairman of the Brotherhood's Grievance Committee, received many letters demanding to know if the circular was spurious or else strongly protesting the use of violence. Hoge or his secretary informed the brotherhood's members that the circular was authentic and that the methods outlined were to be followed.

One of the strongest protests Hoge received came from George H. Baker, chief engineer of the Brotherhood of Locomotive Engineers at Decatur, Illinois. Baker, described as "one of the best engineers on the line and a man of great force of character," bitterly predicted that once the brotherhood employed violence it would lose public sympathy and the strike would be lost. In May, 1888, rumors were so strong that dynamite was to be introduced into the strike that General Manager Stone and his two daughters traveled on separate trains from Chicago to Burlington.

It is evident from the Pinkertons' secret reports, that one of their informants held a position of authority in the brotherhood. For example, a report, dated June 21st, from Pinkerton to Stone, quotes "our informant" as meeting the Grand Master of the brotherhood, who denounced the Hoge circular "asking the men to destroy engines and other property."

> It was a d——d infamous [*sic*] that was ever perpetrated. It was done without the knowledge of either myself or Arthur [the head of the brotherhood] and it was only discovered by Arthur who at once took heroic steps to stop them. I believe only a few got off before we stopped them; and we are trembling lest the C.B.&Q should get one of them. It would create a tremendous feeling against us and would be a terrible weapon in their hand.
>
> I asked carelessly if he was here only on a visit or had some special business on hand. He said his business was to enlighten his Order throughout his section on the true state of the strike; that they had done all the laws of the Order required for the strikers; had advised the strikers there was not a ray of hope of any settlement with the C.B.&Q. . . . and that the strike should be called off at once. . . .[9]

But the strike dragged on, with both sides refusing to grant concessions. Then, in early May, 1888, dynamite was used to tear up lengths of track, shatter bridges, and overturn engines. In Chicago, William Pinkerton ordered his men to the scene of the blasts immediately after they had been reported to the line's main office. Tiny scraps of brown paper from the outside wrappings of the explosives were gathered and painstakingly pasted together. Operatives traced the brand of dynamite, but found it was not sold locally. A wholesaler was finally pinpointed, and a company official identified the wrappings. A list of retail outlets in the Midwest was obtained and checked one by one. In June, William telegraphed to Robert in New York City; the coded message said they had located two stores in Noblesville and Westfield, Indiana, that had sold the dynamite. Descriptions of recent buyers at both stores were obtained, and compared with members of the brotherhood's grievance committee. One seemed to fit J. A. Bowles, who was put under a twenty-four-hour surveillance. Undercover operatives, meanwhile, had located Aurora as the meeting place for the dynamiters. A day-and-night watch was kept on an Aurora boardinghouse, with William Pinkerton keeping in touch with his operatives by coded telegrams. In July, the operative tailing a James Broderick alerted William that he was sure the strike leader was on his way to buy dynamite. Hours later word came into the Pinkerton office that Broderick and a group of union leaders were going to Chicago for a meeting. The operative told Pinkerton that he would follow Broderick and the others onto the train and try to get a nearby seat. He would take off his hat and wipe his face with a handkerchief if Broderick and the others still had the dynamite in their possession.

Pinkerton, who realized he would be immediately recognized, sent his assistant Chicago superintendent to accompany Chicago detectives and United States marshals to make the arrests. One by one the law officers entered the cars. When the Pinkerton operative sitting behind Broderick took off his hat and slowly wiped his face, the police and marshals moved in. Broderick and the others were found to be carrying a package of dynamite. One threw a letter out a window, but an operative found it by retracing the train's route. It established a conspiracy to use the dynamite for sabotaging trains on the struck line.

When the arrests were announced in Chicago, Baker the union leader, offered to testify against the defendants, "as we are unalterably opposed to such violent methods."

Bowles confessed his part in the conspiracy, and, accompanied by a Pinkerton operative, went to Galesburg and dug up a cache of dynamite that he claimed was to have been used to blow up trains, machine shops, and roundhouses. Three of the strikers were later found guilty and sentenced from one to two years in Joliet. During the trials it was revealed that the private secretary to one of the brotherhood's officials had been on the Pinkerton payroll, while two "suspects" jailed in the roundup of dynamiters were a Chicago detective and a Pinkerton operative.

Before the summer ended, the strike was broken. In the bitter aftermath, labor charged the Pinkertons with fabricating the dynamite plot to serve their own purposes. The evidence in the records of the strike shows that this is improbable. The Pinkerton reports in the Burlington Archives reveal that the company was consequently put to a great deal more expense than would have been necessary if fabricating evidence had been their objective. In addition, the confession of one of the conspirators confirms the details of the plot. What also must be considered is the corroborative testimony of independent witnesses, such as that of the merchant who sold the dynamite, bank drafts and letters found on the defendants that they had thrown from the train at the time of their arrest.

In 1889, one of the prisoners wrote from Joliet to Illinois Governor Joseph W. Fifer, asking for a parole, and confessing to "the enormity of my offenses."

If the Pinkertons committed any offense in this strike, it was merely by being there. By the 1880's, they were retained by most of America's big business to protect its property during a strike, and its operatives were used to gain evidence of wrongdoing on the part of the union. The mere sight of a Pinkerton watchman's blue uniform in a strikebound area was enough to enrage the union men. Yet, viewing the complex problem of the 1880's from the employers' side, they had a right to use private law enforcement to protect their property from the violence and savagery of labor. The inefficiency of the nineteenth-century law-enforcement organization must also be considered.

The Pinkertons, of course, always maintained that they were acting within the scope of the law of their time, and in that they were correct; that they were acting morally was another question. The unions, who considered this to be legalized strikebreaking, regarded the Pinkertons as their deadliest enemy. It was inevitable that they would someday clash head on. Their long-awaited confrontation took place on the muddy banks of the Monongahela in 1892.

CHAPTER 28
The Works on the Monongahela

An entire book could be written on who was right and who was wrong on that muggy July morning in 1892 on the banks of the Monongahela River, but a brief understanding of the political, economic, and social conditions of the times is necessary to place the events in their proper perspective; Homestead cannot be separated from its own world.[1]

The riot took place at the beginning of an era that linked the old frontier with the new America. The country was leaving behind the log cabin, coonskin cap, Indian wars, orthodoxy in religion, philosophy and, in some areas, a gentle, romantic way of life. What the nation faced was a tougher, dirtier, more aggressive environment, clouded in smoke from belching chimneys. Stirring with unrest in the ghettos, it was feeling the first convulsive changes in population, technology, and labor. America was now a nation no longer isolated from world politics and its wars. Appomattox was only a quarter of a century old, but already the ranks of the Gray and Blue were thinning. The reunions outside Gettysburg Cemetery were getting smaller each year. The voices of political figures of the war still echoed in Congress, but each election brought new faces and louder voices, like that of William Jennings Bryan, who was born during the year of secession.

The key issues of this momentous decade were reform and expansion. Businessmen, workingmen, and farmers had seen only hard times in the late eighties. They were disillusioned with the old leaders and their orthodox politics. Somewhere, somehow, the American dream had become a nightmare. It was now apparent that the distribution of the nation's wealth was shockingly unequal. Thomas G. Sherman, in his *Owners of*

America, which stirred the country at the time of its publication in 1889, estimated that 200,000 people controlled 70 percent of the country's wealth.[2] Other economists concluded that 80 percent of Americans made a bare living, while the remaining 20 percent controlled the power and wealth of the land.

Poverty was everywhere, and in its shadow stalked crime. Labor conditions were unspeakable, and women and children worked incredibly long hours in mills and mines. The Negro was free in name only, for the white man's arm still barred the doors of education, industry, and politics. The census showed 6,000,000 illiterates. Except for the brief, exciting World's Fair, there was little gaiety in what is popularly known as the Gay Nineties. Rather it was a time of grim questioning of rigid, traditional authority, of reforming many aspects of our social, economic, and political life.

The 1890's opened with the last of the Indian battles, the Ghost Dance War, which was really a massacre by the cavalry instead of a war. Benjamin Harrison was in the White House, a man whom Henry Adams considered the best President the Republican Party had put forward since Lincoln's death, but the majority considered him to be a cold, aloof man.[3] One hundred thousand settlers had run for the land in the Cherokee Strip and Chickasaw Reservation. Farmers had taken over most of the large grazing tracts in the deep West to end the ranching frontier. Immigration was at an all-time high. More than 3,500,000 immigrants came to the United States between 1891 and the turn of the century. Machine-made products were now common, while urban growth was rapidly making the United States a nation of cities. Industrial consolidation and monopoly had begun in railroads, and "trusts" were already established in oil, sugar, whiskey, and lead. Industrialism was not only altering the face of America; it was also deeply affecting the relationship between labor and capital.

As the decade began, about 4,000,000 women and 23,000,000 males over ten years of age were working. Only a small percentage belonged to unions. The Knights of Labor, organized in 1888, had dwindled from 700,000 to 100,000 in 1890; unstable organization, weak leadership, and dabbling in politics had led to its decline. The American Federation of Labor had a total membership of 225,000 in 1890, but that would grow to 545,000 by 1900. Scarcely a month passed without a major strike. In five years, over 7,000 strikes were called that put hundreds of thousands of workmen out of jobs.

On June 10, 1890, the McKinley Tariff bill, a major factor in the Homestead story, became a law. Duties on raw sugar were repealed and those on iron and steel reduced, but duties on a large variety of commodities were prohibitively increased. The Democrats, with former President Cleveland as their leader, denounced Harrison and the Republican administration for the tariff law that "banishes from many humble homes the comforts of life in order that the palaces of wealth and luxury may more abound."

The elections of 1890 did not go well for the Republicans. In the West, they took on the aspect of a social and political revolution, with Wall Street pictured as a money-hungry ogre enslaving millions of American workingmen. June, 1890, saw the emergence of the People's Party, the nation's third party, and the birth of Populism.[4]

In June, 1892, little more than a month before Homestead, Cleveland, who had left the White House in 1889, was selected as the Democratic presidential nominee. The McKinley Tariff was bitterly attacked in the party's platform. Harrison was the Republicans' choice; General Weaver, a Civil War veteran, was the choice of the Populists. There was little doubt that the McKinley Tariff would be one of the leading issues of the day.

It was against this background of political and social unrest, with a third party born in defiance of the monopolies and trusts, and a growing bitterness against the arrogance of the entrenched wealthy that the first rumblings of discord at Homestead were heard. Physically, Homestead covered forty-two acres along the Monongahela River, six miles from Pittsburgh. The "works," as it was called, was part of Carnegie Company, Ltd. At the time this was a company of limited copartnership, with a capital of $25,000,000, formed under the laws of Pennsylvania and composed of Andrew Carnegie, Henry C. Frick, G. Henry Phillips, Jr., George Lauter, H. M. Curry, M. J. Abbott, John G. A. Leischman, T. Lovejoy, Otis H. Childs, and others.

There were 3,800 workmen at Homestead at the time, engaged in manufacturing structural iron for fireproof buildings and plate armor for warships. Of the total employed, 800 were members of the Amalgamated Association, a labor organization of iron and steel workers. In 1889, the company entered into an agreement with the association for a three-year contract. By the terms of the contract, the wages of the members of the association were based upon tonnage rates, regulated by the market price of steel billets, with a minimum limit of $25. The wages of the other employees such as engineers, water tenders, pressure pumpmen, traveling-crane operators, narrow-gauge locomotive engineers, river pumpmen, and so on, were not regulated by the union's contract.

The expiration date of the three-year contract was June 20, 1892. In January, new scales were submitted by the spokesman of each department covered by the union to their negotiators, who presented them to the company. The company in turn handed the union leaders a counter-offer with three new essentials:

1. A reduction in the minimum limit of the market price of steel billets from $25 to $23.

2. A change in the expiration date of the contract from June 30th to December 31st, when a strike was less likely to be called.

3. A reduction of tonnage rates because new and improved machinery gradually being installed in the plant would enable the workers to increase their output.

The reduction in tonnage rates would have affected the wages of 280 men, and the reduction of the tonnage rates and the minimum limit of the market price of steel billets, about 325, inclusive of the 280.

Negotiations continued until June 24th. As the congressional committee's report said: "Both parties seemed to have no confidence in their ability to come together and their relationship became more strained as the time approached for the final termination of the contract."

When Frick handed his final offer to the union, the report pointed out, "There were new signs that each side was preparing to test the strength of the other, and, if possible, by a resort to extreme measures force them into submission." [5] Commenting on the wage scale at Homestead, the committee's minority report, which included a survey of wages paid to ironworkers throughout the world, showed that "wages paid under the old scale ran from $278.50 paid to H. McCrorey, a roller, for twenty days work in May, 1892 ($12.65 per day), to $1.40 to James Torgasgo, a laborer, for one day's work that month." The report also revealed that "many" of the Homestead workers owned their own homes "and lived in comfort and plenty; that taking the lowest possible earnings under the new scale, the rates would be still more than double the rates paid in Europe for similar labor, much of it working longer hours." [6]

Automation in the form of new and expensive machinery the company was installing was one of the major obstacles in the negotiations, one of the first times this issue was raised in labor-management dealings. Curiously, this aspect of the Homestead story, has been overlooked or ignored in many historical tracts and histories. The Amalgamated also knew that Carnegie was determined to get rid of many of the crucial job rules for which the union had fought to prevent speedups. Carnegie wanted to abolish the rules that, as he wrote, "required far too many men." Getting rid of the Amalgamated, he wrote to his officials, would provide the company "with a chance to reorganize the whole affair, and exact good reasons for employing each man." From his hunting lodge in Scotland came orders from Carnegie to break the strike.

The union's reply to the automation plans of the company was simply put: "If the improved machinery produced larger tonnage, there was no reason why the workers' should be reduced."

Wage scales, union demands, automation, and the company's counter-offers, of course, had nothing to do with the Pinkertons. Frick, unfortunately, was Carnegie's chief spokesman at the negotiations. The committee's report estimated Frick as "a business man of great intelligence and energy but he seems to have been too stern, too brusque and somewhat autocratic, of which the men justly complain, and which led to rather abrupt termination of the negotiations." [7] Frick also "was opposed to the Amalgamated Association, and had no anxiety to contract with his laborers through this organization." Frick's attitute was clearly demonstrated when he ordered that the plant be surrounded by a plank fence, topped by barbed wire. The workers immediately dubbed it "Fort Frick."

Inside the plant, Frick and John C. Potter, the general superintendent who would play a melancholy role with the Pinkertons, were hanged in effigy. When foremen tried to tear the figures down, they were driven off by workers using fire hoses. On the 29th, the plant was shut down. On the morning of July 1st, Potter and several foremen walked up to the main gate to face a crowd estimated at between fifty and a hundred. When they tried to enter, they were "persuaded to leave."

It was then that the union swung into action to take over the plant. Chief Justice Paxson of the Pennsylvania Supreme Court, in addressing an Allegheny County Grand Jury, described what happened:

> It [the union's Advisory Board] allowed no persons to enter the mills of the Carnegie Steel Company, and even permitted no strangers to enter the town of Homestead without its consent; that it arranged and perfected an organization of military character, consisting of three divisions, with commanders, captains, etc., the captain to report to the division commanders and the latter to report to the Advisory Committee; that a girdle of pickets was established by which the works and the town were guarded like a military encampment; that these pickets arrested every man who attempted to approach either the town or the plant until he could give an explanation that was satisfactory to the Advisory Committee. . . .[8]

On July 2nd, Carnegie's attorneys, Knox & Reed, writing from Pittsburgh, advised Frick to

> particularly charge Mr. Potter that no matter what indignities he may be subjected to in the performance of his duty at Homestead, that neither he nor any of the company's employees should do any act of aggression, but should confine themselves to protecting themselves and the company's property. They should under no circumstances resort to the use of arms, unless it should be for the protection of their lives.

On July 5th, William H. McCleary, the high sheriff of Allegheny County, posted four hundred copies of his proclamation about Homestead, which read:

A PROCLAMATION

TO WHOM IT MAY CONCERN:

Whereas it has come to my knowledge that certain persons have congregated and assembled at and near the works of the Carnegie Steel

Works, Ltd., in Mifflin Township, Allegheny County, Pennsylvania, and upon the roads and highways leading to the same, and that such persons have interfered with workmen employed in said works and obtaining access to the same, and that certain persons have made threats to injure employees going and coming from the said works, and have threatened that if the owners of said works attempt to run the same property will be injured and destroyed. Now I, William H. McCleary, High Sheriff of said county, do hereby notify and warn all persons that such acts enumerated are unlawful, and that all persons engaged in the same are liable to arrest and punishment.

And I further command all persons to abstain from assembling and congregating aforesaid, and interfering with the workmen and said business of the operation of said works, and in all respects to preserve the peace and to retire to their respective homes and places of residence, as the rights of the workmen to work and the rights of the owners to operate their said works will be fully protected, and in case of failure to observe the instructions all persons offending will be dealt with according to the law.[9]

On July 5th, Knox & Reed sent Colonel Joseph H. Gray, McCleary's chief deputy, to Potter with a letter of introduction. The significant last paragraph to the formal note of introduction was lost in the later rattle of gunfire: "You will understand that Colonel Gray, as a representative of the sheriff, is to have control of all action in case of trouble." [10]

On the same day, Sheriff McCleary tried to recruit a band of one hundred deputies, but could raise only eleven. These he sent under Colonel Gray "to inspect the plant and see that no damage had been done to the property," but they were driven off by the pickets. Hugh O'Donnell, who had been elected chairman of the Advisory Board, sent a message to Potter offering "300 of as good men as could be found in the Allegheny County" to protect the plant.

The offer was undoubtedly made in good faith, but in view of the times, no one in Frick's place would have accepted it. A survey of the newspapers of the period reveals how the extent of the destruction of property by striking workmen was a phenomenon of the decade. Trains were derailed, plants dynamited, and mills and rolling stock burned, to a replacement cost into the millions. This is not to waive any responsibility on the part of management, which had allowed insufferable conditions to prevail in American industry. The injustices of management were countless, and labor fought back with wholesale, senseless destruction. Both sides were caught between unrestricted immigration, an expanding economy, and the greed and shibboleths of men. There was no escape.

In Homestead, when it appeared the union had taken possession of the plant, Frick notified Sheriff McCleary that he intended to place Pinkerton watchmen in the works, and asked if they could be deputized.

The subcommittee's report states: "After obtaining legal advice, he [the sheriff] agreed that if the men were put into the mill as guards and the property was attacked and there was liable to be destruction of the same, he would deputize them but that the determination of the contingency must be left to his judgment.[11]

The question of legal deputization of the uniformed Pinkerton watchmen was very much in the minds of both Robert and William Pinkerton, and they continued to press Carnegie for written confirmation of it.

Philander C. Knox, senior counsel of the plant's law firm, and later Attorney General in Taft's cabinet, finally confirmed, in a longhand letter to Robert Pinkerton, that this would be done:

H. C. FRICK
Chairman
J. G. A. LEISHMAN,
Vice-Chairman and Treasurer

F. T. F. LOVEJOY,
Secretary and Auditor

AGENCY OF CARNEGIE BROTHERS & CO., LTD.
OFFICES, 44–46 WALL STREET
C. H. ODELL, SALES AGENT   NEW YORK, JUNE 30, 1892.

ROBERT PINKERTON, ESQ.:
DEAR SIR:

Confirming what I told you this morning, I beg to say that in an interview with the High Sheriff of Allegheny County, and his counsel yesterday, I informed them that owing to the threats made that Messrs. Carnegie would be prevented from starting up and operating their Homestead Steel Works, that it was proposed by them to supply a large number of watchmen, say about 300, to guard their property from injury and their workmen from violence; that these watchmen would be employed through you and that you desired to know if such an outbreak and disturbance were so employed as to render it necessary to deputize them as Sheriff's deputies for the protection of the company's property, or their own protection, would he do so. He assured me that he would.

Very truly,
P. C. KNOX.[12]

As will be seen from a later letter, Frick wished the Pinkertons brought in without the sheriff's knowledge, and without an arrangement made to deputize them.

CHAPTER 29

The Siege

In late June, the company closed its negotiations with Robert Pinkerton for three hundred watchmen at $5 a day. In accordance with an agreed plan, the watchmen were sent to Ashtabula, Ohio, and on July 5th were taken on the Fort Wayne Road to Davis Island Dam, just below Pittsburgh. About 120 men came from Chicago, another 120 from New York City, and 76 from Philadelphia.

William Pinkerton boxed and shipped from Chicago 250 Winchester rifles, 300 pistols and their ammunition to the Union Supply Company in Pittsburgh. Pinkerton later testified he didn't know the company belonged to Carnegie or that the arms would be shipped to the plant on the barges with his men. He was either naïve or deliberately evasive.

At 11:00 P.M., July 5, 1892, two barges and a towboat captained by W. B. Rogers, who would prove to be a courageous and intelligent riverboat skipper, appeared at the dam to take on the watchmen. Lurid stories later described how the Pinkertons had iron-plated the barges with firing slits, and this was discounted by eyewitness testimony after an examination of the barges by congressional investigators. One barge was equipped as a kitchen; the other had rows of bunks for sleeping quarters. The watchmen were under Captain F. L. Hines, a ten-year Pinkerton employee. Also aboard were Colonel Gray, as the sheriff's representative, and Carnegie General Superintendent Potter. The explosive events would soon reveal them to be two frightened incompetents.

One of the watchmen, recalling the trip down the river, said, "We were told we should fire no arms and if we got a few bricks on the head or thrown at us, that we should not say much about it." There were a number of Civil War veterans among the guards who, the same watchman recalled, "did not attempt to exercise authority but carried themselves very professionally."

Word of the movement of the barges ran through the night. As the towboat neared the plant, which loomed against the dark sky like a grim, medieval castle, a siren was set off. When the barges swung into the riverbank on the Carnegie property, a huge crowd stripped down the plank fence and poured through, shouting, cursing, and jeering.

As Roberts, a heater at Homestead, put it: "In our minds the workmen were confronted by a gang of loafers and cutthroats from all over the country, coming here as they thought to take over their jobs [and that is why] they naturally wanted to go down and defend their homes and their property and their lives if necessary."

Captain Rogers later testified of the events that followed:

> We proceeded to land just above the railroad bridge, on the property of the Carnegie Steel Company which was fenced in. We went right on against the shore and there were met by an armed mob, I think about fifty to one hundred, whose numbers were being reinforced by the crowd on the bank following the boat, until there were about a thousand there within five minutes after we had made our landing.
>
> The first crowd attacked and tried to prevent us from putting our boat ashore and putting out a stageplank. As they came it was something like a charge over the river bank with the evident intent to get on the barges. They got on the stage and were met by the Pinkerton men. One young man threw himself flat on the stage, when Captain Hines of the Pinkerton Corps went forward to push him off. His lying there looked like a piece of bravado, and the others were trying to crowd in over and pass him. While another Pinkerton man was endeavoring to keep the crowd back with an oar, the man lying on the landing stage fired the first shot at Captain Hines, wounding him twice in the thigh.
>
> Immediately the crowd began firing from the river bank, as well as the river's edge near the barge. Two men of the Pinkertons were shot at this time, one at the head of the barge and one was reported to me to have been shot at the stern. All this occurred before the Pinkerton men fired but immediately upon it they fired a general volley, that is about twenty at the head of the boat with revolvers principally and the mob retreated behind their entrenchments which they had provided of pig iron and iron plate.[1]

Rogers told the committee that the stage was pulled back aboard the towboat and that a conference was held. At this point Hines, lying on the deck of the boat, his men trying to stop the flow of blood, demanded that Colonel Gray, as representative of the sheriff, deputize his men immediately. Gray refused, explaining that "there was no necessity at this time." When Hines pressed for a definition of where he and his men now stood legally, Gray passed the responsibility to General Superintendent Potter, whom he called "the representative of the company." But Potter, aware of the letter inside his jacket from Carnegie's attorneys warning him not to commit any "overt acts," nervously tossed the responsibility back to Gray. Surely it was an incredible scene of the two representatives of big business and the law debating whether or not the watchmen could defend themselves. Finally, when Hines again pressed Gray for an answer, the sheriff's deputy reluctantly told him, "Potter had a perfect right to put them [the watchmen] on the property and [the Pinkertons] had a perfect right to defend themselves in the prosecution of their duty." [2]

When the strikers momentarily retreated up the bank, it appeared that the watchmen could storm the works and take possession; but Hines pointed out the women and children milling in front of the barricades. Later testimony indicates there was little leadership besides that of the wounded Hines and the towboat's Captain Rogers. Potter later explained: "It was a question of whether we should get into the works by force or let things take their course. Mr. Gray didn't feel like taking the responsibility, nor did I." [3]

After a conference among Captain Hines, Captain Rogers, Colonel Gray, and Potter, it was decided to take the badly wounded back upriver and let the barges of men remain at the riverbank. Potter's reasoning was that "we would let the barges where they were, the crowd seemed to be breaking up, and we thought, in an hour, two or three, we would be able to make a peaceful landing. Mr. Gray, the deputy, refused to take any action in this matter, and I felt my instructions had been carried out. I had letters on my person at the time that cautioned me against any overt act, and I did not propose to order any change."

Captain Hines at first decided to stay behind with his men, but he collapsed from loss of blood. As he lay on the deck, Captain Rogers recalled Hines saying that he would go on if he could, but "I don't like the idea of lying here on a boat deck and bleeding to death." The towboat soon departed with Hines, three dead Pinkertons, several wounded, the nervous Colonel Gray, and Potter who had the carefully worded lawyer's letter in his pocket.

It was deep in the morning when Captain Rogers set out again for Homestead. Aboard was a crew of six and a Pinkerton watchman who had volunteered to return. Neither Potter nor Gray returned. As Rogers later recalled, as he neared the works he raised "colors bow and stern in anticipation of being fired on again." When the towboat appeared, Rogers later told the committee, "The shore was lined with thousands all of whom seemed bent on destroying our lives and the boat."

The strikers by this time had obtained artillery, and heavy cannon fire blew holes in the hull above the waterline. As the boat came abreast of the two barges with the Pinkerton watchmen, a continuous volley of gunfire forced the pilot and crew to hug the decks, and the boat slowly drifted downstream. One crewman was shot, and later died. After the tow-boat left, the strikers charged down the riverbank, but the fire of the watchmen on the barges drove them back to their barricades of girders and plates. The cannon was dragged up, and the barges were bombarded. The exchange of gunfire continued all morning and afternoon. At one point, drums of oil were emptied into the river and touched off by the strikers, who hoped to fire the barges, but a slack tide and a strong breeze blew the flames in a different direction, and burned down a wooden water tower.

At five o'clock Hugh O'Donnell, the chairman of the union's Advisory Board, which had originally taken over the plant, addressed the mob, then estimated at between six thousand and seven thousand, and asked for a cease-fire "to let the barges go for the sake of humanity." With O'Donnell were the president and officers of the Amalgamated, holding an American flag as they climbed to the top of a metal bin. O'Donnell proposed they raise a white flag, but this was shouted down. When a proposal to parley was voted, the union leader told the vast sea of faces he would not move a step unless every man in the mob would guarantee that if the Pinkertons surrendered they wouldn't be harmed. As O'Donnell said, "They pledged themselves with a cheer."

O'Donnell and his men then tied a white handkerchief to a gun barrel and walked down to the riverbank. They waved the handkerchief and shouted to the barges that if one of the watchmen would expose himself, they would do the same.

What happened was then described by O'Donnell:

> I must say the Pinkerton man came to the bow first and he exposed himself and waved a handkerchief and some other man came with him. Seeing this we immediately went down to the boat and parleyed. I made the remark, "Are you not sick of this firing?" and he replied, "I am heartily sick of it."
>
> Now I said what are the conditions under which you will surrender?
>
> We will surrender, the Pinkerton man said, if you will give us your pledge from you and your people that you will pack our arms in boxes and give us a safe passage from Homestead.
>
> We promised this. I flattered myself I had sufficient control over our own people to do that, but I did not consider at the time that half the people who had congregated there were from various parts of the vicinity at Homestead. I then placed a guard over the gangplank and told them not to allow anyone to enter. We got some of our best men and placed them and then they commenced to unload the rifles.
>
> Afterwards I went down and asked them if I could have one loaded rifle to prevent the looting of the barges. For I said, we had a mob outside of wholly irresponsible parties and I mounted a table—they had

The Pinkertons, overwhelmed by gunfire and flames, surrender
to the strikers and are marched through the town of Homestead.
Leslie's Illustrated Magazine

a table running the full length of the barge—I got on that table and I superintended the unloading of the rifles. . . . When all was ready I gave the order and they marched out and I remained on the boat until the last man. I will state that by this time the people were coming up, down and across the river and the barges were in the hands of rabble.[4]

The union guards marched the Pinkertons to the center of the town and to Labor Hall, where before they were released they were forced to swear that they would never again hire out to Carnegie. As they marched out, they were engulfed by the screaming, hooting, and cursing mob. Some men were stripped of their clothing. Watches, wallets, and cash, even shoes, were stolen and rings taken. Then the watchmen were forced to run an Indian-type gauntlet. When wounded men fell, they were beaten to death. O'Donnel claimed that the Amalgamated Union's leaders fought to protect the Pinkertons, but they were swept aside.

O'Donnell told the congressional committee: "Men, women and boys formed on either side and I must say the Pinkerton men were subjected to every inhuman treatment which our men were powerless to protect them from."

The committee's report states:

> The character of the injuries inflicted upon the Pinkertons in some cases were too indecent and brutal to describe in this report. Whatever may have been the character of these men or the offense which they had committed against the feelings of the people at Homestead, the indignities to which they were subjected when prisoners and defenseless is not disgraceful to the town but to civilization as well; and there is no evidence that any attempt was made upon the part of their captors for their protection, except as stated by Mr. O'Donnell, who did not see it. No brave man or good woman will mistreat a prisoner who is disarmed and has no chance to defend himself.[5]

When the savagery of the mob was exhausted, the watchmen who were able to walk carried the dead and dying to the railroad station and West Penn Hospital. Two men died from their wounds; another was later committed to an asylum as a result of the beating. Some remained in hospitals for periods of a week to three months. One wounded man had both arms broken by musket butts as he lay helpless on the ground.

The strikers, on the other hand, were not without casualties. As a result of the day's exchange of gunfire, they counted ten dead and several wounded.

The tragic summer day finally came to a close at the riverbank late that night. The barges and a pumping station were burned, casting a lurid glow on the Monongahela while thousands hooted, cheered, and fired rifles whenever a burning timber crumbled to send a shower of sparks up into the night.

On their way to New York, the watchmen read that Senator Palmer described them all as outcasts and remarked that to kill them would be a service to humanity.

In his office, Allegheny County's High Sheriff William H. McCleary, who certainly can't be described as the epitome of courage, received the first report of the initial contact between the Pinkertons and the strikers from his deputy, Colonel Gray, who had hurried from Davis Dam. As additional reports poured in, McCleary realized that the situation in Homestead was now out of control. He sent two telegrams to Governor Robert E. Pattison in Harrisburg, the first describing Homestead as "very grave," and the mob surrounding the plant now numbering "at least 5,000." He warned the governor that "unless prompt measures are taken further bloodshed and great destruction of property may be expected."
In his second and more hysterical telegram he told Pattison:

> The works in Homestead are in the hands of an armed mob, they number thousands. The mill owners attempted to land a number of watchmen and an attack was made on the boats and six men on the boats are seriously wounded. A number of men on shore were killed and wounded, how many I do not know. The boat later came down and was fired on from the shore compelling the pilot to abandon the pilot house. I have no means at my command to meet emergencies; a large armed force will be required. Any delay may lead to further bloodshed and destruction of property. You are therefore urged to act at once.[6]

Governor Pattison was later charged with failing promptly to call out the National Guard or to declare an emergency. As a Democrat with ambitions, he was in a political dilemma: Should he call out the troops and be denounced by labor, whose support his party was frantically seeking in the growing presidential campaign, or should he wait and hope the local authorities would eventually get the situation under control?
But the reports from Homestead were too ominous to ignore; mob rule controlled the community. Pattison reluctantly ordered out the Pennsylvania National Guard.

CHAPTER 30
Investigations and Hearings

The news of the battle at Homestead spread across the nation. There was widespread sympathy for the strikers, while Carnegie, the Pinkertons, and the McKinley Tariff Law were denounced in a barrage of editorials from the West Coast to New York.

Homestead came at a time when the presidential campaigns were in full swing. The McKinley Tariff, which had raised the cost of consumer goods from tin cups to fresh fish, was the leading issue, but not the only one. There was national resentment against the lavish spending of the Fifty-second Congress, the so-called "Billion Dollar Congress," and the Democrats exploited this by pointing out to the voters that if Harrison's Republican administration had wanted to reduce the nation's surplus they could have done so by relieving the taxpayers.

Then came the Homestead riot. The Democrats were quick to link the events at Homestead to the high tariff. Daniel W. Voorhees of Indiana told Congress that "labor battles and blood-stained fields have sprung alone from the doctrine of protection." Cleveland, running ahead of Harrison in national popularity, used Homestead in his acceptance speech, pointing out that the Republicans had long promised that the McKinley tariff would raise wages and reduce taxes, but "while they listen, scenes are enacted in the very abiding place of high protection that mock the hopes of toil and attest the tender mercies the workingman receives from those made selfish and sordid by unjust governmental favoritism." [1]

Whitelaw Reid, candidate for the Vice-Presidency, sent telegraphic appeals through the State Department's cipher code to Carnegie—apparently with Harrison's approval—pleading for a settlement or at least peace terms and recognition for the union, but without success. A representative of the Republican National Committee, acting as spokesman

350

for the party, was sent to Pittsburgh to see Frick, but had the greatest difficulty even in interviewing him. This was a shocking example of the weakness of government authority at the time: that an emissary of the Republican Party, and unofficial representative of the government, could be rebuffed by a Frick. Nothing, it seemed, neither national sentiment nor editorial thunder, could shake the Carnegie Company in its determination not to recognize the Amalgamated or any other union organization. A single corporation held in its iron fist the fate and livelihood of thousands of workers, touched the everyday existence of millions of Americans, and held the power of deciding national elections.

While the nation and the world watched the titanic struggle between Labor and Big Business, the House Judiciary Subcommittee was ordered by Congress to investigate the riots and "to investigate the said Pinkerton detectives, to wit, the character of their employments by corporations engaged in the transportation of interstate commerce or the United States mails; the number so employed, and whether such employment had provoked breaches of peace or caused destruction of property, and of material facts connected with their employment." The resolution to investigate the cause of the riots and the employment of the Pinkertons was passed with the curious amendment that the committees be also instructed to investigate "whether the employment of the Pinkertons has anything to do with the present system of Federal taxation."

One of the principal witnesses was Powderly, president of the Knights of Labor. Powderly, an Irish mechanic and former Mayor of Syracuse, led the Knights through the major years of his life. The Knights, formed in 1869 by a Philadelphia cutter, was in the 1870's a strictly secret organization formed to fight the blacklist and other antiworkingman tactics. Largely because of the opposition of the Catholic Church, the Knights abandoned its secrecy in 1881. Powderly was a bitter foe of the wage system, and advocated a classless social order. He disapproved of strikes, and favored arbitration in all labor disputes. His constant boast was that as head of the Knights he had never called a strike. Membership in the Knights had boomed in the mid 1880's but had rapidly declined by 1890. When Powderly appeared as a witness, his power was fading, and the Knights of Labor were rapidly dwindling to pave the way for the job-and-wage-oriented trade-union movement.

Powderly was a bitter foe of the Pinkertons, and a review of his testimony reveals numerous unfounded charges and hearsay evidence. So serious were the charges that the committee requested he produce witnesses. Powderly promised to return within a few days, but he never again appeared. Both the majority and minority reports of the committee dismissed his testimony:

> Master Workman Powderly of the Knights of Labor, was called before
> us as a witness and he testified generally in condemnation of the man-

ner of the Pinkerton guards and watchmen, alleging them to be irritating to laborers and productive of breaches of the peace. Mr. Powderly also charged them with gross injustice and violations of the law in many cases, but these charges were based almost entirely on hearsay evidence. He also attacked the character of many of these guards and watchmen. Mr. Powderly was requested to furnish the committee with the names of persons who could give testimony against the Pinkertons and their practices to prove his charges but he failed to give the name of any such witness or witnesses.

An example of Powderly's recklessness was his testimony: "During the Denver & Rio Grande strike we employed watchmen to watch the Pinkerton watchmen and discovered them in the acts of placing dynamite on the tracks. I believe you will have no trouble in securing the evidence." [2]

Both Pinkertons testified, Robert, who had originally negotiated the Carnegie contract, more intensively than William. In a general statement read before the House subcommittee, they answered Powderly's charges point by point. For example, the Pinkertons satisfied the committee that the Agency was not hired during the Denver & Rio Grande strike. In another charge, Powderly accused the Pinkertons of having "induced men" to place dynamite on the tracks during the Chicago, Burlington & Quincy strike of 1888; but Robert Pinkerton produced statements from law-enforcement officials that showed that two members of the Brotherhood of Locomotive Engineers had confessed to placing the charges on the tracks, and had become state's witnesses to convict other members of that union. The Pinkertons said:

> It is pretended that there would be no acts of violence during these strikes if they were not caused by the Pinkerton men or the exasperation of the strikers at their presence. This was solemnly urged before the House Committee. Yet shortly after the occurrence at Homestead and while union leaders were professing that the whole trouble came from the employment of Pinkerton watchmen, the community was shocked by the outrages at Coeur d'Alene and Buffalo [scenes of riots in which lives were lost and much property damage done by mobs].
>
> Yet no Pinkertons were employed or were present at either strike. The conduct of the strikers, however, was the same at Homestead. [3]

Before Robert Pinkerton testified on July 22nd in Washington, John Devlin, A. W. Wright, and John W. Hayes, the executive board of the Knights of Labor, presented to the committee a list of questions which they demanded that Pinkerton answer. Congressman William Oates of Alabama, chairman of the committee, informed the Knights no questions would be allowed unless the witnesses agreed to answer them. Pinkerton, after reading the list, told the committee to "fire away." He readily answered the union's questions—about fifty or more—which dealt with the events leading up to the strike and to the night of the riot. He dismissed the published stories that the barges were sheeted with iron, pointing out to the committee that its members had examined the towboat and the barges, and had seen the numerous bullet and shell holes. "The great amount of wounds inflicted on our men should conclusively establish that the barges were not a sufficient protection," he said.

Both Pinkertons insisted they would never have allowed their watchmen to depart from Chicago "had we known they were going to be attacked before landing." The landing at night, Robert explained, was to allow the barges to come aboard on the company's property

> at an hour when we thought the strikers would be in bed, because we felt that after the experience of the sheriff's men, an attempt might be made to forcibly prevent our men from entering the works if they came by railroad. Had we known when the men started, that they could not have landed without a breach of peace we would not have allowed them to leave unless they had been authorized by the governor or by the sheriff.

Pinkerton was careful to point out that "our employers, the Carnegie Company, had duly applied to the proper legal authority and that we were going to Homestead with the consent and approval of the sheriff and our watchmen would be sworn in in case of trouble." Pinkerton, however, did admit they had not been personally in touch with the sheriff of the county, but had taken the word of the company.

In connection with the rifles, pistols, and ammunition that had been aboard the barge Pinkerton testified that they had been shipped to the Union Supply Company on instructions from the Carnegie Company:

> We positively instructed the men and our officers that the arms were not to be used except after they were sworn in by the sheriff and their lives were in danger. I desire to say I did not know the arms were to go up on the boat, but I have understood that the reason they were sent up on the boat was it was impossible to get anything inside the works otherwise.

The arms, he said, were to be issued to the watchmen when they were on the company's property and only to be used in defending their lives. Congressman Charles J. Boanter of Louisiana, who was obviously hostile to the Pinkertons, hammered away at Robert on the questions of the arms and when they were to have been used. The detective quietly insisted that the original agreement stated his men were to land on the company's property, march into the works, and then be armed "only in the protection of their own lives."

After the Washington hearings had ended, Homestead was still a political football, tossed back and forth in the bitter presidential campaign. The Allegheny County coroner's jury in its findings recommended that the question of the "unlawful assembly, which had assembled on the said property of Carnegie-Phipps and Co. Steel Works, to attack the landing of the said barges, be certified to the September session of the Grand Jury."

On October 26, 1892, Chief Justice Paxson of the Pennsylvania Supreme Court, on invitation of the county judiciary, sat as Judge of Oyer and Terminer of Allegheny County to charge the grand jury investigating the riot. Justice Paxson reviewed the disagreement between Carnegie and the Amalgamated Association, the strike, and the activities of the union's "Advisory Board" that had shut off Homestead "by an organization of a military nature by which the works and the town were guarded like a military encampment."

Justice Paxson's charge, which was widely published, loudly praised or strongly denounced, must be viewed against the findings of the grand jury that indicted 176 strikers for treason! As the New York *Sun* editorial writer asked: Treason against whom? Frick?

After reviewing the preliminary steps to the negotiations of the contract and the siege of the Pinkertons, who, Justice Paxson pointed out, "were in charge of a deputy sheriff . . . their business and their only business was to protect property of their employers," he detailed the calling up of the National Guard,

> which has resulted in the humiliating spectacle of a business plant surrounded by the army of the state for its protection at an expense of several hundred thousand dollars [actually $440,000] to the taxpayers and the business of the country, disturbed to some extent, and for what?
>
> We can have some sympathy with a mob driven to desperation by hunger, as in the days of the French Revolution, but we can have none for men receiving steady employment of exceptionally high wages in resisting the law and in resorting to violence and bloodshed in the assertion of imaginary rights, and in entailing such a vast expense upon the taxpayers of the Commonwealth. It was not a cry "of bread or blood" from famished lips or an ebullition of angry passions from a sudden outrage or provocation. It was a deliberate attempt from men without a grievance to wrest from others their lawfully acquired property and to control them in their use and enjoyment of it.
>
> The existence of such a state of things in a government of law indicates a weak spot somewhere. It is not in the law itself. That is sufficient for the preservation of order. All that is needed is its proper enforcement. To accomplish this it is only necessary that every one connected with its administration shall do his duty.

Paxson then told the grand jurors the rights of the company "to protect its property:

> For this purpose it could lawfully employ as many men as it saw proper, and arm them, if necessary. Many of our banks and other places of business are guarded by armed watchmen. The law did not require it to employ as watchmen the men from whom it anticipated the destruc-

tion of its works. When a man seeks to protect his house from burglars it would be unreasonable to require him to place the burglars in possession for that purpose. So long as the men employed by the company as watchmen to guard and protect its property acted only in that capacity, and for that purpose, it mattered not to the rioters, nor to the public, who they were, nor from whence they came. It was an act of unlawful violence to prevent their landing upon the property of the company.

The rights of the men, as before stated, were to refuse to work unless their terms were acceded to, and to persuade others to join them in such refusal. But it will sustain them no further. The moment they attempted to control the works, and to prevent by violence, or threats of of violence, other laborers from going to work there, they placed themselves outside the pale of the law, and became rioters.[4]

In the last paragraph of his lengthy charge, Justice Paxson, perhaps without even realizing it at the time, struck at the heart of what had brought about the bloody events at Homestead, when he told the jurors that American business could not "concede to the agrarian doctrine that the employee may lawfully dictate to his employer the terms of his employment." Homestead, as we know now, was far more complex than a strike riot: It was the first major confrontation of the growing revolt against social Darwinism—the survivor of the fittest in business— and all it stood for.

In Homestead, union leaders disclosed that the strike had cost three-fifths of the struck jobs and a wage loss of $1,250,000. Congress and the nation's press still echoed with the defense or the denunciation of the Pinkertons. *Harper's Weekly* solemnly pointed out that the events at Homestead hinted at a darker flaw in the American character when it condemned the strikers, while the nation could not let the Pinkertons "operate without confessing to conditions of things among us, which we must be ashamed of. A truly civilized community would not have to look to a Pinkerton force to do under private pay that which is obviously the business of the regulated constituted authority." The Populists demanded the abolition of "all private armies," and included this proposal in the preamble to its 1892 Omaha platform. *The Nation,* in a widely discussed editorial, defended the Pinkertons, and condemned the national press for criticizing the defenders of property while rioters were subjects of sympathy. The majority of America's religious press condemned the strikers, assailed the union, and justified the employment of the Pinkertons, while a number of Protestant clergymen publicly declared their support of the strikers.

In December, 1892, the House subcommittee handed down its long legal report. It found that the presence of the Pinkertons was entirely legal, that the testimony of witnesses, some hostile to the Agency, agreed that the watchmen did not fire or by armed threat provoke the first shot; that the mob was assembled unlawfully, and that, under the law, Carnegie had a right to protect its property. As to the use of the Pinkertons, the report pointed out in this significant paragraph:

"The practice of employing Pinkerton guards or watchmen by corporations in case of strikes or labor trouble has grown very largely out of the sloth and inability of the civil authorities to render efficient and proper protection in such cases."[5]

In commenting on the "unspeakable tortures" inflicted on the watchmen by women and boys in the mob—"rabble" as Hugh O'Donnell, the head of the union's Advisory Board described them—the house report said:

"We are loath to believe that any of the women are native Americans."

It was typical of the attitude of the Establishment of that time toward "foreigners."

Another section, referring to Hugh O'Donnell's bitter denunciation of the Pinkertons in his testimony, said:

> Will anyone deny that it is a privilege of any citizen of Pennsylvania to accept employment from Carnegie & Co. either to work in their mills at Homestead or be a watchman therein or be an armed guard, so that he commits no trespass or breach of the peace on the person or property of any other person? It is equally the right of each of the strikers, yes, of every citizen of Homestead, to employ a Pinkerton watchman or any other person to stand guard over his house, his property, his premises, if he chooses to do so. If the washerwoman of Burgess McLuckey or Hugh O'Donnell refuses to wash for what he is willing to pay, that is her right, but she has no right to stand in the front of his door and fling stones at another woman who comes in her place to do the work under a new scale of pay which he is willing to pay.
>
> One may be lawfully employed to guard the property of his employer, even to the extent of shooting down an incendiary or another person who approaches the same with the intent of destruction, after warning such trespasser to desist.

Congress, the report went on, did not have the constitutional authority to pass any laws to regulate or prohibit the hiring of watchmen or guards; it was strictly within the legal framework of the state's legislative machinery to enact such laws.

The minority report, describing the Pinkerton watchmen as men "of superior courage but doubtful discretion," urged that the prohibition of

> any foreign force in a local community, except by manner of law, is a danger to the peace and good order of any society. No principle in our form of government is more firmly embedded in the hearts of our people than local administration. The citizens of every community are imbued with the same spirit of local government and view with great jealousy the presence of any other than the force which they have provided for the protection and preservation of their lives and properties . . . the presence of a force not called in the regular manner, even if

clothed with the semblance of authority, is more likely to impress the peaceful citizen, much more the excited workman with the conviction that his home, his rights, his liberties are being invaded, than that the laws are being upheld for his preservation.

The execution of the laws by high officials, the report sternly warned, should "not be farmed out to private individuals in the employ of private persons or corporations." Both majority and minority reports dismissed the charge that the Pinkertons had anything to do with the tariff.

In view of both Pinkertons' strongly held opinions, and the assumed Bourbon cast of their minds, it is interesting to note that on December 4, 1892, before the congressional committee had reached its lengthy decision, the Agency issued a public statement: "Work of supplying watchmen [in labor troubles] is extremely dangerous and undesirable and for that reason we prefer not to furnish watchmen in such cases."

Announced at a time when their services of the sort were more than ever in demand, and when they could command very high prices, the decision seems to indicate a perception of the changing social and economic conditions.

Two letters might close the Homestead incident and its bitter aftermath.

Though they are little known, they are important, revealing Frick's intention to try to slip watchmen into Homestead without first notifying the sheriff:

H. C. FRICK, Esq.,   July 19, '93
Chairman, Carnegie Steel Co.,
Pittsburgh, Pa.

DEAR SIR:

We have delayed bringing up the subject of our losses at Homestead until now, hoping that some of the property would be recovered and that some suggestion might be made by your company to reimburse us for the heavy losses sustained by us.

We respectfully request that your company reimburse us for the property shipped by us to the Union Supply Company, Pittsburgh, and taken on the boats at Homestead, and for the other damages sustained by us by reason of accepting employment in this matter.

No doubt you will recognize that our foresight in insisting that the sheriff should be made aware of the intention of Carnegie & Co. to bring our men to Homestead and to deputize them should there be an indication of trouble before we would send them there, placed your company in much more favorable light than they would have been placed had they been sent to Homestead as originally requested without the sheriff being consulted as to their coming.

I think there can be no doubt that we have stood by your company loyally throughout all this trouble and Congressional and State investigations, and that as a matter of fairness we should be reimbursed our actual out-of-pocket losses.

> For the almost irreparable injury our business sustained, we make
> no claim whatever, although it seems to us some recognition of the
> sacrifice we made might be suggested.
>
> Yours truly,
>
> ROBERT A. PINKERTON [6]

On September 14th, Pinkerton sent a second note to Frick, calling his attention to the July letter.

Despite the pleas of high Republican leaders to Carnegie and Frick to recognize the union and come to an agreement, they refused. They held out until November, when the strike collapsed. It broke the Amalgamated Association of Iron and Steel Workers in this country, and destroyed unionism in the steel industry for neary fifty years.[7]

Other strikes during that summer, of railroad switchmen at Buffalo, of soft-coal miners in Tennessee, and the silver miners at Coeur d-'Alene, all helped to discredit Harrison's administration. But the bloody events of Homestead were one of the principal rallying symbols of the Democrats. In November, Cleveland was elected, with the voters casting 5,556,545 votes for him as against 5,175,582 for Harrison.

In looking back over the years since that July morning, and summing up the events that took place, it is difficult to find a single hero or villain. That the Pinkertons were acting within the law is incontestable; that they were acting morally is another question. Rather than the Carnegies and Fricks, the inflamed workers and the Pinkertons, the evil present that morning was the law itself, which protected the advocates of social Darwinism, the tooth-and-claw philosophy of ruthless business rivalry and unprincipled politics. During the 1870's and 1880's, the American middle class accepted the dream of personal conquest, the legend of the self-made man through pluck and hard work. Even Walt Whitman, the poet of democracy, viewed the "maniacal appetite for wealth" as part of American progress. "My theory demands riches and the getting of riches," he wrote in 1872.

In time the American middle class shrank from the principle it had gloried in, and as Richard Hofstadter writes, "turned in flight from the hideous image of rampant, competitive brutality, and repudiated the once heroic entrepreneur as a despoiler of the nation's wealth and morals and a monopolist of its opportunities."[8]

Homestead was one of the first major confrontations between these two philosophies. On the part of the workers, it was a savage battle for survival, "survival, naked and abstract," to use William James's description; for Frick and Carnegie it was a defense of their autocratic world where the survival of the fittest was the iron rule, a world already tottering. As for the Pinkertons, they were caught in the middle, seeking to carry out commitments that had steadily grown more lucrative and, as they belatedly realized, more antisocial.

BOOK 7
The Pinkertons in the Wild West

CHAPTER 31
The Train Robbers

From the 1860's to the early years of the twentieth century, the Pinkertons chased, captured, and killed—and were themselves killed—in the apprehension of countless stagecoach, bank, and train robbers in the American West. In that sparsely populated, majestic land, they were a major law-enforcement agency in the era after the Civil War. Sometimes together, many times alone or leading posses of deputies, townspeople or farmers, William and Robert Pinkerton trailed gangs of desperadoes on horseback, train, buggy, spring wagon, or even on foot. Their record in the West is impressive: In every major train or bank robbery, they either captured or killed the thieves, and gathered the evidence that led to scores of convictions of outlaws who were imprisoned in territorial or federal jails, and recovered large percentages of the stolen monies. The Pinkertons' activities in outlawry linked the American frontier to the years just preceding World War I. They began by chasing outlaws on horseback. They ended rounding up posses by telephone.

Most Americans, influenced by television or motion pictures, view the American outlaw through a romantic haze that pictures them to be happy-go-lucky Robin Hoods, engaging, handsome men who had been forced into a life of banditry because of evil railroads, miserly foreclosing bankers, or tyrannical beef barons. The letters of Robert and William Pinkerton, the laconic reports of their superintendents, and the memories of frontier lawmen—some of whom were still alive and active in the early 1940's—present the majority of gunmen and bandits in the cold light of eyewitness reality as illiterate, conscienceless, cold-blooded, contemptuous of law and society, and oftentimes cowards who gladly became state's witnesses in return for lesser sentences.

Yet, curiously, the same reports, the same memories, along with photographs and daguerreotypes from the early Pinkerton Criminal Gallery help to confirm the legends, at least in part. Some of the western bravoes were indeed lean and handsome; many had a marvelous sense of humor; nearly all were superb riders, crack shots, had courage, and at times appeared to possess an unbelievable amount of endurance. But never were they Robin Hoods; weeping widows were never handed a sack of gold to pay the mortgage. There was little or no grandeur to their lives; their motives were simply greed and excitement. As William Pinkerton pointed out to a convention of International Police Chiefs in 1907: "Outlaws and holdup men were made of men too lazy to work, with enough bravado to engage in robbery and in the Southwest and Middle Border of daredevils from the Civil War."[1]

The first outlaw band the Pinkertons chased were the Reno Brothers of Indiana, then the Jameses and Youngers. From the 1870's to the turn of the century, there was scarcely an American railroad that had not been robbed. The Adams Express Company and the Southern Pacific Express companies were the usual targets. The combination of kinship, fear, apathy, and the breakdown of local law enforcement, either through fear or bribery, presented enormous obstacles for a detective.

A phenomenon of American outlawry was its family makeup: The Jameses, Youngers, Renos, Daltons, Evans, McCoys, Farringtons were brotherhoods. Some of the early bands were composed of former Quantrill riders who used guerrilla techniques of harassing a small town or village with gunfire, piled logs on tracks to derail trains, or "hurrahed" passenger cars with volleys while the express-car door was being blasted open.

Western train robbers did not use dynamite until about 1890; before that, black powder was employed to blast open the heavy wooden doors of the express cars. From 1890 to 1893, dynamite was used in several train robberies, but as William Pinkerton pointed out, while it saved the outlaws precious time, handling of the explosive by amateurs increased the risk. Train robbers in the West became so frequent in this period that express companies were urged to build steel cars. Pinkerton answered this proposal by quoting the general manager of the San Francisco Railroad:

> I frequently received suggestions to have steel express cars built and to send guards with the trains. But why should we do that when anyone may buy a quarter's worth of dynamite, and blow to pieces the strongest metal ever put together?
>
> Great treasure is carried by every line, and dynamite will open the

best of safes. In many states anyone may buy that dangerous explosive and no questions are asked. Law should first restrict the sale of it as it does poison. Men who hold up passenger trains are armed, and if it is necessary to carry out their designs, they will kill. Aside from the liability of an engineer or a curiously-inclined passenger to be shot, there is a greater danger that another train may come along and wreck the passenger train, standing alone on the track in some dark cut or lonely piece of woods.

By 1892, train robberies in the West had become so numerous and costly that the general managers of the major American railroads met in Denver to draft a resolution asking Washington to place the crime of train robbery under federal jurisdiction. The Pinkertons helped to draft this proposal, although they must have been aware that a good percentage of their business could be lost. Congressman Caldwell of Ohio introduced the bill that same year, but it died in committee. It wasn't until after World War I that train robbery finally became a federal crime. Pinkerton wrote:

> If it becomes a crime against the United States government to hold up a train, it is almost certain that this class of work will soon come to an end. The government should take charge of these cases, as the robbers are not likely to be able to control the United States officials as they control the local authorities. The latter will frequently drop pursuit at the State or county lines, claiming that they have no authority to go further. A State or county line would not act as a barrier for a United States officer.[2]

Until train robbery became a federal crime, Pinkerton said, his operatives, along with express-company detectives, would continue "to relentlessly hunt down train robbers if it means traveling across the country twenty times."

The mounting numbers of train robberies in the 1880's and 1890's threatened seriously to affect the transporting of bank funds and the rates of money. To force government action, express companies in 1893 seriously considered raising the rates so high that major banks would be forced to use the United States mails to transport their money. To western outlaws this would mean holding up the government, not a privately owned corporation. That same year, at the suggestions of both Pinkertons, and despite the misgivings of the San Francisco railroad's general manager, extra guards, "known for their determination and nerve," and armed with the "latest improved style of revolvers and Winchesters," were placed in express cars crossing the western plains. Safe companies also produced so-called "burglarproof safes, constructed so it will take the robbers hours to get into them, and if they are blown up the money will be destroyed so that it will not do the robbers any good." The safes, locked in New York or Chicago, were not opened until the point of destination. The guards were not given the combination.

Yet, despite the "nervy" guards, their high-powered Winchesters, and the alleged burglarproof safes, the western outlaws continued to plunder the railroads and their express cars. Black powder—according to a Pinkerton operative who traced a scrap of powder bag to a Denver company, Number Four, Coarse Grain, was their favorite brand—and dynamite were used to blow the cars and the safes. There were times the inexperienced outlaws used such heavy charges the roof and sides of cars were blown out. Miraculously, only a few guards were killed.

Most of the Pinkerton operations were conducted from Denver, where James McParland, the nemesis of the Molly Maguires, was superintendent. When word was telegraphed that a train had been robbed, William or Robert Pinkerton, sometimes both, would rush to Denver to supervise the search with McParland.

Aiding them was a network of reward-eager sheriffs the Pinkertons had established during the 1870's. In a way it was a primitive, interlocking police state-to-state system. Each sheriff or peace officer sent descriptions of local outlaws, their associates, friends, hideouts, and if possible a photograph to the Chicago or Denver offices. The latter request may appear foolish, but the Pinkertons had found from experience that outlaws possessed enormous egos and that they loved to pose for frontier photographers. One Pinkerton Rogues' Gallery photograph of an outlaw has him on horseback, aiming a six-shooter at the photographer. A Pinkerton or Union Pacific Railroad detective discovered the famous group photograph of Butch Cassidy and the Wild Bunch in a Fort Worth studio. The Pinkertons distributed the photograph in thousands of wanted posters, both in the West and in South America, where Cassidy later introduced outlawry, American style, in the pampas. Individual photographs were also pulled out of the group by the Pinkertons, and, accompanied by a detailed physical description, were distributed with rewards to almost every sheriff in the West. Before the Fort Worth photograph, the Wild Bunch riders were faceless. The extensive circulation of the posters undoubtedly helped in their apprehension.

Informers, who cooperated either out of greed, fear, or a sincere desire to seek justice in an area terrorized by a gang, were also recruited into this network by the Pinkertons. Railroad men, saloonkeepers, sheepherders, cattlemen, mine operators, and small-town bankers constantly fed information into the Pinkertons' Chicago, Denver, or New York offices. Nothing was ever too trivial. The scraps and bits of fact or gossip were carefully put together and cross-indexed to form a whole picture of a hard-riding gang—a system used by modern law enforcement. The identities of all informers were closely guarded, and only code names were used in official communications. Thus we find "Birdstone" sending a brief note that Will Roberts, alias Billy Roberts, who rode with Butch

Cassidy and the Wild Bunch, "is about 36 years old, height, 5 ft. 7½ in., weight, 133 lbs., complexion real dark like a Mex, he has dark eyes and a good nose. He has a tooth out in front, eyes appear bloodshot but are natural. A good cook, Mexican blood, talks good Mex. His residence is either in Mexico or America. He's a breed, carries a lot of hardware [six-shooters] and knows how to use same."

Only death closed the Pinkerton file on an outlaw, but there were occasions when even that didn't satisfy the Agency, who had the corpse disinterred and extensively photographed, with an operative putting on and taking off the dead man's hat. Copies of these gruesome but necessary photographs were then distributed to the wardens of state and federal jails, prison physicians, members of the jury that had convicted the dead outlaw, informers, and hostile relatives. Only when the dead man was positively identified, did William or Robert dispatch a round-robin telegram to all branches, ordering the file of that outlaw transferred from the "active file" to the "dead and removal file." As the files of the Agency grew to mountainous proportions, the dead-and-removal files were condensed; fortunatey, many of the old photographs and daguerreotypes of the criminal gallery were kept.

In their investigations of outlaw bands, the Pinkertons' favorite method was assigning an operative to play a role to infiltrate a group. Operatives worked as ranch hands, trainmen, bartenders, sheepherders, stagecoach drivers, hobos, and riverboat hands. In some cases elaborate preparations were made to turn an operative into a wanted man. He was given a new identity, a carefully prepared police record, and perhaps a much folded wanted poster.

Charlie Siringo, whose autobiography is a minor western classic, was a Pinkerton operative for years. When he was chasing the Wild Bunch, he successfully posed as a silent, mysterious gunman in order to make his way into the outlaw community of Hole in the Wall. To locate the hideout of one desperado, he courted the outlaw's girl friend in Montana. Another operative trailed a stolen horse herd thousands of miles to pick up the trail of an outlaw who had taken part in a train robbery. And another, who posed as a drummer with a suitcase filled with men's articles, traveled from town to town gathering bits of information across boardinghouse breakfast tables, in saloons or in livery stables. Every man was under strict orders to send in a daily report; some are still extant, in notebooks, on sheets of western hotel stationery, or on old-fashioned lined paper: "Man answering Logan's [Harvey Logan, a notorious western desperado] description was in the Star Saloon last week. He said he was going North to work the mines. The livery man says the gang's hideout is at the WS ranch which is owned by the McCoys, all disreputable characters. . . ."

Then suddenly the frontier was gone—almost overnight, as some men remembered. There was no more free range, and sodbusters were everywhere. Barbed wire fenced off huge sections; villages grew into towns, towns into cities. The longhorns vanished; telephone poles appeared, then the telephone. The gunmen became myths.

The balladeers sang of Jesse James and Sam Bass, but the lone Pinkerton operatives who entered hostile communities, rode countless miles, and faced fast-shooting outlaws in stand-up fights had helped immeasurably to bring law and justice to a ruthless land that suffered no cowards.

Though Jesse James had been riding for four years, he had yet to rob his first train, and the Renos were buried when a five-man outlaw band held up the Mobile & Ohio Railroad, near Moscow, Kentucky. A total of $1,600 had been taken from the Southern Express Company's safe, and the express messenger had been shot in the lungs. Robert and William Pinkerton interviewed the dying messenger, who gave them a description of the outlaws. The Pinkertons spent the next few weeks "canvassing the township for known disreputable characters." The people of the community were unanimous in their choice: the Farrington brothers, Levi and Hillary.

The Farringtons had worked a ramshackle farm near Gilliam Station in West Tennessee with their mother before they had started to ride about the countryside, drinking in the rough log saloons or country stores, engaging in shooting brawls, and terrorizing the communities through which they passed. Both were big, powerful men, but Levi towered over Hillary. He wore his coal-black hair shoulder length, "and dressed like a mountain man," as his wanted posters said. He was a superb marksman who could hit a squirrel at fifty yards, "if the light was right." When they left their farm, they persuaded their hard-riding young neighbors, also brothers, William and George Barton, to join them. The fifth man of the gang was William Taylor, an excellent woodsman and hunter.[3]

William and Robert found the Farrington farmhouse and the mother of the clan, a stone-faced backwoods woman who cradled a rifle as she talked to the detectives. She insisted her sons had ridden off, a fact the Pinkertons confirmed. They had picked up the trail of the outlaws when the Farringtons robbed the Southern Express Company's safe aboard the Mobile & Ohio at Union City, Tennessee, of $20,000.

The press of business forced Robert to return to New York, and William continued on alone. He finally found an old planter who told how he had "shared a jug" with five strangers as he passed their camp. Near Hickman, Kentucky, Pinkerton discovered an abandoned skiff, and from another planter heard about the five strangers who had opened a general store near Lester's Landing, a desolate, weed-choked, woodchopping depot, twenty miles from Hickman.

They were a strange lot, the gossipy planter said. They never had a customer, and they drank up the store liquor supply, but always seemed prosperous. Pinkerton, accompanied by Pat Connell, a former Memphis policeman whose distinguishing feature was a fiery-red moustache, set out for Lester's Landing, at the time a desolate swamp country inhabited by "cane-fed whites," so called from the use of cane to feed their hogs. They were hostile to strangers, "and had two accomplishments, woodcraft and marksmanship, both of which they excelled in to a remarkable degree." William Pinkerton hired two guides, and the party set out. After a tortuous journey through the swamps, they arrived at Lester's Landing the following evening.

As Pinkerton later reported, it was a weird place, damp and gloomy, with night birds screeching in the deepening twilight, while the muddy river swirled sluggishly past the woodyard and landing. Set back from the banks was a crude log cabin with a door and skin-covered window. The cabin had been built on stilts to protect it from the periodical floods, while behind it were cleared fields. There were no signs of life. When one of the guides told William the cabin had a rear door, the detective ordered Connell to go to the rear while he went to the front entrance. Pinkerton tried the door; it was unlocked. He found himself in a narrow hall that ran the length of the house. When he heard voices coming from a room on his left, he stepped in. The only light came from the smoldering logs in the fireplace. Five roughly dressed men, a young girl, and a woman were seated about the fireplace. The men, one huge, jumped to their feet.

"What do you want?" one shouted.

William explained that they were strangers, and were looking for the Tiptonville Road.

The big man raised a tallow dip, and the wavering light fell first on Pinkerton's face, then Connell's.

"It's Connell," the big man shouted, and leaped for the rear door. Both Pinkerton and Connell fired, but missed. The outlaw, Levi Farrington, whirled about, fired his navy Colt, and disappeared into the darkness. The heavy slug grazed Pinkerton's left side, and hit Connell in the stomach. The red-haired detective was bowled over but bounced back to his feet. The small dark room became a bedlam, with Pinkerton and Connell flailing about with their fists and pistols "while constantly calling for the outside, making the men believe there was a posse surounding the cabin." They finally clubbed the four men into submission, then tied them up. The woman and the girl, both Lesters, were ordered to sit in a corner and remain quiet. Pinkerton was bleeding profusely from the bullet wound, which, however, turned out to be superficial. When he tore open Connell's shirt, they discovered that the slug had been defected by a thick button on his heavy Kentucky jeans" and had traveled under the skin to his back. While the girl held the tallow wick, Pinkerton removed the slug "with a corn knife."[4]

For the next few hours Pinkerton questioned the bound men, who were later turned over to a Missouri sheriff as fugitives from robbery and murder charges. Before they left with the posses to escort the thieves to Union City, Pinkerton carefully searched the cabin. He found a scrap of paper with the name of a woman in Farmington, Illinois. Pinkerton and Connell talked to the woman, a distant cousin of the Farringtons, and learned that Mrs. Farrington was driving by wagon across the Indian Territory to western Missouri, where she intended to settle on a farm.

Pinkerton had arranged for an expressman who worked near Gilliam Station, where the Farrington homestead was, to alert him if Mrs. Farrington returned. In St. Louis, he received a telegram not only advising him the mother had returned to the farm but also that she had left the following day to meet a farmer named Duram near Verona, Missouri. By train and horse, Pinkerton, Connell, and operatives George W. Cottrell and Arthur C. Marriott hurried to Verona. With the help of a local land agent, they located the Duram farm several miles out of town. The Durams consisted of the farmer, his wife, and a young daughter, Kate. Recently, the land agent said, two men had stopped off at the Durams'. In fact, the agent said, the bigger of the two had been in town only that day for supplies for a trip to the Indian Territory. Their descriptions fitted Hillary Farrington and George Barton.

Pinkerton, Connell, and his two operatives, leading a posse of eleven townspeople and farmers, surrounded the farmhouse. Pinkerton shouted for Farrington to come out with his hands up. There was a pause; then Farrington called out that if they wanted him and Barton, they would have to come and get them. After an hour of trading shots, Pinkerton studied the house. It was built on logs about three feet off the ground. Behind it was a small grassy slope. When Pinkerton discovered that one of his possemen owned the cabin, he bought it on the spot for $200, along with a wagonload of hay from a nearby farm. Dodging the crashing volleys from the cabin, they hauled the wagon up a slope. Once set afire, Pinkerton explained, the wagon would be a blazing juggernaut that would crash into the cabin and set it afire.

"First, we are going to give them a chance to let the women get out," "Pinkerton said. When a posseman crawled through the grass to a point near the cabin and shouted the warning, there was a long silence. Pinkerton told Connell that he would wait five minutes. Suddenly one of the posse shouted that a white rag was waving at a window, and Pinkerton yelled that he was ready to parley.

Kate Duram, a slim young girl, walked out the door, down the few steps, and toward the kneeling posse men with their rifles. As a contemporary account described her, "She was a pretty young thing with an anguished heart."[5] She told Pinkerton she was a cousin of the Farringtons, and pleaded to be allowed to try to persuade Hillary Farrington and George Barton to surrender. Inside the cabin, the Durams were pleading with the outlaws to give up. Pinkerton agreed. The girl returned to the house waving a handkerchief. Minutes passed. Then the door opened "and she came out, her arms loaded down with pistols and rifles."

Behind her came Farrington and Barton, their hands held high. When the Pinkertons searched the cabin they found an arsenal of Winchesters, revolvers, and boxes of ammunition. Asked why he had surrendered, Hillary said that they would have gone down fighting but that they didn't want to endanger Cousin Kate's piano, which had been hauled in a wagon all the way from Farmington, Illinois.

The hay and wagon were returned to the farmer; the posseman returned the $200—minus $5 for his cooperation—and Connell and Pinkerton started on the long trip with both outlaws to Union City. Arriving in St. Louis too late to catch the train, they had to stay over until the following evening to get a train to Cairo. From there they had to travel by riverboat to Columbus, Kentucky, and then by Mobile & Ohio to Union City. Pinkerton took advantage of this layover to separate the outlaws. With the assistance of St. Louis Police Chief Harrigan, they persuaded Barton to confess and become a state's witness. An important part of Barton's confession was Levi's plan to visit the cousin in Farmington, Illinois, "as this was a good place to keep under cover." Robert Pinkerton, who had returned to Chicago, was ordered to Farmington with Operative W. T. Brown.

Robert first got in touch with the sheriff, who, he recalled, looked him up and down after the detective had told him he was in town to arrest Levi Farrington.

"Sure you can do it, young man?" he asked.

"I'm sure. Why?" Robert asked.

" 'Cause he whupped the whole town in the last few weeks," was the reply.

Late that afternoon the sheriff told Pinkerton, who was sitting in his office, "Well, here he comes, young feller."

When Pinkerton and Brown walked down the town's main street, they saw the giant backwoodsman getting off his horse. Pinkerton flung himself at Farrington, and Brown attempted to disarm him. Brown almost had his head snapped off by a pile driver blow, but hung on doggedly, and managed to get the train robber's pistols. After a savage fight, the detectives managed to pistol-whip the big robber into submission. Another difficulty arose when it was discovered that no available handcuffs were large enough for Farrington's wrists.

Farrington was taken to Chicago, where he was held in the Pinkerton office overnight. Because there was no cot big enough to hold him, the train robber sat up most of the night, chatting with the Pinkertons and hopefully offering bribe after bribe. The next day Pinkerton and Operative Brown started the trip to Union City, after an extra-large-size pair of handcuffs for Farrington had been found.

Meanwhile, William Pinkerton and Connell had left Cairo with Hillary Farrington and George Barton for Columbus, Kentucky, aboard the stern-wheeler *Illinois*. During the night, Farrington asked to be taken to the ship's bar, "pleading he was very cold and needed a drink." The saloon could be reached either through the barbershop or from a door leading onto the deck immediately in front of the paddle wheels. Pinkerton agreed to take the outlaw for a drink; but at the entrance to the barbershop Farrington asked Pinkerton to use the other entrance, "as there were some people in the shop, and he didn't like to be seen under the circumstances."

Pinkerton, curiously considerate of a train robber's sensitive nature, agreed, and followed Farrington to the open deck. They reached the barroom door, where Pinkerton, with his hand on the butt of the revolver in the right-hand pocket of a loose greatcoat, took his hand from the gun to open the door. Farrington grabbed the gun, and Pinkerton clutched his wrist and whirled around. They struggled up and down the moonlit deck, with Pinkerton fighting to keep Farrington's hands stretched to the limit of his handcuffs to prevent his thumbing back the hammer of the weapon with a free hand.

Pinkerton, managing to back his prisoner against a rail, shouted for help. Connell, who had a cabin nearby, ran out in his underwear as Farrington jerked one hand free and pulled back the hammer. He fired as Connell lunged at him, and the bullet grazed Pinkerton's scalp. Connell struck the outlaw across the head with his revolver, and Farrington, with a wild cry, slipped over the rail, into the churning paddles. An alarm was sounded and the boat turned about. The body was never found.[6]

Barton was brought back to Union City and placed under heavy guard. The next day Connell and Pinkerton set out for Reelfoot Lake to arrest William Taylor. The train robber was discovered on the edge of the lake, "shooting ducks." The two detectives, posing as hunters, dismounted and called out an invitation to have a drink. Taylor said that he would, and put his rifle against a tree. When he lowered the flask, he was looking into Pinkerton's pistol while Connell was ejecting the shell from his rifle. Taylor also confessed, and the trio set out for Union City, "going through the canebreak swamps, for if they had been found with the prisoner in their hands it would have gone hard with the two detectives."

Pinkerton and Connell took Taylor and Barton to Memphis to stand trial, but a mob broke into the Bracken House in Union City, where Levi Farrington was held—there was no jail in the town—and riddled him with bullets. The action of the night riders would have pleased Allan Pinkerton; how it touched his son is not known, for William never mentioned the incident.

In April, 1878, the Agency was retained by the Texas Express Company after the Sam Bass gang had robbed the Texas & Pacific at Mesquite, Texas. Pinkerton and several operatives put up at the La Grande Hotel in Dallas to join the Texas Rangers in their hunt for the Indiana farm boy who had adopted the technique of the Renos.

The Pinkertons always insisted that Sam was the classic example of a young farm boy influenced by the exploits of the postwar outlaws. Sam had never forgotten the details of the Marshfield robbery he had read in the Cincinnati *Enquirer,* "when he was a hand on the Sheeks farm, only forty miles west of Seymour, stronghold of the Renos."

Not all the Pinkerton operatives were at the La Grande Hotel. One day a new bartender appeared at Wheeler's Saloon in Denton. Operative Tooney Waits, who had been on Sam's trail since he and his gang had robbed the Union Pacific at Big Springs, Nebraska, in 1877, was working closely with Tom Gerren, Denton's deputy sheriff, and Sheriff William C. Everheart of Grayson County, northeast of Denton.[7]

In the fall of 1877, Sam, Henry Underwood, and Frank Jackson were in San Antonio spending what Sam called the "177 pieces," gold eagles taken at Big Springs. Waits, Deputy Gerren, and Sheriff Everheart arrived in San Antonio early in December, but before the two sheriffs could arrest Waits, they got into a loud argument in a saloon. A dance-hall girl who knew Sam tipped him off that the Pinkertons and the lawmen were in town with a warrant for the Nebraska train robbery. Sam, Underwood, and Jackson slipped out of town and rode north to Fort Worth, holding up a stagecoach near Mary's Creek on their way. The loot was only $43, with the kindhearted Sam giving each passenger a dollar for breakfast. They continued north, stopping off at Fort Worth, then riding into Denton County. Sam and Jackson went on to Cove Hollow, while Underwood spent Christmas eve with his wife.

On Christmas morning, a posse led by Operative Waits and Sheriff Everheart surrounded the Underwood house. Rather than endanger his family in a gun battle, Underwood threw out his six-shooters, and surrendered. Waits and several other possemen escorted him to Kearney, Nebraska, where he was jailed on a charge of train robbery. During the following spring he escaped. That same year Sam Bass was killed by Texas Rangers, and became a legend of the Southwest.

In October, 1886, William Pinkerton had just broken up a ring of beef thieves in the Chicago stockyards, when he received word that the Adams Express Company car had been robbed of $59,000 in cash and $29,000 in nonnegotiable securities, fifteen miles outside St. Louis. After four months of plodding police work, William led a posse of his own men and Chicago police to arrest Fred Wittrock, a Chicago coal man, as the brains of the gang. Other arrests were made in various parts of the Midwest. As the St. Louis *Republican* observed, "This is the busiest Christmas at the Pinkertons in many a year."[8]

A few months later the Pinkertons were on the trail of another outlaw brotherhood. In the fall of 1886, Rube and Jim Burrows, two farm boys from Lamar County, Alabama, had joined the rustling and horse-stealing gangs operating in the Indian Territory. A newspaperman who had talked to Rube described him as a "tall, muscular man, straight as an Indian. He has deep set, grayish blue eyes that flash like an animal's, a square and heavy chin, a heavy drooping mustache . . . he has a Winchester rifle in his hands, two large revolvers in his belt and over his shoulder a belt of cartridges." The reporter found Rube to be "a man of great determination, will power and a wild recklessness." The reporter's eyewitness account praised Rube's marksmanship; the outlaw "hit a knot 100 yards away, every time and hit a rope tied between two trees, as far as he could see it distinctly." [9]

In the fall of 1887, the gang left the Indian Territory, chased by a posse of Indian police and federal marshals. While riding through the Panhandle, the Burrows came upon the Fort Worth & Denver Express at a watering stop. As Rube Burrowses later said: "There were only two cars. Jim kept the passengers covered while I took up the collection. There were four soldiers but they were so scared I didn't have much trouble disarming them. I think we only got two hundred dollars on that raise."

Two weeks later the Burrowses held up the same express at Ben Brooks, this time cleaning the passengers of about $4,000. Rube, now enthusiastic about train robbery, held up another train at the same spot, this time collecting $500. After hiding out in Lamar County for a few weeks, "to let things blow over," Rube gathered his gang together and robbed the Texas Pacific at Gordon. Four days later they held up the same train; this time it was going in the opposite direction. The express car yielded $8,000.

They next appeared in December, 1887, when the brothers, aided by another local farmhand, Jim Brock, held up the St. Louis, Texas, and Arkansas train at Genoa, Arkansas, a few miles north of Texarkana. The Southern Express Company's safe was looted of $2,000.

The express company, protected by the Pinkertons, telegraphed the Agency. Operative McGuinn, who had played the role of a card and pool hustler in an earlier train-robbery investigation, was assigned by William Pinkerton. Three days after the holdup, McGuinn, who had to swim his horse through several miles of bottomland flooded by days of rain, reached Genoa. He made a wide tour of the countryside, talking to farmers, railroad men, saloon and livery owners, boardinghouse landladies, and local peace officers. One deputy told McGuinn he had fired on three suspicious-looking men hiding in the woods shortly after the train had been robbed. After a sharp exchange of rifle and pistol fire, the trio had ridden off. "I didn't wing 'em but I came damn near it," the deputy said as he held up a hat and a raincoat: both had bullet holes.

McGuinn examined the garments, and found the label of a Dublin, Texas, store on the raincoat. He went to Dublin, but was told that hundreds of the same type of hats and coats had been sold that winter, which had been a particularly rainy one. Acting on a hunch, he began traveling from town to town, exhibiting the garments and asking if anyone knew the owner. At Alexander, Texas, his hunch paid off. A salesman identified the coat as the one he had sold to "Bill Brock who lives with his father-in-law five miles from Alexander, on the road to Dublin."

The salesman also said that when Brock made the purchase, he had been accompanied by a man who said he was from Alabama. McGuinn went back on his trail, and on December 31st, twenty-two days after the robbery, arrested Brock at his Dublin home. The highwayman was taken to Texarkana to be identified by the engineer. He made a full confession, giving details of the train robberies, and naming Rube and Jim Burrows as the gang's leaders.[10]

Rube wrote to Brock from Lamar County, but the outlaw's mother turned the letter over to McGuinn. Chicago ordered McGuinn to set out for Alabama at once. On January 8th, McGuinn arrived at the Lamar County sheriff's office, where several other operatives were waiting. Despite a sleet storm, a posse of Pinkertons and local deputies set out for the Burrows farmhouse, twenty miles away. In the windy, icy darkness the party lost its way several times. Finally, at dawn, wet and chilled to the bone, the manhunters rode up to the rickety farmhouse, only to see Jim Burrows fleeing from the back door. Several rounds were fired, but the train robber escaped.

The county abounded with Burrows' kinfolk, and word passed from cabin to cabin that detectives were looking for Rube. The outlaw was hiding out at Kennedy, eighteen miles away, and by noon was out of the county. McGuinn now had a good description of the outlaws, which he wired to Chicago. The Agency made several hundred posters, and distributed them throughout the countryside. On January 22nd, an alert conductor on a Louisville & Nashville train spotted Jim and Rube coming aboard at Brock's Gap, and wired ahead to Montgomery. Police surrounded the train when it came in, and arrested Jim, but Rube shot his way out of the trap. Jim boasted to William Pinkerton: "My name is Jim Burrows and the other man is my brother, Rube, and if you give us two pistols apiece we are not afraid of any two men living."

Because McGuinn was now known, another operative, disguised as a peddler, was sent into Lamar County in a rickety old wagon with boxes of wearing apparel. Apparently he was a fine actor, because he stayed the night at the Burrows farmhouse and even sold a pair of pants to Rube's brother-in-law. But the operative, for all his fine dramatic ability, never discovered that Rube was hiding out in the cabin of John Thomas Burrows, an uncle who lived deep in the forest less than a mile from the outlaws' farm. Later, the Pinkertons searched the house and found a hidden room, three feet by nine, in which Rube had slept. He had dug out firing slits in the thick log walls and fashioned ports from pine slabs which could be opened from the inside. It was Clay County all over again. As one contemporary account said: "Rube thought he was safe from any attacks made on him, and his friends and relatives were constantly on guard, ready to give him notice of the approach of any stranger in the county."

During his stay in Lamar County, Burrows killed the local postmaster over a package addressed to him. He had sent his brother-in-law to claim his mail—it was the same relative who had bought the pants from the Pinkerton operative—but the postmaster insisted Rube had to claim the package and sign a receipt. Burrows, in a towering rage, rode up to the post office, called out the postmaster, and shot him before the eyes of his horrified wife. An account of the shooting said, "Rube then tipped his hat and rode off."

Later, a member of the gang told the Pinkertons that the package contained a false beard that Rube had intended to use in his next robbery.

The cold-blooded crime horrified the state. The sheriff telegraphed to the governor that the Burrows gang "has the county in a state of siege." Two companies of troops, acompanied by a posse of deputies and several Pinkertons under McGuinn, met at Vernon, the county seat. The Burrows farmhouse was surrounded, and several of Rube's kinfolk were arrested for conspiracy to hide a fugitive. Three days later they were all released "because not a man in the county had the courage to testify against them."

Rube began riding the following year with a new recruit named Joe Jackson another farm boy from Lamar County. On September 29th, the pair held up the Mobile & Ohio train a few miles from Buckatunna, Alabama. This time the loot was $11,000. In November, the Pinkertons picked up their trail in Blount County, Alabama, where they were hiding out in a mountain cabin. For two days the Pinkertons and a posse engaged the outlaws in a running battle. At Sand Mountain the outlaws made a stand, with Rube's superb marksmanship claiming the lives of two young farmers in the posse. By late afternoon another was badly wounded, and two others less seriously. The sheriff telegraphed the news of the battle to Birmingham, asking for more men, rifles, and bloodhounds. On a Sunday morning, post-office supervisors and two hundred townspeople, some with bloodhounds, joined the battle. But Rube and Jackson had slipped off into the forest. The force trailed them past the small town of Oneonta to Snead's Mill at the base of a range of mountains where the hounds picked up the outlaws' scents. With the hounds' frantic baying filling the gathering twilight, the posse moved in for the kill. Suddenly there were sharp yelps. Rube had picked off the dogs. The battle continued until nightfall, with Rube shouting and taunting the posse for their poor marksmanship. Finally he and Jackson disappeared into the darkness. Legend has him making a circle and joining the posse for a time. For the next three days, the possemen, some on horses, others on mules, in wagons, or walking, trailed Burrows and Jackson across the mountains until the trail petered out, and the posse disbanded.

When he heard that his brother was to go on trial in Texarkana, Rube swore to storm the jail. But the ring of armed men about the courthouse changed his mind. When Jim was ordered arraigned, Rube made one last attempt to free his brother. As Jackson later recalled for the Pinkertons, Rube rose in his stirrups as they galloped along the dark roads, shouting that he would "shoot all the detectives down and make Jim a free man or die in the attempt."

They rode to Okolona, Mississippi, on to Sardis, through Tate County, crossing the Mississippi at Helena, Arkansas. Swinging off southwest, they rode into Pine Bluff, then to a way station on the Iron Mountain Railroad, sixty-five miles south of Little Rock. With cocked revolvers under their coats, they searched the two trains leaving Little Rock.

Then they rode to Curtis, where they discovered that Jim was on a train that did not halt at the little flagstop and that their only hope was to catch it at Arkadelphia, fifteen miles away. They rode, "killing our horses," as Jackson later said, but arrived at the station as the train disappeared down the tracks. On September 10th, Jim was delivered by the Pinkertons to Miller County circuit court, and arraigned. His case was put over to the spring, and a guard of heavily armed Pinkertons returned the outlaw to the state penitentiary at Little Rock. In October he died "from a fever."

Rewards for Rube, dead or alive, now totaled $7,500. Letters and telegrams from reward-hungry sheriffs, farmers, and townspeople, informing the Agency where the gang was supposedly hiding, poured into the Chicago office. "It appears," William Pinkerton said wearily, "Rube Burrows has a thousand twins."

The pressure of the Agency, plus the reward, whittled down the gang. Jackson was finally captured by the Pinkertons, and was sent to prison after he confessed. In his last train robbery, Rube was alone. At Flomanton, fifty miles northeast of Mobile, he held up the Louisville & Nashville train, cleaning the Southern Express Company's safe of several thousand dollars.

Rube's end came in the tiny village of Linden, where a sharp-eyed storekeeper named C. Carter recognized the outlaw from a wanted poster he had seen in a railroad depot. With another storekeeper and a Negro handyman, Carter got the drop on Rube as he examined a new rifle in Carter's store. A few hours later, Burrows broke out of the one-room jail and went looking for Carter, who was waiting in a grain store for a reply to his telegram to the Pinkerton office in Chicago. When both men saw each other, they opened fire simultaneously. Carter's left arm was shattered, while his bullet tore open Rube's stomach. Half bent over,

Rube backed down the street, followed by the staggering Carter, "both men emptying their revolvers at each other until they both fell to the ground."

Rube was dead when the townspeople ran up. Though Carter was seriously injured, he survived.

The Pinkertons, like Rube's kinfolk in Lamar County, refused to believe that the big outlaw had been killed. William Pinkerton sent Operative McGuinn to Marengo, the county seat, to have the corpse photographed. The picture, still extant, shows the outlaw in a rough pine box. In accordance with the Agency's rules, McGuinn first identified the dead man as Rube, then had his identification confirmed by law officers and relatives in Lamar County. Only then was the Burrows file closed.

In April, 1891, Carter, Rube's killer, was found by a reporter in the National Surgical Institute. The storekeeper's left arm, shattered by the outlaw's bullet, was completely paralyzed. The reporter asked Carter the usual journalistic cliché as to whether he would do it all over again. Carter replied simply that he would. "Before I killed Burrows I had never quarreled with another man in my whole life," he said. "But it is like gambling. I have had a taste of it, and I feel pretty sure I would do it again." [11]

In a curious way, Carter was also summing up the wild, rough life of the Lamar County farmhand who once said that outlawry was like drinking whiskey: After the first glass there's no stopping.

In the fall of 1893, $70,000 was stolen from the Adams Express Company safe on the Mineral Range Railroad at Calumet. The money, all cash, was the payroll of the huge Hecla Cooper Company.

When William Pinkerton arrived on horseback at the isolated crossroads, the logs that had been piled on the tracks by the robbers in the best Jesse James fashion were still there. As the engineer told him, he and his crew had started to remove the logs when a masked man wearing a linen duster held them up. They were ordered back into the cab, and the train robber took over the throttle. Two other masked men in dusters broke into the express car. With a pistol at his head, the messenger had opened the safe. After the payroll was dumped into a bag, one bandit fired a shot as a signal, and they jumped out. Before he disappeared into the brush, the train robber in the cab waved his pistol and shouted, "Tell them in Calumet they'll be going without their pay for a while."

After questioning the crew, Pinkerton and his men fanned out across the countryside. This was routine in every train robbery. Pinkerton's theory was that the loneliness and vastness of rural areas actually emphasized the unusual for its inhabitants. Even a farmer's purchase of a new hat or gun was known about the county in a day, with the gossip transmitted by farmers and their wives, hungry for the slightest morsel of news about their neighbors.

In a few hours, a Pinkerton operative was served a hearty breakfast by a farmer's wife who eagerly told him she had seen a "strange red buggy with red wheels and a horse blanketed to its fetlocks" tied to a tree near the crossing only a few hours before the robbery.

Pinkerton found the spot where the horse had been tied. Several long strands of horsehair were caught in the bark of the tree. But it was the outline of the horse's hoofprints that interested the detective. An expert on horseflesh who owned his own racing stable, Pinkerton knew the print had been made by a horse shod with racing plates instead of the heavy shoes commonly used in that hilly and rocky farming country. Pinkerton then followed the tracks into the woods to measure the gait of the horse, which he judged to be a pacer. That afternoon the Pinkertons searched the county for a pacer shod with racing plates. Within two hours one of his men reported he had found the animal. Everyone in Calumet knew that Jack Kehoe, a saloonkeeper, owned a fine pacer named Champ K— and a red-wheeled buggy.

Operatives also learned that Jack King, a friend of Kehoe and a former Cornish wrestling champion, had ridden the pacer and buggy out of town at eight o'clock on the morning of the robbery. He had returned about ten. Neighbors near the livery stable had agreed that the horse "looked hard driven." A local madam added the information that Kehoe and King had met one night at her place with Dominick Hogan, the express messenger in the looted car.

Another routine assignment in all train robberies was to ascertain if any railroad employees had been seen in the neighborhood of the robbery. The night following the holdup, an operative reported to Pinkerton that a man named George LaLiberty, "an ex-fireman claiming the privileges of an old railroader," had begged a ride from Marquette to Houton. At the Houton depot, the baggageman told Pinkerton he had "rough words" with LaLiberty who wanted to check his trunk without paying. At one point, the baggageman said he thought he saw LaLiberty throw something behind a pile of packages and trunks, but paid no attention. Pinkerton and his men emptied the baggage room, and in a corner behind a trunk they found a rough mask, made from the lining of a coat. Pinkerton, the local sheriff, and officials of the Duluth, South Shore & Atlantic Railroad arrested LaLiberty in Marquette. The young fireman, who claimed he had been cheated out of his share of the loot, readily confessed. He named Kehoe, King, Dominick Hogan, the express messenger, and his brother, Edward, as the train robbers. The stolen money had been taken to Houton in the red-wheeled buggy and hidden near Marquette. All but $65 of the $70,000 was returned to the company by Pinkerton. The case had taken only seventy-two hours to solve. The following spring, the quartet was tried and convicted and sentenced to five years in the penitentiary.[12]

June, 1894, found the Pinkertons solving a series of train robberies in Illinois and Virginia. Several thousand dollars were taken from the Adams

 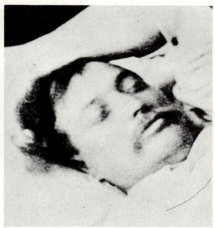

Charles "Texas Jack" Searcy, in a photograph taken just after he had been captured. *Pinkerton's, Inc.*

Charles Morgan, photographed in the hospital after he was shot in a train robbery. *Pinkerton's, Inc.*

Express Company safes before two professional gamblers, turned outlaws, "Texas Jack" Searcy and Charles Morgan, were flushed out of their hideout in Cumberland, Maryland, by a posse of Pinkertons and sheriff's deputies. Two months later a particularly vicious gang of train and bank robbers left a trail of looted vaults and trains from Kansas City to Marcus, Illinois, where they held up the Chicago, Burlington & Quincy Express and cleaned out the Adams Express Company safe.

During the robbery, one of the gang was wounded when his six-shooter accidentally discharged. The leader of the gang shot him in the head and killed him.

"Dead men can't talk to detectives," he told the others.

The Pinkertons removed the bandit's body to a local mortuary, "where it was photographed in every fashion: standing, lying down and dressed in many fashions of clothing," as one newspaper reported. The pictures show the dead highwayman, a gaping wound in his head, leering at the camera with half-closed eyes. Copies of the photographs were rushed by special train to Chicago, Denver, New York, and Philadelphia offices. In Chicago, Assistant Superintendent William Irle reported to William Pinkerton that a check of the Pinkerton Criminal Gallery revealed that the dead man was George Gordon, a veteran train and bank robber, who had been arrested by the Pinkertons several times in the Midwest. His "associate," as Irle wrote, was known as Conn Eddie, a young western desperado whose photograph was in the gallery.

Operative Charles J. White of the Chicago office was assigned to find Conn Eddie, alias Edward Estelle. For six months White worked along the Mississippi as a clammer, riverboat man, and baggage handler, living, as he reported, "with the scum of the river." Whenever possible he showed the photograph of Estelle—"Conn Eddie, my pal who I'm looking for," as he would explain. A fisherman finally told White that Estelle was a "hard character" who had hired his boats several times. White traced Estelle to Kansas City, where he "put up" at the same boardinghouse. He trailed the train robber to a Memphis boardinghouse, where he again became Estelle's next-door neighbor. With the local sheriff, the Pinkertons surrounded the boardinghouse. When the train robber went for his gun under a pillow, William Pinkerton knocked him out. In Chicago, the train crew identified Estelle and his gang. They were tried and convicted, with Estelle getting life.

"The boys left in good spirits," wrote the Mount Carroll, Illinois, *Mirror* reporter, "with one of the gang wondering what sort of job he would have in prison and Estelle swearing to Bill Pinkerton that no matter what they would have him do he would be a good boy." [13]

In the West, train and bank robberies continued at an alarming rate. Gangs of rustlers, former cowhands, horse thieves, and killers were raiding banks in small communities in almost every western state and territory, while train robbery was no longer a novelty. In the early 1890's, a family of outlaws, similar to the earlier outlaw gangs of the Middle Border, had established an outlaw community at their ranch on the Arkansas River between Texas Creek and Cotopaxi, Fremont County, Colorado.

Young Tom and Joe McCoy and their father, "Old Dick," publicly threatened to kill any man who helped the law. When a local cattleman, Edward Watkins, with the aid of an old miner, swore out rustling warrants against the McCoys, a posse took the gang at gunpoint to the county seat, where they were released in bail to await trial. In Canon City, the McCoys bushwacked Watkins, looped a noose about his neck, and dragged him for half a mile. The battered corpse was found the next day. In Cotopaxi they killed the old miner as he was entering a store to buy supplies. An intimidated jury released the three on their alibi of self-defense.[14]

The Rio Grande also knew the elder McCoy for his many demands of restitution for cattle killed by trains. When his requests were ignored, railroad bridges were burned. At the peak of Colorado's political campaign of 1884, a barbecue was given at Canon City to honor Joseph Maupin, the town's popular young attorney, who would later be named Colorado's attorney general. A few years earlier, as the local prosecutor,

Tom McCoy

P. N. D. A. *Chicago.* Agency.
Name *Tom McCoy.*
Alias
Residence
Nativity
Occupation
Criminal Occupation *robbery*
Age *16*   Height *5ft 8in.*
Weight *135*   Build
Complexion *light*   Eyes *gray.*
Color of Hair *light.*
Color of Mustache
Color of Beard
Style of Beard
Date of Arrest *Nov 13" 1891.*
Where Arrested
Crime charged *robbery.*
Peculiarities of Build, Features, Scars
Marks, etc.

he had brought up the elder McCoy on rustling charges. After his speech young Maupin stepped down from the platform to face McCoy and his sons, all armed. Maupin tried to brush past the trio, but the older McCoy grabbed a knife from a nearby table and slashed the attorney. In the wild brawl, Maupin was rescued, but bore the scars until his death. McCoy was never arrested.

In 1888, the Cattlemens Association, desperate to stop the wholesale rustling, hired an ex-convict, W. J. Arnold, as an informer to gather evidence against the McCoys. Arnold built a cabin near the McCoy ranch, and began sending reports to the ranchers. A few months later, McCoy shot and killed Arnold as the ex-convict was driving cattle into his corral. In 1889, the McCoys were put on trial for Arnold's murder, but the first trial ended in a disagreement. Before the second trial began, "Old Dick" McCoy bought a wagonload of ice in Canon City and sat on it for hours while his sons rode into town to notify the court their father was helplessly paralyzed from a fall. A court-appointed doctor found the old man stretched out on his bed, his "lower limbs cold as ice." The doctor, whose decision was probably influenced by the fact that McCoy's sons escorted him back to town, informed the court that McCoy was helplessly paralyzed and could not stand trial for some time. Joe McCoy, however, was rearrested on the murder charge, but broke jail before he could be tried.

On September 1, 1891, the Rio Grande Express was robbed by the McCoys near Cotopaxi, and a bag of gold retorts and $3,000 were removed from United States mail pouches. Riding with the McCoys was another notorious Colorado outlaw, Thomas Eskridge, dubbed Peg Leg by the cowhands because of his wooden leg. The limb had been amputated after a gun battle in Texas. Peg Leg, a slight, wiry ex-cowpuncher, rustler, train robber, and gunfighter, was known to have been living at the McCoy ranch, along with several other desperadoes, at the time of the robbery.

When the Agency was retained by the railroad, William Pinkerton telegraphed instructions to turn the case over to Tom Horn, who had recently joined the Agency. Horn, one of the most fascinating and colorful figures of the West, had been an Indian fighter, under General Nelson A. Miles, and a stockman's detective before he joined the Pinkertons. But above all he was a cold-blooded, merciless killer for hire. As he once boasted: "Killing is my specialty; I look at it as a business proposition, and I think I have a corner on the market." [15]

Horn teamed up with W. C. ("Doc") Shores, the sheriff of Gunnison County, Colorado, who also worked for the Pinkertons. Shores was a superb western lawman, of whom McParland wrote to William Pinkerton, "There is no better than Doc." The lawmen covered hundreds of miles on horseback, as the Denver *Times* said, "without changing a saddle." They trailed Peg Leg and another member of the gang, Red Curtis, a young Texas desperado, across the Sangro de Cristo range, down by the Villa Grove Iron Mines, back to the east side of the Sangro de Cristo at Mosca Pass, through Huerfano Canyon, where the train robbers came out by Cucharas, and then continued east of Trinidad. Horn and Shores rode into Clayton, New Mexico, shortly after Peg Leg and Curtis had left, following a saloon shooting.

After a brief stop to feed and rest their horses, Horn and Shores continued the manhunt. They picked up the train robbers' trail near the Indian Territory, and followed them into Ochiltree County, Texas. Again they missed Peg Leg and Curtis by hours. Without stopping, Shores and Horn crossed into the Indian Territory near Canadian City. Passing cowboys and settlers remembered the rider with the wooden leg and his companion with bright-red hair riding toward the Washita River in the Territory. In Paul's Valley, the Pinkerton operatives captured Curtis; Shores took Curtis back to Denver, leaving Peg Leg for Horn. Several days later the outlaw, whom McParland called a cold-blooded killer, rode up the trail to the hideout cabin in the valley. Horn stepped out of the bushes and said quietly that someone had come for him. Few men, on either side of the law, argued with Horn. As he recalled, "I had little trouble with him."

When Horn wired to the Pinkerton office in Denver that he was bringing in Peg Leg, McParland's answer was brief: "Good. Old Man McCoy
got eighteen years today." As Peg Leg told Horn on the long journey
back, the train robbery had been staged at the suggestion of the McCoys
to raise funds to pay their father's legal fees and "carry McCoy's case up
to the Supreme Court."

When Horn learned that young Joe McCoy was wanted for murder, he
told McParland he could find him in the northwestern part of the state.
After an exchange of telegrams with Robert Pinkerton, Horn was assigned to bring in McCoy. On Christmas Eve, Horn and Sheriff Stewart
of Fremont County, where McCoy was wanted, left Denver for Rifle by
train. From there they took the stage to Meeker, fifty-five miles north.
After a bitter journey in ten-degree-below-zero weather, the lawmen
reached Meeker, only to learn that McCoy was in Ashley, Utah, "for the
Christmas festivities." There was no connecting stage, so they rode across
the foothills of the Rockies in a driving snowstorm. The Green River
was crossed on ice, and late at night they reached Ashley. The following
morning Horn learned that McCoy was eating breakfast at "Mrs. Col-
throp's, where he took his meals." Horn followed the young outlaw into
the log-cabin boardinghouse, and took him at gunpoint. As Horn said,
"He had a big Colt's pistol on him but did not shoot me." After a hard
ride back across the mountains, Horn and his prisoner caught the Denver
& Rio Grande to Denver, where he turned McCoy over to McParland.

Within a few weeks, the rest of the gang, including another brother
team of outlaws named Price, "who had been making a name for themselves in the hardware department," as one newspaper put it, had been
jailed and held in high bail for trial, all owing, as the Denver *Times*
said, "to the marvelous work of Sheriff Shores and the Pinkertons."

But the Agency's investigation wasn't ended. In November, Operative
W. H. Valette, who had been hunting the gold retorts stolen in the robbery, swore out a warrant in Leadville, Colorado, for the arrest of
Thomas Walker, owner of Leadville's principal express company. Walker,
the Pinkerton man testified, had been paid by the Price Brothers to make
a tour of Leadville "in order that they might dispose of the gold retorts."

After the Rio Grande robbery, Horn left the Agency. His autobiography gives the reason: "My work for them was not the kind that exactly
suited my disposition; too tame for me." [16]

Horn was hanged in Wyoming for the murder of a fourteen-year-old
boy he had mistaken for his father, a sheepherder. Rumors were so strong
that powerful cattlemen, afraid of the secrets Horn knew, were ready to
storm the jail to free their favorite killer that the governor ordered in the
state militia. Horn broke out once, but was retaken almost immediately.
He died, lips sealed, on November 20, 1903.

Three years after Horn's death, Robert Pinkerton informed William
that he had sent a copy of a book the Agency had compiled on racetrack

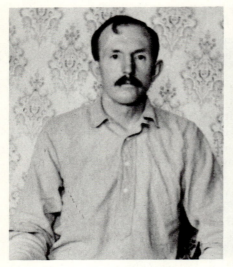

Tom Horn, just before his execution. *Denver Public Library Western Collection*

An early photograph of Butch Cassidy

"ringers" to F. R. Hitchcock, the famous steward of the Jockey Club. In
addition, he said, he had forwarded a copy of Tom Horn's brief autobiography to Hitchcock, "who had known of Tom Horn through a party who
used to bring polo ponies from Wyoming to sell in South Carolina."
Robert wrote:

> I have always been sort of sore at myself that I did not look a little
> more thoroughly into Tom Horn's case, as since reading this book I
> have an idea he might have been innocent. I also gave a copy of the
> book to Mr. Knapp, one of the Jockey Club Stewards and it has also
> made him doubtful as to whether Tom Horn was guilty.
>
> Horn was a peculiar, unique Western character, a man seen fre-
> quently in the Indian fighting days. He was at one time in our employ,
> having come to us with good army references as a brave man and a
> first class scout and tracker. Also some references from some Western
> sheriffs which he gave me, certifying to his honesty and bravery. He re-
> mained with us for about five or six years. We used him principally
> to follow up rustlers, cattle and horse thieves, stage and holdup men.
> We found in Horn a most thorough plainsman and trailer; a man of
> unquestionable courage and good judgment in all that pertained to his
> class of work. He left our employ to enter the employ of a cattle com-
> pany in the Sweetwater County, Wyoming, as stock detective. This
> company had been having a great deal of trouble with rustlers. In
> trying to clear the company's range of rustlers, cattle thieves and un-

desirable characters, it finally came down to open war between the ranch owners and stock detective Horn on one side and the rustlers on the other. We only occasionally heard of Horn but these were rumors that he had been connected with the death of several rustlers. This was the condition of the affairs out there when he was arrested for the killing of that boy. Our managers at the time believed that Horn was guilty and recommended to me that we offer him no assistance but since reading his book I have had some doubts as to his guilt. If you find the book of sufficient interest I would like to get your views when we meet in the Spring. Knowing Horn as I did I would judge the language he used to be entirely his. He was not an educated man; just a common grade school education, such as he could pick up in the West but he had read considerable western literature and during the time he was with us when he had leisure to do so, I found him inclined to read fairly good books.[17]

The evidence that United States Marshal Joe LeFors gathered against Horn was overpowering, but in the West the question of the celebrated killer's guilt or innocence is still debated in biographies, magazine articles, and pamphlets.

Robert, like William on other occasions, had refused to be convinced by "evidence," insisting that their operatives divorce themselves from established investigations, and continue on their own. One wonders what would have happened had the Pinkertons "looked more thoroughly into Horn's case."

Horn's execution and the shattering of the Wild Bunch ended the long and melodramatic chapter of the Pinkertons' war on outlawry in the West. In the classic tradition, the Bunch disappeared in the dust of hoof-beats and the crash of six-shooters. While the relentless pressure of the Pinkertons and railroad detectives helped to break up this fast-riding gang of desperadoes and train robbers, credit really belongs to the color-less efficiency of the twentieth century. Before they were killed, jailed, or driven from the West, the Wild Bunch riders had taken to riding bicycles, while their pursuers were using the telephone to round up a posse.

From the early 1890's to the turn of the century, the miles covered by the Pinkertons in chasing the gang were staggering. Bandits were chased from Montana to New Mexico, from Knoxville to New York City, and then to the rain forests of South America.

Telegrams, letters, wanted posters, reports, logs written by operatives during the chases, along with memories of Pinkerton men still living after World War II, tell an exciting story of the last years of the Wild West. Cassidy, the leader, was a happy-go-lucky ex-cowboy in the best Robin Hood tradition; the unconscionable killer was Harvey Logan, alias Kid Curry. For comedy relief, there was Tom O'Day who had a battle with a skunk on his way to help rob the Winnemucca, Nevada, Bank. As the Pinkerton wanted poster pointed out, "One smelled like a polecat."

Tom O'Day

The Wild Bunch riders frequently changed in personality and numbers, but the hard core usually included Butch Cassidy, the gang's leader; Elza Lay, Harvey and Lonny Logan, Tom O'Day, Harry Longbaugh, the Sundance Kid; Ben Kilpatrick, the Tall Texan; and Will Carver. There were two known women, Laura Bullion and Etta Place, along with a number of prostitutes. The gang's hideout was a ranch in Alma, New Mexico, where Cassidy was known as Jim Lowe. Some historians of the outlaws have insisted that Cassidy never robbed a train, but his original photograph in the Pinkerton Criminal Gallery lists him as "Bank Robber, Train Robber and Outlaw." Agency reports also connect him with at least one Wyoming train robbery.

The Wild Bunch riders were tough ex-cowboys, mostly illiterate, like Ben Kilpatrick, the Tall Texan, who never ordered anything but ham and beans because he couldn't read the whitewashed menu on the bar mirrors in frontier saloons. Elza Lay, from men who knew him, had some education, and was a highly intelligent man. He is listed as the discoverer of one of Utah's big oil fields, but gave up his claim before it could be worked.

The favorite hideout for Cassidy and his men was Fanny Porter's Sporting House in San Antonio's "Hell's Half Acre." Lillie Davis and Maud Walker, two of Fanny's better girls, were the favorite companions of Kid Curry and Will Carver. In the winter of 1901, William Pinkerton

Bertillon Measurements.

Height,	Head length,	L. Foot.
59.4	19.3	
Outer Arms,	Head width,	L. Mid. F.
60.0	14.1	10.8
Trunk,	Length,	L. L. P.
85.1	5.8	9.0
	Cheek,	L. Fore A.
	13.0	41.5

Name Della Rose
Alias Clara Hays
Alias Laura Casey & Bullion
Crime Forgery
Age 28   Height 5.3
Weight 113   Build Slender
Hair Black   Eyes Hazel
Born Ky.   Beard
Complexion Sallow
Occupation Prostitute
Date of arrest Nov. 6/1901
Officer Guion. Brady. Burke
McGrath. J. Shevlin &
Geo. Williams.

REMARKS:

Scar above L. elbow. Scar on L. elbow.
Small scar on L. forearm. 2 cuts on L. middle
finger. Cut on L. thumb. Cut on R. little finger.
Blue dot & small mole on center forehead.
Small scar above center of upper lip.
Teeth Full.

Della Rose, alias Laura Bullion. A good example of the early Bertillon measurement chart. This, from the St. Louis Police Department, was sent on to Pinkerton for cross-reference. *Pinkerton's, Inc.*

persuaded Lillie Davis to talk. The interview with the frontier whore presents a less popular, but more realistic, version of the life of our western outlaw. As Lillie revealed, the Wild Bunch riders had taken to riding bicycles, used the telephone, and complained bitterly when another thief stole their guns.

In the fall of 1900, Lillie and Maud accompanied Kid Curry and Carver on a trip to Denver, and then to Shoshone, Idaho. Lillie, who came from Palestine, Texas, married Carver, and the four went on a wild honeymoon. At Denver the outlaws left their girls at the McFall House "to go on an errand." When they returned, five days later, Will Carver explained to his week-old bride, "We were up the road." When Carver and Logan, who had been in on the Winnemucca robbery, opened their trunk, Lillie recalled seeing "6 or 7 sacks of gold . . . the gold

being in twenty dollar pieces. Will also had a big pile of paper money.
. . . Then they had a satchel stolen from them which contained a big gun
and they did considerable complaining and grieving over the loss of this
satchel." Lillie identified Butch Cassidy as the Jim Lowe she had known
in Fanny's place. Cassidy, she said, "was an athletic looking fellow and an
expert bicycle rider."

When the Pinkertons and railroad detectives moved into Texas on
the trail of the Wild Bunch, Lillie said that Will Carver kissed her
goodbye and sent her home to Palestine with $167, "a set of diamond
earrings which he bought for $225 and a fur sack which cost him $30.
But I have traded the earrings away and raised money on them to pay
debts, and today I am in debt to $65 to Kid Fox [a local loan shark].
All the good clothes I got from Carver are gone with the exception of the
fur sack."

Fanny Porter, the frontier madam, also loved to play the genteel
lady, Lillie said, using only sheets from Fort Worth's best store. She
went into a rage one night when Kid Curry came in drunk and staggered
into her "guest room." Because Kid Curry had forgotten to remove
his spurs, the "Fort Worth sheets," as Lillie said, were torn to shreds.

Lillie was slightly contemptuous of Maud, Kid Curry's girl. She was
not Maud Walker, as she told Pinkerton, "but Beulah Phinburg . . .
her mother lives in St. Louis and her brother runs some kind of a dry
goods store." Lillie ended her long chat with Pinkerton by telling him:
"I did not know what kind of men they [Carver and Kid Curry] were, or
I would not have gone with them, but if I had known the kind of men
they were, I would have worked him for all I was worth. I did not love
Will and did not marry him for love. I married him to clear my name
at home and show them I was respectable." [18]

The major robberies committed by the Wild Bunch included the
Union Pacific Train Number 3 at Tipton, Wyoming, on the evening of
August 29, 1900, and the holdup of the First National Bank of Winnemucca, Nevada, when they stole $32,640. The UP robbery netted them
only a bag of watch parts and $50.14 in cash.

In 1900 Cassidy undoubtedly realized there would be no more Wild
West in the twentieth century; the open range was gone; the manhunters
were growing more numerous with every robbery, and the criminals'
avenue of escape was narrowing. In the Denver office of the Agency,
Superintendent McParland, William Pinkerton, and the United States
marshals were now dispatching posses on flatcars to the nearest point
where they could close off the famous relay of horses used by the Wild
Bunch.

At the turn of the century, either an operative or a Union Pacific
detective dicovered a group picture of the Wild Bunch in the studio of
John Swartz, 705 Main Street, Fort Worth. On a whim, the Wild Bunch
had their pictures taken while they were dressed in derby hats, wearing

watch chains and store suits. Kid Curry, who had recently traveled two hundred miles to kill a man, even sported a boutonniere. In the photograph were Will Carver, Kid Curry, Harvey Longbaugh, the Sundance Kid; Ben Kilpatrick, the Tall Texan; and Butch Cassidy. The photograph was rushed to Chicago, where William Pinkerton ordered hundreds of wanted posters made from individual pictures chosen from the group shot. This was in addition to furnishing every bank in the country with a list of the serial numbers of stolen bonds. In Nashville an alert teller spotted one of the bonds, and notified the Pinkertons, who captured Kilpatrick and Laura Bullion. The Tall Texan and his girl friend were later sent to federal prison. The Pinkertons continued to chase Cassidy, Longbaugh, and Etta Place, who may have been a schoolteacher or a new girl at Fanny Porter's place when she met the Sundance Kid. In February, 1901, Cassidy, Etta Place, and the Kid came to New York City, where they stayed for a time at an East Twelfth Street boardinghouse.

The Pinkertons later discovered that the outlaw trio had had a gay holiday in the big city. They had celebrated Etta's birthday at a champagne supper, attended the theatre, bought Etta a hundred-dollar watch at Tiffany's, while Etta and the Kid, both in formal attire, had had their portraits taken by De Young, the society photographer of his day. By the time the Pinkertons had picked up the trail in New York, they had sailed on the S. S. *Pioneer Prince* for Buenos Aires. The bowlegged Sundance Kid and the tall, stately Etta Place occupied the honeymoon suite.

Nearly twenty years ago, Operative Frank Dimaio, then ninety years old, and still wonderfully alert, told how he had chased Cassidy, Longbaugh, and Etta from Buenos Aires to Cholila, Province of Chubut, District 15 de Octubre, in the interior, where they staked out a homestead ranch. Dimaio was told that it would take months to reach the seaport nearest the place and that there would still be a fifteen-day ride to the outlaws' ranch. The fact that the rainy season had set in, he was told, would make the trip impossible.[19]

On instructions from Robert Pinkerton in New York, Dimaio had hundreds of posters made up in English and Spanish. He distributed these up and down the South American coast, to banking firms, provision and mining supply houses, police, and steamship companies, requesting that information about the *bandidos* be sent to Buenos Aires Chief of Police Beasley. At the time, Cassidy and the Sundance Kid had committed so many gold-train and bank robberies in Argentina that official protests were lodged with Ambassador Lord in Buenos Aires, who forwarded them to Washington. In Lord's initial reports Kid Curry was listed as among Cassidy's riders in South America, a rumor still accepted as fact by some frontier historians. Cassidy and the Sundance Kid were later killed near San Vincente, Bolivia, by a detachment of Bolivian cavalry. Etta Place, in the meantime, had returned to the States, and vanished.

Pinkerton detective Francis P. Dimaio.   Harvey Logan (Kid Curry)
Pinkerton's, Inc.

The tenacity with which the Pinkertons insisted on chasing an out-law even beyond the grave to confirm his identification for the law is underscored in the nationwide manhunt of Kid Curry after he had broken out of the Knox County, Tennessee, jail, just before his transfer to the federal penitentiary at Columbus, Ohio, to serve a life term.

On June 7, 1904, three masked men had held up the Denver & Rio Grande Express at Parachute, Colorado, and dynamited the express car, but found the safe empty. That night a posse cornered the trio in a gully near Rifle, and wounded one. As a sheriff later said: "We heard one of them in the darkness call out, 'Are you hurt, Tom?' And the other answering, 'I'm all in, I'm going to end it here.' Then there was one shot."

In the morning the posse found that two of the train robbers had slipped through their lines, leaving behind a dead man identified as Tap Duncan, a drifter who had worked at some of the local spreads for over a year. He was known as a loner and a fast man with a gun. Tap Duncan was buried in a cheap pine coffin in the cemetery at Glenwood Springs. As usual, the local sheriff telegraphed the Denver office of the Pinkertons, giving a description of the dead man. McParland sent the report on to Chicago, where it was circulated among the operatives working in the West. Lowell Spence telegraphed to William Pinkerton that the dead man was undoubtedly Kid Curry. When the Pinkertons released the story that the shabby cowhand in the obscure cemetery was the infamous gunfighter and outlaw, several railroad detectives publicly denied Spence's story. To clear up the confusion, the State Department asked Pinkerton to confirm the identification of the body as that of Logan or Tap Duncan.

Accompanied by Chief Agent Canada of the Union Pacific, Spence went to Glenwood Springs. The body was disinterred and closely examined by a physician in the presence of both men, and photographed. Spence took the pictures and the description to several Knox County jail guards, federal prosecutors, wardens, and even to outlaws "no longer on the dodge" to confirm his suspicions. All agreed that the body in Glenwood Springs cemetery was that of Kid Curry.

Lowell Spence said:

> I was laughed at a number of times because of my identification, but I knew it was Logan's body. Mr. Canada only saw Logan but once and then behind bars in the Knoxville jail. I had seen and talked to Logan a dozen times. I had seen him awake and asleep in the jail, on the streets of Knoxville, going and coming from his trial and I had observed him for many hours as he sat in the courtroom. I have seen a number of reports that Logan was known to be here, there, everywhere, including South America, but I know his body is buried in Glenwood Springs, Colorado, marks, scars, old bullets holes and all.[20]

Not all the outlaws of the closing years of the twentieth century rode horses and wore spurs. William and Robert's letters reveal that their operatives once hunted a New York train robber in a derby and kid gloves whom the New York *World* described as "one of the most spectacular train robbers the country has ever known."

Superintendent Bangs wrote to William Pinkerton: "The man who committed the train robberies here [New York] is one of the nerviest I ever heard of. There are few if any men who possess the daredevil courage to accomplish what this train robber did yesterday." [21]

The gentleman-desperado's first robbery took place on the evening of September 29, 1891, as New York Central's crack Train Number 31 left the Albany station. The express car had just cleared the depot when a slender hawk-faced man ran out of the shadows and swung aboard. Using a thin, sharp saw, he cut out a square in the wooden end of the car and crawled inside. After tying and gagging the messenger, he broke open the safe and filled a small grain sack with $5,000 in cash and $3,000 in jewelry. With the sack tied about his middle, he lowered himself between the swaying cars, the saw between his teeth. While he held on to one end of the car's platform, he cut the train's air brakes. The train slowed down with a series of grinding jerks. Before the cars came to a halt, the train robber had disappeared into the darkness.

Operatives under Robert Pinkerton canvassed the towns along the tracks for two weeks. It was the usual dogged, leg-tiring police work. In Rochester, operatives picked up the trail of a man answering the bandit's description, "who was spending money freely in the hook shops." Though Pinkerton missed him in Syracuse, he learned his name and background from underworld informers. Nineteen days after the robbery, Pinkerton identified the train robber as Oliver Curtis Perry, ex-convict, ex-cowboy, and former train engineer. Pinkerton's minute description of Perry included his open-faced stem-winder "with the name, Samuel G. Tappen, Troy, N. Y. on the works." [22]

Several months later, on a Sunday morning, Perry held up Train 31 for the second time. Instead of the thin saw he used a rope ladder equipped with sharp hooks at one end. As the train pulled out of the Syracuse depot, Perry climbed to the roof of the "money car." It was a bitterly cold, windy Sunday. The roof was icy, and he clung to the grillwork of the ventilator as the train clicked along. Despite the swaying of the car, Perry clamped his ladder to the roof's edge and let it dangle against the upper glass part of the car's sliding door. Kneeling and clutching the grillwork with frozen fingers, Perry waited until the train reached a straight section of track, then slid down the rope ladder foot by foot until his toes rested on the window's edge. Through the grimy glass he could see the American Express messenger sorting his packages. With the butt of his gun, Perry smashed the glass, then fired a shot over the messenger's head. The messenger grabbed his gun, and fired blindly. Perry's next shot shattered the messenger's arm. Clinging to the swaying ladder, the train robber reached in and opened the heavy latch. The messenger, still full of fight, lunged at Perry and managed to yank the bell rope. Perry fired twice, each time wounding the courageous messenger, who finally collapsed.

The train ground to a stop, but Perry leaped out and intimidated the crew and passengers with several shots. At his command the train started out again. He ran back to the end of the train as if running toward a clump of woods; but as the last car passed, he swung aboard again. Back in the express car he took the cap and spectacles from the unconscious messenger, and when the train pulled into Lyons, its whistle tied down, Perry jumped off to mingle in the gathering crowd. As he started to push his way through, a switchman who had seen him leap from the express car grabbed his arm. Perry twisted free and pulled his gun. As the crowd backed away he ran across the tracks and jumped aboard an old steam engine at the head of a line of coal cars. He forced the engineer and fireman off at gunpoint, uncoupled the locomotive, pulled the throttle wide open, and started down the tracks. The crew of Train 31 also uncoupled their engine, and started off in pursuit, with a posse of passengers clinging to its side.

It was one of the strangest chases in outlaw history. When the speedier express engine caught up with the freight locomotive, Perry threw the throttle in reverse. As the engines rushed past each other, the train robber leaned out the cab window and fired at the passengers. Some who had shotguns blazed away, but there were no casualties. When the express engine also reversed throttle, both engines raced back down the track. They met and again exchanged shots. Up and down the tracks, reverse and forward, they flew, the train yards echoing with the heavy

Oliver Curtis Perry

Newspaper sketch showing how Oliver Curtis Perry robbed the Express car in New York

slam of the shotguns and the sharp bark of Perry's six-shooter. When his steam supply dropped, Perry leaped from the locomotive and took to the woods.

A Wayne County posse under Deputy Sheriff Jeremiah Collins, who, curiously, was unarmed, chased Perry into the swamps. Perry finally agreed to surrender to Collins "rather than to those damn Pinkertons." [23] As Perry later told a reporter, "I had to take a bold stroke with big chances and I guess I lost."

Like most outlaws, Perry had a strange attraction for women. With the help of a middle-aged missionary worker, he broke out of Dannemora, New York, State Prison in 1895, only to be captured a few weeks later. As the New York *World* reported, "The gentleman-desperado was captured in, of all places, Weehawken, N.J." Perry had taken refuge in a watchman's hut, and was surprised by Edward C. Clifford, a railroad detective, and Weehawken patrolman Bernard McAlseese. Perry died in Dannemora on September 5, 1930, completely forgotten as the man who, the New York *World* claimed, "electrified the nation with his daring exploits."

The outlaw saga in the Pinkerton's fading records ends on a quiet, almost whimsical note, when "Old Bill" Miner, certainly the oldest outlaw in western history, was captured for the last time by the Pinkertons in 1909. Miner's life story reads like a frontier legend: He held up his first stagecoach in 1866. Three years later he escaped from the vigilantes, who had lynched his partner after they had robbed the famous Del Norte Colorado stage. In 1881, he was leading a three-man outlaw band that was holding up trains in Oregon and California. Captured by a posse, he was sentenced to twenty-five years, only to scale the prison walls.

In 1901, the Pinkertons reported by letter and telegram to all western lawmen that Old Bill had held up the Oregon Railroad & Navigation passenger train at Mile Post 21, near Corbett, and had fled to Canada. Five years later, the Royal North-West Mounted Police notified William Pinkerton that Miner had been found guilty of train robbery and sentenced to life imprisonment.

But because Pinkerton suspected prison walls couldn't hold Miner, on June 1, 1906, he ordered his Oregon superintendent to obtain the photographs of Miner and his two fellow road agents from the Royal Mounted Police, to be circulated throughout the Agency, together with a complete dossier on Miner, including newspaper accounts of his trial.[24]

Pinkerton detective Lowell Spence.   Old Bill Miner, when he was al-
Pinkerton's, Inc.   most ninety years old

Offices of Pinkerton's National Detective Agency at 57 Broadway, New York City, in the early 1900's. *Pinkerton's, Inc.*

A few months later, Miner escaped and fled to the States. At the request of the Royal Mounted, the Pinkertons alerted its network of lawmen and informers across the West and the South. Rewards for Old Bill now totaled $12,500. As Pinkerton warned his people, "Miner will undoubtedly try to rob a bank or train in the Northwest."

In June, Pinkerton's prophecy came true when Miner walked into a Portland, Oregon, bank and scooped up $12,000. Operatives traced him across the Northwest, and for a time it appeared he had returned to Canada. For the next two years the usual letters and telegrams from bounty hunters and small-town sheriffs trickled into the Pinkerton offices, insisting they had Miner in their sights; operatives always proved them mistaken.

On February 16, 1911, Miner held up the Southern Express car near Sulphur Springs, Georgia, and took $3,000 from the safe. White-haired and arthritic, his gun hand trembled so violently the messenger was afraid the old-fashioned six-shooter would accidentally go off. Since Miner's first stage robbery, an entire way of life had vanished in America. In his early days, the posses and vigilantes were his only dangers; this time he was trapped by the telephone.

At the time of the robbery, Henry W. Minster, Assistant Superintendent of the Pinkerton Philadelphia office, was in Atlanta, preparing to open a branch office. Detailed to the case, he hurried to Gainesville, Georgia, to question the crew. As he listened to the conductor's description of the ancient train robber, Minster suddenly recalled Miner's wanted poster. Minster and the local sheriff studied a local map, "deciding that the robber would work his way to the Blue Ridge Mountains and come out in Pennsylvania. We used the telephone freely advising all sheriffs and law officers of Miner's description." [25]

Two days later, the sheriff of Lumpkin County received a tip that a strange man was camping in the woods. The sheriff, who had been called by Minster, rounded up his deputies, and arrested the camper. Miner angrily denied he was a train robber until Minster arrived with his picture and dossier.

"You know," he said sadly to Minster, "I'm getting too old for this sort of work."

BOOK 8
Murder
Is a
Little
Thing

CHAPTER 32
America's Bluebeard

The last decade of the nineteenth century and the first of the twentieth are the "mystery" years of the Pinkertons. In Chicago their guard work was firmly established, in New York there was an increase in their security on racetracks, beaches, and fairs of the period. Train robbery cases which had composed 5 percent of the business were down to 1 percent. After December, 1909, the Pinkertons no longer represented the American Bankers Association, and that business was taken over by William J. Burns whose reputation as a detective had been increasing since his successful work on the Oregon timber scandal, the San Francisco graft arrest of Abraham Ruef, the political ruler of that city, and other Secret Service cases.

Railroads were building up their own detective forces—by 1914 there were 14,000—and reorganizing them along modern and efficient methods. Records of metropolitan police departments reveal that from 1894 to 1906 there was a noticeable increase in the hiring or appointments of detectives, partly as a result of the cleanup of police administrative procedures and organization following the various public criticisms and investigations. In New York the Lexow Committe uncovered shocking police abuses and corruption. Lincoln Steffens, America's muckraker, was an important critic of police departments, but there were also many little-known research investigations such as the New York Bureau of Municipal Research, which examined police procedures across the nation.

Competition among private police agencies was intense during these years. The tightening of controls on the procedures of licensing some forms of private policing—mainly watchmen and private detective firms— had begun, yet their numbers increased. The police departments under censure were increased in size and re-formed in management organization, under public pressure.

On the surface it would appear that the loss of an important segment of its work, increased competition from both private police agencies and the increased efficiency of formal police organizations would have resulted in a crisis of the Agency's financial life. On the contrary, a study of their letterheads of the period reveals that fifteen new offices had been added across the country from a base line of only six. What type of new work had the Pinkertons picked up? A study of the changing patterns of crime of the last year of the Victorians and the first decade of the new century fail to supply an answer. Regretfully there are no internal Agency records to help.[1]

Possibly, the increase in business for the Pinkertons came from undercover or surveillance work for big business. This type of retainer was 30 percent in 1937, yet it could hardly have been that in the 1890's or early 1900's. The congressional investigation of Homestead did not lead to any changes in the laws permitting industry or utilities to employ private police for this purpose. No real curtailment came until the late 1930's. However, some states did pass laws forbidding agencies to bring in employees from outside the state. Perhaps this may be one answer why the Pinkertons established branch offices in such states so they could recruit locally. Another reason for their expansion may be in their increased work on insurance claims.

However, state and local authorities did occasionally retain the Pinkertons during this time of severe public police criticism. An example was the hiring of the Agency by the New York County District Attorney for an investigation of "Maw" Mandlebaum, probably the country's most colorful receiver of stolen goods. A huge woman with apple-red cheeks, Maw held daily court in the Thieves Market in the Five Points Section of lower Manhattan, as she established the rates to be paid for stolen goods.

She lived in a ramshackle tenement, but her apartment was lavishly furnished with rare paintings, objects of art, and imported rugs—all stolen from Long Island estates. Legend has her entertaining politicians and police officials while a string orchestra played behind a screen of palms.

Through her connections with Tammany Hall, Maw was untouchable. Several times crusading police or a district attorney arrested her but failed to find any stolen goods in her apartment, necessary for a conviction. The Pinkertons were secretly retained, and operatives, playing the role of thieves, vanished into the underworld. After months of investigation, Robert Pinkerton presented the evidence his men had uncovered to the district attorney. A party of Pinkerton operatives and trusted DA detectives raided Maw's apartment early one morning. She was arrested, and several wagonloads of stolen property were removed. While waiting trial, she skipped her bail and fled to Canada where she established one of the largest department stores in Toronto.

During this time of mysterious transition, the activities of the Agency were blurred but the public image of William, more than Robert, grew clear and distinct. By degrees, as he received reporters in his charming, bric-a-brac cluttered office in Chicago, or spoke to them in various cities or at some lonely western depot or bank where a robbery had been staged, he stood revealed as a huge, brooding, moustached giant symbol of America's lawmen, a man of ultraconservative ideas, a vigorous defender of nineteenth-century economic orthodoxy, outmoded views, but interesting, witty, and likable nonetheless.

Elsewhere there was the other William Pinkerton, settling down to his duties as the trained detective, plodding, methodical, and even brilliant. He was at his best in crimes of national attention such as the murder-for-profit case of "Doctor" Holmes, America's Bluebeard, and the international hunt for the shabby, wild, young desperado who held up a Missouri bank in the wrong century and committed the unpardonable sin of killing a Pinkerton.

Of his many aliases, Herman Mudgett liked Holmes best of all. He had used it in several bigamous marriages to finance his medical studies. In 1881, he was a second-year student at the Ann Arbor Medical School when one day he noticed that a cadaver assigned to him bore a striking resemblance to his roommate, who had recently taken out a $1,000 insurance policy. Holmes peruaded the other student to make him his beneficiary; then he dressed the body in his roommate's clothes and had the corpse "discovered dead in bed." He collected the insurance, split with his roommate, and left college.[2]

In the 1880's, Holmes wandered about the country, marrying scores of women whom he left after stealing their savings. In 1885, he settled in Chicago, where he built a four-story gabled house at the corner of Sixty-third and Wallace streets, later Chicago's famous "Holmes Castle."

It was a weird house, with winding passages ending where they began and stairs leading to blank walls. Some rooms, doorless and windowless, could be entered only by trapdoors. Swindled furniture companies supplied the castle's furnishings. Agents sent to collect the money or the furniture later reported that the house was empty; Holmes had the furniture stored in his secret rooms.

One corner of the rambling house was a drugstore where Holmes sold spurious drugs and "rheumatism machines." As he later told a Pinkerton superintendent, "My motto is, never put off for tomorrow, the man you can do today."

His best-known swindle was the "invention of a machine that turned water into gas." The intricate gadget looked so impressive, a representative of a Canadian utility gave Holmes $2,000 for the rights. The not so naïve Chicago Gas Company sent inspectors, who broke down the castle's door to discover that Holmes was making gas by simply tapping the city's gas lines. The company dug out the machine, leaving a gaping hole in the cellar of the castle, which Holmes promptly filled with water. Newspaper ads advertised the water as "natural soda water from a natural spring accidentally discovered in my basement."

Barnum's adage was proved when long lines formed outside his drugstore to buy a glass of water for ten cents. City health inspectors exposed this fraud when they discovered that Holmes was tapping the city's water mains. After settling suits brought by both utilities, Holmes disappeared for a time. He returned to Chicago about 1890, introducing the tall, attractive blonde on his arm as his wife. She was Miss Minnie Williams, of a well-known Fort Worth, Texas, family. Only one thing about Minnie impressed Holmes. She had inherited $60,000 in real estate. Their marriage was stormy. Holmes refused to stop hiring his pretty "secretaries" or to answer Minnie's questions about his secret rooms. When she found her handsome husband and his latest "secretary" in a compromising position among the bottles in the back of his drugstore, Minnie packed her bags. She relented, however, after Holmes eloquently begged forgiveness, and made empty promises.

The next day he installed a buzzer system. A wire, hidden under the carpet of the top step, sounded a soft alarm in his drugstore whenever his wife tiptoed down to see what was going on. Their quarrels continued until Minnie's sister, Nannie, a teacher in the exclusive Fort Worth Academy for Young Ladies, came to live with them. For a time life went on smoothly in the Holmes "Castle," as the neighbors now called the grim, gabled house. Then neighbors noticed that the sisters had disappeared. Holmes explained that he had sent them on a "European vacation."

In 1893, he closed his drugstore and began traveling again, leaving a trail of bigamous marriages across the country. In Philadelphia he joined another swindler, Benjamin F. Pitezel, a mousy little man who appears to have been a born loser. By now, Holmes was running out of money. He outlined the insurance fraud of his medical college days to his partner, and suggested they stage the whole thing over again, only this time for bigger stakes. Holmes would find a cadaver and plant it in a rented office as Pitezel's body; the props would be an exploded bottle of benzine and a pipe that supposedly had touched off an explosion. An added gruesome touch to the plan was for Pitezel's fourteen-year-old daughter, Alice, to identify the remains as her father's. Mrs. Pitezel urged her husband not to go through with the fraud, but he refused. Holmes and Pitezel took out a $10,000 life-insurance policy with the Philadelphia Fidelity Mutual Insurance Company on the latter's life; Mrs. Pitezel was the beneficiary.

In August, 1894, Pitezel and Holmes leased a combination patent and chemist's office on Callowhill Street, Philadelphia. After he had hired a sign painter and bought office furniture, Holmes left for Fort Worth and St. Louis to dispose of property owned by his "late" wife, as he told Pitezel. En route to the Southwest, he briefly visited his dusty Chicago castle—to bury the lime-clean bones of Nannie and Minnie Williams, as the Pinkertons later discovered. In Fort Worth, Holmes disposed of the Williams property, but became entangled in a series of real-estate swindles.

There is an incongruous note to his escape from the Fort Worth police: The always immaculately dressed Holmes, who usually sported a monocle or pince-nez, rode out of town on a stolen horse. In St. Louis he sold a heavily mortgaged drugstore, and was arrested. In the St. Louis jail Holmes met Marion Hedgepeth, a notorious train robber, to whom he promised $500 for recommending a "slick lawyer." In late August, 1894, Holmes was back in Philadelphia, ready to finish his "urgent business," as he had described it to Hedgepeth.

On September 3rd, a passerby discovered a charred, unrecognizable corpse in the combination patent and chemist's office on Callowhill Street. Alongside the corpse was a shattered bottle of benzine and a pipe.[3]

Holmes, Mrs. Pitezel, and the "slick lawyer" from St. Louis later put in a claim, after the Pitezels' terrified fourteen-year-old daughter tremblingly identified the charred body as that of her father. The Fidelity Insurance Company of Philadelphia paid the $10,000, and Holmes gave the St. Louis lawyer $2,000. Mrs. Pitezel refused to be calmed by the bundles of money Holmes spread out on the table before her; she demanded to see her husband. Holmes's explanations were elaborate: Insurance company investigators were everywhere; the family must be separated to avoid prison. He would take Alice and the other two children "to a nice old lady in Covington, Kentucky," and he advised the distraught incredibly naïve woman to visit her family in Galva, Illinois. Before he left with the three children, Holmes counted off $7,000, which he took "for expenses."

Holmes, as the later Pinkerton investigation showed, made an incredible tour of the country, visiting his various "wives," while he parked the three Pitezel children in hotels and boardinghouses. The gullible, infatuated women apparently never asked any questions. Holmes later explained that he rushed from wife to wife, while taking time out to have dinner with the three bewildered children.

In his St. Louis jail cell, Hedgepeth, the train robber, had finally decided that it was useless to wait any longer for the $500 Holmes had promised, and turned informer in the hope of getting a lesser sentence. He wrote a letter to St. Louis Police Chief Harrigan, exposing Holmes's Philadelphia scheme. The case took another bizarre twist when the Pinkertons, retained by the Philadelphia insurance people, sent one of its St. Louis operatives to interview Hedgepeth about his former cellmate. It was the Pinkertons who originally had put Hedgepeth behind bars. Hedgepeth talked, and signed a statement describing Holmes's insurance fraud. The evidence was turned over to Fidelity Mutual, but the company's insurance officials informed Robert Pinkerton that they considered

Hedgepeth's story "to be a fake, manufactured by a criminal who hopes to have his sentence reduced."

Pinkerton, who believed Hedgepeth, ordered an investigation of the train robber's statement. Ironically, the detectives who had jailed the outlaw now set out to prove he wasn't a liar.[4] The "slick" St. Louis lawyer was arrested by the Pinkertons, and confessed his knowledge of the plot. Operatives from the Philadelphia office located the sign painter hired by Holmes and the salesman who had sold him the office furniture, and both identified a St. Louis Rogues' Gallery picture of Holmes.

Another operative, C. T. Leviness, was assigned the staggering task of finding the swindler. Boston Superintendent John Cornish could only suggest that Holmes was believed to be traveling somewhere in New England under one of many aliases. It was the old story of common sense, dogged legwork, and tenacity. In the depot at Gilmanton, New Hampshire, Leviness finally found what he was looking for—a piece of luggage with the name "Howard," one of Holmes's favorite aliases.[5]

With Operative Leviness sitting behind him on the train, Holmes journeyed to Boston, where he was arrested by Superintendent Cornish. While the swindler was being "sweated" by police, Robert Pinkerton alerted all branch offices to see if Holmes was wanted in their cities. Fort Worth promptly replied that Holmes was wanted for questioning in the disappearance of the Williams sisters and for stealing a horse.

"I don't want to be lynched for horse stealing in Texas," Holmes told Cornish, and confessed the insurance fraud. Pitezel, he said, was "somewhere in San Salvador."

"All they can get me for in Philadelphia is insurance fraud, but in Texas they hang you for stealing a horse," Holmes told Cornish. The Pinkerton superintendent spent a great deal of time with Holmes, whom he found "well read, and full of stories about his days as a medical student." One afternoon the murderer asked Cornish to deliver a note to a "Mrs. Cook, a friend of mine in Burlington, Vermont." Cornish, of course, was only too happy. The next day an operative arrested "Mrs. Cook," who turned out to be Mrs. Pitezel.

"This is all a mistake," she told Cornish. "Where is my husband? I know he is alive. How do I know? Mr. Holmes told me. I'm also worried about my three children."

When Cornish questioned Holmes about the Pitezel children, he just shrugged and replied, "Oh, they're in Europe in the custody of Miss Minnie Williams, formerly of Fort Worth, Texas." [6]

The Agency turned Holmes, his confession, and Mrs. Pitezel over to Philadelphia District Attorney Graham, along with a confidential memorandum from Robert Pinkerton that Superintendent Cornish and the operatives who had worked on the case were positive Holmes had murdered the Pitezel children. Pinkerton urged Graham to assign his best man to locate the corpus delicti. Graham selected Detective Frank Geyer, a superb detective, for the task. For months, Geyer, a human blood-hound, traced the erratic journey of Holmes from city to city, through real-estate agents, hotel and boardinghouse keepers, trainmen, and livery-stable operators. His journey ended in a Toronto cellar, where he dug up the bodies of the Pitezel children.

When his Toronto office telegraphed him the news, Robert Pinkerton wired to William, who alerted the Chicago police. Operative Frank Wind, who had helped slove the Dr. Meyers insurance ring, another famous Victorian murder case, accompanied Chicago detectives on their search of the Holmes Castle. With candles casting wavering shadows on the dusty walls, and the empty house echoing with their footsteps, Wind and the detectives explored the strange labyrinth of dead-end stairways and suffocating, windowless rooms. A portion of Wind's report reads:

> We found a trap door leading to the cellar. Extending to the base-ment was a wooden chute leading to a lime kiln about six feet long and three feet deep. In the rear of the kiln was an opening where anything that was not consumed could be raked out. There was a barrel with extra heavy iron hoops which we discovered contained acid. There were also ties connected to the Englewood City Water Company. This was the water Holmes sold to the Chicago residents for ten cents a drink. There were a great deal of human bones and parts of a female body.[7]

For the next few days Wind and the Chicago police dug out the cellar. Baskets were filled with charred bones, women's and children's clothing. A gold watch chain and metal buttons from a woman's dress were taken to Fort Worth by the Pinkertons, where a jeweler identified the chain as one he had sold to Minnie Williams, and friends said the metal buttons were identical to those of her favorite dress.

In Philadelphia, Holmes told a weird story of how Minnie had killed her sister in a fight over his affections. To protect her, he had sent her to Europe and sunk Nannie's body in a western lake. He had "forgotten" the name of the lake, he told detectives and "wasn't sure" where the other sister was staying in Europe. He kept changing his confession until at last he admitted that the burned corpse found in the Callowhill Street office was Pitezel's body. His partner had died, he insisted, in a benzine explosion touched off by an ash from his pipe.

The sensational newspaper stories about the gruesome discoveries in the Holmes Castle brought to the Pinkerton offices numerous tips and clues that were turned over to Graham. Months of investigation produced a harrowing tale of Holmes's butchery of women and children from Toronto to Chicago.

On May 7, 1896, Holmes was hanged in Philadelphia. On the day before his execution, he confessed to murdering twenty-seven women and children. The Pinkertons and Chicago and Philadelphia police had accounted for twelve. The others were unknown.

CHAPTER 33
The Blackest of Days

The Pinkertons always dreaded a day when they received word that one of their own had been killed in the performance of his duty. William once wrote:

> Every day when I come to the office that dread hangs over me. In our business we daily meet men and women who are carrying arms. If they are guilty of a crime it is our duty to turn them over to the law. Few submit to the hand on the shoulder. The first thought they have is to use their concealed weapon, uppermost in their mind is how they can kill you and go free. . . .[1]

One such day came in 1902, in the wake of a bank robbery that brought back "Memories of the Missouri Bandit Days," as the headline of the St. Louis *Post-Dispatch* observed. In the early hours of December 28th, two men on horseback rode into Union, Missouri, the county seat of Franklin County, about fifty-five miles of St. Louis. One took a position across the street, while the other quickly jimmied open the bank's door. Minutes later, a roar shook the small town. As windows flew up, and men ran out of their houses, the man across from the bank opened fire with a six-shooter. One citizen answered with his rifle, but was silenced when the bank robber shattered his window. Townspeople who peered through their curtains could see a man stumble through clouds of brownish smoke pouring out of the bank door. He threw some heavy sacks across the back of his horse, and then was joined by the other man, who sprayed the buildings with bullets before riding off into the darkness.

When the people of Union finally emerged, they found the bank's vault looted of $16,000 and $12,000 in nonnegotiable bonds. No attempt was made to follow the robbers, nor was there any attempt to raise a posse by Sheriff Thomas Burch, who explained that "he had been ill for the past week." As one townsman put it, "The robbers blew the vault, blew the safe, blew out of town and got enough money to blow themselves." [2]

The violent blast had been felt for miles around Union, stopped the clock in the town square at 1:26, and tossed several people out of beds. More than fifty .45-caliber cartridges were collected near the spot where the lone gunman had calmly hurrahed the sleeping town.

The bank, a member of the American Bankers Association—the Agency was still representing it—notified the St. Louis Pinkerton office, and Operative Charles J. Schumacher was assigned. Schumacher, brother of the superintendent of the Pinkerton Chicago office, arrived in Union late the same day. After studying the remnants of the vault door, he informed St. Louis that the robbery was obviously the work of a professional who had used nitroglycerine. From St. Louis came dozens of photographs of known professional "yegg" burglars, transient tramp robbers who had taken the place of the traditional outlaw train and bank robbers in the 1890's and early 1900's. Schumacher painstakingly showed the Rogues' Gallery photographs to the townspeople who had watched the robbers at work, but none could identify them.

For the next several days Schumacher toured neighboring towns and villages, questioning hotel men, livery-stable owners, saloonkeepers, merchants, and clerks to see if they had noticed any strangers in town during the week of the robbery. In St. Clair, Schumacher found a livery-stable owner who had rented a buggy and horse "to a young man who explained he once lived in Union and wanted to visit some friends." In Union a hardware merchant belatedly recalled the young stranger in the buggy who had stayed in town overnight, turned in his horse to a local livery to be returned to St. Clair, and then had set out on foot, "followinging the Frisco tracks to Stanton." Before the stranger had left town, the merchant told Schumacher he had observed him studying the bank.

Schumacher hired a horse, and rode to Stanton, where the sheriff told him that the description of the young stranger fitted Bill Rudolph, the "Missouri Kid," who lived with his mother, father, and sister in an old miner's boardinghouse outside town. "He's the worst I've ever saw," the lawman told Schumacher. "If he wasn't shooting somebody's hogs for devilment, he was in other scrapes. When we went for him he was never home." Several years before, the sheriff said, the county had been shocked by the brutal robbery of an old farm couple. The robbers had tortured the old people with white-hot pokers to force them to reveal the hiding place of their supposedly buried money, later revealed to be a backwoods myth. Rudolph was suspected, but vanished soon after the crime, and had not been seen since, the sheriff said.

Schumacher, in the disguise of a hunter, took up lodging in a local boardinghouse, and began roaming about the countryside. He discovered that Rudolph had returned with a younger companion named Fred Lewis.

Schumacher, like every Pinkerton operative, knew William Pinkerton's firm rule to listen to local gossip because it might contain a lead. Over the boardinghouse table he learned that "Old Man" Rudolph had bought a suit and a new hat for himself and a gown for his wife. The trivial incident was the talk of the backwoods, the landlady explained to Schumacher, because the older Rudolph, since they had first come to the county, had not bought his wife a new hat, much less a gown.

Schumacher decided to visit the Rudolph place, which was three miles from Stanton. On a late afternoon, shotgun over his shoulder, he approached the lonely, weatherbeaten house built on a small rise. At his repeated knocking, the door swung open and a pretty young girl asked what he wanted. Schumacher said he was a hunter who had been out all day without much luck and wished to buy some supper. A man suddenly appeared behind the girl, stared at Schumacher for a moment, then invited him into the house. Before the door closed behind him, the operative knew he was facing Bill Rudolph. Sitting off to one side was Fred Lewis, who nodded silently. The elder Rudolph, a reticent backwoodsman, said little. His wife, "a woman worn with years," offered to serve Schumacher supper for fifty cents.

It was a terse meal. Rudolph insisted that Schumacher remove the shells from his shotgun "because a loaded gun makes me nervous." They watched the Pinkerton operative as he ate, ignoring most of his small talk. As Schumacher later told the sheriff, he felt that at any moment he might be shot. When he finally left, the Missouri Kid and Lewis stood in the doorway to watch Schumacher make his way across the fields.

That night Schumacher told the sheriff he was sure the pair were the Union bank robbers. While there was no prima facie evidence to enable him to take them into custody, he reminded the sheriff of the old torture-robbery charge, and a warrant was sworn out for Rudolph's arrest.

The next day Schumacher, the sheriff, and three deputies rode out to the Rudolph house. Before they could dismount, shots rang out, and a deputy slipped from his saddle. Schumacher swung down and started to run toward the man. There were several more shots, and Schumacher fell, wounded in the stomach and groin. The rest of the posse, including the fallen deputy, who was later described as "scared not hurt," rode off into the woods, leaving Schumacher to crawl toward a rail fence. Inside the house someone called out, "That damn detective isn't dead yet!"

"Well, I'll make sure he is," Rudolph cried, and ran outside to fire five more shots into Schumacher's body. "I hope the son of a bitch is a Pinkerton detective," Rudolph said when he returned to the house. "That's one I wanted to get."

The posse, certainly not the bravest in the world, apparently were satisfied to peg occasional shots at the ramshackle house; they were instantly
answered by a crash of six-shooter fire. As the winter twilight closed in,
Rudolph and Lewis made their way to a neighboring farmer's stable and
took two horses, leaving $200 on the feedbox. Another and much more
courageous posse met them in the woods that night. As one farmer
recalled: "It was the wildest fight I had ever been in since the time I
helped run off some of Quantrill's boys. All we had to go on was their
gun flashes. You could hear the bullets whiz overhead and take the bark
from the trees."

When Lewis was slightly wounded, the two young bank robbers pushed
deeper into the woods. After searching the night and part of the next
day, the posse wearily returned to town with Schumacher's body. The
physician at Union later testified that seven bullets had been fired into
the detective.

On January 23, 1903, Superintendent Schumacher, stunned and fighting to control himself, walked into William Pinkerton's office, handed
him the telegram, and said very quietly, "They killed my brother."

Within a few hours, William and the pick of his Chicago office were
on their way to St. Louis by special train. After a grim meeting of his
St. Louis staff, and local and state officials, Pinkerton issued a terse statement: "The world is not big enough to hide Bill Rudolph. We'll get
both of them, we will never stop looking for them as long as I live." [3]

In the spring and summer of 1902, the country had eagerly followed
the manhunts for two notorious western outlaws and killers who had
escaped from prison—Harry Tracy and Kid Curry. Pulitzer, Hearst, and
Scripps had sent special writers and artists to accompany the posses. But
the manhunt launched by the Pinkertons for Rudolph and Lewis overshadowed the other two by its intensity and scope. The most obscure
railroad depot had a Pinkerton wanted poster. Descriptions of the pair
were sent to American consulates in Europe, South America, Canada,
and Mexico. Teams of operatives, expert at playing the roles of yegg
burglars, moved across the country, living in hobo camps, while informants from Spokane to Spanish Honduras sent in tips to where the fugitives were hiding. All information, regardless of distance, was checked
out; all proved false.

More than 260 freight and raliroad warehouses were also covered after
it was learned that Rudolph had once worked in a midwestern warehouse. Thirty-five operatives were assigned exclusively to watch steamship
and sailing vessels leaving East and West Coast ports. Every liner that
left New York had aboard a Pinkerton operative who stayed until Ambrose Light was cleared, when the search was usually finished. Ships
bound for South American ports were searched until they left Quaran-
tine. Operatives were detailed to railroad yards; armed guards searched
trains leaving Missouri; and posses with bloodhounds crisscrossed the

state. One newspaper estimated the hunt was costing the Pinkertons $35,000 a month.[4]

The excitement of the international manhunt, the mounting rewards now obscured the ramshackle house on the hill where Schumacher had been killed. Rudolph's mother, father, and sister had been taken into custody after some of the cash had been found in the well, along with the bank's bonds and securities. The dripping bags of silver and gold coins were escorted back to the town by the posse, but Pinkerton operative George D. Charlesworth stayed behind, "just to give things a second look over," as he told the St. Louis office.

George D. Charlesworth

In the cold stillness of the old house that was creaking in the winter wind, Charlesworth wandered through the rooms, his shoes crunching on shattered window glass. It was a typical backwoods house, the furniture worn and homemade. The wall decorations were yellowing calendars or cheap, water-stained "scenes" of Niagara Falls or Chicago. Charlesworth, a short, rather heavy man who looked like a banker rather than like a detective, ignored the sofas and bedding that had been torn apart in the earlier search for the bank's money. Instead, he carefully poked through the trash that littered the floors. In one pile he found an old medicine bottle. On its label was the name of a Hot Springs pharmacist. In the kitchen he went through every jar and can. The stove came next. Charlesworth, whom a fellow operative recalled as a most fastidious man, took off his coat, rolled up his sleeves, and emptied the stove. Each piece in it was carefully examined. Suddenly he grunted with satisfaction. In his soot-dirty hands was a tiny charred scrap of paper covered with handwriting "scrolls" and the words of a popular ballad, "How Would You Like to Have a Dinner with Covers for Two?"

In St. Louis, William Pinkerton and Superintendent William Minster agreed that Charlesworth should check on the medicine bottle. The Hot Springs pharmacist gave Charlesworth a description of the two men who had waited for the prescription to be prepared. One had a venereal disease, and both descriptions fitted the Missouri Kid and Lewis. The bathhouses yielded a massager who recalled Rudolph and Lewis because of the latter's elaborate tattooing, which he said had been done in the Philippines when he was in the army. This information was telegraphed to Pinkerton in St. Louis. That same night, a coded message was delivered to Robert in New York. The next day an operative was assigned to check the War Department's army records.

In Hot Springs, the precise, portly Charlesworth visited every one of the resort's countless hotels and boardinghouses. He finally found the one where Rudolph and Lewis had stayed a week. Charlesworth carefully took the charred scrap of paper from his wallet and compared the flowing penmanship with the names in the register; the same hand had written both. Rudolph was under his own name, but Lewis had used the name George Ladoux. This information was forwarded to Washington. "The handwriting is neat and flowing," Charlesworth reported to Pinkerton, "like that of a person proud of his penmanship."

The army records produced a retired army sergeant named Ladoux, living in a small village outside Montreal. He told a Pinkerton operative they should look for a man named George Collins, who had served with him in Company M, Thirty-fifth Infantry, in the Philippines. Collins, he said, had been used as a company clerk because of his penmanship, which he boasted was the best in the army. He was young, wild, and no stranger to the stockade, the sergeant observed.[5]

The pieces were slowly falling into place. After an exchange of coded messages with his brother in St. Louis, Robert assigned Assistant Superintendent George S. Dougherty and the operatives James Gabay and F. H. Davis to Hartford to find George Collins, who was proud of his tattooed chest and his neat, almost feminine penmanship. In Hartford, Detectives Garrett J. Farrell and John F. Butler joined the Pinkertons in their hunt for the Missouri bank robbers and killers.

Collins was discovered to be the stepson of a French Canadian woodworker. To avoid arrest for a minor robbery, he had left town several years before and joined the army. Washington now had forwarded Collins's army record to New York. A detailed description of Collins, including his tattoos, birthmarks, and scars, was telegraphed to Dougherty in Hartford.[6]

The Pinkerton operatives and Hartford detectives located Collins in a house on Allyn Street. He was now smartly dressed, with a new diamond ring, stickpin, and gold watch. "Don't take Collins until he meets Rudolph," Robert Pinkerton ordered Dougherty in a coded telegram. "Take them both alive if possible."

George Collins.
Pinkerton's, Inc.

Bill Rudolph, the Missouri Kid.
Pinkerton's, Inc.

For a week the Pinkertons and the detectives tailed Collins day and night, even to the extent that one of the operatives—not Dougherty, who was huge and heavy—took dancing lessons with Collins at the academy of H. T. Marsh, "Master of Dancing and Deportment," in Hartford's Goodwill Hall. When Collins paid $5 for a month's lessons, Marsh gave him a card receipt, which the bank robber put into his coat pocket. After a brisk set, Collins hung up his coat in the washroom. The jolly young dancer who joked with him about the quality of the girls that evening was as sleight of hand as he was light on his feet. Collins searched for the card, but it was in Dougherty's hand before the evening was over.

When Collins began courting a young secretary, one of the Pinkerton operatives got a job in her household as a cook. Another was a livery-stable attendant who groomed Collins's horse; a third worked in a saloon, where Collins never failed to buy a round from a thick roll of bills.[7]

After ten days of close surveillance, the Missouri Kid appeared, and the bank robbers began "living in style" at the Allyn Street boarding-house. They hosted champagne parties and were the favorite customers at a local brothel. On a Saturday night when the pair was "popping corks in Madam May's," the Pinkerton operatives and local police surrounded the house, and moved in. Collins went for his gun but was sent sprawling; the Missouri Kid was tougher. He fought savagely, once almost getting his six-shooter free before he was finally subdued. In their valise Doughterty found $8,685 in gold and bills.

The capture of the pair was a sensational news story, with many of the bigger dailies comparing the twentieth-century outlaws with the Jameses and Youngers. If they were not in the same league with Jesse and his men, Collins and Rudolph still attracted crowds who cheered them as they hobbled aboard a special car bound for Missouri. As the *World* reported. "There were as many people to cheer the Missouri desperadoes as they were taken away, as they were to cheer President Roosevelt when he stopped over in Hartford."

The Missouri Kid continued the role of the fearless desperado on the trip to St. Louis. He told the New York *World*'s reporter: "You may bet your life I won't wilt if they hang me. They won't have to drag me to the scaffold. I'll march up to it like a man and take my medicine, that's the kind of chap I am."

There was no braggadoccio in Collins, who, the New York *Times* observed, "has none of the appearance of a criminal." He stared out of the window, and said little.[8]

Rudolph and Collins were quickly arraigned in Union, where they were held without bail on the murder and bank-robbery charges. The Union jail was a small one-story brick building, and at the suggestion of William Pinkerton the pair were transferred under heavy guard to the St. Louis jail. Their arrival at Four Courts produced the usual mobs of curiosity seekers and admiring women. Bags of "scented" letters were delivered to Rudolph's cell; he acknowledged them in public statements to the press. "I have always admired and respected womanhood," he solemnly told a reporter.

During the winter the Pinkertons continued their investigation. By early summer a team of operatives had gathered impressive evidence against the two killers for the state's attorney. A trial date was finally set in early July.

From the moment Rudolph and Collins had been captured, William Pinkerton had urged that strong security measures be taken, twenty-four hours a day, to prevent escape. "These men are desperate and will take the smallest advantage to escape," he wrote to St. Louis Superintendent H. W. Minster. "Suggest to the warden he put good men on guard."[9]

For the first few months the prison took elaborate measures to guard Collins and Rudolph; but gradually, as the summer wore on, the bank robbers were given more freedom. As William Pinkerton had suspected, they were plotting an escape—"three days after we got into the jail," Rudolph later admitted.

On the third day of his arrival in the Four Courts, the Missouri Kid noticed a skylight directly above the top tier. Leading up to the large pane of glass was a series of girders. Rudolph carefully plotted their escape. He counted the number of steps from his cell to the stairway, the number of steps to the top tier, then the distance from the floor of the last tier to the skylight. He also sought out other convicts who could give him a description of the slanted roof that dropped to a chapel roof. Beyond that were a yard and the jailer's house.

Rudolph selected the afternoon of July 6th for their break. Two convicts were paid to stage a fight at the far end of the prison hall. At three o'clock the fight broke out. When guards hurried to the far end of the hall, Rudolph raced up the stairs to the top tier and, like a gymnast, scaled the girders. Collins had started after him but turned back, explaining later, "I just didn't think I could make it." High above the floor, Rudolph clung to the last girder and swung upward, smashing the glass with his feet. He crawled out onto the roof, slowly slid down its slanted sides to the gutter, hung for a moment, and dropped to the chapel roof.

What the other convicts didn't know was that a network of wires stretched across the second roof. When Rudolph fell, he became entangled in the wires, and for a few minutes hung upside down. He finally freed himself and fell to the roof. Badly bruised, and with blood streaming down his face from a deep gash, the Missouri Kid crawled to the edge of the second roof to drop twenty feet into the yard. He now scaled a twenty-foot iron fence—he hadn't been told about that, either—and fell into the jailer's garden. The back door was unlocked. Rudolph entered the house, bowed to the jailer's aged mother as she looked up from her ironing, then walked out into the street. At the corner of Spruce and Eleventh streets he stole a butcher boy's bicycle and "took off fast enough to keep out of the way of the jail people and the man who owned the bicycle."

Rudolph made his way across the city, once gallantly stopping to let a woman shopper cross the street, and waving to a policeman standing on a corner. At North St. Louis, he crossed the Mississippi in a stolen skiff, rode a freight car to Memphis, where he stole a horse and rode to Arkansas and the Indian Territory, the traditional hideout for wanted men.[10]

In July, Collins went on trial. The dramatic highlight was the testimony of Nellie Rudolph, the Missouri Kid's sister, "a young and buxom girl," who tried to save the life of "the man I love" by insisting her brother had killed Schumacher. But the jury wasn't swayed by either her buxom beauty or tearful pleas, and found Collins guilty of murder. While he waited for his execution, Collins wrote numerous letters on two subjects; one was his hatred of the Pinkertons—"I would like to have Billy Pinkerton in the sights of my .45"—and the other was the best way to prepare nitroglycerine: "Get 75 sticks of Dine, thaw it out in a warm room or close to a stove. Then crumble it up like sawdust, then pour hot water on it and stir it up. Then squeeze it through a rag, then pour water off the top and you have your soup in the bottom of the can. A little kid can do it so I know you can if you try. . . ."[11]

Nellie, who had sacrificed her brother, was ignored.

After the escape of the Missouri Kid, William Pinkerton joined his brother in New York. It was a bitter hour, William wrote to F. H. Tillot-

son, his superintendent in Kansas City, but there was no time for recriminations or criticism of the jailers—all energies and resources of the
Agency must be combined for one purpose: recapturing Rudolph.

When Rudolph was traced to the Indian Territory, William Pinkerton, who hadn't been on a horse in years, rode with the posses searching
the badlands. Weary and saddlesore, he returned to New York with new
orders:

> We are contacting every sheriff where possible to send us a telegram
> at our expense to advise us of every bank robber or yegg burglar they
> get. There is little doubt in my mind that Rudolph will come out of
> the Indian Teritory and return to crime. If he is caught he may be
> arrested and sentenced under an alias. We must be alert and compare
> all yegg burglar photographs and measurements with Rudolph's
> charts.[12]

In addition to sending photographs and Bertillon charts to sheriffs, the
Pinkertons distributed the Missouri Kid's likeness and charts to sixty-two
prisons and 160 workhouses in the United States, Canada, and England:
"A careful examination of prisoners now in your custody or received by
you may result in obtaining information concerning Rudolph's whereabouts."

Members of the American Bankers Association were also warned that
Rudolph was on the loose and would probably try to rob a rural bank.
On January 19, 1904, Pinkerton's hunch came true when Rudolph tried
to hold up the Louisburg, Kansas, National Bank. This time he was captured by a "posse of farmers armed with pitchforks." He was arraigned
under the name Charles Gorney, and jailed. The sheriff of Paola, Kansas,
where Rudolph was held, got in touch with the Kansas City Pinkerton
office, but the operative reported back that the dirty, bearded tramp who
had surrendered without firing a shot, could not be the dapper, aggressive
Missouri Kid.

Rudolph, alias Charles Gorney, was found guilty, and sentenced to
an indeterminate term in the Kansas State Prison at Leavenworth. As a
result of the Agency's canvass of American prisons, the warden ordered
Gorney's Bertillon chart and photograph sent to Pinkerton's New York
office. In his office, William stared at the photograph that dropped from
the warden's letter. He compared it with the one of Rudolph that he
had on his desk, then walked into his brother's office. "I think we have
Rudolph," he said.

When Assistant Superintendent Dougherty and the other two operatives who had arrested Rudolph in Hartford also identified the photograph, the Pinkertons knew they had their man. Within the hour F. H.
Tillotson, Kansas City Superintendent, had deciphered an urgent telegram, which read:

Charles Gorney under arrest Paola, Kansas, for burglary safe Louisburg, Kansas, positively identified by Asst. Superintendents Dougherty and Murphy as William Rudolph. Call up without delay Sheriff Paola on telephone. Notify him who Gorney is, the amounts of rewards offered and the possibility of his breaking jail, and to instruct him without delay to place special guard over jail if necessary at our expense as he might escape tonight. Guards should be men who can be absolutely depended upon. Request sheriff make no publication of any kind, regard as confidential. Better go yourself and investigate immediately. Arrange to have Rudolph held for Schumacher murder. Use utmost caution against escape. Satisfied we can arrange with Kansas authorities for his return to Missouri. Act promptly and carefully. Avoid all publications until identification is absolutely confirmed.

Pinkerton was sending one of the most important telegrams in the history of his Agency, yet his attempts to gain what publicity he could from the sensational disclosure and to prevent the local sheriff from beating him into print are shocking. The rest of his telegram is devoted to cautioning Tillotson how to deal with the press. Then he ends: "Delay all publication until Sunday morning newspapers. Request sheriff to avoid all publications until for Sunday papers. Cold day."[13]

The telegram was dated 1:40 P.M. February 12th, a Friday. Pinkerton's reference to "cold day" meant the Saturday newspapers, traditionally thin and with small circulation. He knew from experience that the Sunday papers in the United States had larger circulation than the dailies, and a story published on Sunday about Rudolph being found by the Pinkertons would be read by millions, adding enormous prestige to the business. It was Justice triumphant and a publicity coup at the same time— a package William Pinkerton dearly loved.

Tillotson didn't go himself to Paola, which would bring William's wrath down upon him, but sent Assistant Superintendent Nelson W. Bush, who "hurried out of St. Louis on the first trolley car," as the St. Louis *Republic* reported. It was still telephones and trolley cars, no matter how much the manhunt brought memoirs of the "old Missouri bandit days."

In Paola the sheriff told Bush that the bank robber Gorney was in Leavenworth. At the state prison, Bush found the Missouri Kid in the prison coal mine.

"Hello, Bill," Bush called out.

Rudolph whirled about, his coal-streaked face alive with surprise. "I'm not Bill, I'm Charles Gorney," he said. "You have the wrong man."

The warden ordered a physical examination. Bush wired the results to New York. Several scars, a small mole on his upper lip, and two gold teeth of the Charles Gorney in Leavenworth, along with his Bertillon measurements, tallied with Rudolph's in New York. Later that night, two St. Louis detectives arrived at Leavenworth to confirm Pinkerton's identification.

"I guess it's all up with me," Rudolph told them. "I'll admit I'm Rudolph to you fellows, but don't let those God-damn Pinkertons get any credit."

Despite the Missouri Kid's objections, almost every major newspaper in the country gave the Pinkertons credit for finding Rudolph, with the St. Louis *Post-Dispatch* headline, "Bill Rudolph Run to Earth by the Pinkertons."[14]

By now William Pinkerton knew as much about publicity as any public-relations director today. After Rudolph's identity had been confirmed, he prepared a lengthy release decribing the role the Agency had played. He had the good sense not to exaggerate but to confine himself to facts, and always included the names of local cooperating police officers.

The release was telegraphed to every branch office from Montreal to Boston. William ordered that superintendents, not operatives or assistants, personally deliver the handout to the editors in their city. As Pinkerton had ordered originally, the story broke nationally in the Sunday, February 14, 1904, newspapers.

In New York, William was jubilant at the arrest of Rudolph but furious with his Kansas City office for almost missing the bank robber in Paola. But something else was bothering Pinkerton besides the carelessness of his branch office. While most of the New York and midwestern newspapers had lengthy stories praising the Pinkertons, Chicago, his favorite town, "was the only city that had no publication of the arrest in its newspapers . . . there is not one word reported in the Chicago newspapers and I am at a loss to know how this happened when the newspapers were so crazy for news of this man. I would like an explanation of this immediately. . . ."

Superintendent Tillotson replied in a three-page letter that apparently mollified Pinkerton. Subsequent extensive coverage in the Chicago newspapers undoubtedly helped.

Rudolph was back in the St. Louis jail only a few weeks, when Collins was executed, on the afternoon of March 26, 1904.

Before Collins was led out, the warden asked what he wanted most.

"A drink," Collins said.

"Booze or beer?" the warden asked politely.

"Both," was the prompt reply.

The deputy returned with a pint of whiskey and a bottle of beer.

"What will it be first?" he asked.

"Oh, push along the booze," Collins said. As the reporter noted:

"Collins drained the tin cup as though it was coffee."

"Now push along the chaser," he said. That also went down like coffee, "and then the prisoner said he felt better."

At the foot of the gallows, Collins told the prison chaplain, "No praying for me; I die game," then slowly walked up the steps to the hangman. The fall failed to break his neck, and he slowly strangled to death as spectators perched on the tops of fences, trees, and rooftops watched in silence. When the prison physician pronounced him dead, a "wild cheer rose from the morbid throng."[15]

Rudolph's trial was a major midwestern criminal trial. The courtroom was packed every day, with hundreds waiting to get in. The strange American phenomenon of women attracted to outlaws was so prevalent that Jailer Danson of Four Courts announced that bouquets of flowers sent to Rudolph would not be delivered. Because of the lack of secretarial help, he urged women not to write "scented and silly letters" to the Missouri Kid.

"A disgusting spectacle," William wrote to Robert in a brief, outraged note. "Here is a man charged with murder and robbing a bank. Why would any self-respecting woman want to write to such a desperate character?" In New York Robert scrawled a penciled note to his superintendent:

"File with Rudolph's criminal record." Apparently he didn't know the answer either.

After a lengthy trial, Rudolph was found guilty and sentenced to hang. In April and May, he wrote to William Pinkerton, begging the detective to help get his death sentence commuted to life imprisonment. In his second letter, Rudolph pulled out all stops, pleading with Pinkerton to act "not for my sake but for a dear old mother's sake . . . to use your powerful influence to spare a young life that no more evil can ever enter into."

"I certainly don't wish to see a young man die on the gallows," William wrote to Robert, "but I will not interfere in this case. I can only see him standing over poor Schumacher and pumping bullets into his body."[16]

The Missouri Kid played the gallant desperado role to the last minute. On the morning of May 8, 1905, when the warden and his deputies stepped into his cell to read the death warrant, Rudolph "removed his hat and announced to all that he had no malice toward anyone—even the Pinkertons. Just be sure you do a good job of it," he told the sheriff, "and everything will be all right."

The hanging of Rudolph, the killer, attracted more spectators than the execution of Collins. Large groups of women waited all night to catch a glimpse of the handsome bandit, who waved aside the hands of the deputies and mounted the gallow steps alone. It was a bungled execution, and, like Collins, he died slowly, with the crowd "waiting patiently until life was extinct."[17]

The moment the prison physicians pronounced Rudolph dead, a spectator hurried from the crowded courtyard to the nearest Western Union office. Within minutes, W. B. Laughlin, Assistant Superintendent of the Pinkerton office in St. Louis, had telegraphed every branch office of the Agency in the United States and Canada. The message was brief:

"Rudolph hung at ten o'clock."

In St. Louis, Operative Charlesworth reviewed the long and intensive investigation for reporters, "modestly" pointing out that it had been the scrap of paper he found in the stove that had led to the capture of Schumacher's killers. "It's the little things that count," he told a reporter for the St. Louis *Star*.

The hunt for Rudolph had been international, the cost unprecedented. The capital crime itself apparently had not been the sole motivation; it was just as important to uphold the honor of the Agency. The Victorian criminals knew the Pinkertons never ceased to hunt them down if they robbed an Agency client. Now it had been demonstrated that the world was not big enough to hide the murderer of a Pinkerton operative. It was not only the killing of a man but also the smirching of a business escutcheon that had to be avenged.

BOOK 9
Operations Against the Mafia in the United States, 1890-1906

CHAPTER 34
Operative Dimaio: "The Raven"

As America stood on the brink of the twentieth century, the Pinkertons continued to play their dual, paradoxical roles as a private, national police force that worked only for profit, and as the protective arm of big business.

It was an age when industrialism was the dominant economic factor of American life. Business was now more important than agriculture in shaping the destinies of the nation and its citizens. The new moguls of industry insisted that money is culture. J. Pierpont Morgan, with his partners, organized as a private bank, was the country's leading investment banker. It was the golden age of railroad transportation, with the lines killing most of the internal water transportation with the exception of that on the Great Lakes. Jay Gould, after almost destroying the Erie, invaded the West, bought up small roads, and helped to drive the Union Pacific into bankruptcy.

An unprecedented number of immigrants had helped to bring about the ultimate triumph of industry. In one year alone, 800,000 entered the United States. Unskilled and unfit for a mechanized society, most of them were assigned to the roughest and simplest work. The vast majority settled in the cities and the industrial and mining centers of the North and the West, where they had to accept the least desirable jobs. Though the difficulties of the new immigrants were greater than those who had come to the United States earlier, they received little understanding or assistance—even from the children of established immigrants of the old stock.

With the exception of the Jews, who had conducted their own internal

418

affairs in the Old World, many of the immigrants of the 1880's and 1890's had no concept of self-government or any experience with the liberty of choosing one's own religion, politics, or civic leaders. They brought over their ancient feuds, hostilities, fears—and secret societies. With the Italians came the Mafia.

Italy's so-called Honorable Society was first established in New Orleans in the late 1870's when Giuseppe Esposito, a notorious Sicilian outlaw, fled to the United States. He had touched off an international furor when he had kidnapped an English clergyman and held him for ransom. Esposito forced the clergyman to write a ransom note to his brother in England, begging him to send an emissary with the money. The British Parliament protested to the Italian government, but Esposito, to show his contempt for Rome, cut off the clergyman's ears and sent them to England. This time the British protest was so severe, Rome ordered troops into Sicily. Esposito escaped to the United States and was smuggled ashore at New Orleans. As the most southerly of American ports, New Orleans had long been a haven for fugitives from the Italian law. They hid in the harbor city and worked on the piers and fruit lines. In a few years, Esposito had formed an American branch of the Mafia. He operated a small logger in the harbor. Flying from its masthead was a pennant with the letters "Leoni," the name of the Mafia chieftain in Sicily. Corruption and fear protected Esposito. In a few years his terrorists controlled the New Orleans fruit piers and the hiring of longshoremen. In one year eighty-nine murders were attributed to Esposito's assassins.

In her "Mafia Riots in New Orleans," Margaret Adams depicts the city:

> The evidence of the existence of a Mafia in New Orleans is overwhelming . . . in the year 1881 certain Italian prisoners were turned loose upon the community. The people went mad with fear. They saw themselves helpless and in the power of the Mafia. They saw the machinery of the law stopped by bribery, the juries corrupted by money, witnesses' lives endangered and the witnesses of future years terrified into silence. They saw every man at the mercy of a band of organized assassins . . . they saw the Italians at large tear down the American flag, spit upon it and trample it underfoot, and then hoist it, Union down, beneath the flag of Italy.[1]

Signor Corte, Italian Consul at New Orleans, denounced the Mafia, and warned newly arrived immigrants to avoid it. Priests in Italian parishes denounced it, and pictured the special spot in Hell reserved for the Mafiosi, but in the ghetto warnings and advice were weak and ineffectual against the killers who swaggered down the twisted streets of the New Orleans Italian quarter, similar to those in squalid Sicilian towns. Here were the same wretched buildings, the filth in the muddy streets, the shrill voices and endless chatter, ancient superstitions, old country feuds, love of family, the code of silence—and dread of the Mafia.

In 1881, David Hennessy, who had once operated a private detective agency, was appointed police chief of New Orleans by a reform administration. Hennessy's charisma as a Victorian racket buster who personally led his raiders in breaking up gambling and vice spots attracted a large following. Romantic stories said he was following in the steps of his father, also a New Orleans police chief, who had been murdered while in office. Physically, Hennessy was a tall, powerful man, with a bristling moustache and cold gray eyes. He was well known to law-enforcement officers throughout the country as incorruptible and fearless. One of his closest friends was William Pinkerton.

A short time after he had taken office, Hennessy publicly vowed to arrest and deport Esposito, and he did. The swarthy, knife-scarred Mafia boss was exhibited to reporters and newspaper "artists" at New Orleans Police Headquarters, with Hennessy promising to break the Mafia's grip on the city. Hennessy and his men delivered Esposito to a steamship in New York. Aboard were several Italian Army officers who turned the Mafia leader over to the authorities in Sicily, where he was convicted of extortion and sent to prison.

A report, issued by Hennessy at the time, described the Mafia in New Orleans as a tightly knit band of Sicilian immigrants who employed stabbings, shootings, and bombings to control the dock areas. However, he reported, the domestic form of the Mafia was not "supported" by the parent organization in Italy.

In the spring of 1890, two rival factions of the New Orleans Mafia waged a war for control of the piers and the unloading of bananas from Honduras. On May 6, 1890, a gun battle took place between the two mobs at Clairborne and Esplanade streets, with gunmen turning the area into a battlefield. Men on both sides were wounded and killed, and pedestrians were hit by flying bullets. Newspapers and public officials demanded action. Hennessy made several arrests, and vowed to take the witness stand in the forthcoming trials "to expose the secrets of the Mafia society." Then the *Times-Democrat* revealed that Hennessy in recent months had quietly received documentary proof from the police in Naples and Palermo "that more than one hundred escaped convicts are in New Orleans." Hennessy, confirming this report, said flatly, "I am now prepared to break the Mafia in New Orleans." Neither threats nor offers of large bribes could make him change his mind.

During the summer and fall of 1890, Hennessy waged a deadly war of attrition against the Mafia. He led his raiders into saloons, coffeehouses, and brothels, arresting scores of men. Death threats were nailed to his door and sent in the mail. "The Mafia doesn't scare me," he said scornfully. "I will tear it out by the roots before I'm finished."

On the evening of October 15, 1890, Hennessy said good night to the men in his office and, as usual, walked toward his home. A thin drizzle was falling. As he approached Girod and Basin streets, a boyish whistle, muted by the rain, rose and fell. Hennessy, his head bowed and apparently deep in thought, paid no attention. At the corner, several shadowy figures, one wearing a strip of oilcloth for a raincoat, surrounded him. There was a brief scuffle, followed by a shotgun blast, a cry, and then silence as the shadows melted away in the mist. Hennessy staggered a few feet to a nearby porch, and fell across the lower step. To a neighbor he whispered, "The Dagos did it," and died.

Hennessy's murder came at the peak of antiforeign sentiment, directed principally against the Italians, whose nationality now unfortunately suggested the stiletto, the Black Hand, the deed of impassioned violence. "The disposition to assassinate in a revenge for a fancied wrong is a marked trait in the character of this impulsive and inexorable race," declared the Baltimore *News*. Hearst and Pulitzer in New York viewed every routine knifing in New York's "Little Italy" section of the Lower East Side as the beginning of a vendetta or a family feud continued from the Old Country. By the 1890's the stereotype of the Italian immigrant as a swarthy-faced, skilled "knifeman" conditioned every major outburst of anti-Italian sentiment.

Like the Negroes in the 1930's, the Italians became victims of lynching parties. In West Virginia, a rumor that drunken Italian laborers had cut the throats of a miner's family started a chain of tales that had sheriffs' posses fighting the alleged assassins in the hills. In the strike-torn Colorado mining country, a mob lynched several Italians implicated in the death of a saloonkeeper.[2]

Widespread unrest and hostility in New Orleans erupted after the murder of the police chief. In the hysterical atmosphere, Mayor Shakespear said, "We must teach these people a lesson they will not forget for all time." The City Council appointed a citizens' committee to suggest ways of preventing the influx of European criminals.

In the convulsive days that followed, nineteen alleged Mafia leaders were arrested for Hennessy's murder. Among the prisoners were Joe Macia, head of the Macia Steamship Line; Charles Matranco, known to the city as "Millionaire Charlie"; and Rocco Gerace, another wealthy Italian businessman. Racial disturbances followed their arrest, with "Italians afraid to leave their houses." Two days after the nineteen were arraigned and held in Old Parish Prison, the eighteen-year-old son of a prominent New Orleans businessman slipped into the jail and shot one of the prisoners.

"I'm willing to hang if one of those Dagoes die and I wish there were seventy-five men more like me," he told the warden.

An indication of the sentiment in the city is reflected in the New Orleans *Times-Democrat* headline: "Assassination Attempt of One of the Accused Dagoes."[3]

In turn, the Mafia underworld openly boasted that the prisoners would never stand trial. Witnesses began changing their stories; others disappeared. About the time District Attorney Charles J. Luzenberg was privately informing Mayor Shakespear that the state's case was crumbling day after day, Colonel Wright Schaumberg, Shakespear's secretary and an old friend of William Pinkerton, was reading a letter he had received from the detective. It read in part:

> The murder [of Hennessy] dazed me. I could not collect my thoughts. Why anybody as courteous and brave and gentlemanly as Hennessy should be assassinated in the brutal manner in which he was, is a mystery to me. . . . I have know him since he was a boy in Chief Badger's office and watched him through the years develop into a fine man and wonderful police officer. Again all I can say is I am stunned, my heart goes out to his mother who I know he adored. Please give her my condolences. . . . I am in touch with Chief of Detectives Gastner to offer the full facilities of our organization to help track down, arrest and convict these criminals. . . .[4]

Schaumberg passed on Pinkerton's letter to the mayor, who replied, thanking Pinkerton. A few days later, Pinkerton wrote to the mayor:

> I will do everything in my power to bring this murderer to justice, placing my whole Agency at your call. If you wish, my brother and I will personally come out and assist Chief Gastner [chief of New Orleans detectives] in any way possible. If Dave Hennessy were my younger brother I could not feel deeper sorrow at the news of his death. If I had all the eloquence of Ingersoll, I could not pay a fitting tribute to his memory.[5]

Pinkerton's offer, tantamount to J. Edgar Hoover being willing to place the facilities of the FBI at the disposal of a city police force to help solve a local homicide, was no idle gesture. Hennessy and Pinkerton had been close friends for years. As William once said, "He's my type of man." They were alike physically, and both were devoted to their own peculiar philosophy of law and order. Neither was interested in the reasons for the racial unrest and social conditions in the city. The existing records do not make clear whether William's gratuitous offer was accepted or if the city officials hired the Agency. However, under either circumstances, Pinkerton's officially entered the Hennessy murder case in October, 1890.[6]

At the time, the state had little or no case against the nineteen defendants. What witnesses remained in the city were terrorized. There were no eyewitnesses to the crime, and, as the district attorney had notified the mayor, his office had not been able to ascertain which defendant had actually killed the police officer.

William and Robert conferred in New York, and agreed on a plan to have an operative arrested as a crimnal and jailed in the same cellblock that held the nineteen Mafia prisoners. It was a delicate, dangerous assignment, and both Pinkertons spent a day studying the list of their best operatives: they stopped at one name—that of Frank Dimaio.

At the time, Dimaio was in his early twenties, slight, olive-skinned, with dark eyes and a coxcomb of thick black hair that would one day win him his Mafia nickname of "The Raven." In 1886, he had resigned as assistant manager of a Philadelphia insurance company "because a desk job bored me." He explained: "I wanted a job with a variety of experiences." As an operative working out of the Philadelphia office, he had successfully played the roles of a Portuguese seaman, a Latin dance instructor, an Italian immigrant, and an organ grinder. He spoke fluent French, Italian, and Portuguese. In October, 1890, he had received a commendation from William Pinkerton for the undercover work he had done to expose a Philadelphia insurance fraud ring. The report of Assistant Superintendent Harry Minster called his performance "excellent— he could be an actor."

On Saturday, October 22, 1890, Dimaio and his bride of six months were packing for their long-delayed honeymoon when a messenger delivered a note from Philadelphia Superintendent Robert J. Linden: "Report to the home of Principal Robert Pinkerton, 81 Eighth Avenue, Brooklyn, Tomorrow, Sunday, promptly at 2 P.M."[7]

Dimaio reluctantly put aside the travel folders, kissed his wife goodbye, and left for New York the next morning. Promptly at two he rang the doorbell of the large Victorian brownstone on Eighth Avenue. To his surprise the door was opened, not by a servant, but by Minster, who ushered him into the front parlor. Years later, Dimaio could still recall the sunny room with the heavy velvet drapes and the oil painting of Allan Pinkerton staring down at him. William Pinkerton entered a few minutes later, and, without any preliminaries, the two men gave their orders: Dimaio was to travel to Chicago and register at the Brevoort Hotel. Minster and Pinkerton would join him after a meeting with the heads of the Secret Service in Washington.

"I will give you the whole plan and assignment when we meet in Chicago," Pinkerton said. He turned to Dimaio, "By the way, Dimaio, I want you to go over to the Bowery and buy a complete outfit, including a derby. Make sure they have their label in everything. Mr. Minster will give you the necessary funds. Then come back and we'll have dinner. You'll both stay here tonight and leave for Chicago in the morning."

Dimaio, still wondering what the assignment could be, bought a new suit, shirt, shoes, derby, and returned to Brooklyn. Dinner, a discussion of Dimaio's work in the insurance case, which Pinkerton highly praised; a fine cigar, and a drink followed.

"Are you married, Dimaio?" Pinkerton asked abruptly.

"Yes, sir. Just six months."

"He was a big man with a thick moustache," Dimaio remembered, "and he just stood there for a minute before he told me that the assignment facing me would be very dangerous and that when I heard the details in Chicago I could refuse and it would not be held against me in the Agency. I had the confidence of ten men in those days and I just told Mr. Pinkerton there wasn't any assignment I wouldn't accept."

In Chicago, Dimaio registered under an assumed name at the hotel, and waited. Three days later, he was joined by Minster and Pinkerton. Pinkerton asked him what he knew of the Hennessy murder, and Dimaio sketched the newspaper accounts he had read.

"Chief Hennessy was one of our oldest friends," Pinkerton explained. "When he was murdered, my brother and I vowed we would do anything to get his murderers. I was considering going out there myself when they arrested the nineteen men. However, the disturbing information I have received indicates the state's case will fail because witnesses are being threatened or bribed. The gang is boasting openly to the prison guards they'll be back in business before long and there will be more killings, including those of police officers." He opened a folder and began reading a report he had received from the New Orleans police outlining the activities of the Mafia. When he finished, Pinkerton threw the folder on the bed and walked to the window.

"There is only one way of really solving this murder and getting the prima facie evidence that could break the Mafia in New Orleans," he said, turning to Dimaio, "and that is why I brought you here, Dimaio."

"Yes sir," said the wondering operative.

"That one chance is to get one of the men to confess, to reveal some details of the crime that have not been revealed before."

"But hasn't that been tried, Mr. Pinkerton?" Dimaio asked. "I'm sure I've read where they laugh at the police."

"That's true," Pinkerton said. "However, my plan is not for you to go into New Orleans as a police officer; you're going in as a criminal. You will be arrested with a great deal of fanfare, and put into the same cellblock with these people. Somehow you may be able to get something on them. Even if you do secure a confession in a way that makes it not admissible in a jury trial, it will provide the means of a grand jury investigation and open the door for the subpoenaing of witnesses." He threw up his hands. "Anyway, it's the best we can do." He opened the file and recited police reports of conditions in the city. "These will tell you that certain people in New Orleans will not hesitate to order you killed if they find out who you are. I must warn you, you will be treated as a criminal from the first moment you are arrested. Only six people will know your real identity, myself, my brother, Minster, District Attorney Luzenberg, the head of the Secret Service in Washington, and their New Orleans superintendent. That's why I went to Washington, to get the cooperation of the Secret Service."

Dimaio found Pinkerton and Minster studying him intently, waiting for his decision. Even though he had enormous confidence in his ability to get out of close scrapes, this would be different. He would be *inside* the jail looking out . . . and it would be eleven against one. . . .

On the other hand, Dimaio was flattered that out of the whole Pinkerton organization he had been selected to try to bring off this difficult, dangerous task. More than sixty years later, Dimaio recalled how he had said very quietly, "with my heart in my throat, 'Well, sir, when do I start?' "

Pinkerton spread a map of Louisiana on the bed. Circled in red were Hammond and Amite.

"You and Minster will travel to Hammond. From there, Dimaio continues alone to Amite, a distance of approximately ten miles. In Amite, Dimaio will register at a boardinghouse that is run by a Mrs. Rogers." From a folder he handed Dimaio a Rogues' Gallery photograph, along with a report written by the New York office. It was headed RUGGIERO, ANTHONY, CRIMINAL REPORT.

"You will be Ruggiero from the moment you leave Minster and start from Amite," Pinkerton told him. "This is his complete criminal record, background, *modus operandi*, criminal associates, and so on. Minster will help you memorize the facts. Remember, your life may depend on how well you know this man."

"Where is Ruggiero now, sir?" Dimaio asked.

"The Agency has received confidential information from the Italian police that he has been caught in a small town in northern Italy and will be out of circulation for many months. However, he's an international counterfeiter and has many friends both here and abroad. Some may be in New Orleans."

"You said I was to be arrested?"

"After you register at Mrs. Rogers's boardinghouse," Pinkerton went on, "Minster will return to Chicago and inform Captain A. F. Wilde, of the Secret Service in New Orleans, that you are hiding out at the boardinghouse, with a suitcase of counterfeit money." He handed Dimaio a photograph of a tough-looking man with a walrus moustache. "That's Wilde, a fine officer. As I said, he's cooperating with us. Minster will deliver the counterfeit money." He turned to Minster. "You will pick up the suitcase of counterfeit money; it's the best work of the Dutchman [Charley Becker, the most famous counterfeiter of his age]. After Dimaio has been arrested by Wilde, you will contact this attorney—" he handed Dimaio a card. "We have investigated his background and found him reliable, honest, and one of the city leaders who have been trying to curb crime. If, however, you [Dimaio] are not satisfied with his conduct, drop him at once and send a coded message to Minster in Chicago."

Dimaio looked at the card. It was a French name.

"Will he be my contact, sir?"

"Yes. Do it either by coded letter which he will send on to Minster here, or verbally." He looked at Minster.

"Have I forgotten anything?"

Minster shook his head.

Pinkerton put out his hand to Dimaio. "Good luck, Dimaio. This means a great deal to me personally. If at any time you feel your identity has been breached or you are in physical danger, I order you to contact this attorney or Minster. I have arranged for Luzenberg to issue an immediate writ of habeas corpus."

For the rest of the next few days, Dimaio and Minster studied Ruggiero's background. "It was like playacting," he said. "I would act out a scene and Minster would try and punch holes in it. Hour after hour I stressed habits, special Italian swearwords, the walk and manner of this man I had never met, until they were part of me."

On the third day Minster was satisfied. Dimaio was now a convincing, fiery, sullen little Italian gangster who apparently walked through life with a chip on his shoulder and had a powerful right hand to back up his dislike of the world.

One afternoon, Minster returned from the Pinkerton Chicago office with a battered black valise. When he opened it, they both whistled: Neatly stacked was $6,000 in crisp new bills. Dimaio ripped open the lining of his coat and carefully sewed in a large amount—a favorite trick of Ruggiero's.

On the morning of the fourth day they set out for Hammond. After a last run through his role, Dimaio said goodbye. As Minster recalled:

> Under no consideration were any reports to be kept in my room in Hammond but mailed to Chicago to William Pinkerton at once and at the main post office only. Mr. Pinkerton stated that conditions in New Orleans were such that required utmost caution. Every possible effort had to be made to insure Operative Dimaio would not be exposed. When Operative Dimaio left me for Amite I stayed behind in Hammond and watched the daily papers for news of his arrest. When I finally saw he had been taken by Captain Wilde I contacted the New Orleans attorney and retained him as Dimaio's lawyer with instructions to visit him at least once a week.[8]

Dimaio, after saying goodbye to Minster, took a carriage to Amite. In Mrs. Rogers's boardinghouse, a large, old-fashioned house with a wide veranda, he registered an Anthony Ruggiero of Nashville, and waited for Captain Wilde to appear.

Two days later he was about to enter the dining room when he saw a "rural looking gentleman" studying the guest register. The stranger turned, and Dimaio recognized Captain Wilde. When Mrs. Rogers started to wave Dimaio to his customary seat in the dining room, he shook his head.

"I think I'll buy some cigars first," he said, and walked out. Wilde followed him. Before he reached the front door, Wilde spun him around to hold him at gunpoint. The Secret Service man frisked him quickly, then reached inside Dimaio's jacket, and ripped the lining. A number of new bills fell to the floor.

"This man is one of the most notorious counterfeiters in the country," Wilde dramatically announced to the startled guests.

"Wilde certainly put on a fine show," Dimaio said. "He marched me inside the dining room, and someone brought down my valise with the queer money, which also had a six-shooter. By this time the boarding-house was in an uproar. Mrs. Rogers had fainted, and two of the guests ran to get their shotguns. After he handcuffed me, Wilde then went on to list all the crimes I was wanted for. It certainly sounded impressive."

There were no trains to New Orleans that night, so Wilde bought two tickets for the next afternoon's caboose. Their departure made the afternoon unforgettable in Amite's history. The depot was mobbed with farmers and curiosity seekers. As the train pulled into the station, one man grabbed the handcuffed Dimaio, shouting that he was the man who had given him a counterfeit twenty-dollar bill "at the St. Louis Fair."

Dimaio decided it was time to start acting the part of the quick-tempered Ruggiero. He swung both fists, and knocked the farmer unconscious. Someone cried he was trying to escape, and the crowd rushed forward, this time with chains and ropes. Wilde kicked and elbowed his way to the caboose, and, as Dimaio said, "threw me into the car before they could string me up."

There were six fellow passengers: two newspapermen who were on their way to New Orleans to write about the Hennessy murder, two priests, and two drunks. The reporters interviewed Dimaio at length; the priests tried to save his soul; and the drunks fed him whiskey. Wilde helped to create the legend of Ruggiero as the toughest man he had ever encountered, with wild tales of how he had taken Dimaio prisoner after a gun battle.

The advance publicity produced another crowd at the New Orleans depot. In the Old Parish Prison, at Conti and Orleans streets, Dimaio was stripped of his new clothes and given a striped suit. Because the warden told Wilde the cells were all filled, Dimaio had to be put in with the other "Dagos."

It was late at night when Dimaio was finally assigned a bunk. Tense, he lay on the straw, wondering what the next day would bring, when the door of the cellblock opened, and he heard someone whisper in Italian, "Who is it?"

The answer came. "It's me, Joe. A government man brought in a counterfeiter; watch out, he may be an informer." Then the door clicked. As Dimaio would later discover, a prison clerk was on the mob's payroll.

Dawn finally arived. Dimaio was given a small wooden toilet with the horrible nickname of "ice-cream freezer," and assigned to a cell. Joe was revealed to be a slender, good-looking young prisoner named Emanuel Politz.[9]

Politz—also spelled Polizzi—was one of the nineteen charged with Hennessy's murder. The others—older, dark, hard-looking Joe Macia, the steamship-line owner; Millionaire Charlie Matranco, Rocco Gerace, and the rest of the prisoners—sat in a circle at the end of the block.

After a miserable breakfast, a guard opened the cell door and threw in a newspaper. "There you are, Ruggiero; read all about yourself," he shouted.

As the newspaper fell on his lap, Dimaio gave it a vicious swipe and cursed in Italian. The paper landed at the feet of Politz, who picked it up, read it hurriedly, and gave it to the others. They huddled together, with Millionaire Charlie reading the account of Dimaio's arrest aloud to the others in Italian. Dimaio's cellmate, Billy Weems, an old-time burglar, was impressed, and told the others, "This little guy is real big in New York. I heard about him. He passes the best queer you can make."

That afternoon Frank Romero, one of the defendants, walked up to Dimaio. He started to greet Dimaio in Italian, but the operative had already devised his strategy. Without a word he swung from the floor. His fist caught Romero on the jaw, and sent him spinning across the cellblock.

"Keep away from me," Dimaio snarled in Italian. "The next time . . ." He drew his finger across his throat.

Two of the other prisoners dragged Romero to his cell and threw water on him. When he was revived, Romero shouted that he would tear the New Yorker into little pieces. Dimaio, who had now decided on the offensive, walked down the cellblock and stared at the raging Romero.

"You talking about me?" he asked.

Romero looked up, then shook his head. One of the others grabbed Dimaio's arm, and whispered, "We only want to be friends," but Dimaio threw off the man's arm and walked back to Weems, who admiringly observed:

"You certainly told those Dagos off, Tony!"

Dimaio, who wasn't interested in Weems's observations, studied Politz's reactions out of the corner of his eye. What he saw satisfied him. For the next two weeks, Dimaio swaggered about the cellblock. Weems was a help to Dimaio. To improve his own status, the wizened old burglar invented stories of Dimaio's connections in the New York underworld, his viciousness, and hair-trigger temper. Dimaio soon found himself a prison celebrity, and the small-time thieves in the block were only too eager to run his errands. The Mafia group had many visitors, and from the snatches of guarded conversations in Italian, Dimaio overheard orders given to outside gunmen to intimidate state witnesses.

Pinkerton detective Frank Dimaio at the time of the Mafia investigation

Courtroom scene when the Mafia leaders were acquitted. New Orleans *Times Picayune*

The scene of Hennessy's murder: (a) where he was killed, (b) where his killers hid. New Orleans *Times Picayune*

Weeks passed. The miserable food gave Dimaio severe atacks of dysentery. He walked bent over with cramps, and began to lose weight. One day a New Orleans madam, who had the run of the prison, asked to see the notorious New York counterfeiter.

"My God, kid, you look like you can stand a good feed," she cried, when a jailer brought her to Dimaio. The next day she sent in fried chicken and a bottle of wine. This was followed by a delivery twice a week from the madam's kitchen. Dimaio always insisted this was not by any prearrangement but simply because "she seemed to like me."

"I don't know why she liked me," Dimaio said, "but I am sure that without it I could not have lasted. In two months' time I was so weak I couldn't knock over a kitten."

Wilde, in the meantime, had been granted a series of adjournments of the case of the "New York counterfeiter," and Dimaio remained in prison. It was only after the first month that Dimaio made his move. He had just received his semi-weekly bottle of wine from the madam when Romero passed his cell.

"Have some wine," Dimaio grunted in Italian.

Romero was so startled, he stopped. For a moment Dimaio thought the squat prisoner would knock the bottle from his hand, but he took it grudgingly. When Dimaio moved over and waved him to the cot, he sat down. In Italian, Dimaio apologized for hitting him, but explained he didn't want any "tinhorns" to start pestering him. By now, Dimaio knew Romero was very proud of his reputation as a tough. As he expected, Romero began boasting how he and the other Italian prisoners controlled the city.

At the end of the recital, Dimaio shrugged. "Well, you have your troubles, and I have mine."

From that day on, the Mafia leaders sought out Dimaio. Grudgingly, he accepted their food and wine. On Sunday, elaborate Italian dinners were brought in, which they shared with Dimaio. But the operative always sought out Politz.

"I made sure I was friendly but not overfriendly," he remembered. "This was an acquaintanceship that had to be carefully nurtured. One abrupt false move, and it could end. He was eager to be nice, but it was clear the boy was in fear of his life from the others."

After several weeks, the New Orleans attorney, at Pinkerton's orders, visited Dimaio. He was shocked at the operative's wasted appearance, and notified Minster, who in turn advised Pinkerton that Dimaio should be released. The operative refused, although he was getting weaker and had started to pass blood. He also contracted malaria. Despite the madam's fried chicken, his prison suit "hung on me like a scarecrow's rags."

By the second month, Dimaio was able to report, through the New Orleans attorney, the names of a private detective and a crooked attorney who were bribing state's witnesses to leave the city until the trial was over. As Dimaio remembered, he sat with the nineteen in the evening, smoking and listening to Millionaire Charlie describe in bewildered fashion how Hennessy had refused their bribes and on one occasion had thrown their courier out of his office.

One day, Dimaio heard he was to be transferred to another prison wing. When the doctor made his rounds, the Pinkerton operative had Billy Weems bring him to the cellblock. "Although I didn't have to put on a great deal, I made a great show of being bent in half by cramps," Dimaio said, "and said I would die if I had to be moved. The doctor, who couldn't care less, agreed, and told the guard to tell the warden I had to stay. But then he gave me a pill as big as a marble, and stood there while I swallowed it. It almost killed me. I found out later it was saltpeter."

As the days passed, the dysentery epidemic in the prison worsened. Dimaio couldn't leave his cot. Most of the other prisoners were in the same condition. The stench in the cellblock became unbearable. What little food Dimaio could eat came from Joe Politz's spaghetti dinners or the madam's chicken. She once came to the cellblock to see Dimaio, but ran down the corridor, pressing a handkerchief to her face.

The attorney told Minster it made him physically ill to visit the prison, but Dimaio still refused to leave. By the end of four months, Wilde notified Pinkerton he couldn't keep Dimaio in prison much longer. By now the operative had lost forty pounds, and he realized that time was running out.

During this period he had begun to experiment psychologically with Politz. He would unexpectedly ask the young prisoner:

"What have the other fellows got against you, Joe?"

Politz, surprised, would shrug, and change the subject.

One day, Dimaio staged a furious argument with Romero, and when Politz asked the reason, Dimaio made a great show of refusing to tell him. Finally, he appeared to relent, and, after swearing Politz to secrecy, Dimaio said the others were afraid Politz "might go to the law." He had tried to tell Romero, he said, that Politz would never be an informer.

As Dimaio kept planting seeds of suspicion, Politz visibly became more nervous as the days passed, and this affected the others, who became brusque with him. Dimaio knew he needed an opportunity to underscore Politz's growing uneasiness dramatically. It came on a Sunday afternoon when the usual spaghetti dinners were delivered. As was his custom, Politz came to Dimaio's cell to share the meal.

The beaming Politz sat down on the cot and unrolled the silverware while Dimaio struggled to a sitting position. When Politz removed the napkin, Dimaio saw that a fine powder of cheese covered the top of the sauce. As he eyed the dinner, a gear clicked in his mind. Politz rolled the spaghetti and was lifting it to his mouth when Dimaio suddenly struck it from his hand.

Politz looked stunned. "What's the matter, Tony? What's the matter?"

Dimaio looked about dramatically, then whispered intently: "Don't eat that, Joe! Don't eat that!"

Politz stared at Dimaio as if he had suddenly gone crazy. The operative yanked the plate toward him, rolled a pinch of cheese between his fingertips, then whispered, "Smell it!" As Politz leaned forward, Dimaio said in his ear: "Poison, Joe! I know poison! That's arsenic!"

Politz raised stricken eyes. Slowly, he put a pinch of cheese to his nostrils. They both turned wordlessly to stare at the others, eating at the far end of the cellblock. By chance, Romero was studying them.

"Why do they want to do that for?" Politz whispered. "Why, Tony? After I done so much for them. Why?"

As Dimaio said later, it took all his control to keep from showing his triumph. He wanted to ask a thousand questions; instead, he lowered himself back on his cot, and said nothing. Politz returned to his cell to lie down for the rest of the afternoon, staring up at the ceiling. Dimaio let him alone, for, as he said, the more Politz brooded and worried, the more receptive he would be to his questions.

The following morning, on the way to empty his "ice cream freezer" Dimaio stopped at Politz's cell. "Don't worry about them, Joe. I'll keep an eye on them for you."

Politz walked with him to the end of the block. "Why me, Tony? Why are they picking on me? I did a lot for them. They know that."

Dimaio decided to begin his questioning. "What did you do for them, Joe?"

Politz groaned, and shook his head. "Murder, Tony, murder."

Dimaio abruptly cut off his questioning. One step at a time, he told himself. From that day on, Dimaio increased his quiet campaign of terror against Politz. He bribed Weems, the burglar, to tell Politz "for a joke," that he had heard the others talking about him, but what it was he couldn't understand, just the man's name. Dimaio insisted on personally tasting every scrap of Politz's food, explaining that a good counterfeiting man must know chemicals and drugs. He kept plucking at the prisoner's raw nerve ends until the slender Mafia prisoner was tense and jumpy. Dimaio also told Politz a terrifying account of a fictitious woman in his grandmother's day who was used by the Mafia to poison landlords in her village. He was quite vivid in his descriptions of the death agonies of the victims after the poison had eaten away the walls of their stomachs.

"I must have been damn convincing," Dimaio said, "or else Politz was in such a condition from the long imprisonment that he would have believed anything. One day he just jumped up and ran from my cell, holding his ears. That ended the stories about my make-believe grandmother.

I was afraid that he would become hysterical and begin babbling accusations to the others. There is no doubt they would have had him killed in short order. Instead, I decided to let nature take its course for a few days."

Dimaio and Politz spent most of their evenings together, sometimes listening to Weems, who spun entertaining stories of yegg burglars he had worked with across the country. They usually shared a bottle of wine left over from the Sunday dinners, and smoked small twisted Italian cigars. As Dimaio watched the struggle waging inside Politz, he knew that the prisoner wanted to talk but that he still feared the traditional punishment for anyone who violated the Mafia's tradition of *omerta—* silence before strangers or the law.

Dimaio at last found his health slipping. He decided on one last bit of stage acting. A bottle of wine had been delivered to Politz, who filled two glasses. Dimaio raised his to his mouth, then flung the wine across the cell.

Politz, who had lifted his glass, froze. His eyes asked the question. Dimaio nodded.

"Cyanide, Joe," he whispered. He took the bottle from Politz's nerveless hand, and poured the wine down the rusty iron sink.

That night Dimaio asked Weems to sleep in Politz's cell and let the Mafia prisoner stay with him. As they lay there in the stench-filled darkness, he kept prodding Politz with questions. Finally, in the early hours of the morning, Politz turned to him and said:

"We murdered Hennessy . . . They think I will betray the Society."

A dam seemed to break inside Politz. In answer to the operative's questions, he told the entire story of the murder. As he babbled on, Dimaio etched dates and names of witnesses and coconspirators on his mind. Sometimes he asked what seemed stupid questions, like those of a man not familiar with the city, to make Politz detail certain scenes.

By dawn, Politz fell into an exhausted sleep. Dimaio stayed awake, going over and over in his mind the elaborate details he had heard. In the morning, when the guards made their tour, he hobbled to the cellblock door and asked that a message be sent to his lawyer to come to see him.

But the guard said: "Write a letter like everyone else, big shot. You know the rules."

"I probably had been going on nerves all those weeks," Dimaio said, "because I had a devil of a time writing a few lines. It was a chore to make the pencil move. Once, Romero strolled over and asked to whom I was writing. I just said, 'A blonde on Basin Street.' He laughed, and called out to the others, who walked down the cellblock to stand around my cell, making obscene remarks while I desperately tried to compose the note that could be their death warrant.

"The next day the guard called my name. 'Hey, big shot,' he shouted, 'your lawyer says he doesn't represent you anymore. He says for you to get another attorney.'

"I was so stunned I couldn't answer. When I hobbled over to the bars and asked him to repeat it, he did. 'He didn't give a reason,' the guard said. 'He just said for you to get another lawyer.' "

Dimaio later learned the reason for the lawyer's decision. Two days before, a witness against the nineteen had been murdered, a murder that probably had been planned in that very cellblock. As a shocking warning from the Mafia, the witness had been butchered, and the corpse dragged to the roof of the police station. The lawyer later explained to William Pinkerton that the sight of the nineteen prisoners sent chills up his back.[10]

Dimaio was desperate. In some fashion he had to get a message to Minster. He was now so weak his head spun when he stood up. Billy Weems and Joe Politz were also ill and confined to their bunks.

On a chance, he took what money he had and wrote out a telegram to "Harry Minster, Attorney at Law, Chicago." The message read, "Can you get me a writ? Tony."

At first the guard refused to smuggle out the telegram, but after Dimaio offered his watch, together with the money, he agreed. A day and night passed while Dimaio wondered if the guard had kept the money and his watch but never sent the telegram. If he had, there was nothing to do but wait until Minster, who knew nothing about the attorney's withdrawal, decided to investigate the long silence from the New Orleans prison. By that time, Dimaio told himself, he might not be alive. Weems and Politz, both concerned about Dimaio's condition, demanded that the guard summon the doctor. The prison physician, after examining the Pinkerton operative, ordered him to the infirmary. Dimaio, who had heard that a trip to that place was certain death, forced himself to totter to his feet and do a little jig to show the doctor he was fit.

"I'm coming around in the morning, and if you're not better I'm giving you one of these again," the doctor said, holding up the marble-sized saltpeter pill.

"If I had taken that pill, the way I was passing blood, I'm sure there would have been a severe reaction," Dimaio said. "But, thank God, that afternoon a young French attorney appeared and said he had been retained by a Mr. Minster of Chicago. When I asked him to file for a writ of habeas corpus, the damn fool shrugged off the suggestion.

" 'It will be a waste of time, monsieur,' he said. 'It is better we ask for an immediate trial and for you to plead guilty.' "

Dimaio had to beg the attorney before he reluctantly agreed to file the writ, which would be the signal for the prosecutor, who in turn was to telegraph to William Pinkerton.

The next day the young attorney returned, surprised and cocky.

"I have done what no other attorney in New Orleans could do," he announced. "I have forced the court to grant a writ of habeas corpus."

"He looked so smug, I had all I could do from laughing in his face," Dimaio said. "The damn fool kept boasting how he had forced the prosecutor himself to grant the request!"

When they heard the news, Millionaire Charlie and Romero sent out for a farewell feast. Joe Politz, who had become morose and melancholy, was the last to say goodbye.

"I don't think I will ever leave here," he said.

When Minster met Dimaio in a carriage outside the prison, he was stunned. "My God, man, what has happened to you?" he asked.

Minster recalled Dimaio's reply as, "I guess I lost a few pounds," before he fainted.

Minster helped Dimaio into a hotel room where William Pinkerton and Prosecutor Luzenberg were waiting. Like Minster, Pinkerton was disturbed when he saw his operative's physical condition. He ordered that Dimaio be put to bed, but his operative insisted on reciting the story as he recalled it from Politz. The prosecutor summoned a stenographer, and Dimaio talked for hours, interrupting his story only to eat ravenously.

"This could be the end of them," Luzenberg told Pinkerton. "I'm going to send out notices tonight to convene a grand jury." He asked Dimaio, "Do you think you're strong enough to testify?"

"Give me a few hours' rest and another supper," Dimaio replied.

Later, Dimaio testified for hours before the grand jury. But his strength gave out, and he actually fell asleep in the witness chair. The next afternoon he resumed his testimony, not only detailing the Hennessy murder as Politz had described it, but also warning the grand jury that Politz had told him the Mafia had unlimited funds and power in the state and that they boasted there wasn't a jury they couldn't buy or bribe. The private detective and the crooked attorney would dispense the funds.

Back in the hotel, Pinkerton brought in a physician, who ordered Dimaio to rest for a least a week in bed. With Pinkerton and Minster gone most of the day, conferring with Luzenberg, Dimaio was left to himself. At first he slept around the clock and ate constantly. But as the days passed he became bored. One afternoon he decided "to get some air." It was the first afternoon of Mardi Gras. Dimaio had slowly walked to the corner of Canal and Burgundy streets, and was watching the parade when someone clutched his shoulder. It was a detective.

"I know you," the officer snapped. "You're that damn New York counterfeiter."

Dimaio was taken to court, where he was arraigned as a professional thief. He pleaded with the judge to believe his story that he was on his way to the railroad station when he was arrested. The judge agreed to dismiss the charges if he would leave New Orleans immediately. Dimaio was only too happy to agree.

"This is hard to believe," Dimaio said, "but I had walked back to Canal and Burgundy streets. I could see the hotel about a block away. I

was so weak I had to cling to a pole and get my breath. Suddenly someone grabbed my arm. Incredible as it may seem, it was another detective.
Again I was arrested, and again I found myself before the same judge, all
within a few hours. This time the judge was apoplectic. He was just
sentencing me to six months when Mr. Pinkerton and Luzenberg appeared. They approached the bench and whispered to the judge, who
turned me over to them. Fortunately, Luzenberg had overheard a detective boasting to another detective near the grand-jury room that he had
just pinched a famous New York counterfeiter named Ruggiero and that
the judge was going to hit him with the book. He found Mr. Pinkerton,
and they both ran down to the courtroom."

Dimaio offered to testify for the state, but Luzenberg refused. "He will
not leave the city alive if he takes the stand," the prosecutor told William
Pinkerton.

On the morning of February 16, 1891, the nineteen appeared in court.
District Attorney Luzenberg was granted a severance, and nine of the
defendants went on trial before Judge Baker in the Old New Orleans
Courthouse. It was a trial without precedence in the history of American
jurisprudence. Through Dimaio's grand-jury testimony, Luzenberg had
subpoenaed numerous witnesses to events leading up to and including
the murder itself. One was a fourteen-year-old boy who had whistled "La
Marica Reale" (The Royal March) to alert the assassins as Hennessy approached the ambush. Bartenders, waitresses, and other witnesses had
been located and questioned after Dimaio had given the grand jury either
their names or the places where they worked.

When the trial began, Dimaio was back in Philadelphia under a doctor's care. Agency observers at the trial telegraphed daily coded reports
to both William in Chicago and Robert in New York. The state assumed
it had an excellent case until the Sunday before the first Mafia trial
began. Then Luzenberg was notified that the Mafia had the names of
every citizen in the city who had been subpoenaed for panel duty. Talesmen disappeared, and others refused to serve, insisting they had been
threatened with murder and bombing. When the trial began, Mafia enforcers appeared in the courtroom. When a talesman rose to be questioned
by the court, the gunmen drew fingers across their throats or held up
thick rolls of bills. More than 1,150 talesmen were examined before a
jury was finally chosen.

Witnesses who could not be intimidated were placed under heavy
guard by Luzenberg. Those brave men actually stepped down from the
witness stand to touch the shoulders of and identify the nine defendants
on trial.

One witness, a Negro, picked out the man he saw firing at Hennessy.
Another identified one of the defendants as the assassin who wore a piece
of oilcloth draped over his shoulders "like a raincoat." The oilcloth, an
important piece of the state's evidence, had been found by police in a raid

on the home of the Mafia prisoner a few hours after the murder. It was produced in court and lay folded on the prosecutor's table, "a silent accuser of the men who murdered Hennessy in the rain that night."

On March 12th, the jury returned a verdict of not guilty. The packed courtroom and halls of the courthouse became a bedlam, with spectators shouting, "Hang the Dagos. Don't let them go!" Bailiffs and patrolmen finally cleared the building. The court then granted Prosecutor Luzenberg's request that the defendants be returned to the Old Parish Prison to join the other Mafia prisoners until his office had thoroughly investigated the verdict.[11]

That night lynch law ruled New Orleans. Torchlight parades wound in and out of the streets, while W. S. Parkerson, a prominent New Orleans attorney, was chosen as "head of the movement to correct justice." Posters urging "all good citizens of New Orleans to appear at Clay Statue to remedy the failure of Justice in the Hennessy case" were plastered about the city. Pinkerton observers telegraphed to William in Chicago that violence was brewing in the city.

At 10:00 A.M. on March 14, 1891, several thousand gathered at the square to listen to the violent vigilante speeches of Parkerson and several other prominent citizens of New Orleans.

"When courts fail the people must act!" Parkerson shouted to the silent, intent mob that stretched out as far as he could see. "What protection or assurances of protection is there left us when the very head of our police department, our chief of police, is assassinated in our very midst by the Mafia society, and his assassins again turned loose on the community? The time has come for the people of New Orleans to say whether they are going to stand these outrages by organized bands of assassins, for the people to say whether they permit it to continue." He paused dramatically; then, his voice rolling over the packed square, he cried: "Will every man here follow me and see the murder of Hennessy vindicated? Men and citizens of New Orleans, follow me! I will be your leader!"

His answer was a chilling roar from the mob. The arsenal was stormed, and rifles and shotguns were issued "to as many as needed them." At the prison a small force of police and deputies were hurled aside. The prison was surrounded on all sides by a hooting, jeering, screaming mob. "Every avenue was jammed from curb to curb. Telephone poles, lamp posts and every available tree held a bundle of human forms," one newspaper reported.[12]

A telegraph pole was cut down and passed, hand over hand to the men at the prison door. In a few minutes the door was smashed in, and the mob, its leaders holding hangman's nooses above their heads, rushed inside. Deputies were beaten and flung into the street. When he had heard of the mob's march on the prison, the warden had frantically hidden the Mafia prisoners in the women's section, but groups searched the floors, cellblock by cellblock, until the ten were found. All were kicked, beaten, and finally riddled with bullets as they begged for mercy. Joe Politz, who had unknowingly signed their death warrants when he whispered to Dimaio in the early darkness some weeks before, ironically suffered the cruelest death. He was clubbed unmercifully, then dragged by ropes to the street, where he was lynched, then shot as he slowly strangled to death. When all the broken, bloody bodies hanging from the lampposts and telephone poles were finally still, the mob quieted. In the strange silence, Parkerson climbed to the driver's seat of a wagon, and for a moment looked out across the sea of tight, hate-filled, triumphant faces.

"I have performed the most painful duty of my life today," he shouted. "Now let us go home, and God bless you and our community."

It was a strange benediction on that savage American morning.

There was no official condemnation of the lynching. The Cotton Exchange, the Border Trade, and New Orleans Chamber of Commerce "promptly passed resolutions commending the citizens of New Orleans."

Mayor Shakespear was quoted as saying:

"No sir. I am an American citizen and I am not afraid of the Devil. These men deserved killing and they were punished by peaceful, law abiding citizens. They [the Mafia prisoners] took the law in their own hands and we were forced to do the same." [13]

Newspapers praised the mob's actions, and some even offered resolutions to that effect. For several weeks, Italian groups held meetings in several large cities, protesting the murders. Baron Fava, the Italian Ambassador, visited the White House and State Department to lodge official protests. Secretary of State James G. Blaine telegraphed to Louisiana's Governor Francis T. Nichols:

> The President deeply regrets that the citizens of New Orleans should have disparaged the purity and adequacy of their own judicial tribunals as to transfer to the passionate judgment of a mob, a question that should have been adjudged dispassionately and by settled rules of the law.

Baron Fava continued to demand that the leaders of the mob be punished by the United States. Blaine patiently explained the embarrassing gap in our federalism—that in such cases the state, and not the central government, has jurisdiction. But Fava pressed for action, until Blaine bluntly replied:

> I do not recognize the right of any government to tell the United States what it should do. We have never received any orders from any other government and we will not begin now . . . it is a matter of total indifferences to me what persons in Italy might think of our institutions. I cannot change them, still less violate them.[14]

At this point jingoism turned the local incident into an international diplomatic affair. On March 31st, Baron Fava was recalled from Washington. However, diplomatic relations between this country and Italy were not severed; each nation left her affairs in the hands of a chargé d'affaires. This exploded the internal hatred in the United States, with Italy now viewed as the villain. Fear of Italian-Americans was enormously magnified. In April, 1891, *New York Illustrated* devoted its entire issue to a review of the Italian fleet, pointing out that Italy had twenty-two capital ships and the United States one, and that one still on the drawing board. This gave rise to rumors that the Italian fleet was moving on the West Coast. Parades and meetings were held by patriot groups, urging America to prepare itself against the "Dagos." Italians were now regarded as potential foreign agents. Stories, usually without foundation, were printed of Italians burning the American flag or engaging in various unpatriotic acts. New York seethed with rumors that a corps of armed Italians was drilling every day. In Wheeling, West Virginia, miners went on strike because their employer had refused to discharge two Italians. A miners' committee drew up a resolution promising "not to work with men allied to a foreign nation that was trying to bring about war with the United States." The *Review of Reviews* pointed out to its readers that America must have a navy to protect itself from "wanton insult," and an Immigrant policy "to keep out the refuse of the murder breeds of Southern Europe." [15]

It was clear, as the *Review* pointed out, that a wave of Americanism was sweeping the country as a result of the New Orleans incident. In his fine *Strangers in the Land,* John Higham states, "Not only Italian immigration but the whole immigration question was dramatized as nothing had dramatized it since the Haymarket affair."

Large dailies were joined by the pulpit in demands for more stringent immigration laws. The influential *Nation* concluded that a secure modern state rested on community of language, and therefore proposed to limit immigration to English-speaking applicants. The severe idea met with general national favor.

On April 3rd, the New Orleans grand jury handed down indictments, naming two trial jurors with accepting bribes in the Hennessy murder case. The jury's report revealed that every member of the Hennessy jury had been "reached" by the private detective and the crooked attorney—both named by Dimaio. This disclosure set off disturbances in Mobile, New York, Kansas City, and other cities where Italians broke out of their ghettoes to battle police and mobs that chanted, "Die, Dagos, die!"

On December 19, 1891, in his annual message to Congress, President Harrison courageously denounced the New Orleans affair as a "most deplorable and discredited incident and an offense against law and humanity." Tempers slowly cooled after an investigation by the government in Rome revealed that of the ten, only three were unnaturalized; "thus no foreign nation could properly object to natural born Americans lynching naturalized Americans."

The incident was finally closed when, "as an act of good faith," Secretary Blaine announced the Italian government had accepted an indemnity award of 125,000 lire ($25,000), which would be distributed among the families of the victims.[16]

This was the fourth historic case in the long career of the Pinkertons in which mob action or lynch law shocked the nation: the Renos, Molly Maguires, Homestead, and now New Orleans. Were the Pinkertons to blame? Obviously neither William Pinkerton nor Dimaio had anything to do with rousing the New Orleans mob. In fact, the Agency had actually done a public service in sending an operative into the prison at the risk of his life. Long before Hennessy's death, there had been evidence of community hostility to the city's minorities. It was clear that police and political corruption had weakened law enforcement in New Orleans so severely that the entire list of jury talesmen had been delivered to the underworld only a few hours after its selection. Those who defied the underworld were intimidated or killed. In this municipal breakdown of law and order, the district attorney and the uncorrupted police eagerly accepted the Pinkertons' offer to step into the case. Dimaio made his report and testified before the grand jury, and that ended the Agency's participation. It was the people who formed the mob and their hands that pulled the ropes.

If anything, the grim events of that March morning in the year 1891 underscore the tragic conclusion that racism and violence are not new and shocking facets of our national character—they are part of our heritage.

CHAPTER 35
Helltown

By 1900, new waves of Italian immigrants swarmed into the slums, the factories, and the mines. In the teeming ghettos, they lived a class apart, the least assimilated and the most impoverished of the immigrants. Viewed as disturbers of the peace, they focalized the fear of foreign-bred discontent. The hostility of the outside world, grinding poverty, and their traditional family clannishness helped to breed the Italian secret societies that preyed mostly on their own people.

By the turn of the century, the Mafia, Comorra, and Black Hand were deeply entrenched in most large American cities. They were particularly strong in Columbus and Akron, Ohio, and virtually controlled the limestone quarries in the Mahoning Valley from Youngstown, Ohio, to New Castle, Pennsylvania. Jobs that paid $5 a day, unusually high for the time, were distributed at gunpoint. Local quarrymen were forced out by beatings, knifings, and bombings, and some later reported they were forced to accept dollar-a-day jobs as streetcleaners in New Castle to survive. Murders became so rampant the police refused to list "Dago killings." [1]

After he had recovered from his New Orleans experience, Frank Dimaio returned to insurance-fraud investigations. In 1902, he had trailed and arrested one suspect in Brazil when William Pinkerton, at the request of the State Department, sent him to Argentina to arrest Butch Cassidy, the Wild Bunch leader and his riders, Harry Longbaugh, the Sundance Kid, and Etta Place, who was posing as the Kid's wife. It was Dimaio's ground-

442

work that later led to the killing of Cassidy and Longbaugh by a segment of the Bolivian cavalry. On his return to the United States, the Pinkertons ordered Dimaio to make a study of the origins of the Italian secret societies, their members, and their strength in this country. Dimaio toured the larger cities, posing as an immigrant laborer. Several months later, he wrote a detailed report for William and Robert Pinkerton. By this time, the Agency had been retained by wealthy Italian businessmen who were threatened by the Mafia. The cases were turned over to Dimaio. In one investigation his undercover work resulted in the arrest and conviction of fourteen Mafia enforcers in Columbus, who had used knifing and bombings to intimidate their victims. For years, Dimaio, "Pinkerton's Mafia expert," would live a precarious life as an undercover operative in the Midwest and Pennsylvania. Lieutenant Petrosino, the famous New York detective and nemesis of the Mafia, paid this tribute to Dimaio: "He knows more about the Society than any other man I know."

In 1905, at William Pinkerton's suggestion, Dimaio formed his own corps of secret agents from Sicilian immigrants who had been former members or victims of the terrorist society. Dimaio played many roles, from a hobo to the black-sheep son of a wealthy, but fictitious, Italian banker.[2]

His favorite role, he said, was that of an Italian laborer dressed in shapeless black pants, checkered shirt, peaked cap, and threadbare coat: "Dimaio's Mafia uniform," as Robert Pinkerton wrote to his brother. Once, while investigating a Columbus, Ohio, bombing threat made to a wealthy Italian cheese exporter, Dimaio was forced to travel to New York and attend a meeting on Mulberry Street—"Little Italy"—where the bombing of a doctor's home was discussed. On the pretext of visiting New Jersey relatives, Dimaio secretly met Robert Pinkerton.

"Dimaio met me yesterday," Robert wrote to William. "He was dressed in his Mafia uniform which makes him a very rough looking character. He had some interesting information which [the New York superintendent] has sent over to the Italian Squad." The bombing was later prevented, and the terrorists were arrested.

The Agency's major investigation of the Mafia took place between 1905 and 1908 in the Mahoning Valley. Assaults, knifings, and threats, and work stoppages took place with such frequency that Charles W. Crook, general manager of the Bessemer Quarry, one of the largest in the valley, met with the other owners and formed an association. The Pinkertons were retained after local police had proved ineffective.[3]

Dimaio, Superintendent J. G. Goodwin of the Philadelphia office, C. H. Young, a New Castle attorney and Lawrence County District Attorney; County Detective Creighton G. Logan, and Robert Pinkerton met in New York. It was agreed that Dimaio and his agents should move into the quarry country—by way of Ellis Island. Dimaio and his men, "part" of an immigrant shipload that arrived at the island, were hired "en masse," as was the custom, by agents of the limestone companies. They were lodged in boardinghouses in Hillsville, Pennsylvania, known locally as "Helltown." Dimaio went to work in the quarry, and for over a year took part in the rough social life of the quarry town.

His never-before published reports parallel in excitement, suspense, and danger James McParland's infiltration of the Molly Maguires thirty years earlier. Like McParland, Dimaio gained a reputation for toughness, drinking, violence, and dancing. Knifemen, rather than gunmen, ruled the villages. As one report revealed, in seventeen murder cases there had not been a conviction: "It is common knowledge that if an Italian wants to prove an alibi all he has to do is express that desire and he can have a dozen men swear to that effect." [4]

In June, 1906, one of Dimaio's agents reported he had "met the head man of the Society at Youngstown, the most expert member in the use of the knife and who is secretly sought by members for training with the knife." Later the operative met another leader, who "over a bottle of wine" said he was worried about the rumors of arrests to be made among the Italians in Hillsville because "a detective is in our midst." The operative quoted the Mafia chief as vowing "to carve out the heart" of any detective they found, "and no one would be the wiser."

A few days later he was reporting from New Castle about an Italian workman who had

> just been relieved of his pay $60 by Black Hand members. This man had received a threatening letter from these people, and on payday had agreed to turn over his pay check. As soon as he was paid, a representative of the group called promptly for the money. Not satisfied with that, that same night they came to his house and relieved him of an additional $30 at gun point . . . there are a number of people here who were afraid of leaving their homes after dark. . . . I find here the worst sort of Italians, many of whom would not stop at anything to accomplish a purpose . . . most of them are armed and carry six or seven inch blades. . . .

In Hillsville, Dimaio carefully cultivated the friendship of a few residents who were known to have defied—and were either shot at or beaten by—the Mafia. One, a crusher for the Carbon Limestone Company, "an intelligent man," gave Dimaio a list of gunmen at the quarry who were taking paychecks from Italian workmen at gunpoint a few feet from the paymaster's window. A Main Street general-store owner became another informant. In one month, he told Dimaio, he had sold 110 pistols to Mafia enforcers.

As the months passed, Dimaio took part in the social life of Helltown. He professed a bitter hatred for the police, and in turn was accepted by the Society as a former *capo* (leader) from Pittsburgh. His reports, many

times scrawled with the stub of a pencil or murmured to a fellow operative posing as a drummer or streetcar conductor, were sent to Pittsburgh,
where Dimaio and his agents had established a central bureau for Mafia
intelligence, then forwarded to Robert Pinkerton in New York, with
copies to William in Chicago. After a time, he was finally accepted by
Sal Candido, known in the mines as Sam Kennedy, Helltown's popular
young capo. In one report Dimaio told how he had traveled to Youngstown with Candido to "buy baby clothing as he was about to become a
father."

The report shows how Candido met with leaders in the villages and
towns they passed through, getting reports on the tribute extorted from
workers in the quarries. Names of the members of the "Honorable Society," as the Mafia was called, its leaders, and their secret meeting places
were sent to Pittsburgh, along with a description of the terrorist organization. Dimaio wrote:

> The Society, as it is known to its members in the Valley, is gaining
> strength numerically each day. It is generally understood that the So-
> ciety is what is known in Italy as the Mafia. There is so far as I have
> been able to ascertain from the various headmen I have met, nothing
> printed or written relative to the Society. And there are different stories
> told by the headmen as to the formation of the Society and the reason
> for its existence. The so-called Black Hand letters are not the work of
> the Society but likely to be the work of an individual member trying
> to get money for their own use.
>
> The headmen do not approve of these letters and severely punish any
> member using them, not so much because some terrorized family or
> individual might have to pay extortion money upon receiving such a
> letter but because the money so obtained would not come to him.

After he had attended the wedding of a quarryman in the company of
Candido and his entourage of enforcers, "with the day given up for cele-
bration," Dimaio reported on the secret rules of the Society:

> Three grades of punishment [are] sanctioned by the Society. One,
> cutting the face. This is done with a razor. When a member is to be
> punished this way it is done at a meeting, generally a special meeting
> and there is no escape for him. He is expelled and can never become
> a member. The knife scar is regarded as a disgrace.
>
> Two, the one-blow fight. Two members may engage in this fight.
> Buttons are placed on the blades of the knife and only one blow is
> permitted. The idea is to draw blood. A member striking the other in
> the back at any time during the fight is killed immediately by order
> of the Capo.
>
> Three, the fight to the death. This fight is with knives furnished by
> the Capo or head man. If either party to the fight is not experienced

with the knife, the head man can give him up to six months to become
proficient with the knife. If there are no efficient knifemen in the district the Capo can send forth and get the best knife man that can be
had. One man must be killed in this fight. Blows can only be struck on
the body so that the dead man can be taken to his home, placed in bed
and covered up so there can be no signs of a violent death. A certificate
of natural causes is then obtained.

The rules for murder, Dimaio discovered, were simple: If anyone in the
Valley was marked for murder, local knifemen were not used.

> Murderers are borrowed from outside the district and after the crime
> has been committed are given $500 to return to Italy for a visit. The
> member of the Society who refuses to obey the order to kill is himself
> killed.[5]

Half a century later, Dimaio's reports would be echoed in the testimony
of Joe Valachi before a Senate committee.

Once, the local police raided Candido's cellar, where Dimaio and some
of the valley's capos were drinking. The riders were led by Detective
Logan. When he frisked Dimaio, the operative muttered a curse and spat
into Logan's face. Logan knocked Dimaio across the room. Before he
could stagger to his feet, he was handcuffed. In his "isolation cell" Dimaio
whispered a report to Logan, who apologized for the mouse under the
operative's eye. When Dimaio was released, he was "greeted with a party
and much wine drinking. I was a hero after that."

In Helltown, Dimaio discovered a local "school for assassination," as he
called it, run by Jatti, a pupil of Giuseppe Musilino, one of Italy's most
famous outlaws, called "the Jesse James of Calabria." In the fall of 1901,
Musilino was captured by troops who found his mountain hideout, but
Jatti escaped to the United States. He settled for a time in New Orleans,
but after the Hennessy murder fled to New York, and from there came
to the valley, where he settled. To get an eyewitness report of the lurid
"school," Dimaio persuaded Candido to introduce him to Jatti, who invited him to join by paying ten dollars in "dues." At several times Dimaio
was a member of a class in which Jatti taught "the use of the knife." As
Dimaio reported, Jatti had a large collection of daggers, knives, stilettos,
brass knuckles, and lead pipes. Several dressmakers' mannequins, with
vital parts of the body outlined in red ink, were used by Jatti to instruct
his "pupils" in the art of "striking a fatal blow from any position, and
how to slice a cheek in such a way as to leave an indelible scar."

In his memories of those tense, precarious days, Dimaio recalled "two
men I will never forget," Dominico, a young Sicilian who would only be
identified, even years later, as Number 89, and a courageous quarryman,
Nicola Cireiglio, who defied the Mafia when he was ordered to become

a member. He was beaten, and almost killed by "accidents" in the quarry, but still shook his head when asked to "take the oath of the Society."

One night he was lured to the home of a friend, where he found himself surrounded by sixteen men, all Mafia thugs. Again he refused to take the oath. He was forced to his knees while every man spat in his face. "I will not swear," he cried. After a night of torture and indignity, he was released. But he had not taken the oath. Some of the younger members promised to kidnap his wife and child; the woman was to be raped repeatedly, and the infant hacked to pieces and delivered in a box. The local capo told his men to wait, for Cireiglio was to be given his last chance. At the next meeting, he would be asked to swear the oath of the Brotherhood. In desperation, the quarryman sought out, first Logan, who in turn brought him to Dimaio, who urged him to join and become their informant.

"Will you testify in court?" Dimaio asked.

"I will not weaken; they cannot scare me," the quarryman said. Night after night Cieriglio went to bed, waited until his wife fell asleep, then slipped out of his house to meet Logan and Dimaio in the hills above Hillsville.[6]

As the months passed, evidence gathered by Dimaio, Operative 89, and Cireiglio implicated a network of thugs, gunmen enforcers, and dynamiters. Prosecutor Young, Robert Pinkerton, Dimaio, and Detective Logan decided to make mass arrests.

Dimaio's plan was accepted. On payday a new payclerk—a Pinkerton operative—appeared at the paymaster's window. On the wall beside him were the payroll numbers of the men to be arrested for extortion, attempted murder, blackmail, and bombing. When the first man showed his brass check, the Pinkerton operative glanced at his envelope, then said with some surprise: "There's a dollar short in your envelope. I haven't time to straighten it out now, but step into the next room and I'll look it up."

The unsuspecting thug opened the door of the room, "and in a twinkling was relieved of his weapons and handcuffed."

Twenty-eight workers, including Jatti, the master of the knife, were lured into the room and arrested in this fashion. Handcuffed and leg-ironed, they were taken to New Castle in a boxcar guarded by Logan, his detectives, and several armed Pinkertons. Almost overnight, Dimaio's agents reported an exodus of the Mafia leaders. To find their hideouts, Dimaio and his men became the most anti-Pinkerton voices in the valley. They denounced all detectives, and suggested publicly they be killed when uncovered.

"Many, many times," Logan later recalled, "I have seen Number 89 [Dimaio's operative] with a Black Hander's wife at his side, a Black Hander's baby on his arm, go to the post office, get the missing Black Hander's mail, and read it to the woman. Many a time he has shaken his fist under my nose and cursed me in the choicest Italian." [7]

Through Dimaio and his men, Robert Pinkerton in New York and William in Chicago "knew what leaders were trying to return to Italy and on what boats they intended to sail. They knew, too, what leaders were in hiding anywhere along the underground of railroad which reaches from Cleveland to Baltimore."

After a long, sensational trial, thirty-three Mafia capos and enforcers were found guilty, and received sentences from three to ten years in the Western Penitentiary. When the time came, Cireiglio had not weakened. Despite threats and bribes, he testified for the state, along with numerous other witnesses recruited by Dimaio and Logan.

On March 6, 1906, State Game Warden Seely Houk, who had gained the enmity of the Mafia for his poaching arrests, disappeared. Rumors had him murdered by the Mafia, but local police were stalemated. They could not find a corpse. The community was terrorized. On April 24th, the thawing Mahoning River yielded up Houk's body; most of his head had been blasted away by a shotgun. Though vigilante talk in the quarry towns flared up, it soon fizzled out. As usual, quarry workers shrugged off questions of the police or refused to testify before grand juries. When the Pennsylvania State Game Commission announced that it had no funds to start an investigation of Houk's murder, a group of wealthy Pennsylvania sportsmen retained the Pinkertons. Dimaio was summoned from Columbus to attend a meeting in New York with Robert and William Pinkerton.[8]

Dimaio insisted that the killer of Houk was among the Mafia gunmen already in the penitentiary, and he maintained that there was one weaker than the others, like Politz in the Hennessy investigation, who could be broken. Dimaio went over each name for the Pinkertons, citing background, police records, underworld activity, and family life. It was finally decided that Candido, the youngest prisoner, whose wife had recently given birth to a son, might break. It was also agreed that Dimaio should reveal his "cover" and confront Candido in prison. Before he visited Western Penitentiary, Dimaio found Candido's wife and took her and her newborn son to a New Castle photographer for a series of pictures of the infant. He also wrote a letter in Italian for the woman, which she signed.

The confrontation took place in a private office of the warden's headquarters. Candido, who was only in his early twenties, denounced and cursed Dimaio as an informer after Dimaio disclosed he was a Pinkerton operative.

"I let him curse me and scream at me," Dimaio said. "When he was exhausted I gave him his wife's letter and dropped the first of the photographs of his child on the table. Then I walked out. The next day I did the same thing. I never discussed the Houk murder. I talked about everything else. At the end of each visit I gave him a cigar and dropped another photograph of his child. Then one day he began asking questions about his son and admiringly showed off the pictures. Day after day I dropped a picture and described elaborately what a fine boy he had and what a beautiful woman he had married. It was like twisting a knife in his heart. After a week I knew he would break. He first started to talk to me about how I could help him.

"I made no promises; in fact at first I just shrugged it off. But when he said, 'Dimaio, you help me and I'll help you,' I went to District Attorney Young and got his agreement; he would get leniency for Candido if he named the murderers."

A week passed. In May, 1908, Dimaio received a letter from Candido:

> Come to prison to see me. I have the facts. The murder was committed by Rocco Racco and Jim Murdocca. There was another person there when they killed him. In order to get this information I had to take three oaths. I am so afraid I cannot eat. Please come at once.[9]

As Dimaio recalled, "I went to the prison as fast as a buggy could get me there," and saw Candido in the warden's office. Candido was trembling and white-faced. He silently handed Dimaio a note writen on a scrap of sugar bag. It was from another prisoner, Surace, a Hillsville capo, warning him, "The Raven [Dimaio] was here and he wants to know about the affair. Don't tell him." The letter was signed by a secret symbol.

"Candido fell to his knees, begging me never to reveal he had been an informer. Then he told me to tear up the note, which I did. But he made me tear it into smaller pieces which he threw in the warden's scrap basket. Then, in the presence of the warden, he told the story of the Houk murder."

Rocca Racco, another capo, he said, had shot Houk with the help of his brother-in-law, Jim Murdocca, who had fled to Italy before the earlier roundup of the Mafia. The murder had taken place after Houk had shot Racco's favorite hunting dog, which he had lent to a friend. Houk had warned Racco he would shoot his dog if he caught him hunting out of season. Racco and Murdocca weighted the body with stones, and with the help of a young quarry worker had thrown the corpse into the river. Racco's wife, Candido said, was hiding the shotgun that had killed Houk.

After Candido had left, Dimaio emptied the wastebasket and collected the tiny scraps of the sugar-bag note. He spent most of the night pasting it together, then returned to the prison to confront Surace, who had written the note.

Surace refused to talk. "I am of the Society," he said. "I will not be a spy."

When Dimaio showed him the note he leaped up, shouting that he had been betrayed. To protect Candido, the warden and Dimaio told Surace that a guard had seen Candido reading the note and had forced the paper out of his mouth when Candido tried to swallow it. Dimaio pointed out to Surace that the note now implicated him in the murder investigation. Surace kept shaking his head, repeating: "I am of the Society. I will not be a spy."

Then Dimaio leaned over and whispered, "Monte Albano." [10]

Surace looked up, startled. "You know of the Society?" he asked.

"I know all your secrets," Dimaio replied.

Surace, trembling, said, "They will kill me if I speak." Dimaio answered, "It is better to speak than to die on the gallows."

There was a long moment of silence; then Surace said hesitantly: "I will tell you all about it. Racco came to me and said, 'I got a sin on my conscience; I want to confess it to you but you will have to swear never to tell it to anyone.' I took the oath. Then Racco, very pale in the face, told me how he and Murdocca killed Houk."

Surace, in his signed confession, said Racco and his brother-in-law had attracted the attention of Houk by firing several shots. The game warden, on the alert for out-of-season hunters, appeared, and was killed. "When he is not drinking, Racco is a saint," Surace told Dimaio, "but when drinking, he is a regular devil, and it was seldom he did not drink."

Once he started talking, Surace revealed all he knew, and his statement required many pages. In addition to the Houk murders, he named the killers of Squire Duff, a local Hillsville official, and the men who had attacked and almost slashed to death a quarry foreman. He also agreed to confront other members of the Mafia in jail who had heard Racco tell of the Houk murder or who knew some of the details. Dimaio reported to Robert Pinkerton:

> Surace was brought to the warden's office to face Giuseppe Cutroneo after the prisoner had adamantly denied he knew anything about the Houk murder. When Surace appeared I stared at him, and never taking my eyes off his face I said, "Giuseppe Cutroneo states here and now he never had any conversation with Rocco Racco about the murder of Houk."
>
> Surace looked at me, then swung about to face the other prisoner, who started to tremble. He gave the sign of the Society to Cutroneo, the same sign which I had given him to persuade him to talk. And then immediately upon receiving the sign, Cutroneo told us how Racco had boasted to him he had killed Houk.[11]

But some of the Mafia refused to break, sign or no sign:

> Another member of the Society, Michael Portolese, was brought into the warden's office to face Surace, but Portolese, even after Surace gave him the sign, said: "I do not care what the others have said or what I know they have said; I do propose to have my soul free from any tarnish [sic] whatever for sending a man to the gallows."

Surace said, pointing to me, "This man is a Pinkerton detective. What is the use of denying that he already knows? An envelope he has in his hands contains the statements of not only myself but other inmates of this prison. It is useless of us to deny any further that Racco did not tell you about the killing of Houk." But Portolese just shook his head and refused to talk.

Dimaio now had three statements, but they were at second hand, and could easily be denied. He needed corroboration. He had to get the shotgun from Racco's wife, and locate the young Italian quarry worker who had helped Racco and Murdocca carry Houk's stone-weighted body to the river. Two more important witnesses to be found were the man who had borrowed Racco's dog, had seen it shot by Houk, and had heard Racco swear he would kill the game warden, "like the dog that he killed," and Mrs. Surace, who had heard Racco describe how he had killed Houk and disposed of his body only a short time after the shooting.

"My wife is somewhere in Buffalo, New York," Surace told Dimaio, "where, I do not know."

Dimaio started with Mrs. Racco. After weeks of searching the villages, he found the frightened woman, lying on the bed, "praying to St. Rocco." Dimaio visited the woman daily, escorting her to the stores, speaking only in Italian, accompanying her to church, and writing letters to her relatives in Italy and her husband in jail. Requests to see her husband's shotgun were answered with shrugs and blank looks. Dimaio was about to give up when he drove Mrs. Racco in a buggy to a pawnshop. He became indignant when he walked inside the shop and found the broker trying to cheat the woman. After threatening to go to Prosecutor Young, he forced the pawnbroker to pay Mrs. Racco a fair price for the jewelry she was selling. Dimaio then drove the woman home. After telling him to wait, she came out of the house and silently handed him a heavy paper-wrapped parcel: the shotgun.

Dimaio returned to the prison, where, "hinting" that he was investigating a poaching case, he showed Racco the weapon. The naïve Mafia leader quickly identified it: "I know it's mine. I know it by the left-handed trigger that works loosely." In Buffalo, teams of Pinkerton operatives searched for Mrs. Surace; then came the telegram that she had been located. Dimaio returned to Hillsville. this time as the Pinkerton operative who had broken the Mafia. In a crowded saloon he stood on a chair to announce: "The Society is dead in the quarries. There will be no more extortions, no more beatings, no more murders if you help me. If you know anything about the murder of Game Warden Houk, come and talk to me."

One of the first to come to him was the local "knifeman" who had boasted to Dimaio's agent months before how he would carve out the heart of any man who betrayed "the Society." He voluntarily signed a

statement describing how Racco told of killing Houk. Dimaio next
found and obtained a statement from the hunter who had borrowed
Racco's dog and obtained a statement from him and from the young
quarry worker who helped him to dispose of the body. Piece by piece,
statement by statement, Dimaio built a case of first-degree murder against
Racco.

"My heart was in my throat every time I walked down a dark street,"
Dimaio recalled. "True, the Mafia big shots were in jail, but the Society was still strong in the fields. Friends warned me they had put a price
on the head of The Raven, as they called me, and every morning I woke
up wondering who was going to try to collect it."

The Agency turned over Dimaio's evidence to District Attorney Young,
who indicted Racco for the Houk murder. Dimaio visited the Mafia
boss in prison many times, pleading with him to implicate Murdocca and
force his extradition. But the short, squat killer only shook his head.

"I will never betray the Society," he told Dimaio. "I will go to the
gallows with my lips sealed."

The New Castle, Pennsylvania, trial of Racco gained national attention when District Attorney Young charged that Mafia gunmen from
New York, Youngstown and Columbus, Ohio, were threatening to kill
witnesses. "Every day I had to buck up our witnesses," Dimaio said.
"All they had to do was see someone in a crowd on the way to court make
the sign of the knife, and they would fall apart. It is really difficult to
know the terror the Society can impose unless you have witnessed it at
first hand."

Surace and others did testify, "swearing on a crucifix." Racco was
convicted and sentenced to hang. Dimaio saw the Mafia boss almost
every day in the condemned cell, but Racco still refused to name Murdocca as the comurderer of Houk.

On a fall morning in 1909, Racco was hanged in the New Castle jail
after the higher courts, including the Supreme Court, refused to reverse
his conviction.[12]

That year saw the collapse of the Mafia in the valley. "Almost daily,
informers came to Young's office," Dimaio remembered. "Murders, assaults, and bombings were solved; and, as I recall, two more Mafia enforcers were executed, and many were sent to prison. After that, there was
a general exodus, and the Society died out."

BOOK 10
The
Undesirable
Citizens

CHAPTER 36

The Murder of Former Govenor Steunenberg of Idaho

In the first decade of the twentieth century, crime was becoming sophisticated. Groups of skilled forgers, embezzlers, and counterfeiters preyed on banks, investment firms, or diamond exchanges. In addition to their extensive Rogues' Gallery and Bertillon files, the Pinkertons had established central bureaus in Chicago and New York to help police departments solve forgeries. Both bureaus contained files of thousands of forgeries classified by groups, so that handwriting experts could pinpoint the gang or individual forger by a sample of the "tracing." By 1900, most American and European police departments were sending samples of forgeries to the two bureaus to be identified, just as present-day law-enforcement agencies depend on the massive files of the Federal Bureau of Investigation.

At the turn of the century, Robert wrote in a weary tone to a friend: "One day we are in a little country village in Maine or Canada, the following month in Havana. There never seems to be an end to man's criminal enterprises. . . ."

Robert may have had in mind the case of William Walter Taylor, state treasurer of South Dakota, who absconded with the state's treasury of $300,000. It was not unusual in this period for states with no central law-enforcement agency, such as the modern state police, to retain the Agency in major criminal cases. The governor hired Pinkerton's when several prominent citizens who had signed Taylor's bond faced financial bankruptcy.

The case was so important, Robert wired to William, that he decided to go after the state official himself. Pinkerton trailed Taylor across the West to Florida, then to Havana, and finally to Vera Cruz, Mexico, where he arrested the fugitive in a small hotel. The money was returned. Before he hung up his guns and "let younger men do the chasing," Robert trailed a well-known New York "man about town," as the New York *World called* him, who had fled with his bank's funds, to Spanish Honduras. Despite an epidemic of yellow fever that was sweeping the native villages of the interior, Pinkerton went into the jungle alone, found his man, recovered the money, and returned prisoner and cash to New York. Robert contracted the fever, and was seriously ill for months.

In the late 1890's and early 1900's, the Pinkertons concentrated on aspects of the Agency's business that eventually brought large profits into the firm. In New York, they developed Pinkerton's Electric Protective Company, a pioneering burglar-alarm system. In New York and Chicago, merchant houses, banks, and express companies were connected to the Pinkerton main office. As one contemporary account pointed out: "After the closing of these places electric connection is made with the safes, vault doors and windows, and the least touch on them will ring a bell in the Pinkerton's office, where a squad of men is daily and nightly kept in reserve." [1]

Another system perfected by the agency, and used in most large American cities of the time, was the armed wagon. The especially built, reinforced wagon—forerunner of today's armored truck—was guarded by Pinkerton men carrying six-shooters and Winchesters. The lumbering wagons were used principally to transfer payrolls from banks to plants, and were a familiar sight in New York City's financial districts.

By 1900, William and Robert were familiar in London, Paris, Havana, Rome, and Constantinople. Foreign governments asked their advice in reorganizing police departments, and there were always letters from Scotland Yard or the Sûreté, seeking assistance in apprehending international thieves. For both Pinkertons, the Agency was still their whole life. Vacations in Saratoga or Paris inevitably were spent with one eye on the sights, the other seeking out crime or criminals. As William told the International Police Chiefs at their Washington convention of 1905:

> One day last Fall, while my brother Robert and I were strolling in a public park in Nice, France, we observed a man in gold cap and knee breeches, who, at a distance, looked like an English tourist, but who, upon coming closer to him, my brother recognized as Becker's [Charles Becker, the famous international forger of the 1890's] adroit middleman, James Cregan, who is eking out a precarious existence in Europe, and who assured us that he has forsaken criminal work. [2]

One day in a London tailor shop, William Pinkerton idly glanced out the window. In a moment he was gone, leaving behind two surprised tailors. The detective had seen an international forger in the passing crowd; he tailed him to his boardinghouse, and notified Scotland Yard. The forger and his gang were later arrested, and a major robbery was prevented. As Robert recalled, his brother returned to the shop, and apologized to the tailors, who went back to taking his measurements.

Little is known of Robert's and William's families. Wives and children were never mentioned in their letters, only crime, criminals, and business. William's wife, the former Margaret Ashland of Chicago, whom he had married in 1866, died in 1895. With his two daughters married, he devoted most of his waking hours to his business. The old Pinkerton homestead at 196 Ashland Boulevard, Chicago, huge and empty, was occupied only by William and a servant. He was a familiar figure in Chicago as he walked from his office on Fifth Avenue to his home in the evening. The Chicago *Observer* saw him as "America's leading detective, the man through whose medium you may know the exact wealth of Li Hung Chang, how much your clerk bet on the election, or what African jungle hides the clerk who ruined the bank of Timbuctoo. His methods, though effective, are painfully matter-of-fact. . . ."

In New York, Robert and his family lived on Brooklyn's Eighth Avenue in what the New York *World* once called "the handsomest mansion in Brooklyn." His wife, the former Elizabeth Hughes of Denver, was a member of an old and prominent western family. She was the sister of Thomas P. Hughes, president of the Colorado Lead Works, and Hendrick Hughes, manager of the famous Keeley Institute of Denver. Robert's two daughters had also married into wealth and position in society: Mrs. Louis Gibb, whose husband was senior member of the lace importing firm of Mills & Gibb, and Mrs. J. Carlisle, whose husband represented the sugar trust on the New York Stock Exchange. The only surviving male Pinkerton, Robert's son, Allan II—of whom his grandfather had once written, "I hope he is worthy of the name"—was brought into the firm in 1896.

As Robert solemnly informed his son, he was "entering service." Robert and William, recalling their own apprenticeships, started Allan as a clerk "to work his way up to learn the business." For several years, the youngest Pinkerton moved about the various branch offices across the country to serve under the famous superintendents, James McParland, David C. Thornhill, George D. Bangs, and others.

Both William and Robert allotted as many hours of a day or night to the Agency's business as possible. William's only form of relaxation was his horses and dogs, "a whole yard of them." The Chicago *Tribune* observed, "He has a fondness for animals to a marked degree." If he went to the theatre, it was a musical comedy, nothing cerebral. One doubts that Robert or William ever bought a work of fiction or poetry. Their letters indicate their reading was confined exclusively to reports of internal business matters, investigations, law-enforcement bulletins, and the daily newspapers. Both William and Robert loved the track, and the only time they grudgingly spared from their business was to attend the races. They were now wealthy men.

Allan Pinkerton's daughter, Joan, then a striking gray-haired matron, was a Chicago society leader, and from newspaper accounts of the time, a busy charity worker. Her father would have been startled to learn that "young Chalmers," who he had predicted at best would be a clerk in his father's countinghouse, had become one of the most important industrialists in the Midwest. In all their letters, from the 1880's to their death, the Pinkertons maintained a curious "Dear Sir" salutation, yet we find a telegram from Robert to the Chicago office: "Don't forget roses for Willie on his birthday."

In 1900, William was forty-four, Robert two years younger. The days in the saddle, chasing outlaws or plodding through jungles on muleback, trailing a bank embezzler, lay in the past. Both were deskbound, content to direct operations from Chicago and New York. Each private office reflected their characteristics. Robert's was neat and businesslike; William's, a hodgepodge of pictures of notables—mostly politicians, sheriffs and marshals, prize-winning dogs, favorite racehorses—and a rolltop desk with bursting pigeonholes. Both were putting on weight, and both had thick black Corsican bandit moustaches. Their Agency was now Big Business, and their political philosophies were decidedly conservative. Before the Homestead Strike of 1892, American labor had viewed the Agency with hostility. By the turn of the century, even though the Pinkertons had adopted a policy of refusing to supply watchmen in strikebound plants, labor still considered them an enemy.

In January, 1906, the Pinkertons were retained by the State of Idaho to solve the murder of former Governor Frank Steunenberg, who had been horribly mangled by a dynamite bomb attached to the gate of his home in Caldwell. The killing was believed to be in retaliation for the occasion when Steunenberg asked President McKinley to send federal troops to restore order after a mob of striking miners had left the huge works at Wardner a flaming ruin. This was not the Agency's first experience in the tough mining country. In 1892, Charlie Siringo, Pinkerton's "cowboy-detective," was sent into the Coeur d'Alene district to alert mineowners for acts of sabotage. Before that, an undercover operative for another detective agency had been discovered, and barely escaped being beaten to death. Siringo joined the miners' union and became its recording secretary. Through a series of reports that he smuggled out of Gem, a mining camp of three stores and six saloons supplying the famous Gem, Helen Frisco, and Black Bear mines, Siringo forestalled some of the bombings and murder plots. However, he was finally recognized, and

Pinkerton detectives James McParland (left) and Charles A. Siringo in Denver at the time of the Steunenberg case. *Pinkerton's, Inc.*

William A. Pinkerton in his Chicago office at the time of the Steunenberg case. *Pinkerton's, Inc.*

after a thrilling manhunt, escaped a mob of miners who intended to "burn him at the stake, as an example of what we do to Pinkerton detectives." [3]

The Pinkertons' reentry into the Idaho mining wars would result in an almost unbelievable tale of professional murder and arson—and one of the most interesting and important trials in the history of American jurisprudence, a trial whose ramifications would be felt for decades in this country's labor movement. The investigation would last two years, with the Pinkertons once again in a whirlwind of controversy, pictured once again as union busters, protectors of scab labor, tools of the capitalists, or defenders of the Republic, shrewd and brilliant detectives, and incorruptible Americans.

Governor Steunenberg's murder came as a climax to the war between the mining unions and the mine operators. For years both sides had indulged in a number of savage acts. The union miners bombed, shot, and mutilated nonunion workers in Colorado, Utah, Nevada, and Idaho mines. The operations in the MOA—Mine Owners Association—paid dismal wages, refused to adopt safety measures, and used their political strength to influence local and state officials to crush the unions. Like the governors of his sister states, Steunenberg had called in troops to restore order in strikebound areas. In doing so, he earned the undying hatred of the WFM—Western Federation of Miners. As James McParland said bluntly, "After he had called in the troops, Governor Steunenberg was a marked man."

How the miners felt about Steunenberg is reflected in a description of his murder that appeared in the federation's magazine, ironically called *Humanity*: "Former Governor Frank Steunenberg of Idaho met his death last Saturday night at his home in Caldwell, Idaho. The press dispatches report his dissolution via the bomb route."

The impact of the former state executives murder was reflected in editorial pages from New York to the West Coast, particularly in the mining country, where the larger newspapers charged that Steunenberg had been murdered at the instigation of, if not personally by, the leaders of the Western Federation of Miners.

The responsibility of solving the killing rested on the local sheriff, who carefully gathered the remnants of the bomb and took the first elementary investigative steps, while numbed state officials made plans to bury the genial, popular son of Holland immigrants, who twice had been elected governor by large majorities.

On New Year's Day, 1906, a capricious fate brought Sheriff Harvey K. Brown of Baker County, Oregon, to Caldwell on other matters. As he walked down the street, Brown, an old-time miner, passed the Saratoga Hotel and caught a glimpse of a man standing outside. Brown sought out Idaho Sheriff Mosely of Canyon County, who was in charge of the investigation.

"I know that fellow," Brown said. "He says his name is Hogan but it isn't. He is Harry Orchard who used to be active in the miners' union in the Coeur d'Alene."

Mosely and his deputies searched Orchard's room while he was out "selling insurance" as Thomas Hogan, and found traces of bomb material and a short piece of fishline that matched the type found on the gate where the bomb had exploded. In Orchard's grip was a trunk check. The officers hurried to the Caldwell depot and opened the trunk: It contained dynamite, a sawed-off shotgun, and a collection of what the local newspapers described as "burglars' tools."

Despite this evidence, Orchard, who insisted that his name was Thomas Hogan, was not arrested; Mosely's only restraint was to tell Orchard not to leave his hotel room. The following day, Orchard strolled into a meeting of the local Citizens' Committee formed by the indignant people of Caldwell to demand action. Incredible as it may seem, he asked for, and was given, an opportunity to address the group "because I understand I am under suspicion and want to clear myself."

He was undoubtedly persuasive, because he left the meeting a free man, strolled back to his hotel, and remained there all day. It was not until late that afternoon that Mosely decided Orchard was a good suspect; so he also strolled over to the hotel, told Orchard he was under arrest, and both men walked to the Caldwell jail.

The next morning Caldwell was deserted, for the townspeople were following the cortege of the man they had sent to the constitutional convention and helped to elect as representative to the first legislative assembly after Idaho became a state in 1890.

Flags flew at half-mast throughout Idaho, and schools and state offices were closed. The funeral was the most impressive the state had ever known. Attorney William E. Borah, soon to make his mark in the United States Senate, delivered the funeral oration; his strong, clear voice sketched Steunenberg's career, "the rarest of men . . . a man of granite hewn . . ." But Borah sensed the groundswell of fear and apprehension that was rolling over the state, making every stranger a potential member of the anarchist, radical unions that had murdered Steunenberg. It is to Borah's lasting credit that he took that somber moment to caution every citizen not to point the finger of guilt "at any class or any portion of our citizens" until evidence had been collected.

"The crime when fastened upon its author, will place him or them beyond the pale of human forgiveness or pity," he told the grim-faced mourners in the Caldwell Cemetery. "Therefore let us not place it unjustly or upon suspicion. Let us not believe it to be the crime of any class or any portion of our citizens or that it finds sympathy with anyone other than the actual perpetrator. . . ." [4]

The press, particularly in the western section of the nation, ignored Borah's words of caution; their editorials continued to charge the Western Federation of Miners with hiring Orchard to commit the murder.

The first detective on the scene was Captain Swain of the Thiel Detective Agency, owned by G. H. Thiel, who had been an operative for Allan Pinkerton in the Civil War and had worked for him in Chicago.

Swain told Idaho's Governor Frank R. Gooding that he had been retained by the Mine Owners Association. Chief Justice E. C. Stockslager, of Idaho's Supreme Court, meanwhile had drafted a telegram to General Superintendent James Nevins of Pinkerton's office in Portland.

Gooding, not wanting to offend the mineowners, hesitated, and the telegram was not sent. On the afternoon of January 4th, the day following Steunenberg's funeral, Swain's assistant informed Superintendent Taber of the Portland office that their client, presumably the mineowners, wanted the Pinkertons to work with Thiel's Agency. Telegrams flew back and forth between William and Robert Pinkerton. Portland was bluntly told that the Agency would work on the case—but only independently. Assistant Superintendent Hasson was sent to Boise to interview Governor Gooding, to ascertain if the state was formally asking the Agency to take part in the Steunenberg murder investigation.

In Boise, Hasson saw Governor Gooding and Chief Justice Stockslager. When the Chief Justice insisted that the Pinkertons be brought into the case, the governor finally agreed. Hasson drew up a contract in which the state agreed to pay the Agency $8 a day for thirty days, after which the rate was reduced to $6. Hasson, "in order to meet competition from the Swain people," had broken the Agency's firm rule of never reducing its set fee. He would hear about his infraction in the weeks to come.

The letters and telegrams exchanged during the following weeks between the Pinkertons, James McParland, then manager of the Agency's Western Division; Governor Gooding, and James Nevins, Portland's general superintendent, give a fascinating insight into the influence and power of the Agency at the time, how it took over a murder case of national importance, eased out its competitors, and then lobbied and jockeyed its way through local politics to carry out its strategy, and finally produce a terrifying confession of professional cold-blooded murder.[5]

After Assistant Superintendent Hasson had been in Idaho for a few days with an undercover operative known only as Number 9, Governor Gooding requested William Pinkerton to send on McParland from Denver. On the afternoon of January 7th, William ordered McParland to Boise to confer with the governor. It was Sunday, and McParland didn't leave Denver until the following evening. Before he left, he sent General Superintendent Nevins a letter explaining his delay, with copies forwarded to William and Robert Pinkerton: "I am highly pleased to note we have been employed on this case although I am afraid that if Swain is still retained in this matter he will be a stumbling block in our path. I will have to take this up with Governor Gooding and Judge Stockslager upon my arrival."

McParland's letter also reveals his philosophy—undoubtedly filtered down from headquarters in both New York and Chicago—that free enterprise could be just as important as justice:

> This is one of the most important operations ever undertaken in the Portland District, and if through our offices we are successful, it will mean a great deal to the Spokane office so far as the mine operators are concerned, in fact all mine operators in the whole district.

McParland arrived in Boise on the tenth, and was met by Hasson and Chief Justice Stockslager. Before dinner, McParland was filled in by Hasson, who told him that Swain of the Thiel Agency had taken over the investigation, with "a number of men in and around Caldwell, all of whom were known to the public." Hasson told McParland that after Swain had demanded copies of his reports, he had gone to the governor and had given him William Pinkerton's direct orders. While the Agency had no objection to Swain working on the case, "still we objected to reporting to him verbally, or to showing him our reports, or otherwise to any other person except the governor."

After this meeting with Gooding, Hasson said, the governor asked that McParland be summoned. A minor, but illuminating, incident took place at the meeting of McParland and Hasson. One of the first things McParland asked Hasson was what kind of "guarantee" he had got from Governor Gooding. The assistant superintendent told him he had the state signed up for $8 a day per operative for thirty days, and $6 per day thereafter. McParland was furious that the Agency's standard rates had been reduced by Hasson without consultation with New York. The harassed Hasson, who had been working day and night bucking Captain Swain's platoon of detectives, explained that he had had to sign up the governor to beat off the competition of the Thiel Agency. In a letter to Portland, McParland curtly demanded that Hasson be "censured" for offering a reduced rate.

After dinner that night, McParland met with Chief Justice Stockslager and Governor Gooding. McParland reported to William and Robert Pinkerton:

> The governor wanted us to work in conjunction with Swain. This I refused to do, telling him we would not do such a thing. We were willing he should continue to retain Swain or anyone else, but if he continued our service he must not show our reports to anyone else save Judge Stockslager or the attorneys for the prosecution and only to the latter when the proper time arrived. Neither did we want to see the reports of the Thiel men, now engaged on the case, that we would work independent or would not work at all.

At this point, Judge Stockslager broke in to tell the governor: "Governor, I told you, you might as well try to remove Plymouth Rock as to change the established rules of the Pinkertons. Their plans are right. Look at the information you have received in the fine reports of Mr. Hasson who has only got on the ground as it were."

"The governor is a strong willed man, as well as strong physically," McParland wrote. "He studied me for as much as five minutes, then said, 'I will accept your proposition. You will work on the same line as Swain but you must stay with us for a week or ten days until we get started. Don't take expense into consideration.' " [6]

While McParland talked to the governor and his chief justice, Captain Swain fumed below in the hotel's lobby. Gooding told McParland he was going to call up Swain and have him sit in on the conference, but the judge warned him, "McParland will walk out."

William's wry observation to Robert was, "The judge was right."

On the following day McParland and Hasson visited the state chemists' shop, and were shown the material taken from Orchard's room and trunk—certainly strong circumstantial evidence: Three sticks of dynamite, a sawed-off shotgun, dynamiters' tools, and a length of fishline matching the kind used to trip off the bomb that had mangled the ex-governor when he had opened his front gate.

"It looks as though Orchard can be convicted and no doubt as to his guilt," McParland wrote to William and Robert. "What is wanted is the parties who instigated him to commit the crime. After the preliminaries he will be brought down to Boise where I will make an effort to break him down."

On January 12th McParland met again with Governor Gooding, who told him that the sheriff at Caldwell was insisting on keeping Orchard in the Caldwell jail after his arraignment, instead of shipping him to the state penitentiary at Boise. The sheriff was supported by a local political power, Judge Frank Smith of the Caldwell District Court. Smith had informed Gooding that "there were a number of citizens of Caldwell who opposed any transfer of the prisoner to Boise, on the grounds it would look as though the people of Caldwell could not take care of him, and still another class who wanted jobs as jail guards."

Gooding, who apparently didn't want to tangle with Smith, asked McParland to see the judge. As McParland reported to New York and Chicago: "He [Gooding] would fetch him [Judge Smith] to my room and he [Gooding] would have it arranged to be called downstairs and leave me to labor with the judge and get him to consent to use his influence with the sheriff to have him fetch the prisoner to Boise after the prisoner had been committed for trial, and to further get the judge to agree not to issue a writ of Habeas Corpus." [7]

McParland was now not only a local political diplomat but also an arranger of justice. From his report to the Pinkertons, McParland evidently was uneasy about this frontier political lobbying, and protested to Gooding that either he "or one of Smith's fellow jurists try to persuade him," but the state executive waved him aside. "He told me he had consulted with Justice Stockslager and he said I was the man to persuade Judge Smith, so I agreed to do the best I could."

The flimsy playacting took place in the rough hotel room, with the governor of the state leaving the room after a prearranged call by a bellboy. When McParland suggested to Smith that Orchard be transferred to Boise, Smith lighted a cigar and asked him bluntly why Orchard should be transferred. Didn't McParland believe the citizens of Caldwell could guard a dynamiter? Smith also reminded McParland that once the move was made, the defense attorneys would file a writ of habeas corpus, "and he would have to grant it and discharge the prisoner."

This was dangerous ground, and McParland knew it. The governor had left, and Smith was obviously nettled. The detective was about to reply when he saw the judge studying his lapel.

"I see you're an Elk, McParland," Smith said.

"So is the governor," McParland replied, "and I never forget my obligation to the Order to use it in any way to forward my plans."

Then Judge Smith asked him if he knew Swain. McParland, still tiptoeing, said he did. McParland reported Smith's reply as: "Old Swain had butted in this case, and he has brought a gang of the dirtiest, low-lived sons of bitches to Caldwell posing as detectives as ever congregated in one place."

McParland, as he reported, knew he was on "good ground," and began questioning Judge Smith about Swain, who called the other detective "a poser" for the newspaper reporters. Smith then revealed that a committee of Caldwell citizens had called on the county commissioners to get rid of Swain, who claimed he had twelve detectives working in the fields, gathering evidence at the rate of $150 a day. The commissioners voted to pay Swain $1,000 and to ask him to leave. A letter had been sent to the governor by the commissioners, advising him they had dismissed Swain. That letter had arrived on the same train that had brought Smith from Caldwell to Boise, the judge informed McParland. McParland wrote to the Pinkertons:

"He charged me not to say anything to the governor about this, but he was sure the governor would advise me as soon as he had received the letter from Caldwell."

The ice was now broken by their mutual dislike of Swain. Judge Smith selected another cigar, and asked McParland to outline his reasons for transferring Orchard to the state pen at Boise. McParland then gave his reasons; he repeated them in his formal report to New York and Chicago:

> First. The jail at Caldwell is insecure. The guard could get careless, and the prisoner having such a strong following, financially and otherwise, might make his escape either by bribery or by having some friends on the outside bribe the guard, or get on friendly terms with them, so they could assist the prisoner to escape by furnishing him the means to do so without being suspected.
>
> Second. Failing to effect his escape in the above mentioned manner, he being the key to the conspiracy and seeing that he was doomed was liable to confess. To prevent this his friends would not hesitate to remove him by either poison or even dynamiting the jail.
>
> Third. Remove him to the penitentiary. Place him in a cell in Murderers Row. (There are two murderers confined there now waiting execution on which the death watch is now placed.) Place guards who

will watch him day and night, who will never take their eyes off
him, either day or night—at the same time never speaking to him, nor
to allow him any visitors except his lawyer. Keep the death watch on
him for about three days and nights after which I will make an
attempt to get a confession from him and hope to succeed but am not
very sanguine.[8]

Whether it was because of the Elks pin, their mutual dislike of Detective Swain, or commonsense reasons, Smith agreed that Orchard should
be removed from Caldwell to Boise Penitentiary. In addition, he promised McParland "he would not issue a writ of habeas corpus unless directed to do so by the Idaho Supreme Court." To guarantee doubly that
the writ would not be issued, Smith urged McParland to have Governor
Gooding "take up the matter with the [Supreme] court."

After a few hours' sleep, McParland called on Gooding at the state
capitol. Together they visited Chief Justice Stockslager, who had originally urged Gooding to retain the Pinkertons, and Justice Sullivan of the
Idaho Supreme Court, and "both agreed that it was perfectly legal to remove the prisoner to the Penitentiary and would sustain Judge Smith in
denying a writ of Habeas Corpus." It was frontier law again.

Three days later Orchard was transferred to the state penitentiary at
Boise and placed in a cell on Death Row. McParland's suggestions were
carried out. Guards peered in at Orchard day and night. They never
spoke, ignoring his questions. His meals were handed to him in silence.
He was given no reading matter. Then one day a tight-lipped guard escorted him to the office of Warden Whitney, where a stranger sat to one
side of the warden's desk. The warden said the stranger wanted to talk
to Orchard, and left the two men alone.

The man facing Orchard was sprucely dressed, about sixty. He had a
fine walrus moustache, wore gold-rimmed spectacles, and carried a heavy
black walking cane. His gray hair, which still held a tinge of red, was
thinning. His face, with its unmistakable Irish stamp, was oddly youth-
ful, but his eyes were cool and searching. Orchard and McParland talked
from two thirty to five thirty. Orchard told the detective he was comfortable, and asked McParland why he wanted to see him. The detective
quietly told Orchard that he was not interested in him as a criminal but
that he represented law and order. He had come, he said, "not to find
out whether he was guilty, and we had positive proof and would hang
him, but as he was but the tool of the inner circle, the hanging of him
would be little satisfaction and (since he was only a tool), he, to a great
extent, had my sympathy."

Then McParland began to talk of the Molly Maguires. Suddenly, Orchard recalled that "this gentle old man" was none other than the famous
Jim McParland.

"You're James McParland of the Pinkertons, aren't you?" he asked.

"I am. And I have come to give you some good advice," McParland replied.

Orchard replied he didn't need any advice, especially from a detective, but McParland ignored the blunt refusal and went on to talk about God and the glory of Heaven. Orchard, one of history's most cold-blooded professional murderers, said he was only vaguely aware of God but knew *He* was there. McParland gave him a kindly tap on the shoulder, and left.

The next day the meeting was repeated. This time Orchard, now curious, demanded that McParland show his Elks card. There is little doubt that Orchard was somewhat awed. McParland's reputation after the Molly Maguires trial had followed him west.

Orchard, almost at once, asked McParland why he had not put the finger on Thomas Hurley, one of the fugitive Mollies supposedly in the Gunnison jail on a minor charge.

"Because Hurley was a tool of Jack Kehoe as you are of Haywood," was McParland's reply.[9]

This was the key to McParland's strategy. Together with the officials of Idaho and Colorado, he believed Orchard was the hired assassin for the inner circle of the Western Federation of Miners, William ("Big Bill") Haywood, George A. Pettibone, and Charles H. Moyer.[10]

The Western Federation of Miners, an industrial union, broke away from the AFL in 1897 because it was too moderate. It conducted a series of strikes in the silver, copper, gold, and lead mines that culminated in the Cripple Creek strike of 1903–1904, one of the nation's bloodiest. Both sides resorted to violence as a matter of course. The miners used dynamiters and rifle teams, while the owners used the state militia, armed strikebreakers, and vigilantes. Mine explosions, shotgun killings on the streets of western towns, and train derailments on one side, and machine-gunning and bombing of miners' meetings on the other made the doctrine that capitalism is a system of class warfare seem an obvious truth to the miners, who worked under the most primitive conditions. After a year they lost the strike only by a sheer lack of firepower.

Their leader was "Big Bill" Haywood, a tough, one-eyed giant who had been a cowboy, homesteader, and a miner. He became the most militant leader of anticapitalist revolutionaries this country has ever produced. Out of the Western Federation of Miners would come the violent IWW, the "Wobblies," as the country knew them, America's first labor organization formally committed to the principle of class warfare. That a labor-union administration must replace the nation's economic and political institutions by revolution was the principle set forth in the preamble of its constitution.

Haywood, Pettibone, and Moyer, McParland was sure, had selected Orchard as the man to kill Steunenberg, and had supplied him with funds and bomb materials. The most McParland could do was try to show Orchard that if he told the truth he would not be worse off than he was—he knew that the evidence found in his room and in his trunk would surely send him to the gallows—and he might do better.

McParland's letters to William and Robert Pinkerton and Governor Gooding in that last week of January, 1906, outlined his persuasive methods:

> I said to Orchard that a man of his intelligence and reasoning power, as his forehead would indicate, had the ability of doing a large amount of good as well as evil. If he had not started out with anarchists and murderers he could have been a shining light. . . . I warned him not to accuse somebody of a crime when he was innocent, for the purpose of ratifying some real or imagined grudge. . . . I showed him that the lawyers were not his but the Federation's and that they would fool him [as to his not implicating Haywood, Pettibone and Moyer] up to the time he took his journey from cell to scaffold.

Orchard, in his autobiography, claimed that McParland finally swayed him by citing St. Paul, the stoning of Stephen, and King David's plot against Uriah the Hittite.

"There is no sin that God will not forgive you—if you repent," McParland solemnly told him. Then he quietly went on to explain to Orchard that there had been many cases where a man had testified for the state and had his own sentence mitigated. . . .

The daily sessions in the warden's office went on, with the gentle, soft-voiced old man who sat at the side of the big walnut desk persuasively talking to the prisoner beside him. The sessions never lasted more than two hours: McParland was too shrewd a judge of men to weary his subject. Every day he planted another seed, and watched it grow in the soil of Orchard's increasing restlessness and apprehension.

In his *Rocky Mountain Revolution,* Stewart H. Holbrook mentions the legend of the organ that was moved into the prison on McParland's orders breaking the grim silence of Orchard's cellblock with the sweet, melancholy chords of hymns familiar to the revival tents of the frontier.

In his darkened cell, Orchard, as he recalled, prayed to God "in a half hearted way." One day, Warden Whitney gave Orchard a religious pamphlet, "left for you by the widow of the man you murdered."

In the last week of January, Orchard cracked. He told McParland he was ready to confess, not only to the Steunenberg murder but also to "my awful life of crime from the beginning."

CHAPTER 37

The Confession of Harry Orchard

The confession of Harry Orchard is one of the most cold-blooded in the history of American crime. What is extraordinary in its fifty-two pages is the lack of human emotion; hate, bitterness, vengeance, or even obvious madness, is totally missing. Instead, there is a terrifying sense of the mechanical, as though Orchard had been a carefully monitored robot who skillfully prepared his dynamite bombs to blow his victims to bits.

The confession, still in existence, has inked corrections, believed to have been made by McParland and Orchard. It shows that McParland did not coach Orchard, but asked him only such perfunctory questions as: "How did the money reach you?" "Who did you live with?" "Can you describe them?" [1]

Orchard began talking on the morning of January 27th, and continued until the evening of the 31st. He began by sketching his early life, his frustrated attempts to become a businessman, his disregard for family life, and his wanderings about the mining camps of the West.

He was born Albert E. Horsley on March 16, 1866, in Northumberland County, Ontario, when that British province was known as Upper Canada. His parents were farmers. His schooling continued through the third grade. He worked at logging until he was about twenty-one, when he became an axman in the Michigan lumber camps. He married, and then opened a small cheese factory. His first venture into crime was bribing local cheese inspectors, and his first arson was putting the torch to his own little factory and collecting $800 in insurance.

He deserted his family, and arrived in the Idaho mining country in 1897, where he obtained a job as a milk deliveryman for the mines in Burke Canyon. It was an era when everyone considered himself a mine operator. Orchard invested his savings in a one-sixteenth interest in the Hercules Mine, paying $300 down and agreeing to pay $300 more. He opened and then sold a fuel business, and finally lost his mine interest in a poker game. Orchard then went into the mines as a mucker, and became a member of the Western Miners Federation. Twenty-nine days after he got his union button, the federation called a strike—the first major test of strength between the federation and the Mine Owners Protective Association of Idaho. Orchard witnessed the dynamiting of the concentrator for the Bunker Hill & Sullivan Mine, then the largest ore concentrator in the United States.

Governor Frank Steunenberg, although he had been voted into office by a fusion party of Democrats and Populists, and had labor's vote, refused to follow the traditional view of previous governors and ignore the trouble in the mining camps. He wired to President McKinley for troops. The military commander of the force arrested miners without preferring charges against them, destroyed miners' camps, cooped the miners in stockades, "deported" hundreds of them out of the state, and confiscated local newspapers. Steadily mounting public protests against the brutalities of the "bullpens" and the suspension of the writ of habeas corpus led to investigations by Congress.

Orchard first became a dynamite assassin when he set a bomb in the Vindicator Mine in August, 1903. Instead of killing nonunion workers, he killed a shift boss and a superintendent. As he solemnly told McParland: "I have since wished a hundred times that it [the bomb] had gone off when I was in there."

Bill Haywood, he said, gave him $300, praised the explosion as a "good job," and then told him "to cut loose and do anything . . . there was nothing too fierce for them. . . ."[2] Before he left the meeting in Denver, Orchard quoted Haywood and the others as saying, "You can get money anytime you want to."

Orchard teamed up with Steve Adams, another union dynamiter, and Pettibone recruited the pair for the murder of Lyle Gregory, a notorious mine detective. Orchard killed Gregory with a shotgun. In Denver, Haywood told him, "it was a damn smooth job."

When some of the locals threatened to leave the federation, Haywood, Jack Simpkins, another member of the executive board and one of Orchard's partners in many murders, "decided something must be done to show their power." They called in Orchard, and told him to "blow up something."

Orchard went to work willingly. He selected the railroad depot at Independence, where he could blow up the Florence & Cripple Creek train bringing in nonunion miners. When McParland asked Orchard to describe his "instrument of death," the murderer gave him a detailed plan of the bomb:

"There was a sort of windlass. Two bottles were attached to the windlass by strips of leather and the bottles were filled with Sulphuric Acid. I used two fifty pound boxes of giant powder and a box of 100 giant caps. The wire ran under the platform and around the corner of the depot."[3]

Orchard's bomb demolished the depot, killing thirteen miners and mangling twenty-four. Steve Adams was his partner that night.

In Denver, Orchard conferred with Haywood and Pettibone about his next murder assignment. Steve Adams and Jack Simpkins had been sent to Wardner, Idaho, to kill two claim jumpers. After that job was done, Adams was to go to Caldwell and kill former Governor Steunenberg. Orchard told McParland this was the first time he had known that Steunenberg was on the list of state officials Haywood and Pettibone wanted murdered.

Haywood also disclosed to Orchard a weird plan of sending Adams— after he had completed his jobs of killing the claim jumpers and the former governor—to seek out Butch Cassidy and his Hole-in-the-Wall outlaws for the purpose of getting them to kidnap Charles McNeil of Colorado Springs, a power in the Colorado Mine Owners Association. Haywood's plan was for the outlaws to hold McNeil for enough ransom to pay the outlaws "for their trouble and to pay the Federation for the cost of the strike it had staged on behalf of McNeil's smeltermen." The fantastic plan, of course, never had a chance to materialize: By 1900, the Pinkertons had broken up the Wild Bunch, and Cassidy and the remnants of his gang were already in the rain jungles of Argentina.[4] "The birds have all flown," Adams sadly wrote to Haywood from Wyoming, advising him he was continuing on to Idaho to kill the claim jumpers and Steunenberg.

Haywood then told Orchard that the next victim was to be Frederick W. Bradley, of the Bunker Hill & Sullivan Mining and Concentrating Company. He had headed the mine when the federation pulled its bloody strike. Now, in 1904, he led the Mine Owners Association in Idaho and California. Bradley had escaped assassination in San Francisco when Steve Adams and another killer had tried to shoot him, but failed to get him in their rifle sights. Bradley was now collecting a huge fund to drive the federation out of California and Idaho, and he had to be killed, Haywood told Orchard. Could he do the job? Big Bill wanted to know. Orchard proudly recalled his past killings, and Haywood agreed he might be able to "pull it off."

Orchard waited three months in and near San Francisco for Bradley to return from an Alaskan mining tour. During this time, he toured the state, drinking and gambling on money sent him by Pettibone. When he read that Bradley had returned, Orchard, in his precise, methodical way, rented a room across from the Bradley home on Washington Street, became friendly with the Bradley cook in a bar, and learned the mineowner's daily routine. For a few nights, with a sawed-off shotgun under his jacket, he stalked Bradley, but the chance to kill him never appeared. Then he set about preparing a ten-stick dynamite bomb, but could not find the opportunity to plant it. Then, when Pettibone sent him a curt letter demanding "action," Orchard bought a quantity of strychnine crystals. After the Bradleys' milk was delivered, he poured the poison into the bottles. It was only by sheer chance that Orchard failed to kill not only Bradley but his wife and their infant sons as well. The cook had tasted the milk, found it bitter, and disposed of the bottles. Orchard now turned again to his dynamite bomb. From his room, he could peer into the Bradley dining room. One morning he watched Bradley finish his breakfast, then order a second cup of coffee. Orchard hurried across the street and attached the bomb to the street mat. Minutes later, Bradley opened his front door. The six-pound bomb, enclosed in lead pipes, exploded in his face, and Bradley and the front of the apartment house were blown out into the street. Miraculously, the mineowner survived, but he was blinded and horribly mangled.[5]

When McParland tried to fix the exact time the Bradley crime had been committed, Orchard helped by insisting "it was just before Christmas."

When Orchard met Pettibone, the federation's violent unofficial adviser and close friend of Haywood, Pettibone told him: "They expressed themselves as they frequently did over such work and said that they were pleased and that if a man did a job like that and was lucky enough to get away he was doing good."[6]

Back in Denver, Big Bill Haywood and the other federation officials insisted that the schedule of murder had to be escalated. When Steve Adams and Jack Simpkins returned with the news that they had killed the two men who had filed on Simpkins' claim, Haywood presented them with a list of state officials he wanted killed. Governor James H. Peabody headed the list. Orchard told McParland: "He said he wished I could get that son of a bitch, meaning the governor, out of the way."

"Did he suggest any way by which you could get him?" McParland asked.

"Yes, he said he thought it would be no trouble for me to go up there [to the state capitol] and shoot him."

"How did you go about it?" McParland asked.

"Well, I went around the capitol and used to sit around in the capitol yard and read the paper, but I would not let Steve Adams sit around there because I was afraid they knew him. I used to sit around there and learn his [Peabody's] habits. I found out who he was and I got to know him. I had not met him before. I also watched him at nights to see his habits and when he went home." [7]

After three weeks of trailing the governor, Orchard and Adams planted a bomb in Peabody's front yard. Adams was drinking heavily, which irritated Orchard, who boasted to McParland that he never drank "while doing a job." Just as Orchard was about to pull the trip wire, two coal wagons appeared, their approach muffled by a heavy snowfall. Before they had passed, the state's chief executive and a bodyguard had stepped past the bomb and jumped into a buggy. Orchard and the fumbling, drunken Adams dug up the bomb and retired to a hotel room to discuss their bad luck over a pint of whiskey. That night the furious Haywood told them, "Why don't you plant the God-damned bomb in Peabody's desk and attach it to the rolltop?"

Orchard's almost unbelievable tour of murder continued. William H. Gabbert, Chief Justice of Idaho's Supreme Court, was next on the list. Orchard planted a twenty-pound bomb in the judge's path, but Gabbert, hailed by a friend a short distance from where the bomb had been planted, turned aside. A young engineer kicked the bomb, and was blown to bits. Once again, the unbelieving police discounted a bomb, and blamed the explosion on a cache of nitroglycerine "buried by yegg burglars."

Shermann Bell, one of Teddy Roosevelt's Rough Riders, and commander of the troops during the Cripple Creek strike, was next selected by Haywood. In a buggy driven by Pettibone, Orchard, a shotgun under his coat, followed Bell all over Denver. But Bell bore a charmed life. Every time Orchard was about to get him in his sights, someone appeared or a vehicle passed between the buggy and the victim. Finally a furious, cursing Pettibone called off the murder attempt.

The rest of the victims on Haywood's list were spared when Moyer appeared in Denver and demanded that the killings be stopped. Unknown to Orchard, Pettibone, or the others, it was the beginning of the historic split between Moyer and Haywood. American labor would feel its reverberations for years to come. It was now the winter of 1905. The Wobblies had been born in Chicago, and Moyer was angry because Haywood was spending more time on the IWW than on the federation. In Denver, they had a violent argument over whom Orchard was to murder. Moyer finally consented to Haywood's fierce insistence that it had to be former Governor Steunenberg.

In the late summer of 1905, Orchard, later joined by Jack Simpkins, set out for Caldwell, Canyon County, to murder Steunenberg. In his trunk and valise he had twenty-five pounds of dynamite, a fishline, alarm clock, and plaster of Paris, his tried-and-true tools for manufacturing bombs. For months, Orchard, Steve Adams, and Jack Simpkins wandered about the state, visiting old friends, and hunting near Wallace. At one point, Simpkins showed Orchard where he and Adams had buried the bodies of the two claim jumpers, "twenty-five miles from Head of Navigation on the St. Joe River." Simpkins laughingly described how they had shot the two men from ambush so it "would scare the layout out of here." A few days after the double murders, the other claim jumpers along the river left hurriedly. As Simpkins told Orchard, there is nothing like murder "to scare people." Orchard, the master of murder, agreed. Between hunting and visiting, Orchard and Simpkins trailed Steunenberg, who was then in the sheep business.

In November, Simpkins, weary of the dreary days in Caldwell when there was nothing to do but watch Orchard lovingly put together his ten-stick dynamite bomb, left for a federation meeting in Denver. Orchard was now alone. He continued to follow Steunenberg, once seeking him on a train. In his confession Orchard casually told McParland that, had he found the ex-governor, he intended to place a valise containing his clock bomb under Steunenberg's seat, and jump off the train. In the quiet, sunny warden's office, the cold-blooded killer shrugged off McParland's suggestion that many other innocent people on the train would also have been killed in the explosion and derailment.

On Saturday, December 30, 1905, Orchard finally caught up with Steunenberg, and hastily planted his bomb at the Steunenberg front gate. While Orchard casually stepped into the bar of the Saratoga Hotel, the building shook with the force of the exploding bomb. Orchard's only reaction was to ask for a drink. The bartender later testified that the hand of the murderous bomber was steady as he downed the shot.

Orchard is a classic and pathetic example of the banality of evil. With innumerable chances to escape capture, he stayed in Caldwell at the Saratoga Hotel, mingling with the crowds in the lobby, listening to the horrified stories, and going in and out of the bar. Though he knew there was enough evidence in his trunk and room to send him to the gallows, for the first time in his career as a professional killer Orchard was paralyzed. He did nothing until the Oregon sheriff spotted him outside the Saratoga Hotel.

CHAPTER 38

The Trial of Big Bill Haywood and the Western Federation of Miners' Officials

Orchard's signed and corrected confession was rushed to the New York office of the Agency, where William and Robert Pinkerton were waiting. With it was McParland's letter of caution: "It is absolutely necessary to corroborate Orchard's testimony as to his travels from the time he first reached Idaho until the time of assassination."

McParland's suggestions were followed immediately. Coded telegrams were sent to the superintendents of every branch office, assigning teams of operatives across the country to dig up evidence to corroborate items in Orchard's confession.

The extent of their investigative work can be seen in some typical reports: "Miss Margaret Smith of Denver and the clerk who received and sent money at Ogden, Utah. She is still in the employ of Western Union at Denver. Miss Florence Miller who made the payment at Ogden is married and her name is Mrs. John O'Brian. James Keenan, telegraph operator at Spokane, is the clerk who received the message over the phone which he subsequently sent by telegraph to Thomas Hogan [the alias Orchard used] at Caldwell."

Or the curtly informative wire from Chicago where operatives were checking the background of Charles H. Moyer, president of the Western Federation of Miners: "Warden, Illinois State Penitentiary, Joliet, informed us that Charles Moyer received February 4, 1886 . . . one year for burglary . . . sworn copies of committal papers sent by . . ."

The confession was kept secret until February 20th. During that time Governor Gooding, State Attorney Hawley, and his associate, William E. Borah, after many conferences with McParland, decided to extradite Haywood, Moyer, and Pettibone in Denver. After McParland conferred with Colorado's Governor J. F. McDonald and the Denver sheriff, Haywood, Moyer, and Pettibone were arrested. On February 19th they arrived at the Boise Penitentiary, the victims of what many charged was an infamous "kidnapping."

Governor Gooding released the confession to shock the country. When Chief Justice Goddard read one paragraph, he dropped his glasses and hurried to his front gate. There in the gatepost was Orchard's rusted screweye. Nearby was a slight depression in the frozen earth. Police were called and gingerly dug up Orchard's bomb composed of thirty-seven sticks of dynamite.

The federation's locals rallied to the defense of their officers, collecting about $21,000. The defense attorneys immediately charged that their clients had been kidnapped in violation of the Constitution, which states that only "fugitives" found in another state may be "removed to the state having jurisdiction of the crime." The union's officers, they told the court, were not "fugitives."

While the lawyers battled through the courts over a writ of habeas corpus, William and Robert Pinkerton conferred with McParland. It was obvious to them that Steve Adams and Jack Simpkins, Orchard's partners in murder, had to be found. Orchard gave McParland directions as to how to take Adams, and his former partner was arrested by Sheriff Brown of Baker County, Oregon, who would play a tragic and still mysterious role in the case. Simpkins was never found.

Adams, at the Pinkertons' suggestion, was placed in a cell with Orchard. Coached by McParland, Orchard went to work on Adams to confess. Between Orchard and McParland, Adams broke, and signed a confession, corroborating Orchard's testimony concerning a number of crimes.

As both sides began to build their cases, President Theodore Roosevelt suddenly and dramatically entered the investigation. At first, he confided to close friends that Haywood, Moyer, and Pettibone were not to be judged as "infamous creatures" but for "this particular and infamous murder." [1] Because interest in the case was now nationwide, Roosevelt ordered his Attorney General, William H. Moody, to conduct an intensive investigation. Moody assigned his assistant, Charles H. Robb. Robb's report to the Attorney General, who turned it over to Roosevelt, favored the prosecution of the defendants, and praised Governor Gooding for his conduct of the case. Gooding, in turn, publicly praised the Pinkertons, and insisted that the state, federal, and United States Supreme Court have "approved the course of our prosecuting office." He described the confessions of Orchard and Adams as "a tale so full of horror as to be almost unbelievable."

"I think the Western Federation of Miners is a body just like the Molly Maguires," Roosevelt wrote to a friend after he had read Robb's report.[2]

Then the Steunenberg murder case emerged as the major issue in Idaho's elections of 1906. Roosevelt identified Governor Gooding's re-election with the interests of law and order, believing the outcome of the trial would come with the results of the election. The President then took the extraordinary measures of sending his Secretary of War, William Howard Taft, into Idaho to campaign for Gooding.

In a major speech at Boise, Taft told a large crowd:

> If in this election Governor Gooding is to be defeated, then the state of Idaho and the people of this state will serve notice on the world that criminals and men charged with crimes, having a wide influence that can awaken sympathy for them, can bring down condemnation upon the officers of the law having courage to bring them to trial.[3]

Taft's mission was greeted with resentment by the miners and anti-Mormon groups, but Gooding was reelected.

The case continued to grow. Maxim Gorky, in the United States to raise funds, had been invited to the White House. Before this meeting of the famous Russian author and revolutionary and the Rough Rider President could take place, Gorky joined in an appeal for Moyers and Haywood.

Radicals and labor leaders joined in the growing national and international movement condemning the jailing of Haywood, Moyer, and Pettibone. The Socialist leader Eugene V. Debs attacked the Pinkertons and capitalism for the jailing of the federation's leaders, with the threat that "a million revolutionists were ready to arm."

On April 2, 1907, Roosevelt, in a letter to a New York congressman, described Haywood, Pettibone, and Moyer as "undesirable citizens."[4] The phrase, which haunted Roosevelt throughout his life, was a rallying cry for labor across the nation, whose members accused the President of prejudicing the case and of being part of a huge conspiracy between the mineowners of Idaho, Standard Oil, and the Pinkertons. Not only radicals condemned the President; so did trade-unionists in the Chicago Federation of Labor who questioned Roosevelt's wisdom in making such a remark. The Democrats, of course, gleefully used the phrase for political gain.

Roosevelt in reply to his critics in labor agreed that it was improper to attempt to influence the course of justice through threats or other means but that he still clung to his opinion that no matter what the jury's verdict would be, he, the President, would not change his judgment of those labor leaders who incited to violence and bloodshed.

Public demonstrations were held in almost every large American city. Thousands in New York heard Elizabeth Gurley Flynn attack both Roosevelt and the Pinkertons. Four days later, twenty thousand packed the Grand Central Palace to hear the same speech. In Boston and Chicago, from three thousand to fifteen thousand marchers shouted their defiance of Roosevelt, and carried banners reading, "I am an Undesirable Citizen but Teddy Roosevent Wants My Vote."

Roosevelt kept in close touch with the investigation through Governor Gooding, who forwarded him reports from Pinkerton's undercover operatives in the mining country. One, Number 24, was recruited by a defense attorney to testify falsely. As a double agent he was reporting almost daily to McParland about the perjured testimony the defense attorney wanted to buy for $1,000.[5]

After Adams's confession, which William told Robert he considered more important than Orchard's, McParland was ordered to corroborate as many facts as possible in the confession, particularly Adams's description of his trip to Pocatello. Adams had sworn he went there on the orders of Charles Moyer, president of the federation, "to look for trains that were bringing in nonstriking miners from Coeur d'Alene to Cripple Creek and to fire those trains and burn them up."[6]

Moyer, Adams said, supplied him with a suitcase of "Greek fire" in bottles packed in a large lard can. His statement tallied with Orchard's that they had experimented with the explosives in the home of Pettibone, an explosives expert. Adams said he had arrived in Pocatello on September 24, 1903, and registered at the Tupper House under the name of J. Ward. But he was not able to carry out his plan, he told McParland, "on account of the fact that no nonunion men were traveling."[7]

At McParland's urging, Governor Gooding, Warden E. L. Whitney of the Boise Penitentiary, and two detectives accompanied McParland and Adams to Pocatello. First, Adams's early visit was confirmed by the hotel register. Then the party, trailed by curious spectators and the local *Tribune* reporter, set out to find the cache of explosives. The town had changed, and Adams walked about, trying to orient himself. He told McParland he remembered a "trench" in the sawmill where he had buried the explosives. The sawmill was now a stable, and someone recalled that a boiler had been removed, leaving deep slits in the dirt floor. The trench was found, and Adams dug up a glass stopper that he said was used to close his bottles. McParland was disappointed that the entire load of explosives had not been uncovered, although he told Gooding he did not doubt that Adams was telling the truth. The next day a Pocatello brick manufacturer explained what had happened. In the fall of 1904, a workman removing lumber from the mill dug up Adams's lard can. When the liquid in the bottles burned his hand, he threw the whole thing into a refuse lot. Six months later, nearby residents noticed a fire smoldering in the refuse. They investigated and found a strange fire in a lard can. Both Orchard and Adams had told McParland about their experimenting with Greek fire under Moyer. The persistent inflammability of the contents of the lard can was now established, McParland wrote to Pinkerton, and Adams's confirmed confession had produced evidence linking the inner circle of the federation with the commission of a crime similar to the one for which they had to stand trial.[8]

Clarence Darrow, who would make his reputation with this case, had agreed to represent Haywood, Moyers, and Pettibone, after labor had raised $300,000 for their defense. Through Adams's uncle, Darrow persuaded the dynamiter to repudiate his confession. The furious McParland worked for months trying to get Adams to revalidate his confession, but the miner refused. It was a shattering blow to the state's case.

Meanwhile, the state supreme court refused to grant the defense a writ of habeas corpus; seventeen months after their arrest, Haywood, Moyer, and Pettibone went on trial for the murder of Steunenberg. Orchard was a superb witness; not even Darrow's thunder and biting contempt could shake the soft-spoken killer. As the *Oregonian* reporter at the trial wrote: "His performance on the stand has been marvelous. At no point has he tripped. On the cross examination he did not vary a hair's breadth of the tenor of what had been said. Old hands around the courts express astonishment."

During the grueling seventy-eight days of court action, Haywood calmly read Voltaire, *Tristram Shandy,* Carlyle on the revolution, Marx and Engels, and sent out flaming declarations "to the workers of America." His split with Moyer grew more bitter, and finally they no longer spoke. The probable reason was the new IWW was now divided into two factions, and the federation had withdrawn its financial report, possibly through Moyer's influence.

Darrow effectively represented the prosecution as not merely a murder case but as part of a vast conspiracy to crucify the American labor movement. His eleven-hour summing up eulogized the righteousness of labor versus the evils of capitalism. Borah was briefer, but he marshaled the state's evidence with great skill, clarity, and dramatic power. As the New York *Times* correspondent wrote: "The case presented by Mr. Borah was terrific, crushing, destroying."

But all the thunder, poetry, clarity, and sound reasoning of both men were less effective than Judge Wood's charge to the jury: "A person cannot be convicted of a crime upon the testimony of an accomplice alone."

As William Pinkerton noted to his brother, when Steve Adams repudiated his confession, he "pulled the plug on the state's case." The jury had no alternative, and a Not Guilty verdict was handed down. However,

Judge Wood told his court the verdict did not mean the defendants were innocent, but rather that their guilt had not ben proved beyond a reasonable doubt as prescribed by law.[9]

Orchard was later sentenced to be hanged, but Governor Gooding commuted his sentence to life imprisonment. When Judge Wood ordered Orchard to the state penitentiary at Boise, he again stated that Orchard's confession was in no way impugned by the fact that Haywood, Moyer, and Pettibone had not been found guilty:

"I want to take the opportunity to say to the associates in crime of this defendant that they cannot terrorize American executives and prevent them from performing their plain duties and they cannot prevent American courts from declaring the law exactly as they find it."

The investigation took another sensational turn when Sheriff Harvey K. Brown of Baker City, who had identified Orchard and who was scheduled to be the principal witness against Steve Adams, was blown to bits with a bomb at the gate of his home, on the evening of September 30, 1907. From his cell, Orchard insisted Brown had been murdered "for helping the state get evidence in the assassination of Governor Steunenberg." The murderer was never found.

Many years later, McParland characterized Brown as "an honest and a very important witness against Adams."[10]

The IWW continued to make its violent passage through the history of the American labor movement. What they lacked in numbers—they organized perhaps 5 percent of all trade unionists—they made up in aggressiveness. Unskilled and semiskilled immigrants formed the greater part of its membership. The significance of the IWW was in its concept of industrial unionism as the basis for the later success of the Committee for Industrial Organization of the 1930's.

Haywood was arrested in the 1917 Palmer raids on IWW halls across the country, and sentenced to Leavenworth Federal Penitentiary. He appealed, and was released on $30,000 bail. After the high courts had upheld his conviction, he fled to Russia. On May 18, 1928, following a party at the home of foreign correspondent Eugene Lyons, he died, embittered and forgotten.

In prison, Harry Orchard recorded Haywood's passing in his diary without comment. Now deeply religious, he was Idaho's most celebrated prisoner. The Pinkertons would hear from him once again.

CHAPTER 39
The Ancient Desperate Men of Stillwater

Although Allan Pinkerton was dead, the frontier gone, and Northfield a lurid, historic footnote, the ghost of Jesse James continued to haunt the Pinkertons and embroil them in controversy into the twentieth century.

The Missouri outlaws appeared briefly to occupy national attention when a campaign to parole the Younger brothers, still making burlap bags in the Minnesota State Penitentiary at Stillwater, gained enough momentum to persuade the State Board of Managers to consider their applications. A new generation regarded the graying, balding desperadoes with curiosity, almost disbelief. In New York some "young gentlemen and ladies" told a reporter they thought "the whole gang had been killed years ago."

Henry Wolfer, warden of the Minnesota Penitentiary and a friend of William Pinkerton, wrote to Frank Murray, superintendent of the Chicago office, asking that he and Pinkerton send letters of commendation for the Youngers to the state parole board. "I would like to have you say all you can consistently in their behalf for a pardon, and direct the letter to Roland H. Harley, Secretary Board of managers, State Capitol, St. Paul," he wrote. He added he had written a separate letter to William Pinkerton, with a request that "he say what he could in favor for a pardon for the Younger brothers."[1]

Wolfer, confident his friendship with Pinkerton would produce the

480

letter for the Youngers, leaked the story of the Youngers' parole applications, adding that Pinkerton had recommended to the parole board that the outlaws be paroled.

The New York *Herald* picked up the story from the Minnesota papers. Evidently the myth makers were still working on the Robin Hood legend of the Jameses and Youngers, for the *Herald* solemnly pointed out: "He [Cole] had studied for the ministry in his youth and will no doubt in the event of his release, take up the calling of a preacher." The story neglected to point out, of course, that Cole had spent most of his youth using a navy Colt and not the Bible.

In her apartment at 100 Pineapple Street, Brooklyn Heights, Mrs. Marion Lull, widow of Captain Lull, the Pinkerton operative who had been killed in the exchange of shots with the Youngers in the battle of Chalk Road twenty-three years earlier, sent a letter to Minnesota's Governor David N. Clough, reviewing the facts of her husband's death, and demanding that the Youngers' parole applications be denied. She also sent a copy of the letter to William Pinkerton, with a note that she was shocked to read that he had recommended parole for the men who had killed one of his own men.

In her letter to the governor, Mrs. Lull wrote:

> I was always glad they [the Youngers] were not hung for I do not believe in capital punishment but they have no claim to anything save a justly measured penalty which they received in a life sentence.
>
> Mercy does not consist in giving ruffians a free rein. There can be no mercy to the community by so doing, for it would simply mean a greater increase of evil and evil doers.
>
> . . . I know today there are many people who believe that immunity to crime is more merciful than repression of it, but it is one of the strangest delusions ever fathered by false sentiment. Pity is for the victims of the wrong, not for the perpetrators of it, just as punishment is for the perpetrators and not for the victims.
>
> If the thief and the violent will not let other people alone they have to be deprived of the freedom which they use only against inherent rights and to be shut up in places where such acts are impossible. . . .
>
> Once more, I, the widow of one of their victims, do protest against a pardon being granted to these men or to either of them.[2]

Five days later, on the thirteenth, William Pinkerton returned to his Chicago office after a six-week vacation in California. On his desk was a folder filled with stories from the Chicago, New York, and midwestern papers, describing the forthcoming parole hearings. Attached to the clippings was the copy of Mrs. Lull's telegram to Governor Clough and her note. Pinkerton was furious. He fired off a telegram to Frank Murray, superintendent of the Pinkerton office in St. Paul, with orders to visit

personally the editor of the *Pioneer Press* and demand a retraction. In
a letter to Mrs. Lull, Pinkerton told her:

> Neither I nor anyone connected with the Pinkerton's National De-
> tective Agency have in any way asked for or do we wish for the pardon
> of these men; that as far as saying that I requested anything of the
> kind it was an absolute falsehood, that I never said anything that could
> be construed in this fashion.
>
> I am too good a hater to do anything of that sort and I respect the
> memory of your husband too much to ask for the release of his
> murderer.
>
> I have also instructed our superintendent to give a copy of your letter
> to Governor Clough to the *Pioneer Press*. You may depend on it that
> anything that we can do to prevent the pardoning of these scoundrels
> will be done. I have written my brother fully on the subject.[3]

Lull's married sister, Mrs. Fanny Lull Henderson, also wrote from Massachusetts to Pinkerton, protesting the Youngers' release. In a letter to
her, Pinkerton revealed that immediately after he had returned to Chicago and learned the news of the Youngers' parole application, he ordered his brother, Robert, to get the powerful American Bankers Association to file a protest with Governor Clough.

As Pinkerton said: "I get very hot at their stating that I in any way
endorsed this pardon and wrote a pretty warm letter to St. Paul on the
subject. . . ." In another letter, a few days later, he added: "I can assure
you that never with the consent of my brother and myself will these
men ever come out of the prison walls until they come out in a wooden
box."

The combined protest of the Pinkertons and the American Bankers
Association, filed with the parole board, undoubtedly influenced the
Board of Managers to deny the Youngers' application. Pinkerton immediately notified Mrs. Lull. Between the lines one can sense the pressure
the Pinkertons and the Bankers Association had put on Governor Clough
and the parole board. As William wrote:

> Capt. Weber [the Pinkerton superintendent at St. Paul] stated to the
> St. Paul papers emphatically that I was opposed to the pardon of these
> people, and also stated it to the Governor. . . . It was through my
> brother's efforts, he being on the ground, that the American Bankers
> Association filed a protest against the pardoning of these men and that
> the protest had great effect in stopping the release of these men,
> as it has in its membership 4/5 of all the banks in the state of Minne-
> sota. This was done through the efforts of my brother and he alone.
> We are the representatives of the American Bankers Association and if

for no other reason are bound to protest against the pardoning of these men.[4]

In his letter to Lull's sister, Mrs. Henderson, advising her that the Youngers had been refused parole, he wrote: "I can assure you and Mrs. Lull that they will never receive a pardon as long as the matter is in the hands of the committee. It means political ruination to any man who signs their release."

The question of the Youngers' pardons would bother the Pinkerton brothers all that summer. In their letters to one another (they still used "Dear Sir") they never failed to repeat that the Youngers were incorrigible, and should remain behind the walls of Stillwater until they came out "in a wooden box." (They never admitted it, of course, but the Youngers were living symbols of the one big case the Agency had failed to bring to a successful conclusion, even though two men had died trying to do so.)

As Robert repeated: "I am glad the Youngers were never pardoned. I hope we will never have anything to do with clemency for either of these men. They should not expect it at our hands, and I hope no employee of ours will ever ask for clemency for them. . . ."[5]

In the following year Cora McNeil, daughter of Dr. D. C. McNeil who attended the dying Captain Lull, wrote a book entitled *Mizzoura,* which a publisher's brochure described as a "work historical, biographical, of fiction and fact, and in some of its chapters a commingling of all these."

On December 15, 1898, Miss McNeil wrote to William Pinkerton in Chicago, advising him of the book and sending him a copy. In one chapter, Miss McNeil revealed the local version of how Lull was "removed" from Roscoe:

> The man who made the box in which the Captain was taken away said, "The Doctor ordered holes bored in it which I did; then asked him why he wanted them. He replied, to let the water out in case I packed the captain in ice but the old doctor did not fool me any; it was to let the air in. . . ."
>
> The coachman (you remember they drove across the country to Sedalia) also had a story, which indicated to them that the captain was alive. These stories and others are traditional in the locality and I made use of them. Papa gave no solution of the problem that vexed the people, either then or thereafter. . . .[6]

It took Pinkerton five days to read the book. Then he sent a letter to Mrs. Lull advising her of *Mizzoura* and describing it as a "ridiculous yarn." He ended the letter with a bitter last line: "Neither I nor my brother will ever be a party to the liberation of those bandits."[7]

Pinkerton's letter to Miss McNeil reviewed how Robert J. Linden, superintendent of the Agency's office in Philadelphia, and Mrs. Lull "removed" Lull's corpse from Roscoe to Chicago.

> Concerning the people who shot Deputy Sheriff Daniels [sic], a worthy, upright officer, and afterwards Capt. Lull, there is no doubt in my mind or anybody connected with us, that the one who shot Daniels was John Younger and the one who fired the fatal shot into Capt. Lull was Jim Younger. Both of these men had virtually surrendered at the time of their assassination, and any attempt to cover these facts up, whether it be in romance or otherwise, would be contradicted by my brother and myself. There is no false sympathy in either one of us for the men who are now in prison; if they had what is their due they would be dead long ago.
>
> The idea of Capt. Lull being brought away from Roscoe alive and holes being bored in the box for the purpose of giving him air is simply too ridiculous to pay any attention to. If your dear father were alive he would tell you how ridiculous a story of this kind would seem. Capt. Lull's dead body was brought from Roscoe to Chicago and is buried in the Knight Templars burial grounds in this city.[8]

For the next three years, popular opinion and political pressure to free the Youngers continued to rise. Finally, over the bitter protests of the Pinkertons and the American Bankers Association, the Youngers were paroled in 1901.

Bob Younger had died in prison, but Cole and Jim, now living legends of another time, left Stillwater Penitentiary to return to Missouri. Jim, then fifty-one, still carried four slugs that had taken away a part of his jaw that bitter day at Northfield, while Cole, whom the New York *World* correspondent found "possessed of a captivating manner," disclosed he had been wounded twenty times rading the outlaw trail, "eleven times the result of the Northfield affair."

"When we came in here," Cole wistfully told a reporter, "there was no electric cars, no telephones, no bicycles. The world certainly must seem very different."

"But we read all the scientific magazines," Jim put in.

"But it isn't like seeing things, Jim," Cole said. "You know reading never is. When I think of myself walking by all those tall buildings and watching those cars . . . I'm afraid I will forget I'm a grown man and act like a country boy. . . ." [9]

They left the pen on a still, hot July day, with tragedy still stalking them as relentlessly as the guns of Northfield. Jim committed suicide when the girl he loved refused to marry him because her family objected to his past.

A year later, Cole returned to Missouri to live out his years by making a living at various jobs; the most ironic was that of selling tombstones.

BOOK 11
The Last Years,
1900-1924

CHAPTER 40
The Eye and the Sport of Kings

One of the last major criminal cases that Robert Pinkerton personally solved centered upon a photograph sent to the Agency's New York office by the Syracuse police in August, 1893. A week before, the man in the photograph and a companion had been captured after killing a young detective during a burglary. The prisoner insisted his name was McCarthy. Although police suspected this was an alias, they could not find a criminal record for the killer. Fingerprinting had yet to replace the Bertillon system of criminal identification.

Pinkerton studied the photograph for a moment, then handed it back to his New York general manager, George D. Bangs, Jr.: "Tell Syracuse this is Dink Wilson who held up the St. Louis and San Francisco line in 1891 with Marion Hedgepeth. From his description the other man in the killing could be his brother, Charles Wilson."

Bangs had the Agency's criminal file on the Wilsons copied and sent to Syracuse. A few days later Pinkerton received a letter of thanks from the Syracuse police chief. Dink Wilson, faced with the Agency's file, had admitted his identity, and on the basis of information furnished by the Agency, his brother had also been captured. Dink was electrocuted in Sing Sing, and Charles was sentenced to life imprisonment.[1]

In the opening years of the twentieth century the western division of the Agency, under William's command, handled the majority of the spectacular criminal investigations, while New York, under Robert, concentrated on the guard and security departments—and the racetracks.

There was no other name, with the possible exception of the Whitneys,

486

Belmonts, or Vanderbilts, better known on the tracks of America than that of the Pinkertons. For a time William had his own stable of thoroughbreds, but he let it go after a few years: "It's a glorious sport," he told a friend, "but it takes too much time away from the business."

Around 1880, the Pinkertons became the nation's first racetrack police at Coney Island. In the 1891 fall and spring meets at Gravesend, they gained immortality in the world of horse racing when they successfully battled a powerful syndicate of New York poolrooms, where most of the betting was done in those days. The skirmishing by both sides made the meets the most unforgettable in turf history.[2]

The war began when the Brooklyn Jockey Club, owners of Gravesend, notified the New York syndicate that it had raised its rate to $4,000 for the privilege of receiving odds and results direct from the track by Western Union. The syndicate in turn informed the club it would not go any higher than $2,500 a day. In that case, the club told the syndicate, there will be no more information. Try to stop us was the return message. The Jockey track owners notified Robert, who called in Bangs to plot their first moves.

The syndicate withdrew their Western Union operators and set them up at spots near the track so the syndicate's legmen could bring them information. The Pinkertons stopped this by locking the track's front gates from twenty minutes before the first race was run until after the last race was over. No one was permitted to leave the track.

The ingenious syndicate heads then bought a supply of tennis balls, pencils, and notepads. The balls were slit, and the syndicate's runners ordered to put the information in the balls and toss them over the fence. Pinkerton ordered his men to catch every ball tosser and escort them out of the park. It was an exciting afternoon, with the crowds in the stands hooting and jeering as the Pinkertons ran down the ball tossers and marched them out by the seats of their pants. The angry syndicate then offered $25 to anyone who threw out the first ball with the results after each race. It made a hilarious afternoon, with the customers furiously scribbling down the results, the air filled with arching tennis balls, and the Pinkertons knocking down the more feeble casts. When this was reported to Robert, he ordered a shift in strategy. Now the Pinkerton operatives threw tennis balls over the fence, but the slips inside contained names of wrong winners, which threw the Manhattan poolhalls into a frenzy. On this ludicrous note the spring meet closed at Gravesend.

In the fall the war continued. Both sides had now devised new plans. Across the street from the track the syndicate had rented the cupola of a large house. Spotters equipped with strong glasses were posted there together with a telegraph operator. When this news was flashed to Robert, he had the track's carpenters build up the fence at this point another fifty feet. After the track closed that afternoon, the syndicate brought out a wagonload of carpenters and built a tower above the cupola. The night echoed with furious sawing and hammering. By dawn the tower was thirty feet and still rising. The syndicate won that round. But immediately after the last race, the track's carpenters were back on the job, and again there was all-night hammering and sawing. By daylight, the fence was sixty feet high, but a strong sea breeze made it sway so much the carpenters dropped their tools and clung for their lives to the rickety structure. After a conference with his men, Robert ordered that tall poles, with canvas stretched between them, be erected about the track. Now all the syndicate's men could see was a vast expanse of billowing canvas. The syndicate then erected higher poles, with its men strapped into a crow's nests, but the Pinkertons countered this with higher poles and more canvas, until the track looked like a section of South Street where the China clippers docked.

Skirmishing continued all that fall. The syndicate rented houses and rooms all around the track, but the Pinkertons cut off their view at every turn. Men were sent into the track armed with elaborate wigwag systems of hats, handkerchiefs, palm-leaf fans, and parasols. The syndicate abandoned this system when the crowds in the stands began making false signs and semaphore signals to confuse the operators. In this mad war it was inevitable that carrier pigeons would be introduced, Pinkerton warned his men. And they were. Men had the birds inside their coats, in top hats or bowlers, and ladies in their bustles. A noted female pickpocket was hired to use her specially made dress to smuggle in a cage of seventeen pigeons, but she was nabbed at the gate. In addition to stopping the pigeon handlers at the gate, Robert also sent up flocks of birds with phony race results, which again created havoc in the poolrooms.

The war became so intense that Robert was at the track every day. It was he who uncovered the syndicate's most elaborate effort. For three days a barouche carrying several expensively dressed men and women arrived at the track. Between races they would wander back to the carriage to dip into the food hamper. Robert noticed that one of the men wore what appeared to him to be a rather large hat. One day, after following the man, Pinkerton snatched off the hat and found in it an electric bulb attached to a battery and telegraph key hidden under a lap robe. The driver, a telegrapher, had used the hat setup to flash results to another telegrapher hidden in the top floor of a nearby house. The meet, later called the "Battle of Gravesend," finally ended with the Pinkertons the victors.

Robert Pinkerton next turned to clearing "ringers" from the nation's tracks. Benjamin A. Chilson, dubbed "King of the Ringers" by the newspapermen in the early 1900's, used this technique:

> His principle was to buy a race horse out of a selling race [a race in which an owner enters a horse and agrees to sell it at a specified price], then get one whose form was miserably poor but looked measurably like

the good horse. This horse would then be doctored with paint and dye where needed and entered at a distant track, the good horse as the bad one. The betting as a rule would be out of town and not at the track so that suspicions would not be aroused. Chilson usually chose either maiden races, or the last race of the last day when the judges would be hurrying to catch trains for the next track and would be less likely to have their attention called to any rumors.[3]

Chilson's most famous coup took place on October 3, 1903, when a horse called Fiddler won the closing race at Morris Park at tremendous odds.

Robert Pinkerton ordered an investigation and confirmed the rumors: The Fiddler was really McNamara, a western racehorse. A few months later Pinkerton went out to New Orleans after he had heard stories of how a sensational horse named Hiram Johnson had won at the fairgrounds. The Johnson horse was also revealed to be McNamara. Chilson, a former veterinarian and expert at dyes and paints, moved about the country's tracks, fixing McNamara to resemble other racehorses. At the time, there were no New York State laws against ringing. While he pushed for legislation in New York through the Brooklyn Jockey Club, represented by the Agency, Bob Pinkerton publicly revealed Chilson's operations. After he sold McNamara, the racehorse of a thousand colors, Chilson bought another horse, called Freckman, reportedly stolen from an Oakland, California, stable. At St. Louis, Freckman was rung in as Buck Wynne, a local horse with a poor record. Freckman came in by a length, and Chilson and his men cleaned up on forty-to-one odds, and hurriedly left town. Buck Wynne was well known to the local racetrack crowd, but so cleverly had Chilson disguised his horse "that horsemen identified the animal as Buck Wynne without a doubt." In October, 1905, Freckman was also used by Chilson at the Jamaica Track under the name of Cartaret, and the ringers staged an enormous betting coup that staggered the New York syndicate.

From 1903 to 1905, Robert Pinkerton conducted an investigation of Chilson, assigning operatives across the country to investigate rumors and reports of any big betting coup. Operatives shadowed Chilson and his jockeys. For the first time, small cameras were used to make a damaging pictorial record of the activities of Chilson and his men. The ringer specialist, whose goatee and courtly manners gave him the appearance of a southern horseman or plantation owner, was as illusive as a wraith. But operatives working about the tracks finally snapped his picture and those of several of his men.

In the winter of 1906, Robert reported to his friend F. R. Hitchcock, the millionaire horseman, that he was urging the Belmonts and Vanderbilts to help him influence the New York legislature to have a bill passed similar to the Missouri and Michigan laws that made ringing a crime.

Pinkerton also informed Hitchcock that the California Jockey Club had recognized the ruling of the Eastern Jockey Club and had barred Chilson from the tracks. "I am greatly pleased to finally see punishment meted out to the ringing crowd," he wrote. "I think the lesson will be very wholesome to certain western people likely to engage in similar business." [4]

As he wrote to his brother, Bob Pinkerton was determined to make the nation's racetracks free of crime. In 1906, with the ringers and the syndicate defeated, he ordered his operatives to concentrate on pickpockets, forgers, confidence men, and other petty criminals. During the Gravesend meets he was a familiar sight, dressed in a tweed suit and wearing his pork-pie-style hat, making his way through the crowds, an operative close by, ready to pounce on a pickpocket lifting a wallet, a known counterfeiter "pushing the queer," or one of Ben Chilson's ringers, hoping he would miss "meeting the Eye." After a day's tour of the track, a feature writer reported:

> There is no place where the swell thieves go more constantly than the races, and probably in the great crowds there are thousands of crooks of one kind or another. Yet robberies are scarcely ever heard of. The reason is that Bob Pinkerton has established the most perfect of systems. Every professional thief knows that if he committed a robbery at the racetrack he would never be safe again. He would be pursued to the end, even his closest friends might betray him, while no pawn broker or other receiver would deal with him. He could commit burglary the night before but he could not rob at the track.[5]

Robert's drive to clean up the nation's racetracks prompted poetry, assassination attempts, and editorial criticism. The New York *Recorder* published a long jingle that their track expert reported was being sung in the grandstands:

> Sing High for the bountiful poolroom man
> Sing low for the politic poolroom man
> But oh, breathe not the name of the Pinkerton man
> In the sensitive ear of the poolroom man!

When the powerful *Sporting World* complained in an open letter to Bob Pinkerton that young hoodlums were annoying "young ladies" leaving the tracks, Pinkerton guards refused to admit them the following day. But the New York *World* indignantly pointed out that the hoodlums should be readmitted "because they are all the sole support of their aged mothers."

When the Eastern Jockey Club, on the recommendation of Pinkerton, continued to pass stricter rules to drive the criminal element from the tracks, the battered New York syndicate decided that Robert had to be killed. A gunman was hired, and for days stalked the burly detective as he made his way through the crowds at the Gravesend track. In July, 1906, he was standing near the rail with a friend from Buffalo when he suddenly turned his head. His friend gave a sharp cry, and dropped, blood pouring from his forehead. Doctors later extracted a rifle slug from under the skin. The bullet, police surmised, had missed the huge Pinkerton as he turned, and glanced off the forehead of his smaller friend.

Every week underworld informants passed along information about a new murder plot against Robert, who shrugged them off. One track plunger he had driven from the Gravesend track was Steve L. Hommidieu, a quick-tempered Creole who swore to kill Pinkerton. During the New Orleans Fair Grounds meet, he followed Pinkerton into Lomothe's, a famous restaurant of its day. "You had me ruled off down east, didn't you?" he shouted as he followed the detective to a table.

Pinkerton took his seat, studied the menu for a moment, then looked up. "Yes, I did. I chased you away because you were corrupting jockeys and owners and I caught you with the goods."

The big Creole pulled a gun, but Pinkerton drove his fist into L'Hommidieu's stomach, knocked him over a table, and "delivered him to the local authorities."

Robert also expanded the Pinkerton's guard and security forces to cover international expositions and world's fairs, a practice that is carried on to this day. The Nashville, Tennessee, Centennial Fair in 1897, the Trans-Mississippi at Omaha in 1898, Pan American at Buffalo, Jamestown in 1907, San Francisco, San Diego, Chicago in 1892—all were protected by the Pinkertons.

Pinkerton operatives were also a part of the great days of circuses, both in the United States and in Europe, where the Pinkerton's identification card read:

> G. V. Bird
> De la
> New York, EUA
> Agent pour
> Le Barnum & Bailey
> Plus Grande Cirque de Monde

Attention was drawn to the card's autre côte, listing officers, divisions, and European branch offices of the Agency and the important fact of "telephone connections."

The operative's duties, as outlined by Robert Pinkerton, were first to get in touch with the police officers in the places where the circus was to play, and establish friendly relations: "The detective usually rides on the first or third train . . . detective on the first [train] should watch for rubbernecks or local ruffians who will swarm into enclosure or horse tents."

On European trips the operatives were warned to expect "very little help from the police who leave their posts and sneak into the tent to see the performance."

Criminal bands followed the circus, and the operative assigned usually maintained a string of informants along the route the wagons were using. The Wells Brothers, Ringling Brothers, Hagenbeck-Wallace—all the great circuses of the late nineteenth and early twentieth centuries before the mergers, as well as Buffalo Bill's Wild West Show—were protected by the Pinkertons. The "route book" of the operative attached to the Buffalo Bill show, 1899, gives a fascinating picture of the pathos, difficulties, and humor of early American show business.[6] It covers the period from April 17th to October 14th, ending at Urbana, Ohio. There are log entries, mileage, railroad connections, and so on, and Buffalo Bill's famous "Order of Parade:" "Col. W. F. Cody and his outriders, Sioux Indians, German Garde-Kurassiers of his Majesty, Kaiser Wilhelm II; Electric Light Engine, No. 1, group of Riffian Arabs . . . famous Cowboy Band Mounted, Old Deadwood Stage Coach . . ."

In May, the operative recorded that in Richmond, Indiana, a howling twister came up suddenly to "make the lot very rough." Battling the billowing, soggy canvas, a man fell from a wagon top and was killed. Johnnie Baker, the famous sharpshooter, injured his hand in Chester, Pennsylvania, "and had to cancel his act, while in Fort Wayne, at the peak of an immense business." Little Mary, a Sioux papoose, died and was buried in the local cemetery, with all hands attending. Impassive Sioux chiefs and warriors, canvasmen and strikers, and perhaps Buffalo Bill in his buckskins and shoulder-length hair crowded the rural cemetery to watch the tiny coffin being slowly lowered. It was a rough season, the operative reported to Robert, so rough that "William Baker, the boy giant," packed his bags, and left.

William and Robert heard from an old adversary in those years, Sophie Lyons, the Lady from Lyons, as the Sûreté called her, the faithful friend of Adam Worth, Baron Shinburn, and other masterful thieves of the Victorian Age. Although they arrested her with regularity, she never failed to call on Robert in New York or William in Chicago whenever she visited those cities. Five foot two, with the aloof air of a president of the DAR, Sophie joined the staff of the New York *World* in the winter of 1897 to become America's first society columnist. Sophie Lyons's total take from blackmailing, swindling, extorting, and shoplifting was about $1,000,000, the Pinkertons estimated.[7]

In 1907, two years before the Pinkertons severed relationship with the American Bankers Association, the Agency had 2,000 employees and safeguarded 4,000 banks in the United States through the association. The Houston *Post* had published the story of the two bank robbers who returned the $50,000 in negotiable bonds they had stolen rather than be pursued by the Pinkertons. The penciled notation to the bank president read:

"Put your ABA sign out where your customers can see it." [8]

Both Pinkertons loved to travel abroad, and in the 1890's and 1900's they frequently toured Europe and the Orient. In the winter of 1907, Robert began to complain about his health, "but usually with a joke," as his New York superintendent recalled. At the urging of William, he finally agreed to visit Germany's Nauheim baths. In August, accompanied by an old male crony, Florence Sullivan, former Washington correspondent for the Chicago *Call,* he left for Europe on the liner *Bremen.*

A few days later, a cablegram was delivered to William at Saratoga, notifying him that Robert had been found dead in his cabin. Two large scrapbooks testify to the news coverage of Pinkerton's death. Every large newspaper in the country and throughout Europe hailed Robert as one of the world's greatest detectives; columns recalled his exploits in such cases as the Northampton bank robbery, his capture of the giant Red Leary, and his fight to clean up the American racetracks.

At the services, held in Brooklyn's First Reformed Church, crowds overflowed into the streets. In Chicago five moving vans took the floral wreaths to Graceland Cemetery, and seven carriageloads of roses were distributed to the city hospitals at William's request.

Not only the famous but also the infamous were among his mourners. One newspaper reporter talked to an old bank robber Robert had befriended when the thief was down in his luck. His eulogy was, "He was a square one." [9]

After the death of Robert, his son, Allan II, succeeded to his father's interest in the Agency. Allan, young and energetic, but always overshadowed by his famous uncle, made many improvements in the sometimes creaky business methods of the Agency.

From the terse notes and memorandums that passed between them, one gets the impression that William glowered and grunted every time his nephew made an improvement, forgetting the days, forty years earlier, when William was sending similar letters to his father.

In 1911, Pinkerton heard from an old friend, Winston Churchill. In June, in response to a cablegram from Churchill, he went to London to assist Scotland Yard during the coronation of Edward VII. G. C. Thiel, Spokane superintendent, reported to New York:

> Extreme steps are being taken to keep out anarchists and dangerous criminals. All steamship landings are being closely watched. The Continental police are cooperating with the Pinkertons. Since his arrival today William Pinkerton has been in constant communication with the Home Office which has the responsibility for the King's safety.[10]

However, not all of the Pinkertons' activities were courageous and exemplary. The role they played in San Francisco's celebrated Tom

Mooney bombing case was ugly and unfair. Their investigation of the rape-murder of fourteen-year-old Mary Phagan in Atlanta in April, 1913, was shoddy and at times despicable. Leo Frank, the factory owner who ironically had hired the Atlanta Pinkerton office to find the killer of his young employee, was himself indicted for the crime. William S. Burns was called into the case, uncovered new evidence, publicly named the killer, and was almost lynched by a mob.

Later the Georgia governor, risking his political life, commuted Frank's death sentence with the observation that the evidence uncovered by Burns was "powerful evidence in behalf of the defendant. But an anti-Semitic mob invaded the Milledgeville Prison Farm with no resistance from the guards, kidnapped Frank, and lynched him at Marietta.

In 1914, the French government retained the Pinkertons to investigate a ring of agents working in New Orleans for the Central Powers. An operative infiltrated the group to become acquainted with a German mechanic named Hans Helle, a saboteur of unusual skill and nerve. Like countless operatives before him, the Pinkerton man obtained rooms in Helle's boardinghouse, drank beer with Helle, and agreed with his violent pro-German arguments. One day, Helle confided to the operative that he had manufactured a bomb, set to detonate in six days, to be hidden on a French ship. At a conference with the district attorney the Pinkertons, in order to make a tight legal case, urged the prosecutor to let them accompany Helle to the ship and make the arrest as he was hiding the bomb. They were overruled on the grounds of public danger.

For several tense hours, the Pinkertons and the New Orleans police waited in Helle's darkened room. As the operative reported: "In the final wait, the size and power of the bomb was magnified in all our minds." One police officer warned the others: "If you grab this guy, lift him right off the ground, he'll be wired like a submarine." With them was a representative of a local explosives company. When he heard that Helle was carrying a bomb he announced that he was only a dynamite expert, and left. Helle finally entered the room, and was surrounded and handcuffed. While the police, frozen to the floor, watched, the operative removed the clock and trigger of the bomb.

Helle was confined in the same prison where Dimaio had been imprisoned with the Mafia twenty-five years earlier. However, he was later released because of a technicality in the indictment.

After America's entry into the war, a Pinkerton operative who had worked on the New Orleans investigation spotted Helle on a Chicago street. He followed him to a wartime munitions factory where he discovered the German saboteur had recently been hired as a foreman. On the Pinkerton's information, Helle was arrested by the Secret Service and detained for the duration of the war.[11]

At the outbreak of the war, Allan Pinkerton, II, enlisted in the army, serving with distinction as a major. He was badly gassed, and invalided back to the States. William, now sole head of the Agency, was summoned to Washington to outline a series of proposals to halt sabotage, but, as he tersely recalled, he left after they failed to "accept my suggestions." It was a striking parallel to 1861, when his father left Washington after Lincoln had kept him waiting.

There are no letters from William explaining the puzzle of why the Pinkerton's, the world's most famous detective agency of its time, was not recruited by the government as it had been in 1861–1862. The answer assuredly lies in Pinkerton's address to the International Association of Police Chiefs in 1919. That speech, which made headlines across the country, revealed that inefficiency, incompetence, a lack of centralization, and jealousy between federal agencies had often "spoiled" important cases of espionage, and were no match for the experienced agents of the German spymasters, Von Bernstorff, Von Papen, Dr. Albert, and others. Although he did not say it in so many words, it had been a case of the amateurs disdaining the professionals or the professionals refusing to work with the amateurs. As he told the police officers:

> Persons selected to perform important Government secret service in the Army and Navy Intelligence Department were often selected from among doctors, bankers, merchants, architects, etc., and I am credibly informed that of these, less than one per cent, or one person in a hundred, had previous police or detective experience. This created separate forces of thousands without training for incredibly important work, which, at all times, requires training and experience to be of real service.
>
> The limited results achieved by these hastily organized Intelligence, or Secret Service Departments, are known to you through your almost helpless efforts to cooperate and assist these inexperienced forces. Their inexperience, zeal and jealousy frequently spoiled important clues of cases of major importance, that otherwise could have been successfully developed.

Pinkerton also denounced the issuance of a list of dangerous alien sympathizers by Army Intelligence:

> This list since its publication has been shown to be so inaccurate and so unjust to persons named therein, that the War Department had to take drastic steps to curb the zeal of the employees of the Intelligence Department and removed the names of the injured persons from this list.

The heart of Pinkerton's speech was his proposal for "a central government agency force of Federal detectives that will centralize, connect up and weave together data gathered by its representatives North, South, East and West.

"This would soon eradicate such elements [enemy agents] as require the attention of our courts."

This organization, he went on, would be beyond the reach of politicians, "and would never be used against labor or against capitalism; never become involved in their differences, an organization to which any suspicious coming to the notice of City, County or State authorities could be reported . . . in other words a centralized clearing house of secret service data for the protection of the people. . . ."

Pinkerton also pointed out that had the United States had such an agency, its experienced operatives would have alerted Washington to the overthrow of the Kerensky government in Russia. War-ravaged Europe, Pinkerton warned, was a fertile ground for the spread of Communism. While the "Reds" were as yet no danger to this country, he predicted they would be in the years to come. The superagency of his dreams, he told the assembled officers, would surely take care of that threat. Pinkerton could have been discussing the Federal Bureau of Investigation.[12]

Pinkerton's strong feeling about the "radicals" of his day was a reflection of the decline, if not the end, of progressivism in the United States, when its leaders failed to unite after 1918. Among the reasons were the flowering of American enterprise under the impact of technical and financial developments and the economic and social status of the urban class, who had begun to realize they were building a new type of America based on mass production and consumption, shorter hours, increasing prosperity. Their country, comparatively untouched by the Great War, was healthier than ever. The middle class had little interest in rebellion or revolt against governments or establishments that might disturb the status quo. It was the age of Babbitt and the solid citizen who feared that bomb-and-whisker Bolsheviks were going to take over Washington. This fear had been heightened by a series of violent strikes that shook the nation shortly after the end of the war. In Pinkerton's time, most Americans were inclined to view them as Red-inspired.

The "Big Red Scare" of 1919–1920 resulted in a national crusade against left-wingers whose Americanism was suspect. More than six thousand were rounded up by Attorney General A. Mitchell Palmer. The nation's fear increased when Palmer's house was bombed in Washington. The fear verged on hysteria in September, 1920, when a bomb, still unexplained, exploded in front of J. P. Morgan's offices at 23 Wall Street, killing thirty-eight and wounding several hundred more.

In these turbulent years, old and familiar faces began to disappear from the Agency's roster. In May, 1918, William wrote to his nephew that he was "going to bury McParland" in Denver. After the funeral he told newspapermen that he "doubted McParland could get convictions today as he did then. Times have changed."

In the postwar years, Pinkerton traveled across the country to campaign for the adoption of national fingerprinting. As he told a convention of law-enforcement officers: "No one who has a practical knowledge of both systems [fingerprinting against the Bertillon system] will for one minute question the superiority of the fingerprint system over the Bertillon system."

Pinkerton also held a series of conferences in London with Sir Edward William, who had introduced fingerprinting in England. In a report to the International Association of Police Chiefs, Pinkerton warned: "You will be behind the times if you do not introduce fingerprinting so that it becomes nationwide."

Fingerprinting had been first introduced in the United States at the World's Fair in 1904, but during World War I and the postwar years it was used only by the military and the Bureau of Immigration. Pinkerton's speeches, as well as the proddings of police chiefs, are credited with helping to bring about national fingerprinting, today one of the most vital parts of local and federal law enforcement.

In the early 1920's, William was a legendary figure on the American scene, a huge man, heavily jowled, with thick gray hair, and brooding black eyes under shaggy white brows. He usually wore an old-fashioned black cravat, a heavy gold watch chain stretched across his large stomach, and a western sombrero-type hat.

Although he often insisted that he didn't care for personal publicity, he never dodged a newspaperman. With young and impressionable female reporters, he played the role of the grim, silent lawman of old. As one wrote, "It is as hard to get him to talk about himself as it is to get him to smile." The more experienced big-city reporters who knew Pinkerton certainly smiled at such naïveté.

Usually the interviews or feature stories were mostly reminiscences of the Old West or the days of Adam Worth, Baron Shinburn, the Molly Maguires, and the colorful thieves of the past, but they also contained many succinct, shrewd observations of American life. When one reporter asked Pinkerton what was America's greatest deterrent against crime, he snapped, "Education and more education." He also suggested that the government, to instill interest in education in the nation's ghettos—"tenement districts" he called them—offer scholarships for the children of the poor, a proposal a half century before its time.

In 1920, when he was seventy-four, Pinkerton created a national stir when he publicly denounced Prohibition as the cause for the national crime wave. He also criticized Hollywood for its flood of "crime movies, a prime motivation for young criminals." [13] William told a Los Angeles *Times* reporter that the postwar years

> have produced an entirely new type of criminal, difficult under our present methods to deal with and have produced conditions that have never before been so rotten in the history of our country.
>
> Everyone is getting big prices for their products. Salaries are high

but so are expenses. This new affluence, following the terrible strain
we have been through during and since the war, has produced the
new criminal element that is providing headaches for the nation's
police.

As for Hollywood's lurid crime movies, he said:

> We [the nation's police heads] have found that this is prime motiva-
> tion of the younger type of criminal. Please don't think I am con-
> demning the movies, for there is no greater movie fan than myself.
> But there are certain types of pictures which I personally think should
> be suppressed. I mean those that illustrate and glorify crime and crimi-
> nals. You and I may forget the pictures we have just seen but the
> young chap with criminal tendencies does not.

In several interviews Pinkerton pointed out that the whipping post in
Delaware had cut down crime in that state. When a reporter challenged
him to prove this, he told the story of a group of Broadway "mobsmen,"
as the racketeers were called in those days, who were caught burglarizing
a banker's home in Wilmington. They were sentenced to ten years and
forty lashes. Pinkterton said:

> The years in the penitentiary were a joke to them. They knew they
> could eventually buy their way free, but the thought of the lashes
> horrified them. They hired the best attorneys but their sentences were
> upheld. They were all tied up in public and given forty lashes, then
> sent to the penitentiary. Word of their terrible humiliation went back
> to Broadway and it was a long time before any New York mobsmen
> paid Delaware a visit.
> Brutal? Perhaps the Whipping Post Law is brutal, but it should also
> be pointed out that crimes, thousands of times more brutal than the
> post, are being committed in this country these days with the innocent
> usually the victim.

It was curious that Pinkerton's sixty or more years on the side of the
law had not taught him that increases in crime often follow disturbances
in human relations, and are caused by them. Thus, crime can almost be
termed the "war after the war."

Pinkerton's proposal was followed by countless editorials praising or
denouncing his ideas of a whipping post for crime-ridden states. Perhaps
the most thoughtful was in the San Francisco *Call-Post*, which pointed
out that while Pinkerton was a necessary part of organized society, sorely
needed to keep it from inner destruction, men of some future civilization
would perhaps look back and remark that the police and the detectives

and the armies of our time were expressions of weakness and not of strength.[14]

Survivors and echoes of famous cases continued to plague William Pinkerton in his last years. In 1920, Harry Orchard, now a cheery, sun-tanned middle-aged man who walked about the prison yard wearing a farmer's straw hat, wrote to a friend in New Jersey, asking him to get the Pinkertons "to write up some kind of record forms" to help him gain a parole. In this letter Orchard revealed that former State Prosecutor James H. Hawley, who had tried Haywood, Pettibone, and Steve Adams, and former Governor Frank R. Gooding were recommending his release.[15]

Orchard recalled how McParland, who had died two years earlier, "used to tell me a great deal about the large cases he had been connected with and how they always recommended clemency for those who had helped them uncover crimes in various degrees."

Orchard's request was sent to William Pinkerton's Chicago office. At the time, Pinkerton was America's legendary detective, and there is little doubt his recommendation could have helped Orchard. But as he wrote to his general manager in New York: "I know that McParland always thought Orchard should have been released for testifying, but I still regard Orchard as a cold-blooded murderer who killed many innocent persons and who testified only to save his own skin." [16]

The Molly Maguires also refused to remain in the past. When A. Conan Doyle published his *Valley of Fear*, a novel based on McParland's famous adventures, William Pinkerton was furious, and sent an angry note to George D. Bangs, Jr., his New York superintendent. As his letter revealed, Doyle had been his shipmate on a transatlantic cruise. One night in the smoking lounge he had told the famous English author the story of McParland's adventures in the Pennsylvania minefields. The late Ralph Dudley, Pinkerton's general manager, recalled:

> W. A. P. raised the roof when he saw the book. At first he talked of bringing a suit against Doyle but then dropped that after he had cooled off. What made him angry was the fact that even if Doyle was fictionizing the story, he didn't have the courtesy to ask his permission to use a confidential discussion for his work. They had been good friends before but from that day on their relationship was strained. Mr. Doyle sent several notes trying to soothe things over and while W. A. P. sent him courteous replies he never regarded Mr. Doyle with the same warmth.[17]

The story was typical of William, his father, and his brother: a wrong, fancied or real, was never forgotten.

Pinkerton continued to be an important news source for London reporters, who crowded about him in the ship's lounge, putting a multitude of questions ranging from America's gang wars to disarmament. Their favorite, which they never failed to ask, was his opinion of Sherlock Holmes, Old Sleuth, or other fictitious detectives of the day.

"Gum shoe detectives of fiction are usually just plain rot," he said in 1922. "Detective work is only using good common sense and nothing else." The *Express,* whose headline read, "The Sherlock Holmes of America Arrives Here," found Pinkerton that year to be "a quiet, gray-haired man full of vigor. He is the antithesis of the popular impression of the great detective. He might be mistaken for a prosperous banker."

On his trips to London, Scotland Yard never failed to give Pinkerton a banquet at the Savoy, with a prominent American as toastmaster or main speaker of the evening. On his 1922 visit, the Savoy's main ballroom was packed with Americans and Britons who listened to Ambassador George Harvey praise Pinkerton as one of the outstanding men of his time.

If anyone thought the old man was quietly dozing in the sun, and tried to trespass on his authority, they always drew back, bloodied. A prominent midwestern police official once claimed credit for the arrest of a gang of notorious criminals. A few days later, Pinkerton sent New York a blistering letter of what he intended to tell the official, "that hog that never fails to try and take credit for the work our Agency has done. . . . I shall not hesitate to tell him at the proper time my opinion regarding this matter."

His nephew, Allan, now back with the Agency as his uncle's partner, also felt the old man's sting. In the 1920's a New York State newspaper published a lengthy article quoting William's story of how a certain President had been swindled in a mine deal while in office. The President was not named, but the wire services picked up the story, which was given prominent space throughout the country. William was in London at the time, and the superintendent in New York wrote a brief note, and enclosed the clipping. Allan had scrawled a few angry lines on the bottom of the note, advising his uncle that he thought the story was "slush" and should never been told. Back came a cold, sharp letter from William saying that he "resented such comments and I don't want you to write me anything of that kind in the future. . . ." The story, he explained, had been given to the paper by an old friend to whom he had told it in confidence many years ago. "If I wanted publicity," he wrote, "God knows I could get all I wanted while I was in Europe."

At seventy-seven William had his own teeth, a thick thatch of iron-gray hair, a healthy appetite, and used old-fashioned rimmed spectacles only for reading. His memory was extraordinary; he could still identify photographs of criminals by a glance. He now enjoyed the theatre, and was an ardent first nighter. As a magazine of the period observed, he was "a patron of the arts." But William's favorite role was that of Principal of the world's greatest detective dynasty. Six months out of the year he toured the country, visiting branch offices, listening to complaints, untangling administrative difficulties, offering suggestions, and examining profits and losses. He could no more stop being a detective than he could breathing. Informers still gave him their tips, rather than talk to anyone else. He would stop on a street and slip a bill to a bedraggled-looking vagrant, explaining to his companion that it was an "old-timer down on his luck." The once great forgers, bank robbers, and confidence men, old, sick, and penniless, never failed to come away with a "loan." Perhaps to Pinkerton they represented an era, the most exciting and triumphant of his lifetime, which inexorable time had swallowed.

When Joe Killoran, a famous paroled bank robber of the 1880's whom the Pinkertons had sent away for a long term, appeared, frail, dying of TB, and with only one leg—the other had been amputated in prison—William gave the old thief a small loan. Judging from his correspondence, he spent many days arranging interviews between Killoran and the representative of a company selling pipe cleaners. Pinkerton bought two hundred of the cleaners to set Killoran up as a salesman. "Let him start out in this way, selling them," William wrote to his New York assistant general manager. "I always like to help these old fellows and put them on their feet."

When George Bliss White, one of the truly cultured bank robbers of the 1890's, who planned and executed the famous robbery of the Ocean Bank of New York in the 1870's, wrote to Pinkerton that he was sick and destitute, William sent an operative to his boardinghouse to confirm the story. When the operative returned with the news that White was seriously ill and broke, Pinkerton paid the bank robber's board bill and gave him a loan "to put him back on his feet to go straight." White, as his New York superintendent wryly reminded William, "had stolen more money than any other human being."

White later returned to thank Pinkerton, the old opponents sitting in the detective's sun-splashed office, reminiscing of men they had known on both sides of the law. White later wrote an autobiographical best seller, and became a popular lecturer. William, who had seen too much of life and men to be surprised by ingratitude, almost jovially told his New York superintendent that "he [White] never fails to put the heat on me or my brother" in his lectures.

William celebrated his seventy-seventh birthday in Hot Springs, and the nation's dailies reported how he had been given a surprise party in the ballroom of the local hotel. Judges, senators, congressmen, millionaire horsemen, old friends, associates, and industrialists jammed the room.

There were many speeches, and telegrams from famous persons, both in the United States and in Europe, were read. At the end, William rose and said simply: "Thank you. This is an evening I will never forget."

In the winter of 1923, he prepared for his annual national tour of the Agency's branch offices. He still spent a full day behind his desk either in New York or in Chicago, reading copies of every report and dictating notes of suggestions, praise, and criticism to his superintendents. Now, from where he sat in that Age of Wonderful Nonsense, he could look back up the long road of history he had traveled that stretched even beyond the Civil War. There was the bitter winter morning when he had helped his father escort the fanatical abolitionist John Brown and the weary slaves to the train that would take them the last miles to freedom in Canada. There was the front-line tent after Antietam where he had sat with his father and the handsome general, while all about them McClellan's army, badly mauled, wearily rested on its arms. And there was the day in the White House when Lincoln had put a hand on his shoulder and admonished his father for using his sons on dangerous missions behind the Confederate lines. There were also many great and grim mileposts along the road: the fires of Homestead, the rattle of six-shooters, and the thousands of miles on horseback, slogging after the outlaws of the Wild West; Victorian London and Adam Worth's dazzling nightclub in the Rue Scribe; gay Havana, where he had captured the Bidwell brothers who had robbed the Bank of England. He had known all the Presidents from Lincoln to Harding, as well as kings, dictators, and criminals of every class. He had experienced countless dangers, from the tangled wildwoods of the Ozarks and the Great Smokies to the mining camps of the West, and had fought for his life in the moonlight on the deck of a riverboat when Mark Twain had worked on the Mississippi.

At seventy-seven he could tell a young reporter: "I guess you can say I lived a full life."

In December, 1923, he arrived in Los Angeles to preside over a series of conferences. On the eleventh, he was stricken with a heart attack, and died in his hotel room.

The obituaries, numerous and lengthy, fill a huge scrapbook, and his funeral was one of the largest in the history of Chicago. He was buried beside his brother and father in Chicago's Graceland Cemetery.

A man and an era had been laid to rest.

CHAPTER 41
The Modern Agency

After the death of William, Allan II became the Principal of the Agency. In the prosperity of the 1920's, business flourished, with more territorial division managers appointed and additional branch offices opened both in this country and abroad. Racetrack, guard, and security duties increased as industrial America expanded. With affluence came crime. The lights, it seemed, never dimmed in the offices of the Agency's Criminal Investigation Bureau. Murder, robberies of all types—including the nation's first armed-truck robbery—increased, with bandits using Model-T Fords instead of horses for their getaways; confidence men and forgery gangs were still hunted and captured by the Pinkertons.

In February, 1923, two officials of a New York utility company retained the Agency to find out who had stolen $500 from the office safe and, later, $2,000 in furs from the penthouse apartment of one of the executives. Operative A. J. Laurent was assigned. After an investigation, he reported that both robberies were undoubtedly connected and had been done from the inside. He began a check of the backgrounds and references of the thousands of utility employees. After weeks of plodding legwork, he discovered that the references of Leo Holland, a clerk, were fictitious.

Laurent and a New York City detective shadowed Holland for days. He was a slight, pug-nosed man, quiet, and well liked among his office associates. He left his office promptly at five o'clock each day, and hurried home by subway, only to appear shortly afterward dressed in an expensive blue suit, pearl-gray hat, and highly polished black shoes. When he left at night, it was always by cab. Laurent and the detective found that Holland visited poolrooms and cigar stores "meeting men who had the appearances of bookmakers—they stand about, carry dope sheets and the general conversation is about horse racing."

After a week of tailing Holland, Laurent and the detective decided that he was a good suspect, and took him into custody. Several keys and $133 were found on him. The arrest was made on a streetcorner, and when the detective said he was going to call the Black Maria, Holland said coolly:

"Oh, please don't do that. Let's take a cab—I'll pay for it."

That night Leo Holland, alias the notorious Willie (The Actor) Sutton took his first ride in a patrol wagon.

During a night of questioning Willie denied everything. A conference was held with the district attorney, who decided there wasn't enough evidence to hold Sutton for grand larceny. The best he could suggest was a charge of giving false business references—a misdemeanor. Sutton pleaded guilty, and was given a suspended sentence.

"Good day, gentlemen," he said to Laurent and the detective as he left the court.

In 1925, a wave of bank robberies took place in the city. In one, the Ozone Park National Bank, the robbers left behind an acetylene torch. The Pinkerton operative reported that the robbers had failed to break into the vault because they did not know how to operate the burner. Later, an investigation revealed that Sutton had suffered a welder's burn and on the drive back to the city had sideswiped a police car. He displayed his characteristic coolness, profusely apologized, and explained that he had got the welder's eye burn while "helping a pal" in the shipyards. Willie had carefully plotted his escape. When the police searched his car, they found overalls and a shipyard badge. Willie, always the meticulous planner, had anticipated a minor auto violation and had ordered his men to leave behind the torch and throw away the burglar tools. Through the serial number on the burner the Pinkertons traced it to the manufacturer, and then to the New Jersey retailer, who identified Sutton's Rogues' Gallery picture. At his West Side boardinghouse, the landlady told the operatives Sutton had left shortly after he had received a package from New Jersey.

On October 28, 1930, Sutton, with a partner, Marcus Bassett, a frustrated poet and author, displayed the technique that would make Sutton the most notorious American bank robber of the postwar years. In the robbery of M. Rosenthal & Sons, fashionable New York jewelers, Sutton used a Postal Telegraph messenger's uniform to gain entrance to the store. After he and Bassett had tied up the porter, they escorted the clerks to the back of the store to be tied and gagged. They obtained the combination of the safe, and cleaned it of $129,000 in gems. After bidding the gagged clerks a cordial good morning, Sutton and Bassett jumped into a stolen car equipped with proper plates and registration, and disappeared into rush-hour traffic.

Allan Pinkerton assigned Captain Herbert S. Mosher, head of Pinkerton's Criminal Identification Bureau, along with Assistant Superintendent Benjamin F. Chambers, and that veteran of countless cases, William Minster, to work with the New York police. The porter and clerks took one look at the Rogues' Gallery picture of Willie's melancholy face, and identified him as the cheery early-morning messenger. The Agency sent out coded messages that morning to all branch offices, assigning operatives to watch known jewelry fences in their cities.

Hundreds of onionskin reports tell how Mosher and his men labored day and night, traveling about the country on Willie's trail. It is a realistic picture of the work of competent private detectives, worlds apart from their counterparts on television. The reports show numerous meetings with informants, tell of checking hundreds of license-plate numbers observed near the jewelry store when it was robbed, of running down endless tips from New York to Canada, of questioning and requestioning witnesses to dredge up forgotten minutiae, of verifying addresses and standing in the shadows to watch a cheap hotel where Sutton was said to be hiding only to find a shoelace peddler who bore a striking resemblance to the bank robber.[1] For three months Mosher and his operatives also checked thousands of messenger boys until they found the one who had sold Willie his uniform. The boy was located on Rikers Island, where he was serving a thirty-day sentence for disorderly conduct.

Finally, a parole-board officer was found who dimly recalled part of a license plate of a car that had been parked near the board where Willie had checked in monthly—until the Rosenthal robbery. Teams of Pinkertons descended on the State Motor Vehicle Bureau in Albany to check licenses. Because they had only part of the number, countless plates had to be checked in all boroughs. One day Captain Mosher picked up the phone in the Pinkerton office on Nassau Street, listened, then told his associate, Captain Jim McCoy: "They found the car. It's registered to Willie's girl. He goes up there every day."

Pinkertons and the city detectives trailed Willie and the girl to a Broadway cafeteria. It was a tense moment, for the place was crowded with diners. Operatives and detectives reading scratch sheets took positions at tables until Willie, lost in conversation with the girl, was encircled. Customers who entered the cafeteria were directed to the far side of the room by an operative in a waiter's coat. Then the trap snapped shut. Sutton and the frightened girl found themselves looking into two guns held by the police.

Willie patted the girl's hand. "It's okay, kid, there won't be any shooting."

Willie, cool and smiling, was questioned by the Pinkertons and the city detectives all night; as always, he denied everything. The girl identified herself as Willie's wife. She told police she thought her husband was a "salesman," a quiet, almost mousy man who had established a trust fund for the "education of the baby when it came." The "trust fund" had been opened a few days after Willie had held up the Rosenthal store.

Weary, plodding canvassing of New York City's streets with the girl finally brought them to a building "with a laundry in the basement" where she had once met Marcus Bassett, Willie's partner. Bassett was gone when Mosher and his men crashed in the door of the rooming house, but they found a collection of many uniforms, auto plates of several states, identification badges, a box of forged job references, telegram forms, handcuffs, pamphlets on pistol silencers, a detailed floor plan of the Rosenthal store, and a timetable of the arrival and departure of every employee. A small card of "The Waverly School of Drama," with a Sixth Avenue address, interested Captain Mosher. His investigation showed that Sutton and Bassett had opened a phony school of drama, had had the business cards and letterheads printed, then rented a number of costumes. Operatives found that the "Waverly School of Drama," operated by J. W. Patterson (Bassett), had closed the day after the costumes, including many uniforms, had been delivered.

A few torn scraps of paper, one with the words: "I will be in Buffalo to spend Christmas with you," sent another team of operatives upstate to watch for Bassett's arrival. The handcuffs were traced to the manufacturer, who informed the Agency that it would "take days to check every shipment we have made to New York. There are 100,000 orders of such type handcuffs." Mosher's order to his men was, "Check every order." Another team of operatives went to the firm's storehouse and checked 100,000 orders "for nickle plated and bluesteel handcuffs."

Another Pinkerton operative was sent to a small Ohio village to interview the owner of a filling station whose name had also been found on one of the torn slips of paper. The operative arrived, only to find that the man had moved. The sheriff of the farming district used the telephone to help trace the filling-station owner, who also owned a kennel, to another town. The kennel owner, finally tracked down in a nearby town, identified Sutton as a man who had bought a pedigreed dog. He had appeared concerned about the AKC papers, explaining, "I want to make sure that when I buy a dog it's the best." Through the registration papers the operative traced the dog to a "well-known woman living in upstate New York." She identified Sutton as a businessman she had known. How Sutton became acquainted with her is a mystery.

In Buffalo, the surveillance by the Pinkerton operatives and city police at airports, railroad, and bus stations finally paid off. Bassett was spotted, trailed, and captured. Handsome, dressed in expensive tweeds, he coolly informed Captain Mosher that "naturally I would have resorted to firearms" if the Pinkertons had caught him in the New York City rooming house.

On November 28, 1930, Bassett confessed to Mosher and Acting Captain Patrick McVeigh of the New York City police that he had been Sutton's partner in eight stickups totaling $214,000.

"Crime doesn't pay," he quipped as he signed his confession. Both Sutton and Bassett were sentenced to thirty years in Sing Sing. As Sutton left the Criminal Courts Building in New York City, he smilingly told Mosher: "Goodbye, Captain. I just want to let you know there is no jail that can hold me."

A year later, Sutton escaped from Sing Sing. He would again meet the Pinkertons.

The jubilation in the Agency over the capture of Sutton and Bassett was overshadowed by the sudden death of Allan Pinkerton in 1930, due, doctors said, to the severe gassing he had received in the war.

Allan's son, Robert II, at twenty-six years of age, became Principal, the fourth generation of Pinkertons to head the Agency. Three years before the death of his father, Robert had graduated from Harvard and attended Columbia Law School. He was a noted horseman and had captained Harvard's polo team for two years. In 1929, he became a Wall Street broker, after his father had bought him a seat on the Stock Exchange. A slender, handsome, and cultured man, he had no intention of joining the detective dynasty. However, under the combined pressure of the executives of the firm and his family, he reluctantly took over.

As he later said: "I really had to start from scratch. I had not specialized in business at college, and the only thing I knew about the Agency was what I had heard my father discuss at home." Robert, however, was reluctant to give up Wall Street, so for the next four years he doubled as a broker and president of the Pinkerton's.[2]

In the 1920's and early 1930's the Agency provided operatives for use in large industrial plants to report on union activities, a practice that resulted in severe criticism and further enmity of labor. By 1936, 30 percent of the firm's business was made up of its industrial services, aside from providing uniformed guards and criminal investigation. In general, it offered to the employer confidential information, secured by the Pinkertons and their sources, as to the degree of unrest in a plant, the presence of outside agitators and organizers, and the general run for what was called labor espionage. The service additionally embraced other aspects of labor-management relations, such as detection of schemes and devices to defraud or rob the employer, endanger the reputation of a product, and create personal and property hazards. These services, used by many of the nation's largest and smallest corporations in the Depression thirties, were usually regarded by management as an indispensable protection.

In 1936, the Seventy-fourth Congress passed Resolution 266, which called for an investigation of violations of the right of free speech, assembly, and of interference with the right of labor to organize and bargain collectively. The Committee on Education and Labor, of which Mr. Justice Black was the chairman, appointed a subcommittee, with Senators Elbert D. Thomas of Utah and Robert La Follette, Jr., of Wisconsin, to conduct hearings.

The issue before the Senate subcommittee was solely that of labor espionage. Two sides to the question were vigorously presented by La Follette and Robert Pinkerton. La Follette pointed out that while the Pinkertons pointed with pride to the fact that they had refused retainers that had any connection with marital infidelity, it was within their code to pay men to spy on fellow workers and that without such work the Agency would collapse.

As to the first, Pinkerton answered: "I feel a man running a business must keep himself posted on how that business is being run." As to the second, he scoffed at the charge that the Agency would fail without labor-espionage work. A huge file was presented to the committee by Pinkerton to bolster his first argument. It contained the court convictions of over two thousand persons "guilty of such crimes as assaults, murders, arson, kidnapping, bombings and all types of criminal offenses in connection with labor disputes." [3]

Robert Pinkerton, as his grandfather had done in 1862, refused to identify their secret sources of information on the ground that it would put the safety of such men in jeopardy. Their counsel, Bruce Bromley, later Justice of the New York Court of Appeals, advised the Agency and the committee that to compel such disclosures was contrary, in his opinion, to the Fourth Amendment. There was a great deal of talk about the threat of Communism, to which the Pinkertons made much reference. There was a comic touch when not one of the officers of the Agency could swear "to ever having seen a Communist." When Senator Thomas declared that Asher Rossetter, then general manager, could not even define Communism, the Pinkerton executive quietly told him he defined it "as a practice calling for the complete abolition of all private properties of every description and the absolute control by committees of organized workers in all matters pertaining to labor, social relationship, religion and so on."

The hearings brought out the scope of labor espionage in the country at the time, when an industrial economist on the National Labor Relations Board furnished the committee with a list showing that 230 private detective agencies had labor informants in over a hundred cities. He estimated an average of $175 a month paid to the agencies per man.

General Motors officials testified that their plants paid $994,855.68 to detective agencies from January, 1934, to July, 1936.

In regard to the Pinkertons, the subcommittee essentially established that when an employer took their service, the Agency, by their own men or through men in the plant whom they paid, provided the employer with reports on what his men were saying or doing, and as to the hazards to the physical welfare of the workers and to the plants, its equipment and its stories, Robert Pinkerton testified that reports came from 303 secret sources, of which 132 were members of trade unions, 43 of company unions, and 31 were executive officers of unions.

The senators, obviously hostile, bullied and baited Robert Pinkerton and his staff of executives, who, on the other hand, were not very responsive, especially concerning their procedures. After the issuance of the committee's subpoena, they forthwith discontinued written reports. The Pinkertons took their traditional stand that what they had done was legal and, given the state of the country at the time, very much in the public interest. It was a strong echo of William's and Robert's defense of their actions before Congress in the House and Senate investigation of the Homestead riots.

After a long and bitter hearing, the Senate, the House of Representatives concurring, passed a resolution that "so called industrial spy system breeds fear, suspicion and animosity, tends to cause strikes and industrial warfare and is contrary to sound public policy."

Pinkerton, then thirty-three, summoned his board of directors and asked that it vote to stop all labor investigations. On April 8, 1937, the management "recognized the change in recent years in the field of employer and employee relations and that the public sentiment generally was condemning any practices which had been in effect for a long time."

On the recommendation of Robert Pinkerton, who had been considering eliminating the firm's labor investigation practices when the Wagner Act was passed, the following resolution was unanimous: "Resolved that the management be authorized and instructed to take such steps as the management may feel necessary that this Agency in the future not furnish information to anyone concerning the lawful attempts of labor unions or employees to organize and bargain collectively."

As Pinkerton said at the time: "Our Agency has always felt that the employer had a right to know what his employees were doing but if the sentiment throughout the country is such as to bring before Congress the resolution that has been passed, it looks as if we were on the wrong side of the fence. Times have changed and we are out of step." [4]

As Pinkerton later told the New York *Times*, "That is a phase of our business that we are not particularly proud of and we're delighted we're out of it. However, there was nothing illegal about it at the time." [5]

In 1938, the first year after Pinkerton's dropped its industrial services, the firm's income dipped to $1,224,661, the lowest it had been since 1921. It continued to mount slowly during the next two years, then rose sharply as World War II neared and industry demanded guards.

The Pinkertons' duties at the nation's racetracks also increased, with ringers still a major problem.

In the 1930's the Pinkertons broke up the operations of another famous racetrack ringer, Peter C. (Paddy) Barrie, an Irishman born in Edinburgh, Scotland. His first job of ringing a horse was on his employer, Lady Mary Cameron, who owned an estate near Edinburgh. He had bought a fading old dapple-gray mare from Lady Cameron for $85. Some time later he sold Lady Mary a spotted, splendid mare for $1,400. Several days after the mare joined the Cameron stables, the animal became docile and listless and the color began to run. Barrie had doctored the mare's teeth and gums, dyed her a bay, and stimulated her with narcotics.[6]

In the United States, he worked for racketeers, doping horses for $5,000 a mount. He also ran ringers on almost every racetrack in the country. The Pinkertons finally caught up with him at Hialeah, and turned him over to the immigration authorities after they had discovered Paddy had jumped ship. He also jumped bail, and it was two years before the Agency found him. This time he was deported, and a Pinkerton operative rode out to Sandy Hook to make sure Paddy returned to Scotland. An investigation by the Agency revealed that between $5,000,000 and $7,000,000 changed hands because of Barrie's ringers.

Paddy's most famous ringer took place at Havre de Grace, on October 3, 1931. He had bought from the Marshall Field stables a three-year-old sorrel stallion named Aknahton for $4,300. From a Long Island trainer he purchased Shem, a dark sorrel with a poor record, for $400. Barrie dyed Aknahton to look like Shem, and entered Aknahton as Shem on the first race of the last day at Havre de Grace. Mrs. Payne Whitney's Byzantine was a heavy favorite, and the lowly Shem got odds of 52 to 1. Shem (Aknahton) got away to a poor start at the gate but caught the field at the two-furlong post. He passed Byzantine and won the race by four lengths. He had done three-quarters of a mile in a minute and thirteen seconds. Barrie and his gambling friends, the Pinkertons estimated, cleaned up more than $1,000,000 on bets.

This swindle and others of Barrie's led Robert Pinkerton and his staff to work out a horse-identification system suggested by Marshall Cassidy, executive secretary of the Jockey Club, whose idea it was. The Pinkerton system includes information on about 30,000 or more thoroughbreds. Whenever a new horse is brought to the track where the system is used, a complete description of the animal is written, including his color markings, disposition, and any other characteristics. The animal is then given a number that is tattooed on the inner upper lip, and included in his record. Six photographs are taken, front, side, and closeups, of the horse's four "nighteyes," the scaly, hardened skin on the inner side of each leg. The surface of the "nighteyes" is made up of distinct ridges and impressions, and never changes after the birth of the horse. They are similar to a human's fingerprints. Before races are run each day, operatives check all horses entered, and compare them with their charts. If any discrepancy is noted, the horse is not allowed to run until the matter is cleared up. The identification system, where it is used, has virtually wiped out the ringing rackets on American tracks.

After the parimutuel system of betting was adopted by all states having racing, bookmakers were persona non grata to the racing associations for the obvious reason that wagers made off the track, with bookmakers, result in the loss of millions for the tracks. In the thirties and years after World War II, the traditional method of studying photographs of bookmakers and shadowing suspects were used; but as advances were made in photography and electronics, the Pinkertons at the tracks were equipped with miniature cameras, walkie-talkies, and computers.

The Agency's business and profits increased sharply during the war years when the Pinkertons supplied protection for war plants. The top year, 1944, saw the gross income from war-plant operations come to $1,748,584 of the Agency's total of $4,089,969. As national business became more security conscious in the postwar years, the Agency's income continued to rise. In 1946, it was $5,309,772, and in the following year slightly under that figure.

Although the reorganization of the Federal Bureau of Investigation, the formation of other federal law-enforcement agencies, state police, and the increased strength and competence of metropolitan police have all been factors in replacing the Pinkertons as the nation's most powerful single law-enforcement body by the 1930's, the Agency still participated in important criminal investigations. In cooperation with the New York police, a team of Pinkertons under Captain Mosher broke up a nationally publicized gang of jewel thieves that numbered among its victims Mrs. James Forrestal, wife of the former Secretary of Defense; Gypsy Rose Lee, and many society figures. The robberies had become so extensive that the police commissioner warned wealthy New Yorkers not to wear their gems to night spots.

Willie Sutton, after making good his boast to Mosher that he would escape, skillfully pulled off a dozen bank robberies throughout the East. Philadelphia police and the Pinkertons finally arrested Sutton in a Philadelphia apartment. He again escaped from prison, and returned to robbing banks all over the country until he was captured through the alertness of a young Brooklyn man, who was later killed by the underworld. Sutton is now in Dannemora State Prison.

The modern Agency, while still engaged in criminal detection work, is now engaged mostly in commercial investigation—which, however, sometimes ends up as a criminal case. A large percentage of the firm's criminal work is done in connection with insurance frauds, especially the fake claim racket.

Numerically, the Agency is now a giant compared to the firm at the turn of the century which the national press routinely called the world's largest. Today there are seventy branch offices across the nation and throughout the world, with 13,000 full-time and more than 9,000 part-time employees. The daily mail at the main offices, still in New York and Chicago, never fails to contain many applications to join the Agency as a "detective." Recruiting is usually done through various media: newspaper advertisements, military recruitment centers, police and fire departments. Operatives—they are now called investigators—must have at least a high school education, but a college degree is preferred. A thorough investigation is made of each applicant. In the old days either Allan Pinkerton himself or the indefatigable George Bangs would take a promising recruit and show him the ropes by on-the-job training. The art of shadowing was demonstrated to young nineteenth-century hopefuls by following another operative. For the modern investigator there is a formal training program consisting of a syllabus and lesson plan, but the old-fashioned way of learning the technique of tailing a suspect is still done by on-the-job instruction under an experienced investigator.

The secrecy that Allan Pinkerton insisted upon in his letter of 1872 to George Bangs is still maintained. Investigators in racial communities—Italian, Negro, Chinese, Irish, Jewish—are under strict orders never to let anyone know they work for the Agency. They never appear at the main offices, and their pay is usually slipped to them by a fellow investigator. Another of Allan Pinkerton's rules, requiring operatives to study Rogues' Gallery photographs, is still followed. New investigators usually work in the criminal-identification department for some time before being assigned to a case. The pay of a Pinkerton investigator is usually commensurate with that of detectives in big-city police departments.

It has long been the custom of the Agency to appoint its executives from the ranks. One of their jobs is to consider whether or not to accept a case. They must judge whether it is compatible with the principles laid down by the founder of the firm more than 150 years ago. The prospective client is interviewed extensively, and his background and reputation are checked out. If the executive is doubtful, he submits the matter to the district head in New York, Chicago, Cleveland, or San Francisco. If a decision is still not made, the report is then sent on to the regional head, either in New York, Chicago, or San Francisco. If the regional head decides it is a policy-making decision, the matter is then sent on to New York for a final evaluation and the ultimate answer.

Pilfering and shoplifting caused a $2,000,000,000 loss to American industry in 1967, despite the existence of an army of 170,000 security guards. Experts, according to *Forbes Magazine,* predict that within a decade the estimate will soar to a shocking $5,000,000,000, a conservative guess. Most companies still provide for their own security needs, but an increasing percentage are turning their work over to the Pinkertons rather than to an "in-house staff." [7]

A random check of the firm's records dramatically demonstrates how the use of private investigation by American business and industry is growing both in scope and in variety of assignments. In a single three-day period, 184 large and small firms authorized investigations in fifty cities in the United States and Canada. Clients ranged from a jet manufacturer to the owner of a shop selling women's apparel. Investigations ranged from a shopping trip by a Pinkerton to determine whether the client's product was being sold under Fair Trade prices to the surveillance of a $50,000-a-year executive whose conduct in his off hours was "detrimental to the corporation's image." Nurses in crime-ridden areas are escorted to their apartments; guards on motor scooters patrol a large campus; and visitors to an atomic-energy project are screened. There is also a Pinkerton Navy. The operatives who lived on horseback in the old West would be startled to see their present-day colleagues patrolling Long Island's Great South Bay, guarding the huge marinas and the clam and oyster seedbeds. Eighty years ago there were wild chases across the western plains; but the modern Agency's Navy, equipped with radar, has engaged in wars with poachers and chases no less exciting.

Almost a hundred years ago Allan Pinkerton had a fierce exchange of letters with his superintendents over the use of female operatives. Allan, as always, won, and the tradition of using women as Pinkerton investigators and security hostesses continues.

In the Agency of the 1960's, its executives have acknowledged the swing toward sophisticated electronics by getting into the manufacturing end of that business. Changing technology apparently has helped the Agency, which made $1.9 million, or $1.40 per share, in 1966 on revenues of $71,000,000, a return on an equity of 28 percent. In the first half of 1967, Pinkerton's earnings were a "thumping"—as *Forbes* put it—50 percent on 19 percent higher revenues.[8]

In 1965, Robert Pinkerton changed the name of the Agency to Pinkerton's, Inc. As he explained, it was done because he believed the new name was a better reflection of the modern Agency's function—supplying uniformed security guards for racetracks and other sporting events, fairs, industrial plants, schools and hospitals and other institutions.[9]

Two years later, for the first time since Allan Pinkerton opened his tiny office in Chicago more than a century ago, a non-Pinkerton was named to the presidency of the Agency. Edward J. Bednarz, executive vice-president and general manager, who joined the firm in 1947 as a special racetrack agent, took over the Agency's top position, while Robert was named chairman of the company. Coleman J. Graham, former vice-president and assistant to the general manager, succeeded Mr. Bednarz. Earlier that same year, the company went public.

Bednarz has played a key part in creating a more sophisticated image for the Agency. He established a research department to study new techniques in industrial security and a school for the study of sophisticated electronic devices. The school was selected by the State Department as the only private agency included in the training program of State's Agency for International Development for Security Officials sent to the United States by other world governments. In 1962, Bednarz arranged for the purchase of a New England company, manufacturing space alarms along radar principles. This subsidiary of the Agency, Pinkerton-Elector Security Company, is now marketing an anti-intrusion device for industry and homes known as Radar-Eye.

Only recently two members of a team of burglars, dubbed the "Walkie-Talkie Gang" by the tabloids, was arrested while burglarizing the property bureau of a Long Island police station. The invisible radar field of the Pinkerton's Radar-Eye equipment triggered the police alarm. The building was surrounded and the gang captured.

It was also Bednarz who gained for the Agency membership in the Ligue Internationale des Sociétiés de Surveillance, with headquarters in London. This international group extends membership to one security agency in each country. Pinkerton's represents both the United States and Canada.

Bednarz also secured the contract for security at the World's Fair, 1964–1965, and drew up the specifications for the fair's elaborate security program.

Pinkerton's, Inc., today is a major American business. The unique, colorful but anachronistic dynasty of detectives had really ended with the death of William Pinkerton in 1923, although the late Robert Pinkerton II had assumed leadership of the firm, replacing its nineteenth-century trappings with modern business methods.

The Agency of today is worlds apart from the one-man business of Allan Pinkerton and his staff of George Bangs, Timothy Bangs, Kate Warne, and James McParland. They would be speechless if they could see the gleaming glass and chrome offices of the firm they had founded. Surely the bearded Bangs and the other superintendents would be uncomfortable detailing assignments to the college-trained staff, many of them former FBI agents.

Any summing up of the Agency's one hundred and nineteen years must begin with the great exploits of its members and employees for over a century—achievements that speak for themselves. And at a time when corruption among city and state police, and even at national levels, is accepted as commonplace by the ordinary citizen, it is indeed remarkable that a private organization could recruit, train, and win enormous loyalty for over ten decades from hundreds of men and women who behaved with such gallantry, bravery, and daring.

The influence of the Pinkertons' techniques on the nation's law-enforcement organizations has been very strong. Allan Pinkerton's early methods of infiltration of organized criminal groups has been imitated and perfected not only by federal agents but also by metropolitan police departments.

The importance of William Pinkerton's plan in the 1890's to centralize Bertillon and photographic records within a national bureau of criminal identification—later the basis for the present FBI's enormous files—is obvious. The Pinkertons' development of a system of identifying lawbreakers through frontier sheriffs and marshals who sent on photographs of dead or captured outlaws and city criminals was a crude but pioneering effort to "weave together the bits and pieces of a crime," as William once said.

William's efforts to link the nineteenth-century Agency to the great European police forces, such as Scotland Yard and the Sûreté, through personal contacts and friendships established the first international exchange of criminal information and mutual assistance, a forerunner of Interpol.

The absence of scandal and corruption in the Agency's history is amazing when one considers that their employees have been exposed for over eighty years to the most contagious of all forms of corruption—gambling. Thousands of men fought and died for the Pinkertons, served them with integrity, and maintained their fidelity against the erosions of jealousy, corruption, and cowardice. Perhaps the times in which Allan Pinkerton and his two sons worked and lived supply a partial explanation. They were men more at home in the field than behind a desk, and gave ample evidence of their own personal courage. Then, too, they had their own charisma: Allan was a friend of Lincoln, McClellan, Grant, Johnson, and many of the famous men of his time; and his sons were active, colorful figures who by the 1880's were household names, familiar to every American and throughout Europe.

On the other hand, all the Pinkertons had a Bourbon cast of mind; they were ultraconservative; and from the very beginning father and sons were devoted to the philosophy that the ends justified the means. Apparently they ignored the question. Was the end worth it? As true believers in the Horatio Alger story, as charter members in the savage world of Social Darwinism, they were susceptible to oversimplification of the principles of free enterprise, and they resisted progressivism. Their darkest hours came when they were ensnared by the inevitable tensions between the two. They seemed awed by the unbridled power of the utilities of their day, and were dedicated to the rule of *status quo*. Perhaps their greatest fault was their unreasoning dedication to an ethical outlook in their time that we, with hindsight, now know was morally corrupt and socially unjust.

Allan Pinkerton's personal drive and ambition are awesome to consider, but for all his self-righteous protests to his children in later years, he ruled his home with a tyrant's hand, as he did his business. There is that significant line in one of his letters to a new employee—"I rule my office with an iron hand. I am self-willed and obstinate . . . *I must have my own way of doing things"*—in which the last five words were underlined.

Allan Pinkerton wrote his famous *Principles* for the Agency, yet although he had fled his native Scotland as a fugitive radical, friend of George Julian Harney, the anarchist; a champion of the exploited workingman, he quickly swung to the other side, once he had tasted success and wealth from his association with big business. His thinking and his philosophy molded his sons, and they never wavered.

Though William and Robert Pinkerton were just as intolerant, vindictive, fiercely opinionated, resentful of criticism, they were also, unlike their father, susceptible to new ideas and social changes. They were not familiar with, nor did they care about, the fine literature or the problems of their day. If Allan read any outstanding book, it was Lytton's *Eugene Aram,* and the subject—the life and discovery of a murderer—rather makes it obvious why he constantly urged the bored George Bangs to buy a copy and read it. William's delight in the theatre was musical comedy. He considered Gillette the great playwright of his day because of Gillette's play—*Secret Service*—about espionage in the Civil War. Robert appeared to be more bookish, and a lover of music. Perhaps it was because of the availability of concerts and opera in New York, where he made his home.

They are an extraordinary trio in our history—possessed of an awesome vigor, industry, capability, and ingenuity. Benevolent in one letter, they could be vindictive and malicious in the next. Though they were controversial—hated, feared, loved, respected—they were never boring.

And what of the Agency's impact, over the span of one hundred and eighteen years, on American society? Many new facts and discoveries have contributed significantly to our historical understanding of the Pinkertons; but, as any good historian knows, it is not finding the facts but finding their meaning that should be the primary objective.

The Pinkertons fulfilled a need in America at a critical juncture in the nation's history—indeed, their growth was in answer to the strict law of supply and demand. They fulfilled it with fidelity to those who employed them and in accordance with their own moral principles and the ethics of their time. However, in the final analysis the tragic blame for that need must rest upon the shoulders of a society that was, and still is, forced to seek out private police to help it enforce its laws and administer its justice.

HORAN'S BOONDOCKS
January 18, 1968

Notes

SOURCES: The National Archives is cited as NA; Library of Congress, LC; Pinkerton's, Inc. Archives, PA; Chicago Historical Society, CHS; Pennsylvania State Historical Society, PHS; The New York Public Library, NYP; Illinois Central Collections, Newberry Library, NL; Chicago, Burlington & Quincy Railroad Collections, Newberry Library, BA; The New-York Historical Society Manuscript Division, NYH; Mitchell Library, Glasgow, ML; The Huntington Library, San Marino, California, HL; Theodore Roosevelt Manuscripts, Library of Congress, TRmms; Scotland Yard Historical Archives, SYA. Newspapers and magazines cited are in the collections of The New York Public Library, Library of Congress, or The New-York Historical Society.

Book One
Barrelmaker, Revolutionist and Detective, 1819–1850
Chapter 1
Glasgow, 1819–1842

1. In a series of letters to his son Robert, then in charge of the Agency's Eastern Division, Allan Pinkerton reviewed some of his family's history; Allan Pinkerton to Robert, May 22, 1879, April 28, 1883, LC. Early-nineteenth-century Glasgow city directories also helped to locate various members of the Pinkerton family and their occupations in the Gorbals. In the fall of 1889, Edgar L. Wakeman, an old friend of Pinkerton, visited Glasgow and sought out facts of the detective's early years from friends, relatives and a Glasgow police chief named Miller. A search of the Glasgow police records does show a police chief named Miller in the 1890's. Wakeman's stories under a Glasgow dateline appeared in the Springfield, Ohio, *Republican,* September 22, 1889. A slightly longer version, probably not edited, was published in the St. Paul *Daily Press,* September 21, 1889. Hereafter cited as Wakeman. See also *Harper's Weekly,* July 12, 1884; the *Inter Ocean,* July 9, 1881; the New York *Star,* July 2, 1884; the New York *Times,* July 2, 1884; the Chicago *Eagle,* October 16, 1897; the *Travelers' Quarterly,* October, 1889; the *People's Journal,* December 23, 1905.

Robert Blair Wilkie, of the "old Glasgow" Museum and Art Gallery, searched the files of the Glasgow Police Department and Glasgow Fiscal Office for Pinkerton's warrant; but unfortunately the reports of the police investigations of the Chartists had long been destroyed. The records of the Glasgow police show Pinkerton's father was attached to that organization, but they do not reveal in what capacity.

2. Wakeman.

3. A description of that rainy morning's raid on Newport can be found in the testimony of the mayor, townspeople, and officers of the 42nd Foot, in *The Trial of John Frost for High Treason, Held at Monmouth, December, 1839* (Saunders & Berry, Book Sellers, London, 1840), NYP.

Accounts of Pinkerton's activities among the physical-force groups of Glasgow can be found in the files of the *Scottish Patriot* [the leading Chartist newspaper] Glasgow *Evening Post,* and Glasgow *Herald,* in the Mitchell Library, Glasgow.

The *Scottish Patriot,* September 7, 1839, has an account of Pinkerton being elected as a member of the board of directors of the Universal Suffrage Association. On December 7, 1839, the same newspaper has Pinkerton's attack on the meeting of the delegates and directors of the Suffrage Association. It would appear that Pinkerton wrote a "scurrilous" letter to the Glasgow *Evening Post* describing that meeting. Unfortunately, the copy of the *Post* containing the letter is not on file in the library. Pinkerton's letter was replied to in the *Scottish Patriot,* January 4, 1840.

There are two references to Pinkerton's career in the Northern Democratic Association Glasgow: the *Scottish Patriot* of February 1, 1840, and March 14, 1840, of the same newspaper when he defended Harney's right to speak. For Pinkerton's resignation from the Universal Suffrage Association, see *Scotland in Chartism* by Leslie C. Wright (London, 1953), p. 89.

Harney's views—"There is no answer like the sword and the musket"—were too radical for the spirit of the movement, and he gradually faded from the Chartists. Around 1854 he moved to Jersey, where there was a branch of the Commune Révolutionnaire; then came to the United States in 1862 or 1863. He remained in the States until 1878, when he returned to England. But it is evident that by this time Pinkerton had no time for Harney. No evidence can be found of any meeting between Pinkerton and Harney in the fifteen or more years the celebrated English radical lived and lectured in the United States.

4. Wakeman.

5. The Marriage Register of the Glasgow City Parish shows that Pinkerton and Joan were married on March 13, 1842. However, Pinkerton always regarded March 28, as his wedding date. The only explanation for the difference in dates is the well-known laxity of early-nineteenth-century registers. See Pinkerton to Joan, recalling their courtship, marriage, and journey from Scotland, March 28, 1878, LC. Hereafter cited as Joan.

6. It has long been accepted by family legend, and has been included

in the numerous error-ridden feature stories written about Pinkerton's life, that Pinkerton and his bride took the bark *Kent* from Glasgow to the United States and that the ship sank off Sable Island. The records of Lloyds of London do not list a ship sunk named the *Kent*. George T. Bates, Provincial Land Surveyor and Secretary of the Halifax Historical Society, pinpointed for me the bark *Isabella* as the only ship leaving Glasgow in that period of March, 1842, that sank off the Nova Scotia coast. The files of the *Acadian Recorder* confirm the sinking of the *Isabella,* the looting of the ship, and robbing of the passengers by the residents of Aspby Bay. Pinkerton never mentioned this incident in his later letters. However, in one to his son Robert, he did recall that he had been robbed of most of his money when he arrived in the United States. To add confusion to the question of what ship they actually took, the files of the Glasgow *Herald* recently revealed a notice that "the fine, fast-sailing Barque, *Kent,* James Gardiner, commanding, is now at berth and ready to receive cargo; will sail pointedly on March 25." A notice of the arrival of the *Isabella* at Cairnyan, in southwest Scotland, was also reported in the *Herald* on March 25. In one letter, Pinkerton wrote that they had sailed on April 9, 1842. The files of the *Acadian Reporter* do not contain the passenger list for the *Isabella*. It is difficult to determine which ship Pinkerton actually took to the United States, but it was probably the *Isabella*.

7. Joan told this story to Wakeman. It has also been handed down as legend.

Chapter 2
How Allan Pinkerton Became a Detective

1. In 1890, George Renwick, then Dundee's superintendent of streets, recalled the story of the arrest to a reporter for the Chicago *Tribune,* on July 1, 1890. Pinkerton also described it in his *Professional Thieves and Detectives* (G. W. Dullingham, London, 1890), pp. 1–54. This book, like many of the volumes of Pinkerton's reminiscences, were put together by "writers," as he once called them in a letter to his son Robert. The license used by the writers and their disregard for facts in many of the books are apparent in *Professional Thieves and Detectives*. There are geographical errors that Pinkerton would not have made. Apparently, after he had supplied the "outline," as he called it, he never bothered to read proof. *Spy of the Rebellion,* his account of the Maroney case, and the *Molly Maguires* I believe are the most factual. His wartime memoirs in *Spy* are colored by his hero worship of McClellan.

Chapter 3
The Frontier Abolitionist and the Move to Chicago

1. In the fall of 1935, the transcript of the Pinkerton trial was discovered in the "Church Book" of the Dundee Baptist Church during research being made for Dundee's centennial.

2. Joan; the Chicago *Eagle,* October 16, 1897; Chicago *Tribune,* July 1, 1890; *The Pinkerton Detective Dynasty,* by Richard W. Rowan (New York, 1931, pp. 6–21); the *People's Journal,* December 23, 1905. See also "Allan Pinkerton, Dundee's World Famous Detective," by Teressa Przeniczny, *Countryside* [Barrington, Illinois] *Press,* September 14, 1967.

Chapter 4
Chicago and the Beginning of the Agency, 1850–1860

1. *Illinois Works Progress Administration State Guide,* p. 197.

2. For an account of the attempts on Pinkerton's life and his service as a postal agent, see the Chicago *Daily Democratic Press,* September 9, 1853, cited hereafter as *Press.*

3. In at least one letter Allan Pinkerton gave 1850 "as the year I started my Agency," yet he once testified in a conductor's trial, he started his firm in 1852. The first letterhead I can locate of Pinkerton's North-Western Police Agency is 1858, although it is listed as "successor to Pinkerton & Co.," with no date given for the latter. In 1852–1853, Pinkerton was working as Special Agent for the United States Post Office in Chicago. It is possible he had formed the Agency with Rucker in 1850 while he was still holding on to his other jobs. However, it is apparent his business did not flourish until he signed the contract with the Illinois Central in 1855. The first paragraph identifies the Agency as "Pinkerton & Co."

4. Obituary of George Henry Bangs, New York *Times,* September 15, 1883.

In his *Expressman and the Detective,* p. 94, Pinkerton tells how he hired Kate Warne, "the greatest female detective who ever brought a case to a successful conclusion." Women were not a part of American Police Departments until 1891, and then only as matrons to care for prisoners. They were first used as investigators in 1903 in New York City, and in 1920 the title "policewoman" was established. The Bureau of Police-women was created in 1923. By 1860, Pinkerton had several female detectives in what he called "my Female Detective Bureau," with Kate as its head. From Pinkerton's letters, Kate was not only a detective but probably an early administrator of the Chicago office.

Pinkerton's affection for Kate is revealed in his books and an 1868 letter to George Bangs in which he informed Bangs that Kate was dying. Her grave is alongside Allan, William, and Robert's in the Graceland Cemetery, Chicago. The original burial records, which I examined, curiously spell her name Warn, as on her headstone, although Pinkerton and Bangs spelled it Warne in their letters and reports. Her death certificate shows she was thirty-five when she died, thus making her about twenty-three when she became America's first female detective in the 1850's.

5. *General Principles,* Pinkerton's National Detective Agency (Jones Printing Company, New York, 1878), PA.

6. Allan Pinkerton to Henry Hunt, October 10, 1856, hereafter cited as Hunt, CHS.

7. In 1946, the voluminous files of the Illinois Central Railroad were turned over to the Newberry Library in Chicago. McClellan's letter books, reports, and personal correspondence number about 5,000 items. See *Guide to The Illinois Central Archives in the Newberry Library, 1851–1906,* compiled by Carolyn Curtis Mohr (Newberry Library, Chicago, 1951); see George Brinton McClellan, "Out Letters," February 1857–July 1860, 10 v. L.P.C.B.; Letters, Ma. 1; for the line's agreement with Pinkerton, see Reports, Legal Contracts, 1851–1852, 2.32. For the violence on the frontier where the line was building, see *ibid.*, The Murder of Superintendent Daniel Short, December, 1853, La Salle, Illinois, NL. See also "Detective Pinkerton" by General R. B. Marcy, U.S.A., *Harper's New Monthly Magazine,* July, 1884, NYH.

Chapter 5
Allan Pinkerton and John Brown

1. "Pinkerton and Lincoln" by Lloyd Lewis, *Illinois Historical Journal,* 1948, p. 376, cited hereafter as Lewis. Pinkerton commented many times in his books and pamphlets on his rabid abolitionist sentiments. See *Spy in the Rebellion* by Allan Pinkerton (Winter & Hatch, Hartford, Conn., 1883), xxxv of Preface, hereafter cited as *Spy.*

2. *John Brown, 1800–1895,* by Oswald Garrison Villard (New York, 1943), pp. 347–390.

3. For an account of Brown's visit to Allan Pinkerton in Chicago, see the Chicago *Times,* September 1, 1882, which describes the reception for Mrs. Brown when Pinkerton, the widow of Jones, and others read their memories of that day and night. See also H. O. Wagoner, Spokane, Washington, *Review,* September 2, 1892; Kagi to Tidd, Detroit, March 13, 1859, Document No. 1, Appendix to (Governor Wise's) Message 1, to Virginia legislature, December, 1859, NYP; also *Old John Brown and The Men of Harper's Ferry, Time,* London, pp. 227–228.

4. Lewis, p. 376.

5. *Spy,* p. xxvi, Preface; Lewis, p. 376. Although Pinkerton hints at a jail delivery at Harpers Ferry, there is scant evidence that he did more than consider the possibility.

Chapter 6
Pinkerton and the Expressman: The Nathan Maroney Investigation

1. Hunt; Allan Pinkerton in a "confidential letter," May 3, 1858, probably to an out-of-town police chief. Both CHS.

2. *Old Way Bills,* by Alvin F. Harlow (New York, 1934), p. 48; hereafter cited as Harlow.

3. In his *Expressman and the Detective* Pinkerton describes the techniques he used in the Maroney investigation. This appears to be a factual

account, and the incidents he cites correspond to contemporary newspaper accounts. See St. Louis *Globe Democrat,* January 9, 1887; Harlow,
pp. 326–328.

4. *Sunday Herald,* Chicago, November 7, 1886.

Book Two
Allan Pinkerton and the Civil War: 1861–1865
Chapter 7
The Baltimore Plot

1. Pinkerton's letter recalling how he was first reached by Felton is in
the Herndon-Weik Collection, LC; Allan Pinkerton to S. M. Felton,
January 27, 1861. See also the manuscript copy of Pinkerton's Record
Book, hereafter cited as Record Book, HL. Pinkerton's letter to Felton, regarding the events of the plot, is in the Felton Papers, PHS.

2. Timothy Webster's reports from Perrymansville to E. J. Allen, February 19, 1861, Record Book, HL. He signed his reports "TW."

In his Record Book, Pinkerton gave as a key to the initials of his
agents: "A.P.," Allan Pinkerton, who used the alias of "J. Hutchinson"
or variants of that name, and "E. J. Allen," later his Civil War nom de
plume; "G.H.B.," George H. Bangs, then listed as Pinkerton's chief clerk,
who apparently remained in Chicago and used no alias; "C.D.C.W.,"
Charles D. C. Williams, the alias used by one of Pinkerton's underground
agents in Baltimore who was either Pryce Lewis, John Scully, or Sam
Bridgman. All three played important roles in Pinkerton's Civil War
activities. "A.F.C." were initials used by Harry W. Davies, stationed in
Baltimore. Pinkerton described him as of French descent and a former
Jesuit seminarian who had traveled extensively abroad; "W.H.S." were
for William H. Scott, whom Pinkerton chose as the agent to deliver the
warning of the assassination plot to Judd, then with the President-elect's
party; "M.B." were initials for Kate Warne; "H.H.L." was Mrs. Hattie
H. Lawton, who was stationed in Perrymansville. Her role in the plot
wasn't significant, but later she would be famous in the North as the
agent who was sentenced to a year in prison by the Confederates for her
espionage work. Webster, her partner in Richmond, was executed.

The Record Book called "The Manuscript Copy of Pinkerton's Record
Book," now in the Huntington Library, is a copy of a copy. The original
was destroyed in the 1871 Chicago fire. It is part of William Henry Herndon's *Source Material for a Life of Lincoln,* 3 vols. Copied by John
Springer with scattered annotation by Herndon. The Pinkerton book is
in Vol. III, starting on p. 258, and the heading is "Operations on Baltimore Conspirators For The Assassination of President Lincoln." The
citation for the page on which Pinkerton denounced Lamon is LN, Vol.
III, p. 321.

Pinkerton also wrote a sixteen-page letter to William H. Herndon on

August 23, 1866, detailing what he and his agents had done in Baltimore, CHS.

3. Record Book, A.P. Reports, February 21, 1861.

4. Pinkerton's remarks about Lamon are to be found in his reports of February 23, 1861, in Record Book, LN 2408, III, 321.

5. George C. Latham's recollections of the *Times* reporter's fabrication of the Scotch hat was made in a statement to Jesse W. Weik, on January 23, 1918, Herndon-Weik Collection, LC.

6. New York *Times,* February 21, 1861. See also John George Nicolay's recollection of that day in his *A Short Life of Lincoln,* 1906, p. 174.

7. Allan Pinkerton to Samuel Morse Felton, March 19, 1861; April 13, 1861, Felton Papers, PHS.

8. *History and Evidence of the Passage of Abraham Lincoln from Harrisburg, Pa., to Washington, D.C., on the 22nd and 23rd of February, 1861,* NYP. See also *Spy,* pp. 45–105; the Chicago *Times,* January 8, 1863; and Colonel McClure's eyewitness account of Pinkerton's role in the Philadelphia *Press,* January 19, 1908. An excellent source book on Pinkerton's role in the Baltimore Plot is *Lincoln and the Baltimore Plot, 1861,* edited by Norma B. Cuthbert (San Marino, Calif., 1949). See also Richard Rowan, *The Pinkerton Detective Dynasty* (New York, 1931), pp. 82–117; *They Had Their Hour* by Marquis James (New York, 1934; *The Spy in America* by George Bryan (Philadelphia, 1943), p. 120; *On Hazardous Service* by W. S. Beymer (New York, 1912), pp. 179–210; *Celebrated Criminal Cases of America* by Thomas S. Duke (New York, 1910), pp. 469–480, hereafter cited as Duke, and "Allan Pinkerton and the Baltimore 'Assassination' Plot Against Lincoln," by Edward Stanley, Lanis, *Maryland Historical Magazine,* 1950.

Chapter 8
Behind Enemy Lines, 1861

1. N. B. Judd to Lincoln, April 21, 1861, Robert T. Lincoln Papers, Vol. 43, No. 9304, LC.

2. Allan Pinkerton to Lincoln, April 21, 1861, *ibid.,* Vol. 43, Nos. 3907–08, LC.

3. *Spy,* p. 139.

4. Allan Pinkerton to Lincoln, *ibid.,* Vol. 48, No. 1042, LC.

5. Allan Pinkerton to General George B. McClellan, Records of the War Department, Army of the Potomac; E. J. Allen to McClellan, June, 1861, NA.

6. Allan Pinkerton to McClellan, July 3, 1861, NA.

Chapter 9
Spy in a Top Hat

1. In 1888, Lewis wrote his memoirs, which were handed down to his daughter, Miss Mary Lewis, the only living descendant. Later they were

legally assigned to Harriet H. Shoen, historian and author and former Associate Professor of History at Davis and Elkins College. The dialogue is as Lewis recalled. See also the Davis and Elkins *Historical Magazine*, March–May, 1949. "What Pryce Lewis Did for the United States Government," *Harper's Weekly*, January 30, 1911, describes Lewis's adventures behind the Confederate lines, and states that Lewis committed suicide by leaping from the dome of the New York World Building. *Spy*, pp. 203–226, also gives an account of Lewis's adventures.

2. Colonel George S. Patton was the grandfather of General George S. Patton, Jr., "Old Blood and Guts" of World War II fame. Patton organized the Kanawah Riflemen in November, 1859, considered to be the first Confederate group formed. It became Company "H" of the 22nd Virginia Infantry Regiment. Patton was made a colonel under General Wise, and served with Jubal Early on the Washington raid. Legend has Patton carrying the slug that either killed or wounded his grandfather, as a good-luck piece during World War II. In a letter to the author in 1955, Mrs. Patton dismissed the story as "one of the many" that surrounded her husband's life.

3. Lewis would have been more alarmed had he known that about this time Wise was writing to Confederate Adjutant General Inspector Cooper that "rigid and harsh discipline" of traitors in the Kanawah Valley would fill all the jails in the Trans-Allegheny. *Official Records*, Series 1, Vol. 2, p. 288, NYP.

4. Pinkerton to Lincoln, July 18, 1861, NA.

5. McClellan to Pinkerton, Wheeling, W. Va., July 25, 1861, CHS.

6. Webster's report to Pinkerton, undated, LC.

7. Pinkerton, August 28, 1861, to his Chicago office (copy), PA.

Chapter 10
Pinkerton and the Wild Rose: The Washington Spy Ring, 1861–1862

1. Brady has mistakenly been given credit for Mrs. Greenhow's picture. Alexander Gardner not only took the photographs of the spies in Old Capitol Prison but photographed the Lincoln Conspirators—also credited many times to Brady. See *Timothy O'Sullivan: America's Forgotten Photographer*, by James D. Horan (New York, 1966).

2. "Mrs. Greenhow and the Rebel Spy Ring," by Louis Sigaud, *Maryland Historical Society Magazine*, September, 1949, hereafter cited as Sigaud. See also *Rebel Rose* by Ishbel Ross (New York, 1954), hereafter cited as *Rose*; and *Desperate Women* ("The Wild Rose," pp. 3–55) by James D. Horan (New York, 1952), hereafter cited as *Women*; and Mrs. Greenhow's memoirs, *My Imprisonment and the First Year of Abolitionist Rule at Washington* (London, 1863); and *Spy*, pp. 250–270. Lewis in his memoirs also details the incident of Pinkerton's arrest in his stocking feet and his encounter with the Wild Rose. See also, *Harper's New Monthly Magazine*, July, 1884; Pittsburgh *Gazette*, January 12, 1913; Richmond

Times Dispatch, September 11, 1932; Baltimore *American,* April 30, 1930; the *Daily News,* August 23, 1911.

3. Wood, who worked very closely with Pinkerton, is a colorful, little-known character of the war. See *The Old Capitol,* by a Lady (1867); *The Prisoner of State* by Dennis Mahoney (New York, 1863); *American Bastille* by John A. Marshall (London, 1872); and *Reveille in Washington,* by Margaret Leech (New York, 1941). William E. Doster, Provost Marshal of Washington, who worked closely with Wood, describes him in his *Lincoln and the Episodes of the Civil War* (New York, 1915), pp. 104, 112.

4. *Spy,* pp. 257, 263; *Women,* p. 21; *Rose,* p. 137.

5. Lewis Memoirs.

6. The material confiscated by Pinkerton and his men can be seen in the National Archives, Captured Confederate Correspondence, Records of the War Department and of the State Department.

7. *Women,* pp. 27–29; *Rose,* pp. 77–81. The brief, feverish notes written by one of the most powerful men in the Senate indicate the influence this flamboyant woman exercised in Civil War Washington.

8. Lewis Memoirs; Sigaud; *Spy,* p. 301.

Chapter 11
The Pinkerton Spies in Richmond, 1861–1862

1. Pinkerton to Scott, July, 1861, LC; *Spy,* pp. 271–300.

2. Pinkerton to Lincoln, July 19, 1861, LC.

3. Timothy Webster to Allan Pinkerton, November 15, 1861 (copy), PA. There was one flaw in Webster's detailed dispatch. It gave the Confederate strength in Virginia as 116,430—over 40,000 too high.

4. *Spy,* pp. 498–560. Pinkerton based his account on what he was told by Hattie Lawton, who was captured with Webster, after she had returned to Washington. In his memoirs Pinkerton said he believed that Lewis, along with Scully, had informed on Webster. Pinkerton's version was later corrected in a now rare pamphlet, published by the Agency on Webster in 1903, which claimed that Lewis "remained staunch and did not confess."

Chapter 12
Escape and Capture

1. This chapter is based on Lewis's memoirs. He kept the Richmond newspaper clippings, with his marginal comments.

Chapter 13
In the Shadow of the Gallows

1. Professor Shoen's research in the Archives of the British Foreign Office confirmed this part of Lewis's story.

Chapter 14
The Execution of Timothy Webster

1. *Spy,* p. 544.

2. *Ibid.,* p. 551.

3. When John Yates Beall and Captain Robert Cobb Kennedy were captured for their part in the fire raid on New York City, Richmond pleaded for their lives, but Stanton refused to commute the sentences. General Dix, who had threatened to hang the Confederate spies to Broadway lampposts, said at the time: "The Rebels should remember Tim Webster." See *Confederate Agent* by James D. Horan (New York, 1954).

4. Richmond *Examiner,* May 1, 1862.

5. Miss Elizabeth Van Lew's diary and papers, Manuscript Room, New York Public Library, describes Captain McCubbin's role as one of Wise's detectives in Richmond. See also *Women,* pp. 146–153. On Pinkerton's instructions, George Bangs went to Richmond and recovered Webster's body.

Chapter 15
Too Many Bayonets

1. Students of the Civil War soon learn to doubt every statement, particularly as to numbers. Especially in the valley campaign, when there was a constant shifting of forces from one command to another, there is a general disagreement as to the strength of the forces engaged. On May 25, 1862 (*Official Records* [hereafter cited as *Off. Rec.*], Ser. 1, XI, Pt. 1, p. 31), Geary reported Jackson's strength at 10,000; while it was stated in a Confederate source that his strength was 13,000 to 15,000 (*Battles and Leaders,* II, 285). G. F. R. Henderson (*Stonewall Jackson,* I, 413) and Frank E. Vandiver, (*Mighty Stonewall,* p. 239) agree on the figure of 16,000. Federal reports place Jackson's forces at Kernstown as about 15,000 to Shields's 8,000 (*Off. Rec.,* Ser. 1, XII, Pt. 1, p. 335); at Winchester (May 25,, 1862) his force was estimated at 15,000 as compared with Banks's force of less than 4,000.

2. Douglas S. Freeman gives Lee's strength after Jackson joined him as 85,000 "of all arms" (*Lee,* p. 116). Lee estimated the Union strength at this time as about 150,000 or more (*ibid.,* p. 117). On May 31, the aggregate number present for duty in the Army of the Potomac under McClellan (on the peninsula) was reported as 98,000 (*Off. Rec.* Ser. 1, XI, Pt. 3, p. 204).

3. Philippe, Comte de Paris, in *Battles and Leaders,* II, p. 118.

4. From his Civil War Record Book dispatches, letters, reports, etc., one wonders how Pinkerton ever accomplished what he did. Bangs, too, evidently was worked to the brink of physical exhaustion. Added to their responsibility of uncovering Confederate spies in Washington was the task of investigating and gathering evidence to convict war marketeers,

soldiers who were stealing food from the military warehouses and selling it to food brokers, crooked cattle dealers, influence peddlers in the War Department, etc. See E. J. Allen, from Colonel F. H. Clarke, Washington, Chief of Commissary, March 12, 1861; E. J. Allen to Colonel H. F. Clark, March 12, 1861; E. J. Allen to Thomas A. Scott, Assistant Secretary of War, August 21, 1861; E. J. Allen (telegram) to George H. Bangs, July 6, 1862, LC.

5. *Diary of Gideon Welles* (New York, 1911), pp. 92–96; 100–105.

Chapter 16
The Washington Cabal, 1862

1. McClellan to Stanton, June 28, 1862; *McClellan's Own Story*, pp. 424–425. The original manuscript of McClellan's book was destroyed in a fire. Ironically, in the book that was finally published Pinkerton is never mentioned.

2. *McClellan's Own Story*, p. 487; William Starr Myers, *General George Brinton McClellan*, pp. 306ff. The letter was for Lincoln's "private consideration." McClellan's motivation for the letter has been bitterly attacked (K. P. Williams, *Lincoln Finds a General*, I, 249–250) and warmly defended (J. G. Randall, *Lincoln the President*, II, 101–104). T. Harry Williams in his *Lincoln and His Generals* believes that McClellan, judged by modern standards, did act improperly (pp. 132–133).

3. Pinkerton to McClellan, August 20, 21, 23, 25, 1865, NA.

4. *Ibid.*, September 1, 1862, NA.

5. Lincoln to McClellan, August 28, 1862; Lincoln, *Works*, VIII, 19; *McClellan's Own Story*, p. 515.

6. In his review of Antietam, Douglas Freeman, while praising Lee's strategy, emphasizes the splendid work of McClellan in the organization of his "demoralized army" and his "unexpected rapidity" in directing federal movements (Freeman, *Lee*, II, chap. VII); while K. P. Williams, on the other hand, endorses the verdict of Peter S. Mitchie, who insisted that no battle containing more errors can be found (*Lincoln Finds a General* [New York, 1949], II, 463–464).

7. *McClellan's Own Story*, p. 648; *Spy*, pp. 561–586; Lewis, pp. 378–379; Myers, *McClellan*, pp. 374–375.

8. McClellan to Pinkerton, July 17, 1863 (copy), PA.

Chapter 17
North to Freedom, 1863

1. Louis Sigaud, *Belle Boyd* (Richmond, Va., 1944, pp. 136–137). When the Lincoln papers were opened in 1952, a letter from Belle Boyd to Lincoln was found in which the Confederate spy threatened Lincoln with "exposure" of certain revelations in his administration unless her husband was released from jail. One wonders if the "revelations" included the story of how she smuggled the gold past Ben Butler.

Chapter 18
Watch on the Western Rivers, 1865

1. R. J. Atkinson, 3rd Auditor, Auditors Office, Treasury Department, Washington, D.C., to G. B. McClellan, Orange, N.J., July 7, 1863; Pinkerton to H. Limouse, New York City, March 10, 1863, both CHS.
2. Nicholay and Hay, *Lincoln*, IX, 196–197.
3. New York *Sun*, June 30, 1889, p. 3, hereafter cited as *Sun*.
4. Thomas Key to Allan Pinkerton, New York, July 29, 1864 (copy), PA.
5. McClellan to Pinkerton, October 20, 1863, Orange, N.J. (copy), PA.
6. John D. Caton to McClellan, Ottawa, Ill., December 18, 1864. Caton MMS., quoted in H. E. Pratt, Life of John Caton (MS) Chap. VIII.
7. Stanton to Pinkerton, April 24, 1865, PA.

Book Three
The Middle Border Outlaws, 1866–1877

Chapter 19
The Overture

1. R. Fels, *American Business Cycles, 1865–1897*, p. 92.
2. Harlow, *Old Way Bills*, pp. 305–325.
3. *The Age of Hate: Andrew Johnson and the Radicals*, by George Fort Milton (New York, 1930), p. 411, footnote describing the source; Note 20, p. 732.
4. Allan Pinkerton to George Bangs, December 22, 1868, LC.

Chapter 20
The Renos of Indiana

1. William Pinkerton to Pat O'Neil, November 25, 1897, PA.
2. The Reno Boys of Seymour (Master's Thesis), by Frederick Volland, hereafter cited as Volland, NYP. Source material on the Renos, research notes, maps, books, etc., of the Reverend Robert W. Shields, are now in the Pinkerton Archives.
3. *John Reno: Life and Career*, Rare Book Room, NYP, hereafter cited as *Reno*.
4. St. Louis *Globe-Democrat*, January 9, 1887, hereafter cited as *Globe*.
5. *Globe*; Chicago *Evening Post*, February 2, 1895; William Pinkerton to Captain Edward Grant, Baltimore & Ohio RR, no date, PA.
6. *Reno*.
7. Unsigned two-page letter, or section, of a report detailing the Magnolia robbery and the gang's escape from jail, dated November 19, 1897, PA. See also Chicago *Evening Post*, February 2, 1895; Detroit *News-Tribune*, November 21, 1897; *New York Globe*, July 9, 1887; *Collier's Magazine*, April 3, 1948; *True Detective Tales of the Pinkertons*, by Cleveland Moffett (New York, 1897), pp. 163–192.

8. Indianapolis *Journal,* December 15, 1868.

9. William A. Pinkerton to Pat O'Neil, November 25, 1897; Pat O'Neil to William Pinkerton, December 3, 1897, both PA.

10. Reno Extradition, Records of the Department of State, Notes to Great Britain, Vol. 14, NA.

11. New Albany *Independent Weekly Ledger,* August 26, 1868.

12. Records, Department of State, Miscellaneous Letters, September 16, 1868, NA.

13. Indianapolis *Journal,* December 15, 1868.

14. Details of the lynching can be found in the daily accounts of the New Albany *Independent Weekly Ledger,* December 19, 1868, to January 12, 1869; Chicago *Evening Post,* February 2, 1895; Louisville *Courier-Journal,* September 10, 1916. The coroner's and doctor's report of Simeon Reno can be found in the Indianapolis *Journal,* December 18, 1868.

15. John Clark Ridpath, *History of the United States* (Cincinnati, 1882), p. 556.

Chapter 21
The Larches

1. Partial letter of Allan Pinkerton to George Bangs (no date), 1868, LC.

2. Operating expenses for Pinkerton's National Detective Agency, Record Book of George Bangs, 1868–1871, LC.

3. Allan Pinkerton to George Bangs, January 5, 1869, LC.

4. Allan Pinkerton to "My Dear Friend," Chicago, February 3, 1872, CHS.

5. "Allan Pinkerton, Pioneer on the Illinois Central," *Illinois Central Magazine,* January, 1946, hereafter cited as *Central; see also* "The Pinkertons of Onarga," by Dorothy M. Long, a paper read before the Iroquois County Historical Society, winter, 1969.

6. *Central,* p. 22; the Iroquois County Historical Society is attempting to raise funds to preserve the Villa and the panels and paintings. Most of the fields now grow corn, and some of the thousands of larch trees planted by Pinkerton still bloom.

7. *Central,* p. 23; *Travelers' Quarterly,* 1888. Some magazines and books have repeated the touching story of how Pinkerton brought his mother to The Larches, but this is a much-repeated error—his mother had died some years before the estate was built.

8. Allan Pinkerton to Chief Justice S. P. Chase, February 3, 1872, CHS. Chase and Pinkerton were friends from the Civil War days. Chase, as Lincoln's Secretary of the Treasury, tried to discredit his President to gain the office for himself. Ben Wade insisted that Chase each morning addressed the mirror, "Good morning, Mr. President."

Chapter 22
Dingus James and His Missouri Bravoes

1. Robertus Love's *The Life and Times of Jesse James* (New York, 1939), is still one of the best source books on the life of the legendary outlaw. While the book is pro-James, Love, a Missouri newspaperman, had the confidence of the family, and "found" Jim Cummings, who had been one of Jesse's riders and, later, a state's witness against Frank James. Homer Croy's *Jesse James Was My Neighbor* (New York, 1955) is entertaining, but a careful work of investigation nevertheless. Croy's story of his interview with Frank Dalton, the phony Jesse of the 1950's, is delightful. My own book, *Desperate Men,* first published in 1949, was reissued in 1962 and is now out of print. The latest book on James and his gang is *Jesse James Was His Name,* by William A. Settle (Columbia, Missouri, 1966).

Curiously, Settle fails to include any letters of the Pinkertons to give them their day in court. For example, he describes Edwin B. Daniel, the St. Clair County lawman killed in the gun battle with the Youngers, as a Pinkerton man, an allegation the Pinkertons denied for years. As late as 1912, William Pinkerton in a letter, which Mr. Settle does not include, insisted that no one in the Pinkerton Agency ever heard of Daniel before he met Lull. The author also failed to consult the Homestead Congressional hearings for both Pinkertons' version of the bomb raid on the James homestead, and apparently was not aware of the Allan Pinkerton and George Bangs Record Books, 1872–1876, in the Library of Congress. Unfortunately, Settle's pedestrian style turns James, one of America's most colorful folklore heroes, into a dullard.

2. The Writings and Speeches of William H. Wallace (Missouri, 1912).

3. Missouri *World,* March, 1874.

4. "Highwaymen of the Railroads," by William A. Pinkerton, *North American Review,* November, 1893, pp. 53–54. See also address of William Pinkerton, Annual Convention International Association of Chiefs of Police, Jamestown, Va., 1907.

5. Robert A. Pinkerton to J. H. Schumacher, Superintendent, Kansas City, November 18, 1898, PA. Hereafter cited as Schumacher.

6. Expense sheet of George Bangs, "Trip to Richmond to Recover Tim Webster's Remains. April 25, 1872"; Bangs to Frank Warner, Superintendent, Chicago, May 6, 1872, referring to his Richmond trip to locate the body. Both LC.

The exact spot where Webster is buried has puzzled historians for years. In 1948–1949, during research for my *Desperate Men,* I accepted early accounts that the Union spy had been buried in Graceland Cemetery, Chicago, on the order of Allan Pinkerton. Recently, Edward J. Bauer, Secretary of the Graceland Cemetery and Crematorium, assisted me in searching old burial records that finally established that Webster's body had been sent on to Onarga. With the help of several Onarga residents, I located Webster's grave in the Onarga Cemetery next to his son's. The stone in the Graceland Cemetery is a "Memorial Stone" erected by Allan Pinkerton. The cemetery records reveal that many of Pinkerton's early operatives, including George Bangs and some of his Civil War agents, are buried there in the Pinkerton plot.

7. George Bangs to Allan Pinkerton, January 12, 1872, LC.

8. *Ibid.,* ———, 1872, LC.

9. George Bangs to Frank Warner, ———, 1872.

10. Allan Pinkerton to George Bangs, August 15, 1872, LC.

11. Allan Pinkerton to Captain Fitzgerald, August 15, 1872, LC.

12. Allan Pinkerton to George Bangs, October 17, 1872, LC.

13. *Ibid.,* November 16, 1872, LC.

14. *Ibid.,* ———, 1872, LC.

15. Allan Pinkerton to William Pinkerton, November 7, 1872, LC.

16. New York *World,* March 28, 1874.

17. William Pinkerton to J. W. Satterwhite, San Antonio, Tex., March 24, 1904, PA. Hereafter cited as Satterwhite. See also Kansas City *Sun,* March 18, 1894; Chicago *Tribune,* April 3, 1874. Daniels's name has different variations. I have used the spelling in the coroner's report.

18. Statement of W. J. Allen, Subscribed and Sworn to before James St. Clair, 18th day of March, 1874, PA. See also Satterwhite; *Jesse James Was His Name* by Settle, pp. 60–62; *Desperate Men* by James D. Horan (1949), pp. 77–87; Statement of Theodore Snuffer, Subscribed and Sworn to James St. Clair, 18th Day of March, 1874; Statement of G. W. McDonald, subscribed and sworn to James St. Clair, 18th day of March, 1874, PA. See also Love, *op. cit.,* pp. 133–144; St. Louis *World,* June 26, 1905; verdict of the St. Clair County Coroner's Jury: members, A. Ray, foreman; G. W. Cox, J. Davis, W. Holmes, R. O. Gill, H. Gleason, the 18th Day of March, 1874, PA.

19. Allan Pinkerton to George Bangs, August 17, 1874, LC.

20. Allan Pinkerton to Robert, September 12, 1872, LC.

21. Robert A. Pinkerton to J. H. Schumacher, Superintendent, Kansas City, Mo., November 11, 1898, PA. See also St. Louis *Globe-Democrat,* July 5, 1902; Kansas City *Sunday Star,* March 11 and 18, 1894.

22. *The Crittenden Memoirs,* by H. H. Crittenden (New York, 1936). The interview with "Old George" Hite is reprinted from the *Courier-Journal,* pp. 152–162. Hereafter cited as *Crittenden.*

23. Chicago *Sunday Record Herald,* May 1, 1909.

24. Jesse James has long been one of America's folklore heroes. Soon after Augustus C. Appler, editor of the Osceola, Missouri, *Democrat* published his book in 1875, the first on the James legend, there has been a flood of books, pamphlets, movies that has never stopped. Don Russell, biographer of Buffalo Bill, has pointed out that Cody is the

only historical figure in American history who has been painted as a hero in more dime novels than Jesse James. The Library of Congress collection numbers over a hundred.

Book Four
The Crucial Years, 1874–1876
Chapter 23
The Molly Maguires

1. Allan Pinkerton to George Bangs, May 17, 1872, LC.

2. *The Molly Maguires,* by Francis P. Dewees (Philadelphia, 1876), hereafter cited as Dewees.

3. *The Molly Maguires,* by Anthony Bimba (New York, 1931), p. 81.

4. *The Molly Maguire Riots,* by J. Walter Coleman (Richmond, Va., 1936), pp. 13–18, 27–28, hereafter cited as Coleman. See also "The Molly Maguires in the Anthracite Coal Fields, 1850–1880," a paper delivered before the Muncy Historical Society by Marshal R. Anspach, NYP.

5. *Official Records,* Ser. 11, Vol. III, pp. 620–629 (Government Printing Office, Washington, D.C., 1880).

6. *The Molly Maguires,* by Wayne G. Broehl, Jr. (Cambridge, Mass., 1964), p. 93, hereafter cited as Broehl.

7. State of Pennsylvania, *Report of the Judiciary General,* the Senate of Pennsylvania, 1871, p. 19.

8. *The Mollie Maguires and the Detectives,* by Allan Pinkerton (New York, 1878), p. 17, hereafter cited as *Mollie Maguires.*

9. Robert Pinkerton, "Detective Surveillance of Anarchists," *North American Review,* November, 1901, pp. 611–612.

10. *Mollie Maguires,* p. 73.

11. *Ibid.,* p. 144; Broehl, p. 167; Dewees, p. 375.

12. James McParland to George D. Bangs (son of the first general superintendent of the Pinkerton Agency, who, like his father, was superintendent of the New York office), February 10, 1914. This is a long and interesting letter that I recently discovered in the Pinkerton files, in which McParland discusses the work he did in the Molly Maguire and ex-Governor Steunenberg investigations. Hereafter cited as McParland.

13. *Mollie Maguires,* pp. 275–278. A memorandum written by Benjamin Franklin, Pinkerton's Philadelphia superintendent, in the Reading Railroad's Molly Maguire papers, dated April 28, 1875, differs from Pinkerton's version of this meeting. Pinkerton had McParland present, but Franklin does not make mention of him. It is doubtful if McParland faced Gowen at that time.

14. *Report of the Case of the Commonwealth vs John Kehoe, et al. . . . For Aggravated Assault and Battery with Intent to Kill Wm. H. Thomas* (Pottsville, Pa., 1876), pp. 25–30, hereafter cited as *Kehoe.*

15. *Kehoe,* pp. 54–63; Coleman, p. 98. John T. Morse, Jr., "The Molly Maguire Trials," *American Law Review,* XI, January, 1877, p. 255.

16. *Mollie Maguires,* p. 400; James Carroll, James Boyle, Hugh McGehan and James Roarity, *vs.* Commonwealth of Pennsylvania, Supreme Court of Pennsylvania, Eastern District, N. 12, January Term, 1877, p. 291.

17. Allan Pinkerton to George Bangs, August 29, 1875, LC.

18. Shenandoah *Herald,* December 11–17, 1875.

19. A secretary's copy of James McParland's letter written about December 10, 1875, PA. In 1948–1949, I discovered this letter, which I have always considered to be one of the most important of the Molly Maguire documents. At the time I strongly recommended to the late Robert Pinkerton II and the late Ralph Dudley, general manager, that the correspondence of Allan Pinkerton and George Bangs in the Record Books, 1872–1876, and the copy of Pinkerton's Civil War Record Book, all of which I had been using, be given to the Library of Congress. After several meetings in which I pointed out the perishability of the documents and the potential loss to future scholars of the period, Pinkerton and Dudley agreed, and the material was sent to the Library of Congress, where the bound volumes are presently in the Manuscript Division. At least one other historian has erroneously stated that he was the first to examine this material. Until my wife and I had dusted off the books in a room set aside by the Agency in their headquarters in the now-demolished New York Tribune Building, New York City, no one had examined them.

20. Benjamin Franklin to Allan Pinkerton, no date. I had copied this letter in 1949. It is now missing. Broehl also reports it missing, p. 265.

21. Dewees, pp. 239–250.

22. Boston *Pilot,* December 18, 1875.

23. *Kehoe,* pp. 92–98.

24. McParland.

25. Allan Pinkerton to George Bangs, November 1, 1874, LC.

26. Official records of the trials are in the Schuylkill County Court House at Pottsville. In addition, the local newspapers the Shenandoah *Herald* and *Miners Journal* published extensive accounts of the testimony. As was the custom of the time, versions of sensational trials were printed in paperback—for example: *Report of the Case of the Commonwealth vs John Kehoe, et al. . . . For an Aggravated Assault and Battery with Intent to Kill Wm. H. Thomas.* This paperback also included the testimony of Jimmy Kerrigan, the Molly informer. Official testimony is available in the cases that went to the Pennsylvania Supreme Court.

Chapter 24
Trials and Tribulations

1. Allan Pinkerton to Robert, February 29, 1876, LC. Pinkerton's books are: *The Mollie Maguires and Detectives*; *Strikers, Communists and Detectives*; *Criminal Reminiscenses and Detectives*; *The Model*

Town and Detectives; *The Spiritualists and Detectives*; *The Somnambulist and Detectives*; *Claude Melnotte as a Detective*; *The Mississippi Outlaws and Detectives*; *Gypsies and the Detectives*; *Bucholz and Detectives*; *The Railroad Forger and Detectives*; *Bank Robbers and Detectives*; *The Burglar's Fate and Detectives*; *A Double Life and Detectives*; *Thirty Years a Detective*; *The Spy of the Rebellion*. All were published, from the 1870's to Allan Pinkerton's death in 1884, by G. W. Dillingham Co., New York publishers.

2. Allan Pinkerton to Robert, September 2, 1875, LC.

3. Allan Pinkerton to George Bangs, September 2, 1875, LC.

4. Allan Pinkerton to Benjamin Franklin, September 2 and 4, 1875, LC.

5. Allan Pinkerton to George Bangs, June 23, 1876, LC.

6. *Ibid.*, September 29, 1876, LC.

7. Allan Pinkerton to Robert, February 29, 1876, LC.

8. *Ibid.*, March 8, 1876, LC.

9. Allan Pinkerton to George Bangs, October 20, 1876, LC.

10. Allan Pinkerton's letters to Robert, in relation to Joan's conduct, November 22, 29, 1876; January 9, 20, 1877, LC.

11. Allan Pinkerton to Benjamin Franklin, January 23, 1877, LC.

12. Allan Pinkerton to George Bangs, March 30, 1877, LC.

13. Allan Pinkerton to George B. McClellan, November 13, 1877, LC.

14. Allan Pinkerton to Robert, March 24, 1879, LC.

15. *Ibid.*, May 15, 1879, LC.

16. Allan Pinkerton to "My Dear Little Wife," March 28, 1877, LC; Allan Pinkerton to "Dear Friend," September 20, 1878, LC.

Book Five
Other Eminent Victorians
Chapter 25
The Scott-Dunlap Ring

1. The Chicago *Tribune*, November 23, 1876; May 29, 1938. For an excellent account of the attempted grave robbing and the Pinkertons' role, see *The Attempt to Steal Lincoln's Body*, by John C. Power (Lincoln Memorial Association, Springfield, Illinois, 1890). Power was the Superintendent of the Lincoln Memorial at the time. The United States Secret Service, which worked on this case and many others in the 1870's and 1880's with the Pinkertons, had its origin in a bill passed in Congress in 1860 which appropriated $5,000 for the suppression of coin counterfeiting. The money was to be paid as rewards to persons furnishing information of counterfeiting activities. When federal currency was adopted in 1864, the government took steps to protect its new money, and $100,000 was made available for the suppression of counterfeiting in this country. Congress was forced to investigate this reward system, and in July, 1865, Hugh McCulloch, Secretary of the Treasury, appointed

William P. Wood, Pinkerton's old Washington enemy, as the first Chief of the United States Secret Service. Elmer Washburn, William Pinkerton's close friend, was Chief from October, 1874, to 1876. James J. Brooks, also a friend of both Pinkertons, headed the Secret Service at the time of the attempt to steal Lincoln's body. Agents did not guard Presidents until after the assassination of President McKinley in Buffalo in 1901. On June 30, 1906, Congress provided funds for the protection of American Presidents by Secret Service agents. Seven years later this protection was extended to the President-elect. Agents also investigated homestead frauds and the famous Louisiana lottery that began in 1862 and ended in 1892.

2. Chicago *Times,* December 20, 1891; New York *Sun* (See Note No. 8), an article written by "E. J. Edwards, Special Reporter," which is one of the best on the Ring. Hereafter cited as Edwards.

3. The Elmira Robbery account is described by William D. Edson in his later testimony. See also Edwards; Wilkes Barre *Record,* July 3, 1889; William Pinkerton to Robert, August 19, 1890, PA.

4. Edwards; John Cornish, Boston, Superintendent, to Robert Pinkerton, January 27, 1892, PA.

5. New York *World,* December 20, 1891. See also Robert A. Pinkerton to Oscar Edwards, president of the Northampton National Bank, February 16, 1893, PA.

6. Edwards.

7. *Ibid.*

8. The facts of the robbery are based on the testimony of John Whittelsey, head cashier of the Northampton National Bank, and members of his household; Oscar Edwards, president; and William Edson, the corrupt safe and bank expert for Herring & Company. Their testimony appears in the rare pamphlet "Trials of Scott and Dunlap for Robbing the Northampton National Bank and Breaking and Entering the Cashier's House; Twelve Days in Court," published by the Gazette Printing Co., Northampton, Mass., 1876, NYP. The Sunday *Sun* article by Edwards is affixed as an appendix.

9. *Evening News,* December 19, 1891.

10. The New York *World,* April 25, 1882.

11. *Evening News.*

12. New York *Herald,* December, 1880.

13. O. M. Hanscom, assistant superintendent, Boston office, to Robert A. Pinkerton, October 4, 1890, PA.

14. The press coverage of Mary Scott's fight to win Dunlap's parole was extensive. See New York *World,* June 20, 1889; December 12, 1889; Boston *Herald,* July 3, 1889; Boston *Evening Record,* July 19, 1889. Mary's own story of her fight to "free poor Jim" was written for the New York *World,* February 23, 1890. See also the Boston *Daily Globe,* July 3, 1890; New York *Sun,* December 29, 1892.

15. Robert A. Pinkerton to Edward F. Hamlin, Esq., Executive Clerk,

State House, Boston, Mass., May 10, 1893; Robert A. Pinkerton to Oscar Edwards, Northampton, Mass., May 10, 1893.

16. Telegrams and letters from William A. Pinkerton to Robert, May 31, 1893; June 2, 1893; William Pinkerton to Robert, July 17, 1893, PA.

17. William Pinkerton to Robert, August 2, 1894, PA.

Chapter 26
Adam Worth: The Other Napoleon

1. Scotland Yard Superintendent Shore's description of Adam Worth after Worth's death, 1903; William Pinkerton's evaluation of Worth is contained in a ten-page letter he wrote to Robert, January 16, 1898, PA, in which he describes three visits of Worth to his Chicago office. The letter is a condensed account of Worth's own review of his criminal career and the men and women who were his associates. Hereafter cited as J16 Letter. See also a pamphlet detailing Worth's life, put out by the Pinkerton Agency at the turn of the century, NYP.

2. New York *Herald*, August 25, 1897.

3. John Cornish, Superintendent, Boston office, to George Bangs, November 23, 1888, PA; *Our Rival, the Rascal* by B. P. Eldredge and William R. Bates (Boston, 1893); *Professional Criminals of America* by Thomas B. Byrnes (New York, 1886), pp. 326–327; Langdon W. Moore's *His Own Story of His Eventful Life* (Boston, 1893), 247–333, hereafter cited as Moore.

4. Moore, p. 247; Report, Merchants' Union Express Robbery, May 4, 1868, PA; "Train Robber and Holdup Men," an address by William Pinkerton, Annual Convention, National Association Chiefs of Police, Jamestown, Va., 1907.

5. St. Louis *Globe Democrat,* January 9, 1887; New York *World,* September 2, 1888; J16 Letter.

6. John Cornish to George Bangs, November 23, 1888, PA.

7. Kitty died on March 14, 1894. Her obituaries, notably that in the New York *World*, March 24, 1894, gave the details of her marriage to Charley Bullard in Liverpool. See also *Memoirs of Sophie Lyons* (McClure's Syndicate, 1915), hereafter cited as *Lyons;* New York *Journal,* August 25, 1894; New York *Herald,* August 25, 1899.

8. Buffalo *Courier,* February 9, 1919.

9. William Pinkerton to Robert, November 9, 1872, PA.

10. George Bangs to Allan Pinkerton, December 12, 1872, PA; "Adam Worth: A Report on His Life," written by William Pinkerton, November, 1902, PA; see also *Inter Ocean,* March 1, 1903; New York *Herald,* March 2, 1894; J16 Letter. According to John Cornish, among the tourists visiting the American Bar was the vice-president of the Merchants Union Express Company, who did not know that his distinguished-looking host was the Charley Bullard who had robbed his company of $100,000 in 1868.

11. William Pinkerton to Allan, January 20, 1873, PA.

12. J16 Letter. In stories written about Worth in the 1890's, much was made of *The Shamrock*. Many of the legends were obviously exaggerated, but there is little doubt he did own a yacht, and used what funds he had to equip it luxuriously. Sophie Lyons, in her memoirs, claims she saw *The Shamrock* docked at a French port. See also Boston *American,* December 18, 1923.

13. Howard Adams (Sesisovich's alias when he was arrested) to "My Dearest Alima," January 29, 1875; William Pinkerton to Robert, January 24, 1888, PA.

14. Worth told some of the details of his Constantinople adventures to William Pinkerton in his last 1898 visit. See also New York Police Department Criminal Identification file on Little Joe Eliott; Byrnes, *op. cit.,* p. 51; Robert A. Pinkerton to Larry Hazen (a Cincinnati detective), April 23, 1878, published in the New York *Tribune,* April 29, 1878.

15. *Lyons;* Robert Pinkerton also suspected that Kitty's daughters were Worth's; see Robert Pinkerton to Donald Swanson, Superintendent, Criminal Investigations Department, Scotland Yard, February 3, 1903, PA.

16. Circular issued by Scotland Yard, Criminal Investigative Division, for Carlos and Anna Sesisovich for questioning in the murder of Lydia Chapman, SYHD.

17. Memorandum of an interview between William Pinkerton and Charles Becker, no date, PA.

18. William Pinkerton to C. Morland, Agnew Galleries, London, ———, 1901, PA; *Lyons;* Circular, "The Theft of the Gainsborough Painting, the Duchess of Devonshire, May 6, 1876, Recovered," PA; Chicago *Tribune,* February 7, 1902; *Evening Sun,* February 7, 1902.

19. *Lyons.*

20. *World,* March 21, 1894; *Lyons;* New York *Herald,* August 25, 1899.

21. "The Kimberly Diamond Mines Robbery," an account written by Max Shinburn, August 5, 1894, at the request of Wililam Pinkerton, PA; "How the Diamond Mine Was Robbed," a report from Scotland Yard, no date, SYHD.

22. J16 Letter.

23. John Shore, Superintendent, Scotland Yard, Criminal Investigations Division, to William Pinkerton, April 8, 1888, PA.

24. Circular, issued October 19, 1892 by Theodore de Corswarem, The Prosecuting Judge, Belgium High Court, District of Liége, PA.

25. J16 Letter.

26. Henry Raymond, c/o Mrs. Strawson, 88th Street, near Shore Road, Fort Hamilton, N.Y., to William Pinkerton, January 24, 1902; William Pinkerton to Robert, February 2, 1902, PA.

27. Henry Raymond to William Pinkerton, February 22, 1902, PA.

28. William Pinkerton to Henry Raymond, no date, PA.

29. After the story of Worth's death broke in the New York *Times,*

nearly every major American newspaper and news syndicate offered William Pinkerton large sums to tell, for the first time, the inside story of the theft of the Gainsborough painting. William at first refused; but after receiving the letter from Worth's son, he wrote his own account, sold it overnight to McClure's syndicate for $700. He thereupon "made the man pay," and sent the money to Worth's son and daughter. A year later the boy hesitantly applied for a minor job with the Agency. He was hired, and Pinkerton circulated a memo throughout the organization, sternly warning its supervisors never to link Worth's name with that of the Henry L. Raymond who had died in London. The employment record still exists, and states that no investigation is to made, since both Pinkertons "know the boy."

A year later, an English convict, then at Dannemora Prison, New York State, about to be released, requested, through his attorneys in New York, the address of Adam Worth or his daughters from William Pinkerton. Pinkerton knew that Kitty Terry, onetime Liverpool barmaid, leader in society, and one of the richest women in America, who had died suddenly in her luxurious East Side apartment, had left two daughters who, the underworld insisted, were Adam Worth's children. Across the bottom of the letter William scrawled angrily: "No information to be given out. The man may think he may get money out of children by thinking to divulge who father was." Robert Pinkerton to Donald Swanson, Superintendent, Criminal Investigation Divisions, Scotland Yard, February 3, 1902; John Cornish to Robert Pinkerton, February 2, 1903.

Book Six
The Great Burlington Strike of 1888; Homestead, 1892

Chapter 27
The Death of Allan Pinkerton

1. Allan Pinkerton to George Bangs, ———, 1881, LC.
2. Allan Pinkerton to the Honorable William Gladstone, ———, 1882, LC.
3. Love, *The Life and Times of Jesse James*, pp. 385–389; Crittenden, *Memoirs*, p. 269.
4. Crittenden, p. 261.
5. Chicago *Times*, September 1, 1882.
6. Allan Pinkerton to C. E. Chapman, Boston, Mass., October 31, 1883, CHS.
7. Last Will and Testament of Allan Pinkerton, filed July 10, 1884, Cook County Surrogate Court, Ill., CHS.
8. Operative's Report, April 8 to General Manager H. B. Stone, May 1, 1888, Pinkerton Reports No. 6, 33, 1888, 9.3 BA. There are large packages of these reports in the Burlington Archives covering the 1888 strike. Nowhere in any of these reports, which were certainly never meant to be read by outsiders, is there any evidence to support Powderly's charges. It is

significant that when the members of the congressional committee investigating the conduct of the Pinkertons at Homestead asked Powderly to return with evidence supporting his charges, he never came back. It is also important to recall that Powderly at the time was desperately trying to regain his power in labor circles. The Knights of Labor, originally an industrial union, had dwindled to little more than a secret lodge, extremely weak, and corrupt as well.

9. Report to H. B. Stone, June 12, 1888; Pinkerton Reports, No. 6, BA.

Chapter 28
The Works on the Monongahela

1. I have based the Homestead chapter on the voluminous testimony, mostly eyewitness and anti-Pinkerton, taken by the House of Representatives Judiciary Subcommittee in its Washington hearings, July, 1892, and its final report, majority and minority, "Labor Troubles at Homestead, Pa., Employment of Pinkerton Detectives," U.S. House of Representatives, Report No. 2447, 52nd Congress, 2nd Session, 1893. Hereafter cited as Report. There was also a Senate hearing, but the House findings were more sweeping and detailed. I have found the newspaper accounts of the riot to be highly inaccurate. Some of the stories had the Pinkertons sheeting the two barges with railroad iron and allowing firing slits and "marching and drilling their army." These reports were discredited by testimony before the committee.

2. Thomas G. Sherman, "The Owners of America," *Forum C*, VIII, November, 1889, pp. 262–273. See also "King Wealth and Income," pp. 72–87; George K. Holmes, "The Concentration of Wealth," *Political Science Quarterly*, VIII, December, 1893, p. 593.

3. *The Education of Henry Adams* (Boston, 1918), p. 321.

4. An excellent study of Populism and its historical significance will be found in *Politics, Reform and Expansion, 1890–1900*, by Harold U. Faulkner (New York, 1959); and *The Populist Response to Industrial America*, by Norman Pollack (New York, 1962).

5. *Report*, pp. xi, xvii.

6. *Ibid.*, "Views of Mr. Buchanan," pp. xxvi to xxxv, includes a scale of wages paid to ironworkers in various sections of Europe.

7. *Ibid.*, p. xi.

8. Charge of Chief Justice Paxson, Supreme Court of Pennsylvania, to the Allegheny County Grand Jury, from the *Pittsburgh Legal Journal*, N. S., Vol. XXIII, O. S., Vol. XL, October 26, 1892. Hereafter cited as Paxson Charge. It must be pointed out that Justice Paxson was hostile to the union leaders later arrested; he advised the grand jury to indict them for treason!

9. Report, p. lxiv.

10. *Ibid.*

11. *Ibid.*, p. xxi.

12. Philander Knox, Pittsburgh, Pa., to Robert Pinkerton, June 30, 1892, PA.

Chapter 29
The Siege

1. HR Report No. 2447, 1893, pp. xxi-xxii.
2. *Ibid.*, p. lxv.
3. *Ibid.*
4. *Ibid.*, p. xxii.
5. *Ibid.*, p. ix.
6. *Ibid.*, p. lxv.

Chapter 30
Investigations and Hearings

1. Democratic National Committee, *Campaign Textbook of the Democratic Party* (New York, 1892), p. 17.
2. *Pinkerton's National Detective Agency and Its Connection with the Labor Troubles at Homestead, July 16, 1892* (New York, 1893), p. 14. Hereafter cited as *Pinkerton's Agency*.
3. *Pinkerton's Agency*, pp. 47–100, takes in the formal statements read by the Pinkertons, their direct testimony, and cross-examination by members of the subcommittee.
4. Paxson Charge, pp. 2–3.
5. HR Report No. 2447, 1893, p. xv.
6. Robert A. Pinkerton to Henry C. Frick, July 19, 1893, PA.
7. "Upheaval at Homestead," by Henry David, in Daniel Aaron (ed.), *America in Crisis* (New York, 1952), pp. 133–170.
8. *Social Darwinism in American Thought* (Philadelphia, 1944), by Richard Hofstadter, pp. 201–202; *The Reconstruction of American History*, John Higham, ed. (New York, 1962).

Book Seven
The Pinkertons in the Wild West
Chapter 31
The Train Robbers

1. Address of William Pinkerton to the International Police Chiefs Association, Jamestown, Va., 1907, NYP. Hereafter cited as Address.
2. "American Highwayman," by William Pinkerton, *North American Review*, 1893, p. 12. Hereafter cited as *Review*.
3. "The Holdup and Robbery of the Southern Express Company, Mobile & Ohio Railroad, October 6, 1871," an Agency brief, PA. See also the Atlanta *Constitution*, September 30, 1936; and Allan Pinkerton's *Mississippi Outlaws and the Detectives*.

4. *Inter Ocean,* February 14, 1909; Memphis *Commercial Appeal,* February 7, 1909.

5. *Commercial Appeal, loc. cit.* See also St. Louis *Globe-Democrat,* January 9. 1887; Address, *Inter Ocean.*

6. *Review,* pp. 530–540; also *Inter Ocean.*

7. *Sam Bass* by Wayne Gard (New York, 1936), p. 139; Robert to William Pinkerton, St. Louis, October 30, 186(?), PA.

8. See also the Denver *Times,* December 26, 1886; Denver *Republican,* December 26, 1886; Cincinnati *Enquirer,* December 23, 1886; "Great American Train Robberies," by Charles Francis Bourke, in *Railroad Man's Magazine,* April, 1906, pp. 512–517.

9. Address; see also the New York *Sun,* October 12, 1890, "The Burrows Brothers," a two-part series.

10. "Rube Burrows," a memoir of the hunt for the outlaw, by G. W. Agee, superintendent, Southern Pacific, PA.

11. "Rube Burrows' Slayer in Atlanta," *Southern Expressman,* Atlanta, Ga., April, 1891.

12. "The Robbery of the Mineral Range Railroad," a memorandum by William Pinkerton, December 6, 1894, PA. See also Chicago *Daily News,* September 21, 1891; Chicago *Evening Post,* September 21, 1893; the Agency's brief, "Holdup and Robbery of the Mineral Range Railroad, Boston Station, near Calumet, Michigan, September 15, 1893, $70,000," PA.

13. Chicago *Chronicle,* January 9, 1903; Memorandum by E. J. Weiss, Assistant Superintendent, Chicago, 19––, PA; Charles Hill, Warden, Folsom State Prison, Calif., to William Pinkerton, March 5, 1894, PA; William Pinkerton to F. H. Tillotson, Superintendent, Kansas City, Mo.; November 6, 1899, PA; Kansas City *Times,* January 7, 1903; *Inter Ocean,* February 10, 1903; Mount Carroll, Illinois, *Mirror,* July, 1903.

14. Colorado *Sun,* November 9, 1891.

15. *The Saga of Tom Horn,* by Dean Krakel (Laramie, Wyo., 1954), p. 4; *The Last of the Badmen,* by Jay Monaghan (New York, 1946), pp. 110–136; Denver *Daily News,* December 10, 1891, Denver *Times,* November 2, 1891.

16. *Life of Tom Horn* (1903), pp. 259–263.

17. Robert Pinkerton to William, New York, January 19, 1906, PA.

18. Memorandum from William Pinkerton on an interview with Lillie Davis, December 5, 1901, PA.

19. I had several long interviews with Dimaio in 1947–1950. The versions he gave me were later checked against his original reports written from 1901–1903, State Department letters, etc., and found to be correct. In the 1950's Percy Seibert, Commissary General of the Bolivian Railroad Commission for the Study of Railroads, a long-time engineer on the Bolivian frontier and the man who hired Butch Cassidy and Longbaugh at the Concordia Tin Mines and probably the only American to have

their trust, detailed for me his long friendship with the outlaws and how they died. J. L. Rawlinson, of New York City, filled me in with accounts of the outlaws in Bolivia, while Victor J. Hampton gave me the version and sketched the Indian village of San Vincente where Cassidy and the Sundance Kid were killed.

20. New York *Times,* New York *Tribune,* New York *Press,* all of January 11, 1904. In 1948, in a series of interviews before his death, Lowell Spence described to me how he had hunted Kid Curry across the West, identified the outlaw for the government after his capture in Knoxville, and then made the final identification in the tiny Glenwood Springs Cemetery.

21. George D. Bangs, Jr., New York, to William Pinkerton, February 22, 1891, PA.

22. New York *Sun,* November 20, 1891.

23. The New York *World,* May 28, 1892, which published Perry's diary, including an account of his surrender to Collins, who Perry insisted was "trembling like a leaf." Collins died on March 10, 1939, in Lyons, with the New York *Tribune* recalling the manhunt.

24. William Pinkerton to all offices, June 1, 1906, PA.

25. Memoirs of Henry W. Minster, Assistant Superintendent, Philadelphia office, June 10, 1936, PA; see also Chicago *Record Herald,* Atlanta *Georgian and News,* and Baltimore *Sun,* all of June 29, 1912.

Book Eight
Murder Is a Little Thing
Chapter 32
America's Bluebeard

1. Allan Levett to James D. Horan, June 25, 1968, and July 3, 1968.

2. Chicago *Evening American,* January 4, 1910.

3. *The Holmes-Pitezel Case,* by Detective Frank Geyer (Philadelphia, 1896), pp. 43–52. Hereafter cited as Geyer; St. Louis *Globe-Democrat,* July 8, 1906; Kansas City *Star,* November 20, 1894.

4. *Celebrated Criminal Cases of America,* by Thomas S. Duke (San Francisco, 1910), pp. 447–467; hereafter cited as Duke; Chicago *Sunday Tribune,* March 21, 1937, hereafter cited as *Tribune.* On July 3, 1940, S. L. Stiles, Superintendent of the Pinkerton's Philadelphia office, sent an operative to make a study of the Fidelity Mutual Life Company's file on the Holmes case. At the request of the late Ralph Dudley, General Manager of the Agency, he submitted a report on July 3, 1940. Hereafter cited as Report. See also the chapter on Holmes in Herbert Asbury's *Gem of the Prairie* (New York, 1942).

5. Report.

6. *Tribune;* Report; Geyer, pp. 43–132.

7. Report of Operative Frank Wind, Chicago, 1894, PA.

Chapter 33
The Blackest of Days

1. William Pinkerton to a sheriff, January 12, 1888, PA.

2. St. Louis *Post-Dispatch,* December 28, 29, 1902; *Inter Ocean,* December 28, 1902; St. Louis *Globe-Democrat,* January 31 and March 21, 1903.

3. Memoirs of H. W. Minster, Superintendent, Pinkerton's St. Louis office (no date), PA; St. Louis *Republic,* January 26–28, 1903; New York *Herald,* March 8, 1903.

4. William Pinkerton to all superintendents, September 2–5, 1903; Joseph Stephens, Consul, Plymouth, England, to William Pinkerton, August 27, 1903; Head Constable, Cardiff, England, Police, to William Pinkerton, September 2, 1903, all PA; the Seattle *Star,* February 8, 1904; St. Louis *Republic,* January 28, 1903; St. Louis *Post-Dispatch,* February 24, 1904.

5. William Pinkerton to Robert, February, 1903, PA; Hartford *Daily Courant,* March 5, 1903; Hartford *Daily Times,* March 2, 1903; Memo of William H. Minster to Ralph Dudley, May 16, 1940, hereafter cited as Dudley, PA.

6. Records of George Collins, Company H, 15th Infantry, Niagara Falls, N.Y., August 10, 1901, U.S.A.

7. Special Report, Operative M. B. Tobin on George Collins, no date, PA.

8. New York *Times,* March 2, 1903; New York *Herald,* March 2, 1903; New York *World,* March 10, 1903.

9. William Pinkerton to W. Minster, March 10, 1903, PA.

10. St. Louis *Post-Dispatch,* February ?, 1904; "Bill Rudolph's Own Story."

11. Confidential memorandum to William Pinkerton, St. Louis, January 11, 1904, PA.

12. William Pinkerton to W. H. Minster, January 9, 1903, PA.

13. Telegram in code, William Pinkerton to H. Tillotson, Kansas City, Mo., February 12, 1904; H. Tillotson to William Pinkerton, February 13, 1904; William Pinkerton to E. S. Gaylor, Manager, Mid-West Division, Chicago, February 17, 1904, all PA; Denver *Post,* February 14, 1904; Kansas City *Journal,* February 14, 1904; Spokane *Evening Chronicle,* February 19, 1904; Spokane *Press,* February 22, 1904; Bridgeport *Herald,* February 21, 1904; telegram, William Pinkerton to H. Tillotson, Kansas City, Mo., February 12, 1904, PA.

14. St. Louis *Post-Dispatch,* February 14, 1904.

15. *Ibid.,* March 26, 1904.

16. William to Robert Pinkerton, May 2, 1905, PA.

17. Franklin County *Tribune,* May 12, 1905; St. Louis *Globe-Democrat,* May 9, 1905; Hartford *Times,* March 11, 1905; telegram, William B. Laughlin to William Pinkerton and other offices, May, 1905, PA.

Book Nine
Operations Against the Mafia in the United States, 1890–1906

Chapter 34
Operative Dimaio: "The Raven"

1. "Mafia Riots in New Orleans" by Margaret Adams, Master's Thesis, Tulane University, 1924. Hereafter cited as Adams. See also House Executive Document, Vol. 1, 52nd Congress, NYP.

2. *Strangers in the Land: Patterns of American Nationalism, 1860–1925,* by John Higham (New Brunswick, N.J., 1962), pp. 90–92.

3. New Orleans *Times-Democrat,* October 17, 1890. For the attempted murder of the Italian prisoners, see Chicago *Times,* October 18, 1890. See also the *Times-Democrat,* October 16–18, 1890, and the *Picayune* of the same date.

4. William Pinkerton to Wright Schaumberg, Secretary to Mayor Shakespear, New Orleans, October 16, 1890, PA.

5. William Pinkerton to Mayor Shakespear, New Orleans, October 19, 1890.

6. There may have been other private detective agencies in New Orleans investigating the Hennessy murder before the Pinkertons arrived. Herbert Asbury, in his *French Quarter,* has the Mooney and Boland Detective Agency also investigating the murder. See "Who Killa de Chief" by John S. Kendall, *Louisiana Historical Quarterly.*

7. The account of Dimaio's experiences in the Hennessy investigation is based on the many interviews I had with him. The quotations I have used are those of his words as he recalled the various incidents. The details of the part Dimaio played in the historic Hennessy case were not known until I interviewed him in the 1940's. I was amazed to discover he was still alive. See also "The Pinkertons in Search for Justice," June 16, 1968, *Dixie Roto Magazine,* New Orleans.

8. Report of H. W. Minster, Assistant Superintendent, Philadelphia Pinkerton office, no date, PA.

9. There are several versions of his name. The indictment listed him as Manuel Politz.

10. Boston *Sunday Post,* March 7, 1943.

11. Adams; New Orleans *Times-Democrat,* November 21, 1891. For accounts of the trial see the daily issues of the *Picayune* and *Times-Democrat,* January to March, 1891.

12. *Picayune,* March 15, 1891.

13. Adams, p. 45; Duke, *Celebrated Crimes in America* (New York, 1910), p. 446; see also "The New Orleans Mafia Incident," by John E. Coxe, *Louisiana Historical Quarterly,* 1937, pp. 1067–1110.

14. Adams includes the letters exchanged between Secretary of State Blaine and Baron Fava. See also New York *Herald,* March 5, 1891; House Executive Document, Vol. 1, 52nd Congress; and James Blaine's

"Twenty Years of Congress," *American Law Review,* May–June, 1891; *The Nation,* January–June, 1891; *McClure's Magazine,* Vol. 38, 71–83, 1911; French Chadwick, *Relations of the United States and Spain,* Vol. 1.

15. *Review of Reviews,* 111, 1891, pp. 443–449; see also "The Present State of Immigration," *Political Science Quarterly,* VII, 1892 p. 232; *The Nation,* LII, 1891, pp. 312–315; "The Evils of Immigration," by W. H. Wilder, *Methodist Review,* LI, 1891, pp. 719–20; "The Mafia and Foreign Immigration," a sermon by the Rev. George W. Cutter, Newport, R.I., 1891; the New York *Times,* April 27, 1891.

16. *A Diplomatic History of the American People,* by Thomas A. Bailey (6th ed.) (New York, 1955), pp. 414–415.

Chapter 35
Helltown

1. *Cleveland Plain Dealer Magazine,* March 28, 1909. This article, by Fred L. Boalt, was probably based on material he obtained from Lawrence County Prosecutor Young and County Detective Logan. However, the author did not have the story of Dimaio's adventures in the limestone country. Hereafter cited as *Magazine.*

2. This account of Dimaio's activities in the Mahoning Valley is based on my interviews with him and some of his original reports.

3. *Magazine.*

4. Report, Operative 89, June 10, 1906, New Castle, Pa.; Report of 89, June 10, 1906, Youngstown, Pa.; Report of 89, New Castle, Pa., June 12, 1906, PA.

5. Dimaio's report, June 20, 1906, to Robert Pinkerton, PA.

6. Reports of Dimaio and Operative 89, May 24–26, 1907, Hillsville, Pa., PA. For a description of the makeup of the Mafia in the quarries, see "The Seely Houk Case, 1908," *Annual Report of the Game Commissioners of Pennsylvania,* and *Magazine.*

7. *Magazine,* p. 14.

8. "A Summary Report of the Houk Murder," written by Dimaio, no date, PA.

9. Note from Salvadore Candido, Western Penitentiary, to Frank Dimaio, May 12, 1908, PA.

10. As Dimaio explained it: Italian legend has Monte Albano, a wealthy banker from Madrid, losing his fortune at cards, and turning outlaw. He called his groups of bandits Camorra, from the name on the back of his playing cards. They traveled down through Italy, to Calabria, the heel of the boot, then crossed into Sicily, where they were known as Mala Vita, which roughly translated means a bad way of making a living. The name Monte Albano was the password among the Sicilian Mafia, and was brought to the Pennsylvania limestone country in the early 1890's.

11. Dimaio's report to Robert Pinkerton, May 25, 1908, PA.

12. Paperbook of Appellant, Archives, Supreme Court of Pennsylvania, Western District No. 82, October Term, 1909: Commonwealth *vs.* Racco Rocco, Appellant. See also Appeal from Court of Oyer and Terminer, Lawrence County, No. 1, June Term, 1908. The decision of the higher courts identified Rocco as "leader of the Black Hand Society" in Hillsville.

Dimaio eventually became superintendent of the Pinkerton Philadelphia office. He retired in the 1930's. When the upper New York State Mafia "convention" took place in 1957, Dimaio, then in a nursing home, was still alert enough to inform a newspaper reporter on the origins and background of the "Honorable Society."

Book Ten
The Undesirable Citizens

Chapter 36
The Murder of Former Governor Steunenberg of Idaho

1. Chicago *Observer,* November 14, 1896.

2. William Pinkerton's address to the National Convention of International Police Chiefs, May 25, 1905, Washington, D.C.

3. *A Cowboy Detective,* by Charles A. Siringo (Chicago, 1912), pp. 135–171. Through a Supreme Court action the Pinkertons delayed the publication of Siringo's autobiography when they forced the publisher to delete some names and change the Agency's name to "Dickinson."

4. William E. Borah's Funeral Oration for Frank Steunenberg, Caldwell, Idaho, January 3, 1906 (no date or copyright), NYP.

5. William Pinkerton to James McParland, January 9, 1906; McParland to James Nevins, January 8, 11, 13, 1906; Nevins to McParland, January 13, 1906; McParland to Assistant Manager Frazier, January 13, 1906, all PA. See also "Reports Relating to Western Federation of Miners, 1906–1907, including Reports to Governor Goodling," microfilmed from James H. Hawley and William E. Borah papers, Idaho Historical Society, including Reports of the Thiel Agency, NYP.

6. The dialogue is as reported by McParland in his January 13 letter to Nevins, General Superintendent of the Portland office.

7. *Ibid.,* p. 2.

8. *Ibid.,* p. 3.

9. James McParland to George D. Bangs, Jr., March 4, 1915; *Rocky Mountain Revolution,* by Stewart H. Holbrook (New York, 1956), pp. 213–224. Orchard also gave his version of his interviews with McParland and later "reformation" in an autobiography, a typewritten copy of which is in the Pinkerton Archives.

10. James McParland to William Pinkerton, January 25, 1906, PA.

Chapter 37
The Confession of Harry Orchard

1. Orchard's fifty-two page confession was published in most of the newspapers in Denver and other towns in the West. Hereafter cited as Confession.
2. Confession.
3. *Ibid.*, p. 32.
4. Holbrook, *Rocky Mountain Revolution,* p. 148.
5. Ironically, the police blamed the explosion on a gas leak. The apartment-house owner sued the gas company, and collected. After Orchard's confession was made public, the company sued the apartment-house owner for recovery of the money.
6. *Confession.*
7. *Ibid.*, p. 31.

Chapter 38
The Trial of Big Bill Haywood and the Western Federation
of Miners' Officials

1. Theodore Roosevelt to George William Alger, March 20, 1906, Theodore Roosevelt Manuscripts, Library of Congress, hereafter cited as TRmms. See also "Theodore Roosevelt's Undesirable Citizens," by Stephen Scheinberg, *Idaho Yesterdays* (Fall, 1960).
2. Theodore Roosevelt to Lyman Abbott, July 10, 1906, TRmms.
3. *Daily Statesman,* November 4, 1906; Denver *Post,* January 8, 1907; *West Mountain Tribune,* November 10, 1906; the files of the Idaho *Daily Statesman* for that period are an excellent record of those politically hectic days.
4. Theodore Roosevelt to James S. Sherman, October 8, 1906. TRmms. See also New York *Tribune,* April 3, 1907.
5. James McParland to Governor Frank R. Gooding, including Operative 24's Reports, April 26 and May 2, 1906, PA.
6. James McParland to George D. Bangs, Jr., March 4, 1915; hereafter cited as Bangs, PA.
7. The combustible was used by the Byzantine Greeks in waging war. Confederate agents under Capt. Thomas H. Hines used Greek fire in their attempts to burn New York City in 1864. According to McParland, Haywood called it "Pettibone's Dope" or "Hell's Fire." The principal ingredients were stick phosphorous, bisulfide of carbon, benzine, alcohol, and turpentine.
8. Bangs, PA, pp. 3–5; Pocatello *Tribune,* March 20–21, 1906; see also "The Haywood Trial, Steve Adams, the Speechless Witness," by Leedice Kissane, *Idaho Yesterdays* (Fall, 1960), pp. 18-21.
9. "The Steunenberg Murder Case and the Haywood Trial," a synopsis by James McParland, PA; Holbrook, *Rocky Mountain Revolution,*

pp. 235–238. The daily issues of the Idaho *Statesman,* Denver *Post,* Denver *Republican,* Spokane *Spokesman-Review,* Colorado *Labor Advocate,* and George K. Turner's articles in *McClure's Magazine* are excellent sources for accounts of the daily court sessions.

10. Bangs, p. 5.

Chapter 39
The Ancient Desperate Men of Stillwater

1. Henry Wolfer, Warden, Minnesota State Prison, Stillwater, Minn., to Frank Murray, Pinkerton's National Detective Office, Chicago, July 7, 1897, PA.

2. Mrs. Marion B. Lull, Brooklyn, N.Y., to the Hon. Davis M. Clough, Governor of Minnesota, July 8, 1897, PA.

3. William A. Pinkerton to Mrs. Marion B. Lull, Brooklyn, July 14, 1897; Marion B. Lull to William A. Pinkerton, July 21, 1897, both PA.

4. William A. Pinkerton to Marion B. Lull, July 25, 1897, PA.

5. Robert A. Pinkerton to William A. Pinkerton, July 27, 1897, PA.

6. Cora McNeil, Minneapolis, Minn., to William Pinkerton, December 15, 1898, PA.

7. William A. Pinkerton to Marion B. Lull, December 20, 1898; William A. Pinkerton to Robert A. Pinkerton, December 20, 1898, both PA.

8. William A. Pinkerton, Chicago, to Miss Cora McNeil, Minneapolis, Minn., December 20, 1898, PA.

9. St. Paul *Globe,* July 11, 1901.

Book Eleven
The Last Years, 1900–1924

Chapter 40
The Eye and the Sport of Kings

1. Address by William Pinkerton, Annual Convention, International Association of Chiefs of Police, Jamestown, Va., 1907, p. 2; Criminal File Record of Dink Wilson, alias George A. Barnes, sent to Syracuse police by W. C. Hanley, Chief, File Clerk, P.N.D.S., August 17, 1893, PA; Charles W. Wright, Chief, Syracuse police, to William A. Pinkerton, March 21, 1894, PA; affidavit of William A. Pinkerton on the character and criminal records of Dink Wilson, March 31, 1894, PA; Syracuse *Journal,* August 13, 1901.

2. "The Pinkerton Story," by Rufus Jarman, *Saturday Evening Post,* Part III, May 29, 1948, p. 28.

3. The New York *Press,* April 23, 1911.

4. Robert A. Pinkerton to F. R. Hitchcock, January 10, 1906, PA.

5. Newark *Call,* August 25, 1907.

6. Route Book for Buffalo Bill's circus, Monday, April 17, Baltimore,

to Saturday, October 17, Urbana, Ohio, PA.

7. The New York *World,* December 3, 1897.

8. Houston *Post,* September 1, 1907.

9. Extensive obituaries on Robert Pinkerton were published in every large newspaper in the world, from the United States to the Orient. Among them were the New York *Times,* New York *Tribune,* New York *World,* Brooklyn *Eagle,* Chicago *Evening Post,* Denver *Post,* Philadelphia *Bulletin,* New York *Telegram,* all of August 17–19, 1907.

10. G. C. Thiele, Superintendent, Spokane office to George D. Bangs, Jr., June 17, 1911, PA.

11. Copy of Operative's Report, New Orleans office, on the arrest of Hans Helle, 1914, forwarded to the New York office, PA.

12. Address by William A. Pinkerton, Annual Convention, International Association of Chiefs of Police, New Orleans, April 15, 1919. The Federal Bureau of Investigation was originally created in 1908 as the Bureau of Investigation, with authority only to conduct investigations for the Department of Justice. After J. Edgar Hoover became director in 1924, Congress gradually added one duty after another until the bureau was reorganized in 1933 as the Division of Justice in the Department of Justice. In 1935, it was formally designated the Federal Bureau of Investigation.

13. *World Magazine,* April 25, 1920.

14. San Francisco *Call-Post,* March 28, 1921.

15. Albert E. Horsley (Orchard's real name) to C. P. Connelly, New Jersey, December 31, 1920, PA. Orchard died on the morning of April 13, 1954. Obituaries in the large city dailies briefly recalled his exploits. But the thunder of his bombs, the horror they inflicted, the turbulent times were now only faint, almost undistinguishable echoes.

16. William Pinkerton to George D. Bangs, Jr., January 3, 1921, PA.

17. An interview with the late Ralph Dudley, general manager, and the author, 1948.

Chapter 41
The Modern Agency

1. Criminal file of Willie (The Actor) Sutton, alias Leo Holland, Julian Loring, Richard Courtney, and Richard Loring, PA. The file contains the voluminous reports of the many investigations of Sutton made by Pinkerton's under Captain Herbert S. Mosher, Criminal Identification Bureau. Hereafter cited as Sutton.

2. New York *Times,* Sunday, August 16, 1964. Hereafter cited as Interview.

3. This file was never returned to the Agency. The text of the hearings before the Subcommittee of the Committe on Education and Labor of the United States Senate, known at the time as the La Follette Civil Liberties Committee, runs to more than 2,500,000 words and eight

volumes, NYP. See also *The Labor Spy Racket,* by Leo Huberman (New York, 1937).

4. Jarman, "The Pinkerton Story," *Saturday Evening Post,* Part III, June 5, 1948, p. 146.

5. Interview.

6. Racetrack Ringers, the File of Peter C. Barrie, PA.

7. *Forbes,* November 15, 1967, pp. 59–60.

8. *Ibid.*

9. Interview. Robert Pinkerton, II, died on October 11, 1967.

Bibliography

MANUSCRIPTS, LETTERS, CORRESPONDENCE, MEMOIRS, ETC.

Association American Railroads Archives, Washington, D.C.

Bangs, George. Letter Book, 1872–1876. Library of Congress.

Burlington, Chicago & Quincy Railroad Archives (Pinkerton Reports). Newberry Library.

Captured Confederate Correspondence, Departments of State and War, National Archives.

Chalmers, Joan Pinkerton (Mrs.), Collection. Chicago Historical Society.

Dahlgren Papers. Library of Congress.

Dimaio, Frank. Interviews owned by the author.

Eastman, Zegina (Pinkerton, Letters). Chicago Historical Society.

Felton, Samuel Morse, Collection (Account by Felton of the plot against Lincoln's life and the role Pinkerton played in it). Chicago Historical Society.

Felton, Samuel Morse, Papers (Allan Pinkerton Letters). Historical Society of Pennsylvania.

Glasgow (Gorbals District) Municipal Records.

Graceland Cemetery, Chicago, Burial Reports.

Halifax Historical Society, File of Shipwrecks.

Herndon-Weik Collection. Library of Congress.

Illinois Central Archives (Pinkerton contract, McClellan Letter Books and Correspondence). Newberry Library.

Levett, Allan. Organization for Order: The Development of Police Organizations in the Nineteenth Century United States (forthcoming Ph.D. dissertation, Department of Sociology, University of Michigan, 1968).

Lewis, Pryce. Memoirs. Owned by Harriet Shoen, Ph.D.

Lincoln, Robert Todd, Collection. Library of Congress.

McClellan, George Brinton, Collection. Library of Congress.

Mitchell Library, Collections, Glasgow.

Pinkerton, Allan, Letter Book, 1872–1876. Library of Congress.

Pinkerton, Allan, Letters (including Allan Pinkerton's will and his contract with the Illinois Central). Chicago Historical Society.

Pinkerton, Allan, Record Book, 1861. Henry Huntington Library, San Marino, Calif.

Pinkerton's National Detective Agency Reports to the American Bankers Association, 1901–1911; Bulletins, Nos. 3, 4, 11, 34, 36, 37. New York Public Library.

Records of the Hearings of State Prisoners Before the Dix-Pierpont Committee, National Archives.

Roosevelt, Theodore, Collection. Library of Congress.

Union Pacific Historical Archives.

Van Lew, Elizabeth, Papers. New York Public Library.

BOOKS, PAMPHLETS, HISTORICAL QUARTERLIES, GOVERNMENT DOCUMENTS, ETC.

It would be impractical to list all the books, historical quarterlies, pamphlets, and so on, that I have consulted during the years I have been working on this subject. Rather than list them all—some have only a peripheral interest in the Pinkertons—I have selected those I have found most helpful.

Aaron, Daniel (editor). America in Crisis: Fourteen Crucial Episodes in American History. New York, 1952.

"Adam Worth, the Greatest Criminal of the Past Century." New York, 1903.

Adamic, Louis. Dynamite. New York, 1935.

Adams, Henry. The Education of Henry Adams. Boston, 1918.

Adams, Margaret. The New Orleans Mafia Riots. Tulane, 1924 (Master's thesis).

Annual Report of the American Historical Association. Washington, D.C., Government Printing Office. 1889 (Vol. II), 1904 (Vol. II), 1905 (Vol. I), 1908 (Vol. I).

Asbury, Herbert. Gangs of New York. New York, 1927.

————. Gem of the Prairie. New York, 1942.

Ashby, Thomas A. The Valley Campaigns. New York, 1914.

Bailey, Thomas A. The American Pageant. Boston, 1966.

————. A Diplomatic History of the American People (6th ed.). New York, 1955.

Bancroft, Frederick. "The Life of William H. Stewart," Political Quarterly, September, 1891.

Barnes, James A. "Myths of the Bryan Campaign," Mississippi Valley Historical Review, Vol. 34, 1947–1948.

Battles and Leaders of the Civil War (4 vols.). New York, 1888.

Beckner, Earl R. A History of Labor Legislation in Illinois. Chicago, 1929.

Beckwith, H. W. History of Iroquois County. Chicago, 1888.

Beymer, William G. On Hazardous Service. New York, 1912.

Blaine, James. Twenty Years of Congress. New York, 1911.

Borah, William E. Funeral Oration for Frank Steunenberg. Caldwell, Idaho, 1906.

Bourke, Charles. "Pinkerton's National Detective Agency." Strand Magazine, London, 1905.

Bowers, Claude. The Tragic Era. New York, 1929.

Boyd, Belle. In Camp and Prison. New York, 1865–1867.

Brayley, Edward A. Vidocq: A Master of Crime. London, 1928.

Bridge, James, Howard. The Inside Story of the Carnegie Steel Co. New York, 1906.

Broehl, Jr., Wayne G. The Molly Maguires. Cambridge, Mass., 1965.

Brown, John A. "Charles A. Siringo," Westerners Brand Book, Chicago Corral, February, 1960, Vol. 16, No. 12.

Burgoyne, Arthur. Homestead 1892. Pittsburgh, Pa., 1893.

Byrnes, Thomas B. Professional Criminals of America. New York, 1886.

Callant, A. G. Saint Murgo's Bells. Glasgow, 1888.

Carman, Harry, Henry David, and Paul N. Gultine. The Path I Trod: The Autobiography of Terence V. Powderly. New York, 1940.

Carpenter, F. B. Six Months at the White House. New York, 1867.

Carpenter, Frank G. Carp's Washington. New York, 1960.

Cash, W. J. The Mind of the South. New York, 1941.

Casson, Herbert. Romance of Steel: The Story of a Thousand Millionaires. New York, 1907.

Chadwick, F. Relations of the United States and Spain, Vol. I, New York, 1909.

Chesnut, Mary Boykin. Diary from Dixie. New York, 1906.

Coit, Margaret L. John C. Calhoun. New York, 1950.

Coleman, J. Walter. The Molly Maguires. Richmond, Va., 1936.

Collier and Westrate. Dave Cook of the Rockies. Denver, 1897.

Commons, John R. History of Labor in America. New York, 1911.

Cook, Dave, of the Rockies, compiled by John W. Cook. Denver, 1897 (new edition and foreword by E. DeGolyer, Jr., Norman, Okla., 1958).

Corliss, Carlton J. Main Line of Mid America: The Story of the Illinois Central. New York, 1950.

Coxe, John. "The Mafia Incident," Louisiana Historical Quarterly, 1937.

Crapsey, Edward. The Nether Side of New York. New York, 1872.

Crittenden, H. H. The Crittenden Memoirs. New York, 1936.

Crowe, Pat. My Life. New York, 1902.

Croy, Homer. Jesse James Was My Neighbor. New York, 1956.

Cruise, J. D. "Early Days of the Union Pacific," Collections of the Kansas State Historical Society (Topeka, 1910), Vol. XI.

Cuthbert, Norma B. (editor). Lincoln and the Baltimore Plot. San Marino, Calif., 1949.

Cutter, George W. The Mafia and Immigration. Newport, R.I., 1891.

Dahlgren, J. V. Memoirs of Colonel Dahlgren. Philadelphia, 1872.

Dave Cook, *See* Cook, Dave.

De Long, T. C. Four Years in the Rebel Capital. Mobile, Ala., 1890.

Denholm, James. History of Glasgow Suburbs. Glasgow, 1798.

Dewees, F. P. The Molly Maguires. Philadelphia, 1877.

Dictionary of American Biography. New York, 1968.

Doster, William E. Lincoln and Episodes of the Civil War. New York, 1915.
Drury, John. Old Illinois Houses. Chicago, 1941.
Duke, Thomas S. Celebrated Crimes in America. New York, 1910.

Faulkner, Harold U. Politics, Reform and Expansion. New York, 1959.
Fine, Sidney, and Gerald S. Brown. The American Past (2 vols.). New York, 1965.
Fisk, John. American Political Ideals. New York, 1885.
————. The Destiny of Man. Boston, 1884.
Frost, The Trial of, for High Treason, Held at Monmouth, December, 1839. London, 1840.

Gard, Wayne. Frontier Justice. Norman, Okla., 1949.
————. Sam Bass. New York, 1936.
Genealogy of the Cutts Family in America. Albany, 1892.
General Principles. Pinkerton's National Detective Agency, New York, 1878.
Geyer, Frank. The Holmes-Pitezel Case. Philadelphia, 1896.
Ginger, Ray. The Age of Excess in the United States, 1877–1914. New York, 1965.
Grant, C. Hartlet. The Three Jameses. New York, 1932.
Grant, Homil. Spies in the Secret Service. New York, 1915.
Greenhow, Rose. My Imprisonment and the First Year of Abolition Rule at Washington. London, 1863.
Guerin, Eddie. I Was a Bandit. New York, 1929.

Hall, John A. The Great Strike on the "Q". Chicago and Philadelphia, 1889.
Harlow, Alvin. Old Waybills. New York, 1934.
Hendrick, Burton J. Life of Andrew Carnegie. New York, 1952.
Higham, John. Strangers in the Land: Patterns of American Nationalism, 1860–1925. New Brunswick, N.J., 1963.
History and Evidence of the Passage of Abraham Lincoln from Harrisburg, Pa., to Washington, D.C., on the 22 and 23 of February, 1861. (See also Magazine of History, No. XXXII, 1935.)
History of Schuylkill County. Pennsylvania, 1881.
Hofstadter, Richard. Social Darwinism in American Thought. Boston, 1944.
Holbrook, Stewart H. The Rocky Mountain Revolution. New York, 1956.
Holmes, "The Concentration of Wealth," Political Science Quarterly, VIII, December, 1893.
Horan, James D. Confederate Agent. New York, 1955.
————. Desperate Men. New York, 1949.
Huberman, Leo. The Labor Spy Racket. New York, 1937.

Illinois Historical Society Journal, December, 1948; December, 1949.
Illinois Works Progress Administration Guide. Washington, D.C., 1937.

James, Marquis. They Had Their Hour. New York, 1934.

Jarman, Rufus. "The Pinkerton Story," The Saturday Evening Post, May 15, 22, 29; June 5, 1948.

Josephson, Matthew. The Politicos. New York, 1938.

————. The President Makers. New York, 1940.

————. The Robber Barons. New York, 1934.

Kagi (John Henry) to Tidd (Charles P.), March 13, 1859, Document No. 4, Appendix to Governor Wise's message to the Virginia Legislature, December, 1859.

Ketchum, Hiram. General McClellan's Pennsylvania Campaign. New York, 1864.

Keyes, E. D. Fifty Years of Observation of Men and Events. New York, 1884.

Krakel, Dean. The Saga of Tom Horn. Laramie, Wyo., 1954.

Lamon, Ward H. Life of Abraham Lincoln. Washington, D.C., 1872; reprinted 1911.

Ledru, Charles. La Vie, La Mort et les derniers moments de Vidocq. Paris, 1857.

Leech, Margaret. Reveille in Washington. New York, 1941.

Lewis, Lloyd. "Pinkerton and Lincoln," Illinois Historical Society Journal, Springfield, December, 1948.

Lomask, Milton. Andrew Johnson, President. New York, 1960.

Love, Robertus. The Life and Times of Jesse James. New York, 1926.

Lowenberg, Bert J. "Darwinism Comes to America," Mississippi Valley Historical Review, XXVIII, 1941.

McClellan, George B. McClellan's Own Story. New York, 1887.

McMurry, Donald L. The Great Burlington Strike of 1888: A Case History in Labor Relations. Cambridge, Mass., 1956.

Mahoney, Dennis. Prisoner of State. New York, 1863.

Malone, Dumas, and Basil Rauch. The New Nation, 1865–1917. New York, 1960.

Marshall, John A. America's Bastille. Philadelphia, 1872.

Miller, F. T. Photographic History of the Civil War (10 vols.). New York, 1912.

Milton, George Fort. The Age of Hate. New York, 1930.

Moffett, Cleveland. True Detective Stories from the Pinkerton Archives. New York, 1893.

Monaghan, Jay. Last of the Bad Men: The Legend of Tom Horn. New York, 1946.

Moore, Langdon W. His Own Story of His Eventful Life. Boston, 1893.

Morison, Samuel Eliot, and Henry Steele Commager. The Growth of the American Republic (2 vols.). New York, 1962.

Morris, R. C. "The Nation of the Great American Desert East of the Rockies," Mississippi Valley Historical Review, Vol. XIII, No. 2.

Nevins, Allan. The Emergence of Modern America, 1865–1878. New York, 1928.

Official Records of the War of the Union and Confederate Armies, 137 vols. Washington, D.C., 1902.
Old Capitol, The. By A Lady. 1867.

Paris, Comte de. History of the Civil War in America (4 vols.). Philadelphia, 1875.
Parkes, Henry Bamford. The American Experience. New York, 1947.
Paxson, Frederick L. History of the American Frontier. New York, 1924.
_____. The Last Frontier. New York, 1910.
_____. "The Pacific Railroad and the Disappearance of the Frontier in America," Annual Report of the American Historical Association, Vol. I, 1907.
Pinkerton, Allan. The Bankers, Their Vaults, and the Burglars. Chicago, 1873.
_____. The Detective and the Expressman. New York, 1888.
_____. The Mollie Maguires and the Detective. London, 1877.
_____. Spy of the Rebellion. New York, 1883.
Pinkerton, William A. "Forgery" (paper read to the Annual Convention, International Chiefs of Police, Washington, D.C., 1905).
_____. "Yeggmen" (Paper read to the International Chiefs of Police, St. Louis, Mo., 1905).
Pinkertons and the Tariff, The, Troubles at Homestead, Views of Mr. Ray. U.S. Judiciary Committee, Washington, D.C., 1893.
Pinkerton's Annual Report to the American Bankers Association, 1905.
Pinkerton's General Information Issued to the American Bankers Association, 1901–1911.
Pinkerton's National Detective Agency and Its Connections with the Labor Trouble. New York, 1892.
Pollack, Norman. The Populist Response to Industrial America. New York, 1962.
Power, John C. The Attempt to Steal Lincoln's Body. Springfield, Ill., 1890.
Przeniczny, Teressa. "Allan Pinkerton, Dundee's World Famous Detective," Countryside, Barrington, Ill. Press, September 14, 1967.

Reno, John. Life and Career.
Rhodes, James F. The Mollie Maguires in the Anthracite Region of Pennsylvania. New York, 1910.
Richardson, Albert Deane. The Secret Service. Hartford, Conn., 1866.
Ross, Ishbel. Rebel Rose. New York, 1954.
Rowan, Richard W. The Pinkerton Detective Dynasty. New York, 1931.

Salmons, C. H., and others. The Burlington Strike. Aurora, Ill., 1889.
Scott, Roy V. The Agrarian Movement in Illinois, 1880–1896. New York, 1926.
Scott and Dunlap, Trials of. Northampton, Mass., 1872.

Seely Houk Case, Annual Report. Pennsylvania Game Commissioners, 1908.

Settle, William, Jr. Jesse James Was His Name. Columbia, Mo., 1966.

Sherman, Thomas G. "The Owners of America," Forum C, VIII, November, 1889.

Sigaud, Louis A. Mrs. Greenhow and the Rebel Spy Ring," Maryland Historical Magazine, September, 1946.

————. "When Belle Boyd Wrote Lincoln," Lincoln Herald Quarterly. Harrogate, Tenn., 1948.

Simkins, F. B. The South Old and New. New York, 1953.

Smith, Edward Conrad. The Borderland in the Civil War. New York, 1927.

Siringo, Charles A. A Cowboy Detective. Chicago, 1912.

Sonnichsen, C. L. Cowboys and Cattle Kings: Life on the Range Today. Norman, Okla., 1950.

Stead, Philip J. Vidocq: A Biography. London, 1953.

Stern, Madeline. Imprints on History: Book Publishing and the American Frontier. Bloomington, Ind., 1956.

Stowell, Myron R. Fort Frick. Pittsburgh, Pa., 1893.

Swiggett, Howard (editor). A Rebel War Clerk's Diary. New York, 1935.

Taussig, F. W. "The Southwest Strike of 1886," Quarterly Journal of Economics, January, 1887.

Tests on Passenger Conductors by the National Police Agency. New York, 1867.

Tests on Passenger Conductors Made by the Pinkertons, Chicago, 1876.

Tillotson, F. H. How to Be a Detective. St. Louis, Mo., 1900.

Webster, Timothy. Spy of the Rebellion. Chicago, 1906.

Worth, Adam. The Greatest Criminal of the Past Century. New York, 1903.

Train, Arthur. An American Lawyer at the Comorra Trials. New York, 1922.

————. Imported Crime: The Story of the Comorra in America. New York, 1912.

Turner, Frederick Jackson. The Frontier in American History. New York, 1959.

Tyler, Gus. Organized Crime in America. Ann Arbor, Mich., 1962.

United States House of Representatives. Executive Document, 1st Session, 1891–1892. Vol. I.

————. Homestead, Labor Hearings, No. 21447, 52nd Congress, 2nd Session, 1893.

Vidocq, Memoirs of (Edwin C. Rich, editor). Boston, 1935.

————. Memoirs of (4 vols.). Paris, 1829.

Villard, Oswald Garrison John Brown, 1800–1859. New York, 1910.

Waterman, A. N. "Washington at the Time of the First Bull Run."

Washington, D.C., Military Order of the Loyal Legion of the United States.

Weik, Jesse. "Allan Pinkerton's Unpublished Story of the Attempt on Lincoln's Life," Magazine of History, LXXX, February 19, 1922 (Foreword by Ida Tarbell).

Welles, Gideon. Diary (3 vols.). New York, 1911.

Wells, Colin. "Social Darwinism," American Journal of Sociology, XII, 1907.

Wilder, W. H. "The Evils of Immigration," Methodist Review, LI, 1891.

Williams, Kenneth P. Lincoln Finds a General (Vols. I, II). New York, 1949.

Williams, T. Harry. Lincoln and His Generals. New York, 1952.

————. Lincoln and the Radicals. Madison, Wis., 1941.

Williamson, James J. Prison Life in Old Capitol. West Orange, N.J., 1911.

Wolf, Leon. Lockout. New York, 1965.

Worth, Adam. See "Adam Worth . . ."

Wright, Leslie C. Scotland in Chartism. London, 1953.

Wyllie, Irvin G. The Self-Made Man in America: The Myth of Rags to Riches. New York, 1954.

MITCHELL LIBRARY, GLASGOW

(Glasgow newspapers during the period of the Chartists, 1839–1842)

The Glasgow Post
Marriage Register, City of Glasgow, 1842
The Saturday Evening Post
The Scottish Herald
The Scottish Patriot

NEWSPAPERS

Baltimore Sun, 1861, 1912
Boston American, 1923
Boston Daily Globe, 1890
Boston Evening Record, 1889
Boston Herald, 1889
Bridgeport Herald, 1904
Brooklyn Eagle, 1907
Buffalo Courier, 1919
Chicago American, 1903
Chicago Chronicle, 1903, 1907
Chicago Daily News, 1898
Chicago Democratic Press, 1853
Chicago Eagle, 1897
Chicago Observer, 1896
Chicago Press, 1895, 1897, 1891
Chicago Record-Herald, 1909

Chicago Sunday Herald, 1896
Chicago Times, 1868, 1882, 1887, 1890, 1891
Chicago Tribune, 1874, 1886, 1890, 1902, 1937, 1938
Cincinnati Enquirer, 1886
Cleveland Plain Dealer, 1904, 1909
Colorado Sun, 1891
Denver Daily News, 1891
Denver Post, 1904
Denver Republican, 1886
Denver Times, 1886, 1891
Detroit News-Tribune, 1897
Franklin County Tribune, 1905
Hartford Daily Courant, 1903
Hartford Daily Times, 1903, 1905
Houston Post, 1907
Idaho Daily Statesman, 1906
Indianapolis Independent Journal, 1868
The Inter Ocean, 1881, 1902, 1909, 1910
Kansas City Journal, 1904
Kansas City Sun, 1894
Kansas City Sunday Star, 1894
Kansas City Times, 1903
Kansas City World, 1889
Louisville Courier Journal, 1916
Morning Advertiser, 1893
New Albany Independent Weekly, 1868
New Orleans Picayune, 1890, 1891
New Orleans Times-Democrat, 1890, 1891
New York Daily and Sunday, 1887
New York Herald, 1880, 1881, 1894, 1898, 1899, 1903
New York Journal, 1894
New York Star, 1884, 1888, 1903
New York Sun, 1881, 1887, 1889, 1890, 1891, 1892, 1902
New York Telegram, 1907
New York Times, 1861, 1884, 1891, 1893
New York Tribune, 1878, 1906, 1907, 1939
New York World, 1874, 1882, 1888, 1889, 1891, 1893, 1894, 1897, 1903
Newark Call, 1907
Philadelphia Bulletin, 1907
Philadelphia Daily Record, 1909
Pocatello Tribune, 1906
Richmond Examiner, 1861
St. Louis Globe-Democrat, 1876, 1887, 1890, 1891
St. Louis Post-Dispatch, 1904, 1905
St. Louis Republican, 1903
St. Louis Star, 1903
St. Louis World, 1905
St. Paul Daily Press, 1889
St. Paul Globe, 1901

St. Paul Pioneer Press, 1897, 1888, 1901
San Francisco Call Post, 1921
Seattle Star, 1904
Spokane Evening Chronicle, 1904
Spokane Press, 1911
Springfield, Ohio, Republican, 1889, 1893
Syracuse Journal, 1901

MAGAZINES

American Law Review
Collier's Magazine
The Eye
The Expressman
Forbes Magazine
Harper's Magazine
Leslie's Magazine
McClure's Magazine
The Nation
North American Review
The People's Journal
Railroadmen's Magazine
Review of Reviews
The Saturday Evening Post
Southern Expressman
Travelers' Monthly

Index